The theme of this book is the crisis of the early modern state in eighteenth-century Britain. The revolt of the North American colonies and the simultaneous demand for wider religious toleration at home challenged the principles of sovereignty and obligation that underpinned arguments and assumptions about the character of the state. These, in turn, were expressed in terms of the 'common good', 'necessity', and 'community' – concepts that came to the fore in late sixteenth- and seventeenth-century European political thought and which gave expression to the problem of defining legitimate authority in a period of increasing consciousness of state power. The Americans and their British supporters argued that individuals ought to determine the common good of the community which they comprised. A new theory of representation and freedom of thought marks the cutting edge of this revolutionary redefinition of the basic relationship between individual and community.

DEFINING THE COMMON GOOD

IDEAS IN CONTEXT

Edited by Quentin Skinner (General Editor), Lorraine Daston,
Wolf Lepenies, Richard Rorty and J. B. Schneewind

The books in this series will discuss the emergence of intellectual traditions
and of related new disciplines. The procedures, aims and vocabularies that
were generated will be set in the context of the alternatives available within
the contemporary frameworks of ideas and institutions. Through detailed
studies of the evolution of such traditions, and their modification by
different audiences, it is hoped that a new picture will form of the
development of ideas in their concrete contexts. By this means, artificial
distinctions between the history of philosophy, of the various sciences, of
society and politics, and of literature may be seen to dissolve.

The series is published with the support of the Exxon Foundation

A list of books in the series will be found at the end of the volume.

DEFINING THE COMMON GOOD

Empire, religion and philosophy in eighteenth-century Britain

PETER N. MILLER

University of Chicago

CAMBRIDGE
UNIVERSITY PRESS

Published by the Press Syndicate of the University of Cambridge
The Pitt Building, Trumpington Street, Cambridge CB2 1RP
40 West 20th Street, New York, NY 10011–4211, USA
10 Stamford Road, Oakleigh, Melbourne 3166, Australia

© Cambridge University Press 1994

First published 1994

Printed in Great Britain by Bell and Bain Ltd., Glasgow

A catalogue record for this book is available from the British Library

Library of Congress cataloguing in publication data
Miller, Peter N., 1964–
Defining the common good: empire, religion and philosophy in
eighteenth-century Britain / Peter N. Miller.
p.   cm. – (Ideas in context: 29)
Includes bibliographical references.
ISBN 0 521 44259 1
1. Great Britain – Politics and government – 18th century.
2. Political science – Great Britain – History – 18th century.
3. Imperialism – Great Britain – History – 18th century.
4. Great Britain – Church history – 18th century.
5. Philosophy, British – 18th century. 6. Common good.
I. Series.
DA480.M627 1994
941.07 – dc20   93–19862 CIP

ISBN 0 521 44259 1 hardback

For Mom and Dad

Again this is apparent to us in daily conversation: that if four or five persons that have lived together be talking, another speaking the same language may come in and yet understand very little of their discourse, in that it relateth unto circumstances, persons, things, times and places which he knoweth not. It is no otherwise with a man having no insight of the times in which they were written and the circumstances unto which they relate, and the reading of ancient books, whether they be divine or humane.

Harrington, Oceana

What is justice? It is constant care for the common good. In what does the science of law consist? In the knowledge of the best government. What is law? It is an art of watching over the public interest. What is law, or 'the just'? It is the useful. What is *natural* law? The private interest of each one of us. What is the law of nations? The common good of all nations. What is civil law? The good of the commonwealth. What are the sources of law and why did the law of nature originate? That many may live in any way soever. Why did *jus gentium* arise? That man might live in security and ease. What reason accounts for the establishment of civil law? The attainment of a happy and prosperous life. Which is the highest law, the standard we are to follow whenever we interpret any legal enactment? The greatness of the state, the preservation of our ruler, the glory of both.

Vico, On the Study Methods of our Time

Contents

Conclusion   413

Acknowledgments

Rabbi Perahia said: 'Appoint for yourself a teacher and acquire a friend.'

Mishna Avot 1:6

Though I have spoken in some detail of the duties of the teacher, I shall for the moment confine my advice to the learners to one solitary admonition, that they should love their masters not less than their studies, and should regard them as parents not indeed of their bodies but of their minds.

Quintilian, *Institutio Oratoria* II.ix

In his *Commentary on the Mishna*, Maimonides suggests that the friendship that exists between teacher and student arises from two people striving for the same end. 'How true', he writes, 'is the statement of Aristotle, "for his friend really is another self".' I feel especially fortunate in no longer being able to distinguish between my teachers and my friends.

My most profound debt is to Quentin Skinner. He inspired me to do this kind of history from afar, years ago, and remains a constant source of encouragement and insight. The final shape of this argument is the product of many enjoyable hours talking about a wide range of ideas with Istvan Hont and Richard Tuck, both of whom took an interest in my work and read this document in its earlier and less happy incarnations. A typically acute question by John Dunn has remained with me and insisted upon an answer. I hope to have given a better one than when first asked. Anthony Pagden and John Robertson examined the dissertation upon which this substantially revised version is based and Michael Sonenscher read a later draft; their questions led me to think fruitfully about other ways of telling this story. My teachers at Harvard, Wallace MacCaffrey and the late Judith Shklar, first nourished my interest in early modern European history and its political thought and encouraged me to keep at it.

In so far as 'conversation is civilization', as Michael Oakeshott has written, my education in Cambridge can be described as one long civilizing process. If my teachers have become my friends, it is as true that my friends have become my teachers. Sam Black, Patricia Clavin, Joan-Pau Rubiés and Norberto de Sousa have been my Virgil. The many hours eating, drinking and talking with Bill Acres, Melissa Calaresu, Cathy Curtis, Richard Fisher, Béla Kapossy, Dean Kernan, Steve Pincus, Jai Ramaswamy, Neil Robertson and Bill Sherman have given these years an extraordinary emotional and intellectual richness. There are no better teachers than people for whom ideas matter – and who can talk about them with a smile.

This project would have neither begun, nor been completed, without material support. I gratefully acknowledge my debt to the Master and Fellows of Trinity College who elected me into an external research studentship, and to the President and Fellows of Clare Hall for first, electing me into a research fellowship, and then making such a hospitable home. Brian Jenkins, Christine Fenn, Gillian Johns and Godfrey Waller have, in turn, made the Rare Books and Manuscript Rooms of the Cambridge University Library the comfortable and alluring places they have been for me. My gratitude to them and to the staffs of that library, of the Wren Library at Trinity College and of the British Library is expressed functionally, in footnotes, but is no less heartfelt for that. I wish to thank Sandra Sider for her help in viewing a manuscript in the collection of the Hispanic Society of America. I am grateful to Professor Jean Bran for assistance with Latin translation. Parts of this argument have been tried out formally at the Social and Political Thought Seminar at Cambridge, the Colloquium on British History at Harvard, the Le Moyne Forum on Religion and Literature, the North American Conference on British Studies Mid-Atlantic Division, the Anglo-American Conference, the American Historical Association Annual Convention and the King's College Research Centre seminar on 'Reason of State'. I thank the hosts for the opportunities, and the audiences for the questions, that have helped give shape to my work.

When Quintilian sought a model for the love of students for teachers, he chose parents. The affection and gratitude I feel for mine can only be acknowledged, never repaid. This book, however, like all human creations, is also a history of its author and in this respect, at least, makes manifest the scale of my indebtedness to them, and to all those who have contributed profoundly to my life these past six years.

Introduction

The idea of a 'common good' is so tightly woven into all thinking
about politics that any change in its content can be investigated as
the manifestation of a significant shift in the conceptual foundations
of political life. This book tells the story of just such a moment of
fundamental change. In later eighteenth-century Britain the cluster
of ideas which constituted the substance of what contemporaries
meant when they talked of a 'common good', and which had taken
its characteristic shape since the sixteenth century, was rearranged
by those who felt it no longer of use in addressing the central issue of
the relation of individuals to community. That the security of the
community was the basic justification for government action was an
ancient idea given its most systematic treatment by the philosophers
and political theorists of the late middle ages; its specific early
modern form reflected the needs of the states that emerged from the
era of Reformation and Counter-Reformation. These were no
longer found to be identical with the needs of eighteenth-century
Great Britain. There was a pronounced discontinuity between the
changed reality of imperial governance, and continuing justifications in terms of the 'common good'. The crisis of relations with
the North American colonies and the renewed demand for wider
religious toleration at home struck at the theoretical foundations of
that type of state. The consolidation of territorial power through
force and the ideological suasion of a state religion both depended
on a notion of community. Distance, dissatisfaction and dissent
shattered this crucial support. Where the British government continued to rely on the older arguments into the nineteenth century,
these late eighteenth-century events had inspired a group of
reformers interested in the causes of America and toleration to
articulate a different vision of that balance between the possibilities
for individual action and the claim of communal necessity. The
scope of this book, then, covers the lifespan of the state shaped by

Reformation and Counter-Reformation, though its particular focus is on the 'end' of the story in eighteenth-century Britain and the specific events and arguments that highlighted the inadequacies of an older approach to politics for a self-consciously enlightened age.

An analytical history of the concept of the 'common good' cannot be told here. But in so far as the ideas of the ancients furnished the arguments and categories in which Europeans thought about politics for the subsequent millennium this heritage is inescapable. The 'common good' was just such a basic category capable of being identified with justice, social policy and liberty. Only very rarely was it perceived to be hostile to the good of individuals; rather, the two ends were believed to coincide. Still, the conceptual priority of the community was unchallenged and was to remain unchallenged for centuries. Aquinas' formulation was typical:

All who are contained in any community are related to it as parts to a whole. The part is what it is in virtue of the whole; therefore every good of the part is to be directed towards the good of the whole ... Since every man is part of a state, it is impossible for any man to be good unless he is well adapted to the common good.[1]

With the revival of vigorous political life in the Italian communes in the thirteenth century, the emphasis on the service of the community took on an explicitly republican hue as writers like Cicero and Seneca, and then Aristotle, were incorporated as authorities. In several recent and important works, Quentin Skinner has traced the centrality of this republican reading of the common good through the thirteenth-century 'pre-humanists' into the *Discorsi* of Machiavelli.[2] The *res publica*, by definition, had as its goal the public good. But it could only be attained when citizens possessed that *virtù* which enabled them to place the well-being of the city above their own. This was the means to *grandezza*; the alternative was deadly and divisive faction. To this way of thinking, the good of the individual was achieved by pursuing the good of the many: 'not the particular good of individuals but the common good is that which makes a city great' (II.2). This is the particular Machiavellian

[1] Quoted in Antony Black, *Political Thought in Europe, 1250–1450* (Cambridge, 1992), p. 32; see pp. 22–34 for a discussion of the common good.

[2] In particular, 'Ambrogio Lorenzetti: The Artist as Political Philosopher', in *Proceedings of the British Academy*, 72 (1986), 1–56; *The Foundations of Modern Political Thought*, 2 vols. (Cambridge, 1978).

tradition whose passage across time and space has been charted by
Zera Fink, Caroline Robbins, Bernard Bailyn and John Pocock.[3] If
the common good necessarily constitutes the centre of gravity for
political thought, in the arguments developed by the publicists and
politicians of these faction-ridden Italian city-republics it was
shaped into an ideological weapon. Not only was the success of the
commonwealth to be sought, but its attainment was made contingent on individuals identifying their private goods with whatever
was determined by the governors to be their common, shared good.
This strong republican argument could appeal to those, like
Machiavelli, who sought a vantage point from which to criticize
current political practice and social decay. The power of this interpretation has led to the conclusion that the message of classical
antiquity to the eighteenth-century was univocal and republican.[4]
The body of this study disputes that claim and argues that greater
attention must be paid to the schools of hellenistic philosophy, as
interpreted by the great Romans, and their much more considerable
impact on the culture of early modern Europe.

But Machiavelli's evocation of Roman republicanism, like
Cicero's own, contained much else that was of value for non-
republicans. The primacy of the political community could be
rendered as an admonition to a prince 'to maintain his state'
(*mantenere lo stato*) as easily as a republican warning for citizens to
take all steps necessary for their common self-preservation.[5] Cicero,
who so ably served the republican theorists of the late middle ages
and Renaissance, conveyed a message as ambiguous as his own
political theory and practice had come to appear in the letters,

---

[3] Zera Fink, *The Classical Republicans* (Evanston, 1945); Caroline Robbins, *The Eighteenth-
Century Commonwealthmen. Studies in the Transmission, Development and Circumstance of English
Liberal Thought from the Restoration of Charles II until the War with the Thirteen Colonies*
(Cambridge, MA, 1959); Bernard Bailyn, *The Ideological Origins of the American Revolution*
(Cambridge, MA, 1967); John Pocock, *The Machiavellian Moment: Florentine Political Thought
and the Atlantic Political Tradition* (Princeton, 1975).

[4] Gordon Wood has argued that 'In the eighteenth century to be enlightened was to be
interested in antiquity, and to be interested in antiquity was to be interested in republicanism. Certainly classical antiquity could offer meaningful messages for monarchy too, but
there is no doubt that the thrust of what the ancient world had to say to the eighteenth
century was latently and at times manifestly republican' (*The Radicalism of the American
Revolution* (New York, 1992), p. 100). It is, of course, arguable whether enlightenment was
coterminous with 'interest in antiquity'. But that is a different question.

[5] See Quentin Skinner, 'The State', in *Political Innovation and Conceptual Change*, ed. Terrence
Ball, James Faar and Russell Hanson (Cambridge, 1989), pp. 90–131, for a history of the
changing character of the concept of the 'state' from the late middle ages to the seventeenth
century.

speeches and tracts whose rediscovery constituted one of the high points of Renaissance scholarship. It was, of course, precisely this ambivalence that Machiavelli exploited.

The history of the political thought of the hundred years following the publication of Machiavelli's works has often been written in terms of the death of republicanism at the hands of princely tyranny. In this story Cicero gives way to Tacitus. It is certainly true that the systematic destruction of the Italian republics and the horrendous dislocation of the civil wars of religion in France and the Netherlands made the search for stability, often in the person of a single ruler with undisputed power, seem absolutely essential. The formulation of prudent, *politique* maxims of policy was the constructive side of Tacitist scepticism about the practice of politics – both republican and princely.[6] Because the writers on statecraft, almost from the very beginning of this later sixteenth-century *genre*, are said to have taken Tacitus as a model at the expense of Cicero, analysis of the literature concerning what contemporaries termed, variously, *ragion di stato, razón de Estado, raison d'état* and 'reason of state' has often become conflated with a discussion of Tacitism.[7]

From Gustav Schmoller and Friedrich Meinecke onwards it has been customary to approach this literature as the ideological consequence of, if not justification for, a process of 'state-building'.[8] The reason of state, to this way of thinking, evolved *because* of and coordinate with the rise of states. Phenomenologically, of course, this is true. There *was* a pronounced alteration in the character and

---

[6] Richard Tuck has recently provided a most compelling account of the relationship of political and moral philosophy in this period. See *Philosophy and Government 1572–1651* (Cambridge, 1993). Some of the basic investigations of this theme can be found in R. de Mattei, *Dal premachiavellismo all'antimachiavellismo* (Florence, 1969); *Il problema della 'ragion di stato' nell'età della controriforma* (Milan and Naples, 1979); *Il pensiero politico italiano nell'età della controriforma* 2 vols. (Milan and Naples, 1982); Etienne Thuau, *Raison d'état et pensée politique a l'epoque de Richelieu* (Paris, 1966); William F. Church, *Richelieu and Reason of State* (Princeton, 1972); Roman Schnur, ed., *Staatsräson: Studien zur Geschichte eines politischen Begriffs* (Berlin, 1975).

[7] See Tuck's illuminating account of the role of Florentine *émigré* writers in the shift from Cicero to Tacitus in sixteenth-century France (*Philosophy and Government*, pp. 40–2). Those accounts perhaps most influential in identifying Tacitism and reason of state with a Machiavellism *manqué* have been those of Giuseppe Toffanin (*Machiavelli e il 'Tacitismo'* (Naples, 1972; 1st edn, 1921) and Friedrich Meinecke. In the latter case, the English translation bears a share of responsibility for adding the word 'Machiavellism' to a title that originally read *Reason of State in Early Modern History*. See also, Peter Burke, 'Tacitism', in *Tacitus*, ed. T. A. Dorey (London, 1969), pp. 149–71; Kenneth Schellhase, *Tacitus in Renaissance Political Thought* (Chicago, 1976).

[8] Gustav Schmoller, *The Mercantile System and its Historical Significance* (New York, 1931; 1st edn, 1895).

quantity of analyses of political practice during this period and contemporaries often remarked on it. More scholastic accounts of the origin of political power gave way to manuals written by and for statesmen about what to do with it. Nevertheless, from a conceptual point of view it is simplistic to assume that the issue of necessity had never confronted a statesman prior to the later sixteenth century. In fact, as will be argued at greater length in chapter 1, when those later statesmen sought guidance for their actions and justifications – for precisely what has come to be called the 'reason of state' – they looked to ancient Roman history, as presented by Cicero and Tacitus. For the particular shape taken by this later sixteenth- and seventeenth-century debate about political necessity owes much to both men as well as to Seneca. Tacitus' scepticism towards the world of politics inculcated a wariness towards appearances and hypostatized values which was complemented by the teachings of Seneca, who taught the ways of preserving oneself in such a world. Cicero, however, remained in use for those concerned with the realm of public order and the principles of communal preservation. In his rhetorical and philosophical works Cicero laid down explicit political principles; in the voluminous surviving correspondence that constituted his *apologia pro vita sua*, readers could gain a sense of the political context of ancient political thought unavailable elsewhere. So, despite the disappearance of those city-states whose greenhouse-like atmosphere nourished a powerful republican reading of Cicero, his usefulness to writers on politics did not lessen. We must, however, look for him in different places.

As the philosophically inclined defender of political legitimacy and the rule of law, there was no greater ancient exemplar of patriotic statesmanship. Cicero's Stoic defence of the good and of religion had enabled the Church Fathers to co-opt him as a pagan authority. But, at the same time, Cicero's recognition that in politics nothing could override the claim of necessity and his philosophical definition of expediency in terms of the public good offered welcome support to civil rulers making tough decisions. At a time when Machiavelli, and even Tacitus, threatened to make statecraft a dangerous word, Cicero's discussion of these issues was, as we shall see, couched in unobjectionable terms. Moreover, the central place occupied by Cicero in contemporary culture – his works formed the nucleus of basic educational programs from the fourteenth century through the nineteenth, at least – served to domesticate arguments which, on close inspection, were potentially no less subversive than those they were designed to marginalize.

The legitimacy of the political entities that emerged from the Protestant Reformation and Catholic Counter-Reformation remained subject to question by internal and external rivals. Its theorists defended the notion of political community that had taken shape in the later middle ages though now focusing on the spiritual and political responsibilities of temporal rulers rather than the value of the universal church.[9] In attempting to hold together this notion of politics at a time of increasing intellectual and political complexity, many of these writers drew on and developed this Ciceronian argument about the pre-eminence of the common good. His analysis of the relationship between the good and the useful (*honestum* and *utile*) in *De Officiis*, after the Bible one of the most widely and continuously read works in the history of Europe, was framed in terms of the needs of the public. This same public utility also mandated support for the religion of the state and its ancient customs, the *mos maiorum*. Several key features of states on either side of the theological and political 'iron curtain' that separated Protestant and Catholic Europe in the later sixteenth century gave especial relevance to Cicero's presentation of this issue.[10]

First, the maintenance of a particular confession, whether Roman Catholic (or Gallican or Venetian) or any of a variety of Protestant creeds, was deemed an interest of state and among the leading responsibilities of the civil magistrate. The Reformation and Counter-Reformation had made a specific moral posture part of the redefined character of civil government.[11] The Tridentine reforms, especially in so far as they affected the relation between governance

---

[9] See, for example, Antony Black, *Council and Commune. The Conciliar Movement and the Fifteenth-Century Heritage* (London, 1979), pp. 162–8. The chapter titles in Black's new survey of medieval political thought (*Political Thought in Europe, 1250–1450*) emphasize the continuity scholars now perceive in the centuries before and after the Renaissance: 'The political community', 'Church and state', 'Empire and nation', 'City-states and civic government', 'Kingship, law and counsel', 'Parliamentary representation', 'The state'. Nevertheless, as regards this last category, it is doubtful that the sense of national identity so characteristic of later periods was at all as widespread in the middle ages.

[10] Though trenchantly characterizing this as a problem for Baroque political thought, Robert Bireley has made Machiavelli the causal agent and read out the antique, and especially Ciceronian, character of this issue. See *The Counter-Reformation Prince: Anti-Machiavellism or Catholic Statecraft in Early Modern Europe* (Chapel Hill, NC, 1990), p. 28. 'Cicero' does not rate even a listing in the index of the book.

[11] Mario d'Addio, *Il pensiero politico di Gaspare Scioppio e il machiavellismo del seicento* (Milan, 1962), p. 330. Also, de Mattei, *Il pensiero politico italiano nell'età della controriforma*.

and spirituality, implied that no separation ought to be effected between morality and the quotidian tasks of policy-making. It is, perhaps, this imperative, at a time in which there *was* an undeniable expansion in the competence and invasiveness of central government, that generated such explicit discussion about the exercise of power. While the needs of governors were no different in the sixteenth century than in the sixth, the public and international dimension of the insistence that Christian princes uphold Christian morality surely complicated the justification of certain necessary, though unsavoury, practices. Cicero had been incorporated into the canon of Christian political thought because he could, quite legitimately, be read as a stoic philosopher. That he had also faced the hard questions which confronted statesmen in every era not only made his judgments more palatable, but deflected any possible allegation of base motives. Cicero had shown how it was possible to integrate the demands of morality and those of policy – precisely the task faced by civil rulers in states washed by the Counter-Reformation and by Protestant princes who had taken upon themselves the supreme headship of national churches. In this sense, contemporary needs forced the Ciceronian issue of *honestas* and *utilitas* to the top of the political agenda.

Secondly, many of these states were themselves composed of smaller entities, absorbed, amalgamated and otherwise retained in a variety of constitutional forms. These 'composite monarchies' or 'multiple kingdoms' were often held together by a fragile equilibrium of laws, privileges, custom and, of course, force. The task of establishing a legitimate central authority coincided with the creation of a single community with a specific vision of the good in place of the variety of pre-existing private goods which reflected differences of religion, region or legal privilege. This, too, lent itself to Cicero's analysis of the relationship between the good and the useful since the public good, or utility, could be used by governments to marginalize people or policies that could be described as serving private gain rather than the public good. In this context, the Ciceronian argument provided a justification for the legitimacy of central power. Though his analysis was framed in terms of personal morality, *De Officiis* was of equally great value for statesmen. For the disagreements between the constituent communities within the early modern state could also be sketched as a conflict between claims of the good and the expedient. In both 'composite' as well as theoretically unified states, the process of welding together a single entity reproduced the circumstances in which the claim of 'public utility' could be used to justify the drive of the single, central authority for a monopoly of political power.

Finally, while Cicero's analysis of this potential clash between the good and the useful was not directly concerned with community, its resolution in terms of the *utilitas rei publicae* obviously depended upon it. Moreover, in works such as *De Amicitia*, he had underlined the particular constitutive bonds the sum total of which comprised the community whose survival and improvement was the statesman's aim.[12] The seventeenth-century revival and adaptation of Stoicism made the concept of friendship the pre-eminent personal relationship and its requisite virtues the core of a new notion of virtue, one which was normative both for rulers and citizens. Scholars have observed that neo-Stoic personal morality provided the ethical training for the increasingly sophisticated bureaucratic infrastructures of increasingly sophisticated states.[13]

Discussions of the common good in the post-Reformation state, whether Catholic or Protestant, relied on a notion of community. For some, its content and shape were determined by a set of religious beliefs. Hence the terrific civil problems engendered by religious diversity, leaving aside their theological impact. For others, however, sheer physical existence, rather than ideological agreement, mattered most. This has been described as a newer argument, and is associated with thinkers like Montaigne and the neo-Stoic Lipsius. Scepticism about universals and despair at the desolation of

---

[12] The theorists of the medieval communes had explicitly put friendship at the heart of the notion of community they sought to inculcate. Henry of Ghent wrote that civil life was impossible without 'the highest friendship, by which each one is held by the other to be another self, and supreme charity, by which each one loves the other as himself, and the greatest benevolence, by which each one wishes for the other the same as for himself' (quoted in Black, *Political Thought in Europe, 1250–1450*, p. 121). An explicitly political history of the concept of friendship would have to recognize the importance of monastic, or spiritual, friendship for medieval writers; an interesting investigation would illuminate the different sources of its early modern role.

[13] This was the gist of Gerhard Oestreich's valuable and posthumously published *Neostoicism and the Early Modern State* (Cambridge, 1982). It is unclear whether Oestreich, had he lived to complete this work, would have wished to put such a strong emphasis on neo-Stoic philosophy as preparation for Prussian absolutism (see esp. pp. 119–26). J. H. Elliott has placed Olivares squarely in the context of Spanish neo-Stoicism, both in terms of the friendships of his early years in Seville and later on when confronted with the death of his daughter and the perils of statesmanship (*The Count-Duke of Olivares: The Statesman in an Age of Decline* (New Haven, 1986), pp. 21–4; 279–80).

their familiar world by ideologically inspired warfare led these men to redefine the character of that *patria* worth defending. Nannerl Keohane has commented that, to this way of thinking, 'Our love of our country is an extension of our love of things that belong to us, bolstered by our awareness that our personal security depends on that of the community.'[14]

National, as a prerequisite for self- , preservation, whether for reasons of ideology or selfishness, made security the measure of policy. There can be no surprise at the prominence in the contemporary literature on politics of Cicero's declaration that the 'well-being of the people is to be the highest law' (*salus populi suprema lex esto*).[15] Well-being was only possible where security was assured. Necessity dictated the means to this end, and, as was well known, necessity knows no law (*necessitas non habet legem*). Thus, even as Cicero argued that what was beneficial to the public determined whether an action was judged good, he also acknowledged that survival was the highest law. But, reflecting his indebtedness to the Greek philosophical tradition, Cicero was also deeply committed to the notion that the life to be strived for was much more than bare existence. In a chapter focusing on the need for a prince to know the art of war, Pedro de Rivadeneira, the Spanish Jesuit, went beyond the application of brute force in time of need to sketch that other, richer vision of a society whose security was, nevertheless, guaranteed by force.

These are what can support religion, give strength and force to justice, maintain peace, give rebuke to the enemy, punish the daring and rebellious; under its tutelage and protection the labourer can go out and sow in the field, cultivate his vine, harvest the fruits of the earth, sleep without fright in the shadow of his vine and fig tree; and the merchant explore, provide and enrich the realm; and the virgin preserve her chastity, the married raise her children in security; and the official work, the scholar study, the monk occupy himself in prayer, the religious contemplate and raise his hands to heaven, the judge do justice, and, finally, the prince be master of his estates.[16]

---

[14] Nannerl Keohane, *Philosophy and the State in France* (Princeton, 1980), p. 131.

[15] J. A. W. Gunn, in his valuable book, concluded that the recourse to this maxim in the seventeenth century was designed to make private rights the basis of the public good (*Politics and the Public Interest in the Seventeenth Century* (London and Toronto, 1969), p. xi). I disagree.

[16] Pedro de Rivadeneira, *Tratado de la religion y virtudes que debe tener el principe cristiano para gobernar y conservar sus estados*, in *Obras Escogidas* (Madrid, 1868), II.43, p. 582.

Sheer survival justified the use of force; but so too did any threat to the welfare of individuals within the well-ordered community. Perhaps the clearest presentation of these two justifications of necessity is found on a wall in Siena. On one side, the figure of *Securitas* floats over the thriving Sienese *contado* guaranteeing freedom of passage on the byways and labour in the fields. In Ambrogio Lorenzetti's (d.1348?) fresco, security is the product of good government and, in turn, makes possible the liberty and flourishing of individuals. On the other side of this very same wall is depicted a blasted countryside in which towns are besieged and the landscape stripped of all life. The allegory of *Securitas* is itself displaced by a larger-than-life hero, the *condottiere* Guidoriccio da Fogliano. No longer a means to an end, the struggle for security is described as the fundamentally grim essence of civic life. The open question, and one central to Post-Reformation political thought, is the one at the heart of *De Officiis*: what cannot be justified in the name of the *utilitas rei publicae*?

Fundamentally, security defined the common good, for, as represented by Lorenzetti and Rivadeneira, without it no other private goods were likely to be attained. It would have been difficult for anyone living in the later sixteenth century to disagree with this judgment. Yet, though the security of the community and the notion of a common good have been recognized as central to the reason of state, and even linked to the Ciceronian tag, this is usually described as the *product* of post-Machiavellian political thought and is often ascribed exclusively to the impact of Tacitus.[17] Surely a more exact evaluation would be that the character of sixteenth- and seventeenth-century politics put new stress on old concepts. Religious schism, warfare, consolidation of territorial power, overseas expansion, commerce, the print revolution, all these – and no doubt other salient features of the time – impacted upon the contemporary understanding of community. Since serving the 'common good' remained the touchstone of political justification, the uncertain nature of community remained a constant threat to the legitimacy of states.

One historian of early modern Europe has consistently argued that the creation of a community was the key to the creation of a viable state. Robert Evans' account of the making of the Habsburg

---

[17] For example, André Stegmann, 'La place de la praxis dans la notion de "Raison d'état"', in *Théorie et pratique politiques à la Renaissance*, ed. Stegmann (Paris, 1977), pp. 483–5.

monarchy has shown how it was possible to weld together a single polity despite such a staggering array of religious, linguistic, legal and political diversity as to sketch almost the limiting case of the Counter-Reformation state. The dramatic, but failed, bid for power by the Bohemian estates leading up to the disaster at the White Mountain (1620) now seems the high-water mark of the attempt to impose a confederal 'solution' on an entity far more complicated than any of the contemporary 'composite' monarchies. Helmut Koenigsberger and Evans argue that such success as was registered by the confederal movement depended on the cultural cohesion of the key group within the estates, the nobility.[18] Where the estates failed, the monarchy triumphed. The re-establishment of order was, however, more an intellectual and cultural than political creation. In fact, Evans argues that 'Had Habsburg supremacy in Central Europe rested on government alone, it would have been very weak indeed.' He notes the specific importance of Lipsian neo-Stoicism and the manifestation of dynastic power and patronage in artistic ventures such as opera and architecture.[19] Sovereigns and citizens were bound together by the powerful ties of Baroque culture. 'The ideals of the Central European Counter-Reformation', according to Evans, 'found their fullest realization in art' since only in art could the tensions of the Counter-Reformation state be reconciled.[20]

Evans' stress on the cultural bonds at the heart of the Habsburg monarchy points to the sufficiency of community for the establishment of stable government. It is no coincidence that at the heart of the modern theory of natural law – Grotius' contribution to the problem of statecraft – lay the notion of a social contract. For this provided a concrete means of constituting a community and indi-

---

[18] Helmut Koenigsberger, 'Epilogue: Central and Western Europe', in *Crown, Church and Estates: Central European Politics in the Sixteenth and Seventeenth Centuries*, ed. R. J. W. Evans and T. V. Thomas (London, 1991), p. 308; Evans, 'Introduction' to *ibid.*, p. xxviii; R. J. W. Evans, 'The Habsburg Monarchy and Bohemia, 1526–1848', in *Conquest and Coalescence: The Shaping of the State in Early Modern Europe*, ed. Mark Greengrass (London, 1991), p. 151.

[19] R. J. W. Evans, *The Making of the Habsburg Monarchy 1550–1700* (Oxford, 1979; rpt, 1991), pp. 113, 152. He also observed that 'The role of the expansive Baroque court as a vehicle for quasi-absolutist regimes in early modern Europe has long been underrated by historians' (p. 152).

[20] *Ibid.*, pp. 443, 446. Evans went on to strike a Musil-sounding note, adding that 'its whole mentality aspired unwittingly to the condition of art, and only there could its scheme be coherent' (p. 443).

cating membership.[21] Alongside the problem of defining community
lay the related problem of defining its supreme power. The search
for a clear notion of sovereignty and obligation is the great drama of
early modern European political thought. That contemporary political debate was conducted in terms of 'common good' and 'necessity' and *not* in terms of sovereignty reflects the slow course of
political transformation. Bodin and Hobbes may have articulated
clear concepts of state and sovereignty but their contributions seem
to have made little impact on the contour of political discussion well
into the eighteenth century.

Though the scope of this book corresponds to the conceptual
lifespan of the post-Reformation state, its emphasis is on Great
Britain in the eighteenth century. For here, I believe, the principles
of this state, namely, uniform confession, territorial consolidation
and, above all, community, were pushed to the furthest extent of
coherence and then shattered. The rebellion and separation of the
thirteen North American colonies, and the revival of a vigorous
movement for wide religious toleration at home set a limit to this
kind of state that was not surpassed. The War of American Independence was not the last war of religion, but the failed attempt, on one
side of the Atlantic, to enforce a feeling of community that had long
since evaporated and, on the other, a cultural revolution that had,
at its core, a new understanding of community.

Like her continental neighbours, early modern England was also
a composite state. In fact, Koenigsberger's terms of analysis are
drawn directly from a fifteenth-century Englishman, John Fortescue.[22] Conrad Russell has taken up this argument and made it
central to his account of the origins of the English civil war, or, as he
terms it, the War of the Three Kingdoms. He has argued that the
skyrocketing cost of war in the later sixteenth century put unbeara-
ble pressure on the fiscal apparatus and delicate balance of communal responsibilities and privileges that held such states together.[23]

---

[21] One might also, at this point, wish to distinguish between those writers on the reason of
state whose treatises closely resembled humanist works on politics, and the natural law
writers, the shape of whose approach to these issues differed so dramatically.

[22] 'He and his contemporaries were observing a real phenomenon, the tendency of kings to
extend their powers, and especially their powers of taxation and legislation at the expense
of the representative institutions of their countries' (*'Dominium Regale* or *Dominium Politicum
et Regale*: Monarchies and Parliaments in Early Modern Europe', in *Politicians and Virtuosi:
Essays in Early Modern History* (London and Ronceverte, 1986), p. 3).

[23] 'The commonest causes of instability in multiple kingdoms were war and the distribution of
offices, both fields in which outlying kingdoms often feared that their interests might be

While the monarch tended 'to give priority to issues of defence and national security', the constituent estates tended to be more concerned with protecting (their) property rights. The conflict between them was often sparked by an assessment of necessity.[24] Since Cicero's argument that the public utility provided the measure of *honestum* was universally accepted, the real issue was not *whether* the *salus populi* could make licit the infringement of basic rights, but *who* was to determine when such a moment of crisis existed. Though sovereignty was at issue, it was approached, in England, through the language of necessity and the common good.

Against this backcloth, seventeenth-century English political arguments closely resemble those in contemporary Catholic states facing the same set of challenges.[25] Religious divisions within England and between the constituent kingdoms placed a large question mark next to any sense of community; the Commonwealth, riding the crest of an anti-monarchical revolution in the name of community, was itself fatally weakened by precisely this type of debilitating political and religious division. Furthermore, the lack of coherent constitutional discussion concerning the bonds within the multiple kingdom meant that there existed, in the very heart of the state, a deep and dangerous ambiguity about its identity. Conrad Russell, in passing, noted that the constitutional thought of mid seventeenth-century Irishmen, like that of colonial Americans, 'carried a certain built-in ambiguity about their relationship with England'.[26] It is the contention of this book that the eighteenth-century crisis of empire was the delayed crisis of the multiple kingdom, staved off after 1649 and 1688, only to be faced with still

---

sacrificed to those of the leading kingdoms' (*Fall of the British Monarchies* (Oxford, 1991), p. 27). Richard Cust and Anne Hughes dispute the value of this European context ('Introduction: After Revisionism', *Conflict in Early Stuart England: Studies in Religion and Politics 1603–1642* (London, 1989), p. 39).

[24] 'If they once allowed that the king had to have money, on grounds of necessity, then the very principle of consent to taxation was put under threat' (Russell, 'Monarchies, Wars and Estates in England, France and Spain, c. 1580–c. 1640', *Legislative Studies Quarterly*, 7 (1982), p. 211).

[25] This point is made strongly by A. D. Wright, *The Counter-Reformation: Catholic Europe and the Non-Christian World* (London, 1982), for example, p. 282: 'The long-term assessment of Catholic development in the Counter-Reformation must also take account of the convergence, to a degree, of the attitudes of states, Catholic as well as Protestant, towards questions of loyalty and obedience, dissent and toleration. The common assumption of states in both parts of Europe, at the beginning of the seventeenth century, was still that religious uniformity was necessary for stable government: experience seemed at the time to confirm this.'

[26] Russell, *Fall of the British Monarchies*, p. 281 note 38.

higher stakes on the table in the new state created after 1707. While it has become fashionable for historians of eighteenth-century Britain to stress continuity over change, the tendency has been to focus solely on the continuing appeal within England of divine-right monarchy, Jacobitism or Country-Toryism. Instead, I would suggest that the most profound continuities between seventeenth- and eighteenth-century British political thought are best seen in the light of early modern European political discussion.

The Union with Scotland generated more contemporary interest north of Hadrian's Wall, and Scottish reactions remain the focus of scholarly interest. That the Union was less discussed in early eighteenth-century England does not diminish its historical value. For it is precisely because it was an 'incorporation' which *failed* to provoke profound self-consciousness about the structure of the state that enabled the core of the problem to pass, unexplored, into the much broader world of the empire. While it is possible to describe seventeenth-century England as a multiple kingdom, it is a still more accurate description of eighteenth-century Great Britain.

Here lies a crucial problem: the state shaped by the Reformation and Counter-Reformation was not an empire. Religious uniformity and territorial consolidation yielded security only in so far as they rested upon the firm, shared basis of community. The circumstances of imperial rule often vitiated, and at the least tested, this pre-condition. The Dutch Revolt had challenged the European agglomeration ruled by Charles V that resembled for a time a mighty empire. Spain's trans-Atlantic empire lasted much longer, but the American territories were not treated like Sicily, Catalonia or Portugal. They were, moreover, the property of Castile, itself only one, though the most favoured, of the Spanish Habsburg crowns. In short, empire in the Western Hemisphere was conducted on principles other than those of composite states, which remained the European norm. The British empire in North America, however, was inhabited by men considered subjects of the British crown, and their status, like so much else, was governed by statute and common law. But the precise character of the relationship between the different colonies and the metropolis remained unclear. They were not explicitly considered a coherent, separate body, like Scotland, though nevertheless increasingly bound up in the legal, commercial and cultural life of the metropolis. The identification of metropolitan interests with an imperial common good remained only implicit. The novelty of the situation led to the wholly understandable, but ultimately disastrous, extension of the early modern principles of the state to the colonial world of North America. The nature of this ill-fitting response is explored in chapter 3.[27]

But the underlying issue remained the one at the heart of the post-Reformation state: the overriding force of the *utilitas rei publicae* only bound those who felt themselves members of the same community. One of the most distinctive aspects of recent scholarship on colonial America has been the attention paid to precisely this issue.[28] Bernard Bailyn's extended project of describing the creation of an American community has made the 'national' question the prerequisite to understanding the creation of an American 'state'. The sense of being part of a community with shared interests had been created in the previous century and made possible the successful articulation of plans, first for confederacy and then for union. Discussions of national identity which declare that 'there is nothing here on political theory' deny themselves access to the range of issues discussed in this book.[29]

In the crisis between Britain and the colonists, the latter protested their Britishness with vehemence. Despite a demographic diversity which questioned the coherence of the notion, shared by Pufendorf and Blackstone, that community transcended the identity of its particular members, and physical mobility which challenged its accepted geographical content, it took a long time for the Americans to cease feeling British. But, at a certain point, this sense of community was pushed to the margins of debate. Friendship and reciprocity, or, as so many contemporaries described it, filial feelings,

---

[27] Bernard Bailyn has likewise commented that 'There had never been any constitutional theory to explain and shape Britain's relations with its dependencies in the West. Somehow the already deficient theory of domestic political and constitutional relations had been stretched to accommodate this burgeoning new world, and the result was a clumsy and inefficient empire which projected in magnified form all the increasingly unworkable compromises that lay at the heart of British life' (*Faces of Revolution: Personalities and Themes in the Struggle for American Independence* (New York, 1990), p. 182.

[28] For example, Bernard Bailyn, *The Peopling of British North America: An Introduction* (New York, 1986); *Voyagers to the West: A Passage in the Peopling of America on the Eve of the Revolution* (New York, 1986). The changing shape of colonial historiography is one of the themes of *Strangers within the Realm: Cultural Margins of the First British Empire*, ed. Bernard Bailyn and Philip D. Morgan (Chapel Hill, 1991).

[29] Linda Colley, *Britons: Forging the Nation 1707–1837* (New Haven and London, 1992), p. 9.

were swamped by the overwhelming sense of diverging interests.[30] At this stage an incipient and vague North American identity, itself only the broadest possible rubric for a host of more particular loyalties, seemed a more obviously true description than the simple 'British colonist'. The government's claim that necessity warranted a colonial taxation was rejected. The metropolitan definition of the common good was no longer persuasive.

Gordon Wood's description of the 'radicalism' of the American Revolution makes clear that the decisive characteristic of this revolution was the wholesale destruction and reconstruction of the ties which held colonial society together. The notion of community that has been described in terms of order, hierarchy, patriarchy or monarchism was overturned by a cultural revolution of colossal proportions. The tory accusations that the revolutionaries sought to shatter the familiar world 'were neither', according to Wood, 'inaccurate nor misplaced. The patriots were indeed trying to destroy the ligaments of the older society and to reknit people together in new ways.' The crucial problem for the revolutionaries was to find a substitute for the existing notion of community, which, as has been suggested, was constituted by a plenitude of personal relationships and friendships.[31] In their stead, the Americans hoped to build on the notion of equality a society bound together by 'love, respect, and consent'.[32]

The colonists' intellectual response to government measures took increasingly more radical forms, culminating in a unilateral declaration of independence on principles peripheral to the contemporary British debate. In Great Britain, the response of those who were moved by the colonial arguments was equally complex. They took up the assertion that there could be no common good without community and then set about exploring the meaning of these concepts.

Here we come to the second limit of this type of entity. If the foundations of the composite state could not adapt to the conditions

---

[30] 'Interest' has long been a key word in the history of the Revolution, though usually approached in terms of political economy; see Michael Kammen, *Empire and Interest: The American Colonies and the Politics of Mercantilism* (Philadelphia, 1970); Alison Gilbert Olson, *Making the Empire Work: London and American Interest Groups 1690–1790* (Cambridge, MA, 1992).

[31] Wood, *The Radicalism of the American Revolution*, pp. 214–15. See also, pp. 12–13, 20, 44, 145, 190.

[32] *Ibid.*, p. 229.

of empire, the existence of religious diversity also challenged the notion of community implicit in the character of the post-Reformation state. Many of those who took up the cause of America were non-conformists and latitudinarian Anglicans. Excluded from the institutional mainstream of English society, they nevertheless were the heirs of an intellectual tradition that stressed liberty of thought and rejected civil interference in religious matters. Their demand for a wider toleration revived during those years in which colonial dissent also grew more insistent, and the two related debates were ultimately, in the 1770s, blended together. What was at stake was a full-scale assault on the principles shaping the post-Reformation state. The notion of community was challenged by the distance and diversity of the American colonies, and the possibility of asserting a common good was thought impossible in the absence of some concrete political representation. But this, in turn, hinted at a distinctly different notion of community, one in which the dissenting theorists played a major role. Their philosophical education described the freely inquiring individual as the ideal citizen, and their ideal community was structured so as to further and enhance the possibility of an individual using his or her mind to explore and choose the proper course of action. The government's response was to argue that the security of the community would be imperilled by the private judgment of individuals just as their response to colonial demands was to stress the utility of taxation for a community which no longer existed.

These writers were not revolutionaries; their goal was reform. They did not reject the notion of a common good. Instead, their arguments constitute an attempt at redefinition. The politics of necessity made the security and survival of the community the primary aim of governments and the prerequisite for a citizen wishing to lead a 'good' life. These reformers, on the other hand, focused on the scope of individual action, and the notion of community was described as subordinate and secondary. In the process, the content of the common good necessarily altered. Since they began from a strong notion of individual liberty, especially intellectual, the construction of community and the determination of its aims was now seen to be the responsibility of citizens and not the decision of their governors.

The American side of this story has been told many times over. The British account seems less noble, in large part because it is a tale of short-term failure. The parliamentary reform movement, which was the most powerful practical manifestation of this new notion of the common good, ran into fierce resistance and took half a century to begin bearing fruit. The drive for wider religious toleration also struggled against the established ideology of the post-Reformation state. The account of winners and losers does not, however, concern us here. Throughout, the focus will be on the constellation of ideas embodied in references to the common good and how this shaped and was shaped by contemporary political events.

Chapter 1 begins by sketching the particular Ciceronian arguments to which later writers on statecraft were to have recourse. The subsequent discussion of the problem of necessity and the justification of extreme action in terms of a common good is built on an examination of Italian, Spanish, French and English political texts. While there certainly were specific regional and cultural contexts in which these arguments were deployed and which had a determinative role in their articulation, that writers across Europe were grappling with aspects of this problem ought to tell us something significant about the nature of the seventeenth-century European political experience. Though the problems of, for example, imperial finance, wartime alliance with heretics and extra-parliamentary taxation are distinct, we must perceive their dependence on the concepts embedded in this Ciceronian discourse if we are to appreciate the *contemporary* character of debates on state sovereignty and its limits. In both Catholic and Protestant Europe the idea of security and the decisiveness of the public utility is seen to provide the context for the justification of policy in terms of the common good. The clash between *honestum* and *utile* is pin-pointed as the debate most characteristic of the early modern state. Chapter 2 continues this investigation, but focusing more and more closely on political conditions in mid eighteenth-century Britain. Discussions of party, patriotism and the science of politics demonstrate the way in which the Ciceronian discourse of the good and the useful served as the touchstone of legitimacy in party politics and in the debate about the limits of liberty between opposition and mainstream defenders of the legitimacy of Hanoverian and ministerial governance. One of the themes linking this chapter and the following one is the intellectual convergence of Commonwealth, or Country, opposition writers and those supporting the government on the importance of security and community. The colonial crisis shattered this agreement and, in the process, introduced a period of distinctly different political argument, conducted on different bases and with different goals. Chapter 3 narrows the investigation to the conceptual relationship between the state and the empire. It also provides an overview of the late seventeenth and early to mid-eighteenth-century British debates on war, conquest and colonization and an explanation of the contemporary use of Greek and Roman classical imagery and history. This survey of the various intellectual resources available to those seeking to understand the political and economic relationship between the colonies and metropolis is necessary in order to perceive just how novel was the situation created by the great territorial acquisitions of the Seven Years War. In chapter 4 the implications of the ambiguous constitutional bond between the colonies and the centre become clearer. The uncertain shape of the empire reflected a grave uncertainty about the nature of the underpinning community. This issue, which I call the 'Realm Question', ties the structural problem to the question of sovereignty. 'Virtual' representation expressed the idea of political community forged in the middle ages and wedded to the notion of a 'common good'.[33] By the 1760s, the challenge to the British theory of 'virtual' representation reflected the collapse of confidence in a common transatlantic good and, correspondingly, a challenge to the sovereignty of the parliamentary state. The concluding chapters document a response to this crisis. Chapter 5 turns to the impact of contemporary events on the other significant characteristic of the post-Reformation state. The issue of religious toleration had provoked debate and massacre in the sixteenth and seventeenth centuries. The British government insisted on civil support for a religious establishment because it believed that uniformity enhanced the security of the state. Some Protestant dissenters and Anglican latitudinarians accepted the thrust of this argument but simply denied that they were a threat. Others made a new and more potent claim. From a theory of natural rights that placed great emphasis on the liberty of the individual and his or her intellectual expansion, they were able to derive a notion of personality to suit the new notion of community that emerged in the course of the debate over representation. This natural rights argument – very different from the fashionable 'natural jurisprudence' – provided the content of a notion of individual good which countered the

---

[33] See Black, *Political Thought in Europe, 1250–1450*, p. 163.

establishment's defence of the security of the community. The implications of both contemporary debates were woven into a coherent challenge to the principles underpinning the state by a group of reformers who are examined in chapter 6. Individuals now take priority and give shape to the notion of community whose good is commensurately redefined. The reform of parliamentary representation, the elaboration of a new notion of both empire and personal liberty and the argument for a free trade oriented away from serving a national to satisfying individual goods are some specific contemporary consequences of this redefinition. The War of American Independence has been termed the last act of the Renaissance. Its revolutionary legacy has been the articulation of an alternative to the kind of state that emerged from the era of Reformation and Counter-Reformation.

CHAPTER I

The figure of Cicero

THE HISTORICAL CICERO

On 4 November 1582 Marc-Antoine Muret, Professor of Rhetoric at the University of Rome, inaugurated the academic year, as was customary, with a lecture introducing a central text. After three years' focus on Tacitus, which have been seen as an important turning point in the history of the later Renaissance, Muret chose to lecture on Cicero's *Letters to Atticus*. There was no clear break between a Ciceronian and Tacitean culture separating a republican Renaissance from a princely Baroque.[1] While Tacitus surely gained in importance, and certainly took on a specific role in contemporary political and social thought, Cicero, far from disappearing, was correspondingly revaluated. Those who turned to Tacitus as a teacher of political prudence and guide through the labyrinthine deception of princely posturing were equally disposed to use Cicero as an authority for the extreme measures that national- and self-preservation often demanded. Moreover, even when used for such purposes, Cicero remained 'respectable' because of the impression generated over the long centuries of European engagement with his rhetorical and philosophical works. Thus, whereas one invariably

[1] For the mainstream view, see especially the early twentieth-century essays of Maurice Croll collected in *Style, Rhetoric, and Rhythm*, ed. J. Max Patrick and Robert O. Evans, with John M. Wallace and R. J. Schoeck (Princeton, 1966). His stylistic argument has continued to dominate treatments of Cicero and Seneca in the sixteenth and seventeenth centuries, for instance, most recently, M. A. Stewart, 'The Stoic Legacy in the Early Scottish Enlightenment', in *Atoms, 'Pneuma', and Tranquillity: Epicurean and Stoic Themes in European Thought*, ed. Margaret J. Osler (Cambridge, 1991), pp. 288–9. Even those interested in stressing the importance of Cicero in early modern culture have got this wrong (see Günter Gawlick, 'Cicero and the Enlightenment', *Studies on Voltaire and the Eighteenth Century*, 25 (1963), 657–82. But for the view argued here, see Jean Jehasse, *La renaissance de la critique* (Paris, 1976), p. 208; J. H. M. Salmon, 'Cicero and Tacitus in Sixteenth-Century France', *American Historical Review*, 85 (1980), 322; Paul Morford, *Stoics and Neostoics: Rubens and the Circle of Lipsius* (Princeton, 1991), pp. 73–4.

speaks of the *new* emphasis on Tacitus, which quickly became *Tacitism*, with Cicero one must, instead, think in terms of different emphases at different times. As the most famous, and best documented, politician of antiquity, Cicero's maxims about the conduct of affairs carried the weight of experience. Moreover, because the affirmation of religious principles and, more broadly, the maintenance of morality, was an explicit fundamental responsibility of the ruler of a Counter-Reformation state (but also in Protestant lands where the civil ruler was head of the national church), the collision between the morally good and the politically useful, a regular event for anyone involved in the *vita activa*, had become a matter of state. This was Cicero's territory.

Muret declared that nothing was more useful than the reading of the *Letters to Atticus* because, aside from questions of style, they allowed the reader to enter into the private political discussions of leading men at a time 'in which the government of the world was changed'. This notion, which was to become central to the seventeenth-century cult of Tacitus, was firmly associated with the reading of Cicero. 'For, especially, the admirable prudence and statecraft [*scientia reipublicae*] of Cicero shows itself never more than in his letters.'[2] Muret's concluding exhortation, that 'the integrity of the Latin language, the knowledge of antiquity and prudence in the management of affairs can be obtained from no book better and more easily than from the letters of Cicero', serves as another reminder that the history of a culture is one of emphases rather than replacement.[3]

In the *Letters to Atticus* Muret's students would have encountered Cicero grappling, not only with the demands of practice in a time of extremely fluid politics, but with basic questions about the obligations of good citizens to bad regimes.

Whether one should remain in one's country, even under a tyranny. Whether any means are lawful to abolish a tyranny, even if they endanger

---

[2] Marc-Antoine Muret, *Opera Omnia*, ed. David Rutinken, 4 vols. (Leiden, 1789), I, pp. 322–5. The moralizing use of Tacitus is signalled in the dedication of Lipsius' 1574 edition: 'Tacitus is a penetrating writer, God knows, and a prudent one: and if ever there was a time when men could profit from reading him, it is now.' For other instances of the argument from the similarity of times, see Antonio Possevino, *Biblioteca selecta* and Juan de Mariana *De rege et regis institutione*, both quoted in Giuseppe Toffanin, *Machiavelli e il 'Tacitismo'* (Naples, 1972; 1st edn, 1921), pp. 125–6; David Halstead, 'Distance, Dissolution and Neo-Stoic Ideals: History and Self-Definition in Lipsius', *Humanistica Lovaniensia*, 40 (1991), 262–74. I thank Bill Sherman for bringing this to my attention.

[3] Muret, *Opera*, I, p. 326.

the existence of the State. Whether one ought to take care that one who tries to abolish it may not rise too high himself. Whether one ought to assist one's country, when under a tyranny, by seizing opportunities and by argument rather than by war. Whether one is doing one's duty to the State, if one retires to some other place and there remains inactive, when there is a tyranny; or whether one ought to run every risk for liberty. Whether one ought to invade the country and besiege one's own native town, when it is under a tyranny. Whether one ought to enroll oneself in the ranks of the loyalists, even if one does not approve of war as a means of abolishing tyranny. Whether one ought in political matters to share the dangers of one's benefactors and friends, even if one does not believe their general policy be wise. Whether one who had done good service for his country, and by it has won ill-treatment and envy, should voluntarily put himself into danger for that country, or may at length take thought for himself and his dear ones and avoid struggles against the powers that be.[4]

The alternatives of 'private safety' or 'the public welfare' were posed on a daily basis.[5] Cicero's own answer, given the following month, employed his own definition of the good as *honestum* and the bad as dishonourable (*turpe*) to argue that nothing was less honourable than one who favoured his 'own high place and private interests' over 'the safety and dignity of the country' (*patriae salus et dignitas*).[6]

For Cicero, there was no greater glory than in seeking the security and welfare of the community. True heroes 'must sweat for the common interests; they must expose themselves to enmity; they must often face storms for the sake of the State".[7] Moreover, when Vatinius sought to cast doubt on the popular support for his recall by insinuating that it was ordered not for Cicero's sake, but for the state's (*rei publicae causa*), Cicero responded that the belief that 'the welfare of the State was bound up with the welfare of my self' was the greatest honour for a statesman.[8] In his speeches, Cicero frequently affirmed that the *salus patriae* was the touchstone of all politics. His 'principle of action' was not unvarying but adapted 'to political circumstances, to the tendency of the times, and to considerations of public tranquillity'.[9] Hence, in his famous defences of

---

[4] Cicero, *Letters to Atticus*, tr. E. O. Winstedt, 3 vols. (Cambridge, MA, and London, 1980, 1984), IX.4, II, pp. 187–9. For a similar set of choices, see VIII.11, II, p. 131; IX.10, II, pp. 227–9.

[5] *Ibid.*, I VII.3, II, p. 21.   [6] *Ibid.*, X.4, II, pp. 283–5.

[7] Cicero, *Pro Sestio*, tr. R. Gardiner (Cambridge, MA, and London, 1966), LXVI.139, p. 227.

[8] Cicero, *In Vatinium*, tr. R. Gardiner (Cambridge, MA, and London, 1966) III.7–8, pp. 249–51.

[9] Cicero, *Pro Plancio*, tr. N. H. Watts (Cambridge, MA, and London, 1979), XXXIX.94, p. 531.

Sestius and Milone, Cicero was to argue that their actions were necessary at the time. Sestio's actions were designed for 'restoring the public safety', while their mutual enemy, Clodius, was 'a far more savage enemy of security and the public safety'.[10] The defence of Milone rested not only on an appeal to natural law to justify all measures necessary for self-preservation (IV.10), but on the ancient tradition of honouring tyrannicides.[11] The legitimacy of extra-legal measures, including violence, in pursuit of the security and well-being of the community was also, of course, the substance of Cicero's actions, as he recorded them for posterity in his orations against Catiline.[12]

Cicero's principle of accommodating his practice to political circumstances (*rei publicae status*), however, raised at least the possibility of a conflict between the morally right and the politically useful. In the teachings of the old Stoa, *honestum* and *utile* were polar opposites, the one embracing all that was honourable, beautiful, virtuous and natural and the other the deficiencies of base reality. Cicero had identified himself as a follower of the late Academy and so allowed himself space for eclecticism. While preserving the language of stoic morality he rejected its dogmatic assertion of human moral self-control and purity. In his address *Pro Murena*, Cicero took the prosecutor, Cato, as an example of the harshness – 'the almost superhuman qualities' – demanded by the old Stoics. Among their doctrines was the belief that 'the wise man is never moved by favour, never forgives anyone's misdeed; only the fool or the trifler feels pity; a real man does not yield to entreaty or appeasement; only the wise man is handsome however misshapen, rich however needy, a king however much a slave'.[13] After confessing to having flirted with these doctrines in his youth, Cicero proclaims himself a follower of the more moderate teachings of Plato and Aristotle. Favour *can* legitimately influence the wise, the good man *can* feel pity, there *are* degrees of evil, and it *is* possible both to forgive and uphold principle.[14] This moderated position, the so-called 'middle Stoa', was

---

[10] Cicero, *Pro Sestio*, VI.15, p. 55.

[11] 'And will you, so far from bestowing any distinctions upon the preserver of a great nation and the avenger of a great crime, even suffer him to be haled hence to a felon's death?': *Pro Milone*, tr. N. H. Watts (Cambridge, MA, and London, 1979) XXXIX.80, p. 95.

[12] For example, *In Catilinam*, tr. and ed. C. Macdonald (Cambridge, MA, and London, 1977), I.3, I.30, II.3 and IV.4.

[13] *Pro Murena*, tr. and ed. C. Macdonald (Cambridge, MA, and London, 1977), 61, p. 263.

[14] *Ibid.*, 63, p. 267; 66, p. 269. See Walter Nicgorski, 'Cicero's Paradoxes and his Idea of Utility', *Political Theory*, 12 (1984), 569.

associated with the arguments of Panaetius (*c.*180–111 BC) and made it possible to broaden the realm of ethical discourse to include spheres in which moral issues were less clear-cut and compromise a normal event.[15] Of all Cicero's philosophical writings, *De Officiis* was the most highly praised by early modern writers.[16] It is also the most obviously engaged with the relationship between these Stoic themes of *honestum* and *utile*. But they are no longer perceived as antithetical. Rather, the book's argument reflects Cicero's 'values of political realism and expediency'.[17] In the investigation of this issue in book III of *De Officiis*, Cicero slides between the middle Stoic values of *honestum* and *utile* and the more purely Roman idiom of public and private interest.[18] According to Giorgio Jossa, the *civitatis gubernatio*, the care of the public, was for Cicero the highest expression of moral life as it alone made possible the conditions favourable to the development of virtue. This task was the responsibility of the prince, and his political activity was identified with the *utilitas rei publicae* or *salus rei publicae*.[19] In this account, honesty and utility are recognized as distinct ethical principles, with the latter as the measure of the former. The *honestum* is itself redefined as 'the intermediate duty of the public man, which can be achieved in the real world and which pertains to the *usus vitae*, the needs of daily life'. Including a

[15] P. Milton Valenté, *L'éthique stoïcienne chez Cicéron* (Paris, 1957), pp. 157, 162. For this reference and several of the following I wish to thank Norberto de Sousa; for a thorough account of Cicero's political thought see his '"Societas Civilis": Classical Roman Republican Theory on the Theme of Justice', unpubl. Ph.D. thesis (Cambridge, 1992), esp. ch.2. Marcia Colish has argued persuasively that Cicero, on occasion, abandoned even the position of the middle Stoic Panaetius for one more closely based on Roman custom, political practice and 'Cicero's own vision of politics' (*The Stoic Tradition from Antiquity to the Early Middle Ages*, 2 vols. (Leiden, 1990; 1st edn, 1985), I, pp. 127, 144, 145, 149).

[16] Jean Barbeyrac characterized him as 'a moderate Academic, who does for the most Part, pursue this Method in his *Book of Offices*; where he is sometimes a Stoic, sometimes a Peripatetic'. He praised *De Officiis* as 'the best Treatise of Morality, that all Antiquity has produc'd; the most regular, the most methodical; and what comes the nearest to a full and exact System' (*An Historical and Critical Account of the Science of Morality*, tr. Carew in Samuel Pufendorf, *The Law of Nature and Nations*, tr. B. Kennet (London, 1749), p. 63).

[17] Marcia Colish, 'Cicero's *De Officiis* and Machiavelli's *Prince*', *The Sixteenth-Century Journal*, 9 (1978), 84.

[18] J. Gaudemet, '*Utilitas publica*', *Revue historique de droit français et étranger*, 29 (1951), 469.

[19] Giorgio Jossa, 'L'*Utilitas rei publicae* nel pensiero di Cicerone', *Studi romani*, 12 (1964), 269–72. Nicgorski has written that Cicero's 'general mode of resolving conflicts between virtues is best seen in his establishing the primary importance of the active political life, or the work of the statesman. The primary importance of the work of the statesman is Cicero's most prominent teaching in his moral and political writings ('Cicero's Paradoxes', 565). See also Ettore Lepore, *Il princeps ciceroniano e gli ideali politici della tarda repubblica* (Naples, 1954), pp. 377–8.

'significant amount of social utility' within the notion of *honestum* constituted a decisive reformulation of the Stoic notion of the highest good.[20] Thus, according to Jossa, the morally right was 'a means for realizing the end of the common good and in this finds its purpose and limit'.[21]

In several instances Cicero affirmed that justice reflected what was useful for the public good: '*sed communis utilitatis derelictio contra naturam est; est enim iniusta*'.[22] Not only is there no single norm that we can call just, but 'there are actions which are called just in some cases but not in others when circumstances or times have changed. Above all, there are actions which could, considered on their own, be called just but are no longer just when they do not serve the common good'.[23] Both Jossa and Marcia Colish uphold Cicero's condemnation of the pursuit of private utility at the expense of justice or friendship and his redescription of justice to accord with the dictates of the public utility. 'Thus', writes Cicero, 'there are many things which in and of themselves seem morally right, but which under certain circumstances prove to be not morally right: to keep a promise, to abide by an agreement, to restore a trust may, with a change of utility, cease to be morally right.'[24] Walter Nicgorski has argued that the centrality of the statesman, or Ciceronian *princeps*, 'brings his idea of utility in the form of the rule of necessity into clear and evident operation'. The very 'rule of nature' was founded on utility and equivalent to the rule of necessity: 'to do what is necessary is to act in accord with duty, that is, to act appropriately'.[25] This is what Colish means by asserting that Cicero 'redefines *honestum* as a species of the *utile*'.[26]

Precisely because of his practical experience Cicero knew that concrete issues, such as the ethics of imperial expansion, did not lend themselves to description as either exclusively just *or* useful. Colish argues that in *De Officiis* Cicero identified the *honestum* with the

---

[20] Colish, 'Cicero's *De Officiis* and Machiavelli's *Prince*', pp. 86–7; Colish, *The Stoic Tradition*, I, p. 148.

[21] Jossa, 'L'*Utilitas rei publicae*', p. 274; the citation is from the *De Officiis*, I.10.31.

[22] Cicero, *De Officiis*, III.6.30. Also: 'This, then, ought to be the chief end of all men, to make the interest of each individual and of the whole body politic identical. For, if the individual appropriates to selfish ends what should be devoted to the common good, all human fellowship will be destroyed' (III.vi.26).

[23] Jossa, 'L'*Utilitas rei publicae*', p. 276; for basic examples see *De Officiis*, I.10.31; III.4.19; III.23.89–90; III.25.95.

[24] *Ibid.*, III.25.95, p. 373.   [25] Nicgorski, Cicero's Paradoxes', p. 565.

[26] Colish, *The Stoic Tradition*, I, p. 151.

'common good' and the *utile* with 'individual interest'. 'The reason why they cannot conflict', she writes, 'is that man is part of a larger social and moral whole, which makes radical individualism unacceptable as a basis for ethical action.'[27] The 'norm of social utility' was decisive. Thus, according to Jossa, 'it is necessary to say that, without doubt, what is just is what serves the *res publica*'.[28] Moreover, the performance of those actions that were 'especially useful deeds of public service' was the mark of the truly magnanimous person.[29] A political theory in which communal necessity provides the justification for action and above which there is no other norm describes what came to be called the reason of state. The justifiable may, indeed, be *just*, as is implied in Cicero's argument, or simply 'necessary'. This built a powerful ambiguity into Cicero's thought and into that of all those who were subsequently to confront the demands of security and right. For, while this *salus rei publicae* could be defined in terms closely compatible with justice and equity, namely the 'peace, security and tranquillity' of citizens, it could also mean the 'interest of the State in the most exclusive and brutal sense, such as power, dominion and imperialism'. Under this heading citizens had to be prepared to expend their lives for the preservation and aggrandizement of the state 'by all available means including the subjugation of other peoples or the sacrifice of her own citizens'.[30]

CICERO AND EARLY MODERN STATECRAFT

The century that began with Muret's lectures on Tacitus and Cicero saw an unprecedented proliferation of political writing on the *conservación y aumento* – the preservation and increase – of the entities contemporaries were calling, with increasing frequency, states.[31]

---

[27] Colish, 'Cicero's *De Officiis* and Machiavelli's *Prince*', p. 89; Colish, *The Stoic Tradition*, I, p. 150.

[28] Jossa, 'L'*Utilitas rei publicae*', p. 281.   [29] Nicgorski, 'Cicero', Paradoxes', p. 566.

[30] Jossa, 'L'*Utilitas rei publicae*', p. 287.

[31] As the English translator of a French treatise put it, rather quaintly: 'You may perhaps wonder (gentle Reader) to see mee adde this little abortive to the importunate spawne of so many Bookes, which (as the Souldiers of Cadmus) rise up, and iusle each other, appearing and perishing in a moment.' E. Molinier, *A Mirrour for Christian States: or, a Table of Politick Vertues Considerable amongst Christians*, tr. William Tyruuhit (London, 1635), sig.2v. Ben Jonson's proposed addition to the 'Cries of London' also acknowledged this phenomenon: 'Ripe statesmen, ripe: They grow in every street./At six and twentie, ripe' ('The New Crie', ll.3–4, in Jonson, *The Complete Poems*, ed. George Parfitt (Harmondsworth, 1988; 1st edn, 1975), p. 64).

Here, too, Cicero spoke directly to men of the sixteenth century. In the youthful *De Inventione* he described two aspects of the *utilitas* of commonwealths, power and security. 'Security', he wrote, 'is a reasoned and unbroken maintenance of safety. Power is the possession of resources sufficient for preserving one's self and weakening another.'[32] While, to be sure, the practice of politics had always brought ethics into conflict with the pragmatic pursuit of these two aims, this particular period of European history generated a robust literature that placed the shrewd management of state on the same level that an earlier – and still healthy – tradition had made the exclusive domain of moral virtue. The emphasis on justice in patristic and Thomist definitions of *honestum* were now matched by a more strictly prudential account. The sceptical, prudential maxims of the reason of state writers draw heavily on Tacitus. This has led to the conclusion that, at a time when Machiavelli remained on the Index, reliance on Tacitus provided a vehicle for both defenders and enemies of Machiavelli to address the issues of hard-edged political life.[33] But many of these same men, as well as those for whom Tacitus' ideas and literary style had themselves come to be associated with danger (especially Jesuits, but not at all exclusively), also turned to Cicero. For Cicero was both ideologically and stylistically acceptable and capable of providing solid support for the politics of late sixteenth- and seventeenth-century European statesmen. He was a defender of rectitude, virtue, conservative customs and the importance of a state religion. The 'Counter-Reformation Prince' was, indeed, none other than the Ciceronian *Princeps*.

But there is, perhaps, another general explanation for Cicero's importance to political thinkers at this time: his searching analysis of the relationship between the *honestum* and the *utile*. This discussion, as we will see, occupied a central place in contemporary political culture for several fundamental reasons. First, the basic premise of the post-Reformation state, both Protestant and Catholic, was that religion was necessary for the maintenance and fulfilment of the purpose of political society. There could, therefore, be no sphere of life to which religious teachings did not apply. Politics might have been recognized as a nasty business, but it too had to be conducted

---

[32] Cicero, *De Inventione*, tr. H. M. Hubbell (Cambridge, MA, and London, 1976; 1st edn, 1949), II.lvi.169, p. 337.
[33] See, fundamentally, Toffanin, *Machiavelli e il 'Tacitismo'*; Peter Burke, 'Tacitism'; Kenneth Schellhase, *Tacitus in Renaissance Political Thought*.

under a moral code of divine origin. In Ciceronian terms, this meant that a policy could not be useful if it were contrary to the divine plan. Conversely, something that served God's purposes was necessarily useful to men. A second reason for interest in this specific debate was that all contemporary European states were struggling with the problems of establishing – or removing – central authority. The rebellion of the constituent parts of what Helmut Koenigsberger has described as 'composite' monarchies devastated Spain and England, but France was also wracked by religious and aristocratic rebellions that had a distinct regional character, Italy remained fragmented and seemingly immune to union, while the idea of the Empire collapsed once and for all in the seventeenth century. This conflict between centre and peripheries often translated into the language of a public as opposed to private goods, or in terms of a public utility against private utilities. In either case, the Ciceronian opposition, originally framed in terms of an individual's relationship to a single community, was readily applied to disputes *between* communities. In this chapter, we will focus on this specific theme, which lies at the heart of the political theory of the post-Reformation state. The remainder of the book turns to the 'end' of the story (if one can speak of 'endings' in history), and the unravelling of this model. Britain's crisis of empire and the increasingly radical demands for a wider religious toleration stressed precisely those points in which the claims of utility and good collided with greatest friction. The scope of this work coincides with the lifespan of the post-Reformation state, and its aim is to detail its crisis and, at least, partial rupture in the English-speaking world in the eighteenth century.

In the opening paragraph of *Della ragion di stato* (1589), one of the earliest and most important treatises on this theme, the Papal diplomat and former Jesuit, Giovanni Botero, defined the reason of state as 'concerned most nearly with preservation, and more nearly with extension than with foundation'.[34] Botero believed that 'preservation' was the most difficult of the prince's tasks because it sought to forestall the natural flux of human affairs.[35] For him, and those who followed, the *origin* of the state mattered little beyond what affected its regular management. Pedro de Rivadeneira, the

---

[34] Giovanni Botero, *The Reason of State*, tr. P. J. and D. P. Waley (London, 1956), I.1, p. 3.
[35] *Ibid.*, I.5, p. 5.

Spanish Jesuit, denounced that 'Satanic sect' of *'políticos'* whose
pursuit of the 'conservation of the state' actually brought about its
ruin and that of its rulers.[36] Yet, he too could not deny that there
was a body of prudent rules with which states 'are founded,
increased, governed and conserved' and 'which all princes had
always to have in front of their eyes'.[37] In the end, where Rivadeneira disagreed with the *politiques* was on the means of conserving
a state.

But before we can turn to the means with which Rivadeneira, and
others, believed states were best conserved, we must first understand
what it was that they hoped to conserve. Helmut Koenigsberger's
analysis of the creation of 'composite monarchies' in Renaissance
and early modern Europe highlighted the inherent tensions in this
gently – though not inexorably – centripetal process.[38] The problems created by the dynastic union of Aragon and Castile were the
target of Olivares' proposed 'Union of the Crowns' and the Portuguese and Catalan rebellions the signs of their intractability. Conrad
Russell's account of the 'War of the Three British Monarchies',
rather than the English civil war, reflects the desire to situate this
seventeenth-century conflict within the trajectory of the history of
the early modern British states.[39] This was a problem that contemporaries could not but be aware of.[40] Financial pressures generated by the high costs of military technology and an increasingly

---

36 Pedro de Rivadeneira, *Tratado de la religion y virtudes, Biblioteca de autores espanoles*, LX
   Madrid, 1868), p. 452.
37 *Ibid.*, p. 456.
38 H. G. Koenigsberger *'Dominium regale* or *Dominium politicum et regale*: Monarchies and
   Parliaments in Early Modern Europe', in *Politicians and Virtuosi: Essays in Early Modern
   History* (London and Ronceverte, 1986), pp. 1–25. Most recently, see J. H. Elliott, 'A
   Europe of Composite Monarchies', *Past and Present*, 137 (1992), 48–71.
39 J. H. Elliott, *The Revolt of the Catalans* (Cambridge, 1984; 1st edn, 1963); Elliott, *The
   Count-Duke of Olivares* (New Haven and London, 1986), pp. 191–202 and 244–55; Elliott,
   The Spanish Monarchy and the Kingdom of Portugal 1580–1640', in *Conquest and Coalescence*, ed. Barry Greengrass (London, 1991), pp. 48–67; Conrad Russell, *The Fall of the British
   Monarchies* (Oxford, 1991), pp. 30, 37.
40 John Eliot, for example, wrote that 'if (as yett the are) the[y] should remaine diuided
   kingdomes, whither should the King have greater respect of, sith he cannot give himself
   wholy to both, should he regard England above Scotland because it is the greater and more
   excellent? but Scotland may alleadge that it is his native Countrey, and hath first right
   unto him; and that he was by oath first bound unto it': *De Jure Maiestatis or, a Political
   Treatise of Government*, ed. A. B. Grosart, 2 vols. (London, 1882), II, p. 49 (all citations will
   be from this volume). Also see Henry Parker, *Observation on His Majesties Late Answers and
   Expresses* (London, 1642), p. 36.

ossified fiscal structure stressed precisely the most vulnerable link within the composite monarchy.[41] Thus, in Spain, the clash between the representatives of the centre and those of the peripheries was shaped by the crown's need for financial assistance and the subordinate monarchies' desire to protect their legal privileges.[42] In England, too, the increasing tendency to describe sovereignty as 'balanced' shaped the conflict into one over *who* was to decide when 'necessity' justified the seizure of private property to serve the state.

The preservation of this entity depended on fending off external enemies and preserving internal cohesion. War, political economy and religion described the space in which states were won and lost.[43] At a time of great international instability, with rebellions and open warfare almost continuous in the seventeenth century,[44] foreign relations were dominated by the theme of security. Michael Roberts' account of Swedish policy during the period of the Thirty Years War has shown the extent to which the related goals of *assecuratio* and *satisfactio* dominated the planning of Gustavus Adolphus and his minister Axel Oxenstierna. Territory and money were deemed the only means of assuring the survival of the state.[45] One contemporary historian reported that the Swedes themselves denied that theirs was a war of religion, as the Habsburgs had alleged in order to pre-empt a possible alliance with France, instead affirming that it was a 'war of state, founded on political reasons'.[46] In the years of negotiation preceding the conclusion of the Peace of

---

[41] See Conrad Russell, 'Monarchies, Wars and Estates in England, France, and Spain, c.1580–c.1640', *Legislative Studies Quarterly*, 7 (1982), 205–20.

[42] Elliott, *Revolt of the Catalans*, pp. 118–19.

[43] Obviously, this is schematic, though perhaps no more so than contemporary analyses. For instance, Pierre Charron broke down the princely prudence required for conservation into seven such categories: 'virtue, manners & fashions, counsels, finance, forces, arms & alliances' (*Of Wisdome* (London, 1651), iii.i.preface, p. 333).

[44] Geoffrey Parker, *Europe in Crisis 1598–1648* (London, 1979), p. 73; G. N. Clark, *The Seventeenth Century* (London, 1947), p. 98.

[45] 'Our basic war is for security', said Gustavus in a council debate in 1630. (*Sweden as a Great Power 1611–1697: Government, Society, Foreign Policy*, ed. Michael Roberts (London, 1968), p. 139.) But see also pp. 141, 143–4, 153, 156–9 and Roberts' own clear accounts in *Gustavus Adolphus: A History of Sweden 1611–1632*, 2 vols. (London, 1958), i, pp. 462–3, 640, where Grotius' intellectual support is highlighted; Roberts, 'The Political Objectives of Gustav Adolf in Germany, 1630–2', in *Essays in Swedish History* (London, 1967), p. 84; Roberts, 'Oxenstierna in Germany, 1633–1636', *Scandia*, 48, (1982), p. 78. Also, J. V. Polisensky, *The Thirty Years War*, tr. R. J. W. Evans, (London, 1971), pp. 509–10.

[46] Gaspar Thuillerio, *Il soldato svezzese: historia della guerra tra Ferdinando II imperatore, e Gustavo Adolfo re di Suetia*, tr. Pompeo Bellanda il Vecchio (Venice, 1634), p. 6.

Westphalia the themes of security and satisfaction reappear in the correspondence of the plenipotentiaries.[47]

All of those involved in politics at the time recognized that security and satisfaction had to be purchased. Thus, while Machiavelli's concern with *mantenere lo stato* was a fundamental principle, his out-dated claim that men, not gold, provided the sinews of war was dropped. Theorists of politics across Europe saw all too clearly that without material resources no nation could long endure. War had simply become far too expensive.[48] Botero wrote that 'the power of a state is today judged as much by its wealth in money as by its size' and that this consisted in the wealth of its inhabitants which, in turn, was the sum of agricultural and commercial riches. Worthwhile expenditure was that which conduced to the 'public good' and its antithesis that which brought 'no security to the state'.[49] The Spanish writers known as *arbitristas* are, perhaps, the best known of these early modern political economists.[50] Pedro Fernandez Navarette entitled his fifty-chapter examination of the causes and remedies for the depopulation and impoverishment of Castile the *Conservación de Monarquías*. Interestingly, in discourse 19 he defended the legality of a forced loan when it did not damage the 'salud publica'.[51] Published in 1626, this appeared at precisely the time when Charles I and his ministers actually implemented such a scheme. It, too, was defended in terms of 'necessity' and the 'public good'.[52] Saavedra Fajardo, whose *Idea de un Príncipe Político-Cristiano* was first published in Munich in 1640 where he had been the long-serving Spanish ambassador, warned princes not to 'disdain

[47] See, for example, *Der Französischen Korrespondenzen*, Band 1, 1644, *Acta Pacis Westphalicae*, ed. Ursula Irsigler (Münster, 1979), pp. 824, 836–7, 840. Also the 'draft protocol' in *Protokolle*, Band 6, *Die Beratungen der städtekurie Osnabrük, 1645–1649, Acta Pacis Westphalicae*, ed., Günter Buchstab (Münster, 1981), pp. 743–53.

[48] Here, as elsewhere, Guicciardini left posterity a more useful heritage. See *Ricordi*, no. 149, ed. Emilio Pasquini (Milan, 1984, 1st edn 1975), p. 176. This is, of course, the main theme of Geoffrey Parker's *The Military Revolution* (Cambridge, 1988).

[49] Botero, *The Reason of State*, VII.3, p. 134; I.15, p. 21; VII.8, p. 139. See also Botero's specific suggestions in book VIII. He was later to devote a tract to the subject of the *Greatness of Cities* in which political economy played a major role (1.3, 1.7, II.9, III.3). See also Charron, *Of Wisdome*, III.ii.21–2.

[50] See José Larraz, *La epoca del mercantilismo en Castilla 1500–1700* (Madrid, 1963).

[51] Pedro Fernandez Navarette, *Conservación de Monarquías ... Discursos políticos* (Madrid, 1626), p. 114.

[52] See Charles' *Declaration of the True Causes which moved His Majestie to Assemble and after Forced him to Dissolve the Two Last Meetings in Parliament*, pp. 22–3, quoted in Richard Cust, *The Forced Loan and English Politics 1626–1628* (Oxford, 1987), pp. 33, 47–9.

economics, because on it depends your conservation'.[53] Beyond a conventional account of the virtues of princes, Fajardo added 'the integrity of the Magistracy, the wise choice of ministers, the maintenance of customs and privileges, the education of youth, modesty or frugality of the nobility, purity of coin, augmentation of commerce and industry, obedience of the people, concord, abundance and wealth'.[54] His contemporary, Fernandez de Villareal, was explicit: 'The high grandeur of a state consists in its armies and navies; these acquire for it riches and conserve its reputation, whether by conquest or by commerce.' Later, he added, that 'Commerce is one of the nerves of the commonwealth, and perhaps it is the most important, for the utility which all receive from it is great. Without it all riches are consumed, all grandeur is finished.'[55] Jonathan Israel has shown how the Spanish government sought to put these ideas into practice by engaging the Dutch in a debilitating commercial war.[56] In his advice-text intended for Olivares, Balthasar Alamos de Barrientos laid out the principles of a maritime economic war and concluded that piracy and boycott were cheap and necessary. All 'great things', he writes, 'have inconveniences and injustices, but are recompensed by the public good'.[57] The republican John Hall, writing in England in 1654, derived national self-preservation from personal, and the quest for national 'plenty' from that for personal advantage. Because the 'particulars' and 'necessity' of each kingdom were different, there would be distinct national aims.[58] This is the basis of the approach to political economy that came to be called mercantilism. D. N. Pearson has described it as, 'after all, really just a policy of economic nationalism in a context of new powerful

---

[53] Saavedra Fajardo, *Idea de un príncipe político-cristiano representada en cien empresas* (Murcia, 1985), no.69, p. 526. This is a facsimile of the expanded second, Milanese edition of 1642.

[54] Fajardo, *Idea*, p. 438.

[55] Fernandez de Villareal, *El político cristiano o discursos políticos* (Pamplona, 1642); citation is from the French translation *Le politique très-chrestien ou Discours politiques sur les actions principales de la vie de seu Monr l'Eminentissime Cardinal duc de Richelieu* (Paris, 1647), p. 137, 145, illustrating that, even though at war, Spanish observations on politics were congenial to French politiques.

[56] Jonathan I. Israel, 'Spain, the Spanish Embargoes, and the Struggle for the Mastery of World Trade, 1585–1660', in *Empires and Entrepôts: The Dutch, the Spanish Monarchy and the Jews, 1585–1713* (London and Ronceverte, 1990), pp. 189–212; Israel, *The Dutch Republic and the Hispanic World, 1606–1661* (Oxford, 1986, 1st edn 1982), p. 205.

[57] Balthasar Alamos de Barrientos, *Advertencias políticos sobre lo particular y público de esta monarchía*, Hispanic Society of America, HC 380/80, f. 101v.

[58] John Hall, *Of Government and Obedience, as They Stand Directed and Determined by Scripture and Reason* (London, 1653), p. 158.

territorial states, an obvious matter of each for itself, designed especially to build up the supply of bullion'.[59]

Finally, theorists of state power in both northern and southern Europe agreed on the necessity of an alliance between the spiritual and secular authorities. The standard claim was that religion complemented the civil ruler's quest for 'conservación y quietud'[60] and therefore 'the state can have no secure foundation without it'.[61] Maintenance of the religion of the state was incumbent upon the ruler.[62] Here the difference with the loathed Machiavelli was a matter of commitment: where the Florentine had addressed the importance of 'civic religion', these later writers demanded of the ruler genuine faith. 'Why then should a Christian prince close the door of his secret council-chamber against Christ and the Gospels and set up a reason of State contrary to God's law, as though it were a rival altar?'[63]

The rulers of composite states used religion to bind together components otherwise kept distinct by law, and often by interest as well. It was precisely the *politique* division between the quest for the *la felicidad pública* and the practice of religion and virtue that threatened the monarch's maintenance of unity, the preservation of his state.[64] In a Britain divided and propelled into warfare by religious and political disagreement between its components, Archbishop Sancroft distinguished between the 'Pseudo-Policy' of those for whom religion and politics were separate and 'that science, which is ever built upon piety and prudence; for upon these solid Bases, your wise Architect delights to raiseth the glorious superstructure of government in a Prince, and subjection in a people: so knitting the Interest of both with reciprocall mixture, that the welfare of the one may be involv'd with the good of the other'.[65] In France, Richelieu's defenders saw the Huguenots as 'a people who were enemies of the

[59] D. N. Pearson, 'Merchants and States', in *The Political Economy of Merchant Empires*, ed. James D. Tracy (Cambridge, 1991), p. 92. Also Nannerl Keohane, *Philosophy and the State in France*, p. 160.

[60] Rivadeneira, *Tratado*, I,1, p. 459.   [61] Botero, *Reason of State*, II.16, p. 66.

[62] John Eliot wrote that, 'Religion being then the Basis, foundation and pillar of the State: wch taken away all States come to ruine, he must haue the charge of religion to whose care & guidance the sterne of State is committed', *De Jure Maiestatis*, p. 135.

[63] Botero, *Reason of State*, II.15, p. 64. Also, Fernandez de Villareal, *Le politique très-chrestien*, p. 33; Fajardo, *Idea*, nos. 24, 27.

[64] See Jeronimo Caballero's dedicatory letter prefaced to Rivadeneira's *Tratado*, p. 454.

[65] Russell, *The Fall of the British Monarchies*, p. 526; William Sancroft, *Modern Policies, Taken from Machiavel, Borgia, and Other Choice Authors, by an Eye Witnesse* (4th edn, London, 1653), sig.A12r.

order and Police' of the realm.[66] The Huguenot rebellion provoked the same recourse to the verses from Romans XIII that recur in English texts of the period.[67] The vigour with which relations with heretics was condemned stemmed directly from the perception that religious disagreement amounted to, or would eventually produce, civil war.[68] This alliance between the 'Ordonnances of Religion and the Maxims of State' was concerned with the appearance of the public space. Sometimes, therefore, private religious diversity could be accepted even by those who denounced it in principle.[69] 'It is not within the purview of the Prince to ferret out the secrets of souls; it is sufficient that the subject obey his Laws, that he observes his commandments without the task of extending his Empire even unto the depths of thought and the secrets of the heart.'[70]

The preservation of the integrity of the community, whether by conquest, commerce or conformity, was the aim of statesmen and those writers most keenly aware of the challenges facing civil rulers. But, when pressed to explain the recourse to the various means employed in the pursuit of *conservación y aumento*, these same writers fell back on what was always the standard justification for the use of political power: the service of the good of the community. Lipsius, in *Politicorum*, gave a succinct definition of the purpose of government: '*the good of the subject* ... which is no other thing then the commoditie, safetie, and preservation of subjects. For "a gouvernour of a state, ought to propose, and set before him, the happie life of his citizens" (Cicero lib.5 De Rep) that the same may be "strengthened

---

[66] Guez de Balzac, quoted in F. E. Sutcliffe, *Guez de Balzac et son temps* (Paris, 1957), p. 99.

[67] For example, see the *Remonstrance salutaire aux rebelles de Montauban, & de la Rochelle ... sur leur desobeyssance & resistance au roy* (Paris, 1621), p. 3.

[68] 'From disloyalty, then, and disobedience are born rebellions against princes, uproar and division of realms and the conflagration and desolation of republics – and it could be no less. For just as discord in matters of faith creates discord in the souls and wills of believers, this same discord and contrariness could not but stir up disagreement and civil wars, like evil children from an evil mother and evil effects from an evil cause' (Rivadeneira, *Tratado*, 1.27, p. 500). Examples of the terrible consequences of the 'false reason of state' which permitted the practice and preaching of heretics could be found in Germany, Bohemia, Poland, Transylvania, Hungary, England, Scotland and, worst of all, in France. Despite his varied condemnations (1.18, p. 484; 1.23, pp. 491–2; 1.25, p. 496), Rivadeneira did admit that if the realm was overwhelmed by heresy 'Christian prudence taught to dissimulate in order not to do more damage than good' (1.26, p. 499).

[69] de Villareal, *Politique très-chrestien*, p. 159. See Paul Morford's discussion of Lipsius' similar argument for public religious uniformity, by coercion if necessary (*Stoics and Neostoics* (Princeton, 1991), p. 108) and his corresponding acceptance of private heterodoxy (p. 114); and Robert Bireley on Rivadeneira's similar convolutions: *The Counter-Reformation Prince* (Chapel Hill, NC, 1990), p. 123.

[70] de Villareal, *Politique très-chrestien*, p. 113.

in wealth, aboundaunt in riches, renowned and magnificent in glorie, honest and venerable thorow vertue (ibid)"'.[71] References to the public or common 'good', sometimes in the preferred seventeenth-century idiom of 'interest' or 'utility', dot the theoretical landscape in seventeenth-century discussions of the basis of political authority, often, like Lipsius, referring back to Cicero. The identification of government with the public good or national interest had the consequence of blackening the pursuit of particular or private interests, which were seen as serving the centrifugal forces that continually beset the early modern composite states. Moreover, the emphasis on security reflected a different notion of liberty.[72]

The lawfulness of a ruler 'is no other then that hee truly thinketh it to bee for the good of the common; that is, for the geatest good, all things considered'.[73] The public good was the only restraint on a prince and constituted 'the essentiall and inseparable quality' of his office.[74] Precisely because it was recognized that 'the princes interest will always override every other argument',[75] both the apologists and the critics of strong rule sought to define that interest in terms of its service of the public good. John Eliot, aware of the composite nature of the Stuart monarchy, warned against the 'transposition of those duties, an inversion of those offices' that put the private interests before the public, the particular before the general. He quoted the authority of Cicero to argue that an outright traitor was no worse 'than hee that, for his owne safetie and advantage, deserts ye common interests'.[76] The 'conservation of the whole, the publick

---

71 Lipsius, *Sixe Bookes of Politickes or Civil Doctrines*, tr. William Jones, (London, 1594), pp. 22–3.
72 'It is not the end of liberty that anyone should govern, because government ought to be by those of merit, but the observance of good laws and good orders, which are more secure in a free society than under the power of the one or the few. And this is the deception which has so tormented our city, because it is not enough to the people to be free and secure, they want also to rule' (Guicciardini, *Ricordi*, no. 109, p. 135).
73 Thomas White, *The Grounds of Obedience* (London 1655), p. 101.
74 Eliot, *De Jure Maeistatis*, p. 85; Molinier, *Mirrour*, ii.17 ('Of love to publick good, being the last duty of Politick Iustice towards the publick'), p. 190.
75 Botero, *Reason of State*, ii.6, p. 41; Roger Manwaring's scandalous judgment was that, because 'the urgent and pressing Necessities of State' could not wait for the meetings of Parliament, if a particular action was for either his 'Security' or the 'Safety and Protection' of his dominions, the king could act unilaterally (*Religion and Allegiance: In Two Sermons* (London, 1709; 1st edn 1628), p. 15. The eighteenth-century reprint was occasioned by the Sacheverell controversy, in which, as will be observed below, this early modern debate is refashioned in the context of the revolution and establishment of the new state.
76 John Eliot, *Monarchie of Man*, ed. A. B. Grosart, 2 vols. (London, 1882), II, p. 182 (all references will be to this volume). This citation, from *De Finibus*, iii.xix, was one of the most common of the era.

utilitie and good' was an obligation incumbent upon rulers and ruled since, 'if the whole ffabricke be dissolv'd, how can a part subsist?'[77] It was precisely because they were no longer tied by a common good that war had exploded 'throughout the Three Nations'. Marchamont Nedham emphasized that the Duke of Rohan's famous dictum that 'Les Princes commandent aux peuples, et l'interêt commande aux princes' was a warning to the private interests that were rending the kingdom. It was, he believed, to no one's interest to support Charles, 'the Interest of a Public Enemy, upon supposition of attaining thereby their own and the Public Welfare'. Instead, agreeing with a polemical opponent, he declared that ' "the real good of the Nation consists not in the private benefit of single men, but the advantage of the Public and that it is made up, not by the welfare of any one Party, but of all." '[78]

This notion of a 'public' or community was the starting point for these discussions of appropriate practice. Because of the priority of the community, it was recognized that there was a danger that the very means of preservation could actually destroy the reciprocal relationships that constituted it by setting off one group against others, all in the name of public utility. 'Friendship', a concept of great importance for the neo-Stoic writers describing a post-republican vision of citizenship, expressed the notion of reciprocity that could be imperilled by the unadulterated pursuit of interest. Innocent Gentillet wrote that 'Friendship (says Cicero) is the true bond of all human society and whoever wishes to eliminate friendship between men (as does Machiavelli between princes) would have to eliminate all pleasure, consolation, contentment and assurance that could exist among men.'[79] Fajardo explicitly declared that 'In republics friendship is more important than justice because if all were friends there would be no need for laws nor judges. Even if all were good, they could not live if they were not friends. The greatest good man possesses is friendship.'[80] And yet, the role of friendship

---

[77] Eliot, *Monarchie of Man*, p. 12.

[78] Marchmont Nedham, *Interest Will Not Lie. Or, a View of England's True Interest* (London n.d.), p. 3. The adaptation of Rohan for English matters was a signal contribution. Many of the numbers of Nedham's *Mercurius Britannicus* and *Mercurius Politicus* dealt with the problem of interest in both international and domestic affairs. Hall noted that the pursuit of private commercial interests was as damaging to the national interest as was the pursuit of private political manoeuvres (*Government and Obedience*, p. 160).

[79] Innocent Gentillet, *Discours, sur le moyens de bien gouverner et maintenir en bonne paix un royaume ou autre principauté* (n.p., 1576), p. 380.

[80] Fajardo, *Idea*, no. 91, p. 670.

was at least slightly subversive of the defence of community, for its most influential spokesmen, Montaigne and Lipsius, used it to mark the limen of private space. True friendship was distinguished from that based on expediency, but it was directed inwards, not towards the *patria*. In this way, the new kind of selfish patriotism described by Keohane and Tuck could be expressed in terms of a common good, but with fewer of the associations that such a declaration would have had for the Jesuit Rivadeneira, for example. The emphasis on friendship in seventeenth-century moral and political thought, bound up as it was with the development of neo-Stoic ideas, marks the incremental step that Nicholas Phillipson has described as the world of sodality, conversation and friendship in the 'coffee houses, taverns and salons' of eighteenth-century Edinburgh and Glasgow.[81] This same passage from a strong, perhaps even 'republican', sense of community, to one in which the public world now stands at a remove can be registered a century earlier in some English attitudes to the disruptions of the civil war and in the academies of Venice.[82]

The dissociation of community into calculating special 'interest' groups was perceived to be such a danger that a number of political commentators took to denouncing the unscrupulous who used the public as a screen for the pursuit of precisely those actions that were inimical to any common good. Rohan had written that no war made in France under the 'pretext of the common good' had anything other than a 'particular interest' as the real object.[83] According to Jean Sirmond the public good was 'a mark that veiled' the fact that great magnates were motivated solely by thought of private

---

[81] Nicholas Phillipson, 'Adam Smith as a Civic Moralist', in *Wealth and Virtue*, ed. Istvan Hont and Michael Ignatieff (Cambridge, 1983), p. 189.

[82] See Adriana McCrea, 'Reason's Muse; Andrew Marvell, R. Fletcher, and the Politics of Poetry in the Engagement Debate', *Albion*, 23 (1991), 655–80; Ruth Nevo, *The Dial of Virtue: A Study of Poems on Affairs of State in the Seventeenth Century* (Princeton, 1963); Maren Rostvig, *The Happy Man* (Oslo, 1954). Also, the prison compositions of John Eliot, *The Monarchie of Man* and Henry Maarten, *Familiar Letter to his Lady of Delight* (London, 1663). For Venice, see Iain Fenlon and Peter N. Miller, *The Song of the Soul: Understanding 'Poppea'* (London, 1992), chs. 5 and 6. I hope to explore the implications of this development in the cultural history of early modern Europe.

[83] Rohan, *Discours politiques du duc de Rohan faits en divers temps sur les affaires qui se passoient* (Amsterdam, 1646), quoted in Salmon, 'Rohan and the Interest of State', *Renaissance and Revolt* (Cambridge, 1987), p. 101. A century earlier, near the beginning of this tradition, Guicciardini advised rulers to bring their aims into line with those of the public good (*Ricordi*, no. 142).

advantage.[84] In one of Nicolas de Campion's dialogues attacking Richelieu's Machiavellian policy an interlocutor suggests that the assertion that the public utility was served by 'these most violent means' was in fact nothing other than a 'manière de parler' and only served to 'authorize injustice'.[85] As for England, L. J. Reeve has written that there, too, it 'was commonly held at court, that critics of Charles' policies were using the language of public interest to disguise their private ends'.[86] Thomas White, writing at the start of the Protectorate, denounced the 'intricate labyrinth of equivocation wherein wee endlessly erre' in using the term common good without recognizing that it included personal good, as well. Without any clarification of its referents, 'to cry, *The Common Good*, is a meere deceit and flattery of words'.[87]

Lurking within this appeal to the common good, though often not addressed directly, was a point of cardinal importance. Public utility could often be purchased only at the price of private utility.[88] The implications of this become clearer if we examine the claim that often lay behind these prolific declarations of the common good: Cicero's declaration that *Salus populi suprema lex esto*. This phrase, from *De Legibus* book III, captured Cicero's own intense commitment to the conservation of a state ruled by law and his recognition that sometimes this required extra-legal measures. William Reynolds' *De iusta reipublicae Christianae in reges impios et haereticos* (1590), a piece of Catholic resistance literature which has been called 'the most comprehensive discussion of political theory' of the Catholic League, preserves this Ciceronian context as completely as in the Catholic and Protestant literature of legitimacy.[89] Starting

---

[84] Jean Sirmond, *Advis du François fidelle au mal-contens nouvellement retirez de la Cour* (n.p., n.d.), p. 3, quoted in Sutcliffe, *Guez de Balzac*, p. 165; *Le Coup d'Estat de Louis XIII* (Paris, 1631), p. 40.

[85] Nicolas de Campion, *Entretiens sur divers sûjets d'histoire, de politique net de morale* (Paris, 1704), pp. 407, 421. These were written between 1640 and 1650.

[86] L. J. Reeve, *Charles I and the Road to Personal Rule* (Cambridge, 1989), p. 98.

[87] White, *Grounds of Obedience*, p. 71. He later explains that while for individuals the common good was determined by 'the good of their private persons', the ruler's 'aime is at the universall good of the whole eternal body of the Commonwealth' abstracted 'from his private good' (pp. 77–8).

[88] For example, Guez de Balzac wrote that 'The public utility often does damage to that of the particular' (*Le Prince* in *Oeuvres complètes*, 2 vols. (Paris, 1665), II, p. 63) and Gabriel Naudé declared that the maxims of state could not be justified by the civil law or the law of nations, 'but solely by considering the good and the public utility, which often supercedes that of the particular' (*Considerations sur les coups d'estat* (n.p., 1639), p. 93.

[89] The book was mined by Robert Parsons for *A Conference about the Next Succession to the Crowne of Ingland* (1594), an oft-reprinted work that Charles McIlwain described as 'the chief

from the declaration in *De Officiis* book I that the claims of the *patria* went beyond even those of children, relations and friends, Reynolds concluded that the defence of the state warranted greater energy even than the defence of one's family; 'It is, therefore right and honourable to kill a tyrant hostile to our country. This is clearly taught by that same good man, and outstanding magistrate and very famous philosopher.' Cicero's comment in book III that no faith need be kept with pirates or those who spurned the law of nature was turned to a rejection of tyranny.[90] Tyrannicide was an example of the highest form of bravery, defined by Cicero (in book I of *De Officiis*) as one possessed by a mind that 'fights not for its own convenience but for the common safety and utility, always clings to justice, does not commit but repels injustice'. Reynolds concludes, in what seems a pastiche of Cicero's own speeches:

> Whoever steadfastly opposes a tyrant fulfills the most important duty of true bravery. For he fights for equality, justice and the laws of the fatherland against the most unjust force of one man, and dutifully wards off injuries offered to the republic, since he himself, as a member of the body politic, is bound by the law of nature to the preservation of the whole, and clearly with danger to his own life achieves the safety of the republic.[91]

Despite its specific role here, this Ciceronian image of the true lover of his country was shared by Christians across Europe.[92] Hence the powerful appeal of the tag *Salus populi*. It graced the title pages and text of so many early modern tracts about the claims of sovereigns and subjects precisely because it captured a set of beliefs about the relationship of individual and community upon which the legitimacy of all governments rested. Moreover, in terms of practical argument it was capable of being used as a justification of either monarchical or aristocratic power.

storehouse of facts and arguments drawn upon by nearly all opponents of royal claims for a century, Protestant as well as Catholic' (Introduction to *The Political Works of James I* (Cambridge, MA, 1918), p. li, cited by F. J. Baumgartner, *Radical Reactionaries: The Political Thought of the French Catholic League* (Geneva, 1975), p. 145).

90 Guilielmus Rossaeus [William Reynolds or Rainalds], *De iusta reipublicae Christianae in reges impios et haereticos* (Paris, 1590), p. 397. See Baumgartner, *Radical Reactionaries*, pp. 146–7, for the question of attribution.

91 Rossaeus, *De Iusta Reipublicae*, p. 404. See also Cicero, *De Officiis*, IV.iv.19.

92 Writing in the Tower, Eliot cited Cicero out of *De Oratore* to the effect that 'those that defend their Contrey to the utmost of their powers, those yt are ready to rescue from all dangers the Commonwealth, & safety, of whatsoever order or degree, however they were borne, are optimates & nobles; ther is noe priviledge beyond them, none yt is equall unto that, but these above the rest, who support it with their necks, as Atlas did the Heavens': *Monarchie of Man*, p. 184.

Pierre Charron, in *De la sagesse*, had adopted Lipsius' argument that sometimes rulers had to 'mingle prudence with justice'. But the exercise of princely power was always restrained, at least in theory, by the necessities of the common good which defined the duty of the prince. The translator inserted, after the Ciceronian tag, the following verses in charming Elizabethan English:

> Salus populi suprema lex esto.
> Princes counsels, love and hate,
> Do homage to the Law of State,
> That people's safety have no mate.
> Other laws do very well,
> But people's safety bears the bell.[93]

It is this same understanding which seems to guide Justice Fleming's decision in Bate's case (1606). He declared that the 'absolute power' of the king could only be 'applied to the general benefit of the people, and is *salus populi*'.[94] The fifth proposition of the Lords' answer to the Commons in 1628 declared that royal discretionary power, here referring to the ability to imprison, existed '*ad communem totius populi salutem, et non ad destructionem*'. Where 'the security of his Majesty's Royal person' or 'the common safety of his people' were threatened, the 'reason of State' gave the king freedom of action.[95] In France, this argument was most powerfully articulated. Philippe de Béthune pronounced that 'It is always the prince's duty to procure the public good. The safety of the people is the supreme law according to which the prince should regulate all his actions.'[96] Louis Machon, in his unpublished *Apologie pour Machiavelle*, was unequivocal: 'A prince, a sovereign, and all the most powerful ministers of state should have no other aim nor guide to their duty than the safety of the people, the public utility, and the preservation of the state. *Suprema lex salus populi*.'[97]

But the belief that the well-being and survival of the populace was the measure of government could easily support claims for popular pre-eminence. Donald Kelley has asserted that in the sixteenth

---

[93] Charron, *Of Wisdome*, iii.ii.4, pp. 337–8.
[94] *State Trials*, eds. W. Cobett and T. H. Howell, 33 vols (London, 1809–26), ii, p. 389.
[95] Quoted in David S. Berkowitz, 'Reason of State in England and the Petition of Right', in *Staatsräson*, ed. Roman Schnur (Berlin, 1975), p. 197.
[96] Philippe de Béthune, *Le conseiller d'estat, ou recueil des plus générales considerations servant au maniment des affaires publiques* (Paris, 1631), p. 399.
[97] Louis Machon, *Apologie pour Machiavelle* (1642), fols. 423–4, quoted in Church, *Richelieu and the Reason of State*, pp. 426–8.

century the tag 'was virtually a code phrase for lese-majesty'.[98] In
the war between parliament and the crown, the *salus populi* could be
found on all sides. In a 'popular state', John Hall affirmed, justice
and equity served the public utility and the ground of equity was
'*Salus populi suprema lex*'.[99] Calybute Downing observed that when
the infringement of law leaves the existing ones 'too short for your
security', the law of nations remains, and its assurance that '*salus
populi* should be *sola, et suprema lex*'.[100] One defender of the
monarchy, John Maxwell, Bishop of Killala, denied that the maxim
could be used to uphold popular control of the monarch.

But this is not that which is meant in *Salus populi suprema lex esto*; The
meaning is, that the Kingdome or State, not onely possibly and probably,
but really and existently may be such, that the Soveraigne must exerce and
exercise [*sic*] an Arbitrary power, not stand upon private mens interest, or
transgressing of Lawes, made for the private good of individuals; but for the
preservation of it selfe and the publick may break thorow all Lawes. This
case may be, and sometimes is, as when sudden forraine invasion, or strong
home-bred sedition threaten King and Kingdome, State and Republique
with present and almost unavoidable ruine.[101]

Looking back from a comfortable distance on the personal rule of
the 1630s, Clarendon observed that the same principles that Charles
had used to extend his authority beyond his bounds were later
employed to deprive him of sovereignty. Necessity served to legitimate the unprecedented steps taken by the adversaries, 'and the
same maxim of *Salus populi suprema lex*, which had been used to the
infringing the liberties of the one, made use of for the destroying
the rights of the other'.[102]

Because of the great value placed on preserving the safety of
the community, it was believed, by both the orthodox defenders of the
state and their critics, that, in time of dire need, statute law could be
temporarily ignored. 'Necessity' was a word that resounded through
the writings of contemporary political councillors. In Spain, Neces-

---

[98] Donald R. Kelley, *The Beginning of Ideology* (Cambridge, 1981), p. 310.
[99] Hall, *Government and Obedience*, p. 147.
[100] Calybute Downing, *A Sermon Preached to the Renowned Company of Artillery* (London, 1641),
pp. 36–7, quoted in J. P. Sommerville, *Politics and Ideology in England, 1603– 1640* (London,
1986), p. 74.
[101] John Maxwell, *Sacro-sancta regum majestas: or, the Sacred and Royall Prerogative of Christian
Kings* (Oxford, 1644), p. 176.
[102] Clarendon, *History*, 6 vols. (Oxford, 1888), II, pp. 85–6, quoted in Robert Ashton, 'From
Cavalier to Roundhead Tyranny, 1642–9, *Reactions to the English Civil War 1642–1649*, ed.
John Morrill (London, 1982), p. 185.

sity was believed to trump the fiscal privileges of the Cortes 'because the salvation of the people is the supreme law'.[103] The French declaration of war on Spain in 1635 made plain that her alliances were determined in accordance with *La necessité de l'Estat*.[104] Arguably, the decisiveness of the unadorned argument from necessity alone distinguishes French from Spanish thinking about the reason of state in the first three decades of the century. In Sweden, Oxenstierna complained that the French were miserable allies, committing hostile acts 'under a mask of friendship'. 'Our late King [Gustavus Adolphus]', he wrote, 'often tore his hair at the impertinences he had to put with from them. But what could he do? Necessity is a great argument, and for a handful of gold one must often sacrifice reputation.'[105] The French, meanwhile, compelled to justify their alliance with the heretical Lutherans, asserted that 'Extreme necessity . . . rejects no type of help, and, without offending one's conscience or scruples, one may make alliances with infidels.'[106]

Whereas in France alliance with Protestants was defended on the grounds of 'necessity', in England 'necessity' lay at the heart of the volatile disputes between parliament and the crown over the latter's capacity to seize private property without the former's consent.[107] John Eliot argued that the power of the prince over the goods of his subjects was limited by the requirement of 'the good of the publicke State. He must not exercise his prerogative over the goods of his subjects *nisi in ordine ad salutem publicam*; where the safety of the State requires it'. Yet, in time of necessity, when the preservation of the state could only be purchased by their private loss, subjects had to cooperate.[108] The question of the time was, as John Sommerville

---

[103] Jeronimo de Ceballos, *Arte real para el buen governo de los reyes y príncipes, y de sus vasallos* (Toledo, 1623), fol. 114, quoted in Elliott, *Olivares*, p. 149.

[104] Jacques Ferrier, *La Catholique d'Estat*, p. 147. For more on this issue see José Maria Jover, *1635: Historia de una polémica y semblanza de una generación* (Madrid, 1949), p. 74.

[105] Quoted in Roberts, *Sweden as a Great Power* (London, 1968), p. 154.

[106] Daniel de Priézac, *Défense des droits et prérogatives des Roys de France*, quoted in Church, *Richelieu and the Reason of State*, p. 373.

[107] See the valuable discussions of Richard Tuck, '"The Ancient Law of Freedom": John Selden and the Civil War', in Morrill, *Reactions to the English Civil War 1642–1649* (London, 1982), pp. 137–62, and David S. Berkowitz, 'Reason of State in England and the Petition of Right, 1603–29', pp. 165–213.

[108] Eliot, *De Jure Maiestatis*, pp. 171–2. 'And private men must patiently sitt downe wth such losse, wch tends to the preservation of the publicke State. And if the State be not able to purchase peace in extremitie, they must exact uppon private mens estates, & take their goods to redeeme the safety of the whole wth all; and lay upon heauy exactions, wch were most uniust in tyme of peace, but allowable in the extremity of the State' (p. 172). See also, Sommerville, *Politics and Ideology*, pp. 149–50.

has noted, *who* was to decide when that moment of extremity had been reached: 'Who is to decide on necessity? who is to determine the common good?'[109] Given the ineluctable forensic power of the *salus populi* claim, these seventeenth-century debates about the legitimacy of reason of state were, in effect, questioning the legitimacy of representation. Could an individual, such as a king, justifiably claim the power to act on behalf of the public? Sorting out the issue of representation is crucial to Hobbes' discussion of sovereignty, for example, and the centrality of the debate on representation in later eighteenth-century Britain marks the crisis for the contemporary understanding of sovereignty.

Perhaps the most articulate exposition of this issue arose in the dispute over ship money. The crown's unilateral decision to issue writs ostensibly designed to provide for the maritime defence of the kingdom highlighted, according to Conrad Russell, two basic issues. First, the breakdown of government by consent and, second, the gulf between the crown's perception of the necessary cost of defence and the population's.[110] The first writs were issued in 1634 though only by 1638 did the level of receipts dwindle. Clarendon observed that 'imminent necessity and public safety were convincing persuasions' at the start, but eventually ship money was perceived to be 'a spring and magazine that should have no bottom, and for an everlasting supply of all occasions'.[111]

The test case brought by John Hampden turned on precisely this issue. The king's letter detailed the threat to the 'safety' of the realm, 'the preservation whereof is only intrusted to our care'.[112] Oliver St John, opening the case for the defendant, agreed that 'in this business of Defence, the *suprema potestas*, is inherent in his majesty, as part of his crown and kingly dignity'. But precisely because the conservation of the state was recognized to be the responsibility of the prince, the question at stake was not '*de persona*', but '*de modo*, by what medium or method this supreme power, which is in his majesty, doth infuse and let out itself into this particular'.[113] In general, he argued, the exercise of the royal prerogative was guided

[109] Johann Sommerville, 'Ideology, Property and the Constitution', in Cust and Hughes, *Conflict in Early Stuart England*, p. 56.
[110] Russell, *Fall of the British Monarchies*, p. 7.
[111] Clarendon, *History*, I, p. 85. For the fullest recent account see, Kenneth R. Andrews, *Ships, Money and Politics: Seafaring and Naval Enterprise in the Reign of Charles I* (Cambridge, 1991).
[112] *State Trials*, III, p. 843.　　　[113] *Ibid.*, III, p. 860.

by the needs of the '*patrimonia et bona publica*, to be employed for the common good'.[114]

Edward Littleton, responding for the crown, addressed himself to the distinction suggested by St John. There was no question that the king could impose a charge 'for conquest or conservation of foreign countries or territories beyond the seas', for responding to foreign aggression, for increase of the royal revenue, and, certainly, 'for preservation of the kingdom'. 'But the question is, *Quando salus regni periclitabatur*', when is the safety of the realm endangered? For, once extremity was admitted, there could be no questioning the king's right to seize private property for the public utility.[115]

> The fundamental reason is the exact rule of the law in the 10th Report cited by that learned gentleman, Mr St John, *salus populi suprema lex*. All other positive laws are subordinate to this law, and are to be regulated by it. We are not to talk of positive laws, till we have a kingdom to use them.[116]

As he explained, there could be no private gain at a time of public loss.[117] Littleton cited the classic examples of an urban fire and storm at sea to illustrate his claim that 'Necessity is the law of the time and action, and things are lawful by necessity which otherwise are not'. The goods of a few could be sacrificed to save the lives and livelihoods of the many since 'the private prejudice that any man hath, is very well repaired by the public utility that comes to the kingdom'.[118]

For the defence, Robert Holborne challenged the crown to demonstrate that the kingdom was, indeed, faced with dire necessity'.[119] This was essential because, in the absence of such clear proof, the bias of the law protected private property.[120] Later in the trial he was to develop this line of argument further by suggesting that *salus populi suprema lex* applied not to emergencies but to peacetime. The question 'is not, what we are to do by necessity, but what is the positive law of the land'.[121] Exception could only be made in

---

[114] *Ibid.*, III, p. 873.   [115] *Ibid.*, III, p. 924.   [116] *Ibid.*, III, p. 926.
[117] 'The public and private are so nearly connext that they can hardly be separated; the public loss falls immediately, and by consequence upon particular persons. Be a man in what condition he would be, if a public loss comes to the state, though it falls on his wedding-day, he shall suffer in it. It is impossible to save private fortunes if the public be lost ...' (*ibid.*, III, p. 927).
[118] *Ibid.*, III, p. 927.   [119] *Ibid.*, III, pp. 965–6.   [120] *Ibid.*, III, p. 970.
[121] *Ibid.*, III, p. 1011.

the most clear-cut of dangers.[122] Holborne's conclusion, that 'a subject, out of fear of an enemy, cannot build a bulwark on another man's land, but when he is a-coming', does, however, seem more motivated by political needs than by the realities of military practice.[123]

The judge's decisions engaged directly with this issue: 'Whether the king, by his right of sovereignty, may charge the subject, in case of necessity, to contribute with him to the necessary defence of the kingdom, without the subject's consent in parliament.'[124] In an English context the invocation of necessity legitimated the exercise of royal discretionary power, or prerogative, but when balanced against parliamentary consent, fed a debate about sovereignty: whose judgment of necessity ought to be decisive? Crawley made the king responsible for the 'prevention of public danger' and recognized that for 'just reason of state' it was impossible to notify parliament. Moreover, he rejected the defence claim that there was, at this time, no pressing necessity.[125] Having admitted extremity, the crown's position was easily defended. '*Salus reipublicae*', wrote Berkeley, 'by all laws, is *suprema lex, et summa necessaria.*'[126] William Jones argued that '*Salus populi est suprema lex*' and so 'when a danger is imminent, the charge must lie upon the whole kingdom, and the burden must be borne by all.'[127] The king's power to seize property in a time of crisis was, of course, *pro bono publico*, for the public good.[128] Sir John Finch's argument was the most extreme since it provided for an inherent royal claim on all private property, even in time of peace.[129] Even the very existence of property rights was based on their putative public role.[130]

The judges' 7–5 decision upheld the king's authority to determine when 'necessity' existed. This power to abrogate property rights parallels the standard post-Reformation claims for the power of the state – one thinks of Balzac and Naudé's well-known contemporary

---

[122] 'So upon the whole, my answer is, Admit the rule of *Salus populi suprema lex*, yet the law of practice doth not yield, till there be an actual enemy, or *flagrans bellum*. It is not enough that there be but an apprehension' (*ibid.*, III, p. 1013).

[123] *Ibid.*, III, p. 1014.   [124] *Ibid.*, III, p. 1078.

[125] 'We see the danger is instant, and admits of no delay. Shall we go home, and sit together in careless security?' (*ibid.*, III, p. 1087).

[126] *Ibid.*, III, p. 1102.   [127] *Ibid.*, III, p. 1184.   [128] *Ibid.*, III, p. 1185.

[129] *Ibid.*, III, p. 1225.

[130] 'First, I say, all private property must give way to the public: and therefore a trespass to private men may be punished by indictment, because it is an offence of the public weal' (*ibid*, III, p. 1231).

arguments. In the *Case of Ship-Money Briefly Discoursed* (1640) Henry
Parker denied that the king was the sole judge of necessity. Strictly
interpreted, *salus populi suprema lex* meant that, when a choice had to
be made, the public good was the highest priority. Using that same
Roman Law example of tearing down houses to impede the progress
of an urban fire, Parker charged that the ship-money went beyond
the containment and extinction of the immediate danger. The
'Ship-scot ... destroys all other Law'.[131] Charles' own recognition
that prerogative supported the liberty of the people implied that its
use was limited by the 'good of the people', or '*salus populi*'. 'To this
law', he wrote, 'all lawes almost stoope, God dispences with many of
his lawes, rather then *salus populi* shall be endangered, and that iron
lawe which wee call necessity it selfe, is but subservient to this
law':[132] In the case of ship-money, the use of prerogative was
illegitimate because there was 'no apparent unavoidable necessity'
that required action or else 'the community inevitably perish'.[133]

Conflict over property rights and the debate about balanced
constitutionalism meant that the European discussion of the
'common good' and 'necessity' was easily translated into the terms of
the English clash between crown and parliament. In his *Treatise of
Monarchie* (1643), Philip Hunton argued that the very purpose of a
mixed polity was to insure the public good. Attacking him, one
writer argued that 'the question is not, whether there shall be an
Arbitrary power; but the only point is, who shall have that Arbitrary power, whether one man or many'.[134] When constitutional
debate degenerated into warfare, defenders of the crown relied on
the conventional early modern view that the prince was the guardian of the *salus populi* and arbiter of necessity.[135] Henry Parker,
having shown that on strict construction the princely argument had
to favour the community, then employed the same argument, but to
devastating effect for the Royalist argument:

Lawes ayme at Iustice, Reason of state aimes at safety; Law secures one
subject from another, Law protects subjects from insolence of Princes, and
Princes from sedition of Subjects, so far as certain rules may be given and
written; but reason of State goes beyond all particular formes and aspects,

---

131 Henry Parker, *The Case of Ship-Money Briefly Discoursed* (London, 1640), pp. 1–2.
132 *Ibid.*, p. 7.
133 *Ibid.*, p. 13.
134 [Sir Robert Filmer], *The Anarchy of a Limited or Mixed Monarchy* (n.p., 1648), sig.A3v.
135 *Ibid.*, pp. 19–20; [Sir Robert Filmer], *The Necessity of the Absolute Power of all Kings*
(London, 1648), 1.

and looks rather to the being, then well-being of a State, and seeks to prevent mischiefe forraign as well as Domestick, by emergent Counsels, and unwritten resolutions. Reason of State is something more sublime and imperiall than Law: it may be rightly said, that the Statesman begins where the Lawyer ceaseth: for when warre has silenced Law, as it often does; Policy is to bee observed as the only true Law, a kind of dictatorian power is to be allowed to her; whatsoever has any right to defend it selfe in time of danger is to resort to policy instead of Law, and it is the same thing in the Replicant, *To deny to Parliaments recourse to reason of State in these miserable times of warre and danger, as to deny them self-defense.*[136]

Parker's defence of a parliamentary reason of state followed directly from his claim that *salus populi* meant that the people were vested with the ultimate authority to decide what constituted 'necessity'.

In the seventeenth century, political communities often fractured over the question of necessity. As Parker suggests in his contrast between the statesman and the strictly legal approach of the lawyer, sometimes the pursuit of the public good required the performance of illegal or immoral acts. Arbitrary imprisonment, secret trials, confiscation of wealth, revocation of privileges and pre-emptive wars 'are in themselves unjust', wrote one seventeenth-century Frenchman, 'but this injustice is counterbalanced by public necessity and utility. Necessity, as it is said, knows no law, and the prince who is reduced to this extremity should be able not only to command according to the laws but even over the laws themselves'.[137] Most writers, however, found it very difficult to endorse outright fraud. So, they resorted to distinctions like Giovanni Botero's between prudence and astuteness. Prudence was 'a virtue whose function is to seek and to find convenient means to bring about a given end'. Astuteness sought the same goal, but whereas prudence pursued 'what is honest rather than what is useful, astuteness takes nothing into account but interest'.[138]

While deception concerned writers on policy and the education of princes, perhaps the most incisive, and characteristically seventeenth-century, presentation of this issue was generated by the increasing importance of a particular bureaucratic manifestion of the state. The ambassador was not a ruler, but he often was put into

---

[136] Henry Parker, *Contra-Replicant* (London, 1643), pp. 18–19.
[137] Philippe de Béthune, *Conseiller d'estat*, pp. 403–4.
[138] Botero, *Reason of State*, II.8, p. 49n. See also II.7, p. 48; IX.22, p. 203. Gentillet had, earlier still, derived the content of 'asuteness' from the needs of war, calling it 'prudence militaire' (*Discours*, p. 388). This distinction was not new; see Dante, *Convivio*, IV.27.

situations in which he, too, was forced to confront the divergent demands of honesty and utility. Juan de Vera y Figueroa's *El Enbaxador* (1620) was the most important of a series of books on the ideal ambassador. Significantly, he drew extensively on both Lipsius' *De Constantia* and *Politicorum* and, as Garret Mattingly observed, 'as De Vera spins the web of his distinctions, the possibility of an ultimate conflict between the honour of the ambassador and the good of the state, between the welfare of the state and the welfare of Christendom only becomes the clearer'.[139] When asked by his interlocutor who invented the first ambassadors, 'Ludovico', de Vera's man, answered: 'Necessity was the inventor'.[140] The ambassadors' task was 'to hear much, see much, consider everything and believe nothing'. Deception and dissimulation were, Ludovico conceded, unjustified in private life, despite being legitimate for the public persona of the ambassador since evil-doing in his professional capacity could actually produce good for his government.[141] In his *Governador cristiano* (1612), the deception perpetrated by Moses and Aaron in their capacity as ambassadors when they demanded from Pharoah only that he let the Israelites journey three days' distance into the desert in order to worship their God provided Juan Marquez with the opportunity to justify such subtlety:

That the Prince, if he was good for the state and was well directed for its temporal conservation, can falsify, deceive, mince words, promise without intent to fulfil, give leave to understand without believing himself and use astuteness and a clever hand for what cannot always be achieved through force.[142]

Thomas White, whose *Grounds of Obedience and Government* bore Cicero's tag on its title page, also defended ambassadorial fraud when it served the public advantage.[143] He recognized, however,

---

[139] Garret Mattingly, *Renaissance Diplomacy* (Boston, 1955), p. 222; G. A. Davis, 'The Influence of Justus Lipsius on Juan de Vera y Figueroa's *Embaxador* (1620)', *Bulletin of Hispanic Studies*, 42 (1965), 160–73. The increasing importance of ambassadors was recognized by the creation of a new diplomatic office, the *conducteur des Ambassadeures*, to address their concerns. See Albert J. Loomie, 'The *conducteur des Ambassadeurs* of Seventeenth Century France and Spain', *Revue belge de philologie et d'histoire*, 53 (1975), 333–56.

[140] Juan de Vera y Figueroa, *El Enbaxador* (Seville, 1620), p. 22v.   [141] *Ibid.*, p. 99r.

[142] Jean Marquez, *El governador cristiano, deducido de las vidas de Moysen y Josue, príncipes del pueblo de Díos* (Salamanca, 1612), I.xiv, p. 73. See also his defence of wartime spying in Jericho, II.vi, p. 227.

[143] 'For, if it bee evident, that the good of the change openly and vastly exceeds the dammage proceeding from the discredit; cleerly hee is bound to admit of the discredit, to purchase the advantage accrewing by the change: But, where there is none or little difference, there

that for those 'who are used to maintaine their credit by custome more than by reason' it was difficult to accept that ambassadors 'must break their word for the common good'.[144] Hence, like Parker in the *Contra-Replicant*, White deprecates the lawyer's view of political reality.[145] Public life was far too complicated and fluid for a simple and fixed moral and legal perspective. 'Although those who recognize no good but utility and no honesty except in appearances are always pernicious', wrote the Frenchman Jean de Silhon, 'those who have unblemished souls sometimes cause no fewer disasters because of their scruples of conscience.'[146]

Rivadeneira rejected Machiavelli's suggestion that religious belief could be used to manipulate political obedience by citing Cicero on the difference between real and false glory.[147] While Cicero was a worthy spokesman for exemplary political conduct, his legacy was, as we have observed, far more subtle. John Eliot's assessment is exact: 'But yett in abrogatinge lawes, he must pceed with good conscience, for the evident utility of the Common wealth, but if he does use fraud in his calling in lawes, his sinn is much greater. For calumnie wch Tully speakes of, is a crafty & malitious interpretation of lawes for his owne advantage':[148] The public utility was the

the ballance hangs upon quietnesse side, and change is not to bee ventured on' (Thomas White, *The Grounds of Obedience and Government* (London, 1655, p. 86).

144 White, *Grounds of Obedience*, p. 87.

145 '... the Lawyer, what can he say? It is against the agreement heretofore made by the Government of the Countrey? The Governour may reply, Yes; but what you say is against the present good of the Countrey, with which I am entrusted. Is the Countrey made for the Lawes, or the Lawes for the Countrey? The Lawes therefore must give place, where the good of the People is against the former Resolutions. If any Law be repealed by the Authority which made it, or by another equal; is it the Lawyers part to plead what was Law before, or what is now? when a supreme Governour speaketh as such, as declaring what the present necessity requires; if any former Law bee against it, it is by his declaration annulled; it was Law before, but it is not now. But the Lawyer will reply, There is no Law in the Land which giveth such authority: It is easily answered; it is not a case for which a Law is to bee made' (*ibid.*, pp. 173–4).

146 Jean de Silhon, *Lettre du sieur de Silhon à Monsieur l'Evesque de Nantes* (n.p., n.d.), in *Recueil de lettres nouvelles*, ed. Nicolas Faret (Paris, 1627), cited in Church, *Richelieu and the Reason of State*, p. 168. Charron added, 'Always to deal simply and plainly with such people [the foxes of the world], and to follow the streight line of true reason and equitie, were many times to betray the state, and to undo it' (*Of Wisdome*, III.ii.4, p. 338).

147 Rivadeneira, *Tratado*, II.2, pp. 520–1.

148 Eliot, *De Jure Maiestatis*, p. 117. The title itself was borrowed from Cicero's discussion of three parts of majesty; Eliot explicitly rejected the alternative locutions used by Livy, Tacitus and the canonists (p. 87). The line Eliot is walking resembles the position of Montaigne in his essay 'Of the Useful and the Honourable', in which he seeks to distance himself as much as possible from the cruder forms of the contemporary infatuation with utility as the measure of decency. 'We poorly argue the honor and beauty of an action from its utility, and we commit a fallacy in thinking that everyone is obliged to perform –

measure of honesty and honesty the only accurate measure of utility. Cicero became the ideal spokesman for the post-Reformation state precisely because he upheld the authority of the state against political and religious dissidents while at the same time providing those who defended the community with the justification for ostensibly extra-legal actions.

When John Eliot sounded the standard theme that kings should be driven by the 'wellfare of their subiects: not their private interests, or faculties, but ye publicke utilitie & good', he emphasized that they were not to be left to act at will, but 'according to a certainty & rule'. While he cites Tacitus' definition of it as 'the chiefe Judgment of all things',[149] it is Cicero, 'yt great Master of intelligence in all the secrets both of Goument & nature'[150] who is brought as an example of the union of theory and practice: 'And Soe Cicero does applie it in this case, & that both intensive for the frame & comprehension of the state, & extensive for the safety & continuance, as in one of his orations against Catiline'.[151] Returning to Tacitus' definition of that *Sumum rerum iudicium*, Eliot concludes that it was 'a Supream Judicature & government of the state for the good and welfare of the subject ... for as Cicero saies, *respublica*, is but *res populi*, & yf the right & interest be the peoples, so should the benifitt & use'.[152]

As a guide to political practice, Cicero could be used to justify overstepping the bounds of law in the pursuit of the common good. As long as utility, or 'interest', coincided with the 'right', or preservation of the community, the measures could be accepted as honest. It comes as no surprise to see that Cicero's crucial discussion of the relationship between *honestum* and *utile* in book III of *De Officiis* is the

and that is is honorable for everyone to perform – an action merely because it is useful' (*The Complete Essays of Montaigne*, tr. Donald M. Frame (Stanford, 1965), p. 610). Moreover, a prince whose conscience was too tender to employ the hard measures of utility 'could not ruin himself more excusably or becomingly' (p. 607). But Montaigne admitted that he would be ruined. Montaigne acknowledged following contemporary usage in calling 'dishonorable and foul some natural actions that are not only useful but necessary' (p. 604). In the final edition, he added that 'Those are dangerous examples, rare and sickly exceptions to our natural rules. We must yield to them, but with great moderation and circumspection. No private utility is worthy of our doing this violence to our conscience; the public utility yes, when it is very apparent and very important' (p. 607). This reading and interpretation has been recently challenged by Robert J. Collins, 'Montaigne's Rejection of Reason of State in *De l'utile et de l'honneste*', *Sixteenth Century Journal*, 23 (1992), 71–94.
[149] Eliot, *Monarchie of Man*, pp. 31–2. [150] *Ibid.*, p. 17. [151] *Ibid.*, p. 34.
[152] *Ibid.*, pp. 38–9.

touchstone for many of these writers. In book IV of the *Politicorum*, Justus Lipsius, who is usually treated as a key progenitor of Tacitism, put forward his discussion of 'mixed or civil prudence'.[153] Despite citing Tacitus 174 times and Cicero only 103, the crux of the argument, the defence of fraud in the service of the public good, is derived almost wholly from Cicero's *De Officiis* (not the more obviously political speeches):

Let some man now come and tell me, 'That we must doe nothing treacherouslie, that we must not use dissimulation, nor doe any thing deceiptfullie'. (de Off 3] O pure men, nay rather poor children. The Philosopher doth note, 'that kingdomes are subverted by subtiltie and guile'. [Ar. Pol. 5]. Does thou say it is not lawfull to conserve them by the same meanes? and that the Prince may not sometimes 'having to deale with a foxe, play the foxe', [Adag] especially if the good and publicke profit, which are always conioyned 'to the benefit, and profit of the Prince doe require it'? [de Off 3] Surely thou art deceived: 'the forsaking of the common profit' is not onely against reason, 'but likewise against nature'. [de Off 3] 'We ought all to stand as it were in some sphere of the commonwealth, which when it is turned about, we ought to choose that part unto which the profit and safetie thereof doth drive us.' [pro Plan.] Does thou beleeve that any unlaefull thing is mixed herewith? There can not be any. For 'that which is commonly reputed dishonest', for this cause 'will not be so'. [de Off 3] 'He who regardeth the societies and benefit of men, doth alwayes that which he ought.' [de Off 3][154]

The problem of a '*Governador cristiano*' was the confrontation between human means and divine laws. Juan Marquez noted in his preface to the reader that the dedicatee, the Duke of Feria, did not want him to join the growing list of writers against Machiavelli, or the equally large squadron of those who wrote discourses on the reason of state. The Duke had informed him that his life had been spent serving the public in tasks dangerous for their contradictions, only some of which could be seen and avoided by others. But the majority of the difficulties were actually invisible save to those involved. As a result, it could seem to observers 'that all is smooth and clear, without seeing the conflicts of the useful with the good [*lo util con lo honesto*], the burden of those things that are not so good, or the human means

---

153 For contemporaries, Lipsius' discussion was fundamental. Charron, for example, when introducing his discussion of princely prudence, acknowledged that 'This matter is excellently handled by Lipsius, according as he thought good: the marrow of his book is here', though adapted to fit Charron's own argument (*Of Wisdome*, III.i.preface, p. 334).

154 Lipsius, *Six Bookes of Politickes*, p. 113. Printed marginalia have been reproduced within brackets. The figures are Bireley's (*Counter-Reformation Prince*, p. 78).

that exceed their limits and that, on the other hand, there is a necessity for some things which the minister neither hears nor approves'. Making these uncertain judgments was the task of governors and ambassadors.[155]

Rivadeneira directly addressed himself to the governors and de Vera to the ambassadors. Prudence had to guide the Christian prince and serve as the 'rule and rate' of all the other virtues. This prudence, 'says Cicero (*De Finibus* bk.v), is the art of life, just as medicine is that for health'.[156] The prince had to be taught how to distinguish between 'what is the true, and that which is only the apparent utility; because, though when an advantage offers itself it may conform or be contrary to the good [*honesto*] and the virtuous, it can be taken for the true'.[157] The difference between moral problems as presented in textbooks and those encountered in the real world raised still another issue. The prince lived in a world filled with 'false friends and true enemies' as well as other princes ready to take advantage of the slightest bit of innocence. Whatever misgivings he might have had about Machiavelli, Rivadeneira was compelled to admit 'that going amidst enemies, it is necessary to go armed, and amidst those who dissemble to employ some dissimulation'.[158] Louis XI was right to say that 'he did not know how to rule who did not know how to dissemble' (*nescit regnare qui nescit simulare*). What was required was to 'measure justice with utility'. Sallust taught that 'there is nothing glorious but what is secure and

---

[155] Marquez, *El governador cristiano*, p. 5v. Charron justified his extended discussion of the legitimacy of mixing justice and prudence 'because of the doubts and difficulties that arise from the accidents and necessities of states, and which do many times hinder the most resolute and best advised' (*Of Wisdome*, III.ii.11, p. 342). Jean de Silhon described this as the 'most sophisticated science of all'. Since it 'consists of dextrously joining the useful and the just and continually resisting evil under any guise that it may assume, one must perfectly understand the conditions of the latter and distinguish between what is evil by nature and what is merely accessory to it' (*Lettre du sieur de Silhon à Monsieur l'Évesque de Nantes*, in *Recueil de lettres nouvelles*, quoted in Church, *Richelieu and the Reason of State*, p. 169). Also [Filmer] *The Necessity of the Absolute Power of All Kings: and in Particular of the King of England*, p. 6: '... it is not onely profitable that a Prince should sometimes abrogate some such Laws, but also necessary for him to alter or correct them, as the infinite variety of places, times and persons, shall require'.

[156] Rivadeneira, *Tratado*, II.23, p. 552.   [157] *Ibid.*, II.31, p. 562.

[158] *Ibid.*, II.4, p. 524. Charron emphasized the legitimacy of deception for defensive purposes: 'It is lawfull by subtiltie to prevent subtiltie, and among Foxes to counterfeit the Fox. The world is full of Art and malicious cozenage, and by deceits and cunning subtilties, states are commonly overthrown, saith Aristotle. Why then should it not be lawfull, nay, why should it not be necessary to hinder, and to divert such evil, and to save the weal publick by the self-same means that others would undermine and overthrow it?' (*Of Wisdome*, III.ii.4, p. 338).

that all that is done for the conservation of the state is good and honourable [*honesto y honroso*]'. Seneca, too, said that a prince who eschewed deception would, in turn, be deceived by other princes 'and to avoid losing his conscience would lose his state, whose conservation was the point of all the laws'.[159] In addition to dissimulation, even inconstancy, otherwise a cardinal vice for late sixteenth- and seventeenth-century moral and political writers, could be accepted when it served worthwhile political ends: 'as Cicero seriously affirms, it is not inconstancy but prudence to change when things change for the better'.[160] Rivadeneira's thin line between acceptable and unacceptable deceit reflected his fear for a fundamental principle of the post-Reformation state. Perfidy 'was the legitimate child of simulation' and was capable of destroying a world sustained by truth and loyalty (*la verdad y fidelidad*). 'This fidelity Cicero calls sometimes public security, sometimes the basis of justice and still other times the conservation of republics'.[161] Under 'fidelity' Rivadeneira has subsumed, but also clearly delineated, the basic purpose of the early modern state, whether Catholic or Protestant: the security, justice and conservation of that community ruled by the prince. While these were pursued variously through conquest, commerce and religion, the specific means to be employed were always to be referred back to the pillars on which the community rested and whose corruption – even in pursuit of its stated aims – would nevertheless lead to its downfall, sooner or later.

---

[159] Rivadeneira, *Tratado*, ii.4, p. 524. Charron developed this argument still more fully. 'Cursed be the doctrine of those, who teach (as hath been said) that all things are good and lawfull for sovereigns: but yet it is sometimes necessary and required, that he mingle profite with honestie, and that he enter into composition with both ['Mais bien est-il quelquefois requis de mesler l'utile avec l'honneste, & entrer en composition & compensation des deux']. He must never turn his back to honestie, but yet sometimes go about and coast it, employing therein his skill and cunning, which is good, honest and lawfull, as saith that great S. Basil *Magna & laudabilis astutia*' (*Of Wisdome*, iii.5, p. 338).

[160] Rivadeneira, *Tratado*, ii.27, p. 557. Also Charron, *Of Wisdome*, iii.ii.17, p. 348.

[161] Rivadeneira, *Tratado*, ii.3, p. 523. Marchmont Nedham, for example, adopted the Catholic Aristotelian distinction between a 'true' and 'false' reason of state. Like Rivadeneira he sought to uphold the principle of 'honesty' as the difference between the two versions. 'A fourth error in policy, and which is indeed epidemical, hath been the regulation of affairs by reason of state, not by the strict rule of honesty. But for fear of being mistaken, you are to understand that by reason of state here, *we do not condemn the equitable results of prudence and right reason*; for upon determinations of this nature depends the safety of all states, and princes; but that reason of state that flows from a corrupt principle to an indirect end; that reason of state which is the statesman's reason, or rather his will and lust, and when he admits ambition to be a reason, preferment, power, profit, revenge, and opportunity to be reason, sufficient to put him upon any design of action that may tend to the present

Juan de Vera had introduced the ambassador as a figure born of 'necessity'. And necessity, to men of this time, meant serving the public utility at the expense of a personal assessment of right or wrong. Iulio asks Ludovico, de Vera's mouthpiece, whether it were not better to assist an enemy whose cause was just than one's own prince when embarked on an unjust course of action. 'In having satisfied this doubt', answered Ludovico, 'I will have overcome the greatest difficulty in this matter', the quotidian clash of '*lo util con lo onesto*'.[162] The ambassador must always strive after the just and put the best gloss on the task he must perform. But, in the end, Ludovico admits, 'there is nothing more difficult than the tasks faced by civil government; because neither the orator in court can be just, neither the Councillor of State, neither the Governor, neither the Captain himself, because one speaks of absolute good. Victory is not held the best end of a war, but only the honest victory; which cannot be, if the war is not just.' And, in response to the question of whether retirement were not the best option for the civil servant, Ludovico agreed that if one 'wanted to imitate the integrity of Aristides, I have no doubt that one should detach oneself from office'.[163] In the imperfect world the ambassador could be trapped between 'the demands of the useful which his King desires, and the *onesto* that the foreigner seeks: since (as Tully says well) they destroy and lose the world who separate the useful from the good'.[164] The Ciceronian argument that the useful was inseparable from the good provided de Vera, like so many others, with a way out: if one could distinguish between them, then the act ought not be performed 'because the utility of the Prince and the Republic must be sought within the terms of *lo onesto* and certainly not in the opposite'.[165]

The second discourse was introduced with Scipio's comment, as reported by Cicero, that 'I am never less alone than when I am alone' (*Nunca estuve menos solo, que quando estuve solo*) followed with Lipsius' affirmation that this should be said in a garden, just as he had opened the second book of his own *De Constantia* in a garden. Ludovico was then faced with the crucial question: could an ambassador lie for a good cause? He offered the various contemporary

advantage; though contrary to the law of God, or the law of common honesty and of nations' (*The Excellencie of a Free State*, ed. Richard Barron (London, 1767, rpt), p. 141.
[162] de Vera, *Enbaxador*, p. 77v.   [163] *Ibid.*, p. 75v [misprint: 78v].
[164] *Ibid.*, p. 75r [78r].
[165] *Ibid.*, p. 76r [79r].

answers. The *políticos* and *estadistas* approved whatever conduced to national advantage. Others took a more moderate line and affirmed that in a world filled with deception one had to be astute. Others argued '"that there is nothing glorious but that which is secure, and everything is just which achieves this security and the *conservación i aumento del estado*", adding, "That where the lion's skin is not enough one should take that of the fox because the public good which it serves is like a sponge, that absorbs and picks up all the dirt that one can have with these means."'[166] Ludovico's initial position is to deny that 'even the public good can justify a lie'. Cicero is again deployed to affirm an upstanding approach to politics, as is Aristotle, though the quote is precisely the one used by Lipsius to argue for the opposite conclusion.[167] 'However', Ludovico felt constrained to add, 'although I approve this doctrine as the basis of my discourses, I know that, though the contrary is the most dangerous part of conscience, it is sometimes the most useful for the state [*la mas util para el estado*]'.[168] Despite a printed postil that refers to Lipsius' argument, Ludovico followed by citing a Ciceronian maxim on the need for everyone in a republic to choose means that conduced to its conservation. He concluded that the ambassador, too, in the management of his offices, had to quiet his conscience and sometimes 'mix the advantageous with the honourable'. Lipsius' own notion of 'mixed prudence (or reason of state)' is then invoked to justify as 'reasonable and licit' the employment of indirect means for political gain.[169]

Lipsius, himself, having distinguished between the three types of mixed prudence, light, moderate and 'great' deceit, endorsed only the first two. And yet, in explaining the appeal of the third category he noted that force was not the sole motive. 'Those words and these precepts are in their minds, *Whatsoeever bringeth much profit, is honest, although it seemeth not so at the beginning* [de Off 3] ... If Princes *should follow iustice and yeeld to euery one that which is his, and that which they have possesed by force of armes, they should be turned to dwell in cottages, in great pouertie.* [de Rep 3].'[170] In *Les Morales* of 1607, Jean Theveneau took up this same reading of the relationship between *honestum* and *utile*

---

[166] *Ibid.*, pp. 86r–7v.
[167] 'Cicero says: "That way alone is just which by means of virtue arrives at honour and glory."' Aristotle is cited from *Politics*, bk. 5: 'That kingdoms are destroyed and ruined by fraud and deception"' (*ibid.*, p. 88v).
[168] *Ibid.*, p. 88v.   [169] *Ibid.*, p. 88r.
[170] Lipsius, *Six Bookes of Politickes*, IV.14, p. 121. The second quotation reflects Carneades' assessment of the implications of a common law of nature; the preceding passage, elided

and concluded that 'Where necessity and public utility appeal, *there is honesty and justice*'.[171] And so, when confronting the same question faced by all these writers on politics, Theveneau declared,

It also must be held as a certain principle in matters of state, that where the injustice is greater than the public utility, one must never commit it: whatever pretext exists. But where the public utility is greater, and it is a counterweight to injustice, one can choose and follow it, so much so that one who gives up and abandons it, as Cicero says, acts not solely against reason, but against nature.[172]

It is precisely the characteristic of the post-Reformation Cicero for him to be used to affirm the distinction between virtue, glory and honour on the one hand, and crude interest on the other, and at the same time provide support for the claim that utility can be a virtue when it is in pursuit of such a glorious and honourable cause – namely the preservation or safety of the community. And so, even Gabriel Naudé, famous as one of the more blunt exponents of the unadulterated exercise of magisterial discretionary power and defenders of *arcana imperii*, supported his crucial argument with references to Cicero, not Tacitus. Theveneau's discussion prefaced an endorsement of dissimulation. Naudé also cited Cicero twice in a passage recognizing the necessity of wilfully misleading political enemies, the aim being, as Cicero phrased it in book I of *De Officiis*, to capture the hearts of men and employ them to your advantage. This, according to Naudé, was the basis of Lipsius' mixed prudence and the everyday practice of political administrators. It did not constitute a secret art of princes, but 'was taught every day in their assessments, employed by ministers and practised without the slightest hint of injustice, as one of the principal rules and maxims for the good police and administration of states and empires'.[173]

In chapter 3, which he himself described as 'the most essential of this discourse', Naudé explained the legitimacy of the *coup d'état*. In a world full of artifice and malice, where, as Aristotle pointed out, kingdoms were overturned by fraud, Lipsius taught that one had to defend oneself by the same means. Against the fox one had to play

here, details his argument in favour of the binding force of utility. This passage was to become central in the reconstruction of this argument by Grotius and then Pufendorf later in the century.
[171] Jean Theveneau, *Les Morales* (Paris, 1607), p. 372. I wish to thank Manuel de Miranda for locating this text in the Bibliothèque Nationale.
[172] *Ibid.*, pp. 373–4.
[173] Gabriel Naudé, *Considerations politiques sur les coups d'estat* (n.p. [Leiden], 1679), pp. 62–3.

the fox and, quoting Sallust, Naudé declared that it was in the nature of all animals to defend themselves and their lives. Hence, Cicero was right to declare, in book III of *De Officiis*, that the dereliction of the public utility was contrary to nature.[174] If the first justification for fraud was to preserve a state surrounded by enemies, the second was when 'necessity or the evident and important public utility of the state or prince obliged following it'. This was, for Naudé, 'a necessary and indispensable' princely obligation, as it 'is always his task to procure the public good':

semper officio fungitur, says Cicero (3 *de Offic*) *utilitati hominum consulens & societati.* (He who provides for the good and society of men always fulfills his duty.) This law is basic and ought to be the principal rule of all the actions of Princes, *Salus populi suprema lex esto* (That the conservation of the people be the sovereign law).[175]

Interestingly, in Naudé's translation *utilitati* becomes *bien*, enforcing precisely that early modern interpretation of Cicero in which the *utilitas* of serving the public is defined as *honestum*. *Salus populi*, moreover, has become the 'conservation of the people', pulling together the central theme of contemporary political thought and its central spokesman and slogan.

In England as well, Cicero served contemporaries as the authority for the exercise of political necessity since his argument in book III of *De Officiis* offered an explanation for the uncomfortable, but seemingly inescapable, daily clash of utility and right. While there could be no profit from evil-doing, what produced an advantage for the state could not, by that very fact, be classified as an evil. John Eliot again:

ubi turpitudo, saies Cicero, *ibi utilitas esse non potest,* where shame and dishonestie inhabitt, there profitt cannot soiourne, & that dishonestie he putts for the violation of a dutie; and again, *nihil utile qd non idem honestum, et nunquam potest utilitas, cum honestate contendere,* what right & office doe impose, can have noe counterchecke by pfitt, nothing being pfitable, that is not likewise right; infinite others might be pduc't for this, but the same Cicero

---

[174] Aristotle: 'Per fraudem & dolum regna evertuntur'; Lipsius: 'tu servari per eadem nefas esse vis'; Sallust: 'Insitum est unicuique animanti'; Cicero: 'communis utilitatis derelictio contra naturam est'.

[175] Naudé, *Considerations,* pp. 127–9. Church cites a tract now believed written under the close supervision of Richelieu which builds political claims on this same foundation: 'To be a most just, loyal and faithful king is to avoid all harm to his state ... When the interest of the state is involved, we must return to first principles and recall that the law of the state compels him to prize it above all his individual acts. Such is the glory of kings and the security of governments' (*Response au Manifeste du sieur de Soubize* (1625), quoted in Church, *Richelieu and the Reason of State,* p. 191).

shall conclude it, who saies, *omnium haec regula est*, it is a rule catholicke & generall, to wch noe posterne lyes open, *aut illud qd utile videtur, turpe ne sit, aut si turpe sit ne videatur esse utile*, that what pfitable shalbe thought, may not be dishonest: and that wch is dishonest may not be thought profitable.[176]

The lurking concern, even for writers disposed to this argument, was that it could become morally corrosive. 'For divers level not their actions and counsels to goodnesse and honesty, but onely to utility', wrote E. Molinier, 'and following that pernicious maxime of the *Pyrrhonians*, that there is nothing just of it selfe, and by its owne nature, but onely out of the opinion and custome of men.'[177] Where the good could be located amidst a constellation of classical and Christian virtues, crude assertions of utility could not be pinned to a single, specific set of referents. Of course, this explained its value for statesmen. But the question remained, for 'those who measure the justice and honesty of things by utility, of what kinde of utility intende they to speake?'[178] The pure pursuit of utility disengaged from any notion of *honestum* threatened the viability of society: precisely what its Ciceronian spokesman sought to preserve:

To take equity from lawes, is of lawes to make them violencies; to violate obedience, is to destroy it, to destroy obedience, is to dissolve union, to dissolve union, is to dissipate society; and to part society is to subvert the State: what followes then, save onely what is just, is the conservation of States, and what unjust, is the destruction thereof.[179]

It was this scenario which faced Hugo Grotius. On the one hand, there was the clear imperative of self-preservation and, on the other, the spectre of utility becoming totally disengaged from honesty. The desire to find some rule with which to balance the needs of the one with the other was referred to by the Duke of Feria, Juan de Vera and Jean de Silhon, among others. Grotius' construction of natural law was the most elaborate of these seventeenth-century responses to a worrying political and intellectual development.

Grotius claimed to have been driven to write about, and so contribute to the creation of, international law from observing 'throughout the Christian World a Licentiousness in regard to War, which even barbarous Nations ought to be ashamed of'. Like Lipsius, he turned to writing as 'the only thing that was left for me to

---

[176] Eliot, *Monarchie of Man*, p. 52.
[177] E. Molinier, *A Mirrour for Christian States*, p. 76 (in a chapter entitled 'That an iniust action cannot be profitable to States, against Machiavill').
[178] *Ibid.*, p. 77.   [179] *Ibid.*, p. 78.

do' after these larger upheavals had led to 'being unworthily banished my Native Country'.[180] The opening sentences of the *Mare
Liberum* (1609), the published fragment of the unpublished tract on
the exploits of the Dutch East India Company (*De Iure Praedae*),
firmly place the work in this seventeenth-century discussion:

> The delusion is as old as it is detestable with which many men, especially
> those who by their wealth and power exercise the greatest influence,
> persuade themselves, or as I rather believe, try to persuade themselves, that
> justice and injustice are distinguished the one from the other not by their
> own nature, but in some fashion merely by the opinion and the custom of
> mankind. Those men therefore think that both the laws and the semblance
> of equity were devised for the sole purpose of repressing the dissension and
> rebellions of those persons born in a subordinate position, affirming mean-
> while that they themselves, being placed in a high position, ought to
> dispense all justice in accordance with their own good pleasure, and that
> their pleasure ought to be bounded only by their own view of what is
> expedient.[181]

The larger work from which this was excerpted sought to address
this issue by following the ancient jurists 'who repeatedly refer the
art of civil government back to the very fount of nature'. Cicero, too,
argued that 'the science of law' had to be derived 'from the inmost
heart of philosophy'. The reacquisiton of the natural source of law
marked, for Grotius, the beginning of any attempt to determine the
proper relationship between *honestum* and *utile*.[182]

The first rule was that 'what God has shown to be his will is
law'.[183] Since the revealed world reflected God's desire, the very
existence of individuals was invested with divine purpose. This rule
endowed what so many had recognized, that self-preservation was a
fundamental feature of the social world, with the force of a law of
nature.[184] Grotius explained just how the useful could be good and
right:

[180] Grotius, 'Preliminary Discourse', xxix and xxxi, *The Laws of War and Peace* (London,
1738), pp. xxv.
[181] Grotius, *The Freedom of the Seas, or the Right which Belongs to the Dutch to Take Part in the East
Indian Trade*, tr. Ralph van Deman Magoffin, ed. and intro. James Brown Scott (New
York, 1916), p. 1.
[182] Grotius, *De Iure Praedae Commentarius*, tr. G. L. Williams (Oxford, 1950), pp. 6–7.
[183] *Ibid.*, ch. 2, p. 8.
[184] See Richard Tuck's works: Grotius, Carneades and Hobbes', *Grotiana*, new ser., 4 (1983),
43–62; 'The Modern Theory of Natural Law', in *The Languages of Political Thought in Early
Modern Europe*, ed. Anthony Pagden (Cambridge, 1987), pp. 99–119; *Hobbes* (Oxford,
1989), pp. 7–11, 20–3; *Philosophy and Government* (Cambridge, 1992), ch. 5. For the sceptic
challenge to Stoicism in antiquity, see Pierre Couissin, 'The Stoicism of the New

From this fact the old poets and philosophers have rightly deduced that love, whose primary force and action are directed to self-interest, is the first principle of the whole natural order. Consequently, Horace should not be censured for saying, in imitation of the Academics, that expediency might perhaps be called the mother of justice and equity. For all things in nature, as Cicero repeatedly insists, are tenderly regardful of self, and seek their own happiness and security.[185]

The implications of this very Ciceronian reading were twofold: individuals could defend themselves and could acquire for them-selves the means for that preservation. 'The latter precept, indeed, we shall interpret with Cicero', Grotius writes, 'as an admission that each individual may, without violating the precepts of nature, prefer to see acquired for himself rather than for another, that which is important for the conduct of life.' This statement is supported with citations from *De Officiis* (i.iv.11; iii.v.22), *Academia* (iv.ii.xiii.131), *De Finibus* (iv.vii.16; v.ix.24) and *Pro Milone* (iv.10).[186]

The next step in the argument was also bolstered by classical authorities: self-preservation depended on social life. The preser-vation of the commonwealth, therefore, took on even greater importance than that of the individual since 'the cargo cannot be saved unless the ship is preserved'. Grotius continued by quoting the Stoic Hierocles: ' "For whatever is beneficial to one's country is likewise of common [advantage] to the various parts thereof" ' (*quod enim patriae utile est, idem singulis etiam partibus commune est*).' Livy was brought to declare that ' "In nowise will you be able to protect your interests by betraying the public interest." '[187] Since self-preser-vation depended on the conservation of the commonwealth, it followed that the defence of society was of the highest priority. 'According to Cicero (*Philippics* xi.xii.28), Jupiter himself sanc-tioned the following precept, or law: All things salutary to the commonwealth are to be regarded as legitimate and just' (*ut omnia quae reipublicae salutaria essent legitima et justa haberentur*).[188] Hence, when Grotius confronted the central issue behind the writing of the entire treatise, the legitimacy of Dutch seizure of Portuguese prizes in the East Indies, the ground had already been prepared.

In an echo of *De Officiis*, Grotius argued in the penultimate

Academy', reprinted in *The Skeptical Tradition*, ed. Myles Burnyeat (Berkeley, Los Angeles and London, 1983), pp. 31–65.
[185] Grotius, *De Iure Praedae*, ch.2, p. 9.   [186] *Ibid.*, ch. 2, p. 10.
[187] *Ibid.*, ch. 2, pp. 21–2.
[188] *Ibid.*, ch. 2, p. 20.

chapter that all things just were also honourable and then, in the final chapter, that all things just and honourable were also useful. Those who denied that 'whatever is just in every respect cannot fail to be honourable' were accused of 'obvious inconsistency' and submerged beneath a tide of references to Cicero.[189] The honourable was, explicitly referring to the Stoics and citing Cicero, that which nature prescribed.[190] Moreover, it was especially honourable to take vengeance on malefactors. Hence there was nothing either unjust or dishonourable in Dutch merchants revenging themselves on the Portuguese, 'the violators of a public right, with the purpose of ensuring greater security for themselves in the enjoyment of that right'.[191] While recognizing that those 'many persons who measure benefit in terms of material gain' did not need to be told that the seizure of prizes was beneficial, Grotius set himself the task of showing that it was beneficial *because* just and honourable. It was 'perverse' to separate these related attributes.[192] Nothing base could be useful, while everything honourable was virtuous and therefore necessarily useful. 'A great many observations in support of this sentiment were made by Cicero in his treatise *De Officiis*, III. In another work by that same author (*De Finibus*, III [xxi.71]), the following argument is presented: "Whatever is just, is beneficial; and whatever is honourable is also just; whence it follows that whatever is honourable is also beneficial."'[193] In this specific case, the seizure of the *St Catharine* by Jacob Heemskerck in 1602, whose value at auction was the equivalent of the annual state budget of England, was obviously exceedingly beneficial.[194]

A few years later, in the midst of the Thirty Years War and after having escaped from prison and fled to Paris, Grotius published *De Jure Belli ac Pacis* (1625). In the Prolegomenon he observed that the general 'despising' of right was reflected in the sayings in 'almost every one's Mouth', that to a sovereign 'no thing is unjust that is

---

[189] *Ibid.*, ch. 14, p. 318. The citations are of *De Inventione*, II.iv; *De Officiis*, I.ix.62; III.viii.33–5; *De Finibus*, I.xvi.50.

[190] Grotius, *De Iure Praedae*, ch. 14, p. 319.   [191] *Ibid.*, ch. 14, p. 327.

[192] *Ibid.*, ch. 15, p. 338.

[193] *Ibid.*, ch. 14, p. 339.

[194] 'Thus spoils are beneficial primarily because the individuals honourably enriched thereby are able to benefit many other persons, and because it is to the interest of the state that there should be a large number of wealthy citizens. Furthermore, inasmuch as a part of the prize in question has fallen to the state at no expense to the latter, a very great and special benefit is involved here, in view of the difficulties confronting the public treasury, which is exhausted in consequence of such arduous war' (*ibid.*, ch. 15, pp. 339–40). For the value of the prize I rely on Richard Tuck's calculation.

profitable' (*nihil iniustum quod utile*), or that 'amongst the Great the stronger is the juster Side', or 'that no State can be governed without Injustice'. Not only the 'vulgar', but 'Men of Wisdom and Learning' claimed that national conflict was 'a Stranger to all Justice'.[195] Hence the choice of Carneades, notorious for having undermined the Stoics' transcendent notion of justice by arguing both for and against it on successive days, as spokesman for contemporary scepticism:

This Man having undertaken to dispute against Justice, that kind of it, especially, which is the Subject of this treatise, found no Argument stronger than this. Laws (says he) were instituted by Men for the sake of Interest [*iura sibi homines pro utilitatem sanxisse*]; and hence it is that they are different, not only in different Countries, according to the Diversity of their Manners; but often in the same Country, according to the Times.

Natural right was 'a mere Chimera' since nature guided all living things to seek their own advantage. 'So that either there is no Justice at all, or if there is any, it is extreme Folly, because it engages us to procure the Good of others, to our own Prejudice.'[196]

In this later work Grotius rejected crude self-interest still more emphatically while placing greater weight on the value of life in community. The 'Desire of Society' was natural to man and led him into life 'in a Community regulated according to the best of his Understanding'.[197] This 'Sociability', or the 'Care of maintaining Society in a Manner conformable to the Light of human Understanding, is the Fountain of Right'. Respect for privacy, property and truthful speech all followed from it.[198] Natural sociability provided a rule with which to ascertain the real usefulness of an action. 'Therefore', Grotius concluded, 'the Saying, not of Carneades only, but of others, "Interest, that Spring of Justice and Right" [*Utilitas Iusti prope mater & Aequi*], if we speak accurately, is not true, for the Mother of Natural Law is human Nature itself, which, though even the Necessity of our Circumstances should not require it, would of itself create in us a mutual Desire of Society.'[199] If the stress was now on nature rather than interest, it was only to emphasize that, in Grotius' handling of this traditional issue, the natural ought not to

[195] Grotius, 'Preliminary Discourse', III, *Laws of War and Peace*, pp. xiii–xiv.
[196] *Ibid.*, V, *Laws of War and Peace*, pp. xiv–xv.
[197] *Ibid.*, VI, *Laws of War and Peace*, p. xv.
[198] *Ibid.*, VIII, *Laws of War and Peace*, pp. xvii–xviii.
[199] *Ibid.*, XVII, *Laws of War and Peace*, p. xx.

be seen in opposition to the useful, but that 'to the Law of Nature
Profit is annexed' (*Sed naturali iuri utilitas accedit*).[200]

If the problem of international lawlessness initially led Grotius to
consider the sceptical challenge to justice and morality as its fundamental cause, his 'answer' to Carneades led him back to the realm of
clashing national interests:

But it is absurd of him [Carneades] to traduce Justice with the Name of
Folly. For as, according to his own Confession, that Citizen is no Fool, who
obeys the Law of his Country, though out of Reverence to that Law he
must and ought to pass by some things that might be advantageous to
himself in particular: So neither is that People or Nation foolish, who for
the Sake of their own particular Advantage, will not break in upon the
Laws common to all Nations; for the same Reason holds good in both.

Thus, just as someone who 'violates the Laws of his Country for the
Sake of some present advantage to himself, thereby saps the Foundation of his own perpetual Interest, and at the same time that of his
Posterity', states which breached the 'Laws of Nature and Nations'
imperilled 'their future Happiness and Tranquillity'.[201]

Individuals and states indeed sought to preserve themselves. But
this self-interest ought not to be narrowly conceived. Rather, the
conduct that was most useful was that which best respected human
nature. Grotius sought to avoid Jean Bodin's error in 'confounding'
discussions of justice and 'the giving Rules about what it may be
profitable or advantageous for us to do'. These, wrote Grotius,
'belong to the Art of Politicks' and were 'of a quite different
Subject'.[202]

Nevertheless, in the world for which Grotius and his contemporaries wrote, the claims of utility and right inevitably collided. Once
states were established with the aim of securing the preservation of
the community, this same logic dictated that damaging internal
dissent be prevented. The decisions of the ruler were not to be
challenged by the populace.[203] Writing after a half century filled
with civil war, international war and rebellion, Jean Barbeyrac
further sharpened Grotius' argument. If citizens, rather than the
government they established, could determine the means of their

---

[200] *Ibid.*, XVII, *Laws of War and Peace*, p. xx.   [201] *Ibid.*, XIX, *Laws of War and Peace*, p. xxi.
[202] *Ibid.*, LVIII, *Laws of War and Peace*, p. xxxv. Nevertheless, Grotius added, 'Yet in some
places I have made mention of the useful, but by the by, and to distinguish it more clearly
from a Question of the Just'. ('*Nonnullis tamen locis eius quod utile est feci mentionem, sed obiter,
& ut idipsum a iusti quaestione apertius distinguerem.*')
[203] Grotius, *Laws of War and Peace*, I.iii.8, pp. 64–71.

collective self-preservation, their *common* good, then they would be supreme. Consequently, not only popular, but even coordinate sovereignty was inadmissible.

That is, if the People had a Right to consider themselves as independent of the King, and proceed against him authoritatively, as often as the King should do any Thing that seems unjust, or prejudicial to the publick Good, a perpetual Source of Quarrels and Disorders would be opened; because it might easily happen, that the People, at certain Times would judge some Things unjust or prejudicial, which are not really so.[204]

International conflict was to be managed in the same terms. The insight that the condition of states mirrored that of individuals was one of Grotius' most enduring contributions. Princes were not obliged to go to war 'unless all or most of his Subjects would be Sufferers . . . For it is a Sovereign's Business to have greater Regard for the Whole than the Part; and the larger the Part is, so much the more does it approach the Nature of the Whole'.[205] Military action was, according to Cicero, only legitimate in the pursuit of security and peace.[206] We know that Gustavus Adolphus rode into battle carrying his copy of *De Iure Belli ac Pacis* since, on his interpretation, it could be used to justify the conquest of territory, especially that of bellicose neutrals.[207] Perhaps, though, recalling Gustavus' insistence on *assecuratio* and *satisfactio*, he was also impressed by Grotius' claim that the king's role was to assure the preservation and security of his state.

Hugo Grotius and Samuel Pufendorf are united across time and space by Sweden and the experience of the Thirty Years War. Grotius' struggle to find a rule with which to calibrate the relationship between the useful and the good accompanied him into politics, prison and a mediocre career as a diplomat, spending much of the Thirty Years War in the crucial post of Swedish Ambassador in Paris. Pufendorf began his professional career in the shadow of Westphalia as an imprisoned member of the Swedish legation in Denmark (1658) and spent much of it in Sweden, in Lund as professor at the new university and then in Stockholm as

---

[204] *Ibid.*, I.iii.9, p. 72, and Barbeyrac, *An Historical and Critical Account of the Science of Morality*, note 3, p. 72.

[205] *Ibid.*, II.xxv.ii, p. 500.

[206] *Ibid.*, III.xvii.2; the citations are from *De Officiis*, I.xi.35 and I.xxiii.80.

[207] Roberts, *Gustavus Adolphus*, II, pp. 422–3. For some of the relevant passages, see *Laws of War and Peace*, III.vi.ii, III.viii.i, III.ix.xiii, and especially II.i. x, III.i.ii.

Historiographer Royal. The experience of politics and international relations informs his major works on jurisprudence as well as his histories and influential works on the interest of states.

In his account of the Thirty Years War, Pufendorf, like Michael Roberts, emphasized the desire for a territorial *satisfactio* and an *assecuratio* that was, fundamentally, to rest upon a union of Protestant states and which was embodied in the final agreement at Westphalia.[208] Pufendorf's first work on law, *The Elements of Universal Jurisprudence* (1660), conceptualized during *his* imprisonment and written just afterwards, supported these same Swedish territorial claims in a far more unambiguous way than had Grotius, Gustavus' rough-and-ready reading notwithstanding.[209] James Tully, in his introduction to Pufendorf's summary *Duty of Man and Citizen* (whose Latin title makes plain its intellectual stirps: *De Officio Hominis*), has characterized him as the theorist of the new, post-Westphalian European order of states who reshaped the familiar reason of state literature into a discussion of comparative politics.[210]

In the chapter of the *De Officio* on 'duty to oneself', Pufendorf stressed that self-preservation was powerful enough to suspend the ordinary force of law 'if that is the only way it can be secured. For this reason, "necessity", it is said, "knows no laws"'.[211] Pufendorf suggested that law was not omnicompetent; there were cases which

---

208 For the importance of a territorial *satisfactio* as the means to procure the security of the Swedish crown and the Baltic littoral, see *The Compleat History of Sweden from its Origin to this Time* (London, 1702), pp. 522, 554, 615, 621, and *Commentariorum de Rebus Suecicis* (Nuremberg, 1686), xx.160, p. 829 and especially xx.128, p. 128. For Sweden's long-term security needs see *The Compleat History*, p. 462; *de Rebus Suecicis*, III.3, p. 42, and III.54, p. 59, and in the discussion of the Treaty of Westphalia, in which the concluding article is entitled 'Punctus Assecurationis', and spells out as the goal of the treaty 'singolorum pactorum firmitudine & securitate' having the force of Imperial law (p. 874).

209 For instance: 'But, when one has to be driven by force to make satisfaction [*ad satisfaciendum est adigendus*], since this very same circumstance renders quite clear his obstinacy in badness, and satisfaction [*satisfactio*] cannot be obtained unless the injured forcibly overpowers the injurers, it rests with the victor to determine just what kind of bond will best provide for his own security [*quali cautione securitati suae quam rectissime judicet prospectum*]. Here he may not merely proceed to taking away arms, demolishing or occupying fortified places, to hostages, perpetual imprisonment, and the like, but even to death itself, if, indeed, it be well enough established that the one restored to liberty will plot our destruction, and no more convenient remedy be found for avoiding that' (*Elementorum Jurisprudentiae Universalis Libri Duo* tr. William Abbot Oldfather (Oxford, 1931), I.xxi.2, p. 200; for another account of the legitimacy of long-term security, see II.iv.13, p. 252).

210 Samuel Pufendorf, *On the Duty of Man and Citizen According to Natural Law*, ed. and intro. James Tully and tr. Michael Silverthorne (Cambridge, 1991), introduction, pp. xx, xiv.

211 Pufendorf, *Duty of Man*, I.5.18, p. 53.

were never presumed to be covered by existing laws. Two survivors of a shipwreck fighting for the same plank or the pulling down of a neighbour's burning house to save one's own were two famous classical examples in which the force of self-preservation created a situation in which necessity was sovereign.[212] In the great work to which *De Officio* was an epitome, Pufendorf had dedicated a chapter to the force of 'necessity' in contemporary arguments: 'The Case of Necessity is a thing in every body's Mouth, and the Force of it generally acknowledg'd in the World; Hence we commonly say, that it *hath no Law*, that 'tis a *suppos'd* or *presumptive* Exception to all human Ordinances and Constitutions; and that, therefore, it gives a Right of doing many things otherwise forbidden.' The force of this argument rested on the natural desire to preserve one's own life. 'And here it is apparent, that the Favour, the Right, the Leave, or whatever it is that in such Cases we attribute to Necessity, springs from this single Principle, that it is impossible for a Man not to apply his utmost Endeavour towards preserving himself; and that, therefore, we cannot easily conceive or suppose, such an Obligation upon him, as ought to outweigh the Desire of his own Safety.'[213] Pufendorf's recognition of the force of 'necessity' took its place in an existing and large body of literature.[214]

Self-preservation and necessity in Pufendorf's account, as in wider seventeenth-century discussions, provided the foundation for a discussion of the scope of sovereign power. As we have observed, in the contemporary idiom the preservation of the community was believed to provide the best guarantee of the security of individuals. Pufendorf cited the fundamental maxim of this approach to political life:

This is the general rule for sovereigns: the safety of the people is the supreme law [*Salus populi suprema lex esto*]. For authority has been given them to achieve the end for which states were instituted. Princes must believe that nothing is good for them privately which is not good for the state.[215]

---

[212] *Ibid.*, 1.5.21, 1.5.24, p. 54.

[213] Pufendorf, *The Law of Nature and Nations*, tr. Basil Kennet (London, 1749), II.vi.1, p. 200. For the shipwreck problem and other instances when self-preservation eliminates the issue of murder, see II.vi.4.

[214] Sometimes necessity was wielded *against* the state, not in support of extra-legal political practice. Christopher Friedrich George Meister lists some sixteen texts published between 1640 and 1740 which engage directly with the theme of necessity, in *Bibliotheca Iuris Naturae et Gentium* (Gottingen, 1757), pp. 208–12. I am grateful to Béla Kapossy for bringing this to my attention.

[215] Pufendorf, *Duty of Man*, II.11.3, p. 151.

The role of the prince as the guardian of the common good made licit
those actions which served to preserve or conserve that community –
the *suprema lex*. This, however, introduced the explicitly Ciceronian
problem that earlier writers had tangled with: how to make sure that
this quest for the useful hewed as closely as possible to notions of
propriety and morality. Tully has noted that Pufendorf was criticized on precisely this point for departing from Grotius' notion of
'sociability' in favour of a notion of utility or interest. But, in fact, as
Tully argues, 'Pufendorf, following Cicero, carefully distinguishes
between rational or long-term utility and depraved or short-term
utility and argues that social duties are consistent with, but not based
upon the former.'[216] This distinction is hammered out in *The Laws of
Nature and Nations*, book II, chapter 3 ('On the Laws of Nature, in
general') in which the Ciceronian union of *utile* and *honestum* is
contrasted with the argument of crude interest: the spectre of Carneades augmented by the presence of Thomas Hobbes.

Recalling the structure of Grotius' presentation, Pufendorf notes
that some alleged that the diversity of customs meant that there was
no single overarching law of nature 'and that all law has arisen from
the convenience of individual states, and cannot be measured in any
other way'. Horace's judgment about utility from the *Satires* is
quoted, as is Carneades' deprecating assessment of a common notion
of the good in a fragment of Cicero's *De Republica* preserved in
Lactantius' *Divine institutions*.[217] Pufendorf's response to Carneades
took the form of Cicero's own rebuttal. 'In clearing up these objections it will not be amiss to begin with Tully's Remark, in his Second
Book of Offices, ch.iii', in which he lamented the pernicious separation of *honestum* and *utile*.[218] Pufendorf adds, very much along the

---

[216] Tully, *Duty of Man*, introduction, p. xxvii.

[217] 'But of all the Antients none disputed this Point so largely as Carneades is said to have
done. His Arguments, as Lactantius hath contracted them, are to this Effect: That Men
first instituted Laws to secure and to promote their own advantage; whence they came to
be so various according to their different Manners, and different Times; but that there was
no such Thing as natural Law in the World. That Mankind, and all other animate Beings,
are by the Guidance of Nature, carried on to the Pursuit of their own Profit; and that,
consequently there can be no Justice; or, if there be, that it must be the highest Folly,
inasmuch as it would make a Man injure himself in consulting the Conveniences of others.
That all nations, famous for Empire and Command, and the Romans themselves, who
then reign'd Masters of the World, if they would be just; that is, if they would restore every
one his own, must return to their antient Cottages, and to their primitive Poverty' (*Law of
Nature*, II.iii.10, p. 125).

[218] 'Profitable,'' says he, ''is a word, which by the Corruption of Time and Custom is
perverted insensibly to the Signification of somewhat that may be separated from
Honesty; so as to make something honest which is not profitable, and something profitable

lines of those post-Reformation writers who sought the defence of the community and faith, that the problem lay in the contemporary abuse of the concept of utility:

For those Masters of false Politicks cheated the heedless Vulgar with the ambiguous Term of Profit; which is of two kinds, as it is rated by different Principles. One sort of Profit is that which appears such to the deprav'd Judgment of ill-composed Affections; these being mov'd chiefly by present and transitory Advantages, and very little solicitous about future Concerns. The other, and the true Profit, is advanc'd so by sound Reason, which doth not only consider Things at hand, but weighs and examines the Effects and Consequences which they are likely to produce. Which therefore must pronounce that alone to be truly profitable, which is universally such, and which gives assurance of Constancy and Duration, but can never judge it a desirable Thing to enjoy a momentary Advantage, drawing after it a Train of endless Mischiefs.

Hence, Pufendorf can conclude that actions performed 'in conformity' with the law of nature had a 'double Excellency', 'not being only Honest; that is, conducive to the Preservation, and to the Increase of the Honour, and good Credit of Men; but likewise *Useful and Profitable*, promoting their Interest and Advantage, and contributing largely to their Happiness'. Turning back to the realm of statecraft, Pufendorf was in a position to assess the validity of claims that certain actions could be justified because they benefited the state:

Therefore 'tis so far from being true, that Civil Laws were first instituted for the sake of this momentary and bastard Profit, that it appears to have been their chief End and Design, to hinder Men from squaring their actions by so false a Measure. For, should any one resolve to direct all his Proceedings to his own private Advantage, without any regard to the rest of Mankind; since all other Men might as well take the same Course; There could not but arise the deepest Confusion, and a kind of War of all against all, a State the most unprofitable, and the most inconvenient in the World.[219]

The 'War of all against all' was the direct result of a misunderstood notion of utility. In the long term, self-preservation was best served by cooperation rather than competition since our 'wonderful Impotency and natural Indigence' militated against our equally natural endeavours, 'by all Ways and Means' to secure our

without being honest: An Error of the most pernicious Consequences to the Life of Man"'
(*Law of Nature*, ii.iii.10, p. 125).
[219] *Ibid.*, ii.iii.10, p. 121.

existence.[220] Self-love was indeed prior to love of others, not because a man should always prefer himself to others or 'measure all things by his own private Advantage' but simply because man was so framed that he perceived his own needs prior to those of others.[221] The version of natural law that reflected the importance of this long-term utility saw in the development and preservation of society the means to individual self-preservation. Pufendorf's assessment closely resembles Richard Cumberland's contemporary conclusions about the 'common Good' which will be examined in chapter 5. According to Pufendorf, 'we, when we maintain that a Man ought to be sociable, do at the same time intimate, that he ought not to make his own separate Good the Mark of his Proceedings, but the Benefit of Mankind in common; that no Person shall pursue his private Advantage by oppressing, or by neglecting other Men; and that none hath Reason to hope for Happiness and Success, who either injures or despises his Neighbours'. Pufendorf concluded with Cicero's famous declaration in *De Officiis* that 'everyone is born, not for himself alone, but for all humankind'.[222]

Just as Cicero himself had suggested, self-preservation and love of one's community were not incompatible. Rather, those were wrong who suggested that men ought each to seek his 'own Advantage to the Injury of others'. Thomas Hobbes was, of course, the most sophisticated of these wrong-headed men. Pufendorf offered him an ironic compliment. 'As for Hobbes's Demonstration, in which he ingeniously enough deduces the[o]se Laws, which we call natural, from the Principle of Self-Preservation, the first Remark that we shall offer concerning it is this; that such a Way of Proof doth indeed clearly enough make out, how conducive 'tis to the Safety of Men, that they act according to these Dictates of Reason', since they would not be protected by Hobbes'. It was, however, not enough to say that a man could employ whatever means were necessary for self-preservation and that therefore he was obliged to pursue them. 'In the next place', Pufendorf adds, 'great Care is to be taken lest any should conclude from such Arguments and Positions, that when he hath once ensur'd his own Safety, and set himself out of Danger, he need not trouble himself about the Security of other Men'.[223] A series of Stoic arguments about the common bond between men supported the assertion that, far from conflicting, 'whosoever hath a

---

[220] *Ibid.*, ii.iii.14, p. 133.   [221] *Ibid.*, ii.iii.14, p. 134.   [222] *Ibid.*, ii.iii.15, p. 136.
[223] *Ibid.*, ii.iii.16, p. 137.

hearty Desire for his own Security, must not, cannot neglect the Care of his Fellows'. This conclusion was punctuated with a telling (and familiar) citation from Cicero's *De Finibus* (iii.xix): 'Nor is a betrayer of his country more to be blamed than one who deserts the general advantage or the general safety on account of his own private advantage or safety.'[224] Pufendorf brought this chapter to a close by going back to Lactantius, who preserved Cicero's account of the force and scope of this natural law: 'Nor will it be different at Rome and at Athens now and hereafter; but will eternally and unchangeably affect all Persons in all Places'.[225]

Pufendorf took the same Ciceronian arguments that were grist for the mill of writers on statecraft and, by emphasizing universal applicability, sought to 'fix' the relationship between 'utility' and 'good'. His account of the 'good citizen', certainly, differs very little from Cicero's own description (usually of himself).

Pufendorf 'meant one who promptly obeys the orders of those in power; one who strives with all his strength for the public good, and gladly puts his own private good second – one, in fact, who believes nothing to be good for him unless it is also good for the state; one, finally, who is well disposed to his fellow-citizens'.[226] Meanwhile, Pufendorf's characterization of the 'general Rule which Sovereigns are to proceed by' as *Salus populi suprema lex esto* and his elaboration of it, were of equally clear derivation: 'For the Authority which Governors bear, was first conferr'd on them, with this Intention, that it might prove a Means of procuring that End for which civil Societies were establish'd. And therefore they ought to esteem nothing as contribution to their own private or personal Good, which is not, at the same time, profitable to the Commonwealth.'[227] After supplying the source of the quote, Jean Barbeyrac, in his comment on the passage, took the opportunity to affirm that 'after all, the Maximes of good Politickes have nothing in them contrary to natural Right', which does seem to be the whole point of Pufendorf's argument.[228]

---

[224] *Ibid.*, ii.iii.16, pp. 137–8.
[225] *Ibid.*, ii.iii.20, p. 143. From *De Republica* ii.xxii.16, cited in Lactantius, *Divine Institutes*, vi.viii.
[226] Pufendorf, *Duty of Man*, iii.5.5, p. 133.
[227] Pufendorf, *Law of Nature*, vii.ix.3, pp. 736–7.
[228] Recognizing that 'the Actions of Sovereigns, and the Body of a State, seem often to depart from the Rules of those Duties, which private persons are obliged to observe towards each Other', Barbeyrac suggested that Pufendorf 'had a Design to compose a Treatise, to shew expressly how far what is called a Stroke of *Policy*, or something done for a *Reason of State*, may be justifiable'. The difficulty of the prince's task was illustrated with the long

Pufendorf was well aware of the strongly prudential cast of many of Cicero's arguments in defence of both individual and community. At times, he even finds them *too* supportive of precisely that raw utility which his idea of natural law sought to ameliorate. Hence, for example, Pufendorf offered that 'Cicero is too free in saying, that "such Promises are not to be kept, as are useless to the Persons to whom they are made; nor if they be less beneficial to him, than prejudicial to the Maker"' (*De Officiis* I).[229] Elsewhere, Pufendorf wrote that 'we can by no means admit of Cicero's rule which he lays down in his third *Book of Offices* (III.vi)' that '"the Law of Nature itself, which preserves and holds together the common Profit of Mankind, does decree, that things necessary for Life and Sustenance may be transferr'd from an idle and useless Person, to a Man of Wisdom, Goodness, and Valour, who, should he be suffer'd to perish, would exceedingly prejudice the Publick by his Death"'.[230] While at one point somewhat disturbed by the broadness of Cicero's explanation for the reason why no faith need be kept with a pirate ('a common foe of all men'), later on Pufendorf took Cicero's side against Grotius.[231] And, where Cicero seemed ambiguous, as in his account of the question of concealment broached in the debate between Antipater and Diogenes (*De Officiis* III.xiii), Pufendorf understood him to be defending flexibility.[232] On the tricky question of dissimulation, Pufendorf acknowledged the inadequacy of Cicero's oft-quoted 'wish', '"That all Simulation and Dissimulation were utterly be banished from human life"'. Sounding like Lipsius and a whole host of predecessors, Pufendorf recognized that this was a recipe for disaster in the 'real world'.[233]

quotation from Charron's *De la Sagesse* (III.ii.2) on the need for prudence to 'be mixed with Justice' (*Law of Nature*, VII.ix.3, Barbeyrac note 1, p. 736).

[229] Pufendorf, *Law of Nature*, V.xii.22, p. 550. Barbeyrac, in fact, has a far less prudential reading of Cicero (note 2).

[230] Pufendorf, *Law of Nature*, III.ii.1, p. 225. And again, Barbeyrac scurried to diminish the impression that Cicero could be seen in opposition to Pufendorf's natural law. 'Cicero', he wrote, 'speaks only of an extraordinary Case, viz. in extreme Necessity, and then, as rigid as he seems to be, builds his Determination, not upon the Right which every one has to preserve himself, but upon the Good of Society' (note 5). Still, this analysis of the principles employed by Cicero to square the needs of the individual and the community, necessity, law and utility only makes clear his value to post-Reformation political thinkers.

[231] Pufendorf, *Law of Nature*, III.vi.11, p. 288; IV.ii.8, p. 345. Grotius had cited – and repudiated – the passages in the *De Officiis* in which Cicero had justified deceiving those in breach of the law of nature (*Laws of War and Peace*, III.xx.1).

[232] Pufendorf, *Law of Nature*, V.iii.4, p. 479.

[233] 'But since he, who is ever freely publishing and declaring his own Concerns, lays himself open to the fraud of wicked Men, and since most Persons are inclined rather to be won

ENGLAND FROM THE RESTORATION TO THE RULE OF WALPOLE

Discussions of statecraft did not take place solely among Catholics, or solely on the Continent. In England, the clash between utility and good was not simply a matter of intellectual discussion. 'Necessity' led, in 1642, to open warfare between crown and parliament, introducing a period of constitutional experimentation and social upheaval that continued until the return of Charles II restored the monarchy. The language of political discussion shows striking continuity. A commitment to the 'Publique Good' constituted the basis of political community and the bond between it and its civil authorities. As Pufendorf and so many before and after him sought to emphasize, there was no discrepancy between the public good and the interest of princes '[because] The Benefit of the Prince being the Advantage of the People, and the Advantage of the People being the Benefit of the Prince'.[234] Monarchs were to be trained up from their youth to 'come to a true Understanding of the great Affairs and secret Reason of State; and therefore more ready in all public dispatches, more quick, apprehensive and sagacious in perceiving what is conducive to the Common Good, and what not, than such who have not been Educated with all those advantages to Govern'.[235] From the mid-1650s English politicians began to argue that war should be fought to protect the national interest and, increasingly, that interest was defined as commerce.[236]

upon by Artifice and Shew, than to be convinced by solid Plain-dealing; therfore it may not be adviseable for us to exclude, from human Society, the Art of innocent Dissimulation, till all the Wickedness, and all the Folly of Mankind is turn'd into Probity and Wisdom' (*Law of Nature*, IV.i.9, p. 324). Grotius had also rejected Cicero's sweeping claim – and then provided references to other places where Cicero had himself admitted that dissimulation 'is absolutely necessary and unavoidable, especially for those to whom the care of the state is entrusted'. See Grotius, *Laws of War and Peace*, III.i.vii, p. 523; the references are to Cicero, *Pro Milone*, xxiv.65; *Pro Plancio*, vi.16; *Ad Familiares*, x.viii.4.

234 Leonard Willan, *The Exact Politician* (London, 1670), p. 150.
235 John Nalson, *The Common Interest of King and People* (London, 1677), p. 113.
236 'Trade ... Being well understood by our neighbours, and made so much the Concerns of them as they now place the very vigilant part of their Interest and Government in it this seems to take away all choice from us, and to lay a necessity not Inevitable upon us; That eyther we must leade this great and generall affayre of State by making ourselves the Masters of Commerce or Keeping up an Equality at least in it; Or we must be content to be lead by it and humbled under the power of them that have the ability to Rule and Governe it' ([Dr Benjamin Worsley], *Some Considerations about the Commission for Trade*, quoted in Robert Conquest, 'The State and Commercial Expansion: England in the Years 1642–1688', in *Journal of European Economic History*, 14 (1985), 155. See Steve Pincus,

Looking back on the experience of the civil war from the perspective of the 'exclusion controversy', one writer devoted a pamphlet to an analysis of *Salus populi*. The rebels of forty years earlier had wielded this tag as their 'Impenetrable Shield', 'preferring the Authority of this sentence to all Authority of Lawes, Kings, Priviledges, and customes what soever'.[237] What did *salus populi* mean, after all? Public safety did not at all imply 'that *no Subject whatsoever, no not the Poorest, the Weakest, the Meanest*, may be injured or wronged by such as are his Equals or Superiors in this World'. Unfortunately this sort of oppression was impossible to prevent. Rather, what was intended obliged rulers to prevent foreign invasion or domestic rebellion.[238] The *populus*, moreover, referred to the entire community collectively, including king and people. In the author's strongly monarchist interpretation, the pursuit of the 'safety of the people' or 'the Publique good' required 'that there be in the Commonwealth a certain *Power Superiour to the Law* to supply their defects' and this power was lodged in the sovereign. The identification of the *suprema lex* with sovereignty and broad discretionary power made it very difficult for the author to comprehend how the tag could be used by rebels:

... in this Axiom is implyed, that the *supream Magistrate hath a certain kind of power over the Laws themselves*, a power *so extensive and unlimited* that he may (as oft as necessity requires it and the present danger will not admit delays) for the defence of himself and Subjects from the suddain incursions or invasion of Foreign, and the Villanies of domestick enemies *by his Prerogative and the fulness of his power* for a while *dispense* with the severe and literal observation of his Laws; or at least *suspend* their force for a time, least by a zealous and unseasonable veneration for, and obedience to them he suffer himself, his people, and the very Laws themselves, to become a Prey to Forreign or domestick Enemies.[239]

A populist spin on Cicero's intent was forestalled by classifying the sentence as one of the Roman *mos maiorum* and addressed specifically to the consuls, or rulers, and not the populace at large.[240]

As for the potential danger of leaving such a fund of unsupervised power under royal control, the author hesitated. Unwilling to concede any popular gloss on the Ciceronian tag, he nevertheless

Protestantism and Patriotism: Ideology and the Making of English Foreign Policy 1650–1668 (Cambridge, forthcoming).
[237] Anon., *Salus Populi, &c., or the Case of King and People* (London, 1681), p. 2.
[238] *Ibid.*, p. 6.
[239] *Ibid.*, pp. 20–1.   [240] *Ibid.*, p. 23.

could not fail to observe that it was this very problem that had propelled England into civil war. The answer to the rhetorical question is fudged magnificently: 'I answer, that if there should occur such a weighty and unavoidable necessity, in such extremity (as is suppos'd) it seems to me *not altogether unlawful* for the subject to *attempt some thing* without the Knowledge of the King, for necessity (as the Proverb runs) has no Law, *yet I utterly deny that that may be attempted or done which some men suppose Lawful to be attempted and done in such Extremities.*[241]

Those unswayed by either strongly monarchist or strongly republican accounts were extremely wary of the claim of 'necessity' and the emotive appeal to the *salus populi.* Since, according to Halifax, a prince always placed himself in danger when he was compelled to rely on someone more powerful than himself, 'so when Prerogative useth *Necessity* for an Argument, it calleth in a stronger thing than itself. The same Reason may overturn it.' Necessity was so dangerous a claim 'since (wherever it is real) it constitutes every Man a Magistrate, and gives as great a Power of dispensing to every private Man, a Prince can claim'.[242] *Salus populi,* too, though an 'unwritten law', could become all too visible, 'and as often as it is so, it supersedeth all other Laws which are subordinate Things compared'.[243] In his *Account of Government* (*c.*1667), Sir Richard Temple (1634–97) argued that the reason of state 'does so formally & essentially render a Prince a tyrant' because it freed him from the bonds of strict justice. But like other 'trimmers' he also believed that by destroying 'the security of the people & the confidence they ought to have in their Prince' it rendered unstable the foundations of civil society. Precisely because the reason of state was supra-legal and 'where there is no law there is no government', its practice by the ruler actually freed citizens from obligation to their governors.

It being as equal that the people may be absolved from the tie of the law in case of necessity as well as the Prince. And *Salus populi* is as good a ground for the plea as *salus principis* if not stronger; since tis most certain if these be

---

[241] *Ibid.,* p. 26. Later, he describes such a well-motivated citizen as a 'Patriot', invoking, perhaps despite himself, precisely that love of community which is absent from his own wholly monarchist account (p. 33).

[242] Halifax, *Political Thoughts and Reflections,* in *The Complete Works of George Savile, First Marquess of Halifax,* ed. and intro. Walter Raleigh (Oxford, 1912), pp. 222–3.

[243] Halifax, *Political Thoughts and Reflections,* p. 210.

opposed, the good of the whole will be preferred even before any of the noblest parts.[244]

Critics of the Stuart regime made these arguments and reached precisely those conclusions feared by monarchists and foreseen by 'Trimmers'. Algernon Sidney's intellectual campaign was conducted in the language of seventeenth-century political practice, defined by 'justice, reason and the public good'.[245] The emphasis on 'interest' and its role in political society was, of course, shared by many contemporary monarchists, who might also have shared Sidney's affiliation with Lipsius and neo-Stoicism.[246] Unsurprisingly, then, Sidney told a friend that he 'esteemed above all ... for perfecting himself [in the] Science ... [of] politics' Juan Marquez' 'Spanish book entitled *El Governador Cristiano*'.[247] Since preservation was the great and universal law it was indisputable that 'no crown is granted otherwise, than in submission to it'.[248] Like Marquez, for example, Sidney asserted that government was for the public good. But for him that good was best secured by a wide scope for public liberty, a liberty that was explicitly incompatible with monarchical sovereignty:

Besides, if the safety of the people be the supreme law, and this safety extend to, and consist in the preservation of the liberties, goods, lands and lives, that law must necessarily be the root and beginning, as well as the end and limit of all magistratical power, and all laws must be subservient and subordinate to it.

What pleased the king was irrelevant; the public good shaped his charge and constrained his actions. As for his discretionary power, Sidney argued that it existed solely to serve the community. The 'utmost extent of his prerogative is to be able to do more good than any private man'.[249] For in Sidney's vision of seventeenth-century European politics the pursuit of the interest of monarchs necessarily constituted the pursuit of a private interest at the expense of the

[244] Sir Richard Temple, *An Account of Government*, Bod. MS. Eng. Hist. C.20.1, fols. 18v–19r. I am very grateful to Steve Pincus for this reference and characterization of Temple's politics.

[245] Sidney's own words of assurance to the Swedish ambassador in 1659, quoted in Jonathan Scott, *Algernon Sidney and the English Republic, 1623–1677* (Cambridge, 1988), p. 128.

[246] For the neo-Stoic background, see Scott, *Algernon Sidney*, pp. 18, 145.

[247] Quoted in Scott, *Algernon Sidney*, p. 151.

[248] Algernon Sidney, *Discourses on Government*, ed. Thomas G. West (Indianapolis, 1990), II.7, p. 117.

[249] *Ibid.*, III.16, p. 403. See also, III.14, p. 395; III.21, p. 440; I.5, p. 17.

public interest. This unhealthy condition was only remedied by the establishment of a republic, in which the public interest would not be constantly threatened by the actions of a royal court. Sidney argued that the clash between public and private interests threatened the constitution of that 'union' of interests which alone defined community.[250] In the *Discourses* he argued that when those rulers 'set up an interest in their own persons inconsistent with the publick good', after being 'created by the publick consent, for the publick good, shall they not be removed when they prove to be of publick damage?'[251] Ironically, resistance based on a defence of the public good was a central argument in mainstream justifications of the Revolution of 1688.[252]

John Locke, like Sidney, stressed the claims of the public interest and good.[253] Societies began when power was entrusted to a single person 'for the publick Good and Safety' alone.[254] Similarly, in the following chapter, Locke commented that, although individuals relinquished the equality, liberty and executive power that they possessed in the state of nature, the 'Legislature constituted by them, can never be suppos'd to extend farther than the common good'.[255] The imperative of individual self-preservation gave content to the 'publick good' as the measure of legitimate government action. This criterion could be applied to the 'Executive', or the state's powers within its borders, and because states remained in a state of nature

---

[250] For Scott's discussion, *Algernon Sidney*, pp. 188, 195, 197, 201.

[251] Sidney, *Discourses*, ii.24, p. 226.

[252] Marquez, in his *Governador Cristiano* had argued that 'No one should doubt that it is licit to resist the injuries of a tyrant, while recognizing that royal power is sacrosanct. Because the moment when he intends force and tyrannizes he does not act like a Lord. The Civil laws account him a private citizen and the Divine a proud, ravenous man against which common agreement arms the people for their own self-defense' (p. 39). Similarly, John Eliot warned rulers to be wary of their great freedom. Therefore, 'saies Seneca, *errat si quis existimat tutum ibi esse regem, ubi nihil a regem tutum*; he errs, saies he, that thinkes a king may there be safe where there is nothing in safetie from the King; *Securitas securitati mutua pascenda est*, securitie must be ballanc'd by securities, it is a *terminus convertibilis*, betweene the Prince & people, a common tearme of safety, wch by mutuall & reciprocall affections one receiues from the other' (*Monarchie of Man*, pp. 56–7).

[253] This has been emphasized by the most recent commentators on Sidney, Jonathan Scott and Alan Houston.

[254] Locke, *Second Treatise*, in *Two Treatises of Government*, ed. Peter Laslett (Cambridge, 1960; rpt, New York, 1965), ii.8.110, p. 386. Locke himself distinguished between two very different kinds of political thought: 'Politics contains two parts, very different the one from the other; the one containing the original of societies and the rise and extent of political power, the other, the art of governing men in society' (quoted in J. P. Kenyon, *Revolution Principles: The politics of party 1689–1720* (Cambridge, 1990; 1st edn, 1977), p. 2).

[255] Locke, *Second Treatise*, ii.8.131, p. 398; also ii.11.135, p. 403.

relative to each other, also to its 'Federative' powers, 'the management of the *security and interest of the publick without*'. The logic of the reason of state, rather than the sure guidance of established precedent and 'standing, positive Laws', dictated the international posture of the state. National self-preservation suggested a different kind of practice, 'and so must necessarily be left to the Prudence and Wisdom of those whose hands it is in, to be managed for the publick good'. While laws could be promulgated to control the actions of one's citizens, 'the variation of designs and interests' of foreign powers put the emphasis on the government's capacity to react and so had to 'be left in great part to the *Prudence*' of governors 'to be managed by the best of their Skill, for the advantage of the Commonwealth'.[256]

Locke's discussion of 'Prerogative', fundamentally a common law category, enabled him to address one of the central themes of contemporary political discussion, 'necessity', in a language familiar to Englishmen. It followed logically from an analysis of the need for prudence and flexibility in an otherwise weak 'Executive' power. Invariably, wrote Locke, there were occasions which could not be anticipated by legislation and had to be 'left to the discretion' of the ruler to be managed 'as the publick good and advantage shall require; nay, 'tis fit that the Laws themselves should in some cases give way to the executive Power, or rather to this Fundamental Law of Nature and Government, viz. That as much as may be, *all* the Members of the Society are to be *preserved*'. Locke illustrated this with the familiar Roman Law example of the urban fire in which public utility (stopping the fire by tearing down houses to create a fire-break) clashed with individual good (the private property that is destroyed for the public utility).[257]

Both Jonathan Scott and Alan Houston have emphasized the points of contact between Locke and Sidney. On the matter of the king's prerogative power, Sidney insisted still more strongly on the fundamentally popular purpose of royal discretionary power. Even Filmer, he wrote, was 'obliged' to admit 'that the king's prerogative is instituted for the good of those that are under it'. Because prerogative existed solely to serve more effectively the public good, 'it can no otherwise subsist than in concurrence with that end'. Hence, Filmer

---

[256] *Ibid.*, II.xii.147, pp. 411–12.   [257] *Ibid.*, II.14.159, p. 421.

himself had to agree that *'the safety of the people is the supreme law'* and the very measure of royal discretionary power.[258]

When William arrived and James fled, Sidney's defence of resistance to rulers who failed the public good was adopted by those who would never have defined that 'good' as the liberty of the people. Supporters of the new regime fought shy of justifying resistance, and so comfortably adopted the view, right from the start, that the deeds of James II had vitiated the legitimacy of his claim. The 'Nobility, Gentry and Commonalty' that assembled at Nottingham declared, on 22 November 1688, that,

We assure ourselves that no rational and unbiassed person will judge it rebellion to defend our laws and religion, which all our princes have sworn at their coronations ... *We own it rebellion to resist a king that governs by law, but he was always accounted a tyrant that made his will his law; and to resist such an one we justly esteem no rebellion, but a necessary defence.*[259]

The war of broadsheets, papers and pamphlets that exploded in its wake spread this argument far and wide.[260] *A Memorial Drawn by King William's Special Direction* (1689) emphasized that the 'revolution' set in train by James' actions 'carries in it no precedent against the security of government' because that 'which an absolute necessity enforced at one time can be no warrant for irregular proceedings at any other time'.[261] Because there was almost no one who disagreed that 'the great and fundamental Law of Nature is *Self-preservation'*[262] it was easily asserted that 'in great Exigencies, and extraordinary Junctures of Affairs, in which the Ruin and Destruction of the Publick is inevitably involv'd', the people had to look to their own survival. This was no sanction for rebellion – what was invoked was a more familiar theme: 'But in extraordinary Cases, these are no Rules; but Necessity has her Laws: As in a time of raging Famine, Propriety of Goods may be forc'd; Corn may by

[258] Sidney, *Discourses*, III.26, p. 470.
[259] Quoted in Kenyon, *Revolution Principles*, p. 6. Also, Anon., *The Advantages of the Present Settlement and the Great Danger of a Relapse*, in *A Collection of State Tracts Publish'd on Occasion of the Late Revolution of 1688, and during the Reign of King William III*, 3 vols. (London, 1705), I, p. 272.
[260] Mark Goldie ('The Revolution of 1689 and the structure of Political Argument', *Bulletin of Research in the Humanities*, 83 (1980), 473–564) contends that 300,000 copies of allegiance pamphlets were in circulation, more than one for every two literate adult males, more than one for every elector and more than eight for every adult with higher education.
[261] Quoted in Kenyon, *Revolution Principles*, p. 45.
[262] Anon., *A Dialogue between Two Friends, A Jacobite and a Williamite, Occasion'd by the Late Revolution of Affairs and the Oath of Obedience*, in *State Tracts*, I, p. 287.

violence be taken from private men, and sold for the publick Relief'.[263] Many of these tracts emphasized the language of 'ruin' and 'destruction'[264] since the admission of this circumstance then triggered the universally accepted natural right to self-preservation. One author cited the rabbinic dictum that *Periculum animae impellit Sabbathum* (danger of death defers the Sabbath) in a discussion of the relationship between necessity and self-preservation.[265] And there were the inevitable references to *salus populi*, now, of course, supporting revolution. Matthew Tindal declared that the 'Consideration of *Publick Good*' is '*the Supreme Law* by which both King and People ought to guide their Actions'.[266] Though conflating 'public good' and *salus populi*, the implication is the same: the 'Fundamental Law' constituted by the public good was set into motion by the threat of 'War and Confusion'.[267] Another wrote, 'I cannot but with *Grotius* believe that *Salus populi est Suprema Lex*. Nor did *Junius Brutus* err in affirming that, *Imperii finis unicus est Populi utilitas* [the public utility is the sole end of government].'[268] A Scottish author even invoked the maxim to support his argument for a quick show of obedience to William and Mary.[269]

Given that the consequences of the Revolution were still being debated a century thence, it is surely no surprise to find these arguments, so basic to the questions of sovereignty and obligation that dogged the new regime in its first decades, recurring again and again. The decision of a group of clergy not to swear allegiance to the new regime but instead give merely 'passive obedience' kept at the forefront of debate the legitimacy of a government installed by

---

[263] Anon., *A Dialogue between Two Friends*, p. 298.

[264] For example, Anon., *An Enquiry into the Present State of Affairs* (1688), in *State Tracts*, I, p. 129.

[265] Anon., *The Proceedings of the Present Parliament Justified by the Opinion of the Most Judicious and Learned Hugo Grotius*, in *State Tracts*, I, p. 182.

[266] Matthew Tindal, *An Essay Concerning Obedience to the Supreme Powers, and the Duty of Subjects in All Revolutions* (London, 1694), p. 15.

[267] Tindal, *Essay concerning Obedience*, p. 19.

[268] Anon., *Some Remarks upon Government, and Particularly upon the Establishment of the English Monarchy, Relating to This Present Juncture*, in *State Tracts*, I, p. 152. Both these references are also made in *The Proceedings of the Present Parliament*, p. 181.

[269] 'But the Kingdom being obliged by the most high Law, to wit, *Salus Populi suprema Lex esto*, and the most cogent necessity of *self-preservation*, to fly and betake it self to his Highness *Heavens-sent* Protection; it is impossible for us to retreat from it, without a most ungrate perfidie toward the Prince, and Damnable folly toward ourselves, in rendering the whole Kingdom obnoxious to a greater Forfeiture, than can be secured against, by any offered Pardon and Indemnity, in our present circumstances' (Anon., *Salus Populi Suprema Lex. Or, the Free Thoughts of a Well Wisher, for a Good Settlement*, (n.p., 1689), p. 5).

revolution. In a sermon on Romans XIII preached before the Lord Mayor of London 29 September 1705, Benjamin Hoadly had sought to justify subjection to the new 'higher powers' by demonstrating the legitimacy of the Revolution. A forceful polemicist, the basis of his argument was the familiar defence of the requirements of the public good. Where Paul commended rulers as God's ministers to whom obedience was due, Hoadly argued 'that the meaning of this can only be, that it is his Will that they enjoy this Power of the public Good'. Consequently, the ruler 'who is not continually watching for the Good and Happiness of Humane Society, is not the Governour whom Paul means in this place, or to whom He here presses obedience'. Moreover, the Apostle's commandment to submit was never intended to ordain subjection to rulers who manifestly violated their charge and misused their authority. In such a case Paul 'plainly leaves nations to the Dictates of common Sense, and the powerful Law of self-preservation'. Hoadly concluded by describing this as Paul's account of 'Governours and Subjects'.[270]

In the preface to the fifth edition of the published version (1718), entitled *The Measures of Submission to the Civil Magistrate Considered*, Hoadly singled out a particular critic, the author of *The Plea of Public Good not Sufficient to Justify the Taking up Arms against our Rightful and Lawful Sovereigns*. In his response, Hoadly asserted the existence of a public good independent of, and prior to, the ruler's. The 'Interest of the body Politic is not tied to one particular Head; and so may be distinct, and sought distinctly from it'. In theory, of course, Hoadly believed that the interests of rulers and ruled *ought* to coincide. If, however, reality were to prove somewhat more intractable, then the public good was to determine the interest of the state and the practice of the monarch:

The True Interest of Kings can never be separated from the *true Interest* of that *Public* of which they are the *Head*; i.e. as long as they are at the Head, it is their chief, and great Interest to promote the *Public Good*: But if they turn aside from this great End, and are endeavouring to overturn and ruine this; in such case (which is ever in my Supposition) the Public Good cannot be the same with any thing inconsistent with it; with the private Advantage,

---

[270] Hoadly, 'The Measures of Submission to the Civil Magistrate Considered', *The Works of Benjamin Hoadly*, ed. John Hoadly, 3 vols. (London, 1773), II, pp. 20–3. See especially Sermon XIII, 'The Nature and Duty of a Publick Spirit', delivered on 1 March 1716, *Works*, III, pp. 638–44. For an assessment of his skill and overview of the subsequent controversy, see Kenyon, *Revolution Principles*, p. 116.

the imaginary, mistaken Interest of any person whatsoever who is attempting the Destruction of it.[271]

This distinction enabled Hoadly to defend the legitimacy of resistance to James II, who clearly pursued his own rather than the public interest. But because only rulers whose actions secured and enhanced the good of the community could command obedience, Hoadly provided an iron-clad support for the new and virtuous rulers of the state.[272] While the critic believed that Hoadly had confused authority, the 'true Ground of Allegiance', with mere convenience, Hoadly contended that Paul had himself made 'Public Good' the basis of authority and hence allegiance.[273]

This definition of 'authority' may itself have been drawn from Locke's argument in the final chapter of the *Second Treatise*, in which William Barclay's defence of absolute monarchy was confuted. Locke claimed that Barclay himself admitted that 'In whatsoever he has no Authority, there he is no King, and may be resisted.' According to Locke, 'The breach of trust, in not preserving the Form of Government agreed on, and in not intending the end of Government it self, which is the publick good and preservation of Property', constituted a forfeit of royal 'authority'.[274]

Others, in the second decade of the century, were employing the very same argument to defend resistance, in principle, to rulers. John Jackson, who is best remembered as Samuel Clarke's intellectual shield-bearer, was defining the limits of obedience in 1718 in the terms forged by the 'revolutionaries' of 1688:

That the *public Good*, in all governments, is the *Supreme indispensible* Law, to which all others must be conformable, or give Place; and that all Governments, of what kind soever, are in their own Natures absolutely *equal* in Power; and that no Government, or *Supreme Legislative* Power, can have a Right to make Laws, or do any thing, that is *destructive* of the public Welfare; and that the community, from whose Consent alone all Power is *naturally* deriv'd, (into whatsoever Hands), for the Preservation of their natural Rights, which is the public Good, must have a Power or Right to maintain and defend those Rights by Force, *whenever* or by *whomsoever* they are invaded.[275]

---

[271] Benjamin Hoadly, 'The Measures of Submission to the Civil Magistrate Considered in a Defense of the Doctrine Preached in a Sermon 29 September 1705', *Works*, II, p. 5.
[272] *Ibid.*, *Works*, II, p. 9.   [273] *Ibid.*, *Works*, II, p. 10.
[274] Locke, *Second Treatise*, II.18.239, p. 474.
[275] John Jackson, *The Grounds of Civil and Ecclesiastical Government Briefly Considered* (London, 1718), p. 7.

The language of 'ruin' and 'destruction' created a 'necessity' in which consideration of the public good could override the existing laws. Citations from scripture showed 'that the grand Principle of *Self-Preservation* and of the *public Good*, being the *Supreme Law*, is not only *natural*, but *Christian*'.[276] Thomas Gordon, writing both as *Cato* and under his own name, contended that the failure of government to serve the public good constituted a deviation from its task and so, while it was 'certainly unlawful to resist Government' it was 'certainly lawful to resist the deviation from Government'.[277] One would want to emphasize that this mainstream defence of the Revolution of 1688 was based on the most mediated understanding of the political role of the individual. While fundamentally the entire argument depended on a notion of self-preservation and *salus populi*, this reliance on the notion of a 'public good' was continually distinguished from republican arguments, which also spoke of a 'public'. Gordon's assessment is most revealing:

Cardinal De Retz says, that with all the arguments and pains he could use, he could never bring the Queen Regent to understand the meaning of these words, *the Publick*: she thought that to consult the interest of the People, was to be a Republican, and had no notion that the Government of a Prince was anything else but Royal Will and authority, rampant and without bounds.[278]

Henry Sacheverell's attack on this set of ideas was the most cogent and damaging of the post-revolutionary period. At the opening of Anne's reign he preached on the subject of *The Political Union: A Discourse Shewing the Dependence of Government on Religion* (1710). This is the standard post-Reformation argument that the mutual support of church and state was the best means to secure the latter's conservation: 'That Religion is the Grand Support of Government; that the Peace, Happiness, and Prosperity of the Secular and Civil Power, depends upon that of the Spiritual and Ecclesiastical.' It was

---

[276] *Ibid.*, p. 13.
[277] The duty of governors was clearly spelled out in *Cato's Letters*, no. 25: 'The Good of the Governed being the sole End of Government, they must be the greatest and best Governors, who make their People great and happy; and they the worst, who make their People little, wicked, and miserable. Power in a free State, is a Trust committed by All to One or a Few, to watch for the Security, and pursue the Interest, of All: And, when that Security is not sought, nor that Interest obtained, we know what Opinion the People will have of their Governors' (*Cato's Letters*, 4 vols. 4th edn, London, 1737), 15 April 1721, I, p. 184. The defence of this kind of resistance is in his *Discourses on Tacitus* (2nd edn, London, 1737), p. 53.
[278] Gordon, *Tacitus*, p. 58.

impossible to speak of one sphere encroaching on the other since they were 'two parts and divisions that both united make up one compounded constitution and body politic'.[279] Without control of the 'Inward State of the Soul' offered by religion, 'All the Arts and Policies of State Government in the world, could not in the least be Able to Preserve Mankind in Safety and Security from one another's Evil Intentions.'[280] Like his seventeenth-century forbears, Sacheverell singled out Machiavelli as 'the founder and Oracle of all Worldly Policy', whose endorsement of deceit and simulated faith had shattered this alliance.[281] Hence his catchy claim that 'Atheism and Anarchy have always went hand in hand'.[282] By undermining the established church with an Act of Toleration and the monarchy with the alteration of succession the Revolution of 1688 threatened that union upon which the state depended.

The argument of this sermon was the basis of the highly flammable text preached and printed as *The Perils of False Brethren* (1710). 'The Grand Security of our Government', Sacheverell declaimed, 'and the very Pillar upon which it stands, is founded upon the steady belief of the Subject's obligation to an Absolute and Unconditional Obedience to the Supream Power, in all things Lawful, and the Utter Illegality of Resistance upon any Pretence whatsoever.'[283] The common view that resistance was permissible under certain conditions, referring to the influence of Hoadly's argument, was extremely dangerous since this 'New fangl'd Notion of Self-Defence' could 'serve to justifie all the Rebellions that ever were, or can be committed in the World'.[284] Moreover, Sacheverell perceived 'Trimming between the Church and Dissenters both in Conscience and Prudence' as a solvent of the alliance between church and state, without which obedience was suspect because based 'upon no Principle, but meer Interest and Ambition'.[285]

Printed without the imprimatur of the Court of Aldermen, *The Perils of False Brethren* quickly sold an estimated 100,000 copies in six printed versions, and according to Geoffrey Holmes, had no equal

---

279 Henry Sacheverell, *The Political Union: a Discourse Shewing the Dependance of Government on Religion in General; and of the English Monarchy on the Church of England in Particular* (Oxford, 1710; 1st edn, 1702), pp. 5–6.
280 *Ibid.*, pp. 10–11.   281 *Ibid.*, p. 15.   282 *Ibid.*, p. 9.
283 Sacheverell, *The Perils of False Brethren, Both in Church and State* (London, 1709), p. 9.
284 *Ibid.*, p. 10.   285 *Ibid.*, p. 12.

as a short-term bestseller in the early eighteenth century.[286] When, no longer able to stomach such a threat to the principle of the new state, the Whigs brought Sacheverell to trial they were outmanoeuvered. By falling back on Grotius' and Pufendorf's defence of extreme 'necessity', the managers of Sacheverell's case were able to affirm the result of 1688 without giving up the principle that resistance was generally inadmissible.[287] The Whigs, meanwhile, were put in the position of either having to endure the embarrassment of being seen to agree with Sacheverell or denying his argument by endorsing the notion of the Revolution as a case of resistance, which they had thus far sought to avoid.[288]

Apart from Sacheverell, even Whigs worried about the implications of 'necessity'. *Cato* warned of sycophants who maliciously advised princes, 'by suggesting Danger where it is not, and urging Necessity where there is none'. They enriched themselves 'pretending the publick Exigencies of the State' and sacrificed political opponents 'under Pretence of publick Security'.[289] John Jackson, whose commitment to the claim of *salus populi* was balanced by an explicitly Stoic belief in natural goodness, emphasized the fine balance between utility and honesty. Facile claims made for immediate political gain were unacceptable and dangerous:

The *Matter* which constitutes *Humane* Law in General, is not to be deriv'd (as some great Lawyers and States-men have thought,) from the meer Will or political Societies consenting to what may most advance, each, their own particular *Interest* and *Power*. This *Machiavellian* Notion too much contracts the *Humanity* of our Nature, and gives too much occasion to unreasonable and inordinate Ambition, and to the unjust Oppression of our Neighbours, and Usurpation of their Rights.[290]

The lions' share of Bernard Mandeville's wit seems to have been reserved for the kind of public-spirited but aesthetic citizen suggested by Shaftesbury and *The Spectator*. His mockery also extended

---

[286] Its readership would have equalled the number of electors in England and Wales. See Geoffrey Holmes, *The Trial of Doctor Sacheverell* (London, 1973), p. 75.

[287] Mark Goldie has observed, that this manoeuvre 'wrecked the case for absolute non-resistance' ('Tory Political Thought, 1689–1714', Unpublished Ph.D. thesis (Cambridge, 1978), p. 321). For more on this defence see Goldie, p. 31, pp. 286–7.

[288] Kenyon, *Revolution Principles*, pp. 138–42.

[289] *Cato's Letters*, no. 62, 20 January 1721, II, p. 254.

[290] Jackson, *Grounds of Civil and Ecclesiastical Government*, p. 3; also, p. 2. Recalling the natural law writers of the previous century, Jackson opposed to the demands of utility, 'the Doctrine of the Stoics that the Original of Law was deriv'd from God and Nature'. Human law was a result of making 'particular Deductions from the general principles of Nature or Reason, or from the reveal'd Law of God' (p. 4).

to those who 'preach up Publick-spiritedness, that they might reap the Fruits of the Labour and Self-denial of others'[291] and those politicians who paraded the public good. Cleomenes' new-found confidence in the politician's pursuit of the public good in the first *Dialogue* drips with sarcasm: 'Formerly I thought, that Chief Ministers, and all those at the Helm of Affairs, acted from Principles of Avarice and Ambition; that in all the Pains they took, and even in the Slaveries they underwent for the Publick Good, they had their private Ends, and that they were supported in the Fatigue by secret Enjoyments they were unwilling to own.' But in the last month, says Cleomenes, 'I have abandon'd that ill-natur'd way of judging: I plainly perceive the Publick Good, in all the designs of Politicians, the social Virtues shine in every Action, and I find that the national Interest is the Compass that all Statesmen steer by.'[292]

Despite the famous Bangorian Controversy which ended his chances of advancement within the church, Hoadly's defence of the British state earned him a pension and employment as a government propagandist under Walpole. Writing as 'Britannicus' in the *London Journal*, Hoadly used the logic of the reason of state to support the policies of the administration. He defended the categorical distinction between rulers and ruled that was manifested in the inaccessibility of the 'Secrets of Statesmen'. Ministerial secrecy and authority was most certainly not to be confused with despotism. In time of need the governors had to have discretionary power to act. The Romans were no less lovers of liberty than the British yet their senate appointed dictators 'to have the last and highest Authority, without Appeal in the City and in the Camp' without constant fretting about conspiracies against their liberty.[293] Hoadly's own sympathy with the dissenters put him at pains to insist that action against enemies of the civil constitution was legitimate only 'as far as the security of the Publick requires it, and for the Sake of their Civil Enmity alone'. Moreover, this threat had to be such 'as immediately affects the State, in distinction to that more Distant, Remote, Accidental Hurt'. He excluded cases in which religious civil issues were interwoven. However, this caution about general practice did not at all restrict the government's capacity to strike pre-emptively against a conspiracy 'as far as present Necessity requires' on 'the Grounds of

---

291 Bernard Mandeville, 'Enquiry', in *The Fable of the Bees*, ed. F. B. Kaye, 2 vols. (Oxford, 1924), I, p. 49.
292 Bernard Mandeville, 'Second Dialogue', *ibid.*, II, p. 41.
293 Hoadly, Letter of 27 October 1722, *Works*, III, pp. 25, 28.

that just Suspicion alone'. In arbitrary governments the prince exercised this discretionary, or prerogative power, while in free states it was procedural and legislated, as in ancient Rome. Hoadly again appealed to the seventeenth-century language of prudential politics:

And the Reason is plainly the same, which bars them from such a Procedure in ordinary Cases, and which runs through every Branch of this Argument, viz. The Interest of the Whole: Because it is undoubtedly for the Interest of the Society, rather to run the Hazard of an Abuse of Power, and suffer Inconveniences from thence, for a Season, upon such extraordinary Occasions; than to be certainly undone, for the want of such a Power lodged somewhere.[294]

Hoadly's justification of extra-legal steps taken to secure the welfare of the public, and indeed, the earlier tradition whose arguments he here rehearses, rests upon the broad inheritance of Ciceronian moral and political philosophy. The conflict between utility and good was not invented in the sixteenth century. The literature of necessity, in so far as it may have been stimulated by the contemporary needs of states and statesmen, drew upon an old and familiar tradition. The specific conditions and needs of contemporary political practice made this an inescapable issue. The complicated relationship between religious, or ethical norms, and politics, difficult in ideal conditions, was put under terrific pressure by the financial, martial and territorial strains confronting nearly every European state in the seventeenth century. English, and then British, history takes its place in this wider European narrative. Just as each of the writers we have encountered was addressing local problems rather than some large and amorphous European tradition to which they, nevertheless, are so obviously connected, there were specific conditions motivating the English and British discussions of necessity and the public good. In the remaining chapters we shall focus on the way in which this language of political thought was used to address a set of political problems in eighteenth-century Britain and how, in turn, its limitations shaped the way in which they were eventually confronted.

---

[294] Hoadly, Letter of 5 January 1722/3, *Works*, III, pp. 59–62. In his *Preservative against the Principles and Practices of the Non-Jurors Both in Church and State* (1716), Benjamin Hoadly defended the seizure of episcopal property and office in cases of disloyalty: 'Every civil Government hath a Right to every thing necessary for its own Defense, and Preservation' (*Works*, I, p. 574). According to Reed Browning, Hoadly's 'central argument was the unabashed invocation of *raison d'état*' (*The Political and Constitutional Ideas of the Court Whigs* (Baton Rouge, LA, 1982), p. 86).

CHAPTER 2

A classical landscape

PATRIOTISM, PARTY AND PITT

The Revolution of 1688 installed a new dynasty. After its failure, parliament legislated for the future of the succession. In 1707 the Anglo-Scottish Union was confirmed by the respective parliaments. These events permanently altered the landscape of political debate in what was now called Great Britain. The events of 1688–9 remained the touchstone of political argument throughout the century that followed. The extent of the aftershocks can be gauged from the new regime's continuing need to defend its legitimacy and assure itself of the loyalty and obedience of its subjects. Thus Edmund Burke, in his *Appeal from the New to the Old Whigs* (1791), affirmed the principles of British politics against the French revolutionaries by explicitly returning to the Whig vision of 1688 and reviewing the arguments of the Sacheverell trial. While the language of the 'public good' and 'necessity' remained current, as politicians dealt with 'normal' rather than revolutionary events, it was now used more and more in its original context, the justification of political practice. Politics in eighteenth-century Britain has conventionally been framed in terms of party: the absence, disappearance, fragmentation or revival of party has structured the most important and incisive examinations of its political culture.[1] The conditions of party politics raised the same questions about the conflict between the useful and the good that, in the seventeenth century, often issued in open warfare.

---

[1] See, for example, J. H. Plumb, *The Growth of Political of Stability in England 1675–1720* (London, 1967); John Cannon, *Aristocratic Century* (Cambridge, 1984); Keith Fieling, *The Second Tory Party 1714–1832* (London, 1951); Louis Namier, *The Structure of Politics at the Accession of George III* (2nd edn, London, 1957); Louis Namier, *England in the Age of the American Revolution* 2nd edn, London, (1961); Jonathan Clark, *Dynamics of Power: The Structure of Politics* (Cambridge, 1985); Linda Colley, *In Defiance of Oligarchy* (Cambridge, 1983).

Loyalty to party was often seen to clash with loyalty to a putative national interest: precisely the seventeenth-century story.[2] In this context, an opposition party could easily be branded a faction and therefore an enemy of the public good. The only option for opponents of the government was to claim that *they*, in fact, had the best interest of the nation at heart while the governors were moved solely by desire for personal gain. The identification of personal with national interest made licit the existence of party. This notional relationship between individual and community closely resembles the patriotic arguments of Cicero. And in this British reshaping of the language of the common good, Cicero provided the model for the squaring of this very circle: the patriotic minister.

The opposition to Walpole sought legitimacy in the name of 'Patriots' while the 'Court Whigs' vigorously contested this claim.[3] The latter identified themselves by their devotion to the constitution and their commitment was to liberty under law as the only guarantee of individual and national self-preservation. Lord Hervey's discussion at the beginning of his *Ancient and Modern Liberty* (1734) reflects the 'line' propounded by mainstream writers in the middle decades of the century:

And as it must be granted, that all Peace, all Order in Society is maintain'd by some Restrictions on natural Liberty, and that the Anarchy of natural Liberty, wholly unrestrain'd, would be as great an Evil as the Slavery of no Liberty at all allow'd; so the best regulated and best concerted Form of Government must be that which avoids the Inconveniences of both Extremes, and at once preserves Mankind from the Oppressions consequent to an absolute Submission to the Will of another, and from the Confusion that would result from an unlimited Indulgence of their Own.[4]

William Arnall's (?1715–?1741) defence of the administration, *Clodius and Cicero* (1727), explicitly linked the Court Whig practice of politics with the radical steps taken by Cicero to quash the Catilinarian conspiracy. Walpole's defence of the common good is described in the language of patriotism, while the ease with which an oppo-

---

[2] Halifax expressed this typical post-Renaissance view: 'That *Parties* in a *State* generally, like *Freebooters*, hang out *False Colours*; the pretence is the *Publick Good*; the real *Business* is, to catch *Prizes*; like the *Tartars*, where-ever they succeed, instead of Improving their *Victory*, they presently fall upon the *Baggage*' (*Maxims of State*, no. 23, in *Works*, p. 182).

[3] See Hugh Cunningham, 'The Language of Patriotism, 1750–1914', *History Workshop*, 12 (1981), 9–11.

[4] [Lord Hervey], *Ancient and Modern Liberty Stated and Compar'd* (London, 1734), p. 3. For more on Hervey, see Robert Halsband, *Lord Hervey: Eighteenth-Century Courtier* (Oxford, 1973).

sition could harangue and accuse is cited as evidence of their commensurate lack of commitment to the state. Such a comparison of the 'Acts of Policy and Power' with 'those of Discontent and Opposition' raised a useful question:

Why may not Zeal (if the Welfare of the State be the drift and Spur of that Zeal) be as well placed in supporting an Administration, as in undermining and assaulting it? Why are not extraordinary Means and Expences justifiable for preserving a Settlement, when extraordinary Methods, and all Methods, are taken to embarass and blow it up? Is it equitable and righteous to inflame, exasperate and distress; but arbitrary and violent to appease, soften and relieve? ... At such a Conjecture, Patriotism is on the Court Side.[5]

The justification of 'extraordinary Means' as patriotic when done in the service of the community is linked to Cicero in an even more suggestive fashion. 'Was there any Comparison between Cicero and Catiline;' Arnall declares, 'any between Cicero and Clodius; or any between the great Cardinal Richelieu and his vain Competitor Cinqmars?'[6] While the identification of Cicero with patriotism was common, Richelieu as model patriotic minister was not. Nor, surely, was the analogy of Cicero to Richelieu intended as a homage to republican liberty.

The most famous and mass-market attempt to identify Cicero with Walpole was Conyers Middleton's blockbuster biography of 1741.[7] He did not lump Cicero together with the old Stoics, whom he describes as 'the bigots or enthusiasts in philosophy', nor, obviously, with the Epicureans. Rather, 'Cicero chose the middle way between the obstinacy of Cato and the indolence of Atticus' accepting the probable when he could not secure the true.[8] In this characteristic early modern presentation, Cicero is depicted as a follower of the New Academy and the Middle Stoa. Middleton's dedication to

---

5 [William Arnall], *Clodius and Cicero. With Other Examples and Reasonings, in Defence of Just Measures against Faction and Obloquy, Suited to the Present Conjuncture* (London, 1727), pp. 6–7. For a recent look at Arnall, see Thomas Horne, 'Politics in a Corrupt Society: William Arnall's Defense of Robert Walpole', *Journal of the History of Ideas*, 41 (1980), 601–14.

6 [Arnall], *Clodius and Cicero*, p. 8.

7 Middleton was a fellow of Trinity College, Cambridge (1706–19), principal librarian of the University (1721–50) and Woodwardian professor (1731–4). George Lloyd Lyttleton's *Observations on the Life of Cicero*, originally published in 1733, was also reprinted in 1741. In the preceding years, the *London Magazine* (VII, 1738, and IX, 1740) ran a series of accounts of parliamentary debates in which the leading figures were all given Roman names. Walpole was called Cicero.

8 Conyers Middleton, *The History of the Life of Marcus Tullius Cicero*, 2 vols. (London, 1742), II, pp. 564–7.

Lord Hervey, Keeper of the Privy Seal and one of Browning's 'Court Whigs', paints the familiar picture of this Lipsian *persona*:

There is another circumstance peculiar to Your Lordship, which makes this task of Study the easier to you, by giving You not onely the greater health, but the greater leisure to pursue it; I mean that singular temperance in diet, in which Your Lordship perseveres with a constancy, superior to every temptation, that can excite an appetite to rebel; and shews a firmness of mind, that subjects every gratification of sense to the rule of right reason. Thus with all the accomplishments of the Nobleman, You lead the life of a Philosopher; and while You shine a principal ornament of the Court, You practise the discipline of the College.[9]

Middleton also read Cicero as a forerunner of Enlightenment natural religion, much as Virgil had been read as a prophet of Christianity.[10] In particular, he was made into a monotheist who believed in Providence, the immortality of the soul, Redemption and the inherent difference between good and evil. Cicero's pagan naturalism was cited by post-Reformation writers because it made him that much more acceptable an authority than, say, Tacitus, with his harsh views of both Jews and Christians.[11] Even more importantly for our story, however, is that the moral system Middleton ascribes to Cicero is precisely what was presented by Samuel Clarke, himself suspected of Arianism and commonly identified as a Stoic, in the name of Cicero in the course of his Boyle Lectures in 1704 and 1705 (see chapter 5):

From this source he deduced the origin of all duty, or moral obligation; from *the will of God, manifested in his works*; or from that *eternal reason, fitness and relation of things*, which is displayed in every part of the creation. This he calls the *original, immutable law; the criterion of good and ill; of just and unjust;*

---

9 Ibid., p. viii. Compare this with Smith's strikingly similar description of the individual shaped by the guidance of that 'man within the breast', which itself closely resembles the Stoic wise man: 'The man of real constancy and firmness, the wise and just man who has been thoroughly bred in the great school of self-command, in the bustle and business of the world, exposed, perhaps, to the violence and injustice of faction, and to the hardships and hazards of war, maintains this control of his passive feelings upon all occasions; and whether in solitude or in society, wears nearly the same countenance, and is affected very nearly in the same manner. In success and in disappointment, in prosperity and in adversity, before friends and before enemies, he has often been under the necessity of supporting this manhood' (*Theory of Moral Sentiments*, ed D. D. Raphael and A. L. Macfie (Indianapolis, 1982), VII.ii.1–48–9, pp. 293–4).

10 But his attack on the superstition of Roman religion was also mined by deists. See Günter Gawlick, 'Cicero and the Enlightenment', *Studies on Voltaire and the Eighteenth Century*, 25 (1963), 657–82; Justin Champion, *The Pillars of Priestcraft Shaken: The Church of England and its Enemies 1660–1730* (Cambridge, 1992), pp. 183–6.

11 See, for example, Rivadeneira, *Tratado*, I.iv, p. 462.

imprinted on the nature of things, as the rule, by which all human laws are to be formed; which, whenever they deviate from this pattern, ought, he says, to be called any thing rather than laws.[12]

But by far the most thorough identification of Cicero with ministerial patriotism was in Thomas Gordon's *Political Discourses* prefixed to his translation of Sallust. The perceived relationship between Sallust and Cicero may have triggered this discussion. Though Sallust actually praised Cicero's handling of matters in his *Catiline's Conspiracy*, eighteenth-century writers often reacted to the 'Invective against Cicero', now believed a pseudo-Sallustian work.[13] Gordon's response was an extended and indubitable encomium. While the history told by Tacitus lent itself to discourses about tyranny and the evil of one-man rule, the story told by Sallust concentrated on faction and corruption.[14] It is a defective account, however, because he treated Cicero 'with the Contempt of a few civil Epithets', a wholly unworthy treatment of 'that great Man, by Right the Hero of his History'. The real Cicero was nowhere to be seen. His 'high Courage, his Penetration, his wise Schemes, his Address and Temporizing, his various and prevailing Eloquence' were treated as ordinary accomplishments. 'He gives you Cicero for a Man of Sense, Experience, and Credit', wrote Gordon. 'But in him you behold not Cicero, the consummate Statesman, the inimitable Orator, the determined Patriot.'[15] These are the basic themes emphasized in Gordon's version.[16]

---

[12] Middleton, *Cicero*, II, pp. 548–58; the quote is on p. 556.

[13] See Richard Steele, *The Tatler*, ed. and intro. Donald F. Bond, 3 vols. (Oxford, 1987), no. 62, I, pp. 430–1: 'I have been just now reading the Introduction to the History of *Catiline* by Sallust, an Author who is very much in my Favour; but when I reflect upon his professing himself wholly disinterested, and at the same Time see how industriously he has avoided saying any Thing to the Praise of Cicero, to whose Vigilance the Commonwealth owed its Safety, it very much lessens my Esteem for that Writer, and is one Argument, among others, for laughing at all who pretend to be out of the Interests of the World, and profess purely to act for the Service of Mankind, without the least Regard to themselves.'

[14] Thomas Gordon, *The Works of Sallust, Translated into English. With Political Discourses upon that Author. To which is added, a Translation of Cicero's Four Orations against Catiline* (London, 1744), sig. Ar.

[15] Gordon, 'Introduction', *Political Discourses*, p. vi.

[16] In the *Letters on the Spirit of Patriotism*, Bolingbroke diminished the importance of eloquence in Cicero's handling of Catiline and instead stressed his political wisdom: '... if he had not united, by skill and management, in the common cause of their country, orders of men the most averse to each other; if he had not watched all the machinations of the conspirators in silence, and prepared a strength sufficient to resist them at Rome, and in the provinces, before he opened this scene of villiany to the senate and the people: in a word, if he had not made much more use of political prudence, that is, of the knowledge of mankind, and of the

Like many seventeenth-century writers, Gordon denied that the common good was broad enough to include the attempts of various politicians and factions to wrap themselves in it. 'Both Sides talk of the Public, and think their own mutual Hate to be Zeal for the Public, whilst they are only weakening and endangering the Public by their eternal Strife. This their Spite to one another, they call Love to their Country.'[17] Contrary to the logic of party, Gordon argued that 'Motives of common Security and Interest' dictated union rather than division. 'A Country divided against itself, cannot stand; nor a Country well united, fall.'[18] The patriot, by contrast,

has always a good Cause, the Cause of his Country and of Mankind, of all others the most important and interesting. His Aim is virtuous, his Ends noble, and therefore all his Pursuits pleasing. The Integrity and laudable Thoughts of his Heart, are a continual Cordial and Support. A Passion for the Public, and the Welfare of Mankind, animates him; the Sense of his Duty fortifies him.[19]

Cicero in action against Catiline was the image of the model patriot 'excited by universal Benevolence to his Country; emboldened by the Goodness of his Cause, and the Approbation of his Conscience, supporting the Interest of public Liberty, and supported by it'.[20] A special obligation was laid on governors to be the 'best' patriots and set an example of patriotism for others since the 'highest and purest Glory is the Freedom and Felicity of their People. To procure this, as it is their Duty and the best Ambition, ought to be the Study and Business of their Lives.'[21]

Cicero's bribery of one of Catiline's co-conspirators raised the old issue about the ambit of necessity. While there was an 'analogy' between public and private morality, it was impossible to deny that sometimes the demands of public office crowded out the considerations of private morals. Sometimes, for example, the public was 'helped, and even saved, by encouraging private Acts of Dishonesty'. Bribery and deception were valid means of uncovering the

arts of government', he would have failed, rhetorical skill notwithstanding (in *Works*, 4 vols.(London, 1844; rpt, 1967), ii, p. 369).
[17] Gordon, *Political Discourses*, p. 22. [18] *Ibid.*, p. 18.
[19] *Ibid.*, p. 37. Also, p. 47: 'He who has a virtuous and tender Regard for the Public; he who wishes and pursues its Welfare; he who rejoices in its Prosperity, and feels its Misfortunes, and is zealous to remove them; he who is jealous of public Liberty as the great Root of all social Felicity; he who dreads and abhors arbitrary Dominion as the most devouring Plague; He, This is the Patriot, the Friend of his Country and deserving its Friendship.'
[20] *Ibid.*, p. 36. [21] *Ibid.*, p. 39.

schemes of one's enemies. If this was an affront to private morals, 'it would be a greater Breach of public Conscience and Morals, to risque the State, or any great public Advantage, for want of it; and, in the Casuistry of a State, the greater Good cancels the smaller Evil'. Gordon had no doubt about the wisdom *and* justice of Cicero's conduct: 'Whatever tends to save or secure the Public, or to mend its Condition, is not Corruption.'[22] By contrast, 'Whatever weakens the Power of a State, is Corruption, however righteous and plausible it may appear.'[23] Thus Catiline's use of bribery 'to promote his Interest against the Interest of the State' was corruption, while Cicero's judicious dispersal of coin was, rather, a demonstration of 'public Spirit'.[24]

Cicero the philosopher and politician was perceived as an exemplar. When William Pitt became the leading minister in 1756 he, too, came to be identified with Cicero. In part, of course, this reflected his reputation for deliberative oratory, but also for his vaunted service to the public (usually referring to his unusual behaviour when, as Paymaster-General during the War of the Austrian Succession, he chose not to pocket as much money as he could get his hands on). In 1761, after Pitt's resignation from office, Richard Cumberland published his *Banishment of Cicero*. The play revived the association of Cicero with prudent patriotism and identified the tribune Clodius with the brutal, impious, passionate and irrational impulses of the masses. Cato was no longer relevant to this story.[25] Rome, meanwhile, was a city 'Rotten at heart, and ripe for dissolution'. It was a diseased 'Public Body' in which magistracies and courts were bought and sold.[26] Clodius' impiety was a characteristic example of this political corruption. 'Whole and untouch'd I mock the wrath of Jove.' In particular, he renounced God's Providence, placing Him beyond worldly cares and yielding 'the reins to chance'.[27]

Cicero was given the task of defining patriotism and it is delivered as a eulogy of his own career.

> By one firm faithful even course of honour;
> By standing forth alone, not Caesar's follower,

---

[22] *Ibid.*, pp. 91–2.   [23] *Ibid.*, p. 96.   [24] *Ibid.*, p. 98.
[25] Richard Cumberland, *The Banishment of Cicero* (London, 1761): 'No more, I sleep o'er Cato's drowsy theme: / He is the Senate's drone, and dreams of Liberty, / When Rome's vast Empire is set up to sale, / And portion'd out to each ambitious bidder / In marketable lots' (p. 11).
[26] *Ibid.*, p. 46.   [27] *Ibid.*, p. 40.

Not Pompey's slave, but Rome's and Virtue's friend:
Sworn to no party; 'midst corruption pure;
Scorning all titles, dignities, and wealth,
When weigh'd against Integrity; remembr'ing
That Patriot is the highest name on earth.[28]

Clodius, however, challenged Cicero's claim, mocking his achievements: 'I have liv'd to laugh at thee, and all thy patriot schemes.'[29]
Cicero is described as a tyrant and turned from a defender of liberty
into an obstacle in the path of greater liberty. The perversion of
language and inversion of political values is a symptom of the
complete corruption that had enveloped Rome:

Is there amongst you one who hates a tyrant?
Your tribune tells you Cicero's a tyrant.
Then crush him, and be free; and in the spot,
Where yon proud palace stands, I'll raise a shrine
To Liberty in memory of your fame.[30]

The story of the decline of Rome would have read, to contemporaries, as one of a series of patriotic laments for a Britain itself
overwhelmed by corruption and political infighting and in danger
of losing her empire as a result.[31] This genre was typified by the
desperate writings of John Brown, discussed later in the chapter.

In Bolingbroke's *Essay on a Patriot King* the end of government is
said to be 'the good of the people' and 'the greatest good of a people
is their liberty'.[32] In Bolingbroke's construction, the defence of this
good was the task of the patriot because liberty was traditionally
linked with the 'good of the people'. In 1745, when Henry Fielding's
True Patriot appeared, the term 'patriot' had become so politicized
that it had first to be cleared of its partisan associations. Its meaning
remained, however, indisputable: 'Love of one's Country carried
into Action'.[33] Consequently, even the lowly ploughman, in so far as
he laboured for the public good, was as much a patriot as the

---

[28] *Ibid.*, p. 64.   [29] *Ibid.*, p. 94.   [30] *Ibid.*, p. 55.
[31] 'O Rome! O Country! once the patriot soil of Freedom; / Parent once of god-like Virtues, /
Mistress of Arts and Empire! now, alas! / The dying victim of unnatural Faction, / And
stage of rank Corruption' (*Ibid.*, p. 63).
[32] Bolingbroke, 'Essay on a Patriot King', *Works*, II, pp. 390–1.
[33] 'Ambition, Avarice, Revenge, Envy, Malice, every bad Passion in the Mind of Man, have
cloaked themselves under this amiable Character, and have misrepresented Persons and
Things in unjust Colours to the Public. We have no Men among us, who have stiled
themselves Patriots, while they have pushed their own Preferment, and the Ruin of their
Enemies, at the manifest Hazard of the Ruin of their Country' (*The True Patriot and Related
Writings*, ed. W. B. Coley (Oxford, 1987), no. 2, pp. 116–17).

grandest senator. The measure of true patriotism was action for the public 'without any selfish Views, or Regard to private Interest'.[34] Party seemed an obvious enemy of patriotism. It was easy to slander the opposition as enemies to the common good.[35] Their defence was to stress the reformist character of party initiative. The anti-Walpolian *Craftsman* described 'party' as a 'national Division of Opinions' on the method of government 'for the benefit of the whole Community, according to the different Judgments of Men'. Their respective 'Principles' distinguished one party from the other. Faction, on the contrary, described political affiliations based on the pursuit of narrow gain 'and acting upon no one Principle of Party, or any Notion of Publick Good, but to preserve and share the Spoils amongst Themselves' often 'contrary to the Interest of the nation'.[36] The government picked up these same arguments. Writing in the *London Journal* in 1732, however, James Pitt defended the existence of a government party on the grounds of its usefulness to the public as a preservative of security:

But then, if the Good of Free Governments be consider'd; as, the absolute Security of Person and Property; full Liberty of examining all Doctrines and Opinions; and that the Liberty of examining is the Root and Source of all Virtue and Happiness; This small Evil of Faction, will be like a Spot in the Sun, not easily discerned, or rather lost in the Glory which surrounds it.[37]

The seventeenth-century language of the common good finds its most characteristic eighteenth-century British usage in these discussions of the legitimacy of party.

Precisely because party was defined, by both government and opposition, as the pursuit of a 'Set of Principles, which they take to be for the publick Good' and faction by the pursuit of 'private

---

34 *Ibid.*, no. 25, p. 266. Patriotism as a *topos* of political debate within eighteenth-century British culture is independent of attitudes towards France or empire, for example, and shows how the very language of politics presupposed a sense of communal identity. The failure of language and perception necessarily coincided.

35 Fielding's caricature of opposition political language is trenchant; 'He then spoke a little lower, and I could only hear in a confused Jargon, the Words POPISH PRINCE; PROTESTANT RELIGION; HEREDITARY RIGHT; LIBERTY AND FREEDOM; with other such Inconsistencies, as made me a little doubt whether the honest Gentleman who uttered them was really in his right Senses' (*ibid.*, no. 19, p. 238).

36 *The Country Journal: or The Craftsman*, no. 674, 9 June 1739, quoted in J. A. W. Gunn, *Factions No More: Attitudes to Party in Government and Opposition in Eighteenth-Century England* (London, 1972), p. 104.

37 *The London Journal*, no. 665, 25 March 1732, quoted in J. A. W. Gunn, *Factions No More*, p. 114.

Advantage', it had become possible to accuse corrupt ministers of themselves comprising a faction.[38] The revelation that government as well as opposition could constitute a faction was a powerful challenge to notions of legitimacy. Coming after two decades of the 'Robinocracy' this serious charge was provoked by William Pulteney's deserting his allies in opposition and joining the post-Walpolian ministry. If party could only be defended in terms of shared principles, how then was such a dramatic instance of inconsistency to be described?

One of the characteristics of the prudent Ciceronian minister was his capacity to evaluate the needs of the state as they changed over time. Arnall accuses the 'Malcontents' of claiming to seek the well-being of the state while at the same moment blocking precisely those correctives set in train by the wise ministry: 'There is no fixing of Power and Property at a certain Stay and Balance; and from the incurable Fluctuation of those, there will be always arising continual Changes in the Manners of the People, and in the Conduct of the Governors.'[39] Recall that Rivadeneira had cited Cicero to prove that it was not inconstancy but prudence for a statesman to shift with changing conditions. More frequently, of course, the language of prudence was employed to block what was perceived as the opposition's desire to innovate for the sake of innovation. The much-scorned 'Modern Patriots' sought to introduce 'notional experimental Systems' 'under the Pretence of Reformation'. This wild and dangerous subterfuge is contrasted with the prudence of those who prefer 'Practice and Experience to Theory and Speculation'.[40] The hack literature amplified this point and redescribed inconsistency so as to make the attachment to principle at the expense of the public good, rather than its abandonment, the mark of faction:

... for a Partyman never deserts his Principle as long as he thinks it for the publick Good, but immediately does, as soon as by Experience he finds it to be destructive of the publick Good: Whereas a factious Man will pursue the Principle he has professed to the Destruction of his Country, if he finds he can no other Way arrive at, or retain power.[41]

---

[38] *The Detector Detected: or, The Danger to Which our Constitution Now Lies Exposed, Set in a true and Manifest Light* (London, 1743), pp. 58–60.

[39] [Arnall], *Clodius and Cicero*, p. 26.

[40] Anon., *The Conduct of the Opposition, and the Tendency of Modern Patriotism* ... (London, 1734), p. 35.

[41] *The Detector Detected*, in Gunn, *Factions No More*, p. 146. Also [John Perceval, Earl of Egmont], *Things As They Are* (3rd edn, London, 1758), p. 31.

According to John Perceval, later Earl of Egmont, writing on the same issue, the circumstances of mid-century politics, in which war and commerce generated enormous sums of money and induced a great deal of jostling for preferment, enabled factions of 'artful Men to raise Murmurs against the most necessary Charges of the State, and to quarrel with the best Means of Publick Security with a manifest Advantage'.[42] The difference between party and faction, then, consisted in their attitude to the 'Publick Security'.

Government and opposition each claimed to be most committed to the service of the public good, whether this was expressed in terms of patriotism or in terms of the legitimacy of party over and against faction. This general convergence on a common vision of politics is nowhere better discerned than in the extraordinary ascendancy of William Pitt. Marie Peters' account of 'City Toryism' and the twists and turns it underwent with Pitt's move from opposition to government perfectly illustrates the resonance and practical possibilities of an appeal to the 'common good' in mid-century politics.

While 'City Toryism' had its origins in a reaction against the transformation of the Whigs into supporters of the 'government, Continental wars, Protestant dissenters, and the new moneyed interest'[43] it was part of a broader current of opposition political ideology. The 'Country' stood against the politics associated with the court; the nation, against the faction that served self-, rather than the public interest. Writes Peters, 'In this sense, the precise eighteenth-century sense of the word, they were "patriots", devoted to the true interests of their country (constitutional as much as foreign) above any selfish ambitions for place.' On the domestic scene they reacted harshly against what were perceived to be Walpole's manipulations and the purchase, by pension or place, of the national interest. Faction and finance coincided. Added to this was the belief that Britain's foreign policy, with its sequence of seemingly interminable and expensive wars, served not the nation but the clique that had installed itself in power. The 'Country' and, indeed, the 'Commonwealth' stood foursquare against these policies.[44]

Pitt rose to power with the support of the City and of Leicester

---

[42] [John Perceval], *Faction Detected by the Evidence of Facts* (3rd edn, London, 1743), p. 5.
[43] Marie Peters, *Pitt and Popularity* (Oxford, 1980), p. 8. See also Linda Colley, 'Eighteenth-Century English Radicalism before Wilkes', *Transactions of the Royal Historical Society*, 5th ser., 31 (1981), 1–20; Nicholas Rogers, *Whigs and Cities: Popular Politics in the Age of Walpole and Pitt* (Oxford, 1989), esp. ch. 3.
[44] Peters, *Pitt*, pp. 25–7.

House precisely because he kept his distance from the government's policies.[45] In the Address in Reply to the King's speech on 13 November 1755 Pitt spoke for one-and-a-half hours against the 'un-British measures' that would lead Britain into another dismal, disadvantageous and deeply unpopular continental conflict.[46] Having staked himself to the role of patriot how could he retain it after joining the ministers whose policies he had excoriated while in opposition? The *Monitor*, published by Pitt's staunch supporter William Beckford, spelled out the problem in the issue of 2 July 1757. Should a 'coalition' form between a patriot and placemen, 'Might not such a coalition induce a belief that he, who was adored for his upright professions, had veered about; deserted the cause of his country; adopted the German measures, was never sincere in his enquiry after the authors of our misfortunes, and only attentive to serve some private passion or interest in preference to his country?'[47]

Perhaps most difficult of all was Pitt's shift on 'Continental connections'. In February and March 1757 he had denied any intention to commit Britain to the German battlefields, but by that summer he had reversed himself. A letter of 9 August 1757 from the Duke of Newcastle to the Earl of Hardwicke quotes Pitt as declaring that ' "we must do what was right and I began to see the situation of affairs was such, that the King would stand in need of some immediate assistance, and that therefore we must depart from the rigidness of our declamations" '.[48]

How were Pitt and his supporters to close the apparent gulf between the politics of opposition, based on principles of patriotism and country, and the prudent tactics of governance while avoiding the obvious accusation of hypocrisy? Their solution was to draw on the redescribed notions of patriotism and party that had been formulated during the years of Walpole's regime by both government and opposition spokesmen in order to affirm that Pitt was, in fact, acting the patriot minister even as he contradicted his earlier patriotic pronouncements.[49] The somersaults and contortions required of

[45] The ground is surveyed in A. N. Newman, 'Leicester House Politics, 1748–1751', *English Historical Review*, 76 (1961), 577–89.
[46] Peters, *Pitt*, p. 39.   [47] *The Monitor*, 2 July 1747, quoted in Peters, *Pitt*, p. 85.
[48] *The Life and Correspondence of Philip Yorke, Earl of Hardwicke*, ed. Philip C. Yorke (Cambridge, 1913), 3 vols., III, p. 166.
[49] For the ideological strain created by Pitt's move, see Marie Peters, ' "Names and Cant": Party Labels in English Political Propaganda c.1755–1765', *Parliamentary History*, 3 (1984), 116; Paul Langford, 'William Pitt and Public Opinion, 1757', *English Historical Review*, 88, (1973), 75–7.

Owen Ruffhead, author of the Pittite journal *The Con-Test*, testify to the stresses of government on an ideology of opposition, and at the same time, the intellectual resources available for use.

In the first number, dated 23 November 1756, which appeared during Pitt's first weeks in the ministry, Ruffhead defined patriotism in such a way as to emphasize its commonwealth interpretation, looking back to Harrington, and at the same time include precisely the kind of flexibility the Court Whigs had sought in their definition:

A true patriot should, in his public capacity, have no personal connections. He should not adhere to men, but measures: And no longer than the latter appear to him to be just, should he continue to co-operate with the former ... But, even with regard to measures, it may become justifiable in him vehemently to oppose the same expedients at one time, which he vigorously promoted at another. The fluctuating state of the political system will not admit of invariable rules of policy.[50]

The argument adduced in defence of William Pulteney some thirteen years before is revived: patriotism often required the sacrifice of principles which no longer served as a means to that end. Because of the swift changes that could befall a nation's affairs, an 'alteration of principles', rather than being an example of 'inconsistency', was evidence of real ministerial prudence, 'of a steady attention to national benefit, free from the narrow prejudice of positive dogmatic maxims, or the servile adherence to the bias of party'. Having thus defined the patriot as the consistent servant of the public good rather than the slave of political necessity, Ruffhead completely exonerated Pitt for joining the government. 'A member of the legislature therefore, ought not to be condemned for standing in opposition to the same measures, which he once earnestly patronized; since a mutation of circumstances, may have operated a laudable change in his conduct.'[51]

Patriotism as the politics of serving the public good could not only redescribe 'consistency' but also take on the colouring of the most bald-faced description of reason of state. Just as the Court Whigs sought, and found, in Cicero's version of patriotism a prudent morality governed by considerations of public utility, Pitt's supporters wrapped themselves in a similar cloak:

But so far as it regards the common good of society, political, is also moral, virtue. And as the general benefit of the public is, or ought to be, the end of all government; all policy therefore ought to be directed to that end. And

[50] *The Con-Test*, 23 November 1756, pp. 2–3.   [51] *Ibid.*, p. 3.

though to attain it, some intermediate acts may become necessary, which may not be strictly reconcileable to the rigid rules of morality, yet if that grand object is invariably pursued, they will ultimately coincide, and the difference will vanish.[52]

In this Ciceronian reconciliation of utility and right the notion of 'self-interest', itself bound up in the early modern vocabulary of prudent politics, was also justified. According to Ruffhead, Soame Jenyns was mistaken when he considered self-interest as the expression of purely factional politics. On the contrary, as with Grotius, self-interest was able to 'connect individuals, so that their union may be made the basis of the common good'.[53]

By the beginning of July, Ruffhead and *The Con-Test* were beginning to prepare opinion for Pitt's climb-down from his steadfast objection to a German War. The statement about consistency was reprinted almost verbatim from the first number of the journal. In addition, Ruffhead incorporated the Ciceronian discussion of means and ends.

When I mention consistency, I am aware that shallow criticks, will object to the expression, and charge the characters I am describing, with what they call, a mutation of principles. But there is a wide difference, between our moral and political conduct. In the one, we may preserve uniformity in the means, as well as the end; in the other, the means will often appear to be inconsistent, though the end is uniform.

'And this art of contemporary accommodation', concludes Ruffhead, 'without prejudice to the projected end, is the capital point, which denotes the skill of the consummate politician.'[54] The extent to which the study of mid-century political thought must constantly weigh political ideas against the reality of practice is rarely better illustrated than by Ruffhead's completely antithetical statement of 1760 – with Pitt still in office. Whereas he had earlier defended the tactics of prudent state management, he now excoriated them:

In essential and fundamental Points of Government, Form, if I may be allowed the seeming Contradiction, is in Fact *Substance*: It is not sufficient that we are right in the End, but we ought also to be regular in the Means: It is not enough that Affairs are well administered, but they ought to be administered by the persons, and according to the Rules which, the Constitution prescribes. Otherwise the Administrators, however they act

[52] *Ibid.*, 5 February 1757, p. 68.   [53] *Ibid.*, 4 June 1757, p. 170.
[54] *Ibid.*, 2 July 1757, p. 195.

with Wisdom and Integrity, do nevertheless exercise an arbitrary and discretionary power; and whenever such Power falls into bad Hands, it must prove fatal.[55]

As was noted in Chapter 1, the defenders of princely prudence and ministerial patriotism were often compelled to argue for a double morality, one for private individuals and one for those whose charge was the preservation of the public good. But this, in turn, raised still another question. Granted that some discretionary power had to be lodged in the sovereign *in extremis*, how was one to insure that statute law not be abused in the name of necessity? In eighteenth-century Britain, the debate about party politics was conducted in the conventional seventeenth-century idiom of the reason of state. Beyond this specific focus, we find that, despite substantial differences, both opposition and government writers converged on the ineluctable logic of security. 'Commonwealthmen' (a somewhat misleading term for an amorphous collection of writers that will be employed here none the less to designate a certain kind of post-'True Whig' discourse of civic politics), 'Sceptical Whigs' and pure monarchists all affirmed the centrality of the public good and *salus populi*, even though they disagreed on the means to its attainment.

COMMONWEALTH AND A COMMON GOOD

The English opposition tradition, whether called True Whig, Country, or Commonwealth, stressed the priority of the public good, suspicion of power, detestation of luxury and standing armies and deep-seated scepticism about the enduring character of all governments. Their commitment to the public good differed from that of government writers, however, in viewing it as the necessary prerequisite to the possibility of human liberty which was both the goal and assurance of prosperity and *paideia*. Because of this great goal, and because of the debased natural condition of man, the only way individuals could secure these aims was by living in society and taking an active role in governing their communities.[56] Left

---

[55] Ruffhead, *Ministerial Usurpation Displayed* (London, 1760), p. 22.
[56] For the relationship of liberty and public service, see Quentin Skinner, 'The Paradoxes of Political Liberty', *The Tanner Lectures on Human Values*, VII, 1986, ed. Sterling M. McMurrin (Cambridge, 1986), pp. 225–50; 'The Idea of Negative Liberty: Philosophical and Historical Perspectives', *Philosophy in History*, ed. Richard Rorty, J. B. Schneewind and

unsupervised there was always the risk of tyranny: 'No Nations ever possessed this Liberty long, where the chief officers were invested with arbitrary sway.'[57] Hence the centrality of proper constitutional arrangements for republicans. Fear of those in power translated into the priority of legal restraint and this sentiment easily made the transition to England where an existing constitutionalist tradition compensated Commonwealthmen for the disappearance of its short-lived republic. This approach to political life was, however, acutely dependent on the existence of a virtuous public:

The freedom of a constitution rests on two points. The orders of it are one: so Machiavel calls them, and I know not how to call them more significantly. He means not only the forms and customs, but the different classes and assemblies of men, with different powers and privileges attributed to them, which are established in the state. The spirit and character of the people are the other. On the mutual conformity and harmony of these the preservation of liberty depends.[58]

Liberty could only be secured by placing the institutions of power, namely government and the military service, into the hands of the people. Yet, unless they already possessed the proper 'manners' the polity would falter anyway. The True Whig and Commonwealthman was faced with an inescapable paradox: without the proper institutions and manners a people could not retain their freedom, yet those manners and institutions could only be found among virtuous people. The absence of any escape from this vicious circle led Commonwealth writers to despair at the first indication that manners or institutions were beginning to slip. It was just this fear that led many to call stability or duration of government the goal of political practice. '*Permanency*, or *Duration* of the State', John Brown wrote, 'is the main Object of these Essays.'[59] This accounts for the vogue for Sparta among Commonwealthmen. From Walter Moyle through Edward Wortley Montagu Jr to John Brown, its prolonged,

Quentin Skinner (Cambridge, 1984), pp. 193–221. For the Augustinian side of Renaissance republicanism, see William Bouwsma's brilliant 'Two Faces of Renaissance Humanism', in *Itinerarium Italicum: The Profile of the Italian Renaissance in the Mirror of its European Transformations*, ed. Heiko A. Oberman with Thomas A. Brady, Jr (Leiden, 1975), pp. 3–60; André Comperat, *Amour et verité: Sebon, Vives et Michel de Montaigne* (Paris, 1983).
[57] Ruffhead, *Ministerial Usurpation Displayed*, p. 18. also, Bolingbroke, 'History of England', *Works*, I, p. 300, and *Cato's Letters*, no. 13, I p. 86.
[58] Lord Bolingbroke, 'The Idea of a Patriot King', *Works*, II, pp. 393–4.
[59] John Brown, *An Estimate of the Manners and Principles of the Times* 2 vols. (London, 1757–8), II, p. 105.

unchanging existence made it an ideal of distant calm amidst the factional political wars of mid eighteenth-century Britain.

For commonwealth or country opposition writers, history was an inexhaustible mine of political prudence. Because 'Men are so much the same in all ages, and in all countries', the history of nations afforded the perspective necessary for 'forming proper principles for the regulation of your future conduct'.[60] The study of history was actually an account of various 'experiments' in the arrangement of individuals and communities which, like scientific experiments, could then be used to deduce more immediate precepts. This lies behind Montagu's melancholy justification of his *Reflections on the Rise and Fall of the Antient Republics*: 'for as the same causes will, by the stated laws of sublunary affairs, sooner or later invariably produce the same effects', the study of the past was the only remedy for potential ills.[61] Within the civic tradition historians had always been esteemed as worthy teachers of politics. As Livy had served Machiavelli and as Tacitus had captured the imagination of an entire European generation, the themes of Polybius channelled the articulation of opposition arguments in the middle decades of the eighteenth century.

Tacitus' central theme, the insidious subversion of Roman liberty, was popular among opposition writers in the first decades of the century, who drew the implicit, and sometimes explicit, parallel with Walpole's regime.[62] Surveying the contemporary scene with some distaste, Bolingbroke suggested that politicians often used luxury to smooth the path to arbitrary power. 'Tiberius', he wrote, 'clearly saw what was the surest instrument of arbitrary power' and refused to act against increasing luxury when the senate had already recognized its deleterious consequences. Subsequently, 'Artful princes have frequently introduced it with that very view.' Such a Tiberian subversion was the thinnest of thinly veiled allusions to Walpole's patronage system and iron grip on parliament. 'This is the finished politician; the darling son of Tacitus and Machiavel.'[63]

---

60 Anon., *Letters to a Young Nobleman* (London, 1762), p. 21.
61 Edward Wortley Montagu, Jr, *Reflections on the Rise and Fall of the Antient Republics* (2nd edn, London, 1759), p. 13. While its author was a noted rake, the book itself was taken very seriously, being translated into French by François René Turpin (1769) and then into Dutch by Simon Styl (1774) as the historical preface to a discussion of 'the rise and flourishing of the Dutch republic'. I am extremely grateful to Stephan Klein for bringing this material to my attention.
62 See Gunn, *Beyond Liberty and Property*, pp. 15–28.
63 Bolingbroke, 'On Luxury', *Works*, I, p. 476.

If comparison with Cicero was a sign of praise, one cursed with Tacitus. With the fall of Walpole the specific object of this critique vanished. While fear of corruption remained a prominent opposition theme, its arena changed subtly in the years that followed. By mid-century, as is clear in the works of Brown and Montagu, the fear of national decline was bound up with the increasing significance of Britain's imperial agenda. As the anatomizer of Rome's rapid rise to Mediterranean *imperium*, Polybius seemed to have new relevance and Tacitus much less. The Greek's older, more familiar role was as the author of the theory of the cyclical alteration of constitutions that had provided republicans with an ominous prophecy about the future of an unvirtuous and unreformed commonwealth. Eighteenth-century readers, though, picked up on another aspect of this constitutional motion, the role of manners in speeding or delaying the inevitable decline and its relationship to imperial expansion. Polybius argued that national prosperity was usually measured in wealth and ease and that these ultimately, but inexorably, subverted precisely those national manners or attributes which helped acquire those riches. James Hampton's translation of 1764 specified that this cycle began after a nation 'arrives at the highest degree of power, and possesses an intire and undisputed sovereignty', a locution that may refer to the just-signed Treaty of Paris and which does not appear in any of the earlier translations.[64]

This corruption was so insidious because it struck at the most successful states and individuals.[65] Each and every government was seen as 'containing within itself the efficient cause of its ruin,' and this cause was 'essentially connected with those very circumstances that had produced its prosperity'.[66] For many commonwealth writers, there existed no more appropriate description of the prospective peril for Britain in its fortunate age of imperial expansion. Set against the backdrop of the ignominious disappearance of the mighty ancient empires they warned of a dismal future in the absence of immediate steps towards a moral reformation.[67]

Perhaps the most profound of these writers was John Brown. In

[64] *Two Extracts from the Sixth Book of the General History of Polybius*, tr. and ed. James Hampton (London, 1764), p. 36.
[65] See, for instance, Soame Jenyns, *A Free Inquiry into the Nature and Origin of Evil* (London, 1757), p. 139.
[66] Jean-Louis De Lolme, *The Constitution of England* (London, 1772; rpt, 1800), ii.18, p. 456.
[67] Francis Hutcheson, *A System of Moral Philosophy*, 2 vols. (Glasgow, 1754–5), ii, p. 378.

two books, one published in 1757 and the other in 1765, he offered first a diagnosis of England's problems and then his remedy. Brown had been a contemporary of Edmund Law's at Cambridge before coming to the notice, and then enjoying the attentions, of William Warburton and his circle. His *Essays on the Characteristicks* were popular, and his plays and poetry a mixture of successes and failures. These political tracts, which sandwiched a fascinating *Dissertation on the Origin of Poetry, Music and Dance*, reveal a man increasingly disillusioned and despairing of politics and life. Brown was to slit his own throat in 1765. In his own lifetime, and since, he has been both ridiculed and called a genius. What is indubitable is that some of Joseph Priestley's most incisive arguments were forged on the anvil of Brown's arguments, taking him as the chief example of a certain vision of political community. Joanna Innes has suggested that there were three sources from which eighteenth-century movements for the reformation of manners drew their arguments.[68] In Brown's 'country' synthesis all three are present. The terrible social consequences of moral lassitude (idleness, improvidence and intemperance), the failure of a disrespected religion to immunize against sin, and the constant peril of national decline are the causes for Brown's lament.

An Estimate of the Manners and Principles of the Times was published in the wake of the disaster at Minorca (1756), an event which only reinforced the author's contention that England was being eaten away from within by spiritual collapse and that it was only a matter of time before it would be overwhelmed from without. In the Britain of the 1750s, 'The Spirit of Liberty is now struggling with the Manners and Principles, as formerly it struggled with the Tyrants of the Time.'[69] Brown believed that what was hailed as the decisive victory of liberty in 1689 was in fact deceptive. The institutional combat of the seventeenth century was, more or less, resolved. Though the liberty of the constitution, to borrow Montesquieu's phrase, may have been established by right, he believed that the liberty of the subject had been guaranteed neither by right nor in fact.

Brown argued that the moral foundation of English liberty had

---

[68] Joanna Innes, 'Politics and Morals: The Reformation of Manners Movement in Later Eighteenth-Century England', in *Transformations in Political Culture*, ed. Eckhart Hellmuth (London, 1990), p. 59.
[69] Brown, *Estimate*, ii, p. 18.

been counterfeited in the half-century since the Revolution. He was profoundly hostile to the 'Modern Whig' argument of Addison and Defoe that commerce and the arts of living were an improvement on the barbarism of the classical farmer. Rather, he proclaimed, by humanity 'is not meant that Smoothness and refined polish of external Manners, by which the present Age affects to be distinguished'. Brown distinguished between the 'manners' of corrupt and virtuous states, and another writer pointed out the superficiality of English society and its departure from the formerly fundamental principles of disinterested pursuit of the 'Interest of the Commonwealth'.[70]

Brown opposed 'the spirit of commerce', that 'begets a kind of regulated Selfishness, which tends at once to the Increase and preservation of Property'.[71] He then developed his arguments against these new spirits of the times: 'external Manners' and 'commerce'. The manners of the times less resembled degeneracy and cruelty so much as 'vain, luxurious and selfish effeminacy'.[72] The end product of the mismanagement of youth was the creation of the 'modern Man of Fashion'. 'Every circumstance of modern use conspires to sooth him into the Excess of Effeminacy: Warm Carpets are spread under his Feet; warm hangings surround him; Doors and Windows, nicely jointed, prevent the least rude Encroachment of the external Air.' The 'modern Man of Fashion' took his greatest pleasure from gaming. It had been believed that books and the arts were requisite hobbies, but no longer; this man's preference for a culture resembling his own interests had turned the theatre, music and painting toward virtuosity and away from true art.[73]

These writers paid attention to the condition of the arts because they believed that it provided the most trenchant indication of the manners of a society. Thus, Montagu spoke of the need to study the objects of 'public applause'. Giving an example of his method in the history of Greece, he traced the origin of the arts to the poems that serenaded the winners of the military tests of virtue that constituted the original form of the Olympic, Isthmian and the other Greek games. Then came the 'fatal alteration' in which the arts themselves became the subject of emulation. As a consequence, 'though the manners of the Athenians grew more polite, yet they grew more

[70] [John Campbell], *Liberty and Right* (London, 1747), ii, pp. 32–3.
[71] Brown, *Estimate*, ii, pp. 22–3.
[72] *Ibid.*, p. 29.   [73] *Ibid.*, pp. 36–7.

corrupt, and publick virtue ceased gradually to be the object of publick applause and publick emulation'. Military training was despised and increasing amounts of money were spent on theatre and festivals. Montagu cited Plutarch's tale of a Spartan visitor at Athens who complained that more time and attention were allotted to theatre 'than to the affairs of the publick'. Montagu concluded this digression by warning of a similar trend in Britain.[74] He likened the 'strong Shakespearomania (as I may term it) which prevailed so lately, so universally amongst all ranks and all ages' to the Athenian preoccupation with the theatre.[75]

Italian opera also aroused intense displeasure. The latest vogue, the so-called *buffa*, with its intrinsically disordered personal relationships and subversion of social hierarchy and aristocratic virtue, would surely have been denounced. Brown commented that '"Our Operas are disgraced with the lowest Inspidity of Composition, and unmeaning Sing-Song." This is a Subject, as much talked of, and as little understood, as the deepest Mysteries of State.'[76] That there was a place for music in the polity was uniformly acknowledged: Brown, after all, did write a treatise on the rise of poetry, dance and music. But music remained a double-edged sword. Plato and the Spartans were right to regulate it closely. Thus, even if music was accepted, italian opera was not, Bolingbroke contending that it ought to be 'noble, manly music', not the 'soft Italian music [which] relaxes and unnerves the soul, and sinks it into weakness; so that while we receive their music, we at the same time are adopting their manners'.[77]

Because a nation's strength depended on her leadership, its increasing effeminacy posed an incalculable threat. Brown's focus on the character of a nation's leaders reflected what he took to be Machiavelli's emphasis. Brown had earlier commented that he would not bother examining the manners of the masses because they were 'a *lifeless Ball* sleeping in the *Cannon*: it depends on some superior *Intelligence* to give it both *Impulse* and *Direction*'.[78]

[74] Montagu, *Reflections*, pp. 125–8.   [75] *Ibid.*, p. 132.   [76] Brown, *Estimate*, II, p. 76.
[77] Bolingbroke, 'On Luxury', *Works*, I, p. 476. In his essay on the 'imitative arts', Adam Smith, too, distinguished between opera *seria* and *buffa*. The latter was 'diverting' and 'enlivening' but the former, when properly performed, was the more powerful vehicle: 'Of the nature of that Imitation which takes place in what are called the Imitative Arts', *Essays on Philosophical Subjects*, ed. W. P. D. Wrightman and J. C. Bryce (Indianapolis, 1982), II. 16,p. 194; also II.28, p. 202. For a discussion of English objections to the Italian opera, see Winton Dean, *Handel's Dramatic Oratorios and Masques* (Oxford, 1959; rpt, 1990), pp. 131–2.
[78] Brown, *Estimate*, II, p. 25.

In classical times the politician was praised for being disinterested. The most inventive eighteenth-century thinkers, on the other hand, had accepted the inevitability of self-interest and instead devised mechanisms to channel self- into public interest. Or they had used this calculating rational self-interest as a brake on the tyranny of the passions.[79] For those like Brown, however, this was simply abetting the moral destruction of Britain. Like the self-centredness of the 'modern Man of Fashion', the legitimacy of self-interest was another sign of vicious, unbridled individualism.

In assaying the causes of the fall of the Roman republic, Montagu stressed the impact of changed manners on the relationship of individuals to their community. His analysis fills out the implications of Brown's argument. While self-love and selfishness were both 'different modes' of the same principle of self-preservation, they had distinct and opposite implications. Self-love was the practice of self-preservation and was, therefore, 'not only compatible with the most rigid practice of the social duties, but is in fact a great motive and incentive to the practice of all moral virtue'. Selfishness, however, was highly destructive because it excluded 'all the social virtues'.[80]

Brown accepted the inevitability of divisions in free society and he distinguished between useful ones based on free exchange of opinions, and factions derived from self-interest. The frequent sessions of parliament since the end of the seventeenth century had made places more valuable. Candidates were more likely to tamper with elections to secure a seat and the court was more likely to try to influence already seated members:

Thus the great Chain of political Self-Interest was at length formed; and extended from the lowest Cobbler in a Borough, to the King's first Minister. But a *Chain of Self-Interest* is indeed no better than a *Rope of Sand*: There is no Cement nor Cohesion between the Parts.[81]

Just as an effeminate government posed a greater danger than an effeminate citizenry, a corrupt, self-interested government was worse than a corrupt, self-interested population. Though Brown's preference was implicit, he gave it tangibleness, citing 'what

---

[79] See Hirschman, *The Passions and the Interests*, (Princeton, 1978).
[80] Montagu, *Reflections*, p. 273.
[81] Brown, *Estimate*, II, p. 111.

Machiavel somewhere delivers as a maxim, "That an ill-disposed Citizen can do no great Harm, but in an ill-disposed City"'.[82]

The attack on self-interest, surely aimed at the calculating language of party political practice, serves as a transition to the second object of Brown's wrath, commerce. In the beginning commerce 'supplies mutual Necessities, prevents mutual Wants, extends mutual knowledge, eradicates mutual Prejudice, and spreads mutual harmony'. As it develops further, 'it provides Conveniences, increaseth Numbers, coins Money, gives Birth to Arts and Science, creates equal Laws, diffuses general Plenty and general happiness'. But in its full maturity it is evil, generating superfluity, luxury, avarice and, most deadly of all, introducing effeminacy into the ruling class.[83] To Brown's way of looking at things, Britain had clearly reached this third stage of commercial development.

Montagu charted this same dreary pattern in ancient monarchies, while, in free states, luxury led to 'degeneracy of manners', destroying virtue and thence liberty itself. Luxury made money the lifeblood of the state, while the masses sold their votes and the rich bought them. Late republican Rome was the best example of this phenomenon. 'There we see luxury, ambition, faction, pride, revenge, selfishness, a total disregard to the publick good, and an universal dissoluteness of manners, first make them ripe for, and then compleat their destruction.'[84]

Yet, Brown was no utopian. He recognized that England was irrevocably committed to commerce and that the only course of action was to try to minimize its effects. The first remedy was to change the nation's manners, but this was acknowledged to be impossible. 'Necessity, therefore, and Necessity alone, must in such a case be the Parent of Reformation.' Like Machiavelli confronted with the reality of Florence's corruption, and like Bolingbroke not long before, Brown placed his hope on the miraculous emergence of a patriotic minister with *virtù*.

Whenever, this compelling Power, *Necessity*, shall appear; then, and not till then, may we hope that our Deliverance is at hand. Effeminacy, Rapacity, and Faction, will then be ready to resign the Reins they would now usurp: One common Danger will create one common Interest: Virtue may rise on the Ruins of Corruption; and a despairing nation yet be saved, by

---

[82] *Ibid.*, p. 72. The source is *Discourses*, 1.17.   [83] Brown, *Estimate*, II, p. 153.
[84] Montagu, *Reflections*, p. 223.

the Wisdom, the Integrity, and unshaken Courage of some Great Minister.[85]

Eight years later Brown was to contradict himself, perhaps too frustrated to wait for the second coming of a classical law-giver, or perhaps heartened by the feats of arms of the later years of the war. His *Thoughts on Civil Liberty, on Licentiousness and Faction* took as its aim the reformation of England's manners and therefore the salvation of her civil liberty. He began by noting that his political principles were consistent with moral and religious ones.[86] Natural, unrestrained liberty was unnatural for humans. Only brutes with 'unerring Instincts' were formed for a life consisting solely of fulfilling appetites. Man's sociability required him to accept limitations on this natural liberty, and the result was a state of 'civil' liberty. The use of this term, which was alien to the participatory ethos of classical politics, is a feature of the convergence of commonwealth and mainstream political thought. Licentiousness, which Brown equated with faction, was the social equivalent of the savage's 'natural liberty'. The control of the 'natural Appetites, Passions, and Desires of Man', the language of the reformation of manners, required the subordination of conscience to polity. If civil liberty required the curbing of natural inclination, then 'without an assistant Regulation of the Passions and Desires, [it] is utterly inadequate to the great Ends either of Private Happiness or public Liberty'.[87] The role of the passions in this discussion of civic manners illustrates how opposition writers drew on the most fashionable contemporary account of human motivation.

The permanent foundations of civil liberty could only rest on the force of manners. These, however had to be 'impressed on the human Mind, as may be an inward Club to every inordinate desire'. The proper sort of manners were those which 'lead to a steady Prosecution of the general welfare'.[88] Unlike Hume, for example, Brown believed that 'salutary Principles and Manners' could 'themselves secure the Duration of State' in spite of bad laws, whereas even the best laws could do nothing with a population whose manners had been corrupted.[89]

The scope of Brown's politics placed a heavy social burden on

---

[85] Brown, *Estimate*, II, p. 221.
[86] Brown, *Thoughts on Civil Liberty, on Licentiousness and Faction* (Dublin, 1765), p. 3.
[87] *Ibid.*, pp. 4–7, 17–18.   [88] *Ibid.*, pp. 21, 22.
[89] Brown, *Estimate*, II, p. 20. Also James Burgh, *Crito. Or, Essays on Various Subjects*, 2 vols. (London, 1766–7), I, p. 49n.

education. Only the indoctrination of the citizenry, beginning at the earliest possible age, could make any progress towards the shaping of good manners. 'Every rising appetite' that was contrary to the 'general welfare' had to be blocked and every effort made 'in forwarding every passion that may promote the Happiness of the Community'.[90] Similarly, it was also true that 'there are many Opinions or Principles, tending evidently to the Destruction of Society or Freedom; and which, therefore, ought not to be tolerated in a well-ordered free Community'.[91] There is, obviously, a deep similarity between this opposition argument and the language of necessity employed by Court Whigs and government supporters.[92]

Brown acknowledged that some will argue 'that This is indeed a system of slavery; that it is building civil liberty on the servitude of the Mind, and shackling the infant soul with early prejudice'. Yet, prejudice was everywhere and inevitable. At least the citizens of his commonwealth would possess socially useful ones. Ancient Sparta provided an example of state-sponsored education which inculcated proper manners and helped maintain liberty longer than in her less well-ordered republican neighbours.[93] And, based on this text, Joseph Priestly, who had great confidence in human reason, did accuse Brown of creating slavery rather than fostering liberty.

Because political life was not determined by laws but by manners, England's longevity was in doubt. All the pagan states except, perhaps, Athens, had 'better' manners than England.[94] The Revolution in 1688 was only possible because of 'the Prevalence of upright Manners and Principles'. However, because 'private licentiousness' was mixed with it disorder was sure to ensue. Vice, poor education and unreformed institutions made a fertile breeding ground for disorder and decline. In the reign of George I irreligion reared its ugly head with the assertion of the doctrines of non-residence and hierarchy. In combatting these evils writers 'assailed *superstition* with such Weapons as destroyed *Religion*: They opposed *Intolerance* by arguments and ridicule which tended to sweep away all public *Establishments*'. The challenge of Roman Catholicism and High Anglicanism had been defeated at the cost of a useful religious

90 Brown, *Civil Liberty*, pp. 23, 24.
91 Brown, 'An Appendix Relative to a Proposed Code of Education', *Thoughts on the Education of Women* (London, 1765), p. 29.
92 See, for example, Pufendorf, *Law of Nature*, VII.ix.4.
93 Moyle, *Essay on the Spartan Constitution*, p. 186.
94 Brown, *Civil Liberty*, p. 87.

establishment. Thanks to *Cato's Letters, the Independent Whig* and Bolingbroke, both revealed and natural religion were undermined.[95] Yet, 'without the more solid Supporters of religious Belief' no scheme of moral reformation could ever succeed.[96]

Brown was haunted by the fragility of the commonwealth, responsive as it was not merely to fortune's whim, but to the still more deadly consequences of human moral weakness. Even the presence of good manners could not overcome the Romans' practice of adopting the good laws discovered amongst their enemies. Brown dubbed this 'the fatal principle of change'. Even as it may have assisted their empire-building, it ultimately destroyed 'That Identity and Integrity of Manners and Principles, which is the Soul and Security of every free state'.[97]

Another point of confusing convergence between the commonwealth and prudent positions was their mutual fear of change and instability. Malachi Postlethwayt, the most systematic exponent of contemporary British political economic policy, recommended that Members of Parliament travel. But he warned them not to bring back any strange customs,

lest we infect the people with the itch of novelty, and corrupt their minds with effeminacy; whereby they will be brought to forget the rigid values and plain honesty, with the good manners, wise laws and customs of their ancestors. For the populace are changeable enough, and nothing is more fatal to a government, than extraordinary innovations.[98]

In a century associated with the 'idea of progress'[99] there was also a belief that progress was a profound threat to human happiness. That both opposition and establishment writers shared this view points to its prevalence and, again, to the convergence and blurring of these two different arguments.

Sparta, rather than Rome, provided commonwealth writers with a model of permanence.[100] For Montagu, as for Brown, the long duration of the Spartan republic testified to its successful constitution. Lycurgus' constitution preserved its liberty and formed 'the minds of his citizens' to enjoy the rational pleasures which were

---

[95] *Ibid.*, p. 102. [96] Brown, *Essays on the Characteristicks* (2nd edn, London, 1751), p. 235.
[97] Brown, *Civil Liberty*, pp. 75, 77.
[98] Malachi Postlethwayt, 'Parliament', *The Universal Dictionary of Trade and Commerce*, 2 vols. (London, 1751–5), II, sig. 5or.
[99] See David Spadafora, *The Idea of Progress in Eighteenth-Century Britain* (New Haven, 1990).
[100] The canonic exposition is Walter Moyle, 'An Essay upon the Lacedemonian Government' (1689), published in *A Select Collection of Tracts* (Dublin, 1728).

independent of sensation and passion.[101] Lycurgus did not 'encourage navigation, strike out new branches of commerce, and make the most of these excellent harbours and other natural advantages which the maritime situation of his country afforded'. Did he promote the arts and sciences and the quest for wealth in the hope that 'he might make his nation, in the language of our political writers, secure, powerful and happy? Just the reverse'.[102] Montagu emphasized how different Lycurgus' constitution was from Britain's. Only when the Spartans violated the laws and 'began to undertake more distant expeditions both by sea and land' did they face the destabilizing consequences of economic inadequacy. The constitution of the state was not geared for commercial and territorial expansion.[103]

Brown admired France as an example of a country which faced the same problems but responded more healthily. Her governors had kept a proper balance between the needs of commerce and society. Brown praised the laws discouraging the nobility from engaging in commerce.[104] Consequently, 'in Contradiction to all known Example, France hath become powerful while she seemed to lead the way in effeminacy'.[105] Her redemption was effected by state-sponsored education. Although as effeminate as the English, the French still possessed strength and glory. Their strength was in their youth. They were trained for public office at the national expense and rewarded on their merit.[106] The consequence of this was noticeable in French military preparedness. They were now contesting Britain for control of the Mediterranean and North America. 'These are the steddy [*sic*] Effects of their Principles and Union; of our Deficiency in both.'[107]

Perhaps the most creative exposition of the commonwealth argument in this period was Montagu's use of Carthage. Rome, Sparta and even Athens were popular sources of political and social truths for didactic writers. Carthage, defeated by Rome and without its own historians, was invisible. Yet, Montagu perceived that the experience of none of these ancient polities really spoke to the condition of Britain during the Seven Years War as directly as did Carthage. Contemporaries marked the innovativeness of this move. In March 1759 a review of Montagu's *Reflections* appeared in the

101 Montagu, *Reflections*, p. 24.   102 *Ibid.*, p. 68.   103 *Ibid.*, p. 35.
104 Brown, *Estimate*, II, p. 115.
105 *Ibid.*, p. 87.   106 *Ibid.*, p. 85.   107 *Ibid.*, p. 89.

Critical Review. The section on Carthage was praised as most 'entertaining' and 'instructive' because of her 'resemblance' to Britain 'in her commerce, opulence, sovereignty of the sea, and her method of carrying on her land-wars by foreign mercenaries'.[108]

For all the perspicuity of the 1759 review, it missed a point of outstanding moment. In rescuing the reputation of Carthage and favourably comparing some of her characteristics with Britain, Montagu had created an extraordinary paradox. His entire book was one long attack on 'luxury' and 'faction' in modern societies, though couched in the language of antiquity. This chapter excepted, he had nothing good to say about commerce. Yet, somehow, the mercantile Carthaginians were different. How is this to be explained? Did Montagu, like Brown in the *Estimate*, recognize that Britain's 'clock' could not be turned back, that commerce had become a permanent part of the nation's manners? If so, then perhaps Carthage, because it resembled Britain most closely, was made into an example of what a commercial republic could achieve. Like Carthage, Britain could be both commercial and virtuous, opulent and patriotic.

In a startling phrase, Montagu broke radically from Montesquieu's typology of republics and revealed the point of the Carthaginian analogy: 'The genius of the Carthaginians was warlike as well as commercial, and affords undeniable proof, that those qualities are by no means incompatible to the same people.'[109] While Rome and Sparta were ruined by wealth, money had no effect on Carthage. No one, not even 'the most partial historian charged any one of them with sacrificing the honour and interest of his country to any foreign power for money'.[110] Since Harrington, English writers had struggled to marry classical exemplars with the dramatically different condition of Britain. For she was a commercial state that was neither an agrarian republic for expansion nor a timid republic for preservation. Carthage survived by ploughing its commercial wealth back into maritime expansion and colonization. They showed no interest in the 'arts of living', leaving these to their more dissipated Greek cousins.[111]

---

[108] Montagu, *Reflections*, p. 176, quoted in *The Critical Review*, March 1759, vol. 7, pp. 249–54.
[109] Montagu, *Reflections*, p. 178. [110] *Ibid.*, p. 321.
[111] *Ibid.*, p. 178. In the *Remarks Historical and Political* (British Library, King's MSS 433), written for the future George III, James Burgh observed that the Dutch had succeeded at becoming wealthy without yielding to indulgence. Their secret was in re-exporting all

The eighteenth-century commonplace, whether one agreed or not, saw luxury and effeminacy as an inevitable consequence of commercial success. For Montagu, Brown and others, commerce did not necessarily civilize. Their understanding of the past had revealed that in so far as the progress of civilization brought luxury and ease it was detrimental to political society. The obvious problem faced by men of this opinion in mid eighteenth-century Britain was the omnipresence of commerce and its effects. Myths of a Spartan golden age provided one solution but only at the cost of rendering their political teachings irrelevant. The alternative was to strengthen the public commitment to manners so as to enable individuals to withstand the blandishments of ease. This was the tack chosen by Brown prescriptively and Montagu historically. The story of Carthage demonstrated that, if riches were put to virtuous use, the manners of a commercial nation could be preserved uncorrupted. Montagu claimed that had Carthage stuck to this policy instead of challenging Rome in Sicily and Spain she would have remained independent.[112]

The centrality of liberty in the opposition account of politics is an obvious feature of eighteenth-century British political discussion. This is that 'Love of Liberty' whose preservation is the aim of Brown's tracts, and whose peril is the cause of his lament.[113] But even the most cursory reader cannot escape the fact that the manners demanded of the citizens of Brown's polity often militate against even a constrained vision of liberty:

For what is more contrary to every gentle and kind Affection, that dwells in the human Breast, than to shed the Blood, or destroy the Life of Man? Yet the ruling Principle above-mentioned, can reconcile us even to this. And when the Necessity of public Example compels us to make a Sacrifice of this Kind; though we may lament the Occasion, we cannot condemn the Fact: So far are we from branding it a Murder, that we approve it as Justice; and always defend it on this great Principle alone, that it was necessary for the public Good.[114]

We know that Brown was not only a careful reader, but a great admirer of Machiavelli, 'who in my Opinion is the greatest political Reasoner upon Facts, that hath appeared in any Age or

their luxury imports. 'Thence it is, that the Dutch are richer than the Spanish, with their goldmines, and their dominions on which the sun never sets' (p. 14.).
112 Montagu, *Reflections*, p. 187.   113 Brown, *Estimate*, II, p. 13.
114 Brown, *Essays on the Characteristicks*, pp. 135–6.

Country'.[115] Brown was deeply engaged with the *Discourses*. The preservation of individual liberty required the preservation of the community and that, in turn, required the kind of virtue which, in Brown's account, deprived individuals of even the most basic freedoms. And yet, we can no longer be sure which Machiavelli Brown is drawing upon. Describing manners as 'the best Security' of a free government blurs the distinction between the service of liberty or necessity. With Brown, the security of the State, the means, in a republican account, seems to have usurped the end of commonwealth politics, the liberty of the citizen.

PRUDENCE AND A SCIENCE OF POLITICS

If the commonwealth argument offered one political interpretation of the relationship between virtue, manners, commerce and history it was also possible to address the problem posed by Polybius in a more sceptical fashion. Where Brown believed that only moral reformation was an adequate response to the challenge posed by the seemingly inexorable decline of political manners, others concerned about national self-preservation formulated a 'science of politics' in order to pre-empt the cycle of constitutional mutation that coincided with inevitable change in society. Moreover, where opposition writers typically depicted commerce and wealth as heralds of the long night of tyranny, these writers envisioned a future filled with greater prosperity and happiness, though perhaps at the expense of some more garish notion of liberty. Polybius' attempt to establish 'fixed principle' for understanding the 'regular sequence' of constitutional change marked him as one who sought to make the study of politics into a discipline. The seventeenth-century analysis of the reason, or interest, of state was transformed into a 'science of politics' since, in the eighteenth century, the attempt to order natural phenomena according to laws transformed any endeavour into a science. Like all other sciences, this one required careful study and involved integrating diverse pieces of information collected from the experiences of polities distant in both time and space. Earlier in the century, *Cato* had written that 'Of all the Sciences that I know in the World, that of Government concerns us most, and is the easiest to be known, and yet is the least understood.'[116] Years later, in the most

---

[115] Brown, *Estimate*, II, p. 47.   [116] *Cato's Letters*, no. 38, ii, p. 35.

famous set of speculations on the possibility of reducing 'politics to a science', Hume emphasized its importance since 'Those who employ their pens on political subjects, free from party-rage, and party-prejudices, cultivate a science, which, of all others, contributes most to public utility . . . '[117] Hume's premise was that laws and forms of government were powerful enough to overcome and even shape the diversity of human temperaments and that one could deduce consequences from them as certain 'as any which the mathematical sciences afford us'.[118] This firm link between the reasons of state and the science of politics is the connection between Tacitus and Polybius. For, while Tacitus was hailed in the seventeenth century as the teacher of politics, a century later a more mature conception of science imposed a more rigorous definition of truth which Tacitus could not meet.[119]

The *Universal History* was a vast enterprise based in London which sought to present the history of the world from the beginning of recorded time through the present in two sections, the *Ancient* and *Modern*.[120] Now, not only was Polybius' method often described as 'universal' or 'general' history, but in one of the volumes he wrote for the *Universal History*, John Campbell referred to both the contemporary discussions of the science of politics and the specific themes associated with Polybius' *History* and the seventeenth-century studies of politics:

Besides, that kind of science, which arises from this reading, is the true political key by which a variety of mysterious events are opened; so that we see clearly the true grounds of the rise of one nation, and the decay of another; the causes why at certain times there are such vast changes even in the exterior appearances of countries, which, from paradises in one age, become desarts in the next.[121]

---

117 Hume, 'Of Civil Liberty', *Essays*, p. 87.
118 Hume, 'That Politics May be Reduced to a Science', *Essays*, pp. 16, 24 and 31. See Duncan Forbes, *Hume's Philosophical Politics* (Cambridge, 1975), p. 227. Montesquieu disagreed, believing that manners were best changed by countervailing manners, not legislation (*Spirit of the Laws*, XIX.14, p. 298). Elsewhere Hume was sceptical about the possibility of ever amassing enough material to perform this 'reduction' ('Of Civil Liberty', *Essays*, p. 87). Others were more optimistic: Priestley, *Lectures on History*, p. 14; Samuel Johnson, 'The False Alarm', *Samuel Johnson's Political Writings*, ed. Donald J. Greene (New Haven, 1977), x, p. 318; John Jones, *Free and Candid Disquisitions Relating to the Church of England* (2nd edn, London, 1750), p. 6.
119 See, for example, Thomas Hunter, *Observations on Cornelius Tacitus* (London, 1752).
120 For some background, see G. Ricuperati, '*Universal History*: storia di un progetto europeo. Impostori, storici ed editori, nella *Ancient Part*', *Studi settecenteschi*, I (1981), 7–90; Abbattista, *Commercio, colonie e impero*, pp. 267–8.
121 *Modern Universal History*, IX, p. 191.

Several years earlier, in the opening paragraphs of his *Present State of Europe*, Campbell had defined the seventeenth-century context of the eighteenth-century's science of politics: 'The kind of Science I mean is Politicks; by which I understand a comprehensive knowledge of fundamental Maxims of Policy, grounded upon the actual and real Interests of the several Governments of Europe.'[122] After citing the Duc de Rohan's famous maxim that 'Les Princes commandent aux Peuples, & l'Interêt commande aux Princes', Campbell restated the seventeenth-century distinction between 'accidental' and 'real' interests.[123] This distinction reflects the similar analysis of public utility into real and fleeting. Only the former provided the measure of *honestum*. The flourishing of a polity depended on a coincidence of interests, understood as the 'Publick Good'.[124] This interpretation also appears in the first number of *The Con-Test* in which Ruffhead was engaged in redefining consistency so as to free Pitt from accusations of inconsistency. The sagacious politician pursued the nation's 'real' interest, which was, of course, synonymous with the public good:

There is in all kingdoms, a real or permanent, and an accidental or immediate interest. If a potent state should be so ill advised as to pursue an accidental or immediate, to the neglect of its real or permanent interest, such an unnatural conduct in them, must influence other powers, to submit to a temporary deviation from those established rules of government, which past experience may have prescribed as most generally essential to public good.[125]

Scientific politics offered the possibility of a more effective use of history than that employed, and largely discredited, by the more vigorous and hyperbolic opposition writers. Those who had actually investigated those exemplary ancient republics, and in practice this meant Rome and Sparta, discovered that there was little to be learned from them. 'Haughtiness of Domination',[126] a rigid social order,[127] perpetual and therefore economically and socially

[122] John Campbell, *The Present State of Europe* (London, 1760), p. 23.
[123] *Ibid.*, p. 9. See J. A. W. Gunn, '"Interest Will Not Lie": A Seventeenth-Century Political Maxim', *JHI*, 39 (1968), 551–64.
[124] Campbell, *Present State of Europe*, p. 77.   [125] *Con-Test*, 23 November 1756, p. 3.
[126] Josiah Tucker, *A Letter to Edmund Burke* (Gloucester, 1775), p. 23.
[127] Priestley, *Lectures on History* (London, 1788), p. 250; Oliver Goldsmith, 'Citizen of the World', *Collected Works*, ed. Arthur Friedman, 4 vols. (Oxford, 1966), II, p. 211.

debilitating warfare,[128] and slave labour[129] could contribute
nothing to a society committed to virtue, commerce and civil liberty.
'But to one who considers coolly on the subject, it will appear, that
human nature, in general, really enjoys more liberty at present, in
the most arbitrary government of Europe, than it ever did during
the most flourishing period of ancient times.'[130]

Until the middle of the eighteenth century, the ancient figures
and the virtues to be emulated were Roman and Spartan, almost
never Athenian.[131] Montagu had praised Sparta precisely because it
was unlike Britain and Athens. If Commonwealth writers found
Athens 'effeminate' and soft in the defence of liberty, most of their
contemporaries saw her as possessing far too much of it. The commonwealth loathed her commercial and cultural ways, while the
mainstream defenders of the community's integrity attacked her
democracy and demagoguery. Bolingbroke, writing 'On the Policy
of the Athenians', managed to unite both strands in a single
diatribe.[132]

Of all Athens' eighteenth-century critics, none rivalled Edmund
Burke in his depiction of democracy as bigger fish eating smaller
fish. In its scope it went beyond democratic Athens to condemn the
entire project of basing political thought on antique models.[133]
Although Athens' constitution was constructed by the 'Poet and

---

[128] Hume, 'Of Commerce', *Essays*, p. 259; 'Populousness of Ancient Nations', *Essays*,
pp. 424ff; 'Of Refinement in the Arts', *Essays*, pp. 29, 278; Goldsmith, 'Review of Guicciardini's *History of Italy*' (1759), *Works*, I, p. 191; Tucker, *The Case of Going to War for the
Sake of Procuring, Enlarging, or Securing of Trade* (London, 1763), pp. 23, 27–9; Samuel
Johnson, *Thoughts on the Late Transactions Respecting Falkland's Island*, *Works*, pp. 370–1.

[129] Priestley, *Lectures on History*, pp. 363, 369; Hume, 'Populousness of Ancient Nations',
Essays, pp. 383–4; Smith, *Lectures on Jurisprudence* (hereafter cited as *LJ*), ed. R. L. Meek,
D. D. Raphael and P. G. Stein (Indianapolis, 1982), A, IV.69, p. 226, A, III.101, p. 181, A,
iv.110, p. 243; *An Inquiry into the Nature and Causes of the Wealth of Nations* (hereafter cited as
WN), ed. R. H. Campbell, A. S. Skinner and W. B. Todd (Indianapolis, 1982),
IV.vii.b.54, p. 587; Tucker, *Tract V. The respective pleas and arguments of the mother country and
of her colonies, distinctly set forth* (Gloucester, 1775), p. iv; John Lind, *Three Letters to Doctor
Price* (London, 1776), p. 157.

[130] Hume, 'Of the Populousness of Ancient Nations', p. 383.

[131] '... between the end of the fifth century B.C. and the eighteenth century A.D. Athens, or
at least Athenian democracy, was as a political idea in almost permanent eclipse'
(Elizabeth Rawson, *The Spartan Tradition in European Thought* (Oxford, 1969), p. 2. For a
contemporary echo, see Hutcheson, *System*, II.v.3, p. 301).

[132] Bolingbroke, 'On the Policy of the Athenians', *Works*, I, pp. 498–501.

[133] Burke, *A Vindication of Natural Society* (2nd edn, London, 1757), p. 64. In subjecting
Athenian democracy to this analysis Burke stood in the company of Hume ('Of the
Original Contract', *Essays*, p. 473) and later Bentham ('Fragment on Government', in *A
Comment on the Commentaries and a Fragment on Government*, ed, J. H. Burns and H. L. A. Hart
(London, 1977), p. 459n).

Philosopher' Solon, 'no sooner was this Political Vessel launched from the stocks, than it overset'. There was no golden age. Because it was a democracy, a demagogue immediately took over and manipulated the people for selfish gain. Hellenistic Athens is so starkly illuminated by the raking chiaroscuro of Burke's description that the passage stands as the most thorough eighteenth-century deconstruction of the myth of the ancient republic:

The people, forgetful of all Virtue and publick Spirit, and intoxicated with the Flatteries of their Orators (these Courtiers of Republicks, and endowed with the distinguishing Characters of all other Courtiers) this People, I say, at last arrived at that Pitch of Madness, that they coolly and deliberately, by an express Law, made it capital for any Man to propose an Application of the immense Sums squandered in publick Shows, even to the most necessary Purposes of the State. When you see the People of this Republick banishing or murdering their best and ablest Citizens, dissipating the publick Treasure with the most senseless Extravagance, and spending their whole Time, as Spectators or Actors, in playing, fiddling, dancing and singing, does it not, my Lord strike your Imagination with the Image of a sort of complex Nero? And does it not strike you with the greater Horror, when you observe, not one Man only, but a whole City, grown drunk with Pride and Power, running with a Rage of Folly in the same mean and senseless debauchery and Extravagance? But if this people resembled Nero in this Extravagance, much more did they resemble and even exceed him in Cruelty and Injustice.[134]

In place of the ancient republics some writers attuned to the political role of commerce sought in a contemporary republic the looked-for blend of the liberty and security of the community. In a passage that was, as we have noted, taken up by Brown, Montagu and James Burgh among others, Montesquieu broke from the tradition anchored in Machiavellian speculation about *virtù*:

True is it that when a democracy is founded on commerce, private people may acquire vast riches without a corruption of morals. This is because the spirit of commerce is naturally attended with that of frugality, economy, moderation, labour, prudence, tranquillity, order, and rule. So long as this spirit subsists, the riches it produces have no bad effect.[135]

The growth of commerce was thought to have introduced property and so created the necessity of law. For 'without security in that respect, the inducements to pursue trade will flag; but with security it will thrive and prosper, and where ever this security is thoroughly

---

[134] Burke, *A Vindication*, pp. 58–61.   [135] Montesquieu, *Spirit of the Laws*, v.6, p. 46.

established, and wisely cherished and promoted' it will lead to an increase in population and thence in wealth.[136] Thus, civilization itself could be said to be a product of commerce.

Guido Abbattista has pointed out Campbell's interest in promoting the 'Dutch Model'. While downplaying any possible republican commitment on Campbell's part, Abbattista has stressed 'that it was also possible to use the idea of a republic as a synonym for government in the interest of the general community'.[137] In reprinting with an introduction Pieter de la Court's *Maxims of Holland*, though attributed to John de Witt, Campbell presented the image of a polity whose governance was committed to the well-being and security of the community. This particular republic existed, unlike the mythical one of English republicans, and was, like Venice, not particularly democratic. Its commitments were to fishing, maritime traffic and manufacturers, not to the acquisition of territory or involvement in balance of power wars. The political theory behind Dutch practice was identified with precisely that cluster of ideas which we have identified with the prudent politics of the reason of state:

... for *fiat justitia & perat mundus*, becomes a judge's mouth very well; for they not being sovereigns, are for the sake of their honour, oath, and office, bound to judge by the laws, and not contrary to them: wherein if they fail, they are in well-ordered republicks to be complained of, and punished. But the proverb does not at all become wise politicians, where *salus populi*, and not the people's ruin, must be the supreme or highest law.[138]

The principle behind this discussion is that politics could not be spoken of abstractly but had to be grounded in practice. Reality was not a game and so 'we ought never in polity (as in playing tennis) to set the ball fair, but must strike it as it lies'.[139]

While Campbell recognized that free governments derived inestimable advantages from the motivation of their citizens,[140] in a later work he was to describe a Dutch polity in which the republicanism was a cipher for the reason of state. 'All the sensible and disinterested part of the Dutch Nation, are by this time convinced, that the

---

[136] *Modern Universal History*, XLIII (1764), p. 333.
[137] Abbattista, *Commercio, colonie e impero*, p. 105. I thank David Armitage for bringing this book to my attention.
[138] [John de Witt], *Political Maxims of the State of Holland* (London, 1743), p. 115. Jonathan Scott (*Algernon Sidney and the English Republic 1623–77*, pp. 210–13) has described this work as a reason of state tract written for republics.
[139] [de Witt], *Maxims of Holland*, p. 14.   [140] *Ibid.*, pp. 300, 417.

Notion of a perfect Democracy, and a Form of Government founded on an Equality of Wealth and Power is mere Delusion' disseminated by a faction. Campbell, instead, placed great emphasis on the office of stadtholder and his position as the 'natural Poize' in the constitution.[141] The practice of the Dutch East India Company, described in his volume in the *Modern Part of the Universal History*, is relentlessly political. The ends are the only justification of the means:

Notwithstanding all this, and notwithstanding that many things in their conduct may not be reconcileable to the nice rules of equity, or the maxims of strict justice; for when did great fortune arise from a close attention to those rules and maxims? In what age, in what country, have there arisen statesmen without vices, or heroes without crimes? Did Rome, did Carthage, nay, did Sparta, grow to be great and famous without censure, without blemish?[142]

Those for whom patriotism consisted in the pursuit of the public good were rarely sympathetic to the opposition's continuing appeal to the spirit of liberty. Campbell's redescription of the Dutch Republic and the seeming irrelevance of personal liberty to John Brown's account of the public good testify to the opposition's difficulty in sustaining a clear-cut republican alternative to the government's insistent identification of themselves with the common good. Defenders of the government often took the offensive, matching the attacks on the liberty of the ancient republics with cutting criticism of the blind worship of British liberty. According to Johnson, 'Liberty is, to the lowest rank of every nation, little more than the choice of working or starving; and this choice is, I suppose, equally allowed in every country.'[143] Goldsmith, himself a historian of Rome, was convinced that the English use of liberty betrayed a complete ignorance of what the word meant: 'Liberty is echoed in all their assemblies, and thousands might be found ready to offer up their lives for the sound, though perhaps not one of all the number understands its meaning'.[144] In an English context, this much-lauded concept was almost historically inapplicable.[145] Only with the establishment of powerful royal authority were the magnates put in their places. Thus liberty was actually the achievement of the despised Stuarts. By comparison, the recent achievements of the

---

[141] Campbell, *Present State of Europe*, p. 496.   [142] *Modern Universal History*, x, p. 440.
[143] Johnson, 'The Bravery of the English Common Soldiers', *Works*, x, p. 283.
[144] Goldsmith, 'Citizen of the World', *Works*, ii, p. 27.
[145] *Ancient and Modern Liberty*, p. 5.

French monarchy made the 'vulgar' view that the English were free while the French were slaves particularly vulnerable to abuse. Hume's praise of the 'civilized' monarchy was directed at this claim which he explicitly associated with the Commonwealth tradition: 'It may now be affirmed of civilized monarchies, what was formerly said in praise of republics alone, *that they are a government of Laws, not of Men*.'[146] The idea that this liberty was a result of an original contract between rulers and ruled was mocked by those, like Hume, Burke, Smith and Tucker, who sought to ground political legitimacy on the reality of social practice.[147]

David Hume is the most famous and powerful critic of the opposition's loose political language. While Duncan Forbes has written felicitously of Hume's 'sceptical' politics, we might as easily describe them as 'prudent'. Hume's discussion of utility and good in the *Enquiry Concerning the Principles of Morals* is part of a distinct philosophical, rather than political account, though his conclusions certainly emphasized the public dimension of utility. Hume's ideal law-giver would legislate according to what 'would best promote public interest, and establish peace and security among mankind'.[148] The nature of this calculation of the public utility explicitly invoked Cicero's example of the shipwreck in *De Officiis* (III.xxiii).[149]

Because circumstances rather than contracts described the nature of justice, history was central to Hume's politics. From this perspec-

---

146 Hume, 'Of Civil Liberty', *Essays*, p. 94; *Letters to a Young Nobleman*, pp. 185–6.
147 Hume, *A Treatise of Human Nature*, ed. Selby-Bigge; 2nd edn, ed. P. H. Nidditch (Oxford, 1978), III.ii.8, pp. 540–1; 'Original Contract', *Essays*, pp. 468, 480–1; Burke, *Vindication*, p. 67. Smith, *LJ*, A, v.115, p. 316, v.119, p. 318, v.135, pp. 323–4; *LJ*, V.13, p. 402, B.15, p. 403; Tucker, *A Treatise Concerning Civil Government* (London, 1781), pp. 41–2, 123. These writers and others opted for the alternative sociological account of the origin of society. For example, Hume, 'Origin of Government', *Essays*, p. 37; Tucker, *Treatise*, pp. 23, 49; Wallace, *A View of the Internal Policy of Great Britain* (London, 1764), p. 166; Henry Winder, *A Critical and Chronological History of the Rise, Progress, Declension and Revival of Knowledge, Chiefly Religious* (2nd edn, London, 1766), p. 12.
148 Hume, 'Enquiry Concerning the Principles of Morals', in *Enquiries Concerning Human Understanding and Concerning the Principles of Morals*, ed. P. H. Nidditch (3rd edn, Oxford, 1975), III.ii.154, pp. 191–2.
149 *Ibid.*, II.ii.143, pp. 180–1; III.1.147, p. 186: 'Is it any crime, after a shipwreck, to seize whatever means or instrument of safety one can lay hold of without regard to former limitations of property? Or if a city besieged were perishing with hunger; can we imagine, that men will see any means of preservation before them, and lose their lives, from a scrupulous regard to what, in other situations, would be the rules of equity and justice? The use and tendency of that virtue is to procure happiness and security, by preserving order in society: but where the society is ready to perish from extreme necessity, no greater evil can be dreaded from violence and injustice; and every man may now provide for himself by all means which prudence can dictate, or humanity permit.'

tive, the *History of England* was the natural endpoint of the philosophical theory with which he began and the essays which developed their implications. His characterization of human nature based
on passion and interest not only redefined justice, but reinforced the
emphasis on unmasking human motivation. The writing of this kind
of history could make sense of social change by explaining the
actions of men:

Mankind are so much the same, in all times and places, that history informs
us of nothing new or strange in this particular. Its chief use is only to
discover the constant and universal principles of human nature, by
showing men in all varieties of circumstances and situations, and furnishing
us with materials from which we may form our observations and become
acquainted with the regular springs of human action and behaviour. These
records of wars, intrigues, factions, and revolutions, are so many collections
of experiments, by which the politician or moral philosopher fixes the
principles of his science, in the same manner as the physician or natural
philosopher becomes acquainted with the nature of plants, minerals, and
other external objects, by the experiments which he forms concerning
them. Nor are the earth, water, and other elements, examined by Aristotle,
and Hippocrates, more like to those which at present lie under our
observation than the men described by Polybius and Tacitus are to those
who now govern the world.[150]

Istvan Hont has described David Hume's attitude towards the
public debt in terms of this fear for the security of the state.[151] The
purpose of the debt was to enhance the interests of the state. When it
no longer did that, or when it actually endangered the state, there
could be no rationale for its maintenance. Hume's view of this
relationship between means and ends could have been taken from
any number of seventeenth-century political treatises:

As the obligation of justice is founded entirely on the interests of society,
which require mutual respect for property in order to preserve peace
among mankind, it is evident that when the execution of justice would be
attended with very pernicious consequences, virtue must be suspended,
and give place to public utility. In such extraordinarily pressing emergencies the maxim *fiat Justitia & ruat Coelum*, let justice be performed,
though the universe be destroyed, is false, and by sacrificing the end to the
means, shews a preposterous idea of the subordination of duties. What

[150] Hume, 'Enquiry Concerning the Principles of Understanding', VIII.i.65, pp. 83–4.
[151] Istvan Hont, 'The Rhapsody of Public Debt: David Hume and Voluntary State Bankruptcy', *The Discourse of Politics in Early Modern Britain*, ed. Nicholas Phillipson and
Quentin Skinner (Cambridge, 1993), pp. 321–48.

governor of a town makes any scruple of burning the suburbs, when they facilitate the approaches of the enemy?[152]

The continuation of that passage turns this definition of the sovereign good into the measure of political obligation in its characteristic seventeenth-century form:

> The case is the same with the duty of allegiance; and common sense teaches us, that, as government binds us to obedience only on account of its tendency to public utility, that duty must always, in extraordinary cases, when public ruin would evidently attend obedience, yield to the primary and original obligation. *Salus populi suprema Lex*, the safety of the people is the supreme law. This maxim is agreeable to the sentiments of mankind in all ages.[153]

The renuncication of politics based on principle for politics based on practice took aim, as we have noted, at the tendency to speak in terms of polarities like liberty and slavery. Hume's claim that 'It may now be affirmed of civilized monarchies, what was formerly said in praise of republics alone, *that they are a government of Laws, not of Men*' reflected his belief that politics could no longer be described in terms of ancient polarities.[154] This kind of government in 'high political rant' was often called 'Tyranny, but which, by a just and prudent administration, may afford tolerable security to the people, and may answer most of the ends of political society'. While republics, rather than monarchies, had generally provided the kind of stability that the rule of law guaranteed, it was now the case that in both forms of government 'people have security for the enjoyment of their property'.[155]

Commerce, redescribed in the early modern language of state-building, was the vehicle of this revolution: 'Trade was never esteemed an affair of state till the last century; and there scarcely is any ancient writer on politics, who has made mention of it.'[156] In the era of state-economics, *conservación y aumento* was an economic imperative:

> The greatness of a state, and the happiness of its subjects, how independent soever they may be supposed in some respects, are commonly allowed to be inseparable with regard to commerce; and as private men receive greater security, in the possession of their trade and riches, from the power of the

---

[152] Hume, 'Of Passive Obedience', *Essays*, p. 489.   [153] *Ibid.*, p. 489.
[154] Hume, 'Civil Liberty', *Essays*, p. 94.
[155] Hume, 'Arts and Sciences', *Essays*, p. 125.
[156] Hume, 'Of Civil Liberty', *Essays*, p. 88.

public, so the public becomes powerful in proportion to the opulence and extensive commerce of private men.[157]

If commerce had become a vehicle for national greatness it also posed a traditional question about the relationship between public and private good, albeit transposed into a new idiom. If improvements in agriculture and industry required a smaller work force, could the sovereign appropriate the surplus labour for the needs of the state? Hume seems to sketch a conflict between 'the greatness of the state and the happiness of the subject'. The former is best served by full employment on public projects while the latter prefers a bigger private sector.[158]

Hume's politics, like those of another early modern prudent politician, Paolo Sarpi, found their final expression in the writing of history. History was important as a means of unmasking the opposition's fabricated history. However, because political legitimacy derived from neither revelation, contract nor form of government, but could only be earned over time, the writing of history also served a crucial political function: it could uphold or undermine the legitimacy of government:

In the particular exertions of power, the question ought never to be forgotten *What is best?* But in the general distribution of power among the several members of a constitution there can seldom be admitted any other question, than *What is established?*[159]

LIBERTY, LAW AND SECURITY

If opposition thought was, and remains, easily stereotyped as a series of economia to liberty, their critics often expressed their political commitment in terms of patriotism and the science of politics. By the middle of the century, security seemed a common theme for all writers on politics. The discourse of natural law, too, following the example of Grotius, seemed to support the integrity of the community. From this perspective, the question of John Locke's value to most eighteenth-century writers seems clear. Whatever use was made of the *Second Treatise* by reform-minded writers, the most pronounced engagement was with mainstream thinkers who found much in common with his Ciceronian description of morality as the

---

[157] Hume, 'Of Commerce', *Essays*, p. 255. Also [Campbell], *Modern Universal History*, xxxviii (1763), p. 1.
[158] Hume, 'Of Commerce', *Essays*, p. 257.   [159] Hume, *History*, iv, p. 354.

very public combination of personal virtue and solicitousness for the common good.[160] In the pivotal account in paragraph 131 of the *Second Treatise* concerning the establishment of society among disconnected individuals, he wrote that the connection with society was made 'only with an intention in everyone the better to preserve himself his Liberty and Property'. Locke insisted that the 'Equality, Liberty, and Executive Power' possessed by all individuals in the state of nature is given 'into the hands of the Society, to be so far disposed of by the Legislative, as the good of the Society shall require'.[161] James Tully has recently identified this public good with 'the end of political power' and defined it as 'the preservation of society and, as far as this is compatible with the preservation of the whole, the preservation of each member'.[162]

William Blackstone not only cited Locke's defence of executive prerogative power in his own general defence of the British constitutional *status quo*, but also stressed the role of prerogative power as an instrument for maintaining the security of the community. 'For', he wrote, 'prerogative consisting (as Mr Locke has well defined it) in the discretionary power of acting for the public good, where the positive laws are silent ...'[163]

Blackstone's constitutionally defined prerogative was bounded by

---

[160] 'For God, having, by an inseparable conexion, joined Virtue and publick Happiness together, and made the Practice thereof, necessary to the preservation of Society, and visibly beneficial to all, with whom the Virtuous Man has to do; it is no wonder, that every one should, not only allow, but recommend, and magnifie those Rules to others, from whose observance of them, he is sure to reap Advantage to himself' (Locke, *Essay*, i.iii.6, p. 69). The standard account of the *Second Treatise*'s eighteenth-century *fortuna* is John Dunn, 'John Locke in England and America', in *John Locke: Problems and Perceptives*, ed. John W. Yolton (Cambridge, 1969), pp. 45–80. But see also Yuhtaro Ohmori, '"The Artillery of Mr Locke": The Use of Locke's "Second Treatise" in Pre-Revolutionary America, 1764–1776, Unpublished Ph.D. thesis (The Johns Hopkins University, 1988).

[161] Locke, *Second Treatise*, ed. Peter Laslett (New York, 1965), pp. 398–9.

[162] James Tully, 'Locke', in *Cambridge History of Political Thought*, ed. J. H. Burns and Mark Goldie (Cambridge, 1991), pp. 619, 625. David Wootton has also recently emphasized the practical political dimension to the argument of the *Second Treatise* ('John Locke: Socinian or Natural Law Theorist', in *Religion, Secularization and Political Thought: Thomas Hobbes to J. S. Mill*, ed. James E. Crimmins (London, 1989), pp. 39–67). While disagreeing with Wotton's conclusion about the relationship between Locke's political and religious positions, James Moore also stressed Locke's deeply political motivations ('Theological Politics: A Study of the Reception of Locke's *Two Treatises of Government* in England and Scotland in the Early Eighteenth Century', in *John Locke and / Und Immanuel Kant: Historical Reception and Contemporary Relevance*, ed. Martyn P. Thompson (Berlin, 1991), pp. 62–82). Both of these works refine John Dunn's argument: Locke's natural rights argument was often interpreted in the light of his explicitly prudential assessments.

[163] Blackstone, *Commentaries on the Laws of England*, 4 vols. (15th edn, London, 1809), I, p. 251. For Blackstone's view of prerogative, see Clark, *English Society*, pp. 202–5.

the 'purpose of society'. Thus, as he writes at the opening of the chapter on 'Prerogative', the 'discretionary power' vested in the crown can 'not intrench any farther on our natural liberties, than is expedient for the maintenance of our civil'. The proper context of this discussion is further clarified by Blackstone's subsequent declaration that in previous ages and places the study of prerogative 'was ranked among the *arcana imperii* and, like the mysteries of the *bona dea*, was not suffered to be pried into by any but such as were initiated in its services'.[164]

The nature of prerogative also defined its limits. Its purpose was most assuredly not the 'private splendour and gratification' of rulers, as was commonly thought by the 'vulgar and ignorant'. Rather, it was designed 'for the security and preservation of the real happiness and liberty of his subjects'.[165] Consequently, if prerogative powers were employed to oppress rather than preserve the lives of subjects and so subverted the maxims of state which defined it, resistance was legitimate.[166] While Blackstone scrupulously denied that support for prerogative joined him to the friends of absolute power, those defenders of passive obedience whom he called 'advocates for slavery', he was equally uncomfortable with the 'commonwealth' willingness to sanction private resistance to private oppression. The defence 'of the being of the state' when endangered was legitimate; individuals determining when the state of legitimate resistance obtained constituted a danger to the state. According to Blackstone it amounted to

A doctrine productive of anarchy, and (in consequence) equally fatal to civil liberty as tyranny itself. For civil liberty, rightly understood, consists in protecting the rights of individuals by the united force of society: society cannot be maintained, and of course, can exert no protection, without obedience to some sovereign power: and obedience is an empty name, if every individual has a right to decide how far he himself shall obey.[167]

Blackstone's effort to define the legal parameters of prerogative is central to his attempt to prevent the civil disorders attendant upon disputed power that typified sixteenth- and seventeenth-century Continental and English history. The maintenance and security of the community required the existence of a power capable of acting in the interests of that community but also one defined clearly

---

[164] Blackstone, *Commentaries*, I, p. 237.   [165] *Ibid.*, p. , 245, n2.   [166] *Ibid.*, p. , 244.
[167] *Ibid.*, p. , 251.

enough to prevent the disorders that destroyed communities. This political definition was given fullest expression, characteristically for the early modern state, in a discussion of the military dimension of prerogative power:

> The king is considered, in the next place, as the generalissimo, or the first in the military command, within the kingdom, the great end of society is to protect the weakness of individuals by the united strength of the community: and the principal use of government is to direct that united strength in the best and most effectual manner, to answer the end proposed.[168]

But a discussion of prerogative raised the questions that had dogged its seventeenth-century analysts. Hume described this particular tension as an inevitable component of political life. 'In all governments, there is a perpetual intestine struggle, open or secret, between Authority and Liberty; and neither of them can ever absolutely prevail in the contest.'[169]

In mid eighteenth-century Britain the conscious attempt to refine the understanding of the constitution, for so many Britons and Europeans alike the glory of the nation, often focused on defining the kind of liberty available under law. This, too, was part of the eighteenth century's conversation with Grotius. One of the singular features of his argument was Grotius' seeming willingness to permit individuals to renounce their liberties. But it was his discussion of the royal right of alienation which actually contributed most powerfully to this later discussion of liberty. His defence of patrimonialism had drawn the contemporary objection that free men could not be bought and sold by their ruler. This led Grotius to make a fundamental distinction:

> But as there is a Difference between the regal Power, and that of a Master over his Slave; so likewise there is a Difference between civil Liberty, and that which is personal: The Liberty of a private Person is one Thing, and that of the whole Body of the People another.

The king's alienation of his people did not affect their personal status since what had changed was the right to govern them as a single people. This argument belongs to the era of Europe's civil wars of religion, when territories and their populations were exchanged and when the loss of political autonomy was not uncommon. Lipsius, for example, exchanged confessions and domiciles

---

[168] *Ibid.*, p., 261.   [169] Hume, 'Of the Origin of Government', p. 40.

several times. According to Grotius, lack of civil liberty would not have affected Lipsius' personal liberty. In the words of Barbeyrac, himself a French Protestant exile,

Now single Persons who are members of a people, are free, though the whole People is not so; for the Liberty of a Man consists in his having no particular Master, who has a Power of commanding his Actions, and even to dispose of his Person and Estate; and those, who are Members of a People not free, have, as such, but one common Master, who has a Right to command them as his subjects. Thus when a King alienates his Crown, we cannot say he disposes of his Subjects, considering each of them in particular; for, after he has sold or given away his Kingdom, each Subject is still as free as before, and has only added another Sovereign. As to the Body of the People, barely by having a King, really such, it ceases to be free.[170]

The distinction drawn by Grotius was to be employed by Hume as the characteristic of the modern era, and so served in his running skirmish with the opposition writers who fancied the ancient republics: 'If we consider the ancient state of Europe, we shall find, that the far greater part of the society were every where bereaved of their personal liberty, and lived entirely at the will of their masters.' The subsequent progress of the arts and commerce eliminated the grounds of personal enslavement. Whereas in antiquity artisans and craftsmen were usually slaves, the increasing demand for consumer and luxury goods had elevated their status and attracted new labourers. 'Thus', concludes Hume, 'personal freedom became almost general in Europe; an advantage which paved the way for the encrease of political or civil liberty', even if only partial.[171]

Grotius' distinction was part of his larger attempt to create a right where the modern Stoics had described a need. Personal liberty was required for self-preservation and security; political or civil liberty was not. In the *Spirit of the Laws* Montesquieu preserved Grotius' motivations intact. Liberty, he recognized, was a word given to a great deal of interpretation. For some it amounted to the right to depose a tyrant, for others the power to choose a new one. Some equated liberty with the right to bear arms while to others it meant being governed by a countryman and familiar native laws.[172] Instead of personal and civil liberty, Montesquieu thought in terms

---

[170] Grotius, *Laws of War and Peace*, i.iii.xii, pp. 76–7.
[171] David Hume, *History of England*, 6 vols. (Indianapolis, 1983), ii, pp. 522–4.
[172] Montesquieu, *Spirit of the Laws*, xi.2, p. 149.

of the political liberty of subject and of constitution. Security continued to define its ambit:

The political liberty of the subject is a tranquillity of mind arising from the
opinion each person has of his safety [*sûreté*]. In order to have this liberty, it
is requisite the government be so constituted as one man need not be afraid
of another.[173]

Ideally, in a free country 'every man who is supposed a free agent
ought to be his own governor'. Nevertheless, this was only possible in
states of small extent.[174] Elsewhere, the liberty of citizens depended
on the constitution. This security was imperilled when two of the
three functions of government, executive, legislative or judicial,
were united in the same person or body. Thus, while the political
liberty of the constitution 'arises from a certain distribution of the
three powers', the liberty of the subject 'consists in security, or in the
opinion people have of their security'. Similarly, in separating
philosophical from political liberty Montesquieu wrote that the
latter 'consists in security, or, at least, in the opinion that we enjoy
security'.[175]

Though Montesquieu described liberty in terms of security he did
not believe it capable of being preserved except under constitutional
government. Thus his distinction between freedom by right and
fact, designed to explain the possibility of either constitution or
subjects being free without the other, vanishes in practice. The tale
of the Gracchi was a cautionary one: 'To favor, therefore, the liberty
of the subject, they struck at that of the constitution; but the former
perished with the latter.'[176] Constitutions did work to uphold personal liberty and so, ultimately, forms of government mattered.

Similarly, describing the condition in which Ireland was sub-
jugated, and then dominated, by Britain, Montesquieu commented
that Britain 'has given this nation of its own laws, yet it holds it in
great dependence: the subjects there are free and the state itself in
slavery'. But the insecurity with which this freedom was held undermined the security of their persons: 'Laws are imposed by one
country on the other, and these are such as render its property
precarious, and dependent on the will of a master.'[177]

The eighteenth-century adaptation and republication of Henry

---

[173] *Ibid.*, xi.6, p. 151.   [174] *Ibid.*, xi.6, p. 154.   [175] *Ibid.*, xii.2, p. 183.
[176] *Ibid.*, xi.18, p. 178.
[177] *Ibid.*, xix.27, p. 311.

Care's *English Liberties* (now updated as *British Liberty*) explicitly lifted the crucial definitions straight out of Montesquieu. Thus, 'Political liberty, consists in security, or at least in the opinion that we enjoy security.' It also repeated Montesquieu's distinction between liberty and independence which will be discussed below.[178] Goldsmith's parody of 'British liberty' can also be read as an attack on the notion that liberty was primarily political rather than personal. The 'Citizen of the World' related the content of a conversation overheard when passing outside a prison:

> The subject was upon a threatened invasion from France, and each seemed anxious to rescue his country from the impending danger. "For my part," cries the prisoner, "the greatest of my apprehensions is for our freedom; if the French should conquer, what would become of English liberty? My dear friends, liberty is the Englishman's prerogative; we must preserve that at the expence of our lives, of that the French shall never deprive us; it is not to be expected that men who are slaves themselves would preserve our freedom should they happen to conquer." "Ay slaves," cries the porter, "they are all slaves, fit only to carry burthens every one of them."[179]

In his *Dissertation on the Mutual Support of Trade and Civil Liberty* (1756), Benjamin Newton wove together the various themes we have been discussing: the reason of state, commerce, manners, security and liberty.

> For Trade increases Wealth; Wealth increases the Arts of Life; and the Arts of Life improve the Manners of a People. Improvement of Manners, by softening the rigour of civil Government, naturally tends to a Diminution of that Power, with which the executive part is invested. For the End of civil Government being the Security of Individuals in their Persons and Possessions; and the means of obtaining this end being a certain degree of Power lodged in the supreme Magistrate, it follows, that in proportion as the End is answered, the necessity of the Means must cease.[180]

Newton argued that economic underdevelopment was the real seedbed of despotism. Invoking the familiar argument that trade required security of property, he suggested that this, in turn, required liberty since 'civil Liberty implies Security to every Individual in his Possessions'.[181]

Where writers like Brown claimed that laws served the process of

[178] Henry Care, *British Liberty* (London, 1766), pp.ii–iii.
[179] Goldsmith, 'Citizen of the World', *Works*, II, p. 28.
[180] Benjamin Newton, *Another Dissertation on the Mutual Support of Trade and Civil Liberty* (London, 1756), p. 14.
[181] *Ibid.*, p. 18.

moral reformation and therefore liberty,[182] the spokesmen for prudence used the locution 'civil liberty' to describe the ability to act within the parameters of law.[183] In Blackstone's formulation,

This liberty, rightly understood, consists in the power of doing whatever the laws permit; which is only to be effected by a general conformity of all orders and degrees to those equitable rules of action, by which the meanest individual is protected from the insults and oppression of the greatest.[184]

Addressing his twentieth-century readers in the preface to volume two of *Crito*, James Burgh described his age as one already removed from the classical view of law as an instrument of social engineering ('police'). The ancient lawgiver 'had a mighty notion of police, or the forming of the minds and manners of the people to certain dispositions, which they thought necessary for securing the happiness of states. We look upon such things as merely Utopian.'[185]

Unlike Burgh, Joseph Priestley felt no remorse at the abandonment of the ancients' preoccupation with manners. For him this was an undesirable facet of the oppressive face of the communal politics of authority. Because law served as the primary instrument of this control, Priestley sought to redefine its scope. The understanding of civil liberty had been distorted 'by an abuse of the maxim, that the joint understanding of all the members of a state, properly collected, must be preferable to that of individuals, and that the greater the presence of the community in the daily lives of its members, the better. 'In truth', Priestley wrote, 'the greater part of human actions are of such a nature, that more inconvenience would follow from their being fixed by laws, than from their being left to every man's arbitrary will'.[186] As an alternative, Priestley suggested that only convincing proof that social intervention was

---

[182] Law 'can act to free us from natural but self-destructive tendency to pursue our selfish interests, forcing us instead to promote the public interest in a genuinely virtuoso style, and thereby enabling us to preserve our own individual liberty instead of undermining it' (Quentin Skinner, 'Machiavelli on the Maintenance of Liberty', *Politics*, 18 (1983), 10).

[183] For contrast, observe the difference between the civic position and that expounded by Robert Filmer: '. . . every law or command, is in itself an innovation, and a diminution of some part of popular liberty: for it is no law except it restrain liberty: he that by his negative voice doth forbid or hinder the proceeding of a new law, doth preserve himself in that condition of liberty wherein nature hath placed him, and whereof he is in present possession' (Robert Filmer, *Observations on Aristotle's Politiques, Touching Forms of Government* (London, 1652), p. 30).

[184] Blackstone, *Commentaries*, I, pp. 5–6.

[185] James Burgh, *Crito. Or, Essays on Various Subjects*, 2 vols. (London, 1766), I, p. 16.

[186] Joseph Priestley, *Essay on the First Principles of Government* (2nd edn, London, 1771), p. 30.

more efficacious than personal action could justify legislation. This conclusion drew on a view of human nature and practical policy that will be fully explored in its more appropriate place (chapter 6). A similar understanding of law is reflected in a passage added by Jean-Louis De Lolme to the 1782 edition of his *Constitution of England*. Englishmen, he wrote, were free until laws were promulgated to limit that basic liberty:

> In England ... It is not the authority of the government, it is the liberty of the subject, which is supposed to be unbounded. All the individual's actions are supposed to be lawful, till that law is pointed out which makes them to be otherwise.[187]

Mark Francis and John Morrow have pointed to the tremendous popularity of the constitutional texts of De Lolme and Blackstone as an indication of the kind of political theory prevalent between 1765 and 1830.[188]

On the matter of 'civil liberty', Blackstone's position was fairly typical. He believed that it was the prized inheritance of all true-born Englishmen and 'no other than natural liberty so far restrained by human laws ...' For Blackstone, law consisted in 'a rule of action' modelled on a Newtonian God who, when He created the universe, 'impressed certain principles upon matter, from which it can never depart, and without which it would cease to be'. These laws of motion, gravitation, optics, mechanics, and nations constituted the 'will' of God and are collectively called 'laws of nature'. And just as God established rules for matter, such as motion, he imposed certain principles of men, among them free-will and the use of reason 'to discover the purport of those laws'.[189]

The rights which this natural law conferred on men could not be enhanced by human law, nor abridged without the possessor's consent.[190] While individuals had a 'natural liberty ... of acting as one thinks fit' commensurate with God's donation of free-will, they relinquished part of it in exchange for the considerable advantages accrued from membership in society. The principal goal of such a society was to protect the individual 'enjoyment' of those natural rights possessed *ab initio* 'but which could not be preserved in peace

---

[187] De Lolme, *The Constitution of England* (London, 1800, 1st edn 1772), p. 436.
[188] Mark Francis and John Morrow, 'After the Ancient Constitution: Political Theory and English Constitutional Writings, 1765–1832', *History of Political Thought*, 9 (1988), 283.
[189] Blackstone, *Commentaries*, I, pp. 38–9.   [190] *Ibid.*, p. 54.

without that mutual assistance and intercourse which is gained by the institution of friendly and social communities'.[191]

Natural and civil law had distinct aims. While natural law was 'the rule of moral conduct', and revealed law 'the rule of faith' as well as morals, the municipal law was 'a rule of civil conduct'. While the former took natural man as a subject, prescribing 'his duty to God, to himself, and to his neighbour, considered in the light of an individual', the civil law regarded him as a citizen, as well. This entailed additional obligations towards his neighbours 'which amount to no more, than that he do contribute, on his part, to the subsistence and peace of the society'.[192]

Natural law and civil law made contact in the logic of legislation. A just law was one which best served the needs of society while diminishing individual liberty as little as possible. 'So that laws, when prudently framed, are by no means subversive but rather introductive of liberty; for (as Mr Locke has well observed) where there is no law there is no freedom.'[193] Here Blackstone was referring to Locke's formulation in paragraph 57 of the *Second Treatise*.

For Law, in its true Notion, is not so much the Limitation as the direction of a free and intelligent Agent to his proper Interest, and prescribes no farther than is for the general Good of those under that Law. Could they be happier without it, the Law, as an useless thing would of itself vanish; and that ill deserves the Name of Confinement which hedges us in only from Bogs and Precipices. So that, however it may be mistaken, the end of Law is not to abolish or restrain, but to preserve and enlarge Freedom: For in all the states of created beings capable of Laws, where there is no Law, there is no Freedom.[194]

Reason had to correctly assess the aims of the municipal and transcendent realms in order to justify legislation.[195] But Blackstone rejected the claim that reason alone could lead one to the abstract principles of this law of nature. Departing from cruder forms of contemporary realism, he contended that just laws were so intertwined with 'the happiness of each individual, that the latter cannot

---

[191] *Ibid.*, pp. 124–5.   [192] *Ibid.*, p. 45.
[193] *Ibid.*, p. 126; also I, p. 438. See [William Knox], *Thoughts on the Act for Making More Effectual Provision for the Government of the Province of Quebec* (London, 1774), p. 35.
[194] Locke, *Second Treatise*, II.6.57, pp. 347–8. On his understanding of law, see James Tully, 'Locke on Liberty', in *Conceptions of Liberty in Political Philosophy*, ed. Z. Pelczynski and J. Gray (London, 1984), pp. 57–82; and *A Discourse on Property: John Locke and his Adversaries* (Cambridge, 1980), p. 45.
[195] Blackstone, *Commentaries*, I, p. 38.

be attained but by observing the former'. By anchoring natural law on the 'paternal precept, "that man should pursue his own true and substantial happiness"', Blackstone, like Smith and Hume, took explicit aim at Samuel Clarke's popular metaphysical theory of natural law.[196] God 'has not perplexed the law of nature with a multitude of abstracted rules and precepts, referring merely to the fitness or unfitness of things, as some have vainly surmised'. None the less, his attribution to God of the characteristics of 'power', 'wisdom' and 'goodness' certainly does indicate acceptance of Clarke's vision, if not the philosophy that followed from it.[197]

Because of his antagonism to fictional or abstract accounts of origin, whether of polities or of law, Blackstone grounded his own natural law on the more secure principle of human happiness. The persistence of natural law arguments in the eighteenth century was not solely the preserve of an opposition. Moreover, the clear relationship between natural law and utility, or between the good and the useful, preserved the context of Grotius' own creation of the modern natural law discourse. If in the wider discussion of politics Cicero's patriotism was emphasized, the moral dimension of his argument was stressed in the writings of the two principal tutors at St John's College, Cambridge, in the mid eighteenth century: Thomas Rutherforth, later Regius Professor of Divinity (1756–71), and James Tunstall (1708–62).[198]

J. H. Burns has defined utilitarianism as 'a form of social theory having as its primary purpose the laying of empirically verifiable foundations for deliberate social change', understood as the maximization of the greatest happiness of the greatest number.[199] As we observed in chapter 1, Cicero's formulation in book II of *De Officiis*

---

[196] Reality rather than transcendence generated the force of obligation (*Enquiry Concerning the Principles of Morals*, III.i.149, p. 188), while Samuel Clarke and his followers were the ones 'who affirm that virtue is nothing but a conformity to reason; that there are eternal fitnesses and unfitnesses of things, which are the same to every rational being that considers them' (*Treatise*, III.i.1., p. 456).

[197] Blackstone, *Commentaries*, I, pp. 40–1.

[198] In the middle of the eighteenth century the fellowship of St John's College included three of the most powerful exponents of the philosophical ideology of the British state: Rutherforth, Tunstall and Thomas Balguy. Important work remains to be done on the place of the college in a university whose best recent account tends to emphasize its 'progressive' character in the eighteenth century.

[199] J. H. Burns, 'Utilitarianism and Reform: Social Theory and Social Change, 1750–1800', *Utilitas*, I (1989), p. 211. For a similar definition, see J. R. Dinwiddy, 'Utility and Natural Law in Burke's Thought: A Reconsideration', *Studies in Burke and his Time*, 16 (1974–5), 105.

was considered an authoritative discussion of the natural desire for 'happiness' and 'utility', and this was taken up by Locke, Samuel Clarke, Shaftesbury, Francis Hutcheson, John Gay and Edmund Law, to name only a handful.

For we all seek to obtain what is to us expedient; we are irresistibly drawn toward it, and we cannot possibly be otherwise. For who is there that would turn his back upon what is to him expedient? Or rather, who is there that does not exert himself to the utmost to secure it? But because we cannot discover it anywhere except in good report, propriety, and moral rectitude, we look upon these three for that reason as the first and the highest objects of endeavour, while what we term expediency we account not so much an ornament to our dignity as a necessity incident to living.[200]

It is precisely the Ciceronian argument about the convergence of utility and transcendent good that can explain the analogous claims of Francis Hutcheson, Thomas Rutherforth and Joseph Priestley.[201] Read against the backdrop of Cicero's own argument as elaborated in the seventeenth century, their formulations reflect a commitment both to the usefulness of the moral law and the impossibility of a moral law that contradicted the *utilitas rei publicae*. J. R. Dinwiddy contrasted this 'utilitarian' natural law with 'intuitional' models;[202] the latter characterized Samuel Clarke's reading of Cicero and that of his followers, among them James Burgh and Richard Price. The difficulty in disentangling the moral and political thought of Price and Priestley can in some measure be attributed to their different understanding of natural law.[203]

James Tunstall's *Lectures on Natural and Revealed Religion* were read at St John's College, Cambridge, from 1745 though published only after his retirement twenty years later. Like Cicero, his premise was that the 'naturally profitable' had always to be 'naturally honest.' Tunstall did not shirk from the implications of this reading:

---

[200] Cicero, *De Officiis*, III.xxviii.101.

[201] James Hoecker, 'Priestley and Utilitarianism, *Enlightenment & Dissent*, 3 (1984), 55.

[202] Dinwiddy, 'Utility and Natural Law in Burke's Thought', pp. 107–8.

[203] In a famous letter to Francis Hutcheson in 1739 David Hume wrote that 'Upon the whole, I desire to take my catalogue of Virtues from *Cicero's Offices*, not from the *Whole Duty of Man* [Pufendorf's *De Officio Hominis & Civis*]' (Quoted in Peter Jones, *Hume's Sentiments: Their Ciceronian and French Context* (Edinburgh, 1982), p. 9). This is indeed the gulf that stands between Hume and Smith on the one hand, and Bentham on the other. For the Scots, utility was public and also good, while for Bentham the useful was defined by the mathematical manipulation of private pleasures (see Douglas G. Long, '"Utility" and the "Utility Principle": Hume, Smith, Bentham, Mill', *Utilitas*, 2 (1990), p. 33).

Sometimes the public is helped, and even saved, by encouraging private acts of dishonesty, such as bribing public and secret enemies with money, &c – in the casuistry of the state, the greater good cancels the smaller evil. The same reasoning holds, when applied to the secret and subdolous means of frustrating domestic traitors and treason. Whatever tends to save or secure the public is not corruption.[204]

Tunstall's reliance on public utility to decide doubtful moral issues was supported by a citation of Pufendorf's declaration that 'it is not at all unjust, that upon an extraordinary Command of the Commonwealth, and in its greatest Extremities, we should hazard that Life in its Defence, which it doth, in Effect, bestow upon us every Day'.[205]

Actions were first declared 'honest' precisely because 'they were found by experience and judgment to be beneficial', and they are called good because 'they are good for something'. Thus, a proper understanding of utility led Tunstall to affirm the Horatian motto invoked by Grotius against the modern disciples of Carneades that 'expediency might perhaps be called the mother of justice and equity' (*Utilitas justi propre mater et aequi*). Literally in the same breath, Tunstall continued:

> But the stoical maxim – *Fiat iustitia et ruat mundus* – is not only faulty, because it puts an impossible supposition, that justice, the strongest cement and support of the whole moral world, may cause its universal dissolution and ruin; but, because it supposes that justice may continue to be a virtue, when its beneficial tendency is removed from it, from which its virtuous quality is derived.

Precisely this Stoic maxim, also repudiated by Hume and Campbell, was invoked, often explicitly, by the leading reformers of the 1770s to justify their proposals. For Tunstall, the just had to benefit both the individual and the community of individuals.[206] Actions which brought advantage to individuals 'to the prejudice of mankind' were dishonest and therefore 'unprofitable'.[207] Private and public utility coincided with *honestum* only in the pursuit of the common good. Directly picking up Cicero's commentary on Panaetius, Tunstall argued that only the service of the common good could prevent any conflict between *utile* and *honestum*:

---

[204] James Tunstall, *Lectures on Natural and Revealed Religion, Read in the Chapel of St John's College, Cambridge* (London, 1765), p. 144, footnote 'b'.
[205] Pufendorf, *Law of Nature*, VIII.2.4, p. 757.   [206] Tunstall, *Lectures*, p. 145.
[207] *Ibid.*, p. 146.

In the pursuit of publick good, all men may agree, and this is the most efficacious cause, and steadiest security for private good too; but, when their views are directed only to their separate happiness, they hardly ever can, nor can private happiness subsist independently of the publick. The rules likewise which morality prescribes will never interfere with each other, when they uniformly tend to one simple end, the good of the whole; to which the consideration of the parts must without exception submit: but they will often interfere, nor could casuistry point out the direct road of duty, had we not the publick good by which to steer, when the complexities of circumstances, and the numerous relations of life carry different ways.[208]

This common good is Tunstall's definition of justice and is equated with 'the primary law of nature', the 'universal good'. By this 'is meant the greatest happiness of all those rational beings' with whom we live in society. The human pursuit of the good was contingent upon the possession of reason, and since 'right is a dictate of reason, there cannot properly be a community of right, where there is no community of reason'.[209] Action without reason was 'below the dignity of a man' and exposed him 'to many inconveniences of life, and miscarriages in conduct'.[210] In this state the irrational rule of the passions dominated. Hence the importance of prudence. 'It is an eminent virtue in itself, and it is the foundation and main security of every other virtue. Where there is no prudence in the direction, there can be no virtue in the execution of any action whatsoever.'[211] Prudence was joined to fortitude.[212] The Lipsian Hercules, depicted by painters from Annibale Carracci to Nicolas Poussin and Benjamin West, was lauded for the 'steady execution of the prescriptions of right reason'. Prudent action was also, as we have observed, characteristic of the eighteenth-century British Cicero:

For human life does chiefly consist not in speculation, but in action; and wisdom is not useful any otherwise than as it is practically applied, no more than art is valuable, but when it actually produces works beneficial to mankind.[213]

In modern times, fortitude was no longer a matter of physical courage and was not displayed to best advantage on the field of battle. Real life with its varied problems posed the true test of

---

[208] *Ibid.*, p. 166.   [209] *Ibid.*, p. 167.   [210] *Ibid.*, p. 149.   [211] *Ibid.*, p. 153.

[212] This was common in many earlier discussions influenced by neo-Stoic ideals, such as the speech of Daniele Barbaro in book II of Paolo Paruta's influential dialogue *Della perfezione della vita politica* (1582) at the beginning of this tradition. Paruta, *Della perfezione della vita politica*, in *Storici e politici veneti del cinquecento e seicento*, ed. Gino Benzoni and Tiziano Zanto (Milan and Naples, 1982), pp. 574–5.

[213] Tunstall, *Lectures*, p. 154.

strength. The politics of the common good was the arena of the mighty sage:

Human life is justly likened to a perpetual warfare, and the fable teaches us that the enemies, and, as it were, monsters, to be subdued in the course of it, must require an herculean strength of mind ... Amongst this trouble of life, and vicissitude of season, great strength of mind as well as steady attention must preserve a direct course, and maintain that composedness and equability of temper, which is the perfection of fortitude, and the sovereign dignity and chief happiness of man.[214]

The model being hammered out by Tunstall was explicitly directed against the old Stoic notion of indifference towards everything that was not virtuous. Instead, citing Cicero's similar repudiation in *De Finibus* IV.12–14, Tunstall argued for a middle Stoic morality that was consonant with the kind of demands generated by the political management of early modern European states and which at the same time enabled citizens to live rich, full lives in communities: 'to put on the saint, it is not necessary to put off the man'.[215]

In ancient and revived Stoicism, temperance, like prudence and fortitude, was associated with the rational regulation of the passions and desires. It is Tunstall's descriptions of this process in terms of 'happiness' which brings us back into contact with the pre-Benthamite Ciceronian discussion of utility. Temperance constitutes,

such measures, as will produce to us the greatest sum of pleasure in the main, together with the least degree of pain; that is, by pursuing pleasure for its own sake, when it may be had without pain either present or future; by forbearing pleasure in such a circumstance, wherein it will be overbalanced with pain, or by chusing to undergo pain in an one, wherein it will be a means of obtaining a greater pleasure.[216]

In Tunstall's moral world, what was useful to the community had to be good and the performance of the good by individuals produced the greatest possible individual and collective happiness. Because he rejected the possibility that purely private advantage could be 'honest', what passed for private happiness was only legitimate when it conduced to that greater happiness which was the community's. An emphasis on usefulness and happiness was not incompatible with a common good. Tunstall minced no words in describing this Ciceronian community: 'The character of this society is, that it

214 *Ibid.*, p. 156.   215 *Ibid.*, p. 158.   216 *Ibid.*, p. 206.

is a society not of equality, but of subordination, in which all rational beings whatsoever are subject by natural right to one universal and supreme moral governour.'[217]

Justice as the pursuit of a common good was the conventional early modern interpretation of Cicero; *utilitas* did not conflict with *honestum* but actually defined its content. The priority and maintenance of the community was the product not merely of expediency, but of the private pursuit of happiness. The Ciceronian reconciliation of utility and right facilitated the unconflicted pursuit of many private ends without recourse to a mighty Hobbesian arbiter since not only had the rights of individuals to 'be consistent with the rights of all others, but the rights of all must be determined by the consideration of the common good'.[218] In all these discussions, it is important to remember their context. Tunstall's larger theme is revealed and natural religion. The sharp edge of this discussion of individual happiness and the common good was an attack on the possibility of religious disssent as a threat to this good.

The defence of this broad Ciceronian theme also motivated Thomas Rutherforth in his *Institutes of Natural Law*, the published version of his lectures on Grotius.[219] Rutherforth's account picked up Grotius' attempt to give the force of natural law to the primacy of self-preservation he derived from Cicero. Rutherforth defined liberty, conventionally, as the power man possessed to act 'where no law restrains him'. He distinguished between this physical liberty and moral liberty, in which the scope of action was reduced. In so far as we are obliged either by divine or human law 'to act in a particular manner, then, as far as we are under such obligations, we have not an independent power of acting as we please'.[220] Com-

[217] *Ibid.*, p. 170.   [218] *Ibid.*, p. 179.

[219] The importance of the 'modern' theory of natural law for eighteenth-century British political thought, and especially the place of Blackstone and Rutherforth in this tradition, has not figured as a central theme in the recent scholarly literature. (See Lieberman, *Province of Legislation Determined: Legal Theory in Eighteenth-Century Britain* (Cambridge, 1989); John M. Finnis, *Natural Law and Natural Rights* (Oxford, 1980); 'Blackstone's Theoretical Intentions', *Natural Law Forum*, 13 (1967), 163–82; John W. Cairns, 'Blackstone, an English Institutionalist: Legal Literature and the Rise of the Nation State', *Oxford Journal of Legal Studies*, 4 (1984), 318–60.) There is, for example, no survey of English natural jurisprudence to parallel Knud Haakonssen's overview of the place of Grotius and Pufendorf in eighteenth-century Scottish legal and philosophical culture (see 'Natural Jurisprudence in the Scottish Enlightenment; Summary of an Interpretation', *Enlightenment, Rights and Revolution: Essays in Legal and Social Philosophy*, ed. Neil MacCormick and Zenon Bankowski (Aberdeen, 1989), pp. 36–49).

[220] Thomas Rutherforth, *Institutes of Natural Law* (Cambridge, 1754–7), 2 vols., I.10.2, I, pp. 146–7.

pared to the other popular Cambridge theory of liberty, popularized by Samuel Clarke and maintained by Edmund Law, this was a
decidedly sceptical position. It is the division between physical and
moral law which enabled Rutherforth to argue that, however free
we may feel, we are never released from the obligations imposed
upon us by the moral law. There could be no liberty to do ill.[221] But
if this protected him against charges of sanctioning licence, his
upholding of coerced promises would have exposed him to the
contrary charge, were this not an explicit comment on Grotius.
According to Rutherforth, coercion did not vitiate liberty; instead,
like Grotius and Hobbes, he argued that one 'is forced indeed to
chuse one part of a disagreeable alternative, either to make the
promise, or to suffer the evil, with which he is threatened'.[222]

The content of morality and obligation is most extensively discussed by Rutherforth in his *Essay on Virtue* (1748). The good is
defined as 'that quality in our actions, by which they are fitted to do
good to others or to prevent their harm'.[223] One of the salient
features of Rutherforth's argument is his insistence that virtue had to
be defined in a social context. Life in society provided the measure of
the good. The effect an action 'may have upon the happiness or
misery of the agent himself, is not what gives the name of virtue to
it'.[224] Rutherforth traces this perspective on virtue back to Grotius:
'he described the natural honesty or virtue of an action so as to make
it at least in part consist in its agreeableness to a social nature, that
is, in its fitness to advance and secure the common happiness of
mankind'.[225]

Rutherforth deployed this argument against several contemporary descriptions of virtue. William Wollaston, who described it as
acting in accordance with truth, is disposed of on the grounds that
using something properly, like using a glass for drinking, cannot
constitute virtue.[226] Hutcheson's moral sense was rejected because it
encouraged a selfish view of virtue: something was judged good
because of individual sensation. For Rutherforth there was no
common ground between self-love and virtue.[227] This is made
especially clear in his comments on Mandeville. He categorically
rejected Mandeville's view that those who 'endeavour the benefit of

---

[221] *Ibid.*, 1.10.4, p. 149.   [222] *Ibid.*, 1.12.16, p. 189.
[223] Thomas Rutherforth, *An Essay on the Nature and Obligations of Virtue* (Cambridge, 1754),
p. 6.
[224] *Ibid.*, pp. 15, 17, 22.   [225] *Ibid.*, p. 10.   [226] *Ibid.*, p. 13.   [227] *Ibid.*, pp. 64–5.

others, or the conquest of his own passions' are acting unnatur-
ally.[228] Instead, he concludes, 'that there is in nature a difference
between vice and virtue; an essential and not an arbitrary distinction between one sort of behaviour and another'.[229]

It is the proximity of this description of 'virtue' to that of Samuel
Clarke and his followers that led Rutherforth to a more precise
delineation of the differences between them. An entire chapter,
entitled 'No eternal and necessary differences, no fitness or unfitness
of things can be the cause of moral obligation', is dedicated to a
repudiation of Clarke's argument. Most of the time, according to
Rutherforth, 'this set of moralists' failed to distinguish between
natural fitness and the moral fitness which alone generated obligation.[230] Moreover, he contended that all of Clarke's talk of
'eternal fitnesses' had not explained how the human perception of
natural good and evil actually guided actions. Clarke had suggested,
employing the famous analogy between God and man, that reason
could fathom God's rational creation. 'But what', Rutherforth
responded, 'obliges us to make that the rule of our actions, which
God has been pleased to make the rule of his?'[231] The rejection of the
logic of the analogy contained at least an echo of Grotius' famous
statement about the possible sufficiency of natural law: 'yet when
out of duty, we imitate God, we are virtuous upon no other principles but those of an implicit conformity to his example. This, if he
does not require it, would be no better than enthusiasm in us.'[232]
And 'enthusiasm', in eighteenth-century parlance, was the property
of those whose individual interpretation of the obligation to the civil
and ecclesiastical authorities constituted a real threat to civil society.

Instead of some 'eternal fitness', Rutherforth argued that there
was 'No obligation to virtue unless it makes us happy. Every man's
own happiness is the end, which nature teaches him to pursue.'
Though virtuous actions were those which benefited others, the
motivation to perform them derived from the performer's happiness.
This origin had been consistently underplayed by philosophers
because of a mistaken understanding of happiness. 'Till a man
understands', wrote Rutherforth, 'that the real good of each particular person is by some means or other so closely connected with
that of all mankind as to make it impossible for him to promote his

---

[228] *Ibid.*, p. 39.   [229] *Ibid.*, p. 59.   [230] *Ibid.*, p. 138.   [231] *Ibid.*, pp. 148–9.
[232] *Ibid.*, p. 152.

own welfare without having a proper tenderness for theirs, he will think it his business to profess himself quite disinterested.'[233]

The reconciliation of the utility of the individual and the good of the community was, as we have already observed, also the goal of Rutherforth's colleague at St John's, James Tunstall. Rutherforth suggested that the source of the common misunderstanding of this relationship derived from an interpretation of ancient Stoicism, in which virtue was identified solely with the good and not with happiness. If, however, it could be shown that the Stoics believed that an action which was good was also good for the person performing it, then virtue could be said to be compatible with happiness. '"Who is there," says Cicero in the person of a Stoic, "that could be elate[d] upon his life being miserable, or that could otherwise upon its being happy? The answer to this question shows us that no one has any reason to glory but in a happy life."'[234] Rutherforth's target was the view of some ancient philosophers, revived by some moderns, that virtue 'is to be approved for its own sake, and that it is to be chosen because it is fit and right'.[235] Because those moderns grounded themselves on a reading of Cicero as an 'old' Stoic, Rutherforth's response led him to argue for the other, prudential interpretation. Rutherforth's question, then, cut to the quick of contemporary debate, not just in morals, but in politics as well: '. . . how shall we make his opinions intelligible, who at one time maintains, that virtue and interest are the very same thing, and at another represents them as quite different, by describing the nature of virtue to be such as will necessarily approve itself to us, even though it should fail of producing our interest?'.[236]

The source of this confusion which, according to Rutherforth, was responsible for the modern attempt to disconnect happiness and virtue, was the ambivalent meaning of 'utility'. In opposition to viciousness or immorality 'it means happiness in general'. This position is attributed to the Stoics and Rutherforth's quotation is from *De Officiis* (iii.xxi), 'that virtue is our only interest and that virtue and utility are different expressions indeed but both mean the same thing'.[237] Alternatively, however, 'the word "utility" was used in a more restrained sense for the advantages of body and fortune in particular'. In so far as happiness or utility referred to the

[233] *Ibid.*, p. 154.   [234] *Ibid.*, p. 180; the passage is cited from *De Finibus*, iii.8.
[235] Rutherforth, *Virtue*, p. 188.
[236] *Ibid.*, p. 189.   [237] *Ibid.*, p. 190.

community, it was legitimate; where it remained private it was not. This was, of course, precisely the distinction drawn by Cicero when endorsing the overriding claims of the public utility and which was frequently recalled by seventeenth-century writers. Thus Rutherforth concluded that the Stoic or Aristotelian 'might represent virtue as recommending itself to our choice though stripped of all utility and not productive of our interest; and yet might affirm without contradicting themselves, that virtue would not be worth our notice, if it could be miserable'.[238] Both groups despised hedonism, but 'neither of them mean being stripped of happiness' entirely. Rather, lasting utility, not transitory corporeal pleasure, constituted 'happiness in general'.

Rutherforth's analysis of 'happiness' was designed to enable him to affirm that the performance of virtue was inevitably 'useful' to the performer even as it benefited another. This 'sociability' was the great advance of the modern over the ancient philosophers.[239] Furthermore, its definition as '*utilitas*' enabled Rutherforth to reconcile the two halves of his argument since both the content and obligation to virtue were directed to the interest of the community in which the individual lived. Thus, like his colleague Tunstall and many, many others, Rutherforth sought to minimize confusion by using public utility as the measure of individual good.

The conclusion of the *Essay on Virtue* is summarized briefly in the *Institutes*. As in Grotius, the use of natural law upheld a view of society dominated by the need to secure a common good. The desire for happiness, for ourselves and others, could only be satisfied in society. Furthermore, since virtue required doing good for others, the goal of social life had to be the service of the 'common interest' or 'general good':

So that although his own particular happiness be the end, which the first principles of his nature teach him to pursue; yet reason, which is likewise a principle of his nature, informs him, that he cannot effectually obtain this end without endeavouring to advance the common good of mankind; but must either be contented to enjoy his own happiness, as a part of the general happiness, or not enjoy it at all.[240]

A society was constituted when a group of men joined together by mutual consent in order to act for a common purpose. The goals of such a civil society were the preservation of the rights men possessed

---

[238] *Ibid.*, pp. 191–2.   [239] *Ibid.*, p. 195.
[240] Rutherforth, *Institutes*, I.1.7, I, pp. 10–11.

by nature and of 'advancing a common good', neither of which individuals could have attained in their earlier, isolated condition. Each individual expected the assistance of the others, and the community which was the sum of its members expected that, in return, each individual would agree to act in the service of that common good.[241] Whether living in nature or in society men could do many things that were neither unjust nor harmful of others. The difference between these states was that in nature individuals decided for themselves in all cases, whereas in society the constituted community prescribed justice.[242] Rutherforth's argument, however attentive to individual happiness, envisioned a vigorous assertion of the supremacy of the common good as a necessary expression of civil society:

... he can have no claim upon the society to act for his security and benefit, where it interferes with the common security and benefit of the whole; because he is obliged to act with the society for this common security and benefit: and whilst he lays himself under this obligation, he cannot be understood to acquire any claim, which is inconsistent with it. He can likewise have no claim upon the society to act for his security and benefit, where it is inconsistent with the security and benefit of any of the other members: because the society is under the same obligation in respect of the others, that it is under in respect of him; and consequently it could not engage to advance his interest at the expence of theirs.[243]

The sovereignty of the community, in Rutherforth's presentation, also made contact with Grotius' claim that civil liberty could coexist with despotism. In Rutherforth's treatment, the difference between natural and civil liberty was that between the moral liberty of men in nature and in society. In practice, this consisted in the difference between individuals who were entirely self-determining and those under law. Therefore, civil liberty constituted as much, or as little, liberty as was consistent with the agreement to establish a government.[244] Although Rutherforth was not suggesting that people would ever contract to establish a tyranny, the thrust of his argument tends to endorse the legitimacy of rulers in possession. In the event, the question that interested him was the importance of civil liberty. Like Hume, Montesquieu and, as we shall see, Priestley,

---

[241] *Ibid.*, II.2.1, pp. 11–12.   [242] *Ibid.*, I.2.4, II, pp. 17–18.
[243] *Ibid.*, II.6.7, II, pp. 230–1.
[244] *Ibid.*, II.8.7, II, pp. 386–7. This seems heavily dependent on Pufendorf's account of law. See J. B. Schneewind, 'Pufendorf's Place in the History of Ethics', *Synthèse*, 72 (1987), 128.

Rutherforth contended that there was no theoretical difference between forms of government, only a practical one. 'Under every form of government their civil liberty is the same in right; but there is not the same security under every form, that it will be so in fact.' It is precisely because the civil liberty of the community as a whole upholds that of its individual members that 'The loss therefore of the former in right will commonly be attended with the loss of the other in fact.'[245]

Rutherforth defined the civil liberty of the community as their right to act in the legislative when they were unable to act as individuals. He denied that this liberty depended on individuals personally taking part in the government and 'much less' in their having some leverage over their representatives.[246] This was explicitly to exclude the act of voting for representatives from civil liberty.[247] Nevertheless, Rutherforth was careful to stress the value of the people's civil liberty, exemplified in a free legislative, as the security for the civil liberty of individuals.[248]

This concern for civil liberty on the collective level led him to reject Grotius' advocacy of non-resistance. Resistance was possible, need not imply a popular supremacy, and could not be opposed, precisely because its occurrence implied the end of the civil compact and therefore the end of the governor's power to oppose it.[249] Furthermore, to deny this right for fear of its abuse could not obviate the existence of the right.[250] However, Rutherforth explicitly rejected Locke's conclusion that the people decide when it was that the governors had failed them. Trying to uphold resistance, on the one hand, without placing this right in the hands of individuals, Rutherforth made the fine distinction between the sources of their different rights. 'But their right of judging is not founded in civil jurisdiction: it is such a right of judging, as all mankind were possessed of in a state of natural liberty.'[251] But if individuals were free to resist because the dissolution of the compact had left them in the state of nature and in possession of natural liberty, its demise also freed the sovereign to act in a similarly unconstrained fashion. Locke's appeal to heaven had become a war of all against one. Each party was both judge and jury to the dispute and there was none to adjudicate between them.[252]

---

[245] Rutherforth, *Institutes*, ii.8.8, ii, pp. 392–5.   [246] *Ibid.*, ii.8.8, ii, p. 398.
[247] *Ibid.*, ii.8.8, ii, p. 400.
[248] *Ibid.*, ii.8.8, ii, p. 401.   [249] *Ibid.*, ii.8.13, ii, p. 413.   [250] *Ibid.*, ii.8.15, ii, p. 452.
[251] *Ibid.*, ii.8.15, ii, pp. 453–4.   [252] *Ibid.*, ii.8.15, ii, pp. 456–7.

Rutherforth's treatise and years of lectures demonstrate the vitality of the natural law tradition in eighteenth-century Britain. The quest for the antecedents of the supposed Locke-inspired radical natural rights arguments of the later part of the century are not found in Rutherforth. On the contrary, the content of his moral theory is an example of the vitality of Grotius' project, the description of basic human obligation in terms of the Ciceronian heritage of prudence and natural law, in the middle decades of the eighteenth century. Finally, one cannot find in Rutherforth support for a polity based on individual rights. These, such as they exist, are immediately subordinated to the sovereign power of the community. Following Pufendorf, the compacters are capable of constructing whatever argument they desire since there was no such thing as an inalienable right.[253] Civil liberty emerges as the communal force of restraint and conservation. The distance between Rutherforth and Blackstone, professors of natural and common law, is much less than that between Rutherforth and another defender of natural law, Richard Price. Our understanding of contemporary political thought and especially of the so-called radical reaction to the American rebellion, turns on this difference.

[253] *Ibid.*, II.6.10, II, pp. 239–45.

CHAPTER 3

State and empire

The 'year one', as computed by most eighteenth-century British political writers, was 1688. At the various centenary celebrations, the era commencing with the Revolution of 1688 was declared 'glorious'. The 'settlement' of outstanding constitutional anomalies had made possible the political consolidation of the British state on the island that had since been united and the simultaneous extension of that state's power across the globe. Politics and empire were obverse and reverse of the formation of this territorial state. Despite general agreement on the purpose of political life, the precise nature of the service of this common good was, as we have observed, a matter of some disagreement. Suspicion of government and a hankering after an ill-defined liberty turned some eighteenth-century opposition writers into enemies of what they perceived to be its debased modern, British version. Parliamentary supremacy had been achieved by corrupting government and population with the wealth drawn from Britain's overseas commerce. Those, however, whose view of politics could be summed up by the word 'prudence' eschewed the politics of moral reformation. They advocated listening to the dictates of necessity; only by securing the well-being of the political community could government earn its legitimacy. Trade, rather than corrupting the nation, strengthened it. The establishment and encouragement of colonies, especially in North America, were components of this political strategy. If the practice of colonization in the seventeenth century occurred under the banner of the reason of state, its eighteenth-century theory reflected the more refined logic of the science of politics. Revolution, union, war and expansion. The transforming events of eighteenth-century British history were precisely those that had convulsed much of continental Europe in the seventeenth century, leading to the articulation of a literature on the power of the state, whose main themes we have tried to discern. In Great Britain, the problems of party were addressed in this language of politics. So were those of empire. But here the dicta of necessity and state power proved less persuasive. The reason for this, and its consequences, are the subject of this and the following chapters.

POWER AND WEALTH

It is a common observation that those who wrote on economic principles and practice in the sixteenth and seventeenth centuries were developing one of the basic themes of the new literature of state necessity.[1] Richelieu's famous aside to Grotius was more a commonplace of this age than previous ones: 'In matters of state, the weakest are always wrong.'[2] These were years of civil war, bureaucratic expansion, overseas exploration, imperial construction and confessional strife. Fiscal power could be ignored only at the prince's risk. That the revolutionary character of these changes made political management a difficult business has been a central theme in recent scholarship, usually linked to the concept of the 'military revolution'.

When the Venetian Tacitist historians, Paolo Sarpi, Enrico Davila and Niccolò Contarini, surveyed the cynical behaviour of their neighbours from the post-republican periphery they reached a common conclusion. The defining characteristic of the modern state was the drive for wealth and power. Their accounts describe the world summed up in the aphorism of their contemporary, Cardinal Richelieu. Contemplating the history of Prussia, Gustav Schmoller at the end of the nineteenth century wrote about the replacement of 'municipal economic policy' by 'territorial institutions', describing the economic dimensions of the reason of state.[3] The coincidence of

[1] For example, Aldo de Maddalena, 'Il mercantilismo', *Storia delle idee politiche, economiche e sociali*, IV *L'età moderna*, ed. Luigi Firpo (Turin, 1980), pp. 640, 647.
[2] Quoted in Tuck, 'Grotius, Carneades and Hobbes', p. 47.
[3] Gustav Schmoller, *The Mercantile System and its Historical Significance* (New York and London, 1896), pp. 12, 14. A survey of the debate over the importance of power or wealth inspired by Schmoller's work provides a rich account of the recent history of economics. J. W. Horrocks, *A Short History of Mercantilism* (London, 1925); Eli Hecksher, *Mercantilism*, tr. Mendel Shapiro, 2 vols. (London, 1935); Jacob Viner, 'English Theories of Foreign Trade before Adam Smith', *Journal of Political Economy*, 38 (1930), 249–301, 404–57; 'Power versus Plenty as Objectives of Foreign Policy in the Seventeenth and Eighteenth Centuries', *World Politics*, 1 (1949), 1–29; Robert L. Schuyler, *The Fall of the Old Colonial System* (Oxford, 1945); William D. Grampp, 'The Liberal Elements of English Mercantilism', *The Quarterly Journal of Economics*, 66 (1952), 465–501; Charles Wilson, 'The Other Face of Mercantilism',

political and economic interests fostered the development of a discrete entity with specific interests. Mercantilism, he wrote, 'is nothing but state making – not state making in a narrow sense, but state making and national-economy making at the same time'.[4] The close association of national power and national wealth 'plunged nations into one war after another, and gave all wars a turn in the direction of trade, industry, and colonial gain, such as they never had before or after'.[5]

The seventeenth-century Dutch threat to engross the world's commerce provoked English fears that they would attain a 'universal monarchy', but their practice was described in the language of state necessity. The Dutch, wrote one contemporary Englishman, had 'made Reason of State their God, and the rule of all their actions'. And, just as Oxenstierna had lamented of Richelieu, the English felt that a Dutchman's 'friendship lasted no longer than till he saw a fit opportunity to make a disagreement more advantageous unto him than his feigned familiarity was'.[6] These fears were subsequently reapplied, in ever broader contexts, to the French policies of Louis XIV and his successors.[7] The increasing vitality and importance of commercial life in early modern Europe channelled the logic of national security from purely political to political-economic matters. Wealth and power coincided in the broadening threat posed by commercial and territorial aggrandizement:

We shall understand this matter better, if we consider the visible change that has been wrought in the manners of most of the European nations since the opening of the trade to the Indies, which may be truly considered as the main wheel of the great machine of commerce; since, by the emulation which the very search of a passage to it raised, America was discovered ... By this means multitudes were brought to devote their time and their labour to cultivating the arts of peace, and to the improvement of the countries which they inhabited; instead of placing all their hopes of aggrandizing and enriching themselves by plundering and oppressing their

---

Revisions in Mercantilism, ed. D. C. Coleman (London, 1969), pp. 118–39; Immanuel Wallerstein, *The Modern World-System II. Mercantilism and the Consolidation of the European World Economy, 1600–1750* (New York, 1980).
[4] Schmoller, *The Mercantile System*, p. 50.   [5] *Ibid.*, p. 64.
[6] Steve Pincus, 'Protestantism and Patriotism: Ideology and the Making of English Foreign Policy 1650–1665', Unpublished Ph.D. thesis (Harvard University, 1990), p. 149.
[7] Steve Pincus, 'Popery, Trade and Universal Monarchy: The Ideological Context of the Outbreak of the Second Anglo-Dutch War', *English Historical Review*, 105 (1992), 1–29; 'The English Debate on Universal Monarchy', in *A Union for Empire: The Union of 1707 in the History of British Political Thought*, ed. John Robertson (Cambridge, forthcoming).

neighbours; and this it was that by degrees, as the many good effects of such a disposition appeared, gave a new turn to politics and induced princes and their ministers to turn their views to the encouragement of industry, as the surest and most effectual means of rendering their subjects, and consequently themselves, rich and powerful.[8]

Writing around 1740, David Hume observed that 'Trade was never esteemed an affair of state till the last century.'[9] The task of *conservación y aumento* could not be accomplished without money.[10] Because commerce provided the best means of acquiring wealth, states seeking the furtherance of their best interests had to exert their force to constantly augment their commerce. Once trade had become an interest of the state, the reason of state had to be employed to gain the greatest share of it, since, in the words of Daniel Defoe, 'Reasons of State are principally the Great Doctrine of Self-preservation.'[11] The economic policies of Charles Davenant, aimed at assuring English strength, glory and independence, have been described as 'eminently Machiavellian in their ruthlessness'.[12] The dominance and scope of ideas of national glory, independence and, above all, security, brought economic means into alignment with political imperatives. This set of ideas underwent little change in the subsequent half-century. This, then, is the proper context for comprehending the intellectual and political resonance of rich passages like this one from Benjamin Newton's 1758 sermon:

The best security against War is national Strength; and the great Source of national Strength is Trade alone, which can at once increase the Treasure and the Numbers of a Nation, which united form the complex Idea of national Strength. Indeed, ere the Mines of India had inspired those improvements in the Arts of War, which, are I know not whether, the Glory or Disgrace of modern Times, the fate of Nations was determined by personal Valour and Strength; but these have in some measure lost their influence. The event of war is now generally decided by Profusion of

---

[8] *Modern Universal History*, IX, p. 172.   [9] Hume, 'Of Civil Liberty', *Essays*, p. 88.
[10] See esp. Istvan Hont, 'Free Trade and the Economic Limits to National Politics: Neo-Machiavellian Political Economy Reconsidered', *The Economic Limits to Modern Politics*, ed. John Dunn (Cambridge, 1990), pp. 41–120; 'Commercial Society and Political Theory in the Eighteenth Century: The Problem of Authority in David Hume and Adam Smith', Paper presented to the Seminar on Cultural History of the University of Amsterdam (June, 1991), p. 12.
[11] Daniel Defoe, 'The Danger of the Protestant Religion, from the Present Prospect of a Religious War in Europe', in *A Collection of the Writings of the Author of the True-Born Englishman* (London, 1703), p. 251.
[12] Hont, 'Free Trade', p. 95.

Treasure; the richest Nation is victorious, and the glorious Wreath of Triumph is become the Price of Gold.[13]

At a time when hopes were high that politics could be 'reduced to a science', some hoped for a similar ordering of the laws of commerce.[14] Though never attaining the precision of a 'science' several principles were recognized as fundamental. Chief among them was the notion of national competition for finite global resources. Thus, wealth was calculated relative to one's competitors and survival guaranteed by keeping the neighbours relatively impoverished. Locke stated this fundamental premise. 'Riches do not consist in having more gold and silver, but in having more in proportion than the rest of the world, or than our neighbours ... '[15] He also perceived the deeply antagonistic political consequences of this theory of relative wealth: Money is 'necessary to us, in a certain proportion to the plenty of it amongst our neighbours. For, if any of our neighbours have it in a much greater abundance than we, we are in many ways obnoxious to them.' Possessors of greater wealth, they would be capable of supporting a more powerful army, of luring talented citizens from other countries, controlling commerce and, ultimately, of cornering the market on strategic goods like naval stores.[16] Malachi Postlethwayt, the leading contemporary theorist in the years of imperial expansion, linked the competition for economic goods to the competition for national power. They shared a common motivation: 'Rivalship'.[17] This wealth was, in turn, calculated as a 'balance' of exports over imports. In his mirror-for-princes manual for George III, James Burgh stressed the competitive nature of the balance of trade. The object was to ensure that commerce did not enrich other nations while 'empoverishing our-

---

13 Newton, *Another Dissertation*, p. 13.
14 See, for instance, [Joseph Massie], *A Representation Concerning the Knowledge of Commerce as a National Concern* (London, 1760), p. 9. These writers also believed that such a redaction was beyond the capacity of any one man (Massie, *Representation*, p. 7; [Joseph Harris], *An Essay upon Money and Coins* (London, 1757–8), 2 vols., I, p. 25).
15 Locke, 'Some Considerations on the Consequences of the Lowering of Interest, and Raising the Value of Money', *Works*, ed. Edmund Law, 4 vols. (London, 1768), II, p. 9.
16 Locke, 'Further Considerations Concerning Raising the Value of Money', *Works*, II, p. 97. Hume had this in mind when he wrote that 'Nothing is more usual, among states which have made some advances in commerce, than to look on the progress of their neighbours with a suspicious eye, to consider all trading states as their rivals, and to suppose that it is impossible for any of them to flourish, but at their expence' ('Of the Jealousy of Trade', *Essays*, pp. 327–8. See also Harris, *Money*, I, p. 26).
17 Malachi Postlethwayt, *Great Britain's True System* (London, 1757), p. 233.

selves'.[18] Depriving competitors of specie, like destroying their armies and fleets, would make British power unsurpassable.[19]

Subscribers to this view of the balance of power did not have to be bullionists since national *gloria* was made of more than specie. Robert Wallace, like Hume, emphasized the value of a range of commodities. 'Riches, in respect to a nation, are the universal plenty of all necessaries, as food, raiment, houses, and furniture, provision for war, &c ... And nothing is so erroneous, as to judge of the riches of a country by the quantity of gold and silver in it.'[20] A common alternative to specie was population: 'If there were any way of having people for money, we could hardly purchase them too dear.'[21] The third source of power was commerce.

A political theory of commerce well served a commercial empire. If the fear of a Dutch and then a French 'universal monarchy' concentrated minds on the economic dimension of state necessity, its continued evocation in the era of eighteenth-century imperial competition is another reminder of the continuity between centuries often split by the vagaries of scholarly periodization:

The Thirst of acquiring Universal Monarchy, has been the Foundation of all the Disputes about Wealth and Power; which Nation is the most wealthy and powerful, has always been the Question. From whence we may conclude it is an establish'd Maxim, That Wealth is the Basis of Power; and, I believe it will be easily allow'd, that Wealth is no way to be acquir'd, but by Commerce; and Commerce no way to be establish'd and ascertain'd, but under the Conduct, and Protection, of a naval Force.[22]

Maritime exploration and the related growth of commerce were two defining characteristics of the new approach to preserving the state. The third leg of Postlethwayt's tripod was colonization. Wealth, measured by the conventional standards of specie, raw materials and population, and the ability to channel it in ways that magnified and secured the power of the state, were both seen as enhanced by the possession of overseas colonies. The management of Britain's North American territories, however undertheorized and disorganized, was conducted with this purpose to the fore. Charles Davenant's *Discourse on the Plantation Trade* (1698)

[18] Burgh, *Remarks Historical and Political*, p. 115.
[19] *Cato's Letters*, no. 87, III, p. 180; Locke, 'Further Considerations', *Works*, II, p. 97.
[20] Wallace, *Internal Policy*, p. 2; also Locke, 'Some Considerations', II, p. 47.
[21] Burgh, *Remarks*, p. 111; Hume, 'Of the Balance of Trade', *Essays*, p. 326.
[22] William Horsley, *A Treatise on Maritime Affairs* (London, 1744), pp. 74–5.

remained widely cited as the most important discussion of commerce, colonies and empire until the events of the mid-century produced a flood of analysis and speculation. These same events also led to the publication of Davenant's *Collected Works* in 1771. As if to leave no doubt about its appropriate context, the editor, Sir Charles Whitworth, dedicated the volume containing the *Discourse* to the Earl of Hillsborough, then Secretary of State for Colonies. Moreover, the editor's preface suggested that Davenant's 'discourses may be properly called the foundation of our political establishment, as several public regulations have taken place from the hints thrown out' by him.[23]

Davenant's assessment of the critical importance of colonies to the political-economic welfare of the state was phrased as a direct consequence of the fear of a possible universal monarchy. Davenant's description of contemporary politics resonated with the language of *ragione di stato*:

We call the false arts of states-men, and the evil faith, perjury, and dissimulation of Princes, wisdom and deep policy; temerity we stile high courage, ambition we call a noble thirst after glory, and they who vex, rob, and disturb the world, we dignify them with the name of conquerors and heroes. And because nothing was set by, esteemed and reverenced, but *wealth* and *power*, the forward part of mankind strove to obtain as much of both as possibly they could; and these, as they grew in strength, formed themselves into particular principalities and commonwealths.

The growth of these states by conquest proceeded 'till they had subdued all round them; and from thence came what we call Universal Monarchy or Empire'.[24] The consequence of falling under the sway of a universal monarchy was truly bleak. While Rome was once used as the model of virtue, in Davenant's argument it had become the towering example of the injustice and danger posed by global tyranny.

The threat of a French universal monarchy was potent in these years of European coalition warfare. The increasing attention shown by the French to their overseas territories held out the possibility that their dominion would extend beyond the confines of Europe and remove all hope of escape from tyranny. As would become common later in the century, even as they feared the

---

[23] Charles Davenant, *The Political and Commercial Works*, ed. Charles Whitworth, 5 vols. (London, 1771), I, sig. A3v.
[24] Davenant, 'An Essay upon a Universal Monarchy', *Works*, IV, p. 5.

French, those who lamented the chronic maladministration and decentralization which afflicted the colonies looked to her with some admiration. In his 'plantations' the King of France gave 'very large appointments to the governors out of his own coffers, not allowing them any perquisites, or to draw any advantages or profit from the inhabitants'.[25]

The French had grasped the fundamental insight that colonies were only 'a strength to the mother kingdom' when their management was efficient and strict, keeping them completely dependent on the metropolis. Mismanagement, on the other hand, would swiftly turn colonies into weapons aimed against the metropolis.[26] In particular, Davenant suggested that colonial economic development should only be encouraged so far as it did not generate local industry since this would ultimately eliminate that dependence on Great Britain which cemented the imperial bond.[27] Most presciently, Davenant argued that size worked against *imperium*, and that Britain might be better off with commercial rather than territorial empire: 'As many empires have been ruined by too much enlarging their dominions, and by grasping at too great an extent of territory, so our interest in America may decay, by aiming at more provinces, and a greater tract of land than we can either cultivate or defend.'[28]

Characteristically, Davenant's commitment to national survival was expressed in both economic and political terms. While the principles guiding colonization were animated by the concerns of the former, the latter directed governors to insure the conformity of manners to political principles:

The welfare of all countries in the world depends upon the morals of their people.

For though a nation may gather riches by trade, thrift, industry, and from the benefit of its soil and situation; and though a people may attain to great wealth and power, either by force of arms, or by the sagacity of their councils; yet, when their manners are depraved, they will decline insensibly, and at last come to utter destruction.[29]

'Vicious' morals sapped the self-discipline that was the basis of healthy, productive industry. This explained why those 'who have

---

[25] Davenant, 'Plantation Trade', *Works*, II, p. 32.   [26] *Ibid.*, p. 29.   [27] *Ibid.*, p. 8.
[28] *Ibid.*, p. 26. 'Extent' is usually considered as a problem for republican theorists of politics, but it received equally significant attention from writers on necessity. See Botero, *Reason of State*, 1.7, p. 11.
[29] Davenant, 'Plantation Trade', *Works*, II, p. 41. Also, pp. 48, 51.

modelled governments for any duration' sought to restrain the passions with a variety of means, especially religion.[30]

This relationship between the 'improvement of manners and publick security'[31] made effective colonial governance of critical importance to national survival. Davenant especially warned of the political consequences of too much free thinking on matters of faith. Loss of reverence would very soon be followed by loss of power and freedom.[32] Thus, he proposed establishing a council to monitor religious affairs in the colonies and insure, among other things, that 'no doctrines are published, destructive to the very fundamentals of religion itself'.[33] In the context of the seventeenth-century *politique* argument about toleration, Davenant's insistence on the civic usefulness of religion was mitigated by the recognition that toleration 'sets the minds of all the people at quiet' and therefore also served the common good.[34] Where toleration did not produce this result, however, it was to be curtailed.

On the contrary, must it not much distract the state, to set the minds of men once more afloat in these mysterious points, which are now believed, and cannot perhaps be examined with any safety to the public? It is hardly to be doubted, but that if the common people are once induced to lay aside religion, they will quickly cast off all fear of their rulers.[35]

In fact, as will be shown below, when this text was reprinted in 1771 the political heirs of Davenant were inveighing against private judgment in religion in just these terms – it was perceived as a threat to the security of the state and the empire.

One of the aims of this prospective council on religion was to nourish a 'love to England their original country'. 'Love of country' was the source of the greatness of the ancient republics and its disappearance one of the symptoms of their decline. Again, contemporary France was used to hold up the mirror to English inadequacy:

In a kingdom but too near us, we may see all sorts of men labouring the public welfare, and every one as vigilant in his post, as if the success of the whole empire depended on his single care and diligence; so that to the

---

[30] *Ibid.*, p. 42.
[31] Anon., *An Application of Some General Political Rules, to the Present State of Great Britain, Ireland and America* (London, 1766), p. 73.
[32] Davenant, 'Plantation Trade', *Works*, II, p. 43.   [33] *Ibid.*, p. 47.
[34] Davenant, 'Peace at Home and War Abroad', *Works*, IV, p. 405.
[35] Davenant, 'Plantation Trade', *Works*, II, p. 46.

shame of another place, they seem more intent upon the prosperity and honour of their country, under a hard and oppressive tyranny, than they are in some free nations, where the people have an interest in the laws, and are a part of the constitution.[36]

The accusation that the French were more 'patriotic' than the English was manifested in Davenant's description of a vicious government in which 'all care of the public is laid aside, and every one is plundering for himself, as if the commonwealth were adrift, or had suffered shipwreck'.[37] The English empire, unlike the French, was managed with little commitment to some putative common good. Echoing Cicero, Davenant argued that favouring one's own goals at the expense of the utility of the community was the antithesis of patriotism. Politics in a just, well-organized and, ultimately, thriving society was best conducted in a Ciceronian key. 'Wherever private men can be brought to make all their actions and counsels, thoughts and designments, to center in the common good, that nation will soon gather such strength as shall rest any home-bred mischief or outward accident.'[38]

COLONIES AND A COMMON GOOD

While Davenant's realistic view of political economy became the received wisdom of government spokesmen, his emphasis on morals and power was inherited by the motley opposition that ranged itself, as Guido Abbattista has suggested, against Walpole's Hanoverian policies and standing army. This alliance of True Whigs and Tories comprised the Country opposition, whose patriotism gloried in the Elizabethan achievement of maritime commerce and commercial empire.[39] While the opposition harangued the government for involving the nation in what they perceived to be expensive, if not wholly futile, balance-of-power wars in Europe, there was little disagreement about the importance of Britain's maritime empire. 'Commerce and liberty' may have been opposition ideology in the 1750s, as argued by Abbattista, but the fact is that government writers were also committed to it. Furthermore, despite its centrality

---

[36] *Ibid.*, pp. 48–9.   [37] *Ibid.*, p. 50.   [38] *Ibid.*, p. 48.
[39] Abbattista, *Commercio, colonie e impero*, pp. 47–62. Also, Jeremy Black, *British Foreign Policy in the Age of Walpole* (Edinburgh, 1985). A striking example of the creation of this 'blue-water' myth is the 'Temple of British Worthies' erected by Viscount Cobham at Stowe in the 1730s.

in the patriotic rhetoric of both government and opposition, there was little concentrated thought on the nature of imperial sovereignty and colonial obligation. Much as the service of the common good was frequently invoked, though remaining largely unexamined, maintenance of the empire was believed to provide the foundation for the security of the state, despite being only vaguely understood.

The opposition that backed Pitt, whether called country, tory, commonwealth, true whig or patriot, brought with it a foreign policy agenda. His supporters believed that 'Concentration on the navy and the colonies would better promote the true English interests of trade and security and serve the common cause of resistance to the ambitions of France.'[40] Abbattista has suggested that Campbell's reissuing of de la Court's *Maxims of Holland* in 1743 and again in 1746, like its initial translation in 1702, marked an attempt to justify a policy of maritime commerce and continental disengagement. Wars of conquest were costly and created dangerous foreign commitments.[41] Writing several years later, Campbell continued to praise the Dutch achievement:

Taking therefore their Fisheries, Manufactures, and foreign Trade together, we may easily account for the Growth of their Naval Power, the Increase of their Wealth, and the Possibility of their sustaining that infinite Variety of Taxes, Customs and Excises, which were necessary to support so long and so expensive a War, as that by which their Liberties were established and secured.[42]

None the less, Campbell and opposition writers like the historian John Entick ended up making their peace with the policies of continental connection, in Entick's case through unswerving devotion to Pitt's own manoeuvrings.[43] Campbell's justification is, perhaps, more interesting since it applied to the politics of empire the notion of 'consistency' first thrashed out in the debates on patriotism and party. The circumstances that made the 'Dutch model' worthy of emulation had changed and so the service of the common good dictated a change in British policy:

The gradual Changes that have happened in the Circumstances of this Nation, may be very rationally supposed to have had a strong Influence upon its Interests, and yet this does not seem to have been sufficiently

---

[40] Peters, *Pitt*, p. 26.   [41] de Witt, *Maxims of Holland*, p. 197.
[42] Campbell, *Present State of Europe*, p. 485; Abbattista, *Commercio, colonie e impero*, p. 102.
[43] John Entick, *The General History of the Late War*, 5 vols. (London, 1763). Compare the defences of maritime (I, p. 206) and continental warfare (IV, p. 315).

considered; for if it had, we should scarce find so many People as there really are, who adhere to the old Notions laid down by some of our Patriots in the Beginning of the last Century, that the true Interest of this Nation consists in keeping their Affairs as distinct from those of the Continent, as their Country is removed from it by nature, who by surrounding it with the sea, seems to have made it a World by itself.[44]

In the previous chapter, Campbell's discussion of interest was linked to the genre of meditations on the practical policies necessitated by a calculating view of the needs of the abstract entity called the state. In Campbell's analysis of empire, the impetus of security remains the driving motivation: 'It is the maintaining the British Empire in this Situation, and thereby providing for the Happiness of this Nation, that as I said ought to be the sole Point of View of our Statesmen and patriots, as of old among the Greeks and Romans.' The flourishing of empire, survival of the state and the happiness of its inhabitants were mutually dependent. Furthermore, Campbell's examination of Britain's imperial 'condition' *c.*1750 drew on the notion of a common good to redefine patriotism and the reason of state. Sometimes Britain's 'real interest' warranted a continental engagement and sometimes only maritime traffic.

It is most evident therefore, that at this Day our Princes can have no Temptation to enterprize Wars of Conquest as in former Times; so that a true Spirit of Patriotism can never be shewn, in opposing Projects that will never be set on foot; and in this lies our great Happiness, that having no Views or Pretensions upon our Neighbours, there is no solid, indeed not so much as a plausible Ground for us to hate them, or they us. This is the true fundamental principle of our Policy; that in respect to the Affairs of the Continent, we are not to be governed by any of those temporary or accidental Conveniences, which very often, and that justly too, pass for reasons of State in other Kingdoms; but by the single Rule, of their acting in Conformity to our natural Interests, so far as is consistent with their own.[45]

In so far as 'Dominion of the Sea' was a British interest, it rested on three legs, colonies, trade and naval strength. Thus, in *The Present State of Europe*, Campbell wrote that 'the Strength and Populousness' of Great Britain was due to the success of its 'Plantations' and that commerce 'is that Tie, by which the several, and even the most distant Parts of this Empire are connected and kept together'.[46]

[44] Campbell, *Present State of Europe*, p. 499.   [45] *Ibid.*, p. 504.
[46] *Ibid.*, pp. 502, 504. See also Malachi Postlethwayt, *The Universal Dictionary of Trade and Commerce*, 2 vols. (London, 1751–5), I, p. 373.

Adam Smith was the most famous advocate of a strategic perspective on colonial policy. Despite harshly condemning mercantile regulation, Smith defended Britain's Navigation Acts precisely because they enhanced the security of the state: 'As defence, however, is of much more importance than opulence, the act of navigation is, perhaps, the wisest of all the commercial regulations of England.'[47] Behind the congeries of legislation that comprised the Navigation Acts[48] stood the familiar commitment to the security and prosperity of the metropolis.

By the middle of the eighteenth century, Britain's overseas trade was oriented squarely towards colonial ports.[49] There, British ships sold finished goods in exchange for raw materials. This autarkic symbiosis was geared to enhance the security of the whole and was seen at the time as the fundamental advantage of colonization.[50] The provision of colonial raw materials in exchange for metropolitan supply of finished goods to the colonial market defined the colony–metropolis relationship. It was believed that Britain's condition as a naval and commercial nation would be jeopardized without the secure access to naval stores and other rare and valuable resources afforded by the North American possessions.[51] Ideally, this relationship benefited both metropolis and colony equally and so eliminated the possibility of future incompatibility. Thus by

---

[47] Smith, *WN*, IV.ii.30, pp. 464–5.

[48] They included customs fees and control of intercolonial trade, enumeration of goods, bounties to encourage particular industries; preferential tariffs for colonial goods, complete monopolies for certain goods in British markets, a ban on the development of potentially competing colonial industries and regulation of colonial currencies to ensure convertibility. Parts went back to medieval times, though the bulk of legislation was passed between 1660 and 1673 (Robert Livingstone Schuyler, *The Fall of the Old Colonial System* (Oxford, 1945), pp. 18–23; Oliver M. Dickerson, *The Navigation Acts and the American Revolution* (Philadelphia, 1951).

[49] Paul Langford, *A Polite and Commercial People. England 1727–1783* (Oxford, 1989), p. 168; Jacob Price, 'The Transatlantic Economy', *Colonial British America*, ed. Jack P. Greene and J. R. Pole (Baltimore, 1984), pp. 18–42; D. K. Fieldhouse, 'British Imperialism in the Late Eighteenth Century', *Essays in Imperial Government*, ed. K. Robinson and F. Madden (Oxford, 1963), p. 28.

[50] Anon., *Considerations on the American Stamp Act* (London, 1766), pp. 20–1. Also Joseph Massie, *A Representation*, p. 21.

[51] John Morgan, *Four Dissertations on the Reciprocal Advantages of a Perpetual Union between Great-Britain and her American Colonies* (Philadelphia, 1766), Anon., no. 3, p. 89, and Morgan, no. 1, pp. 16–17. Also, Matthew Decker, *An Essay on the Causes of the Decline of the Foreign Trade* (London, 1744), p. 106; Thomas Whately, *The Regulations Lately Made Concerning the Colonies and the Taxes Imposed on them* (London, 1765), p. 5.

restricting the avenues of economic development open to colonists Britain pre-empted misunderstanding and jealousy.[52]

Montesquieu's extensive praise of the English constitution included the claim that 'If this nation sends colonies abroad, it must rather be to extend its commerce than its dominion.' The combination of commerce, navigation and colonies yielded what he called the 'empire of the sea'. His description of its implications for domestic politics would have appealed both to opposition writers and defenders of the existing order:

> The ruling nation inhabiting a large island, and being in possession of a great trade, has with extraordinary ease grown powerful at sea; and as the preservation of its liberties requires that it should have neither strongholds nor fortresses nor land forces, it has occasion, for a formidable navy to defend it against invasions; a navy which must be superior to that of all other powers, who, employing their treasures in wars on land, have not sufficient for those at sea.[53]

Malachi Postlethwayt, fountain of mid-century British political economic commonplaces, did not speak of an 'empire' when he described this connection: 'If the dominion of the sea is absolutely necessary to a people who aim at empire, of how much greater moment is it to a nation whose grandeur, whose wealth, whose very being depends upon Commerce and Navigation?'[54] Postlethwayt's two-volume, folio-size dictionary includes no listing under 'Empire'. Instead, under 'Sea English', he wrote 'That empire has always followed trade, travelling (as it were) from one part of the world to another, as commerce has shifted its station: and, in all countries, still growing or declining in power, in proportion as traffic has been encouraged or disregarded.'[55]

The North American colonies were so highly valued because they enhanced commerce and promoted maritime power. Thomas Whately, adviser to George Grenville and one of the most important theoreticians of the colonial relationship (see chapter 4), wrote that Britain was fortunate that 'the Real and Substantial, and those are the Commercial Interests of Great Britain, are now preferred to every other Consideration'. The trade which brought her wealth

---

[52] Postlethwayt, *Universal Dictionary*, I, p. 536.
[53] Montesquieu, *Spirit of the Laws*, XIX.27, pp. 311–12.
[54] Postlethwayt, *Universal Dictionary*, II, p. 308. See also II, pp. 306, 675, 832.
[55] *Ibid.*, II, p. 692. Daniel Baugh's phrase is 'Blue-Water'; see 'Great Britain's "Blue-Water" Policy, 1689–1815', *International History Review*, 10 (1988), 58.

rests upon 'Maritime Power' and this, in turn, 'depends upon a wise and proper use of the Colonies'. They provided population, consumed British goods, supplied necessary commodities and stimulated shipping.[56] Hence Campbell's conclusion, that 'it is to the wonderful Growth of our Plantations that we owe the Strength and Populousness of this Island, which could never otherwise have attained its present Condition'.[57]

The importance of the colonies did not, however, license their acquisition in every circumstance. For many, including for example, Postlethewayt and 'Cato', conquest was 'the most shameless Thing in the World'. The triumph of force of arms, rather than the 'People's Good', conferred no legitimacy and often brought about real harm.[58] Their colonies were to be part of a maritime empire which not only created wealth but cost less to manage. In *Brittania* [*sic*], James Thomson praised it as 'inexpensive power unencumbered with the bulk immense of conquest'.[59] This is the context that makes sense of the imprecise use of 'Empire' for much of the first half of the century.[60]

Eighteenth-century British colonization, reflected in means like the Navigation Acts and notional balance of trade, was based on the fundamental priority of the security of the state identified as the interest of the metropolis. Hence Campbell's declaration, that 'The great design of colonies, considered in a political light, is the advantage of the mother country.'[61] In 1763 a memorialist in the Landsdowne Manuscripts wrote that 'The British Colonies are to be regarded in no other light, but as subservient to the commerce of

---

[56] Whately, *The Regulations Lately Made*, pp. 3–4. For similar views, see Anon., *The Political Balance* (London, 1765), p. 38); Richard Price, *Britain's Happiness and the Proper Improvement of It* (London, 1759), p. 4; John Mitchell, *The Contest in America between Great Britain and France* (London, 1757), p. 140; *Cato's Letters*, no. 64, II, p. 272; Samuel Johnson, 'An Introduction to the Political State of Great Britain', *Works*, X, pp. 141–2.

[57] Campbell, *Present State of Europe*, p. 502.

[58] *Cato's Letters*, no. 74, III, p. 74. Cato added that 'Government is either designed for the People's Good, or else I know not what business it has in the World', and therefore common sense dictated that international disputes ought to be resolved in favour of that party most likely to serve this end.

[59] James Thomson, *Brittania, A Poem*, quoted in Richard Koebner, *Empire* (Cambridge, 1961), p. 82.

[60] For examples of imprecision see, John Ashley *Memoirs and Considerations Concerning the Trade and Revenues of the British Colonies in America* (London, 1740), II, pp. 94–6; Malachi Postlethwayt, *Great Britain's Commercial Interest Explained* (2nd edn, London, 1759), I, p. 469, where the contrast with France is implicit.

[61] [Campbell], *Modern Universal History*, IX, p. 558. Also Anon., *The Justice and Necessity of Taxing the American Colonies, Demonstrated* (London, 1766), pp. 18–19.

their mother country; the colonists are merely factors for the purpose of trade, and in all considerations concerning the Colonies, this must be always the leading idea.'[62] Metrocentric primacy[63] meant that within the colony–metropolis relationship there lurked an intrinsic tension: under no circumstances could the components of the empire ever contest the centre's determination of that 'common' good which seemed to advance the 'national' interest.

While 'empire', 'community' and 'nation' were treated, for all intents and purposes, as identical, they were not. From this lack of congruence arose many of the problems that were to rock the empire. And yet it was precisely the definition of the term 'common' that was most susceptible to pressure. Like the attendant problem of necessity, *who* was to do the determining went a long way towards answering the question. For supporters of the government would not brook the expression of an autonomous colonial judgment that would inevitably fragment the common good. Prudence and necessity inclined towards security above all:

That which chiefly wants to be ascertained is, what is the nature and what the limits of the servitude that is due to the master, or, what it is he has a right to extract from his servant. And here necessity, the foundation of all my reasoning, obliges me to pronounce, that the sole determination of that right rests with the superior; because, if that is not allowed, it cannot under God reside any where.[64]

In the course of his definition of 'colonies', Postlethwayt argued that 'The general good of the community is ever to take place of that of any particular persons ... '[65] He declared elsewhere to 'have endeavoured to make the national Interests my sole Guide; no other Motives whatever have had the least Influence to divert or bias me to deviate from that Principle'.[66] If Britain's might were ever to be undermined, it would be the product of individual selfishness, with the desire for personal gain coming at the expense of the prosperity

---

[62] Quoted in Clarence W. Alvord, *The Mississippi Valley in British Politics*, 2 vols. (Cleveland, 1917), I, p. 50.

[63] Robert W. Tucker and David C. Hendrickson (*The Fall of the First British Empire: Origins of the War of American Independence* (Baltimore, 1982)) may justly lament the historiographical tendency to view the colonial crisis solely from the perspective of Britain. Nevertheless, because the North American colonies were viewed as subordinate domains attendant on British policy-making, the only way to understand those policies is to try and see the world as it looked from the other side of the Atlantic.

[64] Allan Ramsay, *Thoughts on the Origin and Nature of Government* (London, 1769), p. 13.

[65] Postlethwayt, *Universal Dictionary*, I, p. 535.

[66] Postlethwayt, *Great Britain's True System*, p. li.

of the community. Such people showed 'an impatience of those ties, which even the most partial to the claims of the colonies must confess to be necessary for the common good'. The repeal of commercial regulation 'would render the colonies not only of no benefit' but harmful to the welfare of Britain.[67] Finally, imperial writers contended for the same Machiavellian bond between the security of the state and its citizens' maintenance of good 'manners' found in Davenant and later opposition writers: 'yet how will this matter appear, upon trial by that real touchstone of all political disquisitions, *improvement of manners and publick security?*'[68]

While Joseph Priestley is justly hailed for his staunch defence of intellectual and religious liberty, his discussion of European colonization and its theoretical basis in the *Lectures on History* shares far more in common with Postlethwayt. In these lectures, delivered as tutor in languages and belles-lettres at Warrington in the 1760s, though not published for twenty years, Priestley acknowledged that the existence of foreign colonies was a cause of the tremendous increase in trade and shipping in modern times. Like Hume he perceived that this made commerce a matter of political importance. Hence the profusion of 'chiefly commercial wars' where before 'commerce was never made an affair of state'. If colonies now served the state, their management was to be guided solely by its interest. Economic 'subserviency' and perpetual dependence was the price of protection.[69] Ironically, given Priestley's commitment to private judgment, his association with Postlethwayt's position put him on the same side as those who argued that these same 'modern maxims' of mercantilism also militated against individual liberty. 'But as our fondness for the words liberty and freedom sometimes lead to licentiousness and even anarchy in government; so may not a too great eagerness for an universal freedom and liberty of trade carry us such lengths, that we may, at length lose all the trade we have?'[70]

One can also gauge the extent of the British commitment to the importance of national security indirectly, by analyzing contemporary attitudes to France. Her economic policy, incorporating the North American colonies within a national strategy, made her a feared and, at the same time, admired neighbour. Henry McCulloh,

---

[67] Charles Lloyd, *The Conduct of the Late Administration Examined* (London, 1767), pp. 69–70.
[68] Anon., *An Application of Some General Political Rules*, p. 73.
[69] Joseph Priestley, *Lectures on History* (Warrington, 1788), p. 339.
[70] Postlethwayt, *Great Britain's Commercial Interest*, ii, p. 235.

a North American expert and sometime adviser to George Grenville (it was he who first proposed a stamp duty[71]) devoted an entire pamphlet to elucidating French policy. He deduced from a survey of their conduct that they, too, believed that national wealth and strength depended upon the improvement of their North American colonies.[72] Unlike the English, the French treated the colonist with respect, since he was 'undergoing great hardships for the benefit of his country'.[73] The laws administering their colonies were also well ordered and 'calculated for the Improvement of their Trade, and Enlargement of their distant Colonies and Possessions'.[74] And, when French colonial administration was attacked, it was for deviating from this policy and neglecting their colonies in favour of their 'former romantick humour of land-conquests'.[75]

Because France had become a paragon of imperial management, and because it was believed that these policies were sure to secure her aggrandizement, it was feared that the French would prove invincible in North America. This was reflected in many contemporary pronouncements. French outposts in Canada and Louisiana (all the territory drained by the Mississippi River and its tributaries) encircled the British colonies, making their ultimate reduction only

[71] In an essay of 1751 addressed to Lord Halifax, President of the Board of Trade, McCulloh again proposed an extension of the British stamp tax to the colonies (it had been suggested in 1722, 1726, 1728 and 1742). In 1757 he submitted a further scheme for colonial taxation. In 1761 he put the idea of a stamp tax into the *Miscellaneous Representation Relative to Our Concerns in America* sent to Lord Bute. Finally, in 1763, still another proposal reached Charles Jenkinson, Secretary to the Treasury, and through him reached Grenville, who finally lent his approval (P. D. G. Thomas, *The Stamp Act Crisis* (Oxford, 1975), pp. 68–9).

[72] Henry McCulloh, *The Wisdom and Policy of the French in the Construction of their Great Offices* (London, 1755), pp. 78–9. Jeremy Black's account of Anglo-French contacts in the eighteenth century, *Natural and Necessary Enemies: Anglo-French Relations in the Eighteenth Century* (London, 1986), emphasizes British distrust of France and makes no mention of their admiration and desire to emulate her. Still more recently, Linda Colley has reared a vision of the creation of Britain on a presumed Anglo-French antagonism (*Britons*, pp. 1, 5–6). Missing in all these accounts is a sense of the ambivalence of this relationship. The French were an enemy, but also a paragon: not only of imperial policy, but, perhaps still more importantly, of taste. The failure to appreciate the texture of Anglo-French relations is proof of the gulf that still remains between the political and cultural history of eighteenth-century Britain.

[73] [William and Edmund Burke], *An Account of the European Settlements in America* (London, 1757), 2 vols., II, p. 44.

[74] McCulloh, *A Miscellaneous Essay Concerning the Courses Pursued by Great Britain in the Affairs of her Colonies* (London, 1755), p. 14. Postlethwayt also praised the various French legal encouragements to their colonial trade (*Universal Dictionary*, I, p. 870).

[75] William Douglass, *A Summary, Historical and Political, of the First Planting, Progressive Improvements, and Present State of the British Settlements in North-America* (2nd edn, London, 1755; 1st edn, 1749–50), I, p. 2.

a matter of time.[76] Given the common origin of French and British
political economy in seventeenth-century discussions of the best
means to conservation and increase, it is not surprising that the
admiration of the French amounted to praise of the extent of their
devotion to the common good.[77]

Samuel Johnson asserted that, 'The French compose one body
with one head. They have all the same interest, and agree to pursue
it by the same means.'[78] Colbert was able to turn the economy
around because he 'could compel individuals to sacrifice their
private profit to the general good; he could make one understanding
preside over many hands, and remove difficulties by quick and
violent expedients'. However, 'Where no man thinks himself under
any obligation to submit to another, and, instead of co-operating in
one great scheme, everyone hastens through by-paths to private
profit, no great change can suddenly be made; nor is superior
knowledge of much effect, where every man resolves to use his own
eyes and his own judgment ... '[79] It is precisely the logic behind
Johnson's praise that led Adam Smith to make an attack on
Colbert's policies the leading edge of his revision of political
economy (see chapter 6). Because of the nature of French decision-
making procedures, their plan to oust Britain from North America
had been long in the works.[80] The English colonies, by contrast,
were chaotically assembled, maladministered and only loosely controlled from the centre. In their history of Western colonization, the
Burkes observed admiringly that even though the French were the
last to settle North America they had since exploited their gains
vigorously and intelligently.[81] The point of these analyses was to
provide an example capable of rousing Britain to similarly sagacious
practice.[82] Postlethwayt suggested that

every impartial Man must discern the wide Difference there is between the
French and the *British* System of commercial Policy: that the one is calculated, by the utmost Stretch of Wisdom and Sagacity, to raise the Commerce of our principal Competitor to its utmost Pitch of Splendor, and that

---

[76] Postlethwayt, *Universal Dictionary*, I, pp. 444, 536. Also, Postlethwayt, *Great Britain's True
    System*, pp. lxxxii–lxxxiii; Archibald Kennedy, *Serious Considerations on the Present State of the
    Affairs of the Northern Colonies* (London, 1754), p. 3.
[77] Davenant, 'Plantation Trade', *Works*, II, p. 49.
[78] Johnson, 'Observations on the Present State of Affairs', *Works*, x, p. 194.
[79] Johnson, 'Political State', *Works*, x, p. 141.
[80] Archibald Kennedy, *Serious Considerations*, p. 5.
[81] [Burke], *An Account of the Settlements*, II, p. 3.   [82] *Ibid.*, p. 46.

the other is calculated to sink and depress the *British* Trade to its primitive Nothingness.[83]

The absence of centralized, strategic planning was a feature of British politics much lamented during the years of colonial competition at mid-century.[84] In 1759 John Campbell followed his enthusiastic report of Dutch imperial management in Asia with an implicit condemnation of the English East India Company: 'No nation has been less careful than we, of preserving and of digesting into method, the memorials of such occurrences as are absolutely necessary to our design of tracing this great branch of English commerce from its original.'[85] The colonists, too, bore a share of the blame for the absence of any attempt to pursue a single imperial common good: 'The colonies have, in reality, in many cases acted as if they thought themselves so many independent states, under their respective charters, rather than as provinces of the same empire, which consideration necessarily requires a union of the parts for the security of the whole.'[86] At the start of Grenville's administration Lord Bute observed that 'We ought to set about reforming our old colonies before we settle new ones.'[87] The theme of imperial reform dominated the pages of sophisticated observers like Postlethwayt, McCulloh and James Abercromby. Thomas Barrow has aptly described this 'old colonial system' as '[b]ased largely on a patchwork mosaic of measures adopted through expediency or accident' and possessing 'little coherence or uniformity'.[88]

WAR

While the increasing interconnectedness of the world and the economic dependence of Britain on her maladministered colonies had been becoming increasingly apparent to some, only the French bid for a greater North American empire awoke the nation to the weighty task of imperial management. John Mitchell, author of the *Contest in America* (1757) describes the importance of the colonies, and hence the on-going 'Contest', in political-economic terms: 'The

---

[83] Postlethwayt, *Great Britain's True System*, p. 272. Also, McCulloh, *Wisdom*, pp. 124, 128.
[84] [Burke], *An Account of the Settlements*, II, p. 288.
[85] [Campbell], *Modern Universal History*, X (1759), p. 1.
[86] Anon., *State of the British and French Colonies in North America* (London, 1755), p. 57.
[87] Quoted in P. D. G. Thomas, *Stamp Act Crisis*, p. 34.
[88] Thomas C. Barrow, *Trade and Empire* (Cambridge, MA, 1967), p. 1.

great thing to be considered by all states is power and dominion, as well as trade.'[89]

The Seven Years War brought to a close the early modern phase of European expansion. The culmination of an imperial struggle with the French that began in the seventeenth century and in which the Revolution of 1688 finds perhaps its most significant context, this war appears in retrospect as the high-water mark of reason of state economics. The policy of national aggrandizement based on transmarine colonies, commercial expansion and naval support had, seemingly, been vindicated and confirmed.

Crushing victory over the French and the Spanish irrevocably altered the conditions in which this political-economy was expected to function. After dismal failures in the Mediterranean and North American theatres at the outset, by the conclusion of hostilities Britain had taken Canada, Louisiana and India from France, the Caribbean sugar islands of France and Spain, and Cuba and the Philippines from Spain. (These were subsequently exchanged for Florida.)[90] Britain now controlled continental empires in North America and South Asia even after relinquishing still more prodigious conquests in the Caribbean and the South Pacific. One of the consequences of being a global power was, according to the Duke of Newcastle, that 'Ministers in this country, where every part of the World affects us, in some way or another, should consider the whole Globe.'[91] Nevertheless, thinking about empire, as usual, moved much more slowly than events. The war posed a serious challenge to the principles of political economy which guided imperial policy. Could its basically maritime cast and highly metrocentric perspective serve as the foundation for a vast territorial empire?

This fundamental problem has been obscured by the historiographical search for the origins of the War of American Independence. The concatenation of events, moving swiftly from the Treaty of Paris (1763) to Grenville's Acts,[92] the subsequent Stamp Act Crisis, the Townshend Duties, and sliding down the slippery slope of Massacres

---

[89] Mitchell, *The Contest in America*, p. xvii.

[90] For more on the terms see Bernhard Knollenberg, *Origin of the American Revolution 1759–1766* (New York, 1966), p. 32; Zenab E. Rashed, *The Treaty of Paris 1763* (Liverpool, 1951).

[91] Quoted in John Brewer, *The Sinews of Power* (London, 1989), p. 175. The question of Newcastle's interest and involvement in imperial policy-making is dealt with by T. R. Clayton, 'The Duke of Newcastle, the Earl of Halifax, and the American Origins of the Seven Years' War', *Historical Journal*, 24 (1981), 573–80.

[92] Thomas, *Stamp Act*, p. 112; Thomas C. Barrow, 'Background to the Grenville Program 1757–1763', *William and Mary Quarterly*, 3rd ser., 22 (1965), 93–104.

and Tea Parties toward rebellion has tempted historians to see a set of causal links originating with the resolution of the war.[93] Other historians have shifted the focus from post-1763 political events and actors to the institutional structure of British colonial rule. For them, the responsibility for the ultimate fragmentation of empire lay in the disorganized jumble of colonial administration.[94] From this vantage point, 1763 was an ill-chosen landmark in already confused terrain.[95] While this approach pays more attention to the theoretical infrastructure of British colonial rule it, too, fails to recognize that commercial management had a distinct political dimension. Military success might acquire a continental empire, but as contemporaries often noted, citing Roman history, it could not maintain it. The deterioration of governance in North America was not a matter of a changing policy – whether driven from Westminster or the Tidewater – but of a changed physical reality. So the Seven Years War *does* mark a turning point, not necessarily in the content of

[93] This is well-traversed terrain, though often differently shaded. See George Louis Beer, *British Colonial Policy 1754–1765* (New York, 1907); Laurence Gipson, *The British Empire before the American Revolution* (New York, 1967), x, pp. 203–4, and IX; 'The American Revolution as an Aftermath of the Great War for the Empire, 1754–1763', *Political Science Quarterly*, 65 (1950), 100, 103; Jack Greene, 'The Seven Years' War and the American Revolution: The Causal Relationship Reconsidered', *The British Atlantic Empire before the American Revolution*, ed. Peter Marshall and Glynn Williams (London, 1980), p. 94; Knollenberg, *Origin*, p. 17; Schuyler, *Old Colonial System*, pp. 33–4; Oliver M. Dickerson, *The Navigation Acts and the American Revolution* (Philadelphia, 1951); Ian R. Christie and Benjamin W. Labaree, *Empire or Independence* (London, 1976); Fieldhouse, 'Imperialism', p. 26.

[94] Again, the volume of literature prescribes brevity. For forceful presentations of this position, see Alison Olson, *Anglo-American Politics 1660–1775* (Oxford, 1973), pp. 118, 142, 145, 181; Jack Greene, *Peripheries and Center. Constitutional Development in the Extended Polities of the British Empire and the United States, 1607–1788* (Athens, GA, and London, 1986), p. 79; Peter Marshall, 'The British Empire in the Age of the American Revolution. Problems of Interpretation', *The American Revolution: Changing Perspectives*, ed. W. M. Fowler, Jr, and Wallace Coyle (Boston, 1979), pp. 196, 200; Michael Kammen, *Empire and Interest* (Philadelphia, 1970), p. 93; Margaret Marion Spector, *The American Department of the British Government 1768–1782* (New York, 1940), pp. 11–13.

[95] Tucker and Hendrickson, *Fall of the First British Empire*, p. 62. It followed from this that the Grenville administration did no more than make a more determined effort to effectuate what had already been undertaken a decade earlier (Tucker and Hendrickson, *Fall of the First British Empire*, p. 127; Marshall, 'The British Empire in the Age of the American Revolution', p. 191; P. J. Marshall, 'The First and Second British Empires: A Question of Demarcation', *History*, 49 (1964), 14; Ronald Hyam, 'Imperial Interests and the Peace of Paris (1763)', *Reappraisals in British Imperial History*, ed. Ged Martin and Ronald Hyam (London, 1975), p. 30). From the perspective of foreign policy, Scott had also argued that 'The fundamental continuities in British diplomacy were still more important than the discontinuities created by the fighting which had ended in 1765' (H. M. Scott, *British Foreign Policy in the Age of the American Revolution* (Oxford, 1990), p. 52).

policy but in the 'scite and circumstances' for which that policy was being made.

One of the most illuminating moments in contemporary British policy-making was the debate over the relative merits of acquiring Canada or Guadeloupe. As Phillip Lawson has argued, the 'Canada–Guadeloupe debate' cannot be taken as an authentic description of a disagreement at the highest levels of policy-making.[96] There seems to have been little doubt that Canada would be retained. This pamphlet skirmish is, however, indisputably valuable as a presentation of contemporary thinking about the purpose and role of colonies:[97]

The Benefit which accrues to the Mother Country from a Colony on the Continent, principally depends on the Number of its Inhabitants; that of a Plantation in the Islands arises from the Richness of its Commodities: We rely on the former chiefly for the Consumption of our Manufactures: We expect more from the Produce of the latter, for our own Consumption and for Exportation.[98]

The choice between 'imperial' or 'commercial' colonies seems starkly put. In the contemporary debate, the islands were preferred by those who adhered most closely to some vision of state glory which made economic autarky a prerequisite of political security.[99] Canada was seen, from this perspective, as a 'vast, wild, uncommercial, inland Country'.[100] Furthermore, the conquest of Canada removed the French threat, alleviating the colonists' dependence on

96 Philip Lawson, '"The Irishman's Prize": Views of Canada from the British Press, 1760–1774', *Historical Journal*, 28 (1985), 577.
97 Clarence Alvord's comment that 'The final decision on this momentous question was influenced by economic theory and financial interests, and by it the future colonial policy of the British empire was determined' (Alvord, *Mississippi Valley*, I, p. 49; Also, Richard Pares, *War and Trade in the West Indies 1739–1763* (Oxford, 1936), p. 217) may exaggerate the practical political options. But he certainly recognized the inextricability of colonial, economic and political thinking at mid-century. See also Pares' classic, 'American versus Continental Warfare, 1739–1763', *English Historical Review*, 51 (1936), 429–65; David B. Horne, *Great Britain and Europe in the Eighteenth Century* (Oxford, 1967), pp. 59–61.
98 Whately, *Regulations Lately Made*, pp. 5–6.
99 See [William Burke], *Remarks upon the Letter Addressed to Two Great Men* (London, 1760), p. 26; Hardwicke letter to Newcastle, 2 June 1762, quoted in Louis Namier, *England in the Age of the American Revolution* (2nd edn, London, 1961), p. 279; Anon., *Reasons for Keeping Guadeloupe at a Peace, Preferable to Canada, Explained in Five Letters* (London, 1761); [?William Burke], *An Examination of the Commercial Principles of the late Negotiation between Great Britain and France in 1761* (London, 1762), p. 24.
100 [Burke], *Examination*, p. 46; Johnson, 'The Political State', *Works*, x, pp. 135–6; Goldsmith, 'Citizen', *Works*, II, p. 73; Bute letter to Bedford, 12 July 1761, quoted in Tucker and Hendrickson, *Fall*, p. 26.

Britain for protection and thereby attenuating the reciprocal bond of obligation and violating one of the best-known contemporary dogmas.[101] The subsequent choice of Canada, in spite of the powerful economic arguments favouring the islands, has been interpreted as a change in British imperial policy. Correspondingly, those who reject the Canada–Guadeloupe dichotomy, and the division into maritime or continental colonies on which it relies, have sought to minimize the significance of the debate.[102]

While it is surely true that British war-fighting and imperial theory distinguished between continental and maritime,[103] the choice of Canada cannot mark a 'switch' from 'mercantilism', or commerce, to 'imperialism', or power, because, as has been argued, contemporary thinking did not distinguish between power and wealth. Instead, the arguments brought forward on behalf of both Canada and Guadeloupe serve to emphasize that there was but one consideration that mattered in the eyes of those who thought, wrote about and guided British colonial policy, and that was security. In 1748 national security was believed furthered by returning the captured fortress of Louisberg to the French despite its fabulous strategic worth. In 1763 it was deemed more prudent to retain territory despite commercial disadvantages. Marie Peters has argued that between January 1759 and June 1760 Pitt decided that the final peace settlement would include territorial changes in North America. The defeats suffered in Germany during the summer campaign of 1760 increased the pressure on Pitt. He was now forced to assert even more insistently that the 'bloody and expensive' continental war was necessary to secure the more popular gains in North America.[104] Success in North America led Pitt's supporters to expect a peace settlement that would ease the financial demands on the state while the government's continental commitments forbade a simple cessation of hostilities. The problem of redefining the common good again loomed up as the critical task of the patriot

[101] *Remarks upon the Letter*, p. 50; Johnson, 'Taxation No Tyranny', *Works*, x, p. 451; [James Macpherson], *The Rights of Great Britain Asserted against the Claims of America* (2nd edn, London, 1775), p. 15; Morton letter to Hardwicke, 15 June 1761, quoted in Namier, *England in the Age of the American Revolution*, p. 278.
[102] For example, Jack Sosin, *Whitehall and the Wilderness. The Middle West in British Colonial Policy, 1760–1775* (Lincoln, NB, 1961), p. 9.
[103] Richard Middleton, *The Bells of Victory. The Pitt-Newcastle Ministry and the Conduct of the Seven Years' War, 1757–1762* (Cambridge, 1985), p. 23; Tucker and Hendrickson, *Fall of the First British Empire*, p. 33.
[104] Peters, *Pitt*, pp. 168–71.

minister. Pitt's understanding of Britain's leading interest, imperial security, led him to prosecute the war; the opposition, and then the new government led by Bute, believed that Britain's security was actually harmed by the continuation of a war that was not only increasingly unpopular, but terribly expensive.[105] Forced to choose between the risk of Pitt resigning with the war still in progress and the risk of a bankruptcy, Bute joined the 'peace party' in early October after Newcastle could no longer raise finances in the City.[106]

Fear of financial collapse had always been an undercurrent in the flood of credit which accompanied the growth of commerce and empire. Traditional opposition arguments about manipulative City financiers fed naturally into concern over costly continental wars. John Entick projected this concern into French strategic counsels. 'The French ministry' perceived that success in North America could be achieved in either of two ways, either by a maritime campaign to cut the lines of communication to Britain, or 'to draw Great Britain into a continental war' which would exhaust her finances. Ultimately, French cunning aimed to prolong the conflict in the hope that financial attrition would destroy their over-leveraged enemy.[107] Istvan Hont, however, has shown how fear of a collapse of credit could also animate those supporters of government whose rule of action was not moral reform but national survival.[108] Because security and survival remained the focus of eighteenth-century ideas of political economy, both financial and military reverses were believed capable of threatening the well-being of the state. Hume set forth both aspects of the contemporary understanding of 'security'. His words, written during a lull in the imperial wars, would have made grim reading in 1761:

Let the time come (and surely it will come) when the new funds, created for the exigencies of the year, are not subscribed to, and raise not the money

---

[105] Israel Mauduit's fantastically popular *Considerations on the Present German War*, published in November 1760, went through five editions in three months and sold more copies (5,750) than any other pamphlet of the decade. He claimed that, while in 1754–5, 4 million pounds were voted as a subsidy and half of that had to be borrowed, by 1761 the amount had climbed to 19.5 million, of which 12 million was raised by borrowing (Peters, *Pitt*, pp. 183, 197).

[106] Peters, *Pitt*, p. 201.   [107] Entick, *War*, II, pp. 30–1. Also, I, p. 207, IV, p. 294.

[108] Istvan Hont, 'The Rhapsody of Public Debt: David Hume and Voluntary State Bankruptcy'.

projected. Suppose, either that the cash of the nation is exhausted; or that our faith, which has hitherto been so ample, begins to fail us. Suppose, that, in this distress, the nation is threatened with an invasion; a rebellion is suspected or broken out at home; a squadron cannot be equipped for want of pay, victuals, or repairs; or even a foreign subsidy cannot be advanced. What must a prince or minister do in such an emergence? The right of self-preservation is unalienable in every individual, much more in every community.[109]

The 'natural death' of credit resulted from the inability to raise funds, its 'violent death' from the consequences of the failure to fund military defence.

John Bullion has argued that contrary to popular perception, both then and now, the king and Bute were strong supporters of a tough policy towards the French and, in 1761, had pushed to exclude them from all North American fishing grounds and from the St Lawrence estuary. Only when Bute was convinced that the French would not simply lay down their arms, and that the British effort required to compel their surrender would have risked a bankruptcy, in other words, only when faced with David Hume's nightmare scenario, did he accept the reality of hastening towards a peace even at the expense of conceding the sugar islands.[110] Security against the French and Indians remained the primary concern for Bute.[111] Like Hume, he perceived that financial weakness was a political as well as economic danger. Returning Guadeloupe reduced the French incentive to recommence warfare and so preserved British finances.[112]

Bute employed a variety of strategies to assuage the Pittite demands for still more extensive territorial acquisitions. *The Briton*, a weekly essay journal sponsored by Bute and written by Tobias Smollett, consistently framed the argument that in this instance security was assured by peace rather than by renewed conflict. Like the redefinitions of party, patriotism and national interest,

---

[109] Hume, 'Of Public Credit', p. 362. For a similar argument, see Richard Price, *Treatise on Reversionary Payments* (3rd edn, London, 1773), p. 46.
[110] John L. Bullion, 'Securing the Peace: Lord Bute, the Plan for the Army, and the Origins of the American Revolution', *Lord Bute: Essays in Re-interpretation*, ed. Karl W. Schweitzer (Leicester, 1988), pp. 27–32.
[111] *Ibid.*, pp. 19–21.
[112] Anon., *A Letter to the People of England on the Necessity of Putting an Immediate End to the War* (Dublin, 1760), p. 49.

Smollett's essays on Britain's 'real' security constituted another attempt to keep policy in line with a perceived common good.[113]

In the issue of 3 July 1762, Smollett had been attacking the *Monitor* for its convenient shift from condemnation of the German war to condemnation of the government for ending it and breaking a treaty with Prussia. He then turned to the more fundamental issue of credit and security:

Our very existence as a powerful nation, seems to be at stake. Whatever may be urged by a set of infamous usurers, who prey upon the necessities of their country, I insist upon it, the public credit is drawn so fine as to threaten cracking at the very next stretch. We all remember the difficulties of last year, when the high premiums granted by the g--t, tempted every individual who could command a sum of ready money, to leave his just debts undischarged, that he might embrace the proffered advantage. Thus all the cash in the kingdom centered in the capital, and the extreme parts were left almost entirely without circulation.[114]

Like the Pittite Entick, Smollett believed the French more able to prosecute a continued continental war 'without contracting one shilling of debt, or laying any heavy additional imposition on their people'.[115]

The Briton's scorn for the 'preposterous' schemes of 'universal conquest' formulated by irrational men borne by a 'rage of conquest' is an obvious appeal to the traditional wariness of continental warfare and connections.[116] The assimilation of secure credit to security polity is, however, a further clarification of the mid-century understanding of the common good. 'I will venture to say', wrote Smollett, 'we have already made more conquests than it is our interest to retain. Our motive for engaging in this war was to defend and secure our colonies in North America.'[117] Having attained this end, what could justify the prolongation of 'the trade of death and desolation, at the hazard of bankruptcy and ruin to his country'?[118] As for those who opposed a separate peace with France that would violate agreements with Prussia, obvious financial necessity set in motion the standard appeal to the public good:

---

[113] See Robin Fabel, 'The Patriotic Briton: Tobias Smollett and English Politics, 1756–1771', *Eighteenth Century Studies*, 8 (1974), 100–14. In the first number Smollett declared that the purpose of *The Briton* was 'To pluck the mask of patriotism from the face of faction' (quoted in Fabel, p. 113).

[114] *The Briton*, 3 July 1762, pp. 33–4.   [115] *Ibid.*, 10 July 1762, p. 38.

[116] *Ibid.*, 25 September 1762, p. 106; 6 July 1762, p. 34.

[117] *Ibid.*, 3 July 1762, p. 34.   [118] *Ibid.*, 18 September 1762, p. 102.

To return from this digression, the *salus populi*, is certainly the *suprema lex*, which must supercede all other ties and considerations; and this, I apprehend, may be adduced as one reason to detach us from the P--n alliance, if the alliance cannot be retained without our consenting to perpetuate the war.

The calculation of national well-being was straightforward: 'The only question that deserves consideration is, whether we have more to apprehend from that ally's resentment, than we have to suffer by his friendship.'[119]

Finally, Smollett held up the threat that Britain's progress 'towards absolute dominion and despotism by sea' would arouse in her neighbours the same fear of French universal monarchy that had stimulated the establishment of coalitions to wage balance of power wars for almost a century. Facing this impending threat with finances drained and resources at an ebb, Britain would be doomed.[120] As H. M. Scott has shown, the isolation foreseen by *The Briton* finally arrived in 1775, a consequence of the immediate post-war imperative to restore fiscal soundness.[121] From this perspective, Bullion is certainly correct to conclude that 'the origins of the American Revolution may be found in the imperatives of imperial security, as perceived by George III and Lord Bute'.[122]

Opinion may have diverged on the question of prolonging the war and on the fate of the sugar islands, but the importance of Canada to the empire was rarely forgotten. Writers on both sides explicitly insisted that Canada be retained because it enhanced imperial security. If, as John Entick argued, the French planned to expand southwards through the Lakes and down the Mississippi in order to link New France with New Orleans they would both block the future growth of the British colonies and secure a valuable warm-water port.[123] Fred J. Ericson brilliantly organized the contemporary debate around four criteria: economics, security, the importance of territory and political and diplomatic exigencies. Canada proved superior on the latter three points, with the additional security it provided being the decisive advantage.[124] Benjamin

[119] *Ibid.*, 10 July 1762, p. 40. Also 25 September 1762, p. 104.
[120] *Ibid.*, 22 October 1762, p. 131.
[121] Scott, *British Foreign Policy*, pp. 5, 51.   [122] Bullion, 'Securing the Peace', p. 35.
[123] Entick, *History of the War*, I, p. 16.
[124] Fred J. Ericson, 'British Motives for Expansion in 1763: Territory, Commerce, or Security', *Papers of the Michigan Academy of Science, Arts, and Letters*, 27 (1941), 581, 594.

Franklin's elucidation of the 'interest of Great Britain' is summarized purely in these terms:

The security desirable in America may be considered as of three kinds; 1. A security of possession, that the French shall not drive us out of the country. 2. A security of our planters from the inroads of savages, and the murders committed by them. 3. A security that the British nation shall not be obliged, on every new war, to repeat the immense expence occasion'd by this, to defend its possessions in America.

In short, 'all the kinds of security we have mention'd are obtain'd by subduing and retaining Canada'.[125]

The conjunction of power and plenty in the theory of British colonial policy is easily seen in the explicit contention that Britain had a claim to Canada by 'Right of Security' and that 'Canada ought to be retained for our Security.'[126] Postlethwayt declared that it was 'the interest of Great-Britain to preserve, increase, maintain, and encourage its colonies on the continent of America' because the French were actively seeking to acquire or destroy them.[127] 'The immediate Defence of our Colonies from imminent Danger as the sole occasion of the last War'[128] was framed by the overarching rubric of Anglo-French competition for 'the ballance of trade and power'.[129] French success in disrupting the British colonies threatened the future of the British empire[130] and, therefore, the subsequent conquest of the French North American posessions, 'which, by their Situation, gave most Alarm and Annoyance to the British Colonies, laid the foundation of lasting Security to Your Majesty's Empire in North America'.[131] Those hostile to the acquisition of

---

125 Benjamin Franklin, *The Interest of Great Britain Considered* (London, 1760), p. 14; for a taxonomy of 'security' see pp. 8–13. Also, W. Burke, *Remarks on a Letter Addressed to Two Great Men* (London, 1760), p. 19.

126 Anon., *A Candid and Fair Examination of the Remarks on the Letter to Two Great Men* (2nd edn, London, 1760), pp. 9, 13.

127 Postlethwayt, *Universal Dictionary*, I, p. 532.

128 Whately, *Regulations Lately Made*, p. 3. He continued: 'Their permanent security has been effectually obtained by the Peace.'

129 Postlethwayt, *Universal Dictionary*, I, p. 535; McCulloh, *Miscellaneous Essay*, p. 1.

130 William Bollan, *Coloniae anglicanae illustratae: or the Acquest of Dominion, and the Plantation of Colonies made by the English in America* (London, 1762), p. 1.

131 Board of Trade report of 7 March 1768, quoted in C. W. Alvord and C. E. Carter, eds., *Trade and Politics 1767–1769* (Springfield, IL, 1921), p. 184. The acquisition of Canada was often justified in terms of security. For example [Knox], *Thoughts on the Act for Making More Effectual Provision for the Government of the Province of Quebec*, p. 6; [William Douglass], *A Letter Addressed to Two Men*, pp. 29, 31; Anon., *Detection of False Reasons and Facts* (London, 1761); Pitt, Commons Debate, 9 December 1762, *Proceedings and Debates of the British Parliaments Respecting North America 1754–1783*, ed. R. C. Simmons and P. D. G. Thomas, 6 vols. (White Plains, 1981–7), I, p. 422.

Canada recognized the overwhelming power of 'conservation' in the contemporary debate: 'And from hence proceeded that utter Oblivion of all former Maxims of our Policy, whilst, under the Name of Security, we sought with Eagerness extensive and unprofitable Empire, and rejected moderate but lucrative Acquisition.'[132] This criticism was directed at those who, like the author of the *Detection of False Reasons*, envisioned the replacement of the French threat with a British 'Universal Empire on the Continent of North America'.[133] Later still, as events began to get out of control, it was widely believed that the conquest of Canada actually provided the colonists with too much security for Britain's good because it alleviated their dependence on her.[134] The irony of the logic of security recapitulates Sir Richard Temple's observation about the reason of state: success could dissolve the bonds of civic life as readily as failure.

THE NEW WORLD

The dominant idioms of colonial security and of 'rivalship' with France emerge from the language of reason of state economics and its basic goal of *conservación y aumento*. If there is nothing unprecedented in the use of security to justify retaining an empire, contemporary events were interpreted as marking a new epoch in history: 'The sudden emerging of Britain from the contemptible figure she made, to its present astonishing power, fills all Europe with amazement and jealousy.'[135] Adam Smith and David Hume had both stressed that the exploration of the Western Hemisphere was a key moment in world history: 'The discovery of America, and that of a passage to the East Indies by the Cape of Good Hope, are the two greatest and most important events recorded in the history of mankind.'[136] William and Edmund Burke, in their history of European colonization in America, spoke of colonization as one of

---

[132] [Burke], *Examination*, p. 61.   [133] *A Detection of False Reasons*, p. 32.

[134] 'Since the Cession of Canada to Great Britain, the Colonies are less exposed to the Danger of an Enemy; therefore when you talk of Protection, they answer, they have no need of Assistance', dissolving the reciprocal bonds of subject and government (Anon., *An Examination of the Rights of the Colonies, upon the Principles of Law* (London, 1766), p. 36).

[135] Wallace, *Internal Policy of Great Britain*, p. 159.

[136] Smith, *WN*, iv.vii.c.80, p. 626; also Hume, *History of England*, iii, p. 80. Their contemporary, Edward Gibbon, wrote this moment back into his Roman history (*The Decline and Fall of the Roman Empire*, 6 vols. (New York, n.d.) i, p. 139).

the principal events in an era which 'conspired to change the face of Europe entirely'.[137]

The political stresses generated by the colonization of a continent separated by thousands of miles of ocean were unprecedented. ' ... there can be found no similar case in all the records of history to serve as a precedent, or clew, to direct their steps; and all they can do is to grope their way by their own industry, and to employ their reason, as the only compass which can steer their course aright to this land unknown'.[138] The history of the long decade between the Treaty of Paris and the outbreak of the North American rebellion demonstrates the limits of political theory. The conventional wisdom of political economy was found wanting because the changed situation vitiated the fundamental premise of securing for a single political community the furtherance of a common good.

In practical terms, the central problem in managing North American colonial affairs in the period of Anglo-French competition,[139] and one that remained unresolved until 1787, was how to govern what was called at the time, simply, 'the West' (Canada and the Mississippi Basin).[140] As with the Canada–Guadeloupe debate, on the matter of the American interior, policy-making intersected with political theory. Colonies were valued as sources of natural resources and markets for finished goods; distant, unpopulated and untracked wilderness could not satisfy these criteria and even raised the possibility of colonial industrialization, if only to provide the necessities made luxuries by their inaccessible location. But since, in this instance, the claims of security were overriding and Britain opted for the hinterland over the entrepôts, policy had to be sculpted on different principles. The immediate British response was to forbid trans-Appalachian settlement.

---

[137] These included the invention of printing, the making of gunpowder, the improvement of navigation, the revival of ancient learning, and the Reformation (*Account of the European Settlements*, II, p. 3).

[138] Anon., *The Justice and Necessity of Taxing the American Colonies*, p. 6. See P. J. Thomas, 'Imperial Issues in the British Press', Unpublished D.Phil. dissertation (Oxford, 1982), p. iii.

[139] Theodore Pease suggested that in North America the colonial war that commenced in 1739 did not actually end until 1763 (Pease, *Anglo-French Border Disputes in the West 1749–1763*, (Springfield, IL, 1936), xix–xx). He also observed that 'Security is the keystone' of the French North American policy (p. lxi).

[140] Alvord, *Mississippi Valley*, I, p. 15; Philip Lawson, *The Imperial Challenge: Quebec and Britain in the Age of the American Revolution* (Montreal, Kingston and London, 1989), pp. 37–8; Marc Egnal, *A Mighty Empire* (Ithaca, 1988).

American lobbying for the establishment of colonies at the mouth of the Ohio River by the Illinois Company and at the confluence of the Ohio and Mississippi Rivers by the Mississippi Valley Company was blocked by opposition from the Lords of Trade.[141] On 5 May 1763, hard on the heels of the Paris settlement, the Earl of Egremont, Secretary of State for the Southern Department, requested a position paper from the Board of Trade. 'Hints Relative to the Division and Government of the Conquered and Newly Acquired Countries in America', written either by Egremont or his aide Henry Ellis, recommended ruling Canada by charter, not local assembly, and directing settlers into the northern, not western, territory.[142] A 'Sketch' written by John Pownall, Permanent Secretary to the Board of Trade, not the 'Hints', is now accepted as the source of the Proclamation of October 1763.[143] Pownall wanted to bar new settlers because of the basic mercantilist fear that they would 'ingage in the production and manufacture of those articles of necessary consumption which they ought, upon every principle of true policy, to take from the mother country'.[144] Despite Grenville's disastrous attempt to enforce these principles (especially the Stamp Act), the government was still wedded to policies that even they perceived to be inadequate to solve the problems of the Mississippi frontier. Disputes with the Indians in 1768 led the Lords of Trade to report to the Cabinet that the 'provisional Arrangement' of 1763 still needed to be systematized.[145] Lord Hillsborough's Board of Trade report recapitulated the central tenets of British colonial policy: the emphasis on imperial security and the conceptual incompatibility of inland colonies and commerce.[146] 'The Proposition of forming inland Colonies in America is, we humbly conceive, entirely

[141] Jack M. Sosin, *Whitehall and the Wilderness*, pp. 139–41.
[142] 'Hints Relative to the Division and Government of the Conquered and Newly Acquired Countries in America', ed. Verner M. Crane, *Mississippi Valley Historical Review*, 8 (1922), p. 371.
[143] Knollenberg, *Origin*, p. 102; Vincent T. Harlow, *The Founding of the Second British Empire 1763–1793* (London, 1952), I, p. 170. For more information on Pownall, see Franklin B. Wickwire, 'John Pownall and British Colonial Policy', *William and Mary Quarterly*, 3rd ser., 20 (1963), 534–54; P. G. Walsh-Atkins, 'Shelburne and America', Unpublished D.Phil. thesis (Oxford, 1971).
[144] Printed, from Joseph Priestley's handwritten text, in R. A. Humphreys, 'Lord Shelburne and the Proclamation of 1763', *English Historical Review*, 49 (1934), 259.
[145] Alvord and Carter, eds., *Trade and Politics 1767–1769*, p. 184. Also P. D. G. Thomas, *The Townshend Duties Crisis* (Oxford, 1987), p. 54.
[146] The French possessions 'by their Situation, gave most Alarm and Annoyance to the British Colonies, laid the foundation of lasting Security to Your Majesty's Empire in North America ... ' (Board of Trade Report, *Trade and Politics 1767–1769*, p. 184).

new; it adopts Principles, in respect to American Settlements, different from what has hitherto been the Policy of this Kingdom.' Until
1763 the purpose of American colonization was clearly the improvement of British commerce, navigation and industry 'upon which its
Strength and Security depend'. These goals required that Britain
confine 'her Settlements as much as possible to the Sea Coast, and
not to extend them to places unaccessible to Shipping, and consequently more out of the reach of Commerce'.[147] In 1770, settlement of the interior was blocked, again because contrary to the
principles of empire. The twin goals of preserving the security of the
colonies against the French and augmenting 'that peculiar Commerce' with them seemed to demand opposing policies. Lord Hillsborough wrote that, while he wished to take a decision, the only
viable options were 'each of them accompanied with such objections, as leave my Judgement in a State of perplexity I am not able
to get over'.[148] As late as 1776, a paper attributed to William Knox
retained the ban on trans-Appalachian settlement.[149] According to
Pocock, it was first-hand experience of the theoretical and practical
difficulties encountered by the British that helped shape the
Americans' attempt to formulate a new model of sovereignty
capable of coping with expansion.[150]

The failure of the government to do more than recommend that
nothing be done about settling and developing this vast continental
empire[151] testifies to the complete failure of Britain's imperial policy
to answer the needs of the post-war colonial world. Britain's acquisition of territorial empire in 1763 had forced on her one of the great
unresolved problems in political thought: the relationship between
size and liberty. By and large, republicans had been most concerned
with this issue since size obviously complicated the participation of
citizens in government. But the politics of the territorial state shifted
the issue away from the identification of liberty with republics. The
challenge facing the government was to insure the maintenance and
flourishing of the state, understood in contemporary terms, while at

---

[147] Board of Trade Report, *Trade and Politics*, pp. 197–8. See also, [Burke], *Examination*, p. 70:
'Inland Colonies Can Never Prove in any Considerable Degree Beneficial to our Commerce ... '
[148] Hillsborough to Gage, 31 July 1770, *The Correspondence of General Thomas Gage with the
Secretaries of State and with the War Office and Treasury 1763–1775*, ed. C. E. Carter, 2 vols.
(New Haven, 1931–3), II, pp. 107–10.
[149] Spector, *American Department*, p. 148.
[150] Pocock, *The Politics of Extent and the Problem of Freedom* (Colorado Springs, 1988), pp. 6, 17.
[151] Board of Trade Report, quoted in *Trade and Politics 1767–1769*, pp. 201–2.

the same time maximizing the liberty of its citizens. The quest for a common good was often summarized as a relationship of protection in exchange for obedience, or as 'civil liberty'. Acquisition of territorial empire made the possibility of formulating a 'common', shared good in an empire of millions spread across nearly 5,000 miles of wastes and ocean an inescapable question.

The absolute novelty of the situation was seen to pose an immediate challenge to policy-making. George III acknowledged the problem of settling the new territories in his speech opening the first post-war parliament in November 1762.[152] The theme also served as the title for a contemporary pamphlet: *Thoughts on a Question of Importance Proposed to the Public, 'Whether it is Probable that the Immense Extent of Territory Acquired by this Nation at the Late Peace, Will Operate towards the Prosperity, or the Ruin of the Island of Great Britain'?* For the author, the size of the territorial conquest 'must make the Time of Acquisition a remarkable Aera of this Government, and produce a great Change in our Situation and Circumstances as a Society'. Since all parts of a single body were in some relation to one another, the addition of such a huge territory compelled a massive reassessment of the relation of the various parts of the realm.[153] While some writers were concerned that a British continental empire would 'over-reach' national capacity, others believed that a greater population and more far-flung territories would redound to Britain's advantage by increasing the size of that population dependent on British commerce and manufacturing.[154] Moreover, distant colonies stimulated the continued expansion of the navy and merchant marine.[155] Another suggested that 'particular Indulgence' was all that was called for,[156] while still another wrote that the only

[152] *Proceedings and Debates of the British Parliaments Respecting North America 1754–1783*, ed. R. C. Simmons and P. D. G. Thomas, 6 vols. (White Plains, NY, 1981–7), 25 November 1762, I, p. 401; Marshall, 'Incorporation', *Mother Country*, pp. 43–4.

[153] Anon., *Thoughts on a Question of Importance Proposed to the Public, 'Whether it is Probable that the Immense Extent of Territory Acquired by this Nation at the Late Peace, Will Operate towards the Prosperity, or the Ruin of the Island of Great Britain'?* (London, 1765), pp. 11, 14–15; Anon., *An Inquiry into the Nature and Causes of the Present Disputes between the British Colonies in America and their Mother-Country* (London, 1769), pp. 5–6.

[154] Anon., *The Comparative Importance of our Acquisitions from France in America* (1762), quoted in Ericson, 'British Motives for Expansion', p. 583; Anon., *Propositions for Improving the Manufactures, Agriculture and Commerce of Great Britain* (London, 1763), p. 117.

[155] William Young, *Considerations Which May Tend to Promote the Settlement of Our New W. India Colonies* (London, 1764), p. 2.

[156] [John Fothergill], *Considerations Relative to the North American Colonies* (London, 1765), p. 10.

consequence of their distance was 'a difference of expense to the mother country in defending them'.[157] To its defenders, the British empire was a unity composed of many parts, 'let the geographical distance, be what it will'.[158]

In a rare fit of optimism, Hume the historian had suggested that the problem of distance had been discussed and rightly minimized during the reign of James I.[159] Adam Smith, on the other hand, recognized that distance was the overwhelming characteristic of British colonization and one which made it unique in world history. 'But the European colonies in America are more remote than the most distant provinces of the greatest empires which had ever been known before. The government of the English colonies is perhaps the only one which, since the world began, could give perfect security to the inhabitants of so very distant a province.'[160] It is tempting to read his description of the Greek colonies against the contemporary comparison of the British with the ancient colonies.[161] Richard Price's pronouncement on the uniqueness of Britain's situation is still another recognition of the unprecedentedness of the post-1763 world: 'This is a case which is new in the history of mankind; and it is extremely improper to judge of it by the rules of any narrow and partial policy; or to consider it on any other ground than the general one of reason and justice.'[162]

In his famous speech of 22 March 1775, Burke made the most dramatic case for respecting the consequences of distance. No matter Britain's immediate success in dousing the fires of rebellion, 'The Ocean remains. You cannot pump this dry; and as long as it continues in its present bed, so long all the causes which weaken authority by distance will continue.'[163] Burke invoked distance as a natural obstacle which no form of government or metaphor had ever been able to eliminate:

Three thousand miles of ocean lie between you and them. No contrivance can prevent the effect of this distance, in weakening Government. Seas roll, and months pass, between the order and the execution; and the want of a

[157] Arthur Young, *Political Essays Concerning the Present State of the British Empire* (London, 1772), p. 38.
[158] Obadiah Hulme, *An Historical Essay on the British Constitution* (London, 1770), p. 199.
[159] Hume, *History*, v, p. 148.   [160] Smith, *WN*, iv.vii.b.52, p. 586.
[161] *Ibid.*, iv.vii.b.4, p. 566.
[162] Richard Price, *Observations on the Nature of Civil Liberty* (London, 1776), p. 33.
[163] *Speech of Edmund Burke, Esq. on Moving his Resolutions for Conciliation with the Colonies, March 22, 1775* (3rd edn, London, 1775), p. 48.

speedy explanation of a single point is enough to defeat an whole system ...
Nothing worse happens to you, than does to all Nations, who have extensive Empire; and it happens in all the forms into which Empire can be
thrown. In large bodies, the circulation of power must be less vigorous at
the extremities. Nature has said it. The Turk cannot govern Ægypt, and
Arabia, and Curdistan, as he governs Thrace; nor has he the same dominion in Crimea and Algiers, which he has at Bursa and Smyrna ... The
Sultan gets such obedience as he can. He governs with a loose rein, that he
may govern at all; and the whole of a prudent relaxation in all his borders.
Spain, in her provinces, is, perhaps, not so well obeyed, as you are in yours.
She complies too; she submits, she watches time. This is the immutable
condition; the eternal Law, of extensive and detached Empire.

Just as some contemporaries had invoked size as the trigger for a
Polybian descent, Burke, and others, viewed it as a natural brake on
the authority of a central government. Nevertheless, he believed
that no plan of imperial reform could overcome this structural
problem: 'I cannot remove the eternal barriers of the creation. The
thing in that mode, I do not know to be possible.'[164]

Josiah Tucker, ever the astute critic, mocked Burke's inability to
bring himself to follow his own conclusion about the inexorable
consequences of distance: 'The immutable Condition! the eternal
Law! of extensive and detached Empire! Pray, Sir, on which Side of
the Question were you retained? And whose Cause are you now
pleading?' Tucker's conclusion was not, as Burke left it, that distant
colonies had to be treated gently, but that there should be no distant
colonies.[165] In his response to Burke, John Cartwright also predicted
that efforts to ignore or overcome distance would prove nugatory.[166]

Faced with this unprecedented situation, British writers turned to
history and its analysts for guidance. Here again, what is usually
seen as a distinguishing characteristic of republican or commonwealth literature had become, by the mid eighteenth century, part
of the common pool of political arguments. Perhaps this is to be
accounted for by the wider scope of classical education, perhaps
simply by necessity. But, whatever the reason, the effect was the
same as has been observed previously: the convergence of opposition

---

[164] Burke, *March 22, 1775*, pp. 35–6. Distance was to make representation particularly
difficult (Fothergill, *Considerations Relative*, p. 4, p. 17).
[165] Tucker, *Letter to Burke*, p. 39.
[166] Burke should have abandoned 'the impracticable endeavour to prove them to be, and the
equally vain attempt for holding them together as one empire' (Cartwright, 'Letter to
Burke', *American Independence* (2nd edn, London, 1775), p. 14).

and government politics at mid-century appeared to render the former unrecognizable and irrelevant.

While much of the theoretical foundation for the discussion of expansion could be derived from Machiavelli, Harrington and Montesquieu, on specific points of guidance they were of little help. Machiavelli had introduced the distinction between republics for expansion, like Rome, and preservation, of which Sparta and Venice were the usual ancient and modern exempla. His preference was for the former, counselling that

the right way to make a republic great and for it to acquire an empire is to increase the number of its inhabitants, to make other states its allies, not its subjects, to send out colonies for the security of conquered territory, to fund the spoils of war, to subdue the enemy by raids and battles, not by sieges, to enrich the public but to keep individuals poor, to attend with the utmost care to military training.[167]

Those city-states preferring preservation to expansion pursued a bootless quest since in a world governed by fortune it was impossible for a state to remain in perpetual peace, and yet this polity would always be unprepared for the eventual combat. But even republics for expansion faced risks beyond simply those of warfare. Here the example of the Romans was fundamental. If, as was indisputable, the rapid expansion of its territory doomed even the virtuous Roman republic, what hope had less well-mannered states?[168]

Montesquieu rejected this dichotomy between expansion and preservation. Here as elsewhere engaged with Grotius' argument, he asserted that 'All governments have the same general end, which is that of preservation.'[169] Differences between states reflected different means of pursuing their security, what he calls their 'particular object', which, as in ancient Greece, could be either conquest or commerce.[170] Because Montesquieu believed that it was possible to escape Fortune's grasp he could describe as a 'wise republic' one which aspired 'to the perpetuation of its condition'.[171] The right 'conditions' amounted to a republic living in a territory of the appropriate size: 'The long duration of the republic of Sparta was owing to her having continued in the same extent of territory after

---

[167] Machiavelli, *The Discourses*, tr. Leslie J. Walker (Harmondsworth, 1970), II.19, p. 335.
[168] *Ibid.*, II.19, pp. 337–8.   [169] Montesquieu, *Spirit of the Laws*, XI.5, p. 150.
[170] *Ibid.*, V.6, p. 46.
[171] Montesquieu, *Considerations on the Greatness and Decline of the Romans*, tr. David Lowenthal (Ithaca, 1968), p. 92.

all her wars.' As long as a state did not exceed its natural frontiers it would be able to maintain itself successfully.[172] Rome, too, thrived so long as she kept within the Italic peninsula. The great conquests ultimately diminished the 'citizen spirit' of the citizen-soldiers, deprived the senate of 'immediate inspection over the provinces' and destroyed 'the harmony of the three powers'. Montesquieu's conclusion was that 'a conquering republic can hardly communicate her government, and rule the conquered state according to her own constitution'.[173] Despite his ambivalence about the possibility of modern states drawing intellectual sustenance from ancient history,[174] his formula about the relationship between size and liberty was axiomatic for English opposition writers, who invoked it against British imperial practice later in the century.

In an extensive republic the public good is sacrificed to a thousand private views; it is subordinate to exceptions, and depends on accidents. In a small one, the interest of the public is more obvious, better understood, and more within the reach of every citizen; abuses have less extent, and, of course, are less protected.[175]

The third writer who would have been extensively drawn upon was James Harrington, whose collected *Works* was reprinted in 1737, 1747, 1758 and 1771; in other words, straight through the entire period of imperial expansion. Harrington's aim, dismissing Machiavelli's wariness of Fortune, had been to make Oceana a maritime 'commonwealth for increase'. Despite its republican cast, the incorporation of these two real aspects of contemporary British politics, maritime traffic and expansion, might have accounted for some of its eighteenth-century relevance.

The republic in which Harrington wrote was defiantly for expansion. Republics for preservation were, therefore, unacceptable models. Their domestic quiet was purchased at the price of weakness overseas that not only imperilled the security of the state but militated against the important acquisition of glory. But Harrington sharply disagreed with Machiavelli's reasons. Sparta did not fall because she expanded in violation of her constitution; she fell

---

[172] Montesquieu, *Spirit of the Laws*, VIII.16, p. 120. This was a frequent observation: see Anon., *Inquiry into the Nature and Causes of the Present Dispute*, p. 12.
[173] Montesquieu, *Spirit of the Laws*, XI.19, p. 180; *Considerations*, p. 91.
[174] Judith Shklar, 'Montesquieu and the new Republicanism', *Machiavelli and Republicanism*, ed. Gissela Bok, Quentin Skinner and Maurizio Viroli (Cambridge, 1990), p. 266.
[175] Montesquieu, *Spirit of the Laws*, VIII.16, p. 120.

because she became unequal. Hence, a republic for preservation lacking an agrarian law would succumb to the same internecine strife that was the plague of its more tumultuous increase-oriented variant.[176] With this step Harrington diverted the argument about permanence and duration away from Machiavelli's categories of preservation and increase and towards the orders of the government. The fall of Rome, on this reading, was not due to her expansion, but to the slight constitutional foundation on which the huge edifice was reared.[177]

Rome's growth proceeded by unequal leagues and colonization, but these latter never extended beyond the Italian peninsula. Harrington's account of the usefulness of colonies closely followed Machiavelli's.[178] But much of it dealt with the methods required after the conquest of new territories and would have been generally irrelevant to conditions in North America, where there was no settled government like that encountered by the Romans in Greece, and no familiar possession of territory as in Europe.[179]

If the republic for increase could survive and flourish, even at great size, because of its 'equal' orders, this equality had somehow to include its periphery, as well. And yet, Harrington acknowledged that the equality of even the Venetian constitution did not, and perhaps could not, extend to the provinces of the *terraferma*. While provincial inequality was egregious, nevertheless 'every commonwealth that holdeth provinces must in that regard be such' to an extent.[180] In so far as 'equality' implied a balance between the power and property of a polity's inhabitants, it was clear that provinces external to the metropolis posed an acute problem. For their status as provinces meant that they had to be ruled from the centre, implying that power was not based on property-holding in the province. Yet if provincial rule *were* to be 'equal', that is, if power was actually exercised by those who held dominion in the province, 'that would bring the government from provincial and dependent to national and independent'.[181] If this dilemma were not taxing enough, the history of Venice demonstrated that inequality on the periphery ultimately corrupted equality at home. Yet, Venice still could not face the risk of independent 'provincial government' as the

[176] Harrington, *Oceana*, in *The Political Works of James Harrington*, ed. J. G. A. Pocock (Cambridge, 1976), pp. 273–5.
[177] *Ibid.*, p. 320.   [178] *Ibid.*, p. 325.   [179] *Ibid.*, p. 330.   [180] *Ibid.*, p. 181.
[181] *Ibid.*, p. 167.

predominance of the provinces would overwhelm the small circle that ruled the commonwealth.[182] Harrington's friend Henry Neville sharpened this point in his *Plato Redivivus*, reprinted in 1763:

so in provincial governments, if they be wisely ordered, no man must have any the least share in the managing affairs of state, but strangers; or such as have no share or part in the possessions there; for else they will have a very good opportunity of shaking off their yoke.[183]

Thus, provinces could not be ruled 'equally' because this dissolved the necessary bonds of subordination even though the maintenance of unequal provincial administration would ultimately submerge the metropolitan constitution. Provincial government, albeit unequal and life-threatening, still seemed the only means of exercising imperial sovereignty. The changed circumstances of eighteenth-century Britain had made the arguments of seventeenth-century commonwealthmen as open to exploitation by government propagandists as by opposition critics.

If the great modern political commentators on history did not speak to the British case, the historical dimension of the problem of size particularly perplexed British writers because it posed the further problem of defining the identity of the British state. Was the history of the ancient republics at all relevant to the condition of a monarchical empire ruled by law? Was the debilitated condition of the Roman empire actually a worthwhile exemplar for a free and constitutional state like Great Britain?

Writing earlier in the century, *Cato* had begun the process of discussing the politics of empire without reference to classical exempla:

People are like Wire: The more they are extended, the weaker they become; and the closer they are together, the richer they grow, and more potent. This is the Language of common Sense and Experience: But Ambition speaks another and a different Language, for extensive Empire and uncontrouled Dominion; and being too well heard, puts Men upon sacrificing their real Strength to what is only imaginary.[184]

While some writers, like Benjamin Franklin, rejected classical history for having little to say about the new world in the West, for most others, there was a lesson to be learned and it was a sceptical

[182] *Ibid.*, p. 168.
[183] Henry Neville, *Plato Redivivus*, in *Two English Republican Tracts*, ed. Caroline Robbins (Cambridge, 1969), p. 94.
[184] *Cato's Letters*, no. 74, III, pp. 70–1.

one. Samuel Johnson observed that a new empire 'is magnificent in prospect, but will lose much of its beauty on a nearer view',[185] while Oliver Goldsmith described the danger of expansion in Polybian terms: 'It is in the politic as in the human constitution; if the limbs grow too large for the body, their size, instead of improving, will diminish the vigour of the whole.'[186]

The implications of expansion for vaunted British liberty especially concerned opposition writers. The new territorial gains renewed, with urgency, the paradox of a republican empire: political liberty simply did not travel.[187] Despite the beginnings of the move away from ancient models, Rome's story was unavoidable. As it expanded, the disjunction between liberty at home and tyranny in the provinces became more pronounced. This was frequently commented upon by eighteenth-century Britons. Early in the century, Shaftesbury described 'vast empires' as 'unnatural' precisely because great distances inexorably transformed even the most benign overlordship into a self-interested oligarchy.[188] Price, at the height of the imperial crisis, echoed Hume's sceptical observation 'that *free* governments, though happier in themselves, are more oppressive to their provinces than despotic governments'.[189] Gibbon wrote, no doubt ominously to some, that the oppression of the provinces actually made the rule of a single person more appealing to them.[190] The condition of the late Empire was long associated with oriental states: 'If we turn our eyes towards the monarchies of Asia, we shall behold despotism in the centre, and weakness in the

---

185 Johnson, 'Review of Lewis Evans (1756)', *Works*, x, p. 211; 'Extensive Conquests', for Hume and Goldsmith (who was, after all, a historian of ancient Rome), triggered decline and the greater the empire the swifter the downward slide ('The Idea of a Perfect Commonwealth', *Essays*, p. 529; 'Of the Balance of Power', *Essays*, p. 340; Goldsmith, 'Citizen of the World', *Works*, ii, pp. 106–8). Hutcheson, like Montesquieu, stressed the logistical limitations on central control (*A Short Introduction to Moral Philosophy* (3rd edn, Glasgow, 1764), iii.ix.2, p. 319).

186 Oliver Goldsmith, 'Citizen of the World', *Works*, ii, p. 74. Also Edward Spelman, *A Fragment out of the Sixth Book of Polybius* (London, 1743), p. iii.

187 The case of 'a free country branching itself out' was unprecedented (Price, *Observations on the Nature of Civil Liberty, the Principles of Government and the Justice and Policy of the War with America* (London, 1776), p. 33).

188 Anthony Ashley Cooper, Lord Shaftesbury, *Characteristicks of Men, Manners, Opinions, Times*, 2 vols. (Indianapolis, 1964), i, p. 76.

189 Richard Price, *Additional Observations on the Nature and Value of Civil Liberty* (Dublin, 1777), p. 49. See Hume, 'Politics May be Reduced to a Science', pp. 18–19. Joseph Priestley also attacked the republic's imperial policy as condoning the oppression of provinces and the rapine of their governors (*Lectures on History*, p. 26).

190 Gibbon, *Decline and Fall*, i, p. 53; also, Anon., *Application of Some General Political Rules*, p. 7.

extremities ... '[191] This is the context, and these the very metaphors, of Burke's great speech of March 1775 on imperial size.

In the absence of any constitutional equality between the provinces and the centre there was no local recourse against the appointed officials of a distant and largely unresponsive central government. The empire was ruled so as to further the interests of Rome first, Italy second and the provinces last and least of all.[192] Because of the absence of specific constitutional arrangements, provincial needs were assimilated to metropolitan objectives, whether congruent or not.[193] The legal and financial condition of the provinces was so precarious that the advantages of Roman citizenship were often defined in contrast to the status of colonials. Were it not for the citizen's privilege of being judged by the people, 'he would have been subject in the provinces to the arbitrary power of a proconsul or of a propretor. The city never felt the tyranny which was exercised only on conquered nations.'[194] As Polybius would have stressed, this problem became acute only in peacetime when the exigencies of war gave way to the yearning for ease and luxury.[195] Facing these actions, the provinces, ruled as they were ostensibly for their own good, could do nothing.[196] Maladministration in the provinces was itself a sign of political collapse as it often demonstrated that gubernatorial appointments were made on 'party merit, and with no other view than to raise a fortune at the expense of the people'.[197] This classic description of unpatriotic, faction politics was, after all, a not uncommon view of British imperial practice.[198]

Burke perceptively evoked the constitutional difficulties of a continental colonial empire. The problem was the potential conflict between the policy-makers' pursuit of security at all costs and the particular British attachment to constitutional liberty. This dilemma was exacerbated by the conditions of imperial rule, in which a 'strong presiding power' was needed to hold together a 'vast disconnected, infinitely diversified empire' which somehow

---

[191] Gibbon, *Decline and Fall*, II, p. 38.
[192] Anon., *An Application of Some General Political Rules*, pp. 16–17.
[193] Joshua Steele, *An Account of a Late Conference on the Occurrences in America* (London, 1766), p. 11.
[194] Montesquieu, *Spirit of the Laws*, XI.19, pp. 180–1.
[195] Anon., *Application of Some General Political Rules*, p. 17.
[196] *Ibid.*, p. 25.   [197] Montagu, *Reflections*, p. 338.
[198] Brewer, *Sinews of Power*, p. xix.

preserved provincial 'liberty and safety'.[199] Defenders of transmarine commercial empire, like John Campbell, rarely considered the colonies in anything but an economic context. The implications of distance did not affect their assessment of the nature of obligation and sovereignty: the 'Subjects as well as the Soil' were British.[200]

The recourse to history was, however, a recourse to two different histories. Most writers initially looked for exampla in the history of Roman republican and imperial government, but others examined the history of ancient colonization, focusing in particular on comparisons of Roman and Greek models.[201] It is one of our cultural commonplaces that the rise of interest in Greek exempla, the so-called 'Greek revival' of the later eighteenth century, was driven by culture rather than politics. But, while Winckelmann disputed with Piranesi, and Stuart and Revett surveyed Athens, the search for purchase on the new imperial situation had also led British writers to focus on Greek political history. In his famous *Considerations on the Present German War*, Israel Mauduit likened Britain and France to Athens and Sparta, the Seven Years War to the Peloponnesian, and the conquest of North America to a potential Syracusan expedition. 'We shall', he concluded, 'soon, I hope, see the mistake of persisting in any such impracticable attempts.'[202] Greek colonies were understood to be bound to their metropolis' by looser ties. Given their relative weakness, most city-states possessed little leverage over their former citizens. Consequently, the colony was able to choose its form of government and decide on the quality of its connection with the mother-city. For her part, the metropolis rarely thought of taxing the colony 'or of retaining over it any mark of sovereignty; because she could afford it no compensation in the article of defence'. The only link between them was, instead, 'affection or alliance'. The fundamental characteristic of the early modern colonial relation-

---

[199] Burke, 'Letter to the Sheriffs of Bristol', *Speeches on the American War, and Letter to the Sheriffs of Bristol*, ed. A. J. George (Boston, MA, 1898; rpt, 1972), p. 207.

[200] Campbell, *Present State of Europe*, p. 503.

[201] William Bollan, on the other hand, began with the origin of European colonization, focusing on the fourteenth-century Iberian kingdoms (*Coloniae anglicanae illustratae*).

[202] Mauduit, *Considerations on the Present German War* (2nd edn, London, 1760), p. 140. In his address against a motion to raise a standing army for North America, Lord Camden observed that the Sicilian débâcle marked the zenith of Athenian imperial aspirations and illustrated the danger of provoking far-flung colonies (*Proceedings and Debates*, 1 November 1775, VI, p. 151).

ship, obedience in exchange for protection, went unfulfilled in the Greek world. This is an important divergence.[203]

The completely different origin and nature of Roman colonies created a completely different political relationship between colonies and centre. Roman colonies took the form of border garrisons, population vents and housing for superannuated legionaries. They were filled by subscription and established wherever the triumvirs wanted new settlers. They possessed the privileges of Romans and local autonomy, but had no say in imperial affairs, while Latin colonies possessed only the privileges of Latins at Rome and could exercise no local autonomy.[204] Adam Smith described their condition as that of 'a sort of corporation, which, though it had the power of enacting bye-laws for its own government, was at all times subject to the correction, jurisdiction, and legislative authority of the mother city'.[205]

Although the conclusions of modern scholarship would suggest that the history of Greek colonization might have spoken directly to the concerns raised by the Seven Years War,[206] only a handful of contemporaries acknowledged any kinship between Greek and British colonies. In his *Lectures on History*, Joseph Priestley likened the recent imperial wars to the Peloponnesian conflict:

The wars between the Athenians and Lacedemonians, particularly the great Peloponnesian war, which is the subject of Thucydides' history, afford an excellent lesson to the English in their wars with the French, exhibiting in the clearest light all the advantages of a maritime force, and the risk that is run by a popular government (or a government inclining to that form) from aiming at extensive conquests.[207]

While ignorance certainly contributed to the minimal role of Greek history in these debates, an even more likely explanation is that most writers saw a closer political affinity between British and Roman imperial practice and so rejected the model that contradicted the

---

[203] William Barron, *History of the Colonization of the Free States of Antiquity* (London, 1777), p. 32.

[204] *Ibid.*, pp. 84–6.

[205] Smith, *W.N*, iv.vii.a.3, pp. 557–8. For Gibbon's view that 'In their manners and internal policy, the colonies formed a perfect representation of their great parent', see *Decline and Fall*, i, p. 32.

[206] The distance of the colony from the metropolis has been seen to determine the political independence of the colony (A. J. Graham, *Colony and Mother City in Ancient Greece* (2nd edn, Chicago, 1983), pp. 96, 117). The implications of distance, could, however, be mitigated by the maintenance of secure lines of maritime communication, as was the case with Corinth's colonies and the Athenian cleruchies (Graham, *Colony*, pp. 152, 191).

[207] Priestley, *Lectures on History*, p. 214. He had also described the struggle between Britain and the colonies as 'dreadful and unnatural', reflecting, perhaps, the Greek view of such

accepted principles of imperial management. In the House of Commons 'American Committee', Philip Yorke declared that 'Our own colonies are more like those of Rome. They went out upon charter, carrying with them the laws and enjoying the protection of the mother country.'[208] Any deviation from this Roman model was believed to threaten the survival of Britain's empire. William Barron, Professor of Ancient History at St Andrew's, suggested that the Romans had repudiated Greek-style colonization precisely because they feared that the 'prosperity and power' of their distant colonies might ultimately lead them to contest 'the dignity and authority of the parent state', as had the colonies of Tyre (Carthage), Phocaea (Marseille) and Corinth (Syracuse).[209]

Ultimately, however attentive they were to history, many writers were forced to admit that it had failed them. Examples drawn from antiquity, 'can never answer the present occasion'[210] because the settlement of North America 'was undertaken from motives, and attended with circumstances, perfectly singular and dissimilar to the views which influenced colonization in the more early ages of the world'.[211] The biggest difference, of course, was that Britain's were distant commercial colonies.[212] This, surely, explains why the chapter entitled 'Precedents respecting colonies' in James Burgh's 1,500 page source book of commonwealth themes and texts filled only three pages.[213]

strife (Priestley, 'The Present State of Liberty', *Works*, xxii, p. 381; Graham, *Colony*, pp. 10ff; Thucydides, *Peloponnesian War*, 1.24ff, 1.60.1, 1.60.66).

[208] *Proceedings and Debates*, 3 February 1766, ii, p. 138.

[209] William Barron, *History of the Colonization*, p. 119.

[210] Anon., *Application of Some General Political Rules*, p. 82.

[211] Anon., *A Letter to the Right Hon. the Earl of Hillsborough, on the Present Situation of Affairs in America* (London, 1769), p. 3.

[212] Samuel Estwick, *A Letter to the Rev. Josiah Tucker* (London, 1776), pp. 92–3; Richard Bland, *An Enquiry into the Rights of the British Colonies* (Williamsburg; rpt, London, 1769), pp. 11–12.

[213] James Burgh, *Political Disquisitions* 3 vols. (London, 1774–5), ii, pp. 299–301. James Otis explained, in his section entitled 'Of Colonies in General', that 'This subject has never been very clearly and fully handled by any modern writer that I have had the good fortune to meet with, and to do it justice would require much greater abilities than I pretend to, and more leisure than I ever expect will fall to my share. Even the English writers and lawyers have either entirely waived any consideration of the nature of *colonies* or very lightly touched upon it, for the people of England never discovered much concern for the prosperity of the *colonies* till the Revolution; and even now some of their great men and writers, by their discourses of and conduct towards them, consider them all rather as a parcel of *little insignificant conquered islands* than as a very extensive settlement on the continent. Even their law books and very dictionaries of law, in editions so late as 1750, speak of the *British* plantations abroad as consisting chiefly of islands' (*The Rights of the British Colonies* (2nd edn, London, 1764), pp. 35–6).

JAMES ABERCROMBY AND THOMAS POWNALL

The years immediately following the Treaty of Paris were ones of domestic and international political turmoil. The specific disputes between the metropolis and her North American colonies generated a range of responses from a variety of quarters. Among the cadre of those worthy of being called imperial experts, men who had served as officials in both the British and North American colonial infrastructure and understood all aspects of the relationship, the writings of James Abercromby (1707–75) and, especially, Thomas Pownall (1722–1805) must be singled out. Not only do they indicate the extent of a life-long attempt to understand the functioning of empire, but, precisely because of their authors' acuity, they also sharply delineate the available alternatives. Abercromby, like Archibald Kennedy and Henry McCulloh, all of whom were Scotsmen, wrote about the need to reform the bases of imperial obligation in the early 1750s.[214] But only at the end of the crisis, in 1774, did he complete his major work on obligation. Interestingly, he chose to pursue contemporary problems through an historical examination of ancient colonization despite the difficulties others had encountered with this approach. To the extent that Abercromby made history serve a political argument, he is an heir of much Renaissance political writing. Thomas Pownall, on the other hand, may have begun, as Caroline Robbins and Jonathan Clark have observed, from some 'neo-Harrington' premise, but it was his experience as a provincial governor which gave purpose to his political writings. Pownall's commitment to the shape of the post-war world led him to redesign the political relationship between Britain and the colonies to suit the times. His recognition of the necessity of bringing theory into conformity with changes in the world is reflected in the continuous revision of his fundamental work *The Administration of the Colonies* (five times in the decade between 1763 and 1777). Abercromby's sophistication ultimately led him to demand a return to the past, Pownall's to admit the need for an entirely new theory of imperial sovereignty and obligation.

The first words of the *Examination of the Acts of Parliament Relative to the Trade and the Government of our American Colonies*, written in 1752,

---

[214] For more on the Scottish imperial perspective, see Ned Landesman, 'The Legacy of the British Union for the North American Colonies', in *A Union for Empire*, ed. John Robertson (Cambridge, forthcoming).

echo Hume and Davenant. 'Whether our American Colonies are Considered, in a Mercantile view, or through the Eyes of a State', there is no aspect of government more 'interesting to this Nation' than the good regulation of colonies.[215] For Abercromby did not distinguish between the 'mercantile view' and 'the Eyes of the State'; rather, the governance of colonies proceeded from a single, unified perspective, that of 'State' or 'Sound Policy'.[216] These constitute those principles 'with respect to the Mother Country, which comprehends the whole system of Colony Regulations, in matters of Government, as well as Commerce, all being directed, by the Grand Principle of Sound Policy, which is a kind of Law, inherent in, and coeval with the Constitution of every State'.[217]

The most popular model of the colony–metropolis relationship was actually neither Greek nor Roman, but, the family. Here, too, Abercromby was on well-trodden ground when he affirmed that 'uniformity of interest' was an adequate bond between the parts of the empire. What he sought to emphasize was dependence, deference and authority. In early modern English political thought the family had been used, most famously by Filmer, to present a model of sovereignty and obligation that conveyed exactly Abercromby's sense: 'In private life, we find that, amongst Familys, where personal, and particular Interest Interferes, all other Considerations, give way.' In political life, too, colonies tended to diverge from their parents as they grew stronger. How to make the 'Natural, and Political Ties' coincide was the central task of colonial policy, and the purpose of the charter presented in the *Examination*.[218]

The starting point of any discussion of colonization, 'whether amongst antient or Modern Nations' was that its purpose was to make colonies 'Subservient to the Interest of the Principal State'.[219] This required the 'subordination' of colonial to metropolitan interests across the spectrum of legislative, judicial and commercial matters.[220] This idiom of dependence or subordination was char-

---

215 James Abercromby, *Magna Charta for America: James Abercromby's 'An Examination of the Acts of Parliament Relative to the Trade and Government of our American Colonies' (1752) and 'De Jure et Gubernatione Coloniarum, or An Inquiry into the Nature, and the Rights of Colonies, Ancient, and Modern' (1774)*, ed. Jack P. Greene, Charles F. Mullett and Edward C. Papenfuse Jr (Philadelphia, 1986); Abercromby, *Examination*, p. 45.

216 Abercromby, *De Jure*, p. 218.   217 *Ibid.*, p. 216.

218 Abercromby, *Examination*, pp. 45, 73. Gordon Wood has called attention to the pervasiveness of this metaphor for political obligation in colonial America (*The Radicalism of the American Revolution*, pp. 157, 165).

219 Abercromby, *Examination*, p. 45.   220 *Ibid.*, p. 73.

acteristic of the debate of the 1760s. Abercromby incisively declared that the challenge posed by colonial objection to the different sorts of metropolitan regulation cut to the heart of the constitution. The issue was actually sovereignty, and, explicitly, who was to possess it:

Nothing can be more Interesting to the State, than maintaining its Sovereignty: the Moment a State gives up Sovereignty, it becomes *Felo da se*, as a State: the Question, therefore, on the rights of Colonies, with regard to this Nation, is of infinite Importance, in its consequence decisive, whether Great Britain shall give or receive Law, from her Colonies? In other words, where the Sovereignty, or the *Jus Imperii*, is Whether, in Old, or New England?

The confusing character of the public debate derived from the colonists' attempt to split the King's sovereignty in New England from that in 'Old' England in order to claim that settlers residing in the former were subjects to the King alone, while citizens of the latter were bound to King and parliament. This was clearly 'inconsistent with our Constitution'.[221] The King's sovereignty was uniform and extended over all the dominions of Great Britain.[222]

The centrality of sovereignty in Abercromby's exposition is also reflected in the importance he attached to the question of the legality of emigration.[223] Abercromby contended that emigration without royal permission was forbidden under English as well as natural law.[224] If settlement had been sanctioned by an act of a sovereign state then there could be no claiming that emigration altered the status of individuals under British law. He accused the Americans of manipulating history to provide them with support for their otherwise unsupportable and unprecedented claim of a natural right to emigrate. It is precisely on this point that Thomas Rutherforth, Abercromby's contemporary, broke with Grotius, on whose *Laws of War and Peace* he was commenting. Where Grotius allowed members of civil societies to withdraw themselves, Rutherforth argued that the common bond between the members in which

---

[221] Abercromby, *De Jure*, p. 176.   [222] *Ibid.*, p. 210.

[223] Uhmori extensively documents the use colonists made of Locke in order to justify a natural right to emigration (for example, '*The Artillery of Mr Locke*', p. 307). Hume, on the other hand, repudiated this entire account: 'A company of men, who should leave their native country, in order to people some uninhabited region, might dream of recovering their native freedom; but they would soon find, that their prince still laid claim to them, and called them his subjects, even in their new settlement. And in this he would but act conformably to the common ideas of mankind' ('Of the Original Contract', p. 476).

[224] Abercromby, *De Jure*, p. 173.

resided the cement of the community forbade such unilateral dissociation. His rationale, based on the priority of preserving the community of a shared good, surely explains Abercromby's own
position:

If each individual was at liberty to leave the state, to which he belongs,
whenever he pleases; civil society would be nothing but a rope of sand; it
would be impossible for a common good to be effectually promoted, or for a
common mischief to be effectually guarded against. Every member of the
society would be at liberty either to continue in it, and endeavour to
advance the general interest, or to leave it, in order to advance a separate
interest of his own.[225]

The colonists and their friends had made the facile comparison
between their condition and that of the Greek colonies, which, after
their establishment, owed only signs of respect to their parents.[226]
But their use of history was both selective and flawed:

Taking for their Example the Condition of Grecian Colonys, The Colony
Lawyers are at first setting out thus mistaken, in the Principles of the Law
of Nations with regard to Colonys, and it must be attended to, that from
this Error, comes all their false Argumentation, against the Jurisdiction of
Parliament, and their Mother Country over America; had they attended,
to the different Conditions of Colonies ... they had found, that the
Condition of Grecian by no means agrees with British Colonys, in point of
formation, nor Government.[227]

How had they come to make this erroneous comparison? According
to Abercromby, by relying on sources whose scholarship, otherwise
admirable, had slipped up on Greek colonies. By failing to perceive
that equality between metropolis and colony was a condition that
applied solely to the colonies of the Peloponnesian states, whose
departure was a matter of mutual consent, Grotius and Pufendorf
had completely misled the British colonists in America. Their
departure was a matter of state interest, not an example of mutual
consent. Furthermore, 'Grotius, and from him, the Colony Lawyers,
have given us only so much thereof, as makes, in favour of Colonys.'[228]
   One of those 'Colony Lawyers' was surely James Otis, whose very

---

[225] Rutherforth, *Institutes*, II.2.7, II, p. 37.   [226] Abercromby, *De Jure*, p. 185.
[227] *Ibid.*, p. 182, also p. 180.
[228] *Ibid.*, pp. 185–6. Commenting on this same argument in Grotius, Barbeyrac wrote that 'It
is well known that the present Colonies always remain dependent Members of the State,
from which they are sent' (*Laws of War and Peace*, II.ix.10, p. 267).

popular *Rights of the British Colonies* was originally published in 1764 and was reprinted many times in both North America and Britain. And Otis did cite Grotius on the ties of reverence and honour that bound colonists to their former home. Emigrants who settled a new land were, accordingly, to be considered as founding a 'new and independent state'. Otis also cited Grotius' distinction between Greek and Roman practice, adding his own gloss condemning the more invasive Roman policy of retaining jurisdiction over distant lands:

And all that can be collected from those facts or opinions, is, that Greece was more generous, and a better mother to her colonies than Rome. The conduct of Rome towards her colonies, and the corruptions and oppressions tolerated in her provincial officers of all denominations, was one great cause of the downfall of that proud republic.[229]

Abercromby's treatise on imperial political thought took the shape it did because he believed, like Hume, that a more ample historical understanding could dissolve adventitious arguments like these.

While Montesquieu had explained that the European colonization of the New World was conducted under a 'New Law', or new 'principles of policy', Abercromby commented that this consisted in the adoption of the harsh Carthaginian policy which exclusively reserved the colonial trade for the parent.[230] Having turned back to antiquity to discover 'some Universal Maxims of Government', Abercromby concentrated on Rome. For, despite the complete absence of a commercial dimension to Roman colonization, he believed that the grounds for comparison were otherwise quite similar:

There is great Affinity, between this form of Government, and that of ours. Our Colonies receive Laws, from the Legislature of this Kingdom, as theirs did, from the Legislature of Rome; Our Governors Receive Instructions, from the Crown, as the Triumviri did, from the Republic of Rome; And afterwards as Proconsuls did, from the Emperors. Each Colonie had besides the Laws of the Mother Country, Laws of their own Making, and so has ours; In each Colonie, there were, Senatores, Publici Concilii Gratia, besides the representatives of the People, And so it is, with our Colonies, under the Royal Government.[231]

---

[229] James Otis, *Rights of the British Colonies*, p. 40; the reference is to Grotius, *Laws of War and Peace*, VIII.12.5. Otis made the same comparison in *A Vindication of the British Colonies, against the Aspersions of the Halifax Gentleman, in his Letter to a Rhode Island Friend* (1765), p. 31.
[230] Abercromby, *De Jure*, p. 250, also p. 217.   [231] Abercromby, *Examination*, p. 68.

Drawing on the work of Carlo Sigonio, Abercromby presented six reasons for colonization which motivated both Rome and Britain: subduing natives and gaining dominion, preventing enemy attacks, increasing the number of subjects, purging undesirables from the metropolis, diminishing urban tumults and rewarding veterans.[232] The need to avoid focusing too much attention on Roman commerce led Abercromby himself to distort the historical narrative.[233] For surely the barest reference to commerce as a British imperial motive could not account for the widely received view of her empire as fundamentally commercial. Where Abercromby admitted a deviation from Roman practice it was to Britain's disadvantage. Thus, while Roman colonists lost their rights as Roman citizens once they left the city, 'Ours retain all their Rights as Englishmen.' Had they not, there would be no question of colonial representation, or any other manifestation of legal equality.[234] Perhaps most important for Abercromby's analysis was the Roman repudiation of the Greek model of colonization. They themselves had viewed with some distress the history of those colonies settled at a great distance from their metropolis. All had soon outstripped their parents. Even colonies established closer to home, such as Rome's Italic ones, ultimately pretended to greater privileges than they merited.[235]

The threat to British imperial sovereignty posed by the Greek model dominated Abercromby's reflections on the contemporary situation. The dispute with the colonies originally turned on 'Equality of Commerce' but they soon assumed 'like the Grecian Colonys, Equality of State'.[236] In eighteenth-century British political thought, as we will see in the debate over theories of representation, equality and independence were always seen as subversive of sovereignty and productive of anarchy. Hence Abercromby's view that 'We have to contend with the Colonys for National Superiority, in Government and Commerce; they, for Equality and total Independence.'[237]

We are now in a position to summarize Abercromby's reasons for rejecting the comparison with Greek colonies. First, it was based on flawed scholarship. There were Greek colonies that remained dependent on the parent. Second, those colonies that became equal departed with the consent of the metropolis. The establishment of

232 *Ibid.*, p. 198.   233 Abercromby, *De Jure*, p. 203.   234 *Ibid.*, p. 174.
235 *Ibid.*, p. 173.
236 *Ibid.*, p. 249.   237 *Ibid.*, p. 260.

the North American colonies was not only conducted by the state, it was conducted to further state policy and therefore without the slightest intention of creating equal states. Greek and British colonies had nothing in common.[238] If a comparison were to be made, Rome was the real analogue:

Grecian Colonys tended to weaken, Whereas, Roman, and all modern colonys were intended, to add strength to the State, by extending its Dominion; Independence, and Equality therefore, are incompatible with such Views; Grecian Colonys became Confederates, no longer subjects. The Romans, on the Contrary, whether under Kings, Consuls, Senate, or Emperors, as with us, and all other Nations of Europe, retained their Sovereignty over Colonys as Subjects, who migrate, under the Authority of the State, who emit them, not, to cease being Members thereof, but, to inhabit elsewhere, under the same Dominion, and amenable, to the Jurisdiction of the Mother Country.[239]

The primacy of sovereignty and the maintenance of dominion was the lesson of the Romans 'from whom, Modern nations (ours in particular) have borrowed Maxims of State'. Abercromby's uncompromising position on colonial taxation followed from his view that sovereignty was unitary and metropolitan and that taxation was one of the 'particular Acts of Superior Sovereignty'.[240]

Abercromby's historical analysis upheld the contemporary account of the colony as a dependent creation designed to further the dominion of the sovereign according to the principles of 'Mercantile' and 'State' policy. His description of this bond is one of the most powerful eighteenth-century distillations of the political economy of the reason of state:

... by which Policy, Colonists are bound to this Kingdom, and which comprehends the Subjects, of the whole Empire, and which must be of Authority, to direct and Ordain Rules, binding upon the whole in extraordinary cases, where the Well-being of the Universality is concerned; a Sovereign State to be subject to and dependent upon any subordinate Pendicle of that State for what is essentially necessary, for its Preservation, is a solecism in Politics; It is making the Interest of Individuals preponderate over that of the Community; And on such Principles, no State whatever could long subsist.

The 'Laws and Regulations' that European countries had enacted to bind their dominions were 'nothing more, than Political Principles, reduced into form of Laws, promulgated and enforced'.[241]

[238] *Ibid.*, pp. 184–5.   [239] *Ibid.*, p. 203.   [240] *Ibid.*, p. 225.
[241] *Ibid.*, pp. 216–17.

What the colonists were suggesting was the complete overthrow of the interest of state and replacing it with one of their own devising. But could two interests coexist within a single state?

Unlike Davenant, Postlethwayt, or other theorists of economic reason of state, Abercromby made no pretence of upholding some idea of liberty. A rigorous application of the reason of state required the subordination of the interests of individuals to those of the community. In the light of his statement of twenty years before, which fought short of the assertion that colonists ought to be governed by laws 'more strict and severe' than those of other subjects,[242] one wonders if the logical conclusion to which Abercromby had been guided by the reason of state was actually beyond the pale of British politics? Where were the 'rights and liberties of Englishmen' in this story? If this was the price to be paid for maintaining the state, had British colonial policy come up against the limit of its usefulness?

The case of a free, commercial state acquiring a continental empire separated by three thousand miles of ocean was unique. The period immediately following the end of the Seven Years War was a kind of theoretical vacuum. Thomas Pownall was its most attentive and engaged commentator. Abbattista has called him 'one of the most brilliant, acute and knowledgeable writers' in Britain before the outbreak of the colonial crisis and the only one creating a 'politico-administrative thought that was truly imperial'.[243] He immediately recognized the need for a new system of colonial policy and contended that formulating the principles of affiliation between individuals and the community was to be the central issue of the new political epoch.

Pownall was educated at Trinity College, Cambridge, before moving to the Board of Trade, where he rose through the administrative ranks, ultimately serving as Governor of Massachusetts (1757–61). His brother John, it will be recalled, remained at the Board of Trade, becoming its Permanent Secretary and playing an important role in the formulation and articulation of metropolitan policy for the crucial decade and a half between wars.[244] After his governorship, Thomas returned to England, where he joined the literary war over Britain's North American policy. His major contri-

---

[242] Abercromby, *Examination*, p. 162.
[243] Abbattista, *Commercio, colonie e impero*, pp. 326–7.
[244] Spector, *American Department*, p. 35.

bution, *The Administration of the Colonies*, went through six different editions between 1764 and 1777. He stood successfully for a seat in the House of Commons in 1767 and was a supporter of the American cause there. Contemporaries mocked his tortured style, even going so far as to translate one of his works into clearer English prose.[245] He has been seen as somewhat apart from the larger mainstream of philo-American reformist thought because he did not share their 'emphasis on the necessity of guarding individual rights.'[246]

Pownall's importance for the evolution of thinking about the empire, as well as his importance for the history of political thought, can only be properly gauged by examining the relationship between his early, theoretical writings and his later political works. For in the *Treatise on Government* (1750) and the *Principles of Polity* (1752), the latter a dialogue in which the *Treatise* was incorporated as the first of three sections, Pownall sought to describe the nature of the relationship between individuals and political societies. He saw this as a fundamental issue in need of elucidation and all his subsequent work on the relationship between colonies and the metropolis bears the shape of this theoretical discussion. By understanding the dependence of Pownall's idea of imperial sovereignty on his notion of political obligation, we may be able to understand the precise relationship between the trans-Atlantic debate and the contemporary 'radical' critique of British political sovereignty.

In the *Treatise*, Pownall set out to provide an explicitly 'natural' alternative to what he perceived to be Bolingbroke's cynical theory of political obligation anchored in 'the Idea of a Patriot Prince'.[247] For too long, he wrote, it had been 'the Fashion (for there is as much

---

245 ' ... and in his brain, / Which is as dry as the remainder biscuit / After a voyage, he hath strange place cramm'd / With observation, the which he vents / In mangled forms' ([Philip Thicknesse], *The Modern Characters from Shakespeare* (London, 1768), p. 68, quoted in John Shy, 'The Spectrum of Imperial Possibilities: Henry Ellis and Thomas Pownall 1763–1776', *A People Numerous and Armed* (Oxford, 1976), p. 38. For the polished version of Pownall, see Anon., *A Translation of the Memorial to the Sovereigns of Europe* ... (London, 1781).

246 Colin Bonwick, *English Radicals and the American Revolution* (Chapel Hill, NC, 1977), p. 165. Several studies of Pownall do exist: Charles A. W. Pownall, *Thomas Pownall* (London, 1908); John A. Schutz, *Thomas Pownall: British Defender of American Liberty* (Glendale, CA, 1951); Louis Namier and John Brooke, *The House of Commons 1754–1790*, 3 vols. (London, 1964), III, pp. 316–18. See also G. H. Guttridge, 'Thomas Pownall's "The Administration of the Colonies: the Six Editions"', *William and Mary Quarterly*, 3rd ser. 26 (1969), 31–46; Caroline Robbins, 'An Active and Intelligent Antiquary, Thomas Pownall', *Absolute Liberty: A Selection from the Articles and Papers of Caroline Robbins*, ed. Barbara Taft (Hamden, CT, 1982), pp. 247–263.

247 Pownall, *A Treatise on Government* (London, 1750), p. 12; also, p. 10.

Fashion in Thinking as in Dress) to treat, under a pretended Zeal for Liberty, the *Imperium* in such a manner as to loosen all the Ties of it, and to disunite and distract all the Orders and Connections of which it subsists'.[248] Instead, he sought to restore a 'one Whole capable of receiving and being actuated by one united actuating Spirit which is appointed by All'. To this end he looked to relationships grounded in property, roughly following, but also modifying, James Harrington's leading idea. His aim was

> to give such an account of this Impire, as being drawn from Nature and Fact will shew that it is not a mere artificial Form fram'd and made up any how at the Will of every Legislator, but an actual natural System arising by the Vigor of natural Principles from that Balance of Property, which is founded in the Scite and Circumstances of each People and their Country.[249]

Pownall's continuing emphasis on 'Scite and Circumstances' is one of the themes that runs through his writings. In the book *Liberty and Right* (1748), attributed to John Campbell, this phrase is joined to a Harringtonian analysis of property helping him to transform the language of the reason of state to a science of politics: 'An alteration of Interest; different Interests require different Rules and Orders of Conduct; and a Conduct opposite to natural Interest, tends to the Ruin of the Conductor, or the Subversion of the Interest itself.'[250] The 'orders' which embodied the various 'real interests' of a state were three: property, manners and arms. Campbell's analysis of the first order lays bare the basis of Pownall's argument: 'The first of these Orders prescrib'd and fix'd the Scituation and Circumstances of the Aristocratical Constitution.'[251]

Pownall explicitly, and favourably, contrasted power based on property with the notion of a social contract and its implicit view of politics as a series of confrontations between opposing groups or orders. Those who maintained that political society depended upon 'a mere Treaty of Alliance between King and People, and such like political parties' could not explain how an 'alliance' could be transformed into 'one Society or Government'.[252] He cited William Warburton's *Alliance between Church and State* as an example of the

---

248 *Ibid.*, p. 6.   249 *Ibid.*, p. 7.   250 [Campbell], *Liberty and Right*, II, p. vi.
251 *Ibid.*, p. vii.
252 Pownall, *Treatise*, p. 33. Also, *Principles of Polity: Being the Ground and Reasons of Civil Empire in Three Parts* (London, 1752), p. 37.

perverted politics of contract.[253] Pownall's description of the consequences of contractarianism cuts through his often opaque language and brings us back to the problematic nature of patriotism and the common good in contemporary political discussion. 'Politics', he wrote, 'are only calculated for Parties and Oppositions, and indeed were never entertain'd but by such, and in the manner that you have represented them, could never be used to any other Purposes.'[254] The 'social state' was 'the real state of the Nature of Mankind' and only recognition of this condition could prevent the growth of faction.[255]

A real community was one which shared a common interest. It would always be easy for dissident politicians to seek to rely on notions of contract to destroy the fellow-feeling that was the true bond of society: ' . . . we must know that all such Individuals as are associated under one Communion can have but one common interest; and that all the lesser Communities, fram'd upon such a one common Interest, must be all linked together under one continu'd Concatenation'. The destruction of this bond, or 'interest', implied the separation of the polity into its component interests. Where an 'Intercommunity of Right and Interest' is replaced by a social contract, there is no longer a community, only the politicians' much-talked about ' "Independency of the Powers of Government" '.[256]

For Pownall, the interests of all men were naturally 'interwoven', and he expressed this in the visual image of a landscape as one 'intricate and exquisite Piece of Mechanism' in which 'an almost infinite Number of subordinate Powers' contributed 'to the one universal Movement of the Whole'.[257] In such a polity, emigration, like resistance, was inconceivable. From a reading of Hesiod and Greek mythology, Pownall sought to give a genetic account of this 'intercommunion'.[258] After switching to the images of Newtonian science, he went on to liken the properly functioning society to a well-tuned machine[259] and to the solar system.[260] This quest for a natural foundation of politics remained central to all of Pownall's later work.[261]

---

[253] Pownall, *Treatise*, pp. 23–4.   [254] *Ibid.*, pp. 32–3.   [255] *Ibid.*, pp. 47–8.
[256] *Ibid.*, p. 36; also, p. 37.
[257] *Ibid.*, p. 52.   [258] *Ibid.*, pp. 53–4; *Principles of Polity*, pp. 76–89.
[259] Pownall, *Principles of Polity*, p. 94.
[260] *Ibid.*, p. 57.
[261] It explains why his political economy so closely resembles that of Adam Smith, and renders his thoughts about the latter's work so poignant. In his *Letter to Adam Smith* (London, 1776), Pownall commented that human capabilities and desires rather than the trading impulse, as Smith had claimed, formed the basis of the division of labour. 'But as

In Pownall's argument, individuals joined together in 'one Communion, in one common Interest' constitute a 'Society', but because they were lacking a 'natural Principle of acting as one whole, they are in a natural Incapacity of managing this common Interest'.[262] Management was the task of government[263] and its elucidation provided the basis for the two additional dialogues that were published, along with this first one, under the title of *Principles of Polity, Being the Grounds and Reasons of Civil Empire* (1752).

The interlocutor challenged Pownall's spokesman by holding up the dreaded image of universal monarchy. The 'natural' social impulse of man would ultimately lead to 'the stronger drawing the lesser into the Sphere of its Power', culminating in 'one universal Monarchy; where the Interest of all Mankind shall be under one and the same Influence'.[264] The response emphasized the role of private property in blocking this complete authoritarianism. The interlocutor's error was in presupposing some kind of contract and so producing a theory which does not differ 'so widely from Mr Hobb's Errors'.[265]

If private property was the basis of social relations among groups of men,[266] the sum total of these relations in a community characterized its nature, and the power in man that perceived these was 'reason'. As these relations were consistent with the community's 'true Nature', they corresponded to 'right' or 'wrong reason'. This latter could also be described as 'Affection' and 'Will'. For Pownall, the power and reason of the community comprised its 'interest' and 'reside where is found the Ballance of the Property in the Community; which Ballance is determined by the Scites and Circumstances of a Country and it's People'.[267] Political entities were the sum of these various natural relations between individuals and between the community and individuals[268] and could, therefore, be defined functionally, as the intersection of reciprocal needs.[269] Pownall was

some thirty years ago, I had made this Analysis of the Principles of Polity; and as I have, in the practical administration of the powers of government, found, that those powers on one hand do, as from the truest source, derive from these principles of nature, and that the liberties of mankind are most safely established on them ... ' (pp. 5–6).
262 Pownall, *Treatise*, p. 54.   263 See, especially, *Principles of Polity*, pp. 68–9.
264 *Ibid.*, p. 42.
265 *Ibid.*, p. 47.   266 *Ibid.*, pp. 55–6.   267 *Ibid.*, p. 65.   268 *Ibid.*, p. 67.
269 ' ... man requires an Extent of Communion and Interest for his Existence, which his own Powers and Capacities are not able to extend to and fill up; that is, his Necessities require the working and culturing many different and various Branches of the Community, that, altho' the Quantity of the Product of his Labour may be equal to the Quantity of

keenly aware of the difficulty in insuring that obligation to government did not result in unimpeded tyranny. Discerning the appropriate boundaries of communal power remained a fundamental
task.

That is, it cannot circumscribe its Powers and Interest so within itself, as to
withdraw itself from this law on one Hand; nor on the other can it extend
it's Claim of Communion so far over the Powers of the Individual, as to
break the Laws and infringe the Right of his Individuality; that is, as it is
circumscribed by the Obligations of the universal Communion of Nature in
general, so is its Extent limited by the Rights of Man, as an Individual.[270]

If communities could be accounted for as the sum total of natural
causes, then it followed that like all things organic there was an
optimal disposition of parts and an optimal size. Having disposed of
the contractarian scheme, Pownall presented an alternative to the
Polybian meditation on the size and success of a polity. The natural
relationships within a community determined the maximum
number of its inhabitants and their occupations.[271] Pownall spoke of
a 'natural Form and magnitude'. Just as, according to Pownall,
Locke suggested there were natural limits to property-holding 'so
likewise hath he in the same manner set the boundaries to the
Influence of a Community, as one Body, by the Limitation of the
Powers of that Body, and the Support and conveniencies of its
Existence as a community'.

Like Polybius, however, Pownall saw that the size of the state was
intimately linked to what he termed its 'interest':

This state, this point, is the Organization and Union of the community. By
this every Individual that exists, or shall arise within this Communion is
part of it as one Whole . . . and is therefore by nature and Right indispensably and indissolubly connected with it, so long as that particular union and
Organization shall continue.[272]

Ultimately, what determined whether a state would be formed of
one community or of several was the number that shared the
'interest' that was its purpose. Thus, for example, England was one

---

Necessaries sufficient to his Subsistance, yet by the Locality of his Powers, and their being
capable of taking only one direction, the quality of such Product cannot extend to the
several Branches of Food, Raiment, and other Requisites to his Existence. But he is so
constituted by Nature . . . ' (*Principles of Polity*, p. 59; also, p. 60). For an explicitly
economic rendering of this account of the division of labour, see Harris, *An Essay upon
Money and Coins*, I, p. 15.
[270] Pownall, *Principles of Polity*, p. 61.   [271] *Ibid.*, p. 61.   [272] *Ibid.*, p. 113.

state while Italy was many because in England 'the Inland and Maritime are intimately connected and interwove' so that a single interest existed. The various political divisions of the island disappeared as their interests coincided.[273]

Pownall's concept of 'interest' marked a particular development of a term associated with the reason of state and, in the eighteenth century, with the science of politics. It also served him as an English equivalent to Montesquieu's 'spirit' and to his parallel discussion of its relationship to size in the *Spirit of the Laws*, published while Pownall would have been at work on his *Principles of Polity*. Montesquieu wrote that, if it was natural for small states to be republics, middling ones monarchies and empires despotisms, 'the consequence is, that in order to preserve the principles of the established government, the state must be supported in the extent it has acquired, and that the spirit of this state will alter in proportion as it contracts or extends its limits'.[274] Pownall himself referred to 'this Spirit of the Government that vitally unites these Parts that arise within the Community of it' and insisted that this 'Spirit' had a 'duty' to subject citizens to the laws of the polity.[275]

Pownall's achievement in these dialogues was in offering a theoretical description of the grounds of a political community that could easily apply to the empire. The first dialogue in the *Principles of Polity* sought to explain the origins of society and the second the kind of government consistent with the interest of individuals. In the third, the concept of 'interest' was used to ascertain 'where that Point may be fix'd that precisely determines the Powers and Claims which the Government may have over the Individual in particular, and how far his Rights and Liberties, as such, may extend'.[276] Because 'interest' was the source of power as well as its limit, the legitimacy of state intervention could be measured by its infringement of this 'interest'.

The 'interest' of individuals implied their freedom, and Pownall's definition of a 'free government' reflected a conception of human nature that reads like a summary of the theology of Samuel Clarke and was popular with other Cambridge dons during the years of Pownall's student residence:

---

[273] *Ibid.*, p. 63.   [274] Montesquieu, *Spirit of the Laws*, VIII.20, p. 122.
[275] Pownall, *Principles of Polity*, p. 114.
[276] *Ibid.*, p. 107.

Now, as that State, whereby an Agent has within itself a Power to act according to the Relations of the Nature of such Agent, is Liberty: As, in Man, the having within himself a Power to act, according to his own Reason, is Liberty: So is it the very Spirit of Liberty, in this Body, to have got, thus fram'd within itself, a Capacity to act according to the Relations of it's Nature and Institution. To be free, it must reason; and, to reason, it must take this Form, whereby it becomes capable of Reason. To be free, it must have a Power to move or act, as of itself and, to act as of itself, it must become one, so united, and so framed, as to be capable within itself of communicating to all the several Individuals, within their respective Orbs, any one Motion of the whole...This is the true and only Liberty, a Liberty of Law and Reason: Liberty without Law is a slavery to itself, without reason is madness.[277]

In likening the community to a person Pownall also served to emphasize that, while states, like individuals, possessed many 'respective Interests', one was pre-eminent and was defined by the existence of social life itself. Just as 'this Communion is the Creating Cause of Society, the Preservation and Protection of this Interest is the End of Government'. There were other 'adventitious, collateral, and coinciding Goods' but they remained secondary.[278] Twenty-three years later, this same argument brought Pownall to agreement with the colonists' claim that 'there never existed, nor ever can exist, a state this subordinate to another, and yet retaining the slightest portion of freedom'. The subordination of the colonial legislatures deprived them of reason, will and choice. How then could they and those they represented be considered free agents?

That Being which hath not, in its own nature, self-motive power, is not an agent. That moral or political Being which hath not within itself these springs, and that cannot, of itself, act from the internal vigour of these springs, is not free. If the motive power acts from without, and if the Being acted upon has no communion in, no participation with, the will of the governing power – This government may be called, as in fact it really is, external government.[279]

An understanding of Pownall's incisive theoretical discussion of the relationship between individuals, communities and states is, therefore, a necessary introduction not only to his contribution to the colonial debate, but to the common ground shared with other critics

[277] *Ibid.*, p. 101.   [278] *Ibid.*, p. 113.
[279] Pownall, *Administration of the Colonies. Part II, Wherein a Line of Government between the Supreme Jurisdiction of Great Britain and the Rights of the Colonies, is Drawn and a Plan of Pacification is Suggested* (London, 1774), pp. 30–2.

of the contemporary ideology of the state and, in particular, Adam Smith.[280]

According to Pownall, the inhabitants of North America would have had a legitimate claim to the 'Rights' and 'Liberty' of Englishmen.[281] In the concluding paragraphs of the *Principles of Polity* he suggested that emigration 'must be an 'Act of the Community, not of the Persons own'. However, the question, as posed only theoretically in 1752, was what would happen if the 'interest' of the North American colonists were to diverge from that of Great Britain so that there no longer existed any 'Act of Community'.[282] Would a single polity still exist? In fact, as we shall see in the following chapter, this was to provide the foundation of Pownall's central argument about the unity of the 'Realm'.

Writing in the first edition of *The Administration* immediately after the war's end, Pownall declared that Britain's acquisition of empire was a 'revolution of events'. Unless policy-making caught up with these changes, he wrote, 'all that is proposed, is by parts, without connection to any whole'.[283] James Otis might have parodied Pow-

---

280 In this context, Pownall's review of Smith's *Wealth of Nations* draws out the deep similarity between the two men: 'When I first saw the plan and superstructure of your very ingenious and very learned Treatise on the Wealth of Nations, it gave me a compleat idea of that system, which I had long wished to see the publick in possession of. A system, that might fix some first principles in the most important of sciences, the knowledge of the human community, and its operations. That might become principia to the knowledge of politick operations; as Mathematicks are to Mechanicks, Astronomy, and the other Sciences.

'Early in my life I had begun an analysis, of those laws of motion (if I may so express myself) which are the source of, and give direction to, the labour of man in the individual; which form that reciprocation of wants and intercommunion of mutual supply that becomes the creating cause of community; which give energy, motion, and that organized form to the compound labour and operations of that community, which is government; which gave force to trade and commerce, and are the forming causes of the instrument of it, money; of the effect of it in operation, an influx of riches, and of the final effect, wealth and power. The fate of that life called me off from study. I have however at times (never totally losing sight of it) endeavoured to resume this investigation' (*A Letter from Governor Pownall to Adam Smith*, p. 3).

281 'We see thus, that a Man born in a free Country, of Parents that were Subjects of the Government of that Country, is as much, by all Right and Law, consistent with his perfect Rights and full Liberty, a subject of that Government, as his first Ancestors were, who subjected themselves by their own consent, as we have been taught to say. And each Individual is so vitally connected to the Whole, by that universal Spirit which all breathe, that he can no way acquire a separate or independent existence' (*Principles of Polity*, p. 130).

282 *Ibid.*, p. 141.

283 'One cannot but observe, that there is some general idea of some revolution of events, beyond the ordinary course of things; some general apprehension of some thing new arising in the world, of some new channel of business, applicable to new powers ... There

nall's sense of occasion and his language, but he did not misunderstand him:

I pretend neither to the spirit of prophecy, nor any uncommon skill in predicting a Crisis, much less to tell when it begins to be 'nascent' or is fairly midwiv'd into the world. But if I were to fix a meaning to the two first paragraphs of the *Administration of the Colonies*, though I do not collect it from them, I should say the world was at the even of the highest scene of earthly power and grandeur that has been ever yet displayed to the view of mankind. The cards are shuffling fast through all Europe. Who will win the prize is with God.[284]

In line with his earlier theoretical argument, Pownall counselled that proper policy would seek to harness the natural conditions of 'a general kind of lead in commerce' in order to fulfil Britain's political ends.[285] Global commerce had been expanding for some time, and with her conquests Britain was now in a position to harvest the wealth of the entire world. Pownall suggested that 'a grand commercial interest, the basis of a great commercial dominion, under the present scite and circumstances of the world, will be formed and arise' and this period of transition constituted 'the present crisis'.[286]

The concept of 'interest' carried the weight of Pownall's theory. Britain was no longer an island with adjunct parts possessing 'many appendages of provinces, colonies, settlements, and other extraneous parts', but now ruled 'a grand marine dominion consisting of our possessions in the Atlantic and in America united into a one interest, in one center, where the seat of government is'.[287] British ascendancy depended on harnessing the natural commercial relationships that followed from the 'general interest' of the parties involved. Conversely, the failure to govern the empire in accord with what provided a common interest would threaten its integrity. Pownall argued that, while the European colonizing powers had sought to restrict artificially the trade of their western colonies, British policy ought to be to 'dissolve the effect of all artificial

is yet an universal apprehension of some new crisis forming; yet one does not find any one precise comprehensive idea of this crisis: and consequently, all that is proposed, is by parts, without connection to any whole ... ' (*Administration of the Colonies* (1st edn, London, 1764), p. 1). Reference to 'revolution' did not appear in subsequent editions.

284 Otis, *Rights of the Colonies*, p. 61.
285 Pownall, *Administration* (1764), pp. 4–5. See also Harrington, *Oceana*, p. 332.
286 Pownall, *Administration* (1765), p. 4.
287 Pownall, *Administration* (1764), p. 9. In subsequent editions 'a one interest' was, reflecting contemporary policy, replaced by 'empire'.

connections which government would create, and form the natural connections under which these interests actually exist'.[288]

The wars with the French in North America were a contest for this leading role and its attainment the true victory.[289] But the existing metropolis–colony relationship had now to be rationalized according to 'the system which thus lies in nature' based on 'the actual state of things as they arise'. Pownall, correspondingly, opposed the new moves at the Treasury to derive a colonial revenue from the strict enforcement of existing commercial regulations.[290] He also recognized, well before the issue surfaced prominently, that only by founding the larger relationship between the colonies and Britain on the firm, natural basis of interest could the incipient colonial demand for greater political power be brought to a peaceful resolution.[291] In this respect he was more far-sighted than other colonial experts like William Knox, agent for Georgia and adviser to George Grenville, Francis Bernard, who succeeded Pownall as Governor of Massachusetts, and Edmund Burke, agent for New York and confidant of Lord Rockingham. While they suggested temporizing, equivocation and, above all, expediency as the guidelines for colonial policy,[292] Pownall sought to refound the relationship now that its material substrate had changed so drastically. But his language was his own and even as this earned the bemusement of mainstream defenders of the government, he was vilified by philo-Americans for having defended even an attenuated imperial system.

---

[288] Pownall, *Administration* (1766), p. 8. The resemblances to Smith's later work are striking.

[289] 'This lead seemed at the beginning of the late war to oscillate between the English and the French, and it was in this war that the dominion also hath been disputed. The lead is now in our hands, we have such connection in its influence, that, whenever it becomes the foundation of a dominion, that dominion must be ours' (*Administration* (1766), p. 9).

[290] *Administration* (1766), p. 12. Pownall does, however, offer a limited justification of general mercantilist principles (*Administration* (1764), p. 113; (1766), p. 28).

[291] 'It is, therefore that the people do, and ever will, until this matter be settled, exercise these rights and privileges after the precedents formed here in England, and perhaps carried, in the application, even further, than they ever were in England' (*Administration* (1764), p. 28).

[292] For Knox, see *The Claim of the Colonies to an Exemption from Internal Taxes Imposed by Parliament, Examined* (London, 1765), pp. 16–17; *A Letter to a Member of Parliament, Wherein the Power of the British Legislature, and the Case of the Colonists, Are Briefly and Impartially Considered* (London, 1765), p. 23. For Bernard, see 'Principles of Law and Polity, Applied to the Government of the British Colonies in America' (1764), in *Select Letters on the Trade and Government of America* (London, 1774), props. 60–5, p. 80. Burke, while sharply criticizing Knox for failing to argue on principle, writing that he 'is always on velvet' (see *Observations on the Late State of the Nation* (London, 1769), pp. 71–3), nevertheless maintained that expediency was itself a 'principle' (*Observations*, p. 88) and employed it to the hilt in his famous speeches on conciliation with America.

One tract was explicitly written attacking *The Administration of the Colonies*, and its author falsely, but tellingly, assumed that Pownall also wrote the fundamental statement of government colonial policy, *The Regulations Lately Made*, actually written by Grenville's Secretary, Thomas Whatley.[293]

Over the course of the 1760s the relationship between Britain and the colonies was greatly altered. In this period of political crisis, the government discovered that they were confronting a problem whose magnitude they could not have imagined only a few years before. The pursuit of power and wealth had led Britain into a war whose success was so staggering that the limited material and intellectual resources available proved inadequate instruments for the management of what had become a new kind of empire. As long as it could be managed as a purely commercial venture – and this had come to be increasingly questioned during the 1750s – theoretical issues of imperial sovereignty and colonial obligation were rarely tackled head-on. Their unavoidability in the changed circumstances of the immediate post-war period confronted a weakened metropolis with potentially devastating instability, because a challenge to the murky principle of imperial management, the existence and welfare of a common good, was also a challenge to the principles holding together the newly established state of Great Britain. The old problem of the common good in a composite monarchy was made more complicated – and more dangerous – because that composite monarchy now ruled an empire with distant colonies.

[293] Anon., *The Rights of the British Colonies Considered* (London, 1765).

CHAPTER 4

The limits of sovereignty and obligation

The triumphant 'Great War for Empire' stretched the territorial extent of the new British state to its greatest magnitude and its theoretical infrastructure to the breaking point. The making of empire illuminated many issues which the making of the state in 1707 had failed to define. The incorporation of Scotland had dismayed many of those who had hoped for some kind of constitutional accommodation; the wealth and distance of the British North American colonies made the implicit threat of a coerced union less realistic, at least initially. The importance of the colonies in contemporary British political-economic thinking was magnified several times in increasing colonial self-importance. Where most Britons believed colonies owed a great debt to the metropolis for the efforts recently undertaken to guarantee their security from the French and Indian menace, colonists tended to pat themselves on the back for a job well done in defence of the empire for the mother-country. Considerations of imperial security continued to guide British policy in the post-war years and, obviously, reflected the metropolitan view of what was best for Great Britain. Things looked different from the periphery. The frictions which seem to have sprung up immediately after 1763 reflect the colonial challenge to the metropolitan determination of what constituted their 'best interest'. While Yorkshiremen, Welshmen, Londoners and even Scots, for the most part, had accepted the notion of a 'common good' from which they all benefited, colonists had begun to think differently. Because the making of colonial policy had followed general principles designed to enhance the power and wealth of the state, the fundamental position of the 'common good' had come to bear a great weight of argument but without the well-articulated support of legal or constitutional discussion. Almost immediately after the war's end, and for the next decade, Thomas Pownall sought to offer a serious theoretical alternative to Britain's imperial policy. Reliance on a 'common good' that no longer seemed 'good' to a population that was no longer a single 'community' bound by a shared 'interest' seemed a recipe for disaster. Only a new explanation of the relationship of parts of the empire to the whole could put Britain's colonial empire on firm footing. Moreover, as Pownall was slower to recognize and others quicker, this same move to refound the empire could serve to reform anomalies and inequalities in the management of Great Britain itself.

THE 'REALM QUESTION'

British overseas possessions had grown up in a haphazard, unsystematic fashion without ever being justified. There had been, for example, no discussion of the impact of the unprecedented distance of these colonies from their parent. Continental empire held by a maritime commercial power defied any familiar recourse to ancient history. Roman *exempla*, despite being clearly unhelpful, remained more popular than the Greek for obviously self-serving reasons. And most important of all, no one had investigated the political relation between the parts of the empire and the whole. John Pocock has argued that there was no first British empire, but 'rather an extent of territories variously subject to a single head, in ways which could not necessarily be reduced to a single series of definitions'. While the king was an effective symbol of *imperium* in his kingdoms, he was less effective outside his realm.[1] This characterizes the early modern political entity that H. G. Koenigsberger has described as a composite monarchy, in which one kingdom ruled others, often quite distant, as provinces. While some states could legislate and tax without consent, for others some form of representative consent was required. These regimes he terms, following Fortescue's initial evaluation, *dominium politicum et regale* and the former simply *dominium regale*. The nature of *dominium politicum et regale* was well suited to composite states in which the ruler could continue adding provinces possessing their own legislative bodies and privileges without needing to re-orient the laws of the entire state. Where the various collected kingdoms were contiguous it was usually seen to be in the interest of both rulers and ruled to call an 'estates general' of the

---

[1] Pocock, *The Politics of Extent and the Problem of Freedom*, pp. 9–12.

entire realm. However, where the member states were not contiguous, logistical difficulties combined with the natural reluctance of
monarchs often proved decisive. Nevertheless, distance did not
necessarily block the establishment of a *dominium politicum et regale*.
Koenigsberger suggests that the problems of the American colonies
are usually studied *sui generis* but 'that they should be seen in a
European context, for they show all the aspects of the problems we
have discussed so far: a composite monarchy with both contiguous
and overseas components, with colonial problems and with regimes
varying from *dominium regale* to *dominium politicum et regale* and parliamentary government'.[2] This is precisely the entity described by
Francis Bernard, who succeeded Pownall as Governor of Massachusetts:

> The Kingdom of Great Britsin has, belonging to and depending upon it,
> divers external dominions and countries; all which, together with Great
> Britain, form the British Empire. Let, therefore the British Empire signify
> the aggregate body of the British dominions, and the Kingdom of Great
> Britain the island which is the seat of the government.[3]

Because of the extent of their self-rule the Americans effectively
constituted a kingdom within this composite monarchy. Koenigsberger has suggested that within 'the context of *dominium politicum et
regale*, the major confrontations between monarchy and assembly
were due much more often to a political offensive by the monarchy
than by the assembly'.[4] Given the web of law, charter and privilege
that held the 'divers external dominions' together, the possibility of
a metropolitan mis-step, intentional or not, was great.

According to Koenigsberger, the instability and ultimately rebellion that wracked the British empire in the eighteenth century
actually reflected the changes wrought on British politics by the
Revolution settlement. The 'break' with the North American colonies was neither the consequence of gubernatorial excess nor disputed metropolitan patronage. Rather, 'It came because the
English revolution had changed the British regime of *dominium
politicum et regale* into something quite different, parliamentary

---

[2] H. G. Koenigsberger, 'Composite States, Representative Institutions and the American
Revolution', *Historical Research*, 62 (1989), 143. These thoughts were also stimulated by John
Robertson's essay, 'Union, State and Empire: The European Context of British Union in
1707', to be published as the introduction to *A Union for Empire*, ed. Robertson, Cambridge,
forthcoming.
[3] Francis Bernard, Prop. 9, *Principles*, p. 72.
[4] Koenigsberger, 'Composite States', p. 147.

government.' The absolute sovereignty of the parliament had fundamentally altered the seventeenth-century disposition of the composite monarchy. Where the periphery had grown accustomed to the looser ties and restraints with which they had been respectfully ruled, the Westminster parliament had become more assertive and no longer needed to be mindful of colonial sensitivities.[5] Thus, while the recent establishment of the colonies freed Britain from many of the entanglements of accumulated precedent it also deprived imperial policy-makers of the guideposts these traditions had conveniently provided. Thus, as late as the eighteenth century, the Americas remained for European monarchies a *terra incognita*.[6]

The first and obviously fundamental issue was the legitimate ground of British colonization. By far the most widely made claim stressed the legitimacy of Britain's 'first possession'. William Wollaston, for example, writing in 1724, offered a philosophical justification of what was an eighteenth-century commonplace. Possession was seen to establish a claim of precedence without at the same time denying another's needs.[7] In the occasional literature, possession was, however, usually defended by the simple assertion of force and chronological priority: 'This property is that Extent of Dominion claimed by the Kings of England, by right of Discovery, and by the Law of Nations, from the Sea Coast, as far back as the land extends, and not pre-Occupied by any other Christian power.'[8] As Abercromby observed, the 'Right of the Natives was not deemed necessary' to determine questions of territorial right; rather, 'the priority of Discovery' was decisive.[9] For others, 'Discovery' had to be supplemented by possession for it to have binding force.[10] Ironically, though perhaps tellingly, defenders of the Hanoverian

[5] *Ibid.*, pp. 149–51.
[6] I share Koenigsberger's assessment of the conflict: 'My argument is that there was a fundamental conflict between political regimes and that this conflict could not be resolved peacefully because no one had had any experience of it. Many contemporaries understood its nature perfectly well; but, without experience or precedents to guide them no one was able to work out any other solution than that which eventually occurred, the complete separation of the two systems' ('Composite States', p. 151).
[7] William Wollaston, *The Religion of Nature Delineated* (London, 1724), p. 134.
[8] Anon., *A Detection of False Reasons and Facts* (London, 1761), p. 23.
[9] Abercromby, *De Jure*, p. 199.
[10] Douglass, *Summary*, I, p. 110; [Edward Bancroft], *Remarks on the 'Review of of the Controversy'* (London, 1769), pp. 14–15. For Blackstone's agreement, see John J. Jerzieski, 'Parliament or People: James Wilson and Blackstone on the Nature and Location of Sovereignty', *Journal of the History of Ideas*, 32 (1971), 102–3.

succession like Benjamin Hoadley were often constrained to argue that 'Mere *Possession* though of never so long a continuance, gives no *Right*, properly so called', in order to discredit defenders of the deposed Stuarts.[11] This dissonance between Whig constitutional principles and Whig imperial practice neatly illustrates the unsystematic approach to the related issues of state and empire.

In the mid-century decades of theoretical upheaval a strong alternative began to be articulated. From both ends of the political spectrum, writers as different as Samuel Johnson and Richard Price challenged the prevailing wisdom. Johnson's vision of the Seven Years War was of thieves contesting the disposition of stolen property with all the niceties of legal proceedings, though 'neither can shew any other right than that of power, and which neither can occupy but by usurpation, and the dispossession of the natural lords and original inhabitants'. The claims of the European powers 'have no other merit than that of a scrivener who runs in silence over a plunderer that seizes by force; all have taken what had other owners, and all have had recourse to arms, rather than quit the prey on which they had fastened'.[12] Goldsmith, in the guise of the 'Citizen of the World', declared that 'Wherever the French landed, they called the country their own; and the English took possession wherever they came upon the same equitable pretensions.' Cynicism aside, these parodies captured the flexibility of 'possession' as a justification for colonization.[13]

If Scottish writers were among the most perceptive analysts of empire, they were also its most perceptive critics. Francis Hutcheson admitted that 'first occupation' was an 'accidental' category generating a 'trifling' distinction between claims but nevertheless saw no alternative to it. In an important gloss on 'trifling', he commented that 'occupation is understood sometimes first discovering by the eye, sometimes touching with the hand, sometimes securing by any instrument, such goods as before were common'.[14] Hume drew out the dubious implications of this footnote with the example of two sets of Greek colonists claiming a town because while the emissary of the one had physically arrived first, the spear of the second had pre-

---

[11] Hoadly, 'The Original and Institution of Civil Government Discussed', *Works*, II, p. 236.
[12] Johnson, Present State of Affairs', *Works*, X, pp. 187–8. Also, 'Thoughts on the Late Transactions Respecting Falkland's Islands', *Works*, X, pa. 367.
[13] Goldsmith, 'Citizen', *Works*, II, p. 74.
[14] Hutcheson, *System of Moral Philosophy*, II.vi.5, I, p. 318. and 318n.

ceded the body of the other to the city gate. Hume confessed he found 'the dispute impossible to be decided' and the entire issue of first possession impenetrable.[15] Smith commented darkly that the 'utility' of the colonies was not clear at their establishment and remained unclear.[16] Rather than prudence and policy, he suggested that 'Folly and injustice seem to have been the principles which presided over and directed the first project of establishing those colonies.'[17] The most lapidary of the sceptical writers, Gibbon, mused that 'The merit of discovery has too often been stained with avarice, cruelty, and fanaticism; and the intercourse of nations has produced the communication of disease and prejudice.'[18] From the antipode of the political spectrum, Richard Price also denounced the indiscriminate application of possession. If first possession could be justified for North America, it also left the German descendants of the Angles and Saxons sovereign over Britain. Moreover, 'If sailing along a coast can give a right to a country, then might the people of Japan become, as soon as they please, the proprietors of Britain.'[19]

Perhaps the most acute presentation of this issue was crafted by Lord Lyttleton (1709–73), once Secretary to Frederick, Prince of Wales. In his fictitious 'dialogue' between Fernando Cortez, the conqueror of Mexico, and William Penn, Quaker founder of Pennsylvania, Lyttleton sketched a Cortez shaped like a 'classical' political hero:

Does thou not know, William Penn, that with less than six hundred Spanish Foot, eighteen Horse, and a few small pieces of Cannon, I fought and defeated innumerable Armies of very brave Men, dethroned an Emperor who had been raised to the throne by his Valour, and excelled all his Countrymen in the Science of War, as much as they excelled all the rest of the West-Indian Nations? ... Does thou not know, that, in doing these wonderful Acts, I shewed as much Courage as Alexander the Great, as much Prudence as Caesar?

Penn's riposte is drawn from the arsenal of eighteenth-century repudiations of the ancients: 'I know that thou wast as fierce as a Lion, and as subtle as a Serpent. The Devil, perhaps, may place thee

---

[15] Hume, *Treatise*, III.ii.3, pp. 507n–8n.   [16] Smith, *WN*, IV.vii.a.4, p. 558.
[17] Smith, *WN*, IV.vii.b.59, p. 588.
[18] Gibbon, *Decline and Fall*, II, p. 444, n.15.
[19] Price, *Review* (1759), p. 262; *Observations*, pp. 37, 39.

as high in his black List of Heroes as Alexander or Caesar.'[20] Taking
the offensive, Penn asked Cortez 'What Right hadst thou, or the
King of Spain himself, to the Mexican Empire?' All Cortez could
answer was that 'The Pope gave it to my Master.' Against this
blatant assertion that might made right, Penn declared that his right
derived not from brute force, but from 'An honest Right of fair
Purchase'.[21]

Thomas Pownall perceived that the question of legitimate European possession, while fundamental, was based on the false premise
of a 'vacant' hemisphere.[22] The debate on this issue among early
modern natural lawyers has been illuminated by Anthony Pagden
and Richard Tuck.[23] Grotius, and following him, Locke, had
argued that overseas lands not obviously incorporated into a state,
like wasteland, could be considered 'vacant' and claimed as colonies
by European nations, while Pufendorf had averred that leaving land
untended was no indication of cession. Blackstone dealt with three
cases of colonization, occupation of empty land, conquest and
treaty, none of which really applied to America.[24] Vattel, cited by
Abercromby in defence of English colonization, gave one
eighteenth-century justification of European settlement in the
Americas: '... by the law of Nature, it may be allowed, to Nations
overstocked with Inhabitants, to restrain others, within reasonable
bounds, and to occupy, what they cannot of themselves do, otherwise than by Hunting and living upon the wild Produce of the
Earth, alluding to the Americans'.[25] For Pownall, on the other

20 Lyttleton, *Dialogues of the Dead* (Dublin, 1760), p. 58. For more on Lyttleton, see Mary Rose
    Davis, *The Good Lord Lyttleton: A Study in Eighteenth-Century Politics and Culture* (Bethlehem,
    PA, 1939). Spanish colonialism also came under fire from Burgh in the pseudonymous, *An
    Account of the First Settlement ... of the Cessares ...* (London, 1759), p. 2.
21 Lyttleton, *Dialogues of the Dead*, pp. 59–60.
22 *The Right, Interest, and Duty of the State as Concerned in the Affairs of the East Indies* (London,
    1773), p. 29. The 'discovery of countries' by British citizens or 'the cession of them by the
    natives' are the standard paths to legitimacy (Knox, *The Controversy between Great Britain and
    her Colonies Reviewed* (London, 1769), p. 73).
23 These issues preoccupied the traditions of natural law and law of nations in the preceding
    centuries of imperial constitution. For sixteenth-century Spanish 'law of nations' argu-
    ments, see Anthony Pagden, 'Dispossessing the Barbarian: The Language of Spanish
    Thomism and the Debate over the Property Rights of the American Indians', *Languages of
    Political Theory in Early Modern Europe*, ed. Pagden (Cambridge, 1987), pp. 79–98; Richard
    Tuck, *Sorry Comforters: Natural Law and the International Order from Grotius to Kant* (Oxford,
    forthcoming).
24 Blackstone, *Commentaries*, I, p. 106. His greater concern in this passage is with the type of
    legal system binding in overseas colonies.
25 Vattel, *Les droits des gens ou principes de la loi naturelle*, Bk.I, ch.18, cited in Abercromby, *De
    Jure*, p. 200.

hand, colonization could only be legitimate if there were some act of 'interconnection with that land, such as the mixing labour with it'. However, where, as in the case of America, 'the lands were already occupied by the human species, and in the actual possession of inhabitants, it will be very difficult to show what true principle or grounds of justice, the Pope, or any other Christian prince, assumed the right to seize on, dispose, and grant away, the lands of the Indians in America'.[26] This is where Pownall's thoughts on Indian property had their keenest edge. He argued that European concepts of 'labour' and 'occupancy' were inapplicable to the natives of America. The Indians were representative of the first stage of social evolution, that of hunter-gatherers, and Europeans of the last and most commercially sophisticated. The former roamed over large hunting areas and therefore 'never had, any idea of property in land, of that property which arises from a man's mixing his labour with it'. European settlers, on the other hand, actually 'settled' and physically transformed the landscape.[27] At issue was a different concept of property: just as fixed rules of trade were crucial to a commercial nation, 'so an exact and strict observance of the law of sporting, the protection of the game, and the most rigid sanction of the *hunt* (better perhaps understood by our sportsmen than our politicians) become the *laws of nations* to an hunting nation'.[28] The results of the Europeans' wilful ignorance were 'injustice', 'impositions and frauds'.[29]

The standard, albeit purely conventional, categories of 'empty' and 'occupied' land had important consequences. Emigrants who settled in a land already occupied by another nation had to be expected to transfer allegiance. Those who landed in an occupied but politically unorganized territory would become independent colonies like the Greek city-states. Those settling in lands already claimed by their own nation, 'yet being settled on the lands, and within the dominions, although external dominions, of the parent state; these colonies remain under a certain relation of allegiance to its general and supreme imperium'.[30] Even granted the legitimacy of colonial possessions, there remained no clear delineation of the responsibilities and obligations resulting from being 'within the

---

[26] Pownall, *Administration* (1768), pp. 46–7.
[27] Pownall, *Administration* (1765), pp. 157ff.
[28] Pownall, *Administration* (1768), pp. 259–60.   [29] Pownall, *Administration* (1765), p. 162.
[30] Pownall, *Administration. Part II*, p. 25.

dominions' yet 'external' to the parent state. What was the extent of that 'certain relation of allegiance'?

The effort to determine that shape often began etiologically. Colonies were planted to further metropolitan interests, understood, in Johnson's words, 'as ramifications by which the circulation of one publick interest communicated with the original source of dominion'.[31] A citizen overseas was, by definition, 'a colonist, and subsequently subordinate to the mother country in the very Nature of Things'.[32] This followed from the 'first principle of colonization', that the metropolis would benefit from their establishment and not 'be deprived of their services and usefulness'.[33]

As we have observed in the case of Abercromby, the characteristic expression of this natural bond was through the metaphor of mother and child. This relationship reproduced the ties of obligation, dependency and protection most believed inherent in that between colony and home country.[34] There was, however, a trojan horse in the argument: children grew up and became independent. While one expected 'the love of parents and children to be constant and equal' this condition rarely lasted beyond infancy.[35] Sooner or later, the interests of parents and children diverged. Behind this suggestion lay *Cato*'s profoundly important 106th letter on the subject of colonial obligation. Individuals, groups and nations continued together only so long as there was some 'cement' or 'interest' that held them.

But when those Interests separate, each Side must assuredly pursue their own. The Interest of Colonies is often to gain Independency; and is always so when they no longer want Protection, and when they can employ

---

[31] Johnson, 'Taxation No Tyranny', *Works*, x, p. 422.

[32] Tucker, *A Letter to Edmund Burke*, p. 23.

[33] Whately, 'Considerations on the Trade and Finances of this Kingdom', *A Collection of Scarce and Interesting Tracts*, 4 vols. (London, 1787–8), ii, p. 156.

[34] While usually employed to stress colonial obligation, the metaphor could also be used to enforce colonial claims against the British. In a famous speech delivered at the height of the debate on the furore over the Stamp Act, Pitt declared the colonists 'the subjects of this kingdom, equally entitled with yourselves to all the natural rights of mankind and the peculiar privileges of Englishmen. Equally bound by its laws, and equally participating of the constitution of this free country. The Americans are the sons, not the bastards, of England' (*A Collection of Interesting, Authentic Papers, Relative to the Dispute between Great Britain and America*, ed. [J. Almon] (London, 1777), pp. 58–9). See also Hutcheson, *System of Moral Philosophy*, 2 vols. (London, 1755), iii.ii.1, ii, p. 188.

[35] Johnson, *Rasselas*, p. xxvi. Also 'Taxation No Tyranny', *Works*, x, p. 425; Franklin, *The Interest of Great Britain*, pp. 24–5. Other writers also emphasized the restraints on parents that existed prior to the child's reaching the age of discretion (see Wollaston, *Religion of Nature*, p. 162; Hutcheson, *System*, iii.ii.2, ii, p. 189).

themselves more advantageously than in supplying Materials or Traffick to others: And the Interest of the MO–C [Mother Country] is always to keep them dependent, and so employed; and it requires all their Address to do it, and it is certainly more easily and effectually done by gentle and insensible Methods, than by Power alone.[36]

The 'family metaphor' provided one perspective on the colony–metropolis bond. Closely related was that of the condition of settlement. Thus, Johnson wrote that 'it is necessary to consider how a colony is constituted, what are the terms of migration as dictated by nature, or settled by compact ... '[37] If emigration was sponsored by the government and was to the advantage of the settlers then they were to be understood as taking with them not only the privileges, but also the obligations of Britons.[38] If, however, the first settlers fled to escape the grip of persecution then one had to presume their flight from persecution also to be a flight from obedience. This argument could be used to glorify the emigrants as defenders of religious liberty as well as justify their opposition to the further imposition of British legislation.[39] The reclamation of the savage wilderness was also hailed as an example of their contribution to the empire.[40] This lay at the heart of the famous Stamp Act debate. George Grenville's vision was of a pampered child 'nourished by our indulgence' whose every stage of development had been gently nursed by the British navy at a great cost and while now able to begin reimbursing its generous parent had refused to do so. Those opposed to taxing the colonies denied any metropolitan generosity. Colonel Isaac Barré rebuffed Grenville point for point: 'Children planted by your care! No! your oppression planted them in America; they fled from your tyranny' into a wilderness which they reclaimed with their toil.[41]

Pownall's attempt to put imperial relations on sound theoretical footing also had to comprehend a logistical problem. Whether

---

[36] *Cato's Letters*, no. 106, IV, p. 9.

[37] Samuel Johnson, 'Taxation No Tyranny', *Works*, x, p. 419.

[38] Anon., *The Rights of Parliament Vindicated, on Occasion of the Late Stamp-Act* (London, 1766), p. 15. Also, [Richard Phelps], *The Rights of the Colonies, and the Extent of the Legislative Authority of Great Britain* (London, 1769), p. 9; Young, *Political Essays*, p. 36; Hume, 'Original Contract', *Essays*, p. 476.

[39] Anon., *Letters to the Right Hon. the Earl of Hillsborough on the Present State of Affairs in America ... An Appendix in Answer to a Pamphlet Intituled, 'The Constitutional Right of Great-Britain to Tax the Colonies* (London, 1769), pp. 14, 16; [Steele], *Late Occurrences*, p. 1; *Necessity of Repealing the Stamp Act*, p. 8.

[40] [Fothergill], *Considerations Relative*, p. 10; Otis, *The Rights of the British Colonies*, p. 86.

[41] *A Collection of Interesting, Authentic Papers, Relative to the Dispute between Great Britain and North America*, p. 5.

legitimately or illegitimately, as children or adults, willingly or unwillingly, British settlement in North America was conducted at a distance of three and a half thousand miles. The concrete political implications of this distance may actually have been highlighted by the improved maritime communications that had, by the mid-eighteenth century, brought the realities of an Atlantic empire into sharper focus.[42] We have noted the importance of distance in contemporary discussions. Those writers who minimized the political force of the sundering sea usually asserted the unity of 'the ISLAND OF GREAT BRITAIN and the EMPIRE OF GREAT BRITAIN' because of her present possession.[43] This only made sense for those who already accepted that the centre could determine what good was to be shared in common by a community whose legitimate bounds remained vague. But the unity of the 'composite' monarchy, 'extended polity',[44] or, to use the eighteenth-century term, 'realm', rested uneasily on its conceptual foundation. There could be no common good if there were no single community. The absence of a firm definition led to a basic question, 'Are the people in the Colonies British subjects, or are they aliens or foreigners?'[45] Colonists might describe themselves as 'his majesty's liege subjects in the Colonies' while calling residents of the British Isles 'his natural-born subjects, or his subjects born within the realm'.[46] But were these the same? Intelligent debate quickly bogged down in the welter of concepts that held a composite monarchy together. One author spoke of the consequences of 'splitting the widely-extended territories of this yet-compacted empire into so many distinct and separate states, independent of, and co-ordinate with, each other, and connected together by no other tie but that of owing an allegiance to the same Sovereign'.[47]

Yet this was a matter of great urgency. For what I shall call the

---

[42] See Ian K. Steele's important *The English Atlantic 1675–1740. An Exploration of Communication and Community* (Oxford, 1986).

[43] John Campbell, *Candid and Impartial Considerations on the Nature of the Sugar Trade* (London, 1763), p. 73.

[44] Greene defines this 'as an analytic category to apply to the far-flung associations of separate political entities represented by the early modern overseas European empires. Unlike either the unitary or the contiguous confederations of states that then existed in Europe, this new category of modern political organization posed unfamiliar new questions about constitutional relationships among the several distinct units of which such organizations were composed' (*Peripheries and Center*, p. ix).

[45] [Knox], *The Controversy Reviewed*, p. 32.   [46] *Ibid*, p. 29.

[47] [Francis Maseres], *Considerations on the Expediency of Admitting Representatives from the American Colonies in the British House of Commons* (London, 1770), p. 5.

'Realm Question' cut both ways: if settlers were 'of the realm', sharing membership in the same community with fellow citizens in Glasgow and Manchester, then they possessed the liberties of Englishmen but were also liable for its fiscal support. If they were 'without the realm' then they were freed from financial obligations but also forfeited all claims to the 'rights and privileges of Englishmen'.[48] This amounted to deciding whether the colonies were 'distinct independent States, or mere British Corporations, within the Realm and jurisdiction of Parliament'.[49] The condition of the composite monarchy led the anonymous author of the *Application of some General Rules* to argue that nothing was more 'interesting' 'than that of the relation which it [Britain] bears to those people, who are connected with us, in a secondary, or kind of dependent nature; some united, but not receiving our municipal law, others receiving our laws after a struggle of many centuries, and others willing to make laws for themselves, had they a power to execute them'.[50] Lord Lyttleton reflected the increasing awareness of this basic confusion when he said, 'The only question before your lordships is, whether the American colonies are a part of the dominions of the crown of Great Britain.[51]

Thomas Pownall dedicated his work, from 1768 until 1775, to answering this question. As early as the first edition of his *Administration of the Colonies*, the nature of colonies was linked to their status within the realm.[52] But it was only with the fourth edition, published in 1768 and substantially revised to reflect the most recent uproar over the Townshend duties, that the Realm Question came to the fore as the focus of the metropolis–colony relationship. His conclusion was that, despite the anomalous legal status of their existence, British colonies ought to be accorded the same parliamentary status as contiguous British possessions:

---

[48] [Knox], *The Controversy Reviewed*, p. 6.
[49] [Edward Bancroft], *Remarks on 'The Controversy ... Reviewed'*, p. 9. Bancroft (1744–1821) was born in Massachusetts, lived in Guiana and came to London in 1769, when he published *An Essay on the Natural History of Guiana* as well as this response to Knox. The quality of this tract may have caught the attention of Priestley and Franklin. Priestley obtained for him a job on the *Monthly Review* and during the American War Franklin employed Bancroft as his London spy. In 1777 he was suspected in an attempt to burn Portsmouth dockyard and fled to France, where he turned double agent and passed U.S. information to Great Britain.
[50] Anon., *An Application of Some General Rules*, pp. 5–6
[51] Lord Lyttleton addressed the Lords Committee on the late tumults in America, *Proceedings and Debates*, 3 February 1766, II, p. 127.
[52] '... colonies, as corporations within the dominions of Great Britain, are included within the imperium of the realm of the same ...' *Administration* (1764), p. 31.

I show that the Colonies, although without the limits of the realm, are yet in fact, of the realm, are *annexed*, if not yet *united* parts of the realm; are precisely in the predicament of the Countie Palatine of Durham and Chester; and therefore ought, in the same manner, to be united to the realm, in a full and absolute communication and communion of all rights, franchises and liberties, which any other part of the realm hath or doth enjoy, or ought to have, and to enjoy.[53]

Early in the argument Pownall tried to clear a middle ground for colonial dependence with limited autonomy but accepting a subordinate legislative status with allegiance to the king alone; in other words, giving the empire clear-cut status as a composite monarchy. In his marginal comment, Burke (for he had not yet abandoned annotating Pownall's theoretical work for Knox's more polemical, and more politically attuned, *Present State of the Nation*) attacked. If Pownall was to affirm colonial subordination 'and that England is to be the Judge, that is as much as anybody demands – but it is directly subversive of all the other reasonings of the Author. All Questions concerning sovereign rights end at last in this – Who is to be the Judge?'[54]Burke perceived that the 'Realm Question' was about sovereignty. There was a single sovereign authority in every government, and one either obeyed or opted out of the political community. From this unitary perspective, colonial subordination brought with it the other obligations of citizenship. Parliamentary supremacy could not be hedged.

In the absence of constitutional discussion of colonization,[55] such legitimacy as existed was conferred by royal commission or charter. Burke asked, 'suppose he had not done this, had both King and Parlt[*sic*] lost their rights[?]'[56] Pownall was setting a bound to 'the whole imperium of Great Britain' by upholding the subordinate rights of colonial assemblies. Burke commented that popular limits on the sovereign meant popular sovereignty and that was inconceivable.[57]

Ironically, Burke's comments ceased just before Pownall began the serious pursuit of this problem. Having completed his examination of colonial charters and constitutions, Pownall announced that

---

[53] Pownall, *Administration* (1768), p. xiv.
[54] *Ibid.*, p. 54. Burke's copy is in the British Library, shelfmark c.60.i.9.
[55] 'There was nothing in the nature of the constitution providing for such things as colonies, or provinces. Lands without or beyond the realm, could not be the property of the realm, unless by being united to the realm' (*ibid.*, p. 59).
[56] *Ibid.*, p. 59.   [57] *Ibid.*, p. 66.

he would now tell how the colonies 'to the Empire of King, Lords, and Commons, *collectively taken*, as having the whole supream power in them, have become connected to the Realm'.[58] He began by analysing the question of the motives of the first emigrants in the light of the Realm Question. However much North America was believed to be 'without the realm', the settlers could not have broken their 'communion and connection to the Realm' without the approval of the 'then forms of the constitution'. Licence for emigration was conditional on the colonists neither legislating nor acting in any way 'repugnant or contrary to the laws of the Mother Country'. As a result of this subordination, the colonists accepted parliamentary legislation as binding.[59] From the original and undisputed legislative authority of parliament in specifically colonial affairs their regulatory power was gradually acknowledged in other areas as well.[60] The slow, nearly imperceptible creep of parliamentary supremacy across the Atlantic made it equally difficult to survey the borders of the realm.[61] Pownall attributed this conceptual confusion to the 'vague indecisive idea – That the colonies are of, or some parts of the realm; but how or what parts, or whether any parts at all, has never yet been thoroughly examined.'[62]

The alternative position was 'that while they are not of the body of the realm, are no parts or parcel of the same, but bodies corporate and politick, distinct from and without the realm' they remained legally bound by its decisions.[63] The Declaratory Act, with its affirmation of crown supremacy and colonial subordination, was said to reflect this idea of the relationship. Lord Mansfield argued that 'No distinction ought to be taken between the authority of parliament, over parts within or without the realm' because it was an accepted rule that parliament 'had a right to bind parts without the realm'.[64] To Pownall's way of viewing the question, however, those who felt the need to assert the unity of a sovereign possessing force throughout the realm merely begged the question. That there was a sovereign did not explain how territories outside the realm, and therefore separate communities, were still subject to that one sovereign.[65]

The precedent provided by the earliest overseas colonization

---

[58] *Ibid.*, p. 119.   [59] *Ibid.*, pp. 119–20.   [60] *Ibid.*, p. 127.   [61] *Ibid.*, p. 128.
[62] *Ibid.*, p. 128.   [63] *Ibid.*, p. 129.
[64] Lord Mansfield, 3 February 1766, *Proceedings and Debates*, II, p. 130.
[65] Pownall, *Administration* (1768), pp. 130–1.

clearly ruled out the possibility of uniting colonies to the realm or subjecting them to parliamentary jurisdiction 'without their express consent'.[66] Thus, the original charter of the Virginia Company affirmed its existence 'without the Realm' and expressly denied parliamentary competence, admitting dependence only on those named in the patents.[67] But, warned Pownall, if the colonists were not considered within the realm but yet were subject to King, Lords and Commons as sovereign, Britain stood revealed as masters of colonial subjects, not governors of citizens. If this was unacceptable, the alternative, to consider the colonists 'by birthright, by nature or by establishment' of the Realm, and thus entitled to the rights and privileges of Englishmen, did not seem to bother most writers on the subject. Much more common was the assertion that being a subject entailed obedience, plain and simple:

Natural allegiance is such as is due from all men born within the king's dominions immediately upon their birth. For, immediately upon their birth, they are under the king's protection; at a time, too when (during their infancy) they are incapable of protecting themselves. Natural allegiance is therefore a debt of gratitude; which cannot be forfeited, cancelled, or altered by any change of time, place, or circumstance, nor by anything but the united concurrence of the legislature.[68]

Johnson considered the colonies as 'constituent parts of the British Empire' and therefore subject to parliament.[69] William Knox also saw one community, bound by ties of obligation and protection but not rights.[70]

The reciprocal ties of membership in the realm, or shared community, were only visible from the centre; the rhetoric of community failed to comprehend the diversity of actual aspirations. Hence, 'the colonies must now consider themselves as a part inseparable from the grand body of the British empire . . .'[71] Abercromby contended that it was precisely because the colonies were 'out of the Realm' that they required a greater 'degree of Jurisdiction, than People incorporated within the Realm of England'.[72]

Pownall recognized that Britain was inescapably caught on the horns of a dilemma of her own making and given immediacy by the

---

[66] [Bancroft], *Remarks on 'The Controversy . . . Reviewed'*, p. 83.   [67] *Ibid.*, p. 17.
[68] Blackstone, *Commentaries*, I, p. 369; also, p. 370.
[69] Samuel Johnson, 'Taxation No Tyranny', *Works*, x, p. 425.
[70] Knox, *The Interest of the Merchants and Manufacturers of Great Britain, in the Present Contest with the Colonies* (London, 1774), p. 2.
[71] Anon., *Application of Some General Rules*, p. 77.   [72] Abercromby, *De Jure*, p. 211.

Seven Years War. The thrust of this dialectical twist put the fundamental rights of individual citizens into conflict with the claims of the community as a whole. The issue is,

whether this sovereign can disfranchise subjects, so circumstanced, of their rights because they are settled beyond the territorial limits of the realm; whether these subjects, thus circumstanced can, because they are supposed not to be of the realm, lose that interest in the legislative power, which they would have had if they were of, or within the realm. – Whether this natural right which they have to personal liberty, and to political freedom is inherent in them 'to all intents and purposes, as tho' they had been born within the realm:' Or whether 'it is to be understood, with very many and *very great* restrictions'. Whether these people, from the nature of these inherent rights and liberties, are intitled to have, and have a right to require a constitution of the same political liberty as that which they left; or whether 'the whole of their constitutions are liable to be new modeled and reformed,' – at the will of this sovereign.[73]

Pownall believed that a modification of the existing thinking on the composite character of the British realm, recognizing the implications for the political and legal status of its inhabitants, was the natural conclusion to be drawn from his analysis of the Realm Question.[74]

Did political rights and liberties reside in an affiliation with a geographically based community or did they inhere in all men? Although Pownall did not push this particular point, another writer did force the dichotomy between rights generated by membership within a realm and rights of men valid in all places and at all times, though only in order to discredit it. 'That the natural rights of mankind should give any people a right to all the liberties and privileges of Englishmen, is, I believe, a doctrine unknown to all civilians, except the assembly of Pennsylvania.' Natural rights would provide the citizen of the world with the kind of liberties now enshrined only in the British constitution. Knox obviously thought it absurd that 'The native Indians in North America, the Hottentots at the Cape of Good Hope, the Tartars, Arabs, Cafres, and Greenlanders, will all have an equal title to the liberties and rights of

---

[73] Pownall, *Administration* (1768), p. 132.
[74] 'Every subject, born within the realm, under the freedom of the government of Great Britain, or by adoption admitted to the same, has an essential indefeasible right to be governed, under such a mode of government as has the unrestrained exercise of all those powers, which form the freedom and rights of the constitution' (*ibid.*, p. 71).

Englishmen, with the people of Pennsylvania; for all their constitutions of government are founded on the natural rights of mankind.'[75]

Thus, one of the implications of the Realm Question was to prize liberty apart from affiliation with a specific community and to consider it as a property of all men. Through the Realm Question the politics of colonial obligation resolved into an investigation of the foundation of political obligation and, even more specifically, the balance of power between individual and community. As long as Britain exercised sovereignty over territories not part of the realm, the inhabitants would believe they had 'a right to raise these questions; and that it is their duty to struggle in the cause, which is to decide them'.[76] The basic issue is familiar from debate about the post-Reformation state: *who* was to determine the content of that good which individuals held in common and which, therefore, created that community whose survival and prosperity remained the responsibility of government.

Pownall had warned against selective colonial obedience to British law as early as 1765: '... if they once make a distinction of admitting some, and rejecting others, who shall draw the line, and where shall it come to pass?'.[77] Sovereignty remained his primary concern through this long decade; when, in 1774, he added a second part to the fifth, revised, edition of the *Administration*, he entitled it: 'wherein a line of Government between the supreme jurisdiction of Great Britain and the Rights of the Colonies, is drawn and a plan of pacification is suggested'.

In the interim, others came to the same conclusion. Because 'British safety, power and trade, furnish this grand object; Britain, therefore, is the more competent judge'.[78] Joseph Priestley also thought Britain would, inevitably, have to be the judge 'because she has the power of enforcing the sentence'. However, he cautioned that legislation without consent, as much as the use of force, constituted tyranny and oppression.[79] The source of legislation, according

[75] [Knox], *The Controversy ... Reviewed* pp. 11–12.
[76] Pownall, *Administration* (1768), p. 144.
[77] Pownall, *Administration* (1764), p. 50; the much expanded argument appears in *Administration* (1766), p. 70.
[78] Anon., *Application of Some General Rules*, p. 78.
[79] Priestley, 'The Present State of Liberty in Great Britain and her Colonies', *Works*, xxii, p. 397.

to Abercromby, was the issue: 'In other words, where the Sovereignty, or the *Jus Imperii*, is? Whether, in Old, or New England?'[80]

By approaching the subject through the colonial debate Pownall effectively showed how the common understanding of the public good was inapplicable for the simple reason that there was no longer a community of interest. What principle, then, was capable of welding together territories of diverging political wills? Only one which respected the rights of de-racinated individuals, and this logically led to a solution indistinctly described as either federal or confederal:

Every subject, born within the realm, under the freedom of the government of Great Britain, or by adoption admitted to the same, has an essential indefeasible right to be governed, under such a mode of government as has the unrestrained exercise of all those powers, which form the freedom and rights of the constitution ... The government of each colony must have the same powers, and the same extent of powers that the government of Great Britain has, – and must have, while it does not act contrary to the laws of Great Britain, the same freedom and independence of legislators, as the parliament of Great Britain has this right (say they).[81]

Preserving sovereignty while at the same time finding a way to enable the individual to enjoy the fullest possible freedom required a new instrument of power. Thus, the Realm Question led Pownall to representation. An adapted system of representation that recognized the primacy of the rights-bearing individual would be flexible enough for a political community that no longer shared a single vision of the common good while still centring in a single sovereign.

If the colonies were 'without the realm' it would be difficult to find any grounds whatsoever to assert the cohesiveness implied by the existing system of representation: 'The Colonies, from their remote distance, and local circumstances, could not have been incorporated into any country, city or borough; at least so it is said: and yet, at the same time, they are supposed to be, and considered as, within the diocese of London.'[82] The example of the Counties

---

[80] Abercromby, *De Jure*, p. 176. Abercromby had also described colonial governance in terms of a line being drawn, at p. 250. On the centrality of sovereignty in the post-Stamp Act world, see Thomas, *The Townshend Duties Crisis*, p. 3.

[81] Pownall, *Administration* (1768), p. 71. See also, *Considerations on Behalf of the Colonies*, attributed to James Otis, where colonial representation 'implies a thorough beneficial union of these colonies to the realm, or mother country, so that all the parts of the empire may be compacted and consolidated ...' (2nd edn, London, 1766), p. 40.

[82] Pownall, *Administration* (1768), pp. 136–8.

Palatine, without the realm and held directly by the crown, illustrated that parliamentary supremacy as expressed in taxation could only be bought at the price of representation. This precedent, showing that 'the nature of power and the nature of subjection must be reciprocal', had to apply to the North American lands.[83]

Pownall recognized that an expanding and more mobile population rendered it inevitable that parliament 'must necessarily at times, from the nature of things, not be an actual representative'.[84] But Pownall clearly distinguished between this necessarily interim fact and the principle 'that no people ought to be taxed, but by their own consent, freely originating from, and given by themselves or their representatives . . .'[85] Pownall insisted upon the absolute inviolability of consent.[86] It followed from his argument, that, in the words of a contemporary pamphlet, 'if the Colonies are within the Realm and Jurisdiction of its Parliament, every Individual among their Inhabitants, who is possessed of a Freehold of Forty Shillings per Annum, is thereby intitled to an actual Representation in the British House of Commons'.[87] Existing justifications of parliamentary representation were so convoluted as to be useless precedents for a colonial empire. Currently, individuals, 'although *constitutionally represented* in parliament, cannot be said to have there *actually* representatives of their own free election'.[88] In sum, if the colonies were to be considered without the realm then an arrangement that gave them a large degree of autonomy had to be promulgated. And if they were judged to be within the realm then it behooved Britain to integrate North America into the system of parliamentary representation as she had done in the case of Wales, and the Counties Palatine of Chester and Durham. 'There is no other practicable or rational answer.'[89]

If, however, the government chose not to extend 'legislative rights' throughout the extent of her dominions then it would have to

---

[83] *Ibid.*, pp. 140–1.
[84] Pownall's argument is paralleled in Rutherforth's discussion of Grotius' view that 'A state in respect of its members is a fluctuating body; some of them are constantly falling off from it by death, and others are constantly joyning themselves to it' (*Institutes*, II.10.12, II, p. 669). For both men, gradual replacement did not destroy the community, though where Rutherforth and Grotius based themselves on the existence of a compact, however primeval, the coherence of Pownall's state was a matter of the 'intercommunion of interests'.
[85] Pownall, *Administration* (1768), p. 143.   [86] *Ibid.*, p. 147.
[87] [Bancroft], *Remarks on 'The Controversy . . . Reviewed'*, p. 93.
[88] Pownall, *Administration* (1768), p. 148.   [89] *Ibid.*, p. 152.

be content with a diminished, 'ptolomaic' system of government.[90] Against its artificiality and inherent untruthfulness, Pownall juxtaposed the Copernican, reflecting the truth existing in 'the nature of things'. In a century in which Newton was put to many, many uses, here the intent is clearly to assimilate Britain's 'real interest' to what was believed the true and therefore optimal disposition of nature. If statesmen dared to look for truth 'They would see, that by the various and mutual interconnections of the different parts of the British dominions, throughout the Atlantic, and in America; by the intercommunion and reciprocation of the alternate wants and supplies; by the combination and subordination of their several interests and powers, by the circulation of their commerce, revolving in an orbit which hath Great Britain for its center' that there existed a 'real union'.[91]

In 1773, on the occasion of a debate over the future of the East India Company, Pownall published *The Right, Interest, and Duty of the State as Concerned in the Affairs of the East Indies*, and in 1774 he added a second part to the fifth edition of *The Administration*, dealing with the problem of sovereignty. These constitute his last attempt to influence the course of the colonial debate, and possess the keen edge honed over the course of a twenty-five year engagement with the issue. The frustration apparent in the previous edition had, six years later, become despair.[92] Nevertheless, Pownall had decided to offer a plan because he believed that even at this late date there was the possibility that war might be avoided if a reworked model of the metropolis–colony relationship could be hammered out.[93]

The question posed by Pownall at the beginning of his pamphlet on India was equally applicable to the North American question

[90] ' . . . the administration must be content to go on in this ptolomaic system of policy – as long as the various centers and systems shall preserve their due order and subordination: Or to speak in a more apposite idea; if we would keep the basis of this realm confined to this island, while we extend the superstructure, by extending our dominions: We shall invert the pyramid (as William Temple expresses it) and must in time subvert the government itself' (*ibid*, p. 162).

[91] *Ibid.*, p. 163.

[92] 'I do confess, as I sincerely think, that neither this, nor any other line of pacification, will at present take effect, or come into practice . . . ' (*Part II*, p. vii). He expressed the same feeling in a speech in the Committee of Supply in November of this same year, 1775: 'He said, that in the wretched commencement of this sad business, in the year 1769, he had given his opinion against measures of force, and by stating the evils and destructive consequences of such measures, had endeavoured to turn the mind of our leaders from *measures of force* to *modes of policy*; he had never varied from that line either in his conduct or opinion' (*Proceedings and Debates*, 8 November 1775, VI, p. 212).

[93] Pownall, *Administration. Part II*, p. vii.

and indicates the coherence of Pownall's approach to issues concerning Britain's external possessions. The issue at hand was 'the relation and predicament in which these foreign possessions, and in which the exercise of sovereignty over them stands with the supreme government of Great Britain'.[94] Writers and thinkers on both sides seemed to want to consider the colonies at once without the realm for purposes of representation and at the same time equal in privileges and financial obligations to residents within the realm.[95] The immediate implications of Pownall's pronouncement in 1774 were made clear, characteristically for the colonial debate, by rejecting the 'family metaphor'. Pownall wrote that when a son reached manhood the law of the parents was no longer binding, the family 'union' dissolved and the son's independence established. Feelings of gratitude and affection remained, 'but these are the duties of the *inward*, not of the *outward* man, who is the object of politics'.[96] Pownall attributed the collapse of empire to the diminution of the public world of the political community and the corresponding expansion of the private space of the individual.[97]

In *Part II* Pownall returned to the 'Realm Question'. Colonists had, in fact, been settled without the realm, but remained bound by a 'certain relation of allegiance' to Britain's 'general and supreme imperium'.[98] The colonists claimed that 'there never existed, nor ever can exist, a state this subordinate to another, and yet retaining the slightest portion of freedom'. Pownall responded by setting forth a theory of individual sovereignty making the same argument associated more famously with Richard Price:

That Being which hath not, in its own nature, self-motive power, is not an agent. That moral or political Being which hath not within itself these springs, and that cannot, of itself, act from the internal vigour of these springs, is not free. If the motive power acts from without, and if the Being

---

94 Pownall, *E. Indies*, p. 12.
95 '... although offsprings and still British subjects yet as external dominions dissevered and distinct from that organized body, which is called the Kingdom of Great Britain' (*Administration. Part II*, p. 11).
96 *Ibid.*, p. 16.
97 The termination of the 'union' between parent and child marked a watershed in Pownall's thought. Only a year earlier, in his pamphlet on India, he was invoking the familiar idea of commercial union. People were beginning 'to view those Indian affairs, not simply as beneficial appendages connected to the empire, but from the participation of their revenues being wrought into the very composition and frame of our finances; from the commerce of that country being indissolubly interwoven with our whole system of commerce ...' (*E. India*, p. 10).
98 Pownall, *Administration. Part II*, p. 25.

acted upon has no communion in, no Participation with, the will of the governing power – That government may be called, as in fact it really is, external government.[99]

Pownall's repudiation of the social contract in his *Treatise* and *Principles of Polity* left him without the apparatus conventionally employed to generate natural rights. Instead, Pownall's politics were based on a vision of common interest, and his view of persons on a naturalistic account that was seen to reflect Samuel Clarke's metaphysical adaptation of Newton. Similarly, Richard Price's definitions of liberty diverged significantly from the Grotian account restated by Montesquieu because of his reliance on the moral psychology of Samuel Clarke. Price defined 'physical liberty' as the principle of 'self-determination, which constitutes us Agents; or which gives us a command over our actions, rendering them properly ours, and not effects of the operation of any foreign cause'. Civil liberty was, therefore, the power of a community to govern itself 'without being subject to any foreign discretion, or to the impositions of any extraneous will or power'. Civil liberty was lacking when a community was governed 'by some will independent of it . . .'[100]

Colonies neither entirely internally governed nor entirely externally governed were ruled by 'colonial government'.[101] This status amounted to internal autonomy without international sovereignty, offering the colonists everything they demanded except equal standing as a political community. The minimal form of imperial subordination was no longer to consist in commercial regulation, but 'a peculiar state or organization'.[102] The independence of 'colonial government' was squared with the principle of the 'Declaratory Act' through another metaphor borrowed from the imagery of theological Newtonianism.[103]

---

[99] *Ibid.*, p. 32. The passage, in fact, follows a similarly pointed citation from Wollaston's *Religion of Nature Delineated*, itself, as will be observed in the following chapter, a key work in the trajectory that descended from Samuel Clarke to Price and Burgh.

[100] Price, *Observations*, p. 4.

[101] In so far as the metropolis 'respects the acts of the colony operating within its own jurisdiction, on its own body, and in matters respecting its rights only, [it] is *internal* and as such, absolute and sovereign. It is, so far as respects its own jurisdiction, within its own community, national, though not independent. It cannot be independent, because so far as it is a part (under a peculiar state of organization) of the whole empire of Great Britain, it is subordinate' (*Administration. Part II*, p. 36).

[102] *Ibid.*, p. 52.

[103] 'In like manner as the Supreme Being, in the moment that he creates a free-agent, does in that moment, and in that instance, necessarily create limits to his own absolute omnipotence, which *cannot act as an efficient on this free agency: So does the constitution of Great Britain*,

Having first defined 'colonial government', Pownall noted that territories which neither fell under that rubric nor were part of the realm of Great Britain were in fact 'externally ruled'. Pownall proceeded to note that if such colonies impeded the functioning of government, they could be downgraded still further to the status of 'Provinces'. These were governed 'by external or provincial government, which is force'.[104] Such a 'provincial system' was actually sketched out by the author of *The Constitutional Right of the Legislature of Great Britain, to Tax the British Colonies in America*.[105] Abercromby, deeply opposed to colonial 'independency' had explicitly declared that colonies were 'void of Sovereignty' and 'cannot with Propriety be called States, but Provincial Governments'.[106] This status implied, for Abercromby as for Pownall, not merely lack of sovereignty but legal subordination.[107] This followed Pufendorf's definition of provinces as 'the appendages of other states, having no kind of sovereign authority in themselves'.[108]

Harrington, with whose work Pownall shows more than a passing familiarity had used 'provincial empire' to describe the commonwealth's holdings that were not 'national or independent'. Provinces were, therefore, dependent by definition, and were retained in this condition by the metropolis building an artificial 'dominion' (see chapter 3). Whereas the equality of an independent government relied on a relation between property-holding and political power, provincial rule explicitly and necessarily violated this precept. For, once the provincials held the balance of power, their government would become independent of metropolitan control. The Mamelukes in Egypt, the Venetians on the *terraferma* and the Spanish in America provided illustrations of this kind of governance.[109] While Roman provinces were governed by Roman magistrates and had a

---

actuated by the King, in the moment that it creates communities, *having political liberty*, limit and bound its own supremacy' (*ibid.*, p. 49).

[104] Pownall, *Administration. Part II* pp. 38–40. Newly found terminological clarity appeared in his pamphlet on India as well (*E. India*, p. 20). Similarly, in his *Letter to Burke*, Tucker had claimed that the colonies wished 'to be an empire by itself and to be no longer the Province of another' (p. 42).

[105] Anon., *The Constitutional Right of the Legislature of Great Britain, to Tax the British Colonies in America* (London, 1765), p. 12. Contemporary writers also defined 'provinces' as subordinate; see Matthew Whelock, *Reflections Moral and Political on Great Britain and her Colonies* (London, 1770), p. 52; Anon., 'Appendix', *A Letter to the Right Hon. the Earl of Hillsborough*, p. 89.

[106] Abercromby, *De Jure*, p. 211.   [107] *Ibid.*, p. 215.

[108] Pufendorf, *Law of Nature*, vii.v.16, p. 185.

[109] Harrington, *Oceana*, pp. 167–8.

definite administrative structure, the specific shape of a provincial government could alter 'according unto the merit and capacity of a conquered people'.[110] Harrington's discussion of the various Roman changes to the government of Macedonia following a succession of revolts indicated that provincial status, their final condition, was considered a punishment for those deemed incapable of self-rule.[111] If Pownall's understanding of provincial status may have reflected this rather disparaging view, he would surely have shared Harrington's sceptical conclusion: 'As whether such a course be lawful, whether it is feasible and, seeing that the Romans ruined upon that point, whether it would not be unto the destruction of that commonwealth.'[112]

Provincial rule held great risks. The dangers to the metropolis implicit in its imposition concerned the anonymous *Letter to the Right Hon. the Earl of Hillsborough*: 'I will venture to lay it down as an infallible maxim that any kingdom that adopts a system of provincial government, such as that which you have proposed, and which renders one part of the community the vassals of the other, will thereby accellerate [*sic*] its own ruin.'[113] For the colonies, too, this new status was ominous. Becoming a province meant the end of a people's existence as an identifiable group. This was the point stressed by Thomas Rutherforth in precisely the terms that were to be used in the 1770s. To the question 'when does the state cease?', he had answered that the violation of the social compact, whether by the elimination of all compacting members, the enslavement of every member of society or their dispersion, effectively terminated the existence of the state. He added a fourth cause: 'a state will cease, if it is subjected as a province to another state' because it was then deprived of an autonomous will. Thus, if the colonies were to be considered as provinces it would imply the end of their distinct corporate status as 'dominions' within the realm. They would be stripped of any local privilege or right and be ruled directly by a sovereign and unchecked parliament. The establishment of 'provincial' government would have been seen as a change in the constitutional base of the composite state.

A look at Grotius' discussion of this issue illuminates some of the more shadowy implications of Rutherforth's comments. Grotius had argued that 'The Frame and Constitution of the Body is dissolved and broken' when subjects separated either by agreement or by

---

[110] *Ibid.*, p. 325.   [111] *Ibid.* p. 327.   [112] *Ibid.*, p. 328.
[113] Anon., 'Appendix', *A Letter to Right Hon. the Earl of Hillsborough*, p. 112.

force. At this point, that 'Body' lost its distinct and possibly autonomous status. But, just as he had elsewhere argued that royal alienation only affected the people as a collective, here, too, the dissolution of distinct political status did not immediately affect considerations of 'personal liberty':

> The Form of a People is gone when they lose all or some of those Rights they had in common; and this is done, either when every single Person is brought into Slavery ... Or when, tho' they retain their personal Liberty, they are yet utterly deprived of the Right of Sovereignty. So Livy tells us, that the Romans were willing that Capua should be incorporated as a Town, but that there should be no Corporation, no Senate, no Common-Council, no Magistrates, no Jurisdiction, but a dependent Multitude, and that a Governor should be sent from Rome, to dispense Justice among them.[114]

Sceptical writers attacked the colonists and their British supporters for describing the measures adopted over the course of the post-war decade as 'slavery'. Recourse to words like 'liberty' and 'slavery' was deemed hyperbolic. Personal liberty could exist in the absence of 'Senate', 'Common-Council' or 'Magistrates'. Yet even writers of this opinion, including Grotius, had recognized that 'personal liberty' could not be long secured under such conditions. When the spectre of 'provincial' government and dissolution of the community was invoked, the threat of tyranny, however, unintentional and hedged, lurked in the margins.

Because Pownall believed that provincial rule was inherently unjust, he saw only two alternatives, one amounting to incorporation along the lines of 1707, and the other an ambiguous independence without its substance. The option of federation and imperial representation seems to have disappeared: 'either the Colonies be admitted into the Parliament of Great Britain by a general *British Union*; or that they have a *Parliament of their own under an American Union*'.[115] The pursuit of a common good by a sovereign parliament had helped give legitimacy to the new British state, but without

---

[114] Grotius, *Laws of War and Peace*, ii.9.6, p. 265.

[115] Pownall, *Administration. Part II* p. 82. While not resorting to the terminology of the Realm Question, the essence of Smith's attack on British colonial policy was that the colonies were never part of the empire. Because they refused to contribute to the common purse they were 'a sort of splendid and showy equipage of empire'. Beyond this, their relationship was overestimated by the government. 'This empire, however, has hitherto existed in imagination only. It has hitherto been, not an empire, but the project of an empire' (*WN*, v.iii, p. 947).

addressing some of the basic issues raised by the process of creating a consolidated entity out of constituent monarchies. This problem was further complicated by the equivocal status of powerful but distant colonies. To what extent could their interests be assimilated to those of the island community whose good continued to dominate imperial policy-making? The demand for a reformed representation came from those who wished to secure the state but were uncomfortable about the consequences of an indisputable parliamentary supremacy. Only by finding a means to re-establish a common, shared good, whether by direct representation or by federal representation, could, they argued, the claims of sovereignty and obligation be balanced more equitably.

REPRESENTING INDIVIDUALS

The cost of war and the decision to establish permanent garrisons in North America made imperative financial and military, as well as administrative, rationalization: 'The Circumstances of the Times, the Necessities of this Country, and the Abilities of the Colonies, concur in requiring an *American* Revenue.'[116] The various measures of the Grenville government, the Currency, Sugar, and especially the Stamp Act, reflect the conjunction of both older demands for rationalization of imperial governance and immediate post-war necessity.[117]

In his 'Address to Protestant Dissenters' (1774) Priestley described the Stamp Act crisis as a 'fatal period' in British constitutional history because it overthrew the system of 'different realms subject to the same king'.[118] Previously, it had been a 'fundamental maxim' 'that though all the kings of this country, since the conquest, have had several *realms*, or principalities subject to them, each has always had its separate legislative body, its separate laws, and its separate system of taxation'. The institution of this tax, according to Priestley, confounded 'the first and fundamental ideas belonging to the system of *different realms subject to the same king*, and even

---

[116] Whately, *Regulations Lately Made*, p. 56. See Thomas *Stamp Act Crisis*, p. 37; Marshall, 'The British Empire', p. 202; Shy, *Toward Lexington: The Role of the British Army in the Coming of the American Revolution* (Princeton, 1965), pp. 45–83.
[117] For comment on their terms see Tucker and Hendrickson, *Fall of the First British Empire*, p. 115; Langford, *A Polite and Commercial People*, p. 359; Dickerson *Navigation Acts*, p. 52; Knollenberg, *Origins of the American Revolution*, p. 164.
[118] Priestley, *Works*, xxii, p. 493.

introduced *a language quite new to us*, viz., that of *America being subject to England*. For America was never thought to be within the realm of England, any more than Scotland or Ireland.'[119]

In Pownall's conceptual analysis the issue of representation had followed naturally from the Realm Question. So, too, in the tangled political history of the period. Thus, in the critical Commons debates on the repeal of the Stamp Act, in January and February 1766, Chatham's defence of representation relied upon at least a working definition of the realm. As with Pownall, the example of the counties Palatine, Chester and Durham was brought to show the precedent for extending parliamentary representation prior to parliamentary taxation.[120] If residing within the realm, then even if not possessing the capacity to vote, colonists were considered as 'inhabitants, and, as such, are virtually represented. Many have it in their option to be actually represented.' The problem was that even 40s freeholders in North America were unable to vote.[121] The colonial claim was that as long as 'their remote Situation and other Circumstances render it impracticable, they should be represented but in their respective subordinate Legislatures' since Parliament had never before taxed 'other of the Subjects without the Realm'.[122] Attorney General Philip Yorke declared that what was being demanded of Britain made him 'alarmed for the vital principle of your Empire, the sovereignty of this country'.[123] The fundamental issues raised in this debate, the extent of the realm and the limit of sovereignty and representation, indicate the acuity of the challenge posed to the basis of the new British state.

Sovereignty and obligation were linked by the problematic notion of a community of interests. The reciprocal obligations and benefits of the colonial tie were explicitly recognized.[124] The power to tax was a token of sovereign power and brooked little dissent. Hence, 'The whole matter in dispute between Great Britain and her colonies may be reduced to a single point – The right of taxation – The power of disposing of the property of all his Majesty's subjects in

---

[119] Priestley, 'Present State of Liberty', *Works*, XXII, pp. 492–3.
[120] *Proceedings and Debates*, 14 January 1766, II, p. 88.
[121] *Ibid.*, II, p. 89. [122] *Proceedings and Debates*, 27 January 1766, II, p. 109.
[123] *Ibid.*, 3 February 1766, II, p. 139.
[124] [Joshua Steele], *An Account of a Late Conference on the Occurrences in North America* (London, 1766), p. 16.

America.'[125] Those who shared this metrocentric interpretation of the common good viewed the colonies as dependent and subordinate, defended parliament's power to tax, and characterized the Americans' reluctance as a symptom of incipient rebellion:

> Has not every nation a right to colonize? – The plantation of the whole earth is a proof of it. – The practice of all nations, ancient, and modern, confirm it. – Can subjects of a state, transplanting themselves voluntarily; continuing under its influence and authority; governed by its laws; and protected by its power: be said to be slaves, any more than when they were in the bosom of their mother country?[126]

When, on the other hand, James Otis sought to dispute parliament's authority he struck at this received metrocentric commitment to prudence and imperial security. Parliamentary approval, understood as the consent 'of all men within the realm' was a necessary prerequisite to taxation.[127] In the even tones of the preface to the second volume of *Crito*, Burgh recommended that future imperialists not follow Britain's lead and 'lay greedy and all-grasping hands on their pittance; do not rashly tax those, who have no representative in your legislature to plead their cause, or to inform you what burden they are equal to'.[128]

What is new in this eighteenth-century debate is best perceived against the backdrop provided by the most important English discussions of representation. For Hobbes, Lawson, Locke, and Blackstone representation and sovereignty were two sides of the same coin. Their views were the targets of those critics of the government responding to the crisis of the 1760s.

For Hobbes, the multitude was made into one person, one commonwealth, when 'personated' by a man or assembly of its choosing.[129] Against the monarcomach view that government was the result of a contract between a pre-existing and sovereign community and one, or many, governors, Hobbes maintained that only their personation by the Leviathan made them into a community. 'This is more than Consent, or Concord; it is a real Unity of them all, in one and the same Person, made by Covenant of every man with every

---

[125] Anon., *An Argument in Defence of the Exclusive Right Claimed by the Colonies to Tax Themselves* (London, 1774), p. 65.

[126] Anon., *The Constitutional Right*, p. 9.

[127] Otis, *Considerations on Behalf of the Colonies*, p. 3.

[128] Burgh, *Crito*, II, p. 41.

[129] Hobbes, *Leviathan*, ed. C. B. Macpherson (Harmondsworth, 1968), I.16, p. 220.

man ...'[130] Because there was no pre-existing political community, there was no sovereign without the Leviathan, and dissolution of government was also dissolution of society. Representation, as something distinct from the sovereign, did not exist; community began with the creation of government and sovereignty rested in its authorized powers.[131]

George Lawson attacked Hobbes for precisely this new interpretation of the link between sovereignty and representation. Not only did it make no mention of reason, justice or law, but it could not distinguish between the legitimate and illegitimate exercise of sovereign power.[132] Lawson contended for the chronological precedence of community to any political organization.[133] The people considered as a community was sovereign and because their founding consent had to be 'rational and just' the Hobbesian Leviathan could never exist.[134] The chronological priority of community to government meant that in the event of a 'dissolution' or 'failure of succession' the community was considered to 'vertually contain a supream power' and therefore had the 'liberty and right' to reconstruct a government to its specification.[135] With the formation of community, 'the Soveraignty is vertually and eminently themselves',[136] and, consequently, 'The standing Subject by Nature is the community, in whom vertually it resides, and is exercised by a general representative upon extraordinary occasions, or at certain determinate times.'[137] Note that in all these passages Lawson described sovereignty inhering 'vertually' in the people as a whole.[138] This usage remained common in the eighteenth century and the govern-

---

[130] *Ibid.*, II.17, p. 227.   [131] *Ibid.*, II.16, pp. 220–1.
[132] Lawson, *An Examination of the Political Part of Mr Hobbs his Leviathan* (London, 1657), p. 4.
[133] Lawson, *Politica Sacra & Civilis. Or, a Modell of Civil and Ecclesiasticall Government* (London, 1660), pp. 10–11.
[134] Lawson, *Examination*, pp. 59–60.   [135] Lawson, *Politica*, p. 16.
[136] *Examination*, p. 49.
[137] *Ibid.*, p. 10. See, *Politica*, p. 34.
[138] The same usage is found in other seventeenth-century political writers. For example, Henry Parker, in *Contra-Replicant*, observed that 'The Lords and Commons make but one entire Court, and this Court is vertually the whole Nation' (p. 16). Even more tellingly, Halifax used this concept to link representation and consent. Authority could not be obtained by force, 'let it be never so great, there must be their consent too, or else a Nation moveth only by being driven, a sluggish and constrained Motion, void of that Life and Vigour which is necessary to produce great things, whereas the virtual Consent of the whole being included in their Representatives, and the King giving sanction to the united sense of the People, every Act done by such an Authority, seemeth to be an effect of their choice as well as a part of their Duty' ('The Character of a Trimmer', in *Complete Works*, pp. 64–5).

ment's defence in the debate on colonial representation is best understood in its seventeenth-century context.

Lawson developed the notion of a 'compound moral person' to explain how it was possible to have a sovereign community and, at the same time, a unitary and sovereign government.

> For whether the subject be the Community, or the Optimates, they must be considered as one person morally, though they be many physically: and the reason is, they must all go together, otherwise there can be no first mover in a State; for it is one supreme power in it self, and must also be in one subject; yet for the administration it may be divided: because the Soveraign doth exercise this power, and acts severally by several Officers, which are but instruments animated and acted by him.[139]

According to Lawson, Hobbes' incorrect notion of sovereignty had led him to an erroneous notion of representation: 'The word Representative, he either doth not understand, or if he do, he intolerably abuseth his unwary and unlearned Reader by that term.' A representative was simply a delegate having a power to act which was conveyed by the possessor of authority.[140]

Disputes about Lawson's place between Hobbes and Locke have not challenged the latter's dependence on Lawson's theory of community sovereignty.[141] For Locke, precisely because the legislative constitutes 'only a Fiduciary Power to act for certain ends, there remains still in the People Supream Power to remove or alter the Legislative, when they find the Legislative act contrary to the trust reposed in them'.[142] The community established a government whose legitimacy derived from a free act of popular consent. In the absence of such consent one was a slave.[143] Such abuse of the power entrusted to the community's representatives resulted in its loss of legitimacy and the reversion of power to its original in the people.

For George Lawson and John Locke, community sovereignty (with legitimating consent) and democratic consent remained

---

[139] Lawson, *Examination*, pp. 30–1. This is the view that came to be most closely associated with Pufendorf, in particular (*Law of Nature*, 1.i.13, p. 8).

[140] Lawson, *Examination*, pp. 37–8.

[141] See Conal Condren, *George Lawson's 'Politica' and the English Revolution* (Cambridge, 1990), pp. 183–6; Julian Franklin, *John Locke and the Theory of Sovereignty* (Cambridge, 1978).

[142] Locke, *Second Treatise*, II.13.149, p. 413.

[143] *Ibid.*, II.3.17, p. 320. John Dunn has persuasively argued that Locke's 'consent' applied only to the creation of government *ab initio*, and not to the quotidian practice of rule ('Consent in the Political Theory of John Locke', *Historical Journal*, 10 (1967), 153–82; *The Political Thought of John Locke* (Cambridge, 1969), pp. 54, 154, 155, 162, 171, 173; also Tully, *Discourse on Property*, p. 173).

mutually exclusive concepts. The compound moral person that was created to act out the will of the community was an abstraction, distanced from individual constituents by several removes. As described by Pufendorf, this fictitious person was an embodiment of the state, representing its members regardless of the birth and death of the individual, physical components of the community.[144] Pownall had employed precisely this argument to justify temporary inadequacies of parliamentary representation. In principle, however, Pownall did not consider it powerful enough to justify a permanently unrepresentative parliamentary arrangement. The rejection of the existing theory of representation was explicitly directed against its foundation in this view of community sovereignty.

Locke buttressed his argument for the priority of the community by supplying it with the force of the original, natural rights of its constituent contracting members. A version of Locke's argument, but one that placed a greater emphasis on English history, dominated eighteenth-century constitutional speculation.[145] David Lieberman has persuasively argued for the importance of just such a role for natural law in Blackstone's thought; its absence 'eliminates the ethical support for what Blackstone celebrated as the single most important attribute that distinguished and glorified the system of law in England'.[146]

William Blackstone's *Commentaries* is the eighteenth-century *locus classicus* of the integration of common and natural law. He absolutely affirmed the existence of natural rights established by God and nature, including life and liberty.[147] Yet, because societies were formed and existed in order to protect these rights, its enacted laws had to be understood as having the force of natural laws. Thus, the defence of the absolute rights of individuals made them contingent upon the existence of 'friendly and social communities'. The specific nature of the individual's dependence on the community, and hence subordination to it, was made clear in Blackstone's discussion of the propaedeutic function of law. Political or civil liberty 'is no other than natural liberty so far restrained by human laws (and no

---

[144] Pufendorf, *Law of Nature*, i.i.xiii, p. 8.
[145] Martyn Thompson, *Ideas of Contract in English Political Thought in the Age of John Locke* (New York, 1987), p. 47.
[146] David Lieberman, *The Province of Legislation Determined: Legal Theory in Eighteenth-Century Britain* (Cambridge, 1989), p. 39.
[147] Blackstone, *Commentaries*, i, p. 54.

farther) as is necessary and expedient for the general advantage of the public'. Thus, laws could restrain an individual's freedom of action yet increase his liberty by rendering him more secure. Laws that encroached on personal life without enhancing its quality were tyrannical. Blackstone did, however, make one general exception to this rule. In the event that 'any public advantage can arise from observing such precepts, the control of our private inclinations' was warranted.[148] Blackstone's defence of prerogative, it will be recalled, was conducted under this same rubric.

One of Blackstone's aims seems to have been to secure the familiar and stable definition of the common good – the security of the community as determined by its leaders – against the possibility of alternative interpretations and interpreters.[149] Like many contemporaries, notably David Hume, Blackstone derided the original contract as purely fictive. A pre-social state of nature was impossible. Instead, individuals were drawn into social groups because of their 'wants and needs'. In the place of an original contract, legitimacy and obligation in Blackstone's political society, as in Hume's, were derived from the inertia of successful management of affairs. Government was never instituted by society, it developed naturally and persisted or disappeared according to performance. Like earlier writers on the politics of state necessity Blackstone saw no need to explain how this primitive government evolved into its modern version. 'How the several forms of government we now see in the world at first actually began, is matter of great uncertainty, and has occasioned infinite disputes. It is not my business or intention to enter into any of them.'[150] Like Pownall and Hume, Blackstone rejected the fiction of a social contract. Also like them, he believed that the nature of human beings yielded predictable consequences. Blackstone's particular formation is as clear an account of the post-Reformation notion of community as can be gleaned from anyone else: 'the whole should protect all its parts, and that every part should pay obedience to the will of the whole; or, in other words, that the community should guard the rights of each individual member, and that (in return for this protection) each

[148] *Ibid.*, I, pp. 125–6.
[149] Much of what follows was stimulated by Robert Willman's analysis of Blackstone's response to the perceived threat of a Lockean dissolution, 'Blackstone and the "Theoretical Perfection" of English Law in the Reign of Charles II', *Historical Journal*, 26 (1983), 39–70.
[150] Blackstone, *Commentaries*, I, pp. 47–8.

individual should submit to the laws of the community; without which submission of all it was impossible that protection could be certainly extended to any'.[151] Moreover, in accepting the implications of a contract, Blackstone accepted Pufendorf's complementary view of the state as a 'compound moral person':

> For a state is a collective body, composed of a multitude of individuals, united for their safety and convenience, and intending to act together as one man. If it therefore is to act as one man, it ought to act by one uniform will. But, inasmuch as political communities are made up of many natural persons, each of whom has his particular will and inclination, these several wills cannot by any natural union be joined together, or tempered and disposed into a lasting harmony, so as to produce that one uniform will of the whole. It can therefore be no otherwise produced than a political union; by the consent of all persons to submit their own private wills to the will of one man, or of one or more assemblies of men, to whom the supreme authority is entrusted: and this will of that one man, or assemblage of men, is in different states, according to their different constitutions, understood to be law.[152]

Still more ironically, Blackstone followed up this view of community, or popular, sovereignty by referring to representation – as had Lawson and Locke.[153] That the community as a whole, rather than its individual members, was to be understood as the source of power, also found expression in his analysis of the mandate of representatives: 'And every member, though chosen by one particular district, when elected and returned serves for the whole realm. For the end of his coming thither is not particular, but general; not barely to advantage his constituents, but the common wealth.' Consequently, the representative was not to be considered as deputized by his constituents.[154] The underlying assumption was that agency remained free despite its political force being mediated by an intervening communal body. Blackstone consistently applied this argument in his parliamentary speeches.[155] The only exception he made was to uphold property rights, but even this was defended on the grounds that 'the public good is in nothing more essentially interested, than in the protection of every individual's private rights, as modelled by the municipal law'.[156]

---

[151] *Ibid.*, I, p. 47.   [152] *Ibid.*, I, p. 52.   [153] *Ibid.*, I, p. 158.   [154] *Ibid.*, I, p. 159.
[155] *Proceedings and Debates*, 3 February 1766, II, p. 140.
[156] Blackstone, *Commentaries*, I, p. 139. One of the contemporary defences of 1688 argued that the security of British citizens (understood as would Montesquieu half a century later) was upheld by Parliamentary consent: 'We may easily think our Security greater than that of

The sovereignty of the compound moral person was then used to defend the priority of the community's common good (Locke's actual position) against the contemporary exponents of what Blackstone mistakenly believed to be Locke's heritage: the individual as sovereign. 'For this devolution of power, to the people at large, includes in it a dissolution of the whole form of government established by that people; reduces all the members to their original state of equality; and, by annihilating the sovereign power, repeals all positive laws whatsoever before enacted.'[157]

How did Blackstone arrive at such a misconstrual of Locke's position? The *Commentaries* was published in the midst of the furious debate over colonial representation. Blackstone read Locke as the philosophical justification of what actually *was* a contemporary attack on the conventional understanding of the common good, and denounced him accordingly. Because defenders of the colonial position resorted to natural rights to uphold the political sovereignty of the individual, Blackstone mistakenly assumed a continuity between Locke's theory of rights and the contemporary use. However, the colonists and their metropolitan supporters had turned the rights argument from supporting popular sovereignty to defending the individual's sovereignty since only that offered an alternative to the government's identification of the former with a metrocentric determination of the common good. An explanation of this crucial change and of the preconditions that facilitated the articulation of this different rights theory must, however, wait for the following chapters.

The crisis that began with the Stamp Act of 1765 concentrated both metropolitan and colonial attention on the legitimate purview of parliamentary taxation. Because this issue was nested within the on-going discussion over the status and disposition of the empire and that, in turn, within the broader ambit of eighteenth-century British

---

any other Nation in Europe, if we reflect but a moment upon this important Article, that we are never obliged to open our Purses, but by the Order and Consent of our Representatives, whom we have trusted with the Care of our Interest; which being equally theirs at the same time, we have no reason to fear that they ever lay any Taxes upon us, but when it is absolutely necessary for the preservation of our Lives, Liberties, and Religion' (*A Defence of the Proceedings of the Late Parliament of England*, in *State Tracts*, I, p. 214). Clearly, there was little substantive change in notions of parliamentary representativeness in the intervening decades; what was to shatter this model was the dissociation of colonial from metropolitan interests.

[157] Blackstone, *Commentaries*, I, p. 161; also I, p. 212.

political thought, its ramifications spread right through the contemporary political debate.

Speaking in the House of Commons in February 1765, Grenville defended the Stamp Act by invoking the doctrine of 'virtual representation':

> The objection of the colonies is from the general right of mankind not to be taxed but by their representatives. This goes to all laws in general. The Parliament of Great Britain virtually represents the whole kingdom, not actually great trading towns. The merchants of London and the East India Company are not represented. Not a twentieth part of the people are actually represented.[158]

The phrase was first turned, and the government's argument first articulated, by the Treasury Secretary, Member of Parliament and Grenville publicist, Thomas Whately (d.1772), in a defence of government policy entitled *The Regulations Lately Made* (1765). Despite their inability to choose representatives, the colonists, like the similarly unfranchised 'Nine Tenths of the People of Britain' were still represented in parliament. Election was simply an aspect of property-holding and was distinct from the representative consent to law upheld by the constitution. Most men, all women and children, and the great trading cities and companies did not cast ballots. Yet it was impossible to imagine *them* as unrepresented. According to Whately, 'The Colonies are in exactly the same situation: All British Subjects are really in the same; none are actually, all are virtually represented in parliament; for every Member of Parliament sits in the House, not as Representative of his own constituents, but as one of that august Assembly by which all the Commons of Great Britain are represented.' The claim that members had to answer to a specific electorate was demeaning, and substituted 'a partial Advantage' in place of the good of the whole. In other words, it encouraged precisely that flowering of private interest at the expense of the public which the apologists of state power had always invoked as the greatest of dangers. As it is, he wrote, the unfranchised residents 'and the Colonies and all British Subjects whatever, have an equal Share in the general Representation of the Commons of Great Britain, and are bound by the Consent of the Majority of that House, whether their own particular

---

[158] *Proceedings and Debates*, 6 February 1765, II, p. 9.

Representatives consented to or opposed the Measures there taken, or whether they had or had not particular Representatives there'.[159]

At first reading, the government's position seems absurd and self-defeating: affirming that a regime was 'representative' with 90 per cent of the population disenfranchised seems an unlikely means of persuading colonists to abide by the same system. Yet this very observation ought to alert us to the possibility that the British meant something very different by 'representation' from what it has since come to mean. Thus, before we can begin to reconstruct this eighteenth-century debate, we must first bridge a semantic chasm that has opened up between their time and our own.[160]

In the seventeenth and eighteenth centuries, 'virtual' did not mean 'almost' or 'nearly', but rather 'essentially' or 'in effect'. It would seem that the intent of Grenville and Whately is captured in the following definition: 'That is so in essence or effect, although not formally or actually; admitting of being called by the name so far as the effect or result is concerned.' The colonists' objection to the government's argument hinged on a very slight semantic shift. Whately could claim that colonists were 'virtually represented, but not actually' because he believed that they possessed the 'essential quality' of being represented. Yet, at just this point in time, 'virtually' was acquiring a meaning that betrayed the government. What had happened, according to the OED, was that 'by a slight weakening of the sense, the idea of simple equivalence' had become 'more prominent than that of essential qualities'. Thus, the colonists understood the government's use of 'virtually' to mean that they were represented by a system that was distinct from, though perhaps equivalent to, that enjoyed by residents of Great Britain. 'In effect, though not formally or explicitly; practically; to all intents; as good as.'[161]

Though surely complicated by this semantic change, the crisis turned on a different notion of community. The government's 'virtual representation' was tied up with a broad conception of a community that was greater than the sum of all its parts and incapable of analysis into those parts. Because the Americans had

---

[159] Whately, *Regulations Lately Made*, pp. 108–9.
[160] See Ian R. Christie, *Wilkes, Wyvill and Reform: The Parliamentary Reform Movement in British Politics 1760–1785* (London, 1962), p. 2; John Cannon, *Parliamentary Reform 1640–1832* (Cambridge, 1973), p. 82.
[161] *Oxford English Dictionary* (2nd edn, Oxford, 1989), XIX, pp. 674–5.

come to have a different understanding of the coherence of the empire and of the source and location of sovereignty they emerged with a different understanding of representation. This is the basic reason for the seeming incomprehensibility of the government's notion of representation both to the colonists and to ourselves, who have for the most part inherited their revolutionary theory. Because it described a communal bond they thought fictional, if not absolutely pernicious, the word itself gained a new meaning. The government was seen as offering a highly mediated form of representation and the colonists wanted a much more direct version. Their wilful misunderstanding has contributed to the general, but false, impression that 'virtual representation' was nonsense. Metropolis and colonies divided over concepts when they disputed about words.

Lawson had employed 'vertual' to assert that political power was *essentially* and effectively in the hands of the community even when day-to-day executive powers were wielded by individual officers. Similarly, when Grenville's government sought a word for a theory of representation which maintained that the interests of all subjects would be secured by entrusting affairs to the government, there was no better term. Every Briton was represented 'virtually', or 'in effect', because the same actions would be 'effected' even if they were neither physically present nor represented by especially authorized deputies. An extremely clear presentation of this notion was provided ten years later by John Lind, former tutor to the Polish royal family, fellow of Lincoln's Inn, collaborator and close friend of Bentham and harsh critic of the colonies:

What is it to represent a country? The Durham and Chester acts tell us, it is 'to represent' – that is, set forth, – display 'the condition of the country represented.' – Take the word in this sense, and you will allow, I suppose, that the word country includes all the country, all the inhabitants. Take the word in a more extensive sense; let it be to act in behalf, and to watch over the interests, of the country. Here too their function would extend to the interest of all the inhabitants, by whomsoever they themselves be deputed; whether by all the Inhabitants or by certain classes of them only. In either, or in both, of these senses, the House of Commons represents not barely the electors, but *all* the inhabitants of Great Britain.[162]

Thus, 'If the Americans are not nominally, they may be said to be virtually represented in the British Parliament.'[163]

---

[162] Lind, *Three Letters to Dr Price, pp. 120–1.*
[163] Anon., *The Honour of Parliament and the Justice of the Nation Vindicated* (London, 1776), p. 37.

If, as was claimed, taxation was an expression of power made licit by consent, and the form in which that consent was given was a manifestation of sovereignty, then this particular form of representation could be said to express the sovereignty of an abstract community. A British subject 'virtually conceives himself to be truly represented; because the common Interest of the British State or Commonwealth, most certainly includes the Subjects of America, equally with those of every other Part of the Dominion ...'[164] According to Allen Ramsey (1713–84), portrait painter and intimate of Samuel Johnson, 'The question which has been for some time agitated, *Whether the legislative power of Great Britain has a right to tax its American colonies?* is of all questions the most important that was ever debated in this country.'[165] Charles Lloyd (1735–73), a pamphleteer in Grenville's interest, contended that this sovereignty depended upon security: 'The first and great principle of all government, and of all society, is, that support is due in return for protection; that every subject should contribute to the common defence, in which his own is included.'[166] Abercromby, a strong supporter of metropolitan supremacy, had described taxation as one of the 'particular Acts of Superior Sovereignty, of which, every province in particular is debarred' and only the State could hold. In the context of his attack on the colonial reliance on the history of Greek colonization he used this argument to distinguish between a colony's status as *autonomos* but not *autotelos*: legal autonomy did not preclude paying taxes 'for the common good'.[167] And so we return to the political economy of the reason of state.

Within the context of the imperial debate the notion of a common good made the colonial demand for representation seem unreasonable since 'the people of North America, being all subjects of Great Britain, are already represented'.[168] Their demand was extremely dangerous, since its only purpose could be to fracture the transatlantic empire. This was Knox's explicit warning. Colonists already were possessed, 'as Individuals, of every immunity and Privilege of

[164] Anon., *Two papers on the Subject of Taxing the British Colonies in America* (London, 1739; rpt, 1767), pp. 17–18.
[165] Ramsay, *Thoughts on the Origin and Nature of Government*, p. 3.
[166] Lloyd, *Conduct of the Late Administration*, p. 12.
[167] Abercromby, *De Jure*, pp. 222–5. Of course Abercromby did not emphasize the fact that the colonies' contribution to the 'Grecian Association' (actually the Delian League) to arm against the Persians implied a confederative structure that did not resemble the British empire.
[168] Anon., *Constitutional Right*, p. 13.

native Englishmen, but they would attempt to prove themselves entitled to more'.[169]

The job description of Members of Parliament bore the stamp of the dominant view of sovereignty. Once elected, they were representatives of an entire nation. Their obligation to a particular constituency extended only so far as was consistent with the wider good. 'They may indeed support the interest of the particular place which elected them, so far as that interest is consistent with the good of the whole, but no farther.'[170] Burke's speech to the electors of Bristol provides the most eloquent exposition of the theory of representation for the common good. While a representative should have 'the most unreserved communication with his constituents' and 'prefer their interest to his own' he was not expected to sacrifice his good judgment to anyone, for any reason.[171]

Parliament is not a congress of ambassadors from different and hostile interests; which interests each must maintain, as an agent and advocate, against other agents and advocates; but parliament is a deliberative assembly of one nation, with one interest, that of the whole; where, not local purposes, not local prejudices, ought to guide, but the general good, resulting from the general reason of the whole.[172]

The government's trump card in the argument was the assertion that there were no grounds for colonial complaint since the vast majority of Britains did not cast ballots either, and no one doubted their representation. Consent, therefore, could not mean that 'no English Man can be subjected to the Payment of Taxes, who has not a Right to vote in chusing the Representative Body of the People'.[173] Soame Jenyns repeated Lloyd's figure that nineteen out of twenty Englishmen, including entire towns such as Manchester and Birmingham, did not vote for their representatives. Yet, this did not damage the legitimacy of representation. Jenyns continued, pushing his argument towards a *reductio ad absurdum*. If this was in fact, an 'imaginary Representation', what prevented it from including America as well as Britain? 'If it can travel three hundred Miles, why not three thousand? if it can jump over Rivers and Mountains, why cannot it sail over the Ocean?'[174] Moreover, according to

---

[169] Knox, *Letter to a Member of Parliament*, p. 12.
[170] Wheelock, *Reflections Moral and Political*, sig.[Alv]; also, p. 3.
[171] Burke, 'Speech to the Electors of Bristol', p. 81.   [172] *Ibid.*, pp. 82–3.
[173] Anon., *An Examination of Rights*, p. 14.
[174] Soame Jenyns, *The Objections of the Taxation of our American Colonies* (London, 1765), pp. 6–8. Also, *Rights of Parliament*, pp. 38–9.

Abercromby, however much scorn the Americans heaped on the 'legal Fiction' of representative consent, it was this which distinguished their condition from that of aliens.[175] That they felt unrepresented did not alter the reality that their status was no different from that of the vast majority of residents of Brtitain, and far better than that of other colonists.[176]

Their demand for individual voting was deemed historically unprecedented. Knox noted that 'it really is of so novel a Cast, that I am at a Loss to guess from what practical Principles or System of Government they have borrowed it'.[177] In the House of Lords, Mansfield declared that the supremacy of parliament's declared law bound every subject 'whether such subjects have a right to vote or not, or whether the law binds places within the realm or without'. In terms of the specific legal capacity to vote, Mansfield argued that the act of emigration constituted an explicit forfeiture of this right.[178] Explained another writer, 'they can have no personal right of representation in the mother-country, because they are not in possession of the particular qualifications annexed to that right'.[179]

Allen Ramsay challenged the rights argument that had increasingly replaced colonial appeals to historical and legal precedent. He denied its fundamental principle: there was no such thing as the natural equality of men. 'This principle of equal right to liberty, which can hardly be separated from that of an equal right to property, has never been *actually* acknowledged by any but the very lowest class of men ...'[180] In place of the artificiality of contract Ramsay opted for Blackstone's combination of 'desires' and 'weakness': 'The rights of government are built upon something much more certain and permanent than any *voluntary* human contract, real or imaginary; for they are built upon the weakness and necessities of mankind.'[181] As with Blackstone and Rutherforth, Ramsay's natural rights are not to be understood as endowing individuals with inalienable metaphysical properties, but ones that could always be curtailed if 'not tending to the support or safety of government, that is to the protection of the whole'.[182] The Americans' rights argument was flawed since under their interpretation natural rights

[175] Abercromby, *De Jure*, p. 231.   [176] Anon., *Justice and Necessity*, p. 22.
[177] Knox, *Letter to a Member of Parliament*, p. 18.
[178] *Proceedings and Debates*, 3 February 1766, II, p. 130.
[179] Phelps, *The Rights of the Colonies*, p. 13.
[180] Ramsay, *Thoughts on the Origin and Nature of Government*, p. 8.   [181] *Ibid.*, p. 10.
[182] *Ibid.*, p. 21.

could be claimed against the community and so dissolve its bonds.[183] Soame Jenyns distinguished three possible versions of the American argument and explicitly repudiated them all: 'either that no Englishman can be taxed without his own Consent as an Individual; or that no Englishman can be taxed without the Consent of the Persons he chuses to represent him; or that no Englishman can be taxed without the Consent of the Majority of all those, who are elected by himself and others of his Fellow Subjects to represent them'.[184]

As far as the supporters of the government could foresee, this subordination of community to individual was sure to produce anarchy. Its implicit, and often explicit, affirmation of natural equality was simply unassimilable. Because it was accepted that there were basic differences between members of the same political community, equality was seen to threaten the object of government, defined in the familiar prudent terms: 'The publick interest, then, or, the good of the whole, is the standard of liberty, in a free government . . . Not that everyone shall be equally free and independent; but that everyone shall be as free and independent, as his circumstances and situation will admit of, consistent with the good of the whole.'[185]

It was believed that natural equality would eliminate the existing justification for the subordination of individuals to the community. This had nearly become a syllogism: coercion of individuals (or colonies) was the essence of sovereignty, and therefore the capacity of individuals (or colonies) to refuse assent signalled a power 'supreme over the supreme, which implies a contradiction'. And this condition, described politically, was anarchy.[186] Without an agreed-upon notion of a public there could be no public utility and, hence, no means of adjudicating the inevitable clashes between the seemingly *utile* and the *honestum*. The sovereignty of individuals was 'an Absurdity in Government'.[187] It would 'occasion such tumult, disorder, and anarchy, as would necessarily dissolve the constitution; and give rise to some new kind of government, fatal, in all probability, to Britain'.[188] Ramsay, too, described the sovereignty of the

---

[183] *Ibid.*, p. 31.   [184] Jenyns, *Objections*, pp. 4–5.
[185] Anon., *Constitutional Right*, pp. 48–9. Also see Knox, *Letter to a Member of Parliament*, pp. 20–2.
[186] Anon., *The Right of the British Legislature to Tax the American Colonies Vindicated* (London, 1774), p. 5.
[187] Anon., *Examination of Rights*, pp. 40–2.   [188] Anon., *Constitutional Right*, p. 51.

individual as the prelude to a return to the vicious licence of the state of nature.[189] Law required uniform submission and so 'To say then that the Colonists have a right of judging for themselves what Laws they shall obey, and which they may protest against, is, in Effect, to invest them with a Right incompatible with the Officers of Subjects, and utterly subversive of the End of all human Institutions.'[190]

Moreover, in rejecting the possibility of a common good the Americans' claim to natural rights based on the equality of all individuals also destroyed the foundation upon which the empire was built.[191] To deny the parliamentary right to taxation was to deny British sovereignty since the power to legislate had long been seen as the prime characteristic of sovereignty. But hostility to parliamentary taxation was only the first step towards a complete renunciation of parliamentary sovereignty.[192] The next would be to reject all commercial regulation and destroy what remained of the empire. For, if the metropolis could not control the commerce of her North American periphery, it could command no imperial possession. If the legislature only had power over those who actually cast ballots to determine its composition, then 'all our possessions in Asia, Africa and America' were released from obedience to parliamentary law.[193] Just as the debate on representation employed concepts of sovereignty and empire, its ultimate resolution was seen to have consequences for both.

Because of their different notion of what constituted representation, when defenders of the government thought to have clinched their arguments by appeals to the non-consenting status of 90 per cent of the population, they were actually setting in motion a vicious *peripeteia*. For, to American eyes, the plight of Manchester and Birmingham only justified their claim that the existing system of representation was unfair. They and their metropolitan defenders heard no reassurance in the British 'admission' that most citizens were only 'virtually' represented: 'I cannot comprehend, how men,

[189] Ramsay, *Thoughts on the Origin and Nature of Government*, p. 16.
[190] Knox, *Letter to a Member of Parliament*, p. 8.
[191] Anon., *A Plain and Seasonable Address to the Freeholders of Great Britain* (London, 1766), p. 6; *Constitutional Right*, p. 42; Hulme, *Historical Essay*, p. 190; *Rights of Parliament*, p. 11.
[192] John Wesley, *A Calm Address to our American Colonies* (London, 1775), p. 5.
[193] Lloyd, *Conduct of the Late Administration*, pp. 119–20. Also, *Plain and Seasonable Address*, p. 9; Wesley, *Calm Address*, p. 4; *Protest against the Bill to Repeal the American Stamp Act* (London, 1766), p. 11.

who are excluded from voting at the election of members of parliament, can be represented in that assembly; or how those, who are elected, do not sit in the house as representatives of their constituents.'[194] James Otis boggled at Soame Jenyns' calm assertion that only one in twenty Britons cast ballots. 'So a small minority rules and governs the majority. This may for those in the saddle be clever enough, but can never be right in theory.'[195] A metropolitan wrong could not be made a colonial right.[196] As far as the Americans were concerned, taxation required consent and anything other than actual consent was incoherent. Simple common sense often ran aground on this shifty notion:

What I understand by being virtually represented, in the sense it is here to be taken, is, that a people may be represented without any choice of their own, without ever hearing, seeing, or knowing any one of their representatives; and the representatives equally strangers to the persons, circumstances, situation and country of the people they represented; without having any joint property or interest, and without ever being exposed to suffer any inconvenience in common with the people they represent.[197]

One writer described this 'imaginary virtual representation' as a 'fallacious sophistry, in opposition to common sense', while a second called it 'a mock Representative'.[198] Moreover, that counties and some boroughs actually did vote for representatives was seen to undercut the philosophical basis of the government's claim. Another writer sought to expose the emptiness of 'virtual' representation with a thought experiment. On the government's reading, because MPs did not serve constituencies, colonial petitions could be directed to any Member of Parliament. Thus, if New Yorkers wished to petition the House they could confidently submit one to any sitting Member, but could, just as confidently, expect it to be returned with the comment that the Member for Buckinghamshire was not their representative. The author was appealing to the seeming contradiction between the concept of 'virtual representation' and the undeniable fact that in practice British MPs were linked to specific

[194] Bland, *Enquiry*, p. 7.   [195] Otis, *Considerations*, p. 20.
[196] Caleb Evans, *A Reply to the Rev. Mr Fletcher's Vindication of Mr Wesley's 'Calm Address'* (Bristol, [1776]), pp. 31–2.
[197] Anon., *An Argument in Defence of the Exclusive Right*, pp. 82–3.
[198] 'Appendix', *Letter to Right Hon. Hillsborough*, p. 82; [Matthew Robinson-Morris], *Considerations of the Measures Carrying on with Respect to the British Colonies in North America* (London, 1774), p. 29.

constituencies that excluded the colonies.[199] Chatham also challenged the defenders of virtual representation to tell him 'by whom an American is represented here? Is he represented by any knight of the shire, in any county in this kingdom?' Or were the Americans the constituents of one of parliament's rotten boroughs? Concerns about colonial representation and parliamentary reform began to converge.[200] For many writers this problem was as old as the establishment of the 40s freehold requirement.[201]

Yet, even if it could be argued that inhabitants of Britain were protected from legislative tyranny by virtue of the fact that Members of Parliament were subject to the same laws as the nonvoting masses, this certainly was not the case when parliament legislated on bills solely affecting the colonies. The fundamental and widely repeated claim was, simply, that 'If Britain be imperfectly represented, she has but an *imperfect* freedom; but if the Colonies have *no* representation, they have no freedom, at all.'[202] Priestley suggested that the point was best made by analogy: 'A parallel to the present case of the Americans, would be a tax upon those towns who send no representatives, or an exemption of the towns that do send members. In this case, would not Leeds and Manchester make as loud complaints as the people of America do now?'[203]

Being forced to debate the merits of 'virtual' representation brought into the open the dependence of British policy-making on the concept of a common good shared by one community. Not surprisingly, defenders of America rejected the claim that representatives in Westminster could legislate for them, because their interests had grown apart. Hence, virtual representation would not be discredited,

Unless you shewed at the same time, that the interests of all the kingdom was not the same; that the representatives of the third part of the kingdom

[199] *The Crisis. Or, a Full Defence of the Colonies* (London, 1765), pp. 11–12, 14. Also, Evans, *A Reply to Rev. Mr Fletcher*, p. 39.

[200] *A Collection of Interesting and Authentic Papers*, ed. Almon, p. 59.

[201] *Reflections on Representation in Parliament* (London, 1766), p. 8; *Letter to Right Hon. Hillsborough*, pp. 38–9; *Appeal to the Justice and Interests*, p. 9; [Gervase Parker Bushe], *Case of Great-Britain and America* (3rd edn, Dublin, 1769), p. 23.

[202] Bushe, *Case*, p. 23. Variations of this can be found in Priestley, *Essay*, p. 23; Caleb Evans, *A Letter to the Rev. Mr Wesley* (London, 1775), p. 7; *Letter to the Right Hon. Hillsborough*, p. 40; *Late Occurrences in North America*, p. 6; Knox, *The Claim of the Colonies*, p. 28; *A Collection of Tracts, on the Subjects of Taxing the British Colonies in America, and Regulating their Trade*, ed. Almon (London, 1733), I, p. 62; [Hercules Langrische], *Considerations on the Dependencies of Great Britain* (Dublin, 1769), pp. 77–8.

[203] Priestley, 'Present State', *Works*, XXII, p. 394. This is also found in Burgh, *Political Disquisitions*, II, pp. 306, 320; *An Argument in Defense of the Exclusive Right*, p. 78.

had no knowledge of, and therefore neglected or injured the interests of the other two; you must shew likewise, that the interests of minors and women, copyholders and the lowest handycraft man in the kingdom, are not interwoven with the interests of every family and man in the kingdom . . .[204]

By the 1770s, many were beginning to believe that this had already occurred.

The problem of the Realm, posed in fact by the Seven Years War, and analysed in print by Pownall, rendered fantastic the notion of a single community of one interest spanning the Atlantic. The size of the continental empire, on the one hand, and its distance from Great Britain, on the other, destroyed the foundation of 'virtual' representation. 'Should the British empire one day be extended round the whole world, would it be reasonable that all mankind should have their concerns managed by the electors of old Sarum?'[205] Could the current theory of representation sustain a global empire? Hercules Langrische (1731–1801), an Irish politician and friend of Burke, dismissed the possibility of the common good traversing 'a thousand leagues' of ocean.[206] North American society was different from Britain's and had its own political and social requirements. Colonel Richard Bland's language echoed Pownall's, describing colonial politics in terms of 'laws of attraction in natural as well as political philosophy', 'cemented by mutual interests', which produced a natural 'intercommunication' between them.'[207] In their absence 'the very idea of representation' would be destroyed.[208]

Differing interests were intensified by distance. This element alone seemed to make a colonial representation in Westminster logistically unfeasible. John Wesley, for example, declared that, while emigrants did not forfeit any claim to representation in principle, they had effectively made it impossible for themselves to take advantage of their privilege.[209] The author of the *Letter to Wesley* admitted the point, but turned it around: if colonists could no longer vote, they ought no longer to be taxed.[210]

---

[204] Anon., *Late Occurrences in North America, and Policy of Great Britain, Considered* (London, 1766), p. 4.

[205] Otis, *Considerations*, p. 10.   [206] Langrische, *Dependencies*, pp. 76–7.

[207] Bland, *Enquiry*, pp. 17–18 [21–2]).

[208] Estwick, *Letter to Tucker*, pp. 76–7; Bollan, *A Succinct View of the Origin of our Colonies* (London, 1766), p. 23.

[209] Wesley, *Calm Address*, p. 8. Also, p. 5.

[210] Evans, *A Letter to the Rev. Mr Wesley*, p. 14; also Evans, *A Reply to Rev. Mr Fletcher's Vindication*, p. 45.

The solution to this problem was worked out within these debates though it never became British policy. Since size posed such difficulties for an imperial policy designed to obtain the security of the metropolitan state while describing its attainment as a common good, and since the gains of the Seven Years War could not simply be returned to France, the only imperial alternative was to shift the priority from the community, with its geographical associations, to individuals:

The present inequality so much complained of, has arisen entirely from confining the right of representatives to particular places; whereas if it was once conferred on number only, this would prevent the evil from ever recurring again in any degree, as well as remove it for the present.[211]

Behind this argument lay a strong theory of individual rights. Because each and every citizen was considered the 'owner' of political sovereignty[212] they could place representatives, 'under such limitations and restrictions as they may think reasonable. In all this we find no mystery, no occasion for occult qualities, no want of the terms virtual representation as distinguished from a representation in fact, or any other jargon.'[213]

Polybius' warning about the debilitating relationship between size and liberty, which conditioned the way many eighteenth-century Britons thought and wrote about empire, was resolved in this manner. The government neither would, nor perhaps, could implement the solution. The composite monarchy managed, inefficiently perhaps, to hold together disparate strategic interests. But the problem of describing the 'common' good grew with the size and power of the state.

Obadiah Hulme's anonymous and highly influential *Historical Essay on the English Constitution* (1771) stands at the crossroads of imperial theory and what was to become, in the following decades, the drive for the reform of the state. He sketched out the new theory of representation and sovereignty in the influential 'language' of Anglo-Saxon history, abandoning the sorry lessons of the Romans. They and the Greeks had successfully placed 'the supreme power of

---

[211] Anon., *Reflections on Representation*, p. 16.
[212] 'In a free State, Every Man who is supposed a free agent, ought to be in some measure his own governor; and therefore a branch at least of the legislative power should reside in the whole body of the people' (Evans, *Letter to Wesley*, p. 9).
[213] Otis, *Considerations*, p. 46.

the state, in laws made by the mutual consent of the people'.[214] While this had worked within the circumvallated Mediterranean *poleis*, the extension of dominion across a wider expanse of territory often diminished the extent of liberty commensurately. Note how closely his description matches the terms of the contemporary imperial debate. The Romans

seem to have had no conception of the model of government, where the elective power of individuals, could diffuse itself through the whole body of a nation, containing some millions of men, living perhaps a thousand miles distant, from the seat of government. And yet be so conducted, as to unite, into one point of action, parts so numerous, and remote, and form a legislative authority, commodiously fit for action, without anarchy or confusion.[215]

Where the ancients had failed to devise a means of making their rich definition of liberty completely portable, the Saxons had an answer: elective representation. Individual consent to law (i.e. participation) was obviously inadequate in a territorial state. Elected representatives provided the necessary executive flexibility while still making the actions of government dependent upon the sovereignty of the people. Hulme's rule was that 'All government must, in its own nature, be confined to time and place.' Those so ill-placed as to be prevented from being part of government remained dependent on others. The great innovation of the British constitution was that it enabled electors, 'to exercise their natural rights of election', affording 'a plentiful security to every man, let him be placed where, and in what condition soever he may'.[216]

Blackstone had gone over much the same ground in the *Commentaries*, making the standard observations about the limit of size on ancient republican participation and the glorious British constitution repairing this historical wrong through the institution of

---

[214] Hulme, *Historical Essay*, p. 2. Janelle Greenberg has discussed the language of Anglo-Saxon politics for the seventeenth century ('The Confessor's Law and the Radical Face of the English Constitution', *English Historical Review*, 412 (1989), 610–37). For a general survey, see R. J. Smith, *The Gothic Bequest* (Cambridge, 1987). Isaac Kramnick has described the politics of Anglo-Saxon exempla as 'reactionary'. Surely the use of this mythical history in support of radical political change forbids such a characterization? A worthwhile comparison would examine the *different* uses of the Anglo-Saxon heritage by Hulme and Samuel Squire.

[215] Hulme, *Historical Essay*, pp. 3–4. Pocock has commented on the importance of ancient representation for Hume and Smith ('States, Republics and Empires: The American Founding in Early Modern Perspective', in *Conceptual Change and the Constitution*, ed. Terence Ball and Pocock (Lawrence, KA, 1988), p. 70).

[216] Hulme, *Historical Essay*, pp. 5–6.

representation.[217] But there are unmistakable differences between them. Blackstone had not spoken of a 'natural right to election '. Nor had the usefulness of representation been applied as acutely to the problem of size and liberty. In fact, Blackstone, and other defenders of the government, sought to skirt this problem entirely through the abstraction of virtual representation. Because participation was not an *a priori* good for most Britons, they did not confront the relationship between size and liberty constrained by any theoretical need to remain as close to the participatory model as possible. Virtual representation expressed the priority they assigned to the metropolitan community's determination of what was the national interest.

The Saxon practice of individual representation produced, according to Hulme, an ideal polity in which 'the natural rights of mankind were preserved, in their full exercise, pure and perfect, as far as the nature of society will admit of'.[218] By contrast, the defence of representation for the common good took a dim view of the legitimate purview of the individual in political life. Hulme, and contemporaries such as Gervase Parker Bushe, specifically excluded the conventional definition of the representative's role:

By *representatives*, I mean men elected and appointed by others, to *act for* them – In a more extended sense of the words, persons who act for others, may be said to represent them, although they be not elected by them. In this sense of the word, an absolute monarch *represents* all his subjects . . . and the British parliament, when it makes trade-regulations for the Colonies, may be said to represent them, because it *acts for* them. But it is by *real* and *elected* representatives, that liberty must be preserved; when, therefore, I speak of representatives, in general, I mean such only.[219]

The attack on representation *for* some common good by those demanding representation *of* individuals occurred across the fracture separating the politics of communities, whether given a commonwealth or prudential inflection, from those of individuals. That representation was the pivotal issue highlighted the difference with republican representation; this was a political system in which individuals consented, rather than participated.[220] Priestley backed up the argument with a newly created category. By combining the content of his purely private 'civil' liberty (Grotius' 'personal

---

[217] Blackstone, *Commentaries*, i, pp. 138–9.   [218] Hulme, *Historical Essay*, p. 7.
[219] Bushe, *Case of Great Britain*, p. 25.
[220] Priestley, *Essay*, p. 12.

liberty') with the force of a natural right, he derived the 'civil right': 'It is of great importance, that all the subjects of government should have a just idea of their natural and civil rights, and that they should be apprized when they are invaded.'[221] It almost goes without saying that for Priestley, Hulme and other defenders of individual representation, as for Locke, Blackstone and Grenville, individual consent was needed to justify taxation and legitimate what would otherwise be outright theft.[222]

The natural rights which underpinned this argument were simultaneously used to affirm the primacy of the privately judging, freely enquiring individual. For, just as the defence of the common good rested upon a model of civil and national political life, the new argument also possessed a theory of human nature. The defence of the politically sovereign individual presupposed a model that combined a basically Stoic view of the good with a stress on individual enquiry and reason.

The very first sentence of James Otis' slashing attack on Soame Jenyns' defence of virtual representation contrasts these alternative, fundamental images of human nature; 'The gentleman thinks it is "absurd and insolent" to question the expediency and utility of a public measure. He seems to be an utter enemy to the freedom of enquiry after truth, justice and equity.'[223] The colonial argument and, as we shall see, that of their British supporters, explicitly challenged the prudent Ciceronian view of politics and the public utility which formed the cornerstone of eighteenth-century political life. These men opposed the dictates of inalienable natural rights to the prudential maxims of state which were so often invoked to subordinate precisely these defining aspects of individuality to the larger needs of public utility. While these reformers did not discard the notion of a common good, they did seek to replace the demi-oligarchic determination of its content with the specific expressions of individuals' political views. In so doing, men like Otis took over the early modern Ciceronian politics of necessity and turned it to revolutionary use. 'But let the *origin* of government be placed where

---

221 Priestley, 'Present State of Liberty', *Works*, xxii, p. 380.
222 Evans, *Letter to Rev. Mr Wesley*, pp. 3, 20; Bushe, *Case of Great Britain*, p. 26; *Appeal to the Justice and Interests*, pp. 7, 25; Otis, *Rights of the Colonies*, p. 57; *The Crisis*, p. 3; Camden's speech, 7 March 1766, *Proceedings and Debates*, ii, p. 323; Grenville letter to Knox, quoted in Paul Langford, 'Old Whigs, Old Tories and the American Revolution', *Journal of Imperial and Commonwealth History*, 8: 2 (1980), p. 109.
223 Otis, *Considerations*, p. 1.

it may, the *end* of it is manifestly the good of *the whole*. *Salus populi suprema lex esto* is of the law of nature and part of that grand charter given the human race' by God.[224]

In the *Rights of the British Colonies*, Otis had upheld a political version of the 'right of private judgment' homologous to that of the English dissenters, hinting at what will be argued in the following chapters, that these two debates were necessary complements: 'If there is not a right of private judgment to be exercised, so far at least as to petition for a repeal, or to determine the expediency of risking a trial at law, the parliament might make itself arbitrary, which it is conceived it cannot by the constitution.'[225] Government writers warned that private judgment was antithetical to the principles with which Britain was governed. Its increasing prominence in contemporary political and religious literature threatened to undermine the unified determination of the common good that was believed to preserve the security of the state.[226] Just as the concept of private judgment had implications for both public and private life, those defending the monopoly of the community contested the same two fronts. Thus, Knox commented that a 'capital Error' in colonial policy was the failure to establish a state religion in the colonies.[227]

Finally, this new emphasis on the welfare, happiness and fulfilment of an individual's social and intellectual needs matched, in *contrapasso*, the declining intellectual appeal of a state-planned economy. The rejection of the claim of national security had to damage the integrity of its political economy. 'Misled by partial considerations', Britain had long viewed 'the colonies as so many appendages or factories to this kingdom, devoted solely to the improvement of its particular interest, wealth, and power, and without any rights or privileges which are not perfectly consistent with the attainment of these desired objects.'[228] Colonists could not be treated as subordinates merely to satisfy the dictates of a putative common good about whose content they were not consulted.

---

[224] Otis, *Rights of the British Colonies*, p. 13. During the parallel American discussions about representation in the Continental Congress, Benjamin Rush argued that 'The Objects before us are the people's rights, not the rights of States' (quoted in Jerrilyn Greene Marston, *The Transfer of Political Legitimacy, 1774–1776* (Princeton, 1987), p. 200).
[225] Otis, *Rights of the British Colonies*, p. 62.
[226] Anon., *Protest against the Repeal of the Stamp Act*, p. 12.
[227] Knox, 'Considerations on the Great Question, What is to Be Done with America', quoted in Greene, 'William Knox's Explanation for the American Revolution', *William and Mary Quarterly*, 3rd ser. 30 (1973), 303.
[228] 'Appendix', *Letter to the Right Hon. Hillsborough*, p. 100.

Appealing to transcendent, natural ideas of justice provided leverage against the claim of necessity so often invoked by governors. While 'The terms of municipal laws usually favour the Sovereign' since his (or its) power was legislative, 'the law of nature is more commonly in support of the people and the publick'.[229] Hence, safety and security had to be 'actually at stake, absolutely required' to justify the abridgement of any individual liberties. To do so simply in order to 'maintain our sovereignty' was deemed wholly unjustifiable.[230] Limiting the scope of necessity shifted the balance of power away from the crown. Because the determination of necessity was, as much as anything else, an early modern measure of sovereignty, giving this power to representatives expanded the scope of constitutionalism by commensurately constraining the capacity of kings and ministers to act on their discretionary assessment of the public good.

The arguments brought in defence of colonial representation did, in fact, as the government's supporters feared, lead to a much broader revaluation of the political individual. The Virginian, Richard Bland, spoke of the 'rights of a people' and concluded that 'rights imply equality'.[231] Another writer asserted that individuals 'are by nature entitled to welfare and happiness and to seek and pursue those blessings'. These natural rights were inherent in people and prior to political life.[232] Finally, it is within this same context that the social role of law is defined, but now explicitly contrasted with Blackstone's standard:

In what does perfect political liberty consist? Some authors define it to be, *the power of doing what the laws permit.* If I do not mistake the meaning of this definition, it is clearly erroneous. To do what the laws of Turkey permit, certainly is *not* liberty. Perfect political liberty consists, rather – in the not being subject to any laws, but such as we have consented to, by ourselves, or by our representatives. If Britain is but imperfectly represented, it has but an imperfect freedom.[233]

Against Rutherforth's reading of Grotius, Bushe argued, and Price was later to reiterate, that life under unjust but constitutionally promulgated laws constituted not civil liberty, but civil tyranny. Sometimes, men were as important as measures.

---

[229] Anon., *Considerations on the Measures*, p. 27.
[230] Anon., *Enquiry into the Nature and Causes*, p. 50.
[231] Bland, *Enquiry*, p. 19.   [232] Anon., *Considerations on the Measures*, pp. 6–7.
[233] Bushe, *Case of Great Britain*, pp. 15–16.

Precisely because the empire was acquired, governed and conceptualized in the same terms as the state, the challenge to the empire was fundamental. The colonial push for individual representation was a demand of great moment. The political and constitutional history of the early modern European states ripples with the tension between subjects and sovereigns. In seventeenth-century England reformers and revolutionaries sought constraints on the monarch; in eighteenth-century Britain they pressed for reform of parliamentary abuses. In both instances what was at stake was an attempt to construct a sovereign. While Scotland and Ireland could be controlled, by force, if necessary, the American colonies posed a greater problem. Their size dwarfed the metropolis and their distance nearly out-ran her writ. How then, asked the colonists, could the determination of their common good be made solely by legislators in London? The dispute over representation, beginning with the Stamp Act of 1765, introduced the possibility of constructing a new 'common' good, this one built, quite literally, from the political expression of individual citizens.

CHAPTER 5

The common good, toleration and freedom of thought

The ubiquity of prudence and the pre-eminent standard of the public utility are salient features of seventeenth- and eighteenth-century European political thought. This was as true for those writers who stressed liberty and moral reformation as a means to this end as for the more bureaucratic defenders of the aggrandizement of the state. The convergence of opposition and government on the character of the 'common' good and its associated principles may account for the relative absence of theoretical debate about political concepts in Britain in the 1750s.

One of the most important consequences of the Seven Years War was to offer a challenge, at first only logistical, to the uncontested theoretical hegemony of public utility. Subsequently, the debate about colonial representation focused attention on the contest between the claims of the sovereign and the obligations of the citizen. While no one challenged the supremacy of a common good as the end of political life, there were those who questioned the constitution of that 'common' or shared goal. Proponents of 'actual' representation were suggesting that individuals had themselves to determine this shared interest for it to be accepted as the legitimate measure of political practice. In part, this reflected feelings of distance and lack of reciprocity within what was no longer felt to be a single community. But the increasing weight borne by the individual in this anti-ministerial argument depended upon a much stronger theory of personality.

This chapter will set forth the philosophical background as well as the specific arguments for religious toleration that followed from it and which were debated in the 1760s and 1770s. In the following chapter, the positions developed in the debates over colonial representation and religious toleration will be drawn together in the writings of a group of men who explicitly formulated a new definition of the common good. The interpretation of Cicero as a prudent, practical statesman has been argued to lie at the heart of the theory of political practice in the post-Reformation state. The clash between the needs of public and private domains which focused so much attention on Cicero did not challenge his conclusion that the preservation of the community was the highest law. This imperative, which motivated the early natural law writers like Grotius and Pufendorf as well as their contemporaries who wrote treatises on the reason of state, dominated thinking about politics in eighteenth-century Britain.

Cicero was so valuable to public men of this time precisely because he defended a moral approach to social life even as his broader perspective elevated necessity to the realm of the *honestum*. This had enabled Pufendorf to use Cicero against the crude consequentialism of Hobbes, recognizing all the while that Cicero made concessions to necessity that troubled him. A contemporary, Richard Cumberland, defended the service of the common good on the grounds that only by serving the community could the desires of individuals be satisfied. Samuel Clarke's use of this tradition is significant. Citing Cumberland, he too took up Cicero, this time against the sceptical atheists whom he described as the modern followers of Hobbes. And so, he also focused on Cicero's theoretical statements about *honestum*, ignoring the prudential arguments that would have sounded far closer to the kind of politics that he believed followed from his antagonists' Hobbesian moral theology. Moreover, because of Clarke's commitment to reading the Newtonian laws of nature as Divine, Cicero's own defence of a law of nature made him exceedingly attractive. But what emerged was a different Cicero, one no longer of much use to politicians locked in inextricable struggles with the claims of public utility. From Clarke through to Richard Price at the terminus of this study, we can trace an alternative argument, one in which the *utile* is, in fact, read out of the *honestum*.

This sketches the theoretical foundation of the new definition of the common good that was offered by Price and his colleagues. The Americans and their British friends, many of whom were religious nonconformists, drew on an individualist essence of Protestantism augmented by Clarke's metaphysical discussion of human attributes. They attached great importance to rational and free inquiry after the truth. Their interpretation of the quest for a 'good' life stood independent of and prior to the concerns of the state. Inverting the classical Roman model of citizenship based on the minimalist goal of *pax*, they classed as illegitimate the kind of politics which failed to recognize and facilitate the rational intelligent nature of the individuals whose common flourishing was the purpose of organized social existence. The kind of liberty sought by these reformers was, indeed, very different from that desired by those influenced by Cicero's prudent politics. Their extremely novel and radical conclusion was that the common good could be no other than the collective good decided upon by freely inquiring rational individuals, going so far as to admit the anti-political conclusion that this could, at times, entail the destruction of community.

Their political and polemical opponents defended the civil management of ecclesiological matters and limited toleration of dissent, like the subordination of the colonies to metropolitan interests, because they calculated the common good in terms of community. While Britain's eighteenth-century imperial crisis was completely novel, the simultaneous debate on the advantages and risks of toleration renewed one of the most lacerating conflicts in early modern Europe. No state had managed to avoid sanguinary religious wars or persecutions and for many seventeenth- and eighteenth-century writers the prevention of further descents into 'barbarism' was a chief goal.

LAWS OF NATURE AND THE COMMON GOOD

What distinguished this new line of argument was its deviation from the notion of political community that was defended by Cicero and adopted by his early modern interpreters. While individual self-preservation constituted the original position for these writers, they were unequivocal about the priority of the community. Only its preservation could assure the security of individuals. Thus, in its early modern version, by translating the sceptical Stoic emphasis on self-preservation into a right, Grotius sought the most limited possible foundation that would yet prove sturdy enough to uphold civil life. As we have observed, Cicero provided Grotius with both 'halves' of the argument, the priority of self- and national preservation as well as the existence of a common and transcendent law of nature and nations. Nevertheless, even this restricted commitment to self-preservation forced Grotius into acknowledging the force of moral realism. The existence of a natural law, however much described in terms of human psychology or sociology, amounted to a belief that a standard of right and wrong existed in the world prior to human articulation. Writing for sceptics in a very sceptical world, Grotius sought to redescribe and minimize the importance of what would have appeared a very weak link in his argument. Yet, his notorious remark that 'all we have now said would take place, though we should even grant, what without the greatest Wickedness cannot be granted, that there is no God, or that he takes no Care of human Affairs' demonstrates how seriously he took these 'real' moral truths that were reflected in natural law.[1] By the later seventeenth century, however, and as a reaction against a perceived voluntarism and consequentialism in Pufendorf's *Law of Nature*, the balance between moral realism and voluntarism began to swing back. Grotius' approach, reinforced by Newton's laws of nature, was believed capable of supporting a new sceptic-proof 'science of morality'.

An important piece of this strand of argument, both for Barbeyrac in his retrospective construction of a tradition, as well as for the English writers not usually associated with it, was constituted by Richard Cumberland's *De Legibus Naturae Disquisitio Philosophica* (1672; translation published in 1727 as *A Treatise of the Law of Nature*). Here, the emphasis was also on Stoicism, but not its support for the sceptical, prudent maxims of the statesman. Rather, ancient Stoic natural law was stressed in order to provide iron-clad backing for the supremacy of the *honestum* over and against the claims of force and expediency, manifested for Cumberland as for Pufendorf, in the malevolent influence of Hobbes.[2] Barbeyrac asserted that Cumberland had rejected the 'bad' principles of the Stoics and taken only the valuable ones. Thus, where the Epicureans had counselled ease and tranquillity, the 'Stoics, on the contrary, contended, that the Sage, in order to live in conformity with Nature had to be disposed to enter without qualms into the administration of the affairs of

---

[1] Grotius, *Preliminary Discourse*, XI, *Laws of War and Peace*, p. xix. This was one of the characteristics used by contemporaries to distinguish between Grotius and Pufendorf (Tully, Introduction to Pufendorf, *Duty of Man*, p. xviii). For the larger story, see Richard Tuck, *Philosophy and Government 1572–1651*.

[2] In the preface to his translation, Barbeyrac wrote that when Pufendorf first encountered Cumberland's book he praised it and saw that like him it sought to refute '"the hypothesis of Thomas Hobbes and to establish another, antithetical to it, which strongly resembled the dogmas of the ancient Stoics"' (Barbeyrac, Preface, *Traité philosophique des loix naturelles* ... (Amsterdam, 1744), p. iii.

State'. Cicero was brought to buttress this position, characteristic of the modern Stoicism originating with Lipsius.[3] Cumberland's heavy stress on the basic principles of Stoicism differed little, for example, from Pufendorf's similar dependence. It was manifest, he wrote, 'from the Nature of Things, That the chief Happiness which we can procure to our selves, arises jointly from promoting Piety and Peace, mutual Commerce among Nations, civil and domestic Government, and also firm Friendship; and that the care of all these things together is to be found only in his Mind, who studies the common Good of all rational Beings'. The opposite was also true: 'That whoever rejects the care of the common Good, does so far reject the Causes of his own Happiness, and embrace the immediate Causes of his Misery and Punishment.'[4] This led Cumberland to conclude that in nature 'the common Good is the supreme Law'. Barbeyrac added that, while this was true of natural society, in civil society the public, rather than the common, good was at stake. Here, 'the preservation of the People is the sovereign law, according to the well-known maxim: *Salus populi suprema lex esto*'.[5] Barbeyrac had no doubt that 'the Public Happiness and the Particular Happiness are tied together and the Public Good has, in the vast majority of cases, a close connection with the particular interest of everyone'.[6]

Cumberland's discussion of personal morality clearly but subtly inflected Grotius' adaptation of early modern Stoicism, emphasizing still more heavily the role of friendship, which contemporaries often hailed as the primary social relationship.[7] This commitment, itself drawing upon that of the ancient Stoics, made the employment of natural law in the service of self-interest, as in Hobbes, completely anathema. By stressing the centrality of friendship, Cumberland sought to provide a concrete illustration of the sociability inherent in the law of nature since it 'points out that possible Action of a rational Agent, which will chiefly promote the Common Good, and by which only the intire Happiness of particular Persons can be obtain'd'.[8]

---

[3] Barbeyrac, *Traité philosophique*, Discours Preliminaire, pp. 11–12, note 1; I.iv, p. 41n. This is Oestreich's main argument for neo-Stoicism as the philosophical basis for the civil service of the absolutist state.

[4] Cumberland, Introduction, xix, *Laws of Nature*, p. 25.

[5] Barbeyrac, *Traité philosophique*, I.iv, p. 42, note 2.

[6] *Ibid.*, I.viii, p. 48n.

[7] See, for instance, the translator's introductory essay, 'Concerning the Imperfections of the Heathen Morality', included in the 1727 *Treatise on the Laws of Nature*.

[8] Cumberland, *Laws of Nature*, v.i, p. 189. John Dunn has emphasized how 'friendship' provided John Locke with the content of the bond between men ('From Applied Theology

Both the 'Clearness' with which the law of nature is perceived and its purpose in promoting the 'Common Good' were to reappear in Clarke's statement. Where Clarke was to employ an analogy between God and Man to generate the grounds of moral obligation, Cumberland deduced from the specific needs of individuals the general needs of the public. Moreover, and this bears attention, these wants were largely intellectual:

> For public good things are the same with the good things of particular persons; and, from a true Idea of any Man's Happiness, may easily be deduc'd, by Analogy, the happiness to be sought after for any Civil State, or even for all Men jointly consider'd. For a Society, compos'd of particular persons, is only then happy, when each of its members, especially the principal ones, have their Minds endow'd with the natural perfections of the Understanding and Will, and their Bodies sound, and with vigor ministring to their Minds.[9]

Cumberland believed that, while 'every one necessarily seeks his own greatest Happiness', it could not be attained by any one person acting alone and, 'therefore, he *cannot propose* to himself his *own Happiness*, separately from that of others'.[10] The effort to articulate the means by which the pursuit of private good necessarily augmented the common good was an important part of Cumberland's attempt to bring the Stoic commitment to community into line with natural moral law, while avoiding the excessive role of expedience that he associated with the construction of the Leviathan. The 'best Method' was one in which the individual's pursuit of 'his own Happiness (which is a part of the Publick Happiness) also 'constantly promotes the Common Good'.[11] Cumberland acknowledged that the objection could be made that self-love was dominant and that people simply assumed that its pursuit also served the community's good. His English translator, John Maxwell, was quick to

---

to Social Analysis: The Break between John Locke and the Scottish Enlightenment', in *Wealth and Virtue*, ed. I. Hont and M. Ignatieff (Cambridge, 1983), p. 127). Locke's friendship with Molyneux has been described, but its possible use for a description of Locke's version of neo-Stoicism has not usually been attempted. See Patrick Kelly, 'Locke and Molyneux: Anatomy of a Friendship.', *Hermathena*, 126 (1979), 38–54; James Tully, 'Governing Conduct', *Conscience and Casuistry in Early Modern Europe*, ed. Edmund Leites (Cambridge, 1988), pp. 3–71; but see John Marshall's fuller account, 'John Locke in Context: Religion, Ethics and Politics', Unpublished Ph.D. thesis (The Johns Hopkins University, 1990). Contemporaries such as Shaftesbury and Addison also placed great weight on this relationship.

[9] Cumberland, *Laws of Nature*, v.viii, p. 203.   [10] *Ibid.*, v.xxviii, p. 234.
[11] *Ibid.*, v.xliv, p. 270.

insist that, 'According to our Author's Scheme, Private and Publick Good never interpose, but are perfectly connected, and the same Actions are productive of both.'[12] At the heart of Cumberland's argument lay a definition of the greatest good:

Since it is certain, from the Nature of the Will and of voluntary Action, that the effecting the Greatest Good is the Greatest End prescrib'd by Reason; That Good must either be the greatest Common Good (wherein I include whatever is consistent with it,) or the greatest Private Good, which every Man can desire or propose to himself as Possible, and to which he directs all his Actions.

Cumberland left no doubt about his preference. 'Reason will not suffer, that the greatest Private Good should be propos'd as the ultimate End.'[13] The crux of the argument is the potential conflict between goods. How could such a dispute be adjudicated? The conclusion of this discussion appeals to reason, realism and public utility. 'For that only is that one End, which is consistent with, and most promotes, the greatest possible happiness of every particular person. In that End, alone, can agree, both natural Instinct, regarding its own, and Reason, respecting the Common Good.'[14] The public and private goods coincided so that 'when we have added to the Common Stock by our greatest Industry, we may take out our own share with Innocence, and enjoy it with pleasure'.[15] As with Cicero, this reconciliation reflected the pre-eminence of the community. Its establishment at the heart of Cumberland's ethical theory enabled him to employ it, quite literally, as a measuring stick with which to arrange other social commitments:

That the Common Good of all Rational Beings, on this very account, that it is the Sum of all Things naturally Good, and, therefore, the greatest Good, is the fittest natural Measure, by a comparison of other good Things with which, we may safely pronounce, whether they be Great, or Small; and, therefore, whether they ought to have the first Place in our Desires, or should be postpon'd to others.[16]

Unlike Cicero, however, was the exclusion of the *utile* from the content of *honestum*. This, I believe, was a consequence of Cumberland's effort to gain some purchase on Hobbes' argument. The tyranny of the Leviathan *might* have been the necessary cure for a

---

[12] *Ibid.*, v.xliv, p. 271n.   [13] *Ibid.*, v.xvi, pp. 213–14.
[14] *Ibid.*, vxi, p. 213.   [15] *Ibid.*, vxvi, p. 214.
[16] *Ibid.*, vııı.xii, p. 342.

society in which the pursuit of individual good necessarily entailed a war of all against all.[17] This solution was assimilated to the contemporary discussion of the propriety of state power. Cumberland acknowledged 'that a greater care of the *publick* Good, than of the Life of any *particular* Person, may be suppos'd as the Foundation of this Prerogative granted to the ruling Powers in States'.[18] But in Cumberland's world, security could only be attained where public and private goods coincided, namely, under the guidance of natural law. On Cumberland's reading of Hobbes, the force of Leviathan was assimilated to the reason of state tradition and its existence described as dangerous to the security of the individual because it eliminated the option of self-defence which was guaranteed by the laws of nature. The point of this was to show that even on Hobbes' terms, namely security, there was a greater advantage in observing the laws of nature than the insistent demands of expediency.[19]

Having contended that private and public goods necessarily coincided, Cumberland described the 'habits of mind' whose acquisition was required by natural law and which was a prerequisite to the service of the common good. This vital intellectual posture is identified as the virtue that had been made central to the political program of the modern, practical Stoicism: prudence. 'Its Foundation lies in a true knowledge of all Nature, but especially the rational Part thereof; its chief Parts are a Knowledge of the chief Ends, (of which the greatest is that we are inquiring after), and a practical Knowledge of the Means conducing thereto.' If this stress on 'practical Knowledge' and the 'chief Ends' of life, understood as the common good, were not enough to alert us to the relevant seventeenth-century intellectual context, the continuation of this entirely Lipsian passage leaves no room for doubt:

The immediate, most general, and essential Effects of Prudence, are 1. Constancy of Mind, by which we adhere without wavering to its Dictates, as being unchangeable Truth, and fitted to all circumstances. For there is a kind of Immutability in the practical Judgment, concerning the best End and Means, and in the Will consequent thereupon, which proceeds immediately from the Perception of the immutable Truth of those practical Propositions, which relate to the End and the Means necessary. Prudence bears the same relation to Inconstancy, that Science does to the giving assent to contradictory propositions at the same time. Constancy in the Prosecution of this great End, in opposition to foreseen Dangers and

---

[17] *Ibid.*, iii.iv, p. 171.   [18] *Ibid.*, i.xxix, p. 78.   [19] *Ibid.*, v.liii, p. 285.

Difficulties, is Fortitude; the same continuing under present Evils, Patience.[20]

Perfect 'Moral and Political Prudence' constituted a thorough knowledge of the various circumstances in which human actions produced their varied consequences. While undoubtedly a difficult task, Cumberland believed that by converting this tangle of events and repercussions into causes and effects it would be possible to treat moral philosophy like natural philosophy. The basic rules of this new science were two, 'That we alwaies propose a possible End (or Effect,) and, of those which we can attain, the best' and 'That we apply those Actions as Means, which are the most suitable and adequate Causes of the foreseen intended Effect.' Cumberland's conclusion effectively blurred the distinction between contemporary prudential politics and the quest for a science of action guided by natural moral entities. 'The Dictates of Prudence, directing Human Actions every where to the Greatest Possible Good of all rational Agents, are the very laws of Nature.'[21] Since the 'Greatest Possible Good' was clearly identified as the common good, Cumberland's dictum was, effectively, that the prudent maxims which served the common good constituted the laws of nature.

The conjunction of prudence, the common good and laws of nature provided Cumberland not only with the desired science of action but with a model of governance.

That he, who seeks the chief Good of rational Agents, seeks the Good and order of the whole World; and that, from the slightest observation of the natural Determinations of Motion, some notion of Order and dependence is produc'd in the mind; which regular Dependence, as it proceeds from the judgment of a rational mind, is properly called Government.[22]

Analogy between the natural and human worlds suggested the type of prudent 'judgment' needed to manage the affairs of men. This insight, when combined with popular Newtonianism, could produce a defence of limited monarchy or ministerial government. Beginning from many of the same premises shared by Grotius and Pufendorf, Cumberland had shifted the weight of argument away from the prudent, political reading of Cicero and towards a greater emphasis on his pronouncements about *honestum* and natural law. Both threads are found in Grotius, for example; what was involved here was a question of insistence rather than exclusion.

[20] *Ibid.*, vi.vi, pp. 308–9.   [21] *Ibid.*, v.vi, p. 201.   [22] *Ibid.*, v.viii, p. 203.

Jean Barbeyrac's mediation of these classical natural law texts reveals the importance of moral realism in the early eighteenth-century development of this tradition. His comment on Grotius' famous clause, cited above, raising the possibility of an autonomous moral law, not only puts Grotius' moral realism into the theological language that was used by Cumberland, Samuel Clarke and his followers, but frames the central challenge of generating obligation from the rational discovery of natural law:

> This Assertion is to be admitted only in the following Sense: That the Maxims of the Law of Nature are not merely arbitrary Rules, but are founded on the Nature of Things; on the Constitution of Man, from which certain Relations result, between such and such Actions, and the State of a reasonable and social Creature. But to speak exactly, the Duty and Obligation, or the indispensible Necessity of conforming to these Ideas, and Maxims, necessarily supposes a superior Power, a supreme Master of Mankind, who can be no other than the Creator, or the supreme Divinity.[23]

Where Grotius had described a natural right as 'the Rule and Dictate of Right Reason, shewing the Moral Deformity or Moral Necessity there is in any Act', Barbeyrac sharply disagreed, denying that a morality derived purely from human reason could have any force: 'The Author here supposes we should be under an Obligation of doing or not doing certain Things, even tho' we were not answerable to any one for our Conduct.' Grotius' views, while 'not entirely just', were still shared by most philosophers and even those 'otherwise very judicious, and far from being Slaves to the schools'. The traditional, and mistaken, view, according to Barbeyrac, was that 'the Rules of the Law of Nature and Morality do in themselves impose an indispensable Necessity of conforming to them, independently of the Will of God'. While Barbeyrac did not dispute the existence of the natural law, he could not admit the possibility that it had any force other than that imparted by God:

> The Question here is not whether we can discover the Ideas and Relations, from which all the Rules of the Law of Nature and Morality are deduced, abstractedly from the Will of an intelligent Being. It must be acknowledged with the Patrons of the Opinion which I oppose, that these Rules are really founded on the Nature of Things; that they are agreeable to the Order conceived necessary for the Beauty of the Universe; that there is a certain Proportion or Disproportion, a certain Fitness or Unfitness between most

---

[23] *Preliminary Discourse*, xi, *Laws of War and Peace*, p. xix.

Actions and their Objects, which give a Beauty to some, and a Deformity to others. But it does not follow from this Concession, that we are, properly speaking, obliged to do or not to do such a Thing. The Fitness or Unfitness, which may be termed the natural Morality of Actions, is indeed a Reason for acting, or not acting; but then it is not such a Reason as imposes an indispensible Necessity, which is implied in the Idea of an Obligation. This necessity can only come from a superior, that is, from some intelligent Being existing without us, who has a Power of restraining our Liberty, and prescribing Rules for our Conduct.[24]

Barbeyrac, and later Hume, though for a completely different reason, was troubled by the question of how to turn relations discovered by reason into obligations. Since reason 'of itself' could not 'lay us under an indispensible necessity of following those Ideas of Fitness or Unfitness', Barbeyrac saw no alternative but to recognize 'that the Will of God is the Source of all Duties' even though His will manifested itself in Laws of Nature that were conformable 'to the natural and invariable Ideas of Order, Fitness and Justice'.[25]

In the *Historical and Critical Account of the Science of Morality*, appended to his 1706 translation of Pufendorf's *Law of Nature*, Barbeyrac made the problematic relationship between moral realism and moral obligation the centrepiece of his discussion of the modern science of morality. Self-interest, ignorance and the difficulty of applying principles to particulars had vitiated the attempt to put morals on the same firm footing as the sciences. With Barbeyrac, the importance of Newtonian natural philosophy for the history of moral philosophy becomes fundamental. His response to the ever-present threat of scepticism was to invoke the Newtonian deity:

The Idea of a Creator, boundless in power, Wisdom, and Goodness; and the Idea of ourselves, as intelligent, reasonable, and sociable Creatures: These two ideas, I say, if well attended to, and compar'd together in their whole Extent, will always furnish us with steady Grounds of Duty, and sure Rules of Conduct; notwithstanding it may sometimes happen, that, for want of Care, or Attention, we may, in uncommon Cases, not know how to apply them; or cannot methodically demonstrate the necessary Connexion of some remote Consequences, with the first Principles of Morality.[26]

---

[24] *Law of Nature*, 1.i.10, p. 10. For Pufendorf's discussion of obligation as imposed by God, see J. B. Schneewind, 'Pufendorf's Place in the History of Ethics', *Synthèse*, 72 (1987), 123–55; Richard Tuck, *Natural Rights Theories* (Cambridge, 1979), p. 159.

[25] *Law of Nature*, 1.i.10, p. 11.

[26] Barbeyrac, *An Historical and Critical Account of the Science of Morality, and the Progress it Has Made in the World, from the Earliest Times down to the Publication of this Work*, tr. Carew, in Pufendorf's *Law of Nature* (London, 1749), p. 9.

Much as Samuel Clarke was concluding at the same time, the attributes of God could be used to supply secure 'Grounds of Duty' and 'Rules of Conduct'. Newton's God gave the law to individuals framed by the conditions of nature.[27] Barbeyrac's description of the metaphysics of the ancient Stoics bore the outline of the newly discovered Newtonian cosmos. They had divided the world into 'the Soul, or the active Principle; and Matter, the passive Principle', exactly mirroring the contemporary formula. Furthermore, the divinity was described as the 'Eternal, intelligent Being, which produc'd all Things', again very closely resembling the formula employed by English followers of Newton, like Clarke.[28] As they were to make clear, deciding the relationship of men to matter and spirit amounted to describing the possibility of morality.

While the ancient sceptics had provided modern ones like Montaigne and Locke with a foundation for an anthropologizing and hence relativized virtue, and the ancient Epicureans left a legacy of atheism that had been taken up by moderns who believed that there was no substance other than body and that body had only extension, solidity, magnitude, figure and motion, Barbeyrac believed that reason was still powerful enough to discover the universal natural laws of conduct.[29] None the less, he admitted that it needed help to withstand the blandishments of self-interest and passion. This 'requires a Being superior to us in Power; who has a manifest Right to our Obedience and who actually commands us to regulate our Conduct by the Light of our own Reason'.[30] The natural law had to be God's law if the intellectual strategies of the modern sceptics were to be foiled. Where Grotius had sought a common ground between the sceptical neo-Stoicism and divine law, by the end of the century the strains in this position began to show. Barbeyrac's doubt about the possible success of Grotius' anti-sceptic sceptical project and discomfort with Pufendorf's extensive voluntarism led him to place greater weight on moral realism backed by revelation. It was precisely this fear that epistemological scepticism would become theological scepticism that brought Locke's *Essay Concerning Human Understanding* into disrepute, being banned at Oxford in 1703.[31]

---

[27] Hence the possible ideological appropriation of this cosmos. See Margaret Jacob, *The Newtonians and the English Revolution* (Ithaca, 1976), and Simon Schaffer, 'Newtonian Cosmology and the Steady State', Unpublished Ph.D. thesis (Cambridge, 1980).
[28] Barbeyrac, *Historical*, p. 59.   [29] *Ibid.*, pp. 10, 57.   [30] *Ibid.*, p. 13.
[31] Rom Harré, 'Knowledge', in *The Ferment of Knowledge*, ed. Roy Porter and G. S. Rousseau (Cambridge, 1980), p. 15.

Moreover, the dominant contemporary political idiom, the hard-edged, prudent politics of the reason of state employed just those tactics that Barbeyrac believed inimical to the rational discovery of the natural law: self-interest and the manipulation of the passions. Against this formidable pair, divine help was clearly necessary.

This same assimilation of natural laws of Stoic origin to the divine ordering of nature lies at the heart of Samuel Clarke's argument. Like Cumberland and Barbeyrac, he saw the challenge of Hobbes' latter-day sceptical atheist followers as the primary danger to the pursuit of a common good characterized as *honestum*. His two-pronged response is reflected in the titles of the disputation topics for his 1708 Cambridge doctorate of divinity: 'No Article of the Christian Faith Delivered in the Holy Scriptures is Disagreeable to Right Reason' and 'Without the Liberty of Humane Actions There Can Be No Religion'. The sixteen Boyle Lectures of 1704–5 had put these principles to work, blending theological and ethical principles while grounding them on what he hoped would be the equivalent of Newtonian certitude – a description of divine attributes that could be shared by all men because accessible to the common light of reason.

Where Locke drew on the principles of natural philosophy to combat sceptics, Clarke looked to a particular, rational description of God, one designed to appeal to atheists as well as Christians. (It is not clear that he was completely successful with either.) The weight of Clarke's argument rested upon, first, establishing the wisdom and omnipotence of God and, second, affirming the analogy between God and man. In so far as omniscience, omnipotence and benevolence described the Newtonian God, as Simon Schaffer[32] has suggested, we can speak of Clarke creating a Newtonian philosophy. Creation communicated God's attributes to the universe and to mankind. Humans partook of God's Self-Motion, Self-Existence and Intelligence. This is the eighteenth-century analogy between God and man that served such an important philosophical task. James Tully has described this relationship between the creation of the natural and human worlds in the parallel metaphor of the 'Maker'.[33] The basic claim was that, 'Tis Possible to Infinite Power, to Create an Immaterial Cognitive Substance, indued with a Power

---

[32] Schaffer, *Newtonian Cosmology*, p. 236.
[33] James Tully, *A Discourse on Property*, pp. 39–41.

of beginning Motion, and with a Liberty of Will or Choice.'[34] Often, as with Bishop Butler, the analogy worked expressly by comparing 'the Constitution of the World', its appearances and design, with the particular constitution of individuals.[35] It is possible to see the analogy as an inherently conservative device, legitimating the status quo.[36] Thus, according to Steven Shapin, Clarke's defence of a voluntarist cosmos in his epistolary debate with Leibniz was an explicitly political defence of the Whig monarchy against critics both overseas and at home.[37] This may have been Clarke's intent in his other works as well. Yet the ascription of 'Self-Motion' to God also opened up the possibility of a most dramatic assertion of human liberty, one which ultimately helped to subvert the political force of the community and common good he had set out to defend.[38]

Just as God chose to use His freedom to fulfil His goodness, humankind ought best to use its granted powers 'to do all the Good it can to all its fellow-creatures'.[39] The necessary connection between liberty and moral agency was expressed by no one more clearly than by Clarke's follower, Arthur Sykes:

The Question, Whether a Man be a *Free* Agent or not, is of the utmost Consequence in an Enquiry whether Mankind is under any *Obligation* to be *religious*. For if they have no Freedom, but are impelled by *Fate* or *Necessity*; if they are absolutely determined by something either external, or internal, which they cannot controul, they cannot be *accountable* for what they do; nor can there be any Rule of *Action* to them, more than there is to *Stones*; They are, and ought to be considered as, mere *passive* Beings, not answerable for their Behaviour.[40]

Because man was so 'framed' as to possess the power to think and reason, he was able to choose between good and evil. Determinism, whether generated by sensation or the tyranny of the passions, was a threat to be exorcised. Locke's followers were the proponents of both

---

[34] Clarke, *A Demonstration of the Being and Attributes of God* ... (London, 1705), p. 159.

[35] Joseph Butler, *The Analogy of Religion Natural and Revealed, to the Constitution and Course of Nature* (London, 1736), p. 44. Also, Tunstall, *Lectures*, pp. 99, 110.

[36] Clark, *English Society*, p. 80.

[37] Steven Shapin, 'Of Gods and Kings: Natural Philosophy and Politics in the Leibniz–Clarke Disputes', *Isis*, 72 (1981), 187–215.

[38] See the author's '"Free-thinking" and "Freedom of Thought" in Eighteenth-Century Britain', *Historical Journal*, 36 (1993), pp. 599–617.

[39] Clarke, *A Discourse Concerning the Unchangeable Obligations of Natural Religion and the Truth and Certainty of the Christian Revelation* (London, 1706), p. 92.

[40] Arthur Ashley Sykes, *The Principles and Connexion of Natural and Revealed Religion Distinctly Considered* (London, 1740), p. 50.

views. For writers like Anthony Collins the process of perception demonstrated that thought and choice were direct consequences of sensation. Moreover, these sensations often formed themselves into ungovernable passions. Hence, the followers of Clarke resorted to the traditional Stoic psychomachia between reason and passion, defending the pre-eminence of the former. But it is important to note that their attack on 'happiness' was directed against a specific kind of happiness, what they believed was the hedonic or Epicurean argument of Locke's followers. Those influenced by Clarke had themselves embraced happiness, but it was of the sort identified by Rutherforth and Pufendorf with Cicero's notion of real and enduring utility. In so far as happiness was tied to present and evanescent physical goods it provided a poor rule of action and was rejected.[41] The desire to combat Hobbesian expediency led Clarke to so constrain the scope of *utilitas* as to push him over the edge into justifications of Ciceronian *honestum* grounded on a realistic natural law. Of course, as a follower of Newton he believed that one could actually argue rationally for the existence of just such laws. However, when, as in William Wollaston's formulation, 'The way to happiness and the practice of truth incur the one into the other', then the practice of rectitude and the attainment of happiness coincided.[42] What Wollaston called truth, Clarke called 'fitnesses'. This set of relations, or 'fitnesses', created by God described His conduct of the world and marked the self-imposed limits of omnipotence.[43] This voluntary self-restraint was the fundamental means by which Newtonians reconciled divine omnipotence and the laws of physics. These fitnesses constituted that 'Law of Nature' and, because the gift of reason enabled humans to interrogate the world, they could serve as models of human conduct.[44] 'Fitnesses', like Cumberland's 'prudence', identified moral judgment with the content of natural law. The analogy to divine governance added the force of obligation, creating a natural moral law:

This is that right Reason, which makes the principal Distinction betwixt Man and Beast. This is that Law of Nature, which (as Cicero excellently expresses it) is of universal extent [de Rep 3 frag], and everlasting duration; which can neither be wholly abrogated, nor repealed in any part of it, nor

---

[41] *Ibid.*, pp. 15–17.
[42] William Wollaston, *The Religion of Nature Delineated* (London, 1724), p. 40. Recall Rutherforth's distinction between these two kinds of happiness in the *Essay on Virtue*, pp. 189–90.
[43] Clarke, *Discourse*, p. 5.   [44] *Ibid.*, pp. 147–8.

be changed in any instance, nor dispensed with by any Authority: Which was in force [de Leg 1] before ever any law was written, or the foundation of any City, or Commonwealth was laid: Which [de Leg 1] was not invented by the Wit of Men, nor established by the Authority of an people; but its Obligation was from eternity, and the force of it reaches throughout the Universe: Which [de Leg 2] being founded in the Nature and Reason of Things, did not then begin to be a Law, when it was first written and enacted by Men; but is of the same original with the eternal Reasons or Proportions of things, and the Perfections or Attributes of God himself.[45]

References to the 'law of nature' and to Cicero frame Clarke's equation of a Newtonian understanding of an eternal law of nature with Ciceronian moral teachings.[46] Yet, the references to Ciceronian texts (*De Republica, De Legibus* and *De Officiis*) read very differently from the more familiar justifications of prudence. The emphasis on these theoretical works shifts the weight of argument decidedly away from the valid claims of utility – an important step in fighting the threat of Hobbism.[47] If, wrote Clarke, the law of nature 'had its original from the Authority of Men, and could be changed by it' then a whole range of abuses, from tyranny and murder to dissimulation and fraud, could be made licit (de Legibus 1). Clarke referred, without citation, to the same passage from the oration *Pro Plancio* that had been cited by Grotius, but in an opposite sense: 'In which matters if any Man thinks that the Votes and Suffrages of Fools have such Power, as to be able to change the Nature of Things; why do they not likewise decree (as Cicero admirably expresses himself,) that poisonous things may become wholsome; and that any other thing, which is now destructive of Mankind, may become preservative of it?'[48] Transcendent natural law, not political practice, had to provide the definitive picture of just relations. On Clarke's reading, Ciceronian virtue was defined as

---

[45] *Ibid.*, pp. 104–5. In this context it is worth noting Clarke's praise of Cicero, whose moral works must have seemed extremely congenial stuff, as 'the greatest and best Philosopher that Rome, or perhaps any other Nation ever produced ... ' (p. 222).

[46] Justin Champion is right to note that Clarke never abandoned revelation, believing, instead, that Cicero lent authoritative support against Matthew Tindal's claim that reason alone was sufficient (*The Pillars of Priestcraft Shaken*, p. 184).

[47] See J. P. Ferguson, *An Eighteenth-Century Heretic: Dr Samuel Clarke* (Kenton, 1976), p. 29; Gawlick, 'Cicero and the Enlightenment', 661.

[48] Clarke, *Discourse*, p. 108.

acts done 'for their own sakes and intrinsick worth and in expecta-
tion of '"no profit or advantage whatsoever"'.[49] Thus, it was
impossible to imagine that '"a Man, contrary to the eternal reason
of things, should desire to gain some small profit to Himself, by
doing violence and damage to his Neighbour [de Off 3]"'.[50]
Moreover, the practice of virtue was so 'noble and excellent' that the
wisest men 'have always declared, that "Neither Life itself, nor all
other possible injoyments in the World, put together, are of any
value or esteem at all, in comparison of, or in competition with, that
right temper and disposition of mind, from which flows the practice
of this universal Justice and Equity [de Off 3]"'.[51] Clarke applied
this specifically to the affairs of states, rejecting the claims of public
utility:

Only here it is to be observed, that by the publick Benefit must not be
understood the interest of any one particular Nation, to the plain injury or
prejudice of the rest of Mankind [de Off 3]; any more than the Interest of
one City or Family, in opposition to their Neighbours of the same Country:
But those things only are truly good in their own nature, which either tend
to the universal benefit and welfare of all Men, or at least are not
destructive of it.

Clarke argued that the good was naturally, not conventionally,
established.[52] In terms of politics, this vision was represented by an
account explicitly attributed to Cicero. A natural moral law exhort-
ing individuals to place public interest before the particular could
promote the public good as effectively and more 'morally' than
could the pragmatic pursuit of the public utility:

All Men stand upon the same level, and have the same natural wants and
desires, and are in the same need of each others help, and are equally
capable of injoying the benefit and advantage of Society; 'Tis evident every
Man is bound by the Law of his Nature, as he is also prompted by the
Inclination of his uncorrupted Affections, to look upon himself as a part
and member of that one universal body or community, which is made up of
all Mankind; to think himself born to promote the publick good and
welfare of all his fellow creatures; and consequently obliged, as the neces-

---

[49] *Ibid.*, p. 114. Clarke refers to Cicero, *De Finibus*, bks 2 and 3, *De Inventione*, bk 2, *De Legibus*,
    bk 1 and, significantly, *De Officiis*, bk 3.
[50] Clarke, *Discourse*, p. 87.
[51] *Ibid.*, p. 90. 'Non enim mihi est vita mea utilitior, quam animi talis affectio, neminem ut
    violem commodi mei gratia' (III.29).
[52] *Ibid.*, pp. 55–6.

sary and only effectual means to that End, to embrace them All with universal Love and Benevolence ...[53]

Clarke denounced social contracts and prudential politics as divisive artificial creations. Like Cumberland, whom he frequently used as ammunition alongside Cicero,[54] Clarke singled out Hobbes' antagonistic egoism as the consequence of a moral theory in which 'there is no such real Difference originally, necessarily and absolutely in the Nature of Things'.[55] Hobbes' moral and political philosophy was taken as the example of all that was wrong with an artificial morality. Like Pufendorf, Clarke specifically and unfavourably contrasted Hobbes with Cicero on just this issue.[56] Clarke summed up the early eighteenth-century natural law case against Hobbes in spectacular fashion by conflating Cicero and Scripture. ' ... and finally, to comprehend all in one word, (which is the Top and Complete Perfection of this great Duty,) [man] ought to *Love all others as himself.* This is the Argument of that great Master, Cicero [de Leg 1]; Whose knowledge and understanding of the true state of things, and of the original obligations of humane nature, was much greater than Mr Hobbs's.'[57] Similarly, where Locke rejected the existence of moral truths prior to the exercise of reason, Clarke sought to stress the continuity between the natural and moral worlds. Locke's claim that the principles of action alone, uneasiness and delight, were innate was far too weak to support Clarke's version of realism.[58] J. N. Finnis has suggested that Hume's critique of Clarke's use of the analogy to generate obligation (the 'is–ought' problem) marked the endpoint of a tradition of voluntarist, rationalist natural law. While its survival in Clarke's followers belies any definitive notice of demise, Finnis accurately observed that this tradition was attractive to Grotius and Clarke 'not least because of its strong verbal and conceptual resemblances to the Stoicism so much admired in European culture from the Renaissance to the end of the eighteenth century'.[59]

---

[53] *Ibid.*, pp. 95–6. This is supported by passages drawn from Cicero's *De Finibus, De Legibus* and *De Officiis.*
[54] Clarke, *Discourse*, pp. 104–9.   [55] *Ibid.*, pp. 51–6; also, pp. 108, 120.
[56] *Ibid.*, p. 97. Tunstall also found fault with Hobbes, and his rejection emphasizes the line taken by Cumberland and Clarke. The Hobbesian state of war was impossible because the rights of individuals not only 'must be consistent with the rights of all others, but the rights of all must be determined by the consideration of the common good' (*Lectures*, p. 179).
[57] Clarke, *Discourse*, p. 97.
[58] John Locke, *An Essay Concerning Human Understanding*, ed. P. H. Nidditch (Oxford, 1975), I.iii.13, pp. 74–5.
[59] Finnis, *Natural Law and Natural Rights* (Oxford, 1980), p. 47.

Clarke's commitment to natural religion, as expressed in his statement that he would try to persuade atheists in their own language of reason, left him open to high church criticism that he had undermined natural religion in the act of upholding it. At the same time, free-thinkers like Collins argued that he was systematically misinterpreting Cicero.[60] Thus, a follower of Clarke's like Arthur Sykes felt obliged to answer the question 'What is Religion?' with the declaration that it is 'the Belief or Practice of any thing that is right, from the Consideration of God'. Its great advantage was 'that the Rule of Action is now doubly secured, by its own Reasonableness, and by this demonstratively sure Addition'.[61] Hedging of bets in this manner was fairly common: Sykes, Bishop Butler, James Tunstall and Thomas Rutherforth all ended tracts on ethics and religion with discourses on revelation.

John Maxwell's translation of Cumberland's *Treatise* appeared in 1727, at a time when Samuel Clarke's ideas were a focus of English philosophical discussion. In his introduction, Maxwell reduced all the laws of nature to one which closely resembled Cumberland's position, and which was phrased in the very language that Clarke had drawn from Cumberland and then popularized in his own works: 'The Endeavour, to the utmost of our power, of promoting the common Good of the whole System of rational Agents, conduces, as far as in us lies, to the good of every Part, in which our own Happiness, as that of a Part, is contain'd.'[62] Moreover, in his appendix attacking those who united matter and spirit, Maxwell reprinted long passages from Clarke, who set the point 'in a clearer and stronger Light' than in 'any other Writer I have met with'.[63]

Clarke's account, drawing together reason, liberty, community and a natural moral law, provided the basis for a series of philosophical tracts written over the next three quarters of a century, from John Jackson and William Wollaston through Edmund Law, James Burgh and Richard Price. While Locke's epistemology remained crucial in Law's mediating position it was not a central

---

[60] In *A Discourse of Freethinking* (London, 1713), Collins suggested that 'Because Cicero's works are so frequently cited against free-thinkers both from the pulpit and the press, and his example recommended for their conviction, it may not be amiss utterly to disarm the enemies of free-thinking of Cicero's authority', by showing how they had abused their sources (cited in Gawlick, 'Cicero and the Enlightenment', p. 675).

[61] Sykes, *Principles and Connexion*, p. 93.

[62] Maxwell, Introduction, IX, *Treatise of the Laws of Nature*, p. 16.

[63] Maxwell, 'Appendix', *Laws of Nature*, p. 5.

concern of these writers. They remained engaged with the meta-physics and the corresponding description of human nature and capacities. Shaftesbury's paraphrase of Clarke's main point des-cribes the outline of the moral theory to which they were committed:

> For whosoever thinks there is a God, and pretends formally to believe that he is just and good, must suppose that there is independently such a thing as justice and injustice, truth and falsehood, right and wrong, according to which he pronounces that God is just, righteous, and true.[64]

After Clarke was compelled by Convocation to cease polemical writing in 1714, his disciple, John Jackson, took up the cause, and destroyed his chances for clerical advancement as a result. His chief polemical antagonists were Anthony Collins and *Cato*'s authors, John Trenchard and Thomas Gordon. Collins emphasized the deterministic consequences of Locke's theory of sensation at the expense of any hint of liberty.[65] *Cato* also sought to extend mechani-cal sensationalism to the operations of the mind[66] while simultane-ously emphasizing the role of the passions and the commensurate feebleness of reason.[67] Jackson's response turned on defending Clarke's vision of a free and intelligent deity from their claims of cosmic necessity. While his critics had strongly argued that passion, not reason, drove human conduct, Jackson reaffirmed the link between reason and liberty, asserting that greater liberty was a product of 'the Degree of *Reason* with which the mind is endued'.[68] The force of passion disengaged good and evil from nature and hence threatened the moral order. Jackson, like Clarke, believed that, because reason could discern 'the natural and unalterable Congruity and Incongruity of Things', good and evil consisted, rather, in the 'agreeableness' of actions to the fitnesses discovered by reason.[69] Jackson rejected the 'Machiavellian Notion' that law was a matter of 'particular Interest and Power', and, instead, located

---

[64] Anthony Ashley Cooper, 3rd Earl of Shaftesbury, *Characteristicks of Men, Manners, Opinions, Times*, 2 vols. (Indianapolis, 1964), I, p. 264.
[65] Anthony Collins, *A Philosophical Inquiry Concerning Human Liberty* (London, 1727), pp. 31, 71.
[66] *Cato's Letters*, no. 111, IV, pp. 47, 54.   [67] *Ibid.*, no. 39, II, pp. 46–7.
[68] Jackson, *A Vindication of Humane Liberty: In Answer to a Dissertation on Liberty and Necessity; Written by A. C., Esq.* (London, 1730), p. 24.
[69] Jackson, *A Defense of Human Liberty, In Answer to the Principal Arguments Which Have Been Alledged against it; and Particularly to Cato's Letters on that Subject* (2nd edn, London, 1730), p. 3.

justice in an explicitly Stoic law of nature.[70] This same divine natural law assured man's greatest happiness so that, 'whenever any Humane Laws deviate from these Principles they are imperfect, and have no Power and Efficacy to promote the Public Good'.[71] Moreover, because the exercise of reason played an absolutely critical role in establishing the grounds of moral conduct, denying it liberty made moral behaviour impossible. The importance of reason brought Clarke's liberty into new and sharper focus:

... Liberty of thinking and judging for ourselves is the Privilege and Right of all Mankind, as being rational Creatures; and a free impartial Enquiry after Truth is, in Matters of Philosophy, the great Principle of natural Knowledge, and in Matters of Religion and Morality, the Ground and Foundation of true Virtue and sincere Piety ...[72]

William Wollaston's contribution to this argument was to emphasize still more strongly the relationship between the good and the true. Thus, words or deeds that conformed to truth were good and those which did not were evil.[73] Wollaston developed this insight in an insouciant fashion, and contemporaries alternately bludgeoned and mocked it. Nevertheless, read in the context of Clarke's fitnesses and laws of nature, it is clear that Wollaston was trying to formulate an explicit link between moral conduct and the natural order. Furthermore, the emphasis on truth made the alternative endorsement of a practical Ciceronian morality fraught with grave rhetorical peril: how to dispense with truth when determining morality? For writers inspired by Clarke, Wollaston's move provided the kind of security heretofore derived solely from revelation. Writing in the next generation, Arthur Sykes commented that 'very little' could be added to what Clarke and Wollaston had written on the 'Existence and Attributes of God'.[74] This is made manifest in Philip Glover's *Inquiry Concerning Virtue and Happiness*, written in 1728, soon after the publication of Wollaston's tract, though only published in 1751.

[70] Jackson, *The Grounds of Civil and Ecclesiastical Government* (London, 1718), p. 4. 'Hence it was the Doctrine of the Stoics that the Original of Law was deriv'd from God and Nature. So that Humane Laws in General, whether Ecclesiastical or Civil, that have a true and right Foundation, are only *particular* Deductions from the general principles of *Nature or Reason*, or from the reveal'd Law of God; establish'd by common Consent in every political Society for the public Good, according as their Exigencies or the particular State of their circumstances may require.'

[71] *Ibid.*, p. 5.   [72] Jackson, *A Defense*, sig. A2r.

[73] Wollaston, *The Religion of Nature Delineated* (London, 1724), pp. 8–9. Also, Sykes, *Principle and Connexion*, pp. 14–15.

[74] Sykes, *Principle and Connexion*, p. 61.

Following a conventional description of God's attributes and the conformity of His actions to the 'eternal and everlasting Rule of all right Action', Glover proceeded to identify this natural law with Wollaston's truth. 'The Nature of Virtue to all moral Agents is, a Conformity in all their Actions to Truth, to the natures, circumstances, and relations of things, that such Beings can observe, and can affect.'[75] In Wollaston's account, reason had the fundamental task of providing access to truth. In its absence man became an animal, guided solely by the urging of the passions.[76] Where Jackson had seen that the fullness of human moral life required the free exercise of reason, Wollaston's formulation that the good represented some true relation with the world put a premium on knowledge. Only education could alert individuals to the nature of those true relations and therefore 'every man may in some degree or other endeavour to cultivate his nature, and possess himself of useful truths'. To ignore this was to 'apostatize from humanity, and recoil into the bestial life'.[77]

Glover, a contemporary of Jackson and Wollaston, focused their commitments to freedom of thought and pursuit of truth on a particular contemporary problem. The arguments for religious toleration later in the century do not move far from this statement:

Hence it follows, that there can be no Merit in right Opinion, Assent to Truth, or what is called Orthodoxy, but only in the Degree of Virtue with which Truth, or perhaps Error, is embraced; so little Reason is there for persecuting those that we think are in the wrong: and also that Actions cannot be materially Good or Bad, but only as they are conformable or contrary to the Dictates of the Conscience: and further, that all Virtue is essentially private, and an internal Act of the Mind.[78]

Because religion was essentially an 'Act of the Mind', ritual observance inconsistent with belief could not be described as religion. Glover suggested that, having reached this conclusion, the time had come to try 'the Effects of an universal Toleration'.[79]

Glover pulled together several different strands of Clarke's argument to create this extraordinary justification for toleration. Obscured, perhaps, by its prescience is the change wrought to the

---

[75] [Philip Glover], *An Inquiry Concerning Virtue and Happiness* (London, 1751), p. xviii. For nearly the same formulation, see Sykes, *Principles and Connexion*, p. 9.
[76] Wollaston, *Religion of Nature*, pp. 50–1, 169.   [77] *Ibid.*, p. 177.
[78] Glover, *Inquiry*, p. 90.
[79] *Ibid.*, p. 130.

tradition *en route* to this formulation. Clarke's law of nature supported a commitment to real moral truths and the common good while repudiating the prudential morality traditionally associated with the pursuit of social life but which too closely resembled the arguments of his polemical antagonists. Reason, then, had to be free to discover the moral law in nature; over time the emphases on freedom of thought and the acquisition of knowledge displaced the centrality of the quest for these truths. Simultaneously, the moral horizon contracted from the community to the individual. This changed perspective characterizes the moral thought of James Burgh and Richard Price and provides an important context for appreciating their political arguments. By mid-century, as we have had occasion to observe, the opposition tradition offered little to distinguish its politics from the rule of prudence and security set forth by supporters of community security – except an appeal to moral reformation. The later reformers, Burgh, Price, John Cartwright and Joseph Priestley, were able to offer a new, invigorated account of public life precisely because their politics reflected the coherence that this deep metaphysical shift had given to accounts of individual liberty in society. The traditional defence of the security and preservation of the community (*salus populi suprema lex esto*) had given way to a new definition of what was worthy of being defended.

James Burgh's cosmos also depended on Clarke's account of God. The deity's moral character was displayed in creating individuals as 'moral agents', 'capable of distinguishing between good and evil, of choosing the former, and rejecting the latter, and of resembling Him in moral perfection'.[80] Because moral agency was impossible without liberty, no means other than persuasion could be used to direct human conduct.[81] Burgh suggested that this was the foundation of all 'political subjects' and that, therefore, 'Plain sense', rather than 'the sublime geometry or the Newtonian philosophy' would be adequate for most citizens.[82] The close relation between Burgh's argument and that of Scottish 'Common Sense' philosophy is given obvious expression by Priestley's later attacks on Price's similar views on the one hand, and those of Reid, Beattie and Oswald on the other.

Agency, and therefore liberty, was identified with virtue and also

---

[80] Burgh, *Crito*, II, p. 127.
[81] Burgh, *The Dignity of Human Nature* (London, 1754), p. 213.
[82] Burgh, *Crito*, I, pp. 1, 189.

with knowledge. Though showing no specific signs of indebtedness to Wollaston or Glover, Burgh, the dissenting schoolmaster, contended that 'there ought to be no distinction between the love of knowledge and of virtue, it being evident, that the proper improvement and due conduct of the understanding is an indispensable part of the duty of every rational being'.[83] Equating liberty and knowledge with virtue reflected Burgh's broader view of human nature, in which intellectual achievement was evaluated as far superior to the martial valour praised by earlier civilizations.[84] None of this is associated with either the stern commonwealthman of legend nor the bourgeois radical of recent times.[85] It does bear a strong family resemblance, however, to Richard Price's *Review of the Principal Questions in Metaphysics* (1759), which Burgh described warmly as possessing 'as much close reasoning, as ever has been put into the same room by any writer, not excepting Mr Locke himself'.[86]

Price's philosophical masterpiece was the culmination of the line of thinkers working with Samuel Clarke's arguments. His God was self-existent, eternal, necessary and free, all the attributes Clarke had specified of Him. In a short essay appended to the third edition of the *Review*, he acknowledged that his argument about the *Being and Attributes of the Deity* 'is the same with Dr Clarke's; but it will be a little differently represented, and pursued farther'.[87] Price was also considered by colleagues to be an authority on Newton.[88] He upheld Clarke's original Newtonian distinction between passive matter and God's active principle and chose, like his predecessor, to make God act within laws even if not really subject to them.[89]

[83] Burgh, *Dignity*, p. 99.   [84] *Ibid.*, pp. 100–3.

[85] Compare the presentations of Carla H. Hay, *James Burgh, Spokesman for Reform in Hanoverian England* (Washington, DC, 1979), and Isaac Kramnick, *Republicanism and Bourgeois Radicalism: Political Ideology in late eighteenth-century England and America* (Ithaca, 1990). Martha Kaderly Zebrowski's *One Cato Is Not Enough . . .* , unpublished Ph.D. thesis (Columbia, 1982) remains by far the most illuminating examination of Burgh's thought.

[86] Burgh, *Crito*, II, p. 131n. Staughton Lynd is correct to describe these as key texts for understanding the dissenting notion of truth as self-evident (*Intellectual Origins of American Radicalism* (London, 1973), pp. 27–8).

[87] Price, 'A Dissertation on the Being and Attributes of the Deity', *A Review of the Principal Questions and Difficulties in Morals* (3rd edn, London, 1787), ed. D. D. Raphael (Oxford, 1954; rpt, 1974), pp. 286, 290; D. O. Thomas, *The Honest Mind: The Thought and Work of Richard Price* (Oxford, 1977), pp. 12, 19.

[88] Evidence of his high standing within this tradition, Price was offered the task of editing Newton's works: see, J. N. Stephens, 'Price, Providence and the *Principia*', *Enlightenment and Dissent*, 6 (1987), 78; Bernard Peach, *Richard Price and the Ethical Foundations of the American Revolution* (Durham, NC, 1977), p. 13.

[89] Price, *A Review of the Principal Questions and Difficulties in Morals* (2nd edn, London, 1769), p. 141.

Price's distinction between abstract and practical virtue served to introduce the category that he came to call, in the *Observations upon the Nature of Civil Liberty*, 'physical liberty'. Practical virtue presupposed liberty since, in the commonplace formulation, without agency there could be no moral responsibility: 'The true idea of liberty is the same with that of acting and determining: And it is self-evident, that where all active powers are wanting, there can be no moral capacities. A being who cannot act at all, most certainly cannot act virtuously.'[90] Price, like his Scottish contemporary Reid, appealed to a common sense perception that it would be an 'absurdity' to say that 'my volitions are produced by a foreign cause, that is, are not mine'. The 'whole language of men', their 'practical sentiments and schemes' and 'the whole frame and order of human affairs' presumed that human beings could be held responsible for their actions.[91] The entire lexicon of moral valuation presupposed 'agency, voluntary motion, free choice'. This is obviously the proper context for understanding Price's fourfold definition of liberty employed in the *Observations* of 1776, but at the time his baffled and incensed interlocutors simply did not recognize it.

Despite his reliance on Clarke's epistemology, Price had broken free of some of his conclusions. He developed the implications of Clarke's reading of Cicero as the defender of rectitude, which in Clarke had remained anchored to the conventional understanding of the common good, into a defence of the very different primacy of the individual. Locke's theory of sensation, Hutcheson's theory of the moral sense and the strong claims of 'benevolence' and 'sympathy' were all rejected as incompatible with Clarke's support for rectitude – now understood as pertaining to individual conduct.[92]

Though Price accepted the fundamental character of benevolence,[93] he rejected its elevation to a position of moral supremacy. No doubt referring to Hutcheson, he assimilated benevolence to the crude 'utilitarian' service of the greater, common, good and then attacked:

It cannot surely be true, for instance, that promises and engagements are not in any case binding upon any one, any further than he thinks the observance of them will be productive of good to particular persons, or to

---

[90] *Ibid.*, p. 301.   [91] *Ibid.*, pp. 302–3.
[92] Against Locke, *Review*, pp. 16, 19–20, 52; against Hutcheson, pp. 9–11, 98, 119, and as quoted by Priestley in *An Examination*, appendix I, p. 322.
[93] Price, *Review*, p. 114.

society; or, that we are released from all obligation to regard them, as soon as we believe, that violating them will not hurt the person to whom they have been made, or that, if detrimental to him, it will be equally beneficial to ourselves, or, in any other way, will be attended with advantages equal to the foreseen harm.[94]

Here is where Price's criticism of the public good began to bite. He pinpointed Hutcheson's most extreme defence of the community's good as a standard of morality, the assertion that enemies of the public good had forfeited their right to law and conscience.[95] Mirroring Hutcheson's chosen examples, Price rebuffed him point for point. Criminals and rebels could not be dealt with summarily, despite their manifest attempt to destroy the public good. Why, Price asked, were individuals not free 'to practise any kinds of dissimulation' so long as no one was harmed? Because, he replied, there was 'intrinsick rectitude in keeping faith and sincerity and intrinsick evil in the contrary'.[96] Price caricatured Hutcheson's utilitarian calculus as the simple dictum 'that the goodness of the end always consecrates the means'. If that were not enough to raise the ignominious spectre of Machiavelli's *Prince*, Price wondered aloud if, '*caeteris paribus*, it is as innocent and laudable to accomplish our purposes by lyes, prevarication and perjury, as by faithful and open dealing and honest labour?'[97]

Duty to ourselves offered another example of virtue, 'the principle of which is not kind affection, and which no views of public utility, or sympathy with others can possibly explain'.[98] The attack on dissimulation and 'Machiavellian' prudence reveals the true target of Price's redefinition of the good: the Ciceronian standard of public utility. In *De Officiis*, the apparent conflict between utility and rectitude vanished in Cicero's exposition of the *utilitas rei publicae*. In Cicero's argument and in those influenced by him, this was described as the public good. Price sets this against the 'rights of beings':

... if the publick good be the sole measure and foundation of property and the rights of beings, it would be absurd to say innocent beings have a right to exemption from misery, or that they may not be made in any degree miserable, if but the smallest degree of prepollent good can arise from it. Nay, any number of innocent beings might be placed in a state of absolute

---

[94] *Ibid.*, p. 220.   [95] Hutcheson, *System*, ii.ix.11, ii, p. 20.   [96] Price, *Review*, p. 221.
[97] *Ibid.*, p. 223.   [98] *Ibid.*, p. 248.

and eternal misery, provided amends is made for their misery by producing at the same time a greater number of beings in a greater degree happy.[99]

Deriving virtue from notions of public utility undermined the relationship between morality and God. 'Is it only for our own sakes', Price asked, 'or out of a view to public utility, that we obey and honour the Deity?' The consequence of this popular view was not merely that individuals became morally expendable in the interest of the greater good, but that individuals were free to employ whatever means could achieve their private good.

How are we to account for a man's refraining from secret fraud, or his practising truth, sincerity, equity, justice, and honour, in many particular instances of their interfering, or seeming to interfere, with private and publick good, as well as with his strongest natural desires? – Let any one, for example, try what reasons he can find from benevolence or self-interest, why an honest man, though in want, though sure of being never suspected, should not secure a good estate, ease and plenty to himself, and relief and aid to his neighbours, by secreting or interpolating a will by which it of right devolved on a worthless person, already sufficiently provided for, and who, in all likelihood, would use it only to make himself and others miserable?[100]

The objects of Price's condemnation were, of course, precisely those tactics employed by the prudent practitioners of the reason of state. From Barbeyrac and Cumberland, most notably, Samuel Clarke would have inherited moral realism, natural law and the belief that the pursuit of various individual goods would coincide in a common good. Newton and his laws of nature had helped sketch the architecture of the analogy and Clarke's subsequent description of human beings made its discovery the key to moral action. The free exercise of reason and the acquisition of knowledge became, accordingly, vital prerequisites for the moral life. By the middle of the century increasing stress on the means had transformed them into ends of sufficient importance as to recast the very purpose of politics. The common good had been effectively removed to a position of secondary importance. No longer could utility and right be reconciled in favour of public utility: 'It is indeed far from easy to determine what degree of superior good would compensate the irreparable and undeserved ruin of one person; or what over balance of happiness would be great enough to justify the absolute

---

[99] *Ibid.*, p. 265, p. 266.   [100] *Ibid.*, p. 309.

misery of one innocent being ... publick happiness cannot be the sole standard and measure of justice and injustice.' The pursuit of God's truth, nature's law and man's good could not be impeded or even shaped by questions of expediency. Cicero the statesman had to be jettisoned. In a footnote to this passage Price firmly set himself against the argument of contemporaries like Hume and Jenyns, and restated Clarke's reading, even citing the exact same passage in *De Officiis*, bk 3.

> There are some actions, says Cicero, so foul, that a good man would not do them to save his country. – He praises Fab[ric]ius, the Roman general, for sending back to Pyrrhus a deserter, who had offered privately to poison him for a proper reward from the Romans: And also Aristides for rejecting, because not just, a proposal very profitable to his country, made to him by Themistocles. – To the question: Would not a good man, when starving with hunger, force food from another man who is worthless? he answers, by no means; and gives this reason for it: *Non enim mihi est vita mea utilitior, quam animi talis affection, neminem ut violem commodi mei gratia* [Nothing in my life is so useful as to lead me to violate a trust for my benefit] – the like answer he gives to the question, Whether a virtuous man would, in order to save his life in a shipwreck, thrust a worthless man from a plank he had seized.[101]

Where Clarke, however, had nevertheless remained committed to the Stoic vision of community, arguing that the very 'Nature of Man' led to the growth of society,[102] Price's emphasis was on the claims individuals could make against their societies. Perceiving that his repudiation of this fundamental political commonplace and redefinition of the public good was sure to cause him to be pegged as an enemy of society, Price sought to head off the inevitable charges of anarchism. Though the public good could not be the 'sole original of justice', Price conceded that it did give 'a very considerable force to the *rights* of men, and, in some cases entirely creates them'. The happiness of the world required secure property and in the absence of such consideration 'general anarchy, distrust and savageness be introduced'.[103] Price knew his society. After the publication of his *Observations*, which made explicit the political implications of this reorientation of Clarke's metaphysical liberty, the most common accusation was that Price was an anarchist.

Price was wary of the possible diminution of the value of the individual when held in a balance with the public good. With his

---

[101] *Ibid.*, p. 267n.   [102] Clarke, *Discourse*, p. 94, citing *De Finibus*, bk 5.
[103] Price, *Review*, p. 272.

belief that only liberty to think and learn made moral action possible, he could not simply assume that public and private goods coincided. His critique of the contemporary weighting in favour of the security of the community closed with a sensitive appreciation of the political problem of preserving some degree of individual liberty while living in society.

Thus, the pursuit of the happiness of others is a duty, and so is the pursuit of private happiness; and though, on the whole, these are inseparably connected, in many particular instances, one of them cannot be pursued without giving up the other. When the publick happiness is very great, and the private very inconsiderable, no difficulties appear. We pronounce as confidently, that the one ought to give way to the other, as we do, that either alone ought to be pursued. But when the former is diminished, and the latter increased to a certain degree, doubt arises; and we may thus be rendered entirely incapable of determining what we ought to chuse. We have the most satisfactory perception, that we ought to study our own good, and, within certain limits, prefer it to that of another; but who can say how far, mark precisely these limits, and inform us in all cases of opposition between them, where right and wrong and indifference take place?[104]

Price, unlike the republican tradition to which he is often attached, did not despair of discovering the proper balance between individual and community. Again like Burgh, agency was believed to depend upon knowledge of what constituted the proper moral course of action. Price wrote that 'There is no person so ignorant as not to have some knowledge of moral good and evil.' The difficulty was in 'acting up' to this high standard.[105] Because moral ambiguity was not inherent in the concepts themselves but in their complicated manifestations in daily life, clear principles of action depended on clarity of understanding. Recall that Cumberland described prudence as the body of knowledge needed to determine moral action, and tried to describe morality in terms of causes and effects. Hutcheson intensified the drive to clarify moral life by devising formulae that calculated virtuous behaviour based on the fractions of 'virtue' in any given action.[106] Price was in this tradition. He mocked Hutcheson's equations but, like Cumberland, believed that only the

[104] *Ibid.*, p. 277.
[105] Price, *The Vanity, Misery and Infamy of Knowledge without Suitable Practice* ... *a Sermon* (London, 1770), p. 8; also *The Nature and Dignity of the Human Soul. A Sermon* ... (London, 1766), p. 12.
[106] Price, *Review*, p. 278.

possession of 'universal and unerring knowledge' made 'the rule of right' possible. The requisite intellectual effort was immense, requiring knowledge of the 'different heads of virtue' and their often conflicting relationship to one another. The only way to gain some purchase on difficult moral issues was by the laborious process of learning in the hope of finding more secure footing.[107] Hence the great importance of education. In the structure of Price's argument, and here it resembled both Clarke's and Cumberland's, learning helped to discover the principles that guided moral action and which constituted the law of nature. It was this emphasis on reason and learning that necessarily minimized the importance of the community:

Until men can be raised above defective knowledge, and secured against partial and inadequate views, they must continue liable to believe cases and facts and the tendencies of actions, to be otherwise than they are; and, consequently, to form false judgments concerning right and wrong.[108]

As the panacea for moral and social ills, this would be a caricature of Enlightenment social theory but as a piece of moral philosophy it illuminates the underpinnings of the political stance taken by Price and others on America and toleration. The enforcement of a community-oriented standard of virtue was a bad idea, and the history of Christianity proved this, if nothing else.[109] Price clearly follows Burgh and Glover in describing all education as invariably a moral education. But there are also unmistakable echoes of Wollaston's description of morality as truth: 'The desire of knowledge also, and the preference of TRUTH, must arise in every intelligent mind. TRUTH is the proper object of mind, as light is of the eye, or harmony of the ear.'[110] The practice of morality required freedom to think. There was no better example of immorality built upon ignorance than religious persecution. Its prevalence throughout history testified to the danger of shackling the mind. Persecution was a function of 'defective knowledge' and the false belief that it did 'Gods service'.[111] Only more accurate information could eradicate these 'false judgments'.

---

[107] *Ibid.*, p. 283.   [108] *Ibid.*, p. 286.   [109] *Ibid.*, pp. 225–6.

[110] *Ibid.*, pp. 118–19. Again, 'Why, therefore, reasonable beings love truth, knowledge, and honour; is to be answered in the same manner with the enquiry; why do they love and desire happiness? This, we have seen, is, and cannot but be desired for itself' (*Dignity and Nature*, pp. 12, 23).

[111] Price, *Review*, p. 284.

TOLERATION AND FREEDOM OF THOUGHT: AN
INTRODUCTION

Though Britain was, by contemporary standards, a tolerant
country, a publicly preaching non-Anglican was legally liable to life
imprisonment and confiscation of property. The Test and Corporation Acts remained, though mitigated by the Toleration Act of
1689, which exempted dissenting ministers from penal laws on
condition that they declared against Popery and swore to thirty-four
or thirty-five of the thirty-nine Articles.[112] Enforcement of its provisions in the eighteenth century was limited by regular Acts of
Indemnity and of Quieting and Establishing Corporations, as well
as by the practice of occasional conformity.[113] None the less, toleration lacked legal security and attempts to obtain it by repeal of
existing legislation failed conclusively in 1739. For thirty years there
were no organized demands for wider toleration. On 17 July 1770
an Association was established, at the Feathers Tavern in London,
to petition parliament for relief from subscription. Although latitudinarians and dissenters had participated in the contemporary
debate about a wider toleration, the petition aimed solely to relieve
the condition of the former. John Gascoigne has described this as the
high-water mark of the Cambridge latitudinarian tradition which
traced itself back from Richard Watson and Edmund Law to
Hoadly, Clarke and Tillotson. In the course of dismissing the petition on 6 February 1772, Lord North had let it drop that a
dissenting petition would have been more favourably heard. A
Dissenters Relief Bill was hurriedly cobbled together but was
rejected by the House of Lords on a second reading in May of 1772.
This bill would have amended the old Toleration Act by repealing
the section requiring subscription to doctrinal articles and replacing
it with a declaration of belief in the Gospels. The bill was reintro-
duced in 1773 but again failed in the House of Lords in May 1774.
No further parliamentary effort was made until 1779 when a similar
bill was finally approved by parliament.[114]

---

[112] J. N. Stephens, 'The London Ministers and Subscription, 1772–1779', *Enlightenment and
Dissent*, 1 (1982), 43, note 1. They were excused from the first clause of article 20, and
articles 34, 35, 36. Baptists only were also excused from article 27.

[113] James E. Bradley, *Religion, Revolution and English Radicalism* (Cambridge, 1990), pp. 70,
84–5.

[114] See Martin Hugh Fitzpatrick, 'Rational Dissent in the Late Eighteenth Century with
Particular Reference to the Growth of Toleration', Unpublished Ph.D. thesis (Aberyst-

The same obvious question that scholars have asked of radicalism has also been asked of dissent: why was there a hiatus during the middle decades of the century and what was the nature of the argument when it revived in the later 1760s and early 1770s? In terms of toleration, the standard answers have focused on the conditions of national and international politics. The middle of the century saw Britain engaged in external wars and the suppression of domestic rebellion. On this argument, dissenters did not threaten the Whig government because they perceived that they were, generally speaking, beneficiaries of the status quo. Patriotism, whether provoked by the French or the Jacobites, made the dissenters great 'friends of civil liberty', as they were later to boast. A decline in numbers and increase in economic well-being may also have militated against political activism.[115] The revival of dissent in the later 1760s has been attributed, variously, to the challenge of Socinian heterodoxy, raised economic expectations, and an increasingly self-conscious group identity.[116] There is also the realm of the contingent. Francis Blackburne's *Confessional*, which set this debate in motion, was finally published in 1766 after twelve years in the making. Had it appeared sooner the movement for a wider toleration might have begun sooner. But we shall never know.

The basic commitments of rational dissent were to the priority of Scripture over tradition and gathered churches over the Establishment.[117] The sufficiency of Scripture never approached fideism: 'On the contrary, revelation was authoritative because it was the voice of divine reason, which spoke directly and compellingly to human hearts and minds.'[118] The power of reason to discover truth was the weight-bearing element in the structure of dissenting arguments. Reason guaranteed the intellectual autonomy of the individual Protestant's negotiation of a spiritual relationship, led to the recognition that fallibility was preferable to dogma and generated

---

wyth, 1982), p. 192; Gascoigne, *Cambridge in the Age of Enlightenment*, p. 194; Stephens, 'London Ministers', p. 43; G. M. Ditchfield, 'The Subscription Issue in British Parliamentary Politics, 1772–9', *Parliamentary History*, 7 (1988), 51–61; Fitzpatrick, 'Toleration and Truth', pp. 7–8; Ditchfield, 'The Parliamentary Struggle over the Repeal of the Test and Corporation Acts, 1787–1790', *English Historical Review*, 89 (1974), 551–77.

[115] See Fitzpatrick, *Rational Dissent*, pp. v, 18; John Seed, 'Gentlemen Dissenters', p. 306; Bradley, *Religion*, p. 88.

[116] Clark, *English Society*, pp. 316–18; Bradley, *Religion*, p. 89; Kramnick, *Republicanism*, pp. 47–50; Russell E. Richey, 'The Origins of British Radicalism: The Changing Rationale for Dissent', *Eighteenth-Century Studies*, 7 (1974), 179–92.

[117] Bradley, *Religion*, p. 4.   [118] Fitzpatrick, 'Toleration and Truth', p. 4.

tremendous optimism about the possibilities of improvement attendant upon the discovery of truth.[119] All this was obviously supported
by the philosophical arguments which, in Price's work, had matured
into a full-fledged defence of the sanctity of the individual.

One of the most noticeable aspects of the political argument of the
rational dissenters, one which distinguishes them from their predecessors earlier in the century, is the importance of the appeal to
natural rights. Again, as in the colonial debate, this 'innovation' is
typically attributed to the influence of John Locke.[120] In fact,
however, this rights argument, like the one deployed in the colonial
debate, has a very different inspiration.[121] There, the threat of 'ruin'
and 'destruction' triggered what was a conventional and accepted
recourse to necessity, and this, the equally conventional assertion of
a natural right to self-preservation. The difference between colonies
and metropolis turned on the determination of the status of necessity. Here, Clarke's metaphysical argument, not some jurispruden-
tial model, provided dissenters and political reformers with their
inalienable natural rights. Thus, we arrive at the somewhat para-
doxical conclusion that this demand for toleration was built on a
'thick', rather than a 'thin' notion of truth. From Barbeyrac through
men like Clarke and Price realism rather than scepticism was seen to
provide the basis of a tranquil and reforming civil society.[122]

The practice of toleration by connivance pre-empted any dissenting appeal to pragmatic, *politique* policy.[123] Moreover, prudence was
itself the leading justification for the denial of any wider legal
toleration. The security of the community demanded that membership in the national church be a prerequisite for those entering its
service. Many dissenters recognized and even shared this concern.[124] The rift within the General Body of London Dissenting

[119] Seed, 'Gentlemen Dissenters', p. 316; Fitzpatrick, 'Heretical Religion and Radical Political Ideas in Late Eighteenth-Century England', in *The Transformation of Political Culture*,
ed. Eckhart Hellmuth (Oxford, 1990), pp. 342–5; Fitzpatrick, *Rational Dissent*, p. 581.

[120] For a recent example, see Bradley, *Religion*, pp. 142–3.

[121] Similarly, see Fitzpatrick, *Rational Dissent*, pp. 229, 311.

[122] Against Bayle, Barbeyrac had argued that 'toleration of different religious beliefs would
be achieved only when there was universal acknowledgment of the natural rights of all
believers to work up their own rational understanding of God's Providence' (James
Moore, 'Natural Law and the Pyrrhonian Controversy', in *Philosophy and Science in the
Scottish Enlightenment*, ed. P. Jones (Edinburgh, 1988), p. 23). See also Mark Philp,
'Enlightenment, Toleration and Liberty', *Enlightenment and Dissent*, 9 (1990), 62; Richard
Tuck, 'Scepticism and Toleration in the Seventeenth Century', *Justifying Toleration*, ed.
Susan Mendus (Cambridge, 1988), pp. 21–36.

[123] Fitzpatrick, 'Toleration and Truth', p. 30.   [124] Fitzpatrick, *Rational Dissent*, p. 216.

Ministers that began in 1773 turned on the question of whether religion contributed to political stability or whether the two were completely separate. If the former were the case, then there were legitimate grounds for civil supervision of religion.[125] Similarly, while most dissenters accepted Locke's reservation that the extent of private judgment was determined by the civil assessment of national security, the real point of contention was what constituted a threat to the common good.[126] Characteristically, the dissenters took the position that differences of opinion about intellectual matters very, very rarely put the security of the state at risk.

The terms of this debate were set by the requirements of the post-Reformation state and elaborated by its spokesmen and theorists. As in the other early modern states possessing national churches, belief, not to mention practice, was considered an interest of the British state. It might have taken a Machiavelli to stress 'civic religion', but the church's role as a supporter and guide for temporal rulers was part of the history of the West since Constantine. If anything, the English Reformation had given legal sanction to a strengthened alliance of church and state. Those who wanted to challenge the prudent doctrines governing imperial management had to claim the transcendental high ground. They could not effect the changes they wanted by appealing to the same sources of authority as their antagonists. Similarly, in a society in which connivance and indemnity were deeply ingrained, religious reformers had to challenge the principle if they were to alter the practice.

RELIGION AND THE 'UTILITAS REI PUBLICAE'

The defence of the ecclesiastical establishment was not primarily conducted in theological language. Instead, the civic value of a religious establishment was felt to warrant the protection of the civil magistrate. Thus, a threat to the former was construed as a threat to the latter.[127] As Roger Newdigate said in the Commons Debate on the Feathers' Tavern Petition, 'indeed what is religion but the soul that animates the body politic?'[128] This image reflects the influence of William Warburton's *Alliance between Church and State*, published in 1736 at the height of the previous demand for wider toleration. Like

---

[125] Stephens, 'London Ministers', p. 52.   [126] Fitzpatrick, 'Toleration and Truth', p. 5.
[127] Tunstall, *Lectures*, p. 3.   [128] Quoted in Fitzpatrick, *Rational Dissent*, p. 199.

the more famous theorists of the post-Reformation state, Warburton's effort to assure the strength of the state religion often sounded very like the Machiavellian 'civic religion' arguments it was designed to confute. It was precisely the recognition that there was an ineluctably civil role for religion in the modern state that lent his work such weight in the debate with rational dissenters who were advocating a separation of the civil and spiritual powers. Warburton's argument remained formidable over three decades later, as attested to by Joseph Priestley, who acknowledged that 'his *Alliance* was generally considered as the best defence of the present system of church-authority, and that most other writers took their arguments from it'.[129] The *Alliance* set the tone of the ideological response to English dissent. Warburton argued that civil society was alone capable of providing 'the Security of the Temporal Liberty and Property of Man'. Because the salvation of souls, as Locke indicated, could be achieved within civil society or outside of it, religion could be considered neither its cause nor end: 'Whatsoever therefore refers to the Body and its Appendixes is in his Jurisdiction; whatsoever, to the Soul is not.'[130] Warburton, however, excepted three fundamental principles whose observance the civil ruler was charged to uphold as forcefully as any civil law. These were the being of God, His providence in human affairs and the 'essential Difference' between moral good and evil.[131]

Where there was an alliance between politics and religion it was in the 'interest' of the civil ruler to promote this religious truth. In describing the conflict between Henry II and Becket in the volume of the *History* published in 1763, Hume seems to be commenting, in this familiar language, on the contemporary relationship of the Church of England to the state: 'The union of the civil and ecclesiastical power serves extremely, in every civilized government, to the

---

129 Priestley, *Considerations on Church Authority; Occasioned by Dr Balguy's Sermon* (London, 1769), p. vii; John Jebb also singled out Warburton's argument as characteristic of the opponents of wider toleration ('Letters on the Subject of Subscription to the Liturgy and Thirty-Nine Articles of the Church of England', *The Works, Theological, Medical, Political and Miscellaneous of John Jebb*, ed. J. Disney (London and Cambridge, 1787), I, pp. 162–3). Although, as Stephen Taylor has noted, from the perspective of orthodox Anglicanism (though not, one might add, from that of contemporary statecraft) Warburton's argument might appear eccentric, it was surely true that dissenters took him as the most potent of their adversaries (Stephen Taylor, 'William Warburton and the Alliance of Church and State', *Journal of Ecclesiastical History*, 43 (1992), 273, 276).
130 William Warburton, *The Alliance between Church and State* (London, 1736), pp. 21–2.
131 *Ibid.*, p. 24.

maintenance of peace and order; and prevents those mutual incroachments, which, as there can be no ultimate judge between them, are often attended with the most dangerous consequences.'[132] The ruler's capacity to reconcile the potentially discordant demands of utility and right underlined the source of Warburton's argument: 'And, by means of Public Utility which his Office enables him so well to understand, he will never be at a loss to know where such truth is to be met with. So that it is impossible under this Civil Influence that Religion should ever deviate far from Truth.'[133] Warburton's reconciliation, like Cicero's, could only be effected because of a prior commitment to the priority of utility. Thus, 'to abridge a Citizen of his Civil Rights for Matters of Opinion, which affect Society, is no Violation of the Laws of Nature'.[134]

Clarke and his followers had employed a natural law argument founded on the capacity of reason to ascertain the 'real' or 'essential' moral truths. While Warburton, too, remained committed to an 'essential' difference between moral good and evil, he suggested that Clarke's interpretation was incorrect. By defining it as 'that which right Reason, taking in all Circumstances, dictates, in every Case, to be done', his followers had conflated natural and civil law to the clear detriment of the former. Warburton argued that an authentic understanding of the law of nature would define it as the prescriptions of reason, based on human nature, 'whether in or out of Society, without any Regard had to the peculiar Frame, Genius and Constitution of Civil Policy'. While Warburton seems to be defending natural law against its contamination by practical needs, he was actually asserting as a law of nature the most prudent consideration of all: 'What else but public Good, the Peace of Civil

---

[132] Hume, *History of England*, I, p. 311.   [133] Warburton, *Alliance*, p. 35.
[134] *Ibid.*, p. 125, also pp. 32, 113. This theme was prominent in the anti-tolerationist literature. See W. S. Powell, *A Defence of the Subscriptions Required in the Church of England. A Sermon* (London, 1758), p. 5; James Ibbetson, *A Plea for the Subscription of the Clergy to the Thirty-Nine Articles of Religion* (2nd edn, London, 1767), pp. 1–2, 20; Nathaniel Forster, *The Establishment of the Church of England Defended upon the Principles of Religious Liberty. A Sermon* (London, 1770), pp. 5, 9, 13; Benjamin Newton, *The Influence of the Improvements*, p. 11; Thomas Randolph, *An Answer to a Pamphlet, Entituled Considerations on the Propriety of Requiring a Subscription to Articles of Faith* (Oxford, 1774), p. 11; Randolph, *The Reasonableness of Requiring Subscription to Articles of Religion* (Oxford, 1771), p. 6; Josiah Tucker, *A Brief and Dispassionate View of the Difficulties Attending the Trinitarian, Arian and Socinian Systems* (Gloucester, 1774), pp. 11, 14; Tucker, *An Apology for the Present Church of England as by Law Established* (Gloucester, 1772), pp. 3–4.

Society, the avoiding Disorder, and stifling the Seeds of Chicane and Progress.'[135]

The alliance was entered into to serve the public good and, since the upholding of natural religion conduced to this end, whatever the civil authority could do to support religious truth fulfilled the goal of civil society:

We have shewn, and it cannot be too much inculcated, that the State espoused, and entered into Alliance with, the Church for the sake of public Utility: We have proved, and it cannot be too oft repeated, that public Utility and Truth do coincide ... If they do coincide, then, Falsehood, the Reverse of Truth, must be destructive of public Good. The consequence is that the State must for the sake of public Utility, seek Truth and avoid Falsehood: And knowing perfectly in what public utility, which is a sure Rule and Measure of Truth, consists, she will be much better enabled to find out Truth than any speculative Inquirer with all the Aid of the Philosophic Maxims of the Schools.[136]

The 'sake of public Utility' is the key to understanding Warburton's defence of civil establishments in religion. He perceived that the familiar defence of the religious Tests as divine truth left them open to criticism from opponents, who saw them as a violation of a human truth. This was both wrong and, in the circumstances of British political debate, imprudent.[137] The emphasis on truth not only left a flank exposed to dissenters, but it disqualified the civil ruler from lending any support to the religious establishment. Because Warburton upheld Locke's distinction between the spheres and responsibilities of civil and spiritual forces, he did not sanction civil interference in religion on religious grounds, only on those of public utility.[138] In fact, he wrote, were religion to be defended on the grounds of its truth, a Test would actually lead 'to the Destruction of Religious Liberty'. Instead, he argued that the defence of the public good necessarily provided for the authentic truth since, in familiar terms, whatever served the utility of the community obviously had to be true:

... we observe, in the last Place, that our Establishment, made only on the motives of Civil Utility, really gains that End, which in the other Scheme, is the sole View in Establishing a Church, which, yet by pursuing in a vain and visionary manner cannot by that scheme be effected. And that is, the Advancement of Truth. For if public Utility and Truth coincide, then to

---

[135] Warburton, *Alliance*, pp. 126–7.   [136] *Ibid.*, p. 132.   [137] *Ibid.*, p. 148.
[138] *Ibid.*, p. 150.

provide for that Utility, Truth must be provided for. Which will not fail of being found, as being sought after is a sure Method of Success.[139]

A religious test simply demonstrated political loyalty and therefore could be no encroachment. It provided 'some sufficient Security given to the State by those admitted into the Administration of public Affairs, that they are Members of the Religion Established by Law'.[140] The Test was the Warburtonians' reply to the question, 'what security does the establishment require, for its own preservation and defence?'[141] Speaking in parliament, Hans Stanley, Member for Southampton, pledged his respect to the Thirty-Nine Articles, adding, 'But still I have in my creed a fortieth article, in my estimation as important as any of them; and that is public peace.'[142] John Rotheram (1725–89), a prominent Warburtonian in the 1760s, argued that whatever coercive power was retained by the church for its self-defence was granted by the state. Moreover, the punishment it could inflict was 'not on a religious but on a civil account; it is not because they are enemies to the church, but to the state'. The central Protestant value of private judgment could only be infringed upon for these civil reasons. Therefore, 'when the safety of the state shall no longer require or dictate such constraint or such penalties, the church of England will be the first to rejoice at their removal'.[143]

The thrust of Warburton's argument was that 'Obedience and authority are reciprocal terms. A right in another to rule over us, and a duty in us to submit ourselves, are but one and the same thing differently expressed.'[144] Thomas Balguy cited Locke and Warburton in support of limiting the magistrate's task to what 'will best promote the peace, and safety, and happiness of his subjects'. On these same principles Balguy was content to sanction toleration of those dissenters 'whose principles are consistent with the duties of citizens and subjects'.[145] It is important not to underestimate the extent to which it had, in fact, become an interest of the state over the course of the eighteenth century to tolerate religious dissent.

---

[139] *Ibid.*, p. 154. [140] *Ibid.*, p. 110. [141] Forster, *Establishment*, p. 13.
[142] Quoted in Fitzpatrick, *Rational Dissent*, p. 200.
[143] John Rotheram, *Essay on Establishments* (London, 1766), pp. 104–5. Also, Ibbetson, *Plea*, p. 20.
[144] Balguy, *Shipley*, p. 3. Balguy explicitly defends Warburton's *Alliance* (p. 17).
[145] Balguy, *Of Subscription to Articles of Religion*, in *Discourses on Various Subjects; and Charges to the Clergy of the Archdeaconry of Winchester*, ed. James Drake, 2 vols. (Cambridge, 1822), I, pp. 226, 233 note a.

Balguy, himself a strong defender of the 'alliance', also serves to mark the distance that had been travelled:

It was generally conceived before the time of the Revolution that civil governors were obliged by their office to support and propagate true Religion. But this notion is now so fully exploded, that we seldom meet with any man, even in the warmth of controversy, who is hardy enough to defend it.[146]

That defenders of the community were nevertheless prepared to concede a relatively substantial degree of religious toleration is a measure of how fear of the civic consequences of religious dissent had lessened over the course of the seventeenth and eighteenth centuries. While writers on the state like Lipsius and Rivadeneira had left open the possibility of a politique toleration, this remained the less frequently and less insistently argued path. Though still a source of obvious risk, toleration was now more broadly recognized as a means of limiting danger rather than engendering it. The nature of the dissenters' new claim of private judgment, however, meant that it could not be mediated within the ambit of a political theory in which individual flourishing was calculated according to the welfare of the community.

Blackstone's discussion of religion reflected his political concerns. Law was 'to regulate the conduct of man' in society and private judgment threatened this structure.[147] In keeping with a security-oriented perspective, Blackstone permitted private judgment only when it was insulated from any public consequences. Priestley made the connection between Warburton and Blackstone, arguing that Blackstone shared the view of the Bishop of Gloucester that 'religion must be governed by the maxims of civil policy'.[148] In the chapter entitled 'offences against God and religion', Blackstone distinguished between personal, and therefore socially innocuous, 'nonconformity' and public 'reviling', which constituted 'private judgment in virulent and factious opposition to public authority'.[149] 'Pernicious effects' which 'prejudice the community' created 'a

---

[146] Balguy, *On Religious Liberty*, in *Discourses ... and Charges*, p. 182.
[147] Blackstone, *Commentaries*, IV, p. 41, pp. 43–4, 51–2. For this aspect of Blackstone's thought, see Stephen J. C. Taylor, 'Church and State in England in the Mid-Eighteenth Century: The Newcastle Years 1742–1762', Unpublished Ph.D. thesis (Cambridge University, 1987).
[148] Priestley, 'Remarks on Some Paragraphs in the ... Commentaries', *Works*, XXII, p. 309.
[149] Blackstone, *Commentaries*, IV, pp. 49–50.

species of public crimes',[150] not mere intellectual divergence.[151] Blackstone also declared that 'propagating any crude undigested sentiments in religious matters' was a punishable offence. Philip Furneaux glossed, wryly: 'every establishment supposing those sentiments to be crude and undigested, which are contrary to its own principles and practices'.[152] Blackstone excluded Roman Catholics and dissenters on the grounds of their 'zealous' non-conformity. This was a sub-category of nonconformity, one of eleven enumerated public offences against religion. While seeking to ameliorate his view of Protestant dissenters, Blackstone, like Locke and Francis Blackburne, especially singled out Roman Catholics. They could be tolerated 'provided their separation was founded only upon difference of opinion in religion, and their principles did not also extend to a subversion of the civil government'. Their status in civil society, not any theory of human nature, controlled his argument; thus 'if a time should ever arrive' when their religious status did not threaten the realm the laws could be 'softened'.[153] If Roman Catholics were to be mistrusted because their oaths were pledged to a foreign potentate, atheists were to be excluded because their oaths were meaningless.[154] Balguy's defence of opinion, worship and speech explicitly excluded anything that 'disables them for remaining in a society'.[155] Thus, speech that struck at 'the very foundations of society' could be forbidden.[156] Finally, atheism in all its forms was banned as dangerous. No good could be expected from it and, in the absence of any social value, why, Balguy asked, 'should a few skeptical philosophers be allowed to unsettle the minds of men'?[157]

Britain's policy towards Quebec, and the reaction of some circles, most notably Hollis', to the Quebec Act of 1774 has been high-lighted as an example of imperial tolerance and 'commonwealth'

---

[150] *Ibid.*, IV, p. 41.
[151] Blackstone, *A Reply to Dr Priestley's Remarks on the Fourth Volume of the 'Commentaries'* (London, 1769), pp. 12–13.
[152] Furneaux, *Letters to the Hon. Mr Justice Blackstone* ... (London, 1769), pp. 44–5.
[153] Blackburne, 'Considerations on the Present State of the Controversy between the Protestants and Papists of Great Britain and Ireland ... ' *The Works, Theological and Miscellaneous*, ed. Francis Blackburne the Younger, 7 vols. (Cambridge, 1804), IV, pp. 39, 64, 68–72.
[154] Mauduit, *The Case of the Dissenting Ministers* (3rd edn, London, 1773), p. 33; Watts, 'A New Essay on Civil Power', *Works*, 6 vols. (London, 1753), VI, p. 139; Hutcheson, *System*, III.ix.2, II, p. 133; I.i.5, I, p. 219; Smith, *Theory of Moral Sentiments*, VI.ii.3.2–3, p. 235.
[155] Balguy, *Religious Liberty*, I, p. 191.   [156] *Ibid.*, I, p. 195.   [157] *Ibid.*, I, p. 200.

intolerance.[158] It is also an example of religion as state policy. As early as 1763, Shelburne was keen that policy towards Quebec Catholics be conducted on a different footing from that towards domestic ones, 'from the possibility of what may happen, should the times change, should their strength increase, and ours diminish'.[159] Eight years later Alexander Wedderburn, the Solicitor-General, produced a report on Canada which warned against tampering with local religion. The logic was that of the reason of state: 'The safety of the state can be the only just motive for imposing any restraint upon men on account of their religious tenets.'[160]

Where the dissenters thought to persuade English Protestants of the justification for tolerating dissent by offering the examples of Protestants in Catholic or Muslim countries, their opponents actually endorsed the persecution of Protestants – in the name of the state. Thus, while Louis XIV was often condemned for revoking the Edict of Nantes, he also had his defenders: 'Yet had not he the same right to persecute Huguenots, as we have to persecute Papists? Was it not necessary there, as well as here, to restrain the growth and propagation of a sect, which had already done much mischief to the state, and was capable of doing more?'[161]

Toleration stood, to this way of thinking, in an equal and opposite relation to 'sound policy'. Rather than subordinating the individual to the community's need for stability and duration, it threatened precisely these with its exaltation of the individual's right to think for himself. In this upside-down world 'every man shall do what is right in his own eyes, without restraint and without controul'.[162]

The power of reason and the inalienability of private interpretation of texts had led the dissenters into this great error. Their confidence in reason was not shared by their opponents. James Tunstall described it as 'experimentally weak', unable to perform the role required to liberate individuals from revelation. Attempts to strengthen it, however, usually resulted in 'atheism and infidelity'.[163] Furthermore, in addition to the 'want of capacity', most people wanted 'opportunity, to think and judge for themselves'.[164] If the undermining of reason could not completely block the exercise

---

[158] Lawson, *The Imperial Challenge*, pp. 143, 151.   [159] Quoted in *ibid.*, p. 46.
[160] Quoted in *ibid.*, p. 122.
[161] Balguy, *Religious Liberty*, I, p. 193.   [162] Rotheram, *Essay on Establishments*, p. 108.
[163] Tunstall, *Lectures*, p. 74.   [164] Balguy, *Of Subscription*, I, p. 225.

of private judgment, Balguy's claim that Scripture ought not to be interpreted as political thought sought to eliminate this option completely: 'Men consult Scripture for what is not to be found in it; an accurate description of their rights and duties: whereas the knowledge of these is supposed, not taught, by the sacred writers.'[165] Defenders of the community's security generally took a pretty dim view of the intelligence of the mass of subjects. If you expect them to think for themselves, wrote Balguy, 'You might as well expect them to compute an eclipse, or to decide between the Cartesian and Newtonian Philosophy.'[166] Because of the defects of human nature 'subjection to authority' was an obligation laid equally upon the Christian and the citizen. Without public institutions based on 'public authority', neither religion nor government could survive.[167]

The opinions of the people are, and must be founded more on authority than reason. Their parents, their teachers, their governors, in a great measure determine for them, what they are to believe, and what to practice. The same doctrines uniformly taught, the same rites constantly performed, make such an impression on their minds, that they hesitate as little in admitting the articles of faith, as in receiving the most established maxims of common life; and whilst they want the advantages of reflection and study, they are the same time free from the uneasiness and the mischief of dispute and doubt.[168]

Because civil and religious governance rested on long-exercised authority, the 'love of change' was deadly. Hence the title of a sermon Balguy delivered in 1779, 'The Danger of Innovation in Church and State'.[169] Priestley's preference for no establishment rather than a bad one finds its antithesis in Balguy's preference for any state religion, including paganism, rather than none at all: 'In general, we may safely assert that religion, even false religion, is the great bond of human society.'[170]

The result of the weak-witted masses employing themselves in the hopeless exercise of their private judgment would be an apocalypse for the state. Such demands, therefore, could only be a thinly veiled assertion of absolute licence. The state of total liberty resulted in

---

[165] Balguy, *Shipley*, p. 4.   [166] Balguy, *Of Subscription*, I, p. 226.
[167] Balguy, *On Church Authority*, pp. 97–8.
[168] Balguy, *Of Subscription*, p. 224.
[169] Balguy, *The Danger of Innovation in Church and State*, in *Discourses … and Charges*, II, pp. 26, 33. Burke's more famous defense of 'tradition' in the *Reflections* captures this aspect of contemporary political thought.
[170] Balguy, *Of Subscription*, p. 227.

anarchy resembling Hobbes' state of nature and requiring the same firm handling: 'The passions of men are always very strongly engaged on the side of their opinions. And nothing less than the strong and steady hand of law and government will be able to keep them within due bounds, and prevent their running into the most violent and dangerous excesses.'[171]

The more far-sighted, like Nathaniel Forster, warned of the tyranny of an ungoverned society of men all of whom thought they possessed the sole truth. 'Truth is relative. There can be no universal standard to determine it for all mankind. Nothing is to any man truth, but what his mind perceives to be such. If he takes falsehood for truth, it is to be lamented; but where is the remedy?'[172] Gibbon's description of the early Christian office of bishop, appearing in volume I of the *Decline and Fall* (1776), provided ammunition for those who shared Forster's scepticism about the compatibility of free enquiry and social peace:

But the most perfect equality of freedom requires the directing hand of a superior magistrate: and the order of public deliberations soon introduces the office of a president, invested at least with the authority of collecting the sentiments, and of executing the resolutions, of the assembly. A regard for the public tranquillity, which would so frequently have been interrupted by annual or by occasional elections induced the primitive Christians to constitute an honourable and perpetual magistracy, and to choose one of the wisest and most holy among their presbyters to execute, during his life, the duties of their ecclesiastical governor.[173]

Gibbon's timely revision of the history of the period upon which the dissenters had based their claim stressed the centrality of authority even in that phase of free, primitive Christianity. Similarly, in his sermon on the accession of Jonathan Shipley to the bishopric of Landaff in 1769, Balguy emphasized the responsibility of the office of minister:

No minister therefore can depart in any respect from the public institution, much less act in contradiction to it, without usurping a power not committed to him, but residing in the body by whom he is authorized and employed. If he does this, he violates the trust reposed in him, and so renders himself unfit to be trusted.[174]

---

[171] Forster, *Establishment*, p. 7. Also, *A Letter to the Members of the New Association for Altering the Articles and Liturgy of the Church of England* (London, 1772), pp. 3–4.
[172] Forster, *Establishment*, p. 16. Also, p. 8.   [173] Gibbon, *Decline and Fall*, I, p. 419.
[174] Balguy, *Shipley*, p. 10.

Balguy's language is important. He is describing the minister as a representative of the congregation in precisely the terms used in the simultaneous debate over colonial representation. This is the language of virtual representation. Balguy's assertion of authority in religious governance placed him in the same relationship to the dissenters' claims of private judgment as the government was to the proponents of actual representation.

THE NEW TOLERATION

Blackburne's critique of utility

Contemporary sources and modern scholars agree that the revival of demands for toleration began with the publication of Francis Blackburne's *Confessional* in 1766. It has been suggested that the volume was prompted by a university sermon in defence of subscription to the Thirty-Nine Articles by William Powell of St John's College, which we have already seen to be a home to several articulate defenders of the primacy of the community. Where Powell stressed the utility of subscription, Blackburne countered by forcefully emphasizing the priority of Scripture over doctrines of human devising.[175] Blackburne's contribution was to make the debate over wider toleration one in which truth was identified with Protestantism and against crude calculations of utility. In establishing this argument he explicitly challenged the government's fundamental political arguments. '"No body"', according to Powell, '"ever asks concerning a petition or a rule, whether it be true; but whether it be decent, proper, reasonable, useful."'[176] Theorists of the post-Reformation state, both Catholic and Protestant, had abandoned truth as a criterion for evaluating religious matters because they believed that it provided a cover for the dangerous growth of faction: 'The notion that misled our forefathers in this matter was, that, if more than one form of religion should be tolerated in a country where only one form of civil government was established, some disorder and confusion would ensue, pernicious to the peace

---

[175] Gascoigne, *Cambridge in the Age of Enlightenment*, p. 132.

[176] Blackburne, 'Remarks on Dr Powell's Sermon in defence of subscriptions', *The Works, Theological and Miscellaneous*, ed. Francis Blackburne the Younger, 7 vols. (Cambridge, 1804), VI, p. 41. On the nature and importance of Blackburne's argument, see Martin Fitzpatrick, 'Latitudinarianism at the Parting of the Ways: A Suggestion', in John Walsh, Colin Haydon and Stephen Taylor, eds., *From Toleration to Tractarianism: The Church of England c.1689–1833* (Cambridge, forthcoming).

and welfare of civil society.'[177] This early modern argument, which expressed the central commitment to the security of the state and the aggrandizement of its wealth and power, was summed up by Blackburne in a single word. 'The word, *interest*, in the common acceptation of it, is a term relative to some kind of competition for benefits or advantages.' Thus, the 'interest of an individual' was in acquiring such wealth as to limit the power of his rivals and enhance that of himself and his friends:

If we carry this idea from an individual, to bodies and societies of men in combination, we find it is for the interest of their common cause, that its partizans be numerous and powerful, able to controul their rivals and opponents, and that the cause itself be such, as, in cause of success, will derive upon its friends and abettors the several emoluments and advantages, which are proposed by those who enter into such engagements.[178]

Blackburne's clear assessment of the prudential politics of states underpinned his attack on its particularly Warburtonian variant. He accused the defenders of the Establishment of 'dropping indeed the point of *right* to establish them as tests of truth, but insisting largely on their *utility* and *experience* in a variety of cases'.[179] Price's philosophical attack on the subordination of truth to utility in his *Review* was matched by Blackburne. Truth, rather than the 'very expedients of human prudence', was the basis of religion:

No wise man, who hath duly considered the genius and design of the Christian religion, will look for much utility or expedience, where the church or church-governors go beyond their *plain commission*. And, whatever may be left to the prudence and discretion of church-governors, there is *so much more* left to the conscience of every Christian in his personal capacity, that it greatly behoves such governors to beware they incroach not on a province which is without their limits. This consideration has always disposed me to reason in a manner just contrary to these gentlemen, namely, from the authority to the utility of religious measures. My opinion is, that where the methods of promoting christianity are matter of scripture precept, or plainly recommended by scripture-precedents, there such methods should be strictly followed and adhered to, even though the expedience of them should not be very evident *a priori*. We can have no pretence of right or *authority* to alter such methods for others seemingly more expedient, while so very much of the effect of religion, or, in other

---

[177] Blackburne, 'Considerations', *Works*, IV, p. 60.
[178] Blackburne, 'Four Discourses: Discourse III. On the True Meaning of the Phrase, *The Interests of Religion*', *Works*, IV, pp. 358–9.
[179] Blackburne, *The Confessional* (London, 1766; 2nd edn, 1767), p. 57.

words, of its utility, is made by our blessed Master to depend on the inward frame of every man's heart, into which ordinary church-governors can have no farther discernment than any other men.[180]

The effort to regulate religion according to the principles of civil prudence had actually been undertaken by the very Protestants who had wielded the claim of private judgment against the Roman defenders of the civil order in the sixteenth century. Once themselves safely established, the various Protestant sects had all sought to establish *their* version of Protestantism with the help of the civil ruler.[181] Blackburne linked the 'corruption' of Protestantism to the same political argument which made public utility the standard of political justice:

There is one science wherein the reformed churches, perhaps in most countries, have made as remarkable improvements as in any other. I mean the science of Politics, which, as some think, has had no obscure effects upon them all. And church politics, in reformed countries, chiefly aim at accomodating all the peculiarities in their respective systems, as much as may be, to the religion of the magistrate; a conduct, which, out of all doubt, cannot be defended in every instance, upon any principles which are of protestant original.[182]

Just as the public utility overrode the claims of individuals, the needs of the religious establishment impinged on the individual's ability to decide for him- or herself. John Firebrace's attack on subscription illustrates the political nature of this debate on ecclesiology: 'In the first case the Magistrate is judge, and his criterion is number – in the second case every individual is judge, and his criterion is the word of God.'[183] In a published letter to James Ibbetson, Firebrace continued to emphasize the difference between politics guided by prudence, and religion which could only be evaluated in terms of truth: 'But, Sir, the reasonings of a Christian upon cases of conscience are not to be bounded by views of mere utility, whether private or public. The question is, what is right – what wrong? This you have evaded.'[184]

By shifting the debate out of the conventional parameters of statecraft the dissenters hoped to secure what otherwise seemed irrelevant. As long as Acts of Indemnity were issued on a regular

[180] *Ibid.*, pp. 39–40.   [181] *Ibid.*, p. 34.   [182] *Ibid.*, p. lxxiii.
[183] John Firebrace, *A Further Defence of the Present Scheme of Petitioning the Parliament for Relief in the Matter of Subscription* (London, 1771), p. 18.
[184] Firebrace, *A Letter to the Rev. James Ibbetson ...* (London, 1771), p. 18.

basis there was little risk of Anglican persecution. Nevertheless, the demand for toleration on principle rather than pragmatism was based on this recognition that religious truth could not be defined by the needs of political practice: 'Those persons, who think that we ought to have been satisfied with the connivance so long granted us, do not appear to me to have considered the matter with due attention. A state of connivance is not to be compared with a state of legal security.'[185]

Blackburne's demand for wider toleration depended upon first distinguishing between the grounds of civil and spiritual obligation. While prudence had to determine the former, only the truth of Scripture could guide the latter. The separation of these two spheres of authority is one of the most common features of the tolerationist literature that emerged in the wake of the *Confessional*. One can, however, discern two versions of this argument. The first, which drew both explicitly and implicitly on John Locke's writings on toleration, maintained this division based on the perceived inefficiency of civil intervention in spiritual matters. Government had not been created to solve this type of problem and subsequent attempts to do so had failed miserably. This argument retained, much as did Locke himself, the logic of prudence and utility. The second version, which also emerged after the publication of the *Confessional*, and which picked up Clarke's emphasis on truth as the distinctive aspect of the religious experience, turned away from prudence almost completely. It is with these writers, in particular Joseph Fownes and Joseph Priestley, that natural rights claims are used to buttress the independence of the individual enquiring after truth. From the right to judge privately the truth of Scripture came the parallel right to think and judge freely on all issues. The endpoint of this argument was the assertion that freedom of thought was the constitutive human attribute. These positions were built into the manifesto issued by the Feathers Tavern Association in November of 1771. The 'liberty of judging for themselves' was deemed a 'possession' which Protestants had a 'right to enjoy' and which had been fought for by the first generation of reformers. Secondly, subscription gave the doctrines of 'fallible men' an authority with which they could obstruct the general improvement of the times. Finally, subscription did not serve the interests of the state 'Because all the security which

---

[185] Andrew Kippis, *A Vindication of the Late Protestant Dissenting Ministers* ... (2nd edn, London, 1773), p. 49.

the state can reasonably require, is already provided by the oaths of supremacy and allegiance.'[186]

Locke and efficiency

When opposition to legal intolerance stirred again in the 1760s, John Locke's arguments reappeared. The primary target of his observationalism was the concept of authority. The claim (of those literally 'in the know') that humans were predisposed to certain beliefs and actions disintegrated under the microscopic (and telescopic) examination of natural philosophy. But scientific anti-dispositionalism had, at least partly, another target as well: religion. The Roman Catholic church had presumed to arbitrate in fields of enquiry beyond theology and the Protestant Reformation and the scientific revolution constituted a renunciation of this claim:

And it was of no small advantage to those who affected to be Masters and Teachers, to make this the Principle of Principles, That Principles must not be questioned: For having once established this Tenet, That there are innate Principles, it put their Followers upon a necessity of receiving some Doctrines as such; which was to take them off from the use of their own Reason and Judgment, and put them upon believing and taking them upon trust, without farther examination: In which posture of blind Credulity, they might be more easily governed by, and made useful to some sort of Men, who had the skill and office to principle and guide them. Nor is it a small power it gives one Man over another, to have the Authority to be the Dictator of Principles, and Teacher of unquestionable Truths; and to make a Man swallow that for an innate Principle, which may serve to his purpose, who teacheth them.[187]

The attack on authority at the end of book I and beginning of book II of the *Essay* was followed by the unfolding of Locke's theory of sensation which made knowledge dependent not on Authority but on the individual's own perceptions: 'From *Experience*: In that, all our Knowledge is founded; and from that it ultimately derives itself.'[188]

If ' "Suspension and examination" *versus* "trust and authority" ' is the intellectual demand of the Reformation',[189] as James Tully has written, it is even more obviously true for the practice of modern

---

[186] Quoted in Jebb, *Works*, III, pp. 16–18.   [187] Locke, *Essay*, I.24.iv, pp. 101–2.
[188] *Ibid.*, II.i.2, p. 105.
[189] James Tully, 'Governing Conduct', *Conscience and Casuistry in Early Modern Europe*, ed. Edmund Leites (Cambridge, 1988), p. 24.

natural philosophy. In England, Locke propagated this rebellion in the *Essay* and the *Letters* on toleration. The late eighteenth-century tolerationists united both religion and science in their defence of the individual's rational free enquiry. With Locke in mind, Tully has written of 'the 150-year intellectual struggle of the Reformation'.[190] In the context of our examination, his estimate could be amended by the addition of a century. While most socially conservative Britons accepted free enquiry in science, the application of the same principle to religious matters was denied. Until the pursuit of intellectual enquiry was accepted for all affairs of the mind, the Reformation and the scientific revolution can be described as incomplete.

Locke's enduring contribution was the distinction he drew between the spheres of civil government and religion. Political society seemed to Locke 'a Society of Men constituted only for the procuring, preserving, and advancing of their own Civil Interests'.[191] The magistrate was invested with all the power necessary to secure the ends of society. These 'civil interests' included the protection, by means of force when necessary, of 'the just Possession of these things belonging to this Life'. Locke also termed them 'Man's Rights'.[192] Locke's claim was that the requisite degree of social security did not require the magistrate to involve himself in religious affairs. This resulted in a division into separate but parallel spheres of civil and religious affairs.

Locke gave three reasons for excluding ecclesiastical matters from the magistrate's competence. The first was the impossibility of extending authority in spiritual matters over others. Like the preservation of physical life, the quest for salvation could not be renounced and given over to the care of another.[193] This applied to all men. The second reason spoke directly to the civil ruler. He was especially enjoined from interference because his authority 'consists only in outward force', not in coercing the 'inward perswasion of the Mind'.[194] Lastly, even if the ruler could command their thoughts, it would only make their salvation contingent on his, surely no more

[190] *Ibid.*, p. 16.
[191] Locke, *A Letter Concerning Toleration*, ed. James H. Tully (Indianapolis, 1983), p. 26. These included 'Life, Liberty, Health' and general material well-being.
[192] *Ibid.*   [193] *Ibid.*
[194] '... true and saving Religion consists in the inward perswasion of the Mind, without which nothing can be acceptable to God. And such is the nature of the Understanding, that it cannot be compell'd to the belief of any thing by outward force. Confiscation of Estate, Imprisonment, Torments, nothing of that nature can have any such Efficacy as to make Men change the inward Judgment that they have framed of things' (*ibid.*, p. 27).

certain a foundation. Only rational free enquiry, not blind adherence to another's rule, could secure the approach to truth.[195] These all served to distinguish the needs and tasks of civil and spiritual life.[196]

In his *Second* and *Third Letters* Locke returned to the reasons for a distinct civil society. Men entered society for material and not spiritual salvation since the latter could have been attained in Hobbesian solitude: 'Nothing can *in reason be reckon'd amongst the Ends of any Society*, but what may *in reason* be supposed to be designed by those who enter into it.'[197] Since 'The Care therefore of every man's Soul belongs unto himself', it was not the task of government to insure its success. Even 'God himself will not save men against their wills.'[198] Under no circumstances was the use of force compatible with religion.[199]

Though Locke rejected the view that truth could be coerced,[200] he believed that it did exist: 'Truth, whether in or out of fashion, is the measure of knowledge, and the business of the understanding; whatsoever is besides that, however authorized by consent, or recommended by rarity, is nothing but ignorance, or something worse.'[201] Truth could, however, only be ascertained by individuals after a freely conducted enquiry:

'Tis a benefit to have true Knowledge and Philosophy imbraced and assented to, in any Civil Society or Government. But will you say, therefore, that it is a benefit to the Society, or one of the Ends of Government, that all who are not Peripateticks should be punished, to make Men find out the Truth, and profess it. This indeed might be thought a fit way to make some Men imbrace the Peripatetick Philosophy, but not a proper way to find the Truth. For, perhaps the Peripatetick Philosophy may not

---

[195] *Ibid.*, pp. 27–8.

[196] John Dunn has perceptively described Locke's argument in a way that also marks off the gap between Locke and the later dissenters: 'For it is the combination of this apparently sympathetic recognition of the practical responsibilities of rule with a fierce repudiation of any human being's right to impose his religious judgment upon the religious judgment of any other human being which explains the trenchancy of Locke's commitment to freedom of worship and the distinctly more muted support which he felt impelled to give to freedom of thought, or speech, or private conduct' ('The Claim to Freedom of Conscience: Freedom of Speech, Freedom of Thought, Freedom of Worship?', in *From Persecution to Toleration: The Glorious Revolution and Religion in England*, ed. O. P. Grell, J. I. Israel, N. Tyacke (Oxford, 1991), pp. 175–6).

[197] *A Second Letter concerning Toleration* (London, 1690), p. 53; *A Third Letter for Toleration, to the Author of the Third Letter concerning Toleration* (London, 1692), p. 62.

[198] Locke, *Letter*, p. 35.   [199] Locke, *Second Letter*, p. 2; *Third Letter*, pp. 16–18.

[200] Locke, *Letter*, p. 46.

[201] Locke, 'On the Conduct of the Understanding', *Works*, IV, p. 169.

be true ... For just the same reason, it cannot be a benefit to Civil Society, that Men should be punished in Denmark, for not being Lutherans; in Geneva for not being Calvinists; and in Vienna for not being papists; as a means to make them find out the true Religion.[202]

This quest for truth was to be measured according to the standard laid down in the *Second Treatise*. Thus, 'The Publick Good is the Rule and Measure of all Lawmaking. If a thing be not useful to the Commonwealth, tho' it be never so indifferent, it may not presently be established by Law.'[203] While Locke believed that the pursuit of uniformity was not essential to the service of the public good, he did believe that the profession of certain opinions could warrant civil action: 'Opinions contrary to human Society, or to those moral Rules which are necessary to the preservation of Civil Society' were punishable. Under this rubric fell sects ostensibly conforming but secretly 'opposite to the Civil Right of the Community'.[204] Catholics were specifically the target of a third category, since

all who enter into it, do thereby, *ipso facto*, deliver themselves up to the Protection and Service of another Prince. For by this means the Magistrate would give way to the settling of a foreign Jurisdiction in his own Country, and suffer his own People to be listed, as it were, for Souldiers against his own Government.[205]

The final object of Locke's intolerance was atheism. Those 'who deny the Being of God' could not be trusted in a world in which 'Promises, Covenants, and Oaths' upheld the civil power.[206] The social implications of this political assessment of religious diversity are indicated in the constitution drawn up by Locke for the colony of Carolina.[207]

Despite the ambivalence in Locke's account, his attempt to separate church and state provided the later dissenters with their own authority. In the generation after Locke, Benjamin Ibbot and Isaac Watts profoundly restated Locke's position. In a sermon before the

---

202 Locke, *Second Letter*, pp. 51–2. At the start of the *Third Letter* Locke replaced 'Peripatetick Philosophy' with 'Christianity' and re-ran the same argument (p. 3). See also John Marshall, 'John Locke in Context', and James Moore, 'Theological Politics: A Study of the Reception of Locke's *Two Treatises of Government* in England and Scotland in the Early Eighteenth Century'.

203 Locke, *Letter*, p. 39. See James Tully, 'Locke', in *Cambridge History of Political Thought, 1450–1700*, ed. J. H. Burns (Cambridge, 1991), p. 649.

204 Locke, *Letter*, p. 49.   205 *Ibid.*, p. 50.   206 *Ibid.*, p. 51.

207 The difficulty of distinguishing Locke's own views from those of his patron, Shaftesbury, does not diminish its value as an illustration of the continuing fear of atheism (Locke, 'Carolina', *Works*, IV, pp. 534–6).

Lord Mayor of London, based on his earlier Boyle Lectures of 1713–14, Ibbot, the assistant to Samuel Clarke at St James's, Westminster, especially stressed the incompatibility of spiritual involvement with the purely secular purpose of government's existence. The 'nature and design' of government and governors was 'to preserve the external peace of the world, and the temporal good of the community over which he presides'.[208] Because religion did not figure among the motives for giving up natural abilities at the outset of social existence, all men retained their 'natural freedom in religious matters'. Moreover, because religion dwelt in human 'judgment, and the internal persuasion of our minds', there could be no spiritual justification for civil intervention.[209] Ibbot sharply distinguished between 'alienable', 'civil' or 'temporal' rights and 'inalienable', 'religious or spiritual rights'.[210]

Isaac Watts, the influential dissenting educator,[211] also contended that religion had no place in the purpose of government and therefore stood outside the ken of its rulers: 'The design of civil government is to secure the persons, the properties, the just liberty and peace of mankind from the invasions and the injuries of their neighbours.'[212] In addition, Watts suggested that since worship was not threatened in nature it did not have to be relinquished in society. 'It was only for the security of their natural and civil societies, and not that their governors should chuse their religion for them.'[213] Burgh was later to term this blend of civil and religious power a 'mixed-mongrel-spiritual-temporal-secular-ecclesiastical establishment'.[214]

With the renewed demands for toleration, the origin of the division between spheres of civil and spiritual authority was restated. This account of origins usually drew on the language of nature and natural rights. According to the Cambridge baptist Robert Robinson, 'A short detail of the origin, the nature and end of civil government' proved that the civil magistrate was never intended to have ecclesiastical power.'[215] Neither 'The origins of civil government'

---

[208] Ibbot, 'The Nature and Extent of the Office of the Civil Magistrate', *The Pillars of Priestcraft and Orthodoxy Shaken*, ed. Richard Barron (London, 1766), I, p. 213.

[209] *Ibid.*, pp. 224, 214–15.   [210] *Ibid.*, p. 224.

[211] Richard Barlow argues that Watts was the conduit for Locke's views on education and toleration (*Citizenship and Conscience* (Philadelphia, 1962), p. 102).

[212] Watts, 'A New Essay on Civil Power in Things Sacred', *Works*, VI, p. 135.

[213] *Ibid.*, p. 138.

[214] Burgh, *Crito*, II, p. 117.

[215] [Robert Robinson], *Arcana: On the Principles of the Late Petitioners to Parliament for Relief in the Matter of Subscription* (Cambridge, 1774), p. 43.

nor 'the ends of his office' authorized civil interference in religion. The 'preservation of their natural rights' led individuals to seek self-preservation in a 'common security'. But this was not to imply that the individual does 'in reality part with any of his original, primary rights; he only submits to certain conditions and regulations, by which those rights are in a more effectual manner secured'. And since religion did not fall into this category it could not be regulated by the civil government.[216] Where the defenders of the establishment asserted the ultimately civil character of religious observance, the dissenters denied 'that a man's behaviour towards his maker is the immediate object of civil government'.[217]

The limited purview of civil government was seen as a function of its very nature. Authority 'can be neither different in kind from, nor superior in degree to, that which the individuals composing a community entrusted to the Magistrate, upon their entrance into Society'.[218] The extent of civil power was bounded then, and therefore now as well, 'by the unalienable rights of individuals'.[219] Priestley stressed the ruler's limited spiritual efficacy: 'Since no power on earth can affect me beyond the grave, why should the powers of this world, or civil governors, pretend to any authority in things that respect my condition there?'[220] Burgh had drawn on the examples of Holland and Pennsylvania to suggest to George III 'The inutility of religious tests' and the commensurate advantages of their absence.[221] Price, too, sought to exclude the magistrate on the grounds of his lack of competence in affairs spiritual:

The civil magistrate ought not to interpose in the defence of truth, till it has appeared that he is a competent judge of truth. This, certainly, he is not. On the contrary; universal experience has, hitherto, proved him one of its worst enemies.[222]

While it was often suggested that the security of the state forbade any alterations in an already well-ordered constitution, dissenters were prepared to borrow from the language of patriotism and

---

[216] Furneaux, *Essay*, pp. 20–1. Also, Philip Furneaux, *Letters to the Hon. Mr Justice Blackstone* (London, 1770), p. 52; Anon., *Free Remarks on a Sermon, Entitled The Requisition of Subscription* ... (London, 1772), p. 29; Blackburne, 'Four Discourses', *Works*, IV, p. 379.

[217] [Caleb Fleming], *Civil Establishments in Religion, A Ground of Infidelity* (London, 1767), p. 33.

[218] [Richard Watson], *A Brief State of the Principles of Church Authority* (London, 1773), p. 11.

[219] *Ibid.*, p. 12.

[220] Priestley, 'A View of the Principles and Conduct of the Protestant Dissenters, with respect to the civil and ecclesiastical constitution of England', *Works*, XXII, p. 351; also *Essay*, p. 55.

[221] Burgh, *Remarks*, p. 177.   [222] Price, *Four Dissertations* (Dublin, 1777), p. 366.

politics and argue that the ability to react to changing circumstances actually defined the good constitutional order: 'And change of circumstances (which in every State will necessarily happen with the revolution of time) may point out the necessity of altering some things; which otherwise it would have been neither needful, nor perhaps safe to alter.'[223] Dissenters often used arguments like this, addressing the dominant concern with safety and security, in an attempt to subvert the government's position. Toleration of those people once, perhaps justifiably, believed threatening to the state was precisely the kind of change recommended by changing times. It was now the case that toleration actually served the public utility. Those who had been branded as dangers to national security could be safely returned to society if it could be demonstrated that it was inutile to stifle their voices: 'Provided a man loves liberty and his country, what is it to the commonwealth whether he sings his prayers, or says them? Or whether he thinks a *bishop*, or a *presbyter* the nearer relation to St Paul?'[224] If one wanted to make stick the claim that the dissenters sought to endanger the state one would have had to prove 'that any ill consequences can flow from free opinion, in the matter of Religion, to Civil society'.[225]

Dissenters were especially keen to escape the accusation of 'dual loyalty'. In fact, they saw themselves as among the most zealous under-labourers of eighteenth-century Britain, men 'whose learning, dilligence and example are ornaments & advantages to the nation'.[226] There was no way to impugn their loyalty to Britain nor their commitment to civil liberty. Priestley was an especially strong exponent of the view that dissenters were ardent supporters of liberty precisely because of their religious status: 'And it appears to us, that the man will oppose them both with equal firmness, who is as tenacious of his religious as he is of his *civil liberty*.'[227] Addressing fellow dissenters, he warned, 'Be assured that your peculiar privileges, and the general liberties of this country, are inseparably

[223] John Jones, *Free and Candid Disquisitions Relating to the Church of England* (2nd edn, London, 1750), pp. 6–7.

[224] Thomas Gordon, 'The Character of an Independent Whig' (1719), *A Cordial for Low Spirits* (London, 1763), I, p. 199.

[225] Benjamin Dawson, *A Free and Candid Disquisition* (n.p., 1770), p. 10.

[226] Burgh, *Remarks*, p. 195. Also Dawson, *A Letter to the Clergy of the Archdeaconry of Winchester* (London, 1773), p. 10.

[227] Priestley, 'A View of the Principles and Conduct of the Protestant Dissenters, with Respect to the Civil and Ecclesiastical Constitution of England', *Works*, XXII, p. 367. Also, Fleming, *Civil Establishments in Religion*, pp. 27–8.

connected, and that whenever the altar of civil tyranny shall be erected, you will be the first victims. As, therefore, you value the one, contend for the other.'[228] Furthermore, they argued that toleration, rather than persecution, best secured the futurity of the polity. Burgh speculated that, 'if all the truth was known, the tolerating protestant is not in fact a more dangerous enemy to the *religion* of the papists, than he, who is for suppressing, or even for *burning* them'.[229] Hume's hypothetical debate between Gardiner and Pole in the third volume of the *History* was his attempt to contrast the relative benefits of tolerance and intolerance. Pole's argument on behalf of toleration was motivated by generally practical concerns; persecution was the sign of theological failure and no mark of a successful regime. Moreover, uniformity was a chimerical goal to begin with. Toleration, on the other hand, was sure to ease the pressures arising from the natural diversity of human opinions and customs. Gardiner was made to retort with variations on the security argument, the defence of intolerance Hume would have been most familiar with from his own time.[230] Finally, Adam Smith offered both this commonplace argument,[231] as well as a more sophisticated one, resembling closely his view of the 'natural liberty' of trade. He claimed that a complete toleration would encourage the proliferation of sects, and in competition for members this would, in turn, drive them from 'zeal' to 'moderation'. This market metaphor was explicitly directed against the notion of any Warburtonian 'alliance' between church and state.[232]

Dissenters were quick to point out that the needs of security could be wielded as easily against Protestants as by Protestants against Catholics. It was an argument true 'as well from the mouth of the Pope's Professor of Divinity in the University of Bologna, as from the Clarendon Press'.[233] Another writer raised the mocking spectre of

[228] Priestley, 'An Address', *Works*, xxii, p. 485; also *Essay on a Course of Liberal Education*, p. 184. Even Hume had to admit that in Europe as a whole, and in England in particular, civil liberty had been preserved from the encroachment of powerful monarchs thanks to the zeal of dissenting Protestants (In Europe, see *History*, v, p. 80, and in England, *History*, iv, pp. 123–4).
[229] Burgh, *Crito*, ii, p. 191; also, i, p. viii; ii, p. 196. See [Robinson], *Arcana*, p. 46; Furneaux, *Letters to Blackstone*, p. 139.
[230] Hume, *History*, iii, pp. 431–3.   [231] See *Wealth of Nations*, v.i.g.18, p. 798.
[232] Smith, *WN*, v.i.g.8, pp. 792–3; also v.i.g.16, p. 797.
[233] William Paley, *A Defense of the Considerations on the Propriety of Requiring a Subscription to Articles of Faith* (London, 1774), p. 3. Still, Paley conceded that Roman Catholics were simply more dangerous than Protestant dissenters and had to be treated accordingly (p. 24).

Rome taking pleasure that 'some even of those who have hitherto professed to be its greatest Opponents, seem to be reconciled to its claims'.[234] Earlier in the century Molesworth and Watts had similarly defended toleration by transposing the argument to the condition of Protestants in Turkey.[235] Anglican oppression merely repeated the misguided Roman exaltation of 'human authority' in religion. The arguments now being invoked against dissent were the same ones wielded by Rome against the reformers, 'which would have suppressed Christianity, would have stopped the Reformation, and would defer every great understanding to eternity – the danger of innovation'.[236]

The issue of Catholic toleration divided dissenters and reproduced in miniature the larger conflict with the defenders of the Establishment. Some, following the logic employed to secure their own toleration, sought to extend it to Roman Catholics, while others believed this too great a security risk. Joseph Priestley was the most voluble dissenting defender of Catholic toleration.[237] Between the appearance of the first and second editions of his *Essay* he engaged in a long correspondence with Andrew Kippis and Theophilus Lindsey, neither of whom was immediately persuaded by Priestley, Kippis studiously avoiding commenting on this aspect of the argument when he reviewed the *Essay* for the *Monthly Review*.[238] Lindsey was later convinced, and a member of his Essex Street Chapel, Sir George Savile, proposed the Catholic Relief Bill in May 1778, while the dissenters' motion for repeal of the Test and Corporation Acts in 1790 included Catholic toleration.[239] Roman Catholics, with their putative 'dual loyalty', posed most acutely the problem of religion as an interest of state. Mark Goldie's observation that Scottish Catholics were compelled to dispute Locke's account of toleration

---

[234] Samuel Wilton, *An Apology for the Renewal of an Application to Parliament by the Protestant Dissenting Ministers* (London, 1773), p. 105.

[235] Molesworth, *Principles of a True Whig*, p. 10; Watts, 'A New Essay on Civil Power', *Works*, VI, p. 144.

[236] John Firebrace, *Letters to a Member of Parliament &c.* (London, 1772), pp. 113–14. Also, Joseph Priestley, *Considerations on Church Authority Occasion'd by Dr Balguy's Sermon* (London, 1769), p. 84; Philip Bendelowe, *Animadversions on an Essay in Religious Establishments* (London, 1769), pp. 4, 18; Anon., *The State of Subscription to the Articles and Liturgy of the Church of England* (London, 1774), p. 49.

[237] He even mocked those who approved of tolerating Protestant dissenters but not atheists and Catholics (*Balguy*, p. 81).

[238] Fitzpatrick, 'Joseph Priestley and the Cause of Universal Toleration', *The Price-Priestley Newsletter*, 1 (1977), p. 13.

[239] Fitzpatrick, 'Heretical Religion', in *The Transformation of Political Culture*, p. 357.

demonstrates how *his* reliance on the category of security could have made him feared by the persecuted as much as appealed to by them.[240] Catholics could have been no more dangerous to the government than they seemed to Thomas Hollis and Francis Blackburne. In perpetuating many of the political prejudices of the seventeenth century, Thomas Hollis took on the role of anti-Catholic propagandist in the 1760s.[241] Although Blackburne's *Confessional* was a founding document of rational dissent, his challenge was to the practice of the civil establishment of religious truth, not to the value of religion for the state. Catholics posed a hazard that had to be carefully monitored for purely political reasons; it was precisely their 'civil' attachment to Rome that made them dangerous, not their doctrines *per se*.

Mostly, however, criticism of the so-called Roman practice of the Church of England was reflected in demands for a 'further reformation'. The heretofore unexplained proliferation of potted histories of the Reformation attests to the significance of history, contrary to the recent tendency to seek the sources of rational and radical dissent in millenarian utopias.[242] Only with the recognition of the primacy of rational free enquiry in religion, as in science, was the Reformation to be completed. The widely accepted belief was that the first reformers, like the Israelites leaving Egypt, were not able to purge themselves of all traces of idolatry and left it for future generations to complete the task.[243]

Philip Furneaux was an independent minister and leader in the

---

[240] Mark Goldie, 'The Scottish Catholic Enlightenment', *Journal of British Studies*, 30 (1991), 40.

[241] See Caroline Robbins' three essays on Hollis in *Absolute Liberty*, pp. 168–246; Fitzpatrick, *Rational Dissent*, ch. 3.

[242] For the importance of such 'counter-histories', see Amos Funkenstein, *Theology and the Scientific Imagination from the Middle Ages to the Seventeenth Century* (Princeton, 1986), pp. 273–5; for an example of the latter, Spadafora, *The Idea of Progress in the Eighteenth Century*, ch. 2.

[243] Examples of this dissenting counter-history are numerous. See, for example, Dawson, *A Letter to the Clergy of Winchester*, p. 35. Also, Blackburne, 'Considerations', *Works*, IV, pp. 57–8; Priestley, 'A Free Address to Those who Have Petitioned for the Repeal of the Late Acts of Parliament in Favour of the Roman Catholics', *Works*, XXII, pp. 499–501; Firebrace, *Letters to a Member of Parliament*, p. 2; Norman, *Two Letters on the Subject of Subscription* (Winchester, 1773), p. 38; Joseph Towers, *A Dialogue between Two Gentlemen, concerning the Late Application to Parliament* ... (London, 1772), p. 12; John Jones, *Free and Candid Disquisition*, p. 9; *A Collection of Letters and Essays in Favour of Publick Liberty*, ed. Francis Blackburne (London, 1774), I, p. xiii; J. Harris, *Observations on National Establishments in Religion in General and on the Establishment of Christianity in Particular* (London, 1767), p. 36. The most influential of these 'counter-histories' was, of course, Blackburne's in *The Confessional*.

Sheriffs' Case brought against the Corporation of London, whose *Essay on Toleration*, like Priestley's contemporary writings, highlighted the relationship between Blackburne's two arguments. He began from Locke's separation of spiritual and civil needs and responsibilities. The former was 'a concern between God and a man's own conscience' and left man accountable to God alone. Human interposition could not penetrate the inwardness of spirituality and any attempt to do so would destroy 'the purpose of religion, belief in God'.[244]

Furneaux used the metaphor of a contract to exclude conscience from the public domain. Men compacted 'for the preservation of their natural rights', exchanging physical liberty for physical protection. Freedom of thought always remained outside this framework:

Absolute liberty, therefore, in the affair of religion, belongs to us, as reasonable creatures, dependent on, and subject to, the universal Sovereign and Judge. It is a right essential to our nature: whatsoever other rights, therefore, we are supposed to resign on entering into society, this we cannot resign; we cannot do it, if we would; and ought not, if we could.[245]

The 'right of private judgment', on the other hand, was best secured 'by keeping the exercise of that in our own' power. The logic of the argument was clear: 'though we may be safe by the power of others, we cannot be religious by the consciences of others ... '[246]

Locke's argument that a civil role in religion was an inefficient means of fostering Christian spirit was frequently employed by dissenters. Priestley began the section of the *Essay* dealing with religious liberty by asking 'whether the civil magistrate ought to extend his authority to matters of religion'.[247] Government was constitutionally unsuited and institutionally too clumsy to intervene in affairs of the mind, and this marked off, indirectly, the scope of individual liberty.[248] For Priestley the liberty of the individual was fundamentally the freedom to think:

Since all men naturally wish to be at liberty to serve themselves in things in which others are not concerned, and the good of the whole is the great rule by which every thing relating to society ought to be regulated, it is

---

[244] Philip Furneaux, *An Essay on Toleration* (London, 1773), p. 9.   [245] *Ibid.*, p. 13.
[246] *Ibid.*, p. 13; see also, *Letters to Blackstone*, p. 114n.   [247] Priestley, *Essay*, p. 110.
[248] Priestley, 'A Free Address to Protestant Dissenters', *Works*, xxii, p. 253.

evidently desirable that recourse should not be had to the power of the society, except when it can be applied with advantage …[249]

Priestley did not believe there was any 'advantage' to justify the existence of an establishment: 'Because whatever utility there may be in *ecclesiastical establishments*, there is certainly utility in truth' and truth had the best chance of being discovered and discussed in a society possessed of 'the most perfect freedom of inquiry and debate'. Blackburne's opening was thoroughly exploited by Priestley, who was also prepared, rather unusually for his time, to reject the commonplace that even a bad establishment was better than none at all.[250]

Truth and private judgment

The grave difficulty in allowing the magistrate to intervene in religion was the real possibility of 'a perpetual contest between the governors and the governed'.[251] The conflict between the claims of public utility, usually measured in terms of security, and private good, by which these Protestants meant judgment, was the paramount question in the political thought of this period. The defect of the criterion of 'efficiency', designed to facilitate the functioning of a just society, as with any prudential test, was that it resembled an empty box. What the dissenters thought efficient for individuals their opponents thought inefficient for communities. Like the analogous invocation of the 'common good', 'efficiency' still left room for the magistrate to intervene in religious matters. Thus, while all dissenters denied civil authorities the punishment of heresy, some, most notably Blackburne, admitted that 'had heresy and schism been the dangerous frightful things to civil government they were represented to be', then the risk to the community would have justified civil intervention.[252]

At the end of the 1760s and the beginning of the 1770s, a period spanned by the first and revised second edition of Priestley's *Essay on First Principles*, the dissenters turned to natural rights. Appealing to a

---

249 Priestley, *Lectures on History*, p. 230. Priestley's construction of a secular political concept out of freedom of thought in religion will be discussed later in the context of his debate with John Brown.
250 Priestley, *Balguy*, p. 45.
251 Furneaux, *Essay*, p. 16. Also, *Letters to Blackstone*, pp. 51, 54.
252 Blackburne, 'Considerations', IV, p. 61. Also Ramsay, *Thoughts on the Origin and Nature of Government*, p. 24.

transcendent standard enabled them to present an unturnable flank to their opponents' prudential argument. They accomplished this by adding the epistemological windfall of truth harvested by free enquiry to the Protestant notion of private judgment.[253] Having likened private judgment to free enquiry, and perceiving the manifold advantages to European culture brought by the latter, it seemed impossible to deny that there was something both ineradicably human *and* worthwhile about freedom of thought.[254]

Because Locke disdained a historical approach he could be no resource for dissenters seeking evidence for the priority of private judgment within Protestantism. Instead, they had recourse to what was seen as incontrovertible support for the principle of the enquiring individual: the Reformation and the scientific revolution. Dissenting writers often addressed these historical events as if they were indistinct representations of a single 'truth':

> Philosophical truth seems to be better calculated to make its way in the world than truth of a religious nature, because men are not so much interested in opposing it. But it must not be forgotten, that Galileo was put into the Inquisition for maintaining one of the first principles of modern philosophy.[255]

Perceptive contemporaries, like Adam Smith, saw the connection between the exploration of the Western Hemisphere, with its manifold ramifications, and the sixteenth-century revolution in the scope of human enquiry, with its many consequences. Robert Robinson (1735–90), a baptist minister and anti-slavery activist, explicitly drew these events into a defence of the enquiring individual. Though the Spanish ecclesiastical establishment opposed Columbus' voyage because of an objection derived from Augustine, 'The king and Columbus ventured to dissent, judged for themselves, and

---

[253] Richard Ashcraft has made this point and also used it to distinguish between latitudinarians, dissenters and orthodox Anglicans. See 'Latitudinarianism and Toleration: Historical Myth versus Political History', in *Philosophy, Science, and Religion in England 1640–1700*, ed. Richard Kroll, Richard Ashcraft and Perez Zagorin (Cambridge, 1992), pp. 160–3 and 166.

[254] Hobbes' opposition to private judgment in the seventeenth century (Steven Shapin and Simon Schaffer, *Leviathan and the Air-Pump* (Princeton, 1985), pp. 104, 322–3) was matched by Tucker's in the eighteenth (*Letters to the Rev. Dr Kippis* (Gloucester, 1773), p. 7; *A Treatise Concerning Civil Government* (London, 1781)). For more on the fear of the political implications of scientific enquiry, see Maurice Crossland, 'The Image of Science as Threat: Burke versus Priestley and the "Philosophic Revolution"', *British Journal for the History of Science*, 20 (1987), 278.

[255] Priestley, 'Letters to a Philosophical Unbeliever', *Works*, IV, p. 493. For more on Galileo and Copernicus in this role, see Furneaux, *Letters to Blackstone*, p. 76n.

found more ample reward for so doing notwithstanding clerical decisions.' The more recent persecutions of Copernicus and Galileo were also cited as 'some of the fruits of denying the right of private judgment'.[256] Watts, emphasizing the English contribution to the enquiry after truth, had earlier exchanged Columbus and Galileo for Newton, but maintained the emphasis on the challenge to 'human authority though it be never so ancient'. Longevity and power provided 'no certain and undoubted claim to truth'.[257]

The pioneers of both the scientific and protestant revolutions had 'but just emerged out of the dark abyss of Popery, and laboured under very strong prejudices from their education, and preconceived opinions'. Under those circumstances, some residual failure was inevitable. 'But', wrote Benjamin Dawson, 'surely three hundred years have not flowed in vain; every science hath received great light and improvement.'[258] Because private judgment was at the crux of both Protestantism and science, and Britain was the glory of European science, it was to be expected that the exercise of private judgment in religion would generate similar 'improvement'.[259]

The perceived quickening pace of learning in recent years was believed to be the result of more individuals being left free to think. In hindsight, efforts to block the truth of men like Columbus and Galileo were obviously misguided. Defending the recently deceased Price against his detractors, Christopher Wyvill wrote,

Intolerance has a microscopic eye, which can discover danger or criminality in any speculation on any subject. In her view, whether the subject of disquisition be theological or moral, whether it relate to metaphysics or natural philosophy, freedom of inquiry is always dangerous, and novelty of sentiment is never free from guilt. On such reasons, the disgrace of Price may be approved; and on similar grounds, Clarke and Hoadly, Newton and Locke, Churchmen, who were the ornaments of their profession; Philosophers, who were the honour of their Country, might have been condemned as Men of dangerous speculation and disturbers of the Public Peace. And thus the Zealots of Church Power, proceeding step by step from one degree of intolerance to another more severe, might justify, by parity of reason, the imprisonment of Galileo at Rome, the legal murder of Servetus

---

[256] Robinson, *Arcana*, pp. 36–7.
[257] Watts, 'The Improvement of the Mind. The Second Part', *Works*, v, p. 334; also p. 337.
[258] Benjamin Dawson, *A Free and Candid Disquisition*, p. 67.
[259] Robinson, *Arcana*, pp. 31–2.

at Geneva, the burning of Protestants in London, and the massacre of the Hugonots in Paris.[260]

The author of *The Foundations of Religious Liberty Explained* presented a powerful defence of the independence of intellectual enquiry.[261] There was no reason to limit improvement to the 'arts, sciences and philosophy', he wrote.

Indeed for a man to be determined by any thing else in the choice of his religion, but evidence, is a most gross affront to the reason of his own mind: for to what purpose had we our understandings given us, if not to judge for ourselves, and to guide us in the most important of all concerns, that of our religion and salvation? Without an honest impartial enquiry after truth, a man's being of the best religion in the world has no sort of merit in it.[262]

In truest Clarkean idiom, joining observation and moral realism, this enquiry would discover the truth 'by the sense of right and wrong which is original in us, and implanted in every man's breast ... '. The 'foundations of religious liberty' were not to be discovered in any definition of public policy. Rather, 'we must carefully look into the frame and constitutions of our own minds'.[263]

Intellectualism was surely one of the most distinctive characteristics of rational dissent. While this might have derived from a primary commitment to Protestant private judgment, for many, intellectual life was an important end in itself. David Williams' definition of intellectual liberty balanced between the two components, describing it as 'the inalienable and universal right of private judgment; and the necessity of an unrestrained enquiry and freedom of debate and discussion on all subjects of knowledge, morality and religion'.[264] John Jortin (1698–1770), in the preface to his five-volume *Remarks*, emphasized that the freedom of thought in question was not to be confused with free-thinking: 'Polite Learning, or humanity helps to open and enlarge the mind, and to give it a generous and liberal way of thinking, not what is vulgarly termed *Free-thinking*, and belongs to vulgar Understandings.'[265] In his Commencement Sermon at Cambridge in 1756, John Ross, still another

[260] Wyvill, *A Defense of Dr Price and the Reformers of England* (London, 1792), pp. 33–4. Also, Fleming, *Civil Establishments in Religion*, p. 2.

[261] [Samuel Bourne], *The Foundations of Religious Liberty Explained* (London, 1755), p. 27. Bourne (1714–96) held a pulpit in Norwich, like his father Samuel Bourne the Younger, and was a follower of Clarke's Christology.

[262] Anon., *Foundations of Religious Liberty*, p. 11.   [263] *Ibid.*, p. 4.

[264] David Williams, *Letter to the Body of Protestant Dissenters* (London, 1777), p. 23.

[265] John Jortin, *Remarks on Ecclesiastical History*, 5 vols. (London, 1751–73), I, xxxix.

fellow of St John's and Bishop of Exeter, argued that the improvement of learning depended on the 'free exercise of reason' and that
freedom of thought in one sphere of life would 'naturally make men
fond of it in another'. He also, and perhaps more ominously for
some, stressed the liberating aspect of learning:

Let a people be loaded with the heaviest shackles of civil and religious
tyranny; let their bodies be subdued by oppression and violence; and let
their minds be enslaved by the grossest inventions of a blind superstition;
let them esteem their princes and priests as the viceregents of God, and let
them reverence them as the distributors of happiness both here and
hereafter; yet if, through a happy coincidence of circumstances; or the hard
struggles of an extraordinary genius, the dawn of learning once break in
upon them; the face of things will be entirely renewed, and the extravagant
notions, which had hitherto prevailed, will disappear, like phantoms, at the
break of day.[266]

While many contemporaries, like Johnson and Goldsmith, made
similar comments, the danger implicit in the dissenters' panegyrics
to the power of reason was never far below the surface. Abraham
Rees declared that 'To be religious, and yet to be uninspired by a
sacred ardour of affection, to be unacquainted with peace and joy
with that freedom, strength and activity of mind which are the
certain effects of religion, is a contradiction.'[267] It was precisely the
link between the dissenters' theology of 'liberation' and the 'inspiration' so closely associated with the anarchy and regicide of the civil
war years that made this enlightenment threatening rather than
uplifting.

In his pamphlet attacking Blackstone, Priestley chided him for
making public nonconformity a criminal act that would have
suppressed England's greatest thinkers. On Blackstone's reading,
Newton and Locke were 'guilty of great *arrogance*, because they
ought to have considered, that the prevailing opinions which they
called into question, had at least a greater chance to be right than
their *singular* notions'.[268] In the same vein, Anglican obstructionism
would be seen to be false to the essence of Protestantism by denying
the possibility of private judgment and thus pre-empting any
potential benefits. Protestants aimed to 'return to their true uner-

---

[266] John Ross, *Commencement Sermon* (Cambridge, 1756), pp. 7–8.
[267] Abraham Rees, *Acceptable Religion Illustrated and Recommended. A Sermon* ... (London, 1770),
     p. 14.
[268] Priestley, 'Remarks on ... Dr Blackstone's *Commentaries*', *Works*, xxii, p. 324. Priestley
     defended a similar point in the *Essay*, p. 278.

ring guide, which would have conducted them aright from the first, and have kept them all together: they must return to the Principle from whence they set out; the sufficiency of scripture itself'.[269] The only means of asserting the essence of Protestantism was by affirming the foundational role of 'free enquiry' and 'private judgment' against the Romish subordination of individuals to authority.[270] Moreover, because religion depended on mental activity and a person 'cannot but believe, according as things appear to Himself', the alternative to private judgment was tyranny.[271] Subscription to the Thirty-Nine Articles was particularly pernicious because it challenged the dissenters' commitment to Scripture alone and its private interpretation.[272] The content of the articles was less a source of opposition than the principle of human authority in religion.[273]

Watts had argued that because private judgment was an intellectual activity it depended on the possibility of freedom: 'It is this freedom of volition or chusing which is properly the liberty of an intelligent being, and the chief subject of dispute ... '[274] By speaking of a liberty of action, Locke had muddled this point,[275] leading many 'to doubt whether there be any self-moving power at all or no, whether there be any first-moving spirit, that is, a God'. Watts sought to eliminate this uncertainty by fixing 'the guilt of evil actions entirely on the will of the creature, by ascribing to the will of a free power to determine itself, either to chuse or to refuse after any representations of good or evil, fitness or unfitness made by the understanding'.[276]

In the 1770s, these arguments fed into a new debate. Looking over his shoulder, Andrew Kippis observed that 'the question concerning

---

269 *The State of Subscription to the Articles and Liturgy of the Church of England*, p. 55; Dawson, *A Short and Safe Expedient for Terminating the Present Debates about Subscription* (London, 1769), sig. [A1]r.
270 Dawson, *A Short and Safe Expedient*, p. 36.
271 Furneaux, *Letters to Blackstone*, p. 33; Ibbot, 'A Course of Sermons ... ' (Boyle Lectures), *A Defense of Natural and Revealed Religion ...*, ed. S. Letosme and J. Nicholl (London, 1739), p. 797.
272 Mauduit, *Case of the Dissenting Ministers*, pp. 35–6, cited by Fitzpatrick, 'Toleration and Truth', p. 4; Dawson, *A Letter to the Clergy of the Archdeaconry of Winchester*, p. 48. Sometimes these two arguments simply merged: Benjamin Fawcett, *The Encouraging Prospect that Religious Liberty Will Be Enlarged* (Shrewsbury, 1773), p. 7.
273 Samuel Palmer, *The Protestant Dissenter's Catechism ...* (4th edn, Belfast, 1773), p. 67.
274 Watts, 'An Essay on the Freedom of the Will in God and in Creatures', *Works*, VI, p. 376.
275 *Ibid.*, p. 377n.
276 *Ibid.*, p. 393. Also Robert Seagrave, *The Principles of Liberty* (London, 1755), p. 13.

the right, expediency and utility of requiring an assent or sub-scription to human articles of religion hath been, for near sixty years, the frequent matter of debate in this country'.[277] Clarke and his followers had written of human liberty, natural laws and laws of nature. Once private judgment was assimilated to the status of natural philosophic enquiry it was a short step to extend to this seemingly constitutively human activity the term 'natural'. The unfettered exercise of freedom of enquiry had become a natural right:

... no Christian society can have a right to impose articles of human composition on any of its members; because such a right is contrary to the authority of our Saviour ... and because it is equally contrary to the principles upon which Protestantism can alone be defended, which are the liberty of private judgment, and the sufficiency of Scripture.[278]

The dissenters stressed the link between the political and religious dimensions of private judgment. They were supporters of 'the cause of liberty and of the right of private judgment (a right unalienable from us as men and christians)'.[279] Robinson invoked Protestant natural rights against the claim that the security of the community as a whole was the burden of government. Because Christianity depended on a personal relationship between man and God, 'how can the depriving men of the right of private judgment be a lawful mean [*sic*] of obtaining that end'?[280] 'Reason', understood in Samuel Clarke's terms, carried the weight of this argument:

We follow no party, but follow reason only, and the dictates of our own plain and natural understanding; not minding whether others have said the same before us, but whether what we say is just, and ought to be said by us, or by any others ... We are persuaded reason will prevail with men of reason. And reason alone will do it, without the concurrence of any authorities.[281]

Like the followers of Clarke, Priestley argued at the time that, because reason played such a major role, its perfection by constant improvement was mandated.[282] The 'reason' that underpinned the broad notion of private judgment is reflected in the ease with which Priestley moved between demanding rights as a Christian, and as a

---

[277] Kippis, *Vindication*, p. 1.   [278] *Ibid.*, p. 3.
[279] Dawson, *A Short and Safe Expedient*, p. 27.
[280] Robinson, *Arcana*, pp. 32–3.   [281] Jones, *Free and Candid Disquisitions*, p. 72.
[282] Priestley, 'The Importance and Extent of Free Enquiry in Matters of Religion', *Works*, xv, p. 71.

man: 'But when the Christian is satisfied, I cannot forget that I am likewise a man; and the generosity of the man and of the Christian happily concur, in wishing for the toleration of all the modes of thinking in the world.'[283] Dissenters could never allow themselves to succumb to the temptations of misology and irrationality.[284] Ultimately, Priestley placed the universal commitment over the particular: 'Conceal, therefore, the obnoxious name of Christian, and ask for the common rights of humanity.'[285]

The terminology of political contractarianism was employed to convey the assertion of a natural right to freedom of thought. Robinson had suggested that the 'condition of man in the state of nature' demonstrated that the right to private judgment was basic.[286] Joseph Fownes was the dissenting minister whose highly provocative *Enquiry into the Principles of Toleration* pushed this Protestant rights argument to a conclusion far more radical than that of Locke. Of all the 'rights inherent in human nature' private judgment was 'the most sacred'.[287] Consequently, Fownes was prepared to declare that any encroachment on this freedom of thought, 'though inflicted by a law' was still 'an infringement of a right, and a DEGREE OF OPPRESSION'. Protection did not depend 'on the supposed truth or error of the sentiments which men may adopt' but on membership in society.[288] In this tradition, private judgment became an 'inalienable natural right':

For though the people, coming out of a state of nature into a state of society, give up many private rights in order to obtain other and greater rights; yet this is a right which cannot be supposed to be given up; for two reasons. First, the right itself in its nature is inalienable. No man can any more divest himself of private judging than of thinking.[289]

As a consequence, civil and ecclesiastical laws were both to be determined by reference to this natural law. Deviations from the rules of nature and revelation, even if warranted by some

[283] Priestley, 'A Letter of Advice to the Dissenters who Conduct the Application to Parliament for Relief from Certain Penal Laws', *Works*, XXII, p. 450.
[284] Priestley, 'An Appeal to the Serious and Candid Professors of Christianity', *Works*, II, p. 384.
[285] Priestley, 'Letter of Advice', *Works*, XXII, p. 443.   [286] Robinson, *Arcana*, p. 35.
[287] Fownes, *Enquiry into the Principles of Toleration* (2nd edn, Shrewsbury, 1773; 1st edn, 1769), p. 15.
[288] *Ibid.*, p. 22.
[289] Robinson, *Arcana*, p. 46. This was a common argument in the latter stages of the debate. See Joseph Towers, *A Letter to Dr Samuel Johnson* (London, 1776), p. 28; Fownes, *Enquiry*,

determination of public prudence, were 'subversive of the most valuable rights of mankind in their temporal concerns; as it is in Ecclesiastical Governors to contradict by their authority the commands of God, or to oppress the consciences of Men'.[290]

The dissenters' vision of the true church constituted, quite simply, a new political society. The Analogy demonstrated that 'a Being of infinite justice and mercy and the most unbounded Benevolence' could not sanction the right of conquest or heredity: government could only be based on the consent of free individuals.[291] 'A congregation, or voluntary society of christians' had 'a right to transact its own affairs, according to the judgment and conscience of the members thereof, independently of any other societies whatsoever'. The Church of England, on the other hand, was most definitely not a 'voluntary society'. Members were 'obliged by law' not of their own making since they were too numerous to assemble and legislate for themselves. Instead, all were 'obliged to an absolute uniformity in faith, worship and discipline'.[292] Political tyranny, understood as the lack of any voice in legislation, either through participation or representative consent, and the absence of individual liberty with the suppression of private judgment, coincided in the dissenters' image of politics. John Dunn has argued that Locke's account of natural rights, with its wide scope for individual liberty, had as an unstated precondition a society of Christians already sharing a certain view of the world.[293] Only the prior acceptance of the premises shared by believing Christians made possible that broad independence. Specifically, without the common vision of the world provided by shared religious beliefs, private judgment and individual liberty would actually have made social life impossible. Defining the balance between individuals and the community, between public and private, was the nettle described by many in the eighteenth century, but grasped by few. The nature of the safety of the state – the definition of the common good – was precisely the crux of the dispute between John Brown and Joseph Priestley.

p. 21; Henry Norman, *Two Letters on the Subject of Subscription*, p. 19; Fleming, *Civil Establishments*, p. 76; Furneaux, *Letters to Blackstone*, p. 93.

290 J. Sturges, *A Letter to a Bishop Occasioned by the Late Petition to Parliament* (2nd edn, London, 1773), p. 71.

291 Anon., *A Letter to the Rev. Dr Cooper, on the Origin of Civil Government in Answer to his Sermon* ... (London, 1772), p. 15.

292 Palmer, *Catechism*, p. 29.

293 Dunn, 'From Applied Theology to Social Analysis', in *Wealth and Virtue*, pp. 128–9.

JOHN BROWN AND JOSEPH PRIESTLEY

John Brown's plea for Britain's soul during the Seven Years War provides us with a picture of complete commitment to civic prosperity at almost any cost. In itself quite valuable, Brown's arguments also provoked Joseph Priestley's most sustained political theorizing, and a proper understanding of the latter's position and emphases depends on some acquaintance with the former's. But Brown was, as noted by contemporaries, a rather peculiar character, and our sense of him is distorted by focusing on his polemical works. His undergraduate years at Cambridge were followed by an appointment as a minor canon and lecturer in the cathedral at Carlisle. He soon fell in with Warburton's circle. Nevertheless, his early sermons, though collected and published only in 1764, reveal a very different political perspective.

Brown preached at Carlisle in 1746 during the trial of the Jacobites on the connection between religious truth and civil freedom on the one hand, and superstition and tyranny on the other. The obvious argument was the relationship between Roman Catholicism and political despotism. Superstition, understood as the absence of reason, rendered individuals amenable to tyranny. Reason, on the contrary, liberated by dispatching the vain phantoms conjured by superstitious belief:

The Activity of the Human Mind does naturally repel the Impositions of outward Force: But when Thought itself is subdued, and Shackles laid upon the Understanding, then it is that all Possibility of Resistance vanisheth; then it is that Tyranny reigns without Controul, and perpetrates the most horrid Absurdities, not only with impunity but Applause.[294]

The natural operation of the mind, in which the experience of wonder was the 'Seed of Knowledge', depended on freedom to explore. Adam Smith was later to further anatomize the different stages of the acquisition of knowledge as surprise, wonder and admiration. Brown, at this stage in his career at least, sought to emphasize the political consequences of obstructing this progression: 'Where this natural Principle of Wonder is cherished by Freedom, it shoots up and opens into Knowledge; but where checked by the ill

---

[294] John Brown, 'The Mutual Connexion between Religious Truth and Civil Freedom; between Superstition, Tyranny, Irreligion and Licentiousness', *Sermons on Various Subjects* (London, 1764), p. 73.

Influence of Tyranny, it degenerates into Ignorance confirmed.'[295]
The suppression of 'wonder' and enquiry led ineluctably to tyranny.

If the wages of superstition were obscurantism and tyranny,
'Religious Truth' promoted liberty. Knowledge of divine goodness
and a 'just Sense of the Condition and Dignity of Man' elevated the
soul to a love of liberty that Brown was at pains to distinguish from
'that Licentiousness which is the Off-spring of Vice'. Religious
truth, however valuable, could not be imposed on people but had to
be arrived at through individual acts of enquiry: 'Whatever some
may fear from an open and unlimited Enquiry, it seems evidently
the only Means God hath vouchsafed us for the Attainment of
Truth. The Abuse of it may be dangerous, but the Want of it is
fatal.'[296] Ironically, Priestley used this exact same language when
attacking Brown in 1765! 'Unbounded free enquiry upon all kinds of
subjects, may certainly be attended with some inconvenience, but it
cannot be restrained without infinitely greater inconvenience'.[297]

The ancients lacked 'consistent Notions of Freedom' and were
governed by passion not reason. The result, according to Brown,
was a world unworthy of imitation:

Cities were ruined, provinces plundered, and whole kingdoms laid in
Ashes, thro' an absurd and impious Love of their Country; a Principle no
better in many of its Consequences, than the most cruel and accursed
Bigotry. Even among themselves a whole Race of unhappy People, and
innocent Children, were destined to a severe and endless Slavery, robb'd of
all the natural Rights of Men, their Life only excepted, and that too at the
disposal of an arbitrary master. Thus Liberty seemed no more than the
casual Product of high Spirit, often of Pride and Revenge, seldom or never
the result of Rational Opinion.[298]

This extraordinary statement, which Brown's later polemical works
seem to repudiate, reflects a commitment to freedom of enquiry that
would have been current in some Cambridge circles, but which was
peripheral to the concerns of Warburton.

His *Essay on the Characteristicks* defended 'that generous Spirit of
Freedom' which he found so praiseworthy about Shaftesbury: 'The
noble Author every where asserts that natural Privilege of Man,

---

[295] *Ibid.*, p. 75.   [296] *Ibid.*, pp. 78–9.

[297] Priestley, *Essay*, p. 133. See also Burgh, *Remarks*, p. 190, *Dignity of Human Nature*, p. 110;
Blackburne, 'Four Discourses: Discourse 1. On the Duty of a Christian Minister under the
Obligation of Conforming to a National Religion, Established by the Civil Powers',
Works, IV, pp. 300–1; Barron, *Pillars of Priestcraft*, I, pp. v–vi.

[298] Brown, 'The Mutual Connexion', *Sermons*, p. 82.

which hath been so often denied him, of seeing with his own Eyes, and judging by his own Reason.' In earlier days the principle was more controversial, but now most people agreed that 'not only the Perfection, but the very Being of Knowledge depends on the Exercise of Freedom'.[299] The difference between this Brown and the later defender of state management of religious and intellectual life is startling.

Throughout his life Brown would maintain the primacy of Locke's epistemology and theory of sensation. Since human conduct was the result of the actions of the passions, Brown deduced that behaviour could be modified by controlling the sensations which produced the passions. This was best accomplished early in childhood, before habits had formed.[300] A less careful attitude towards the stimuli affecting children would result in citizens who were governed by their passions and not by the laws of reason or the state. This was especially worrisome at a time and in a place where the surrounding attitudes were not conducive to any form of self-discipline.[301]

Brown's remedy for this situation was tight state control over the flow of information and, therefore, special attention to education. In 1765, just before committing suicide, Brown published his systematic thoughts on this matter. In contrast to the views of rationalist followers of Clarke like Price and Burgh, the goal of education was not to expand the minds and enlighten the souls of individuals, but to secure the preservation of the state: 'By a Code of Education, therefore, he means a System of Principles, religious, moral, and political; whose Tendency may be the Preservation of the Blessings of Society, as they are enjoyed in a free State: to be instilled effectually into the infant and growing Minds of the Community, for this great End of public Happiness.'[302] Unsystematic education left individuals to the mores of their time and in eighteenth-century Britain this had resulted in the collapse of female morality. The 'Loss of domestic Union and Happiness' had subsequently produced, according to Brown, a commensurate decline in national morality since mothers with bad manners raised corrupt children.[303] Like

---

[299] Brown, *Essays*, pp. 2–4.
[300] Brown, 'On the First Principles of Education', *Sermons*, p. 82.
[301] Brown, *Essays on the Characteristicks*, p. 234.
[302] Brown, 'An Appendix, Relative to a Proposed Code of Education', *On the Female Character and Education: A Sermon* (London, 1765), p. 25.
[303] *Ibid.*, p. 18.

other defenders of the state, Brown, too, assimilated the family to the larger political society.

In Brown's diagnosis, the decline in public virtue could be traced to the inadequate preparation of women for their role in society. This failure manifested itself in one significant characteristic: ' ... Women, scorning the timid and subordinate Character, affect a self-sufficient and haughty Independency; assert an unbounded Freedom of Thought and Action'.[304] In the world-view centred on the security of the community, freedom of thought was seen to promote 'independence', that solvent capable of undoing the most important social bonds. This led Brown to a most explicit comment, repudiating his own view of twenty years earlier: 'To this the Writer replies, that in his Judgment, there are many Opinions or Principles, tending evidently to the Destruction of Society or Freedom; and which, therefore, ought not to be tolerated in a well-ordered free Community.'[305]

In his *Thoughts on Civil Liberty on Licentiousness and Faction*, also published in 1765, Brown expounded this theory of society in the familiar idiom of classical politics. He held up the social institutions of the Spartan state as an example for eighteenth-century Britain. Its institutions were perfectly suited to promote the success of national policy. Education was the primary instrument for the continuation of the Spartan ideal.[306] Sparta was, as we have seen, an attractive model for defenders of the security of the community. Even writers more usually associated with a freer attitude towards information also acknowledged the advantages of the Spartan system of state education. Thus, Oliver Goldsmith wrote that 'For the state to take charge of all its children, as in Persia or Sparta, might at present be inconvenient; but surely with great ease, it might cast an eye to their instructors.'[307] Sparta was also excluded from Adam Smith's condemnation of the failure of the ancient Greek cities to maintain a public education, which resulted in the decline of their military might.[308] For Brown, as for Smith, Athens' tumultuous and deadly democratic politics were a result of the absence of a public education. The city lacked an 'established Education, suited to the Genius of the State ... '[309]

---

[304] *Ibid.*, p. 17.   [305] Brown, 'Appendix ... Education', *On the Female Character*, p. 29.
[306] Brown, *Thoughts on Civil Liberty*, pp. 40–4.
[307] Oliver Goldsmith, 'On Education', *Works*, I, p. 457.
[308] Smith, *WN*, v.i.f.41, p. 776.   [309] Brown, *Thoughts on Civil Liberty*, p. 61.

A discussion of Joseph Priestley's politics must proceed with caution. Clearly, there is some connection between his philosophical, scientific, theological and political writings. But because he wrote so widely and so much – 150 books and pamphlets, many of them of several volumes, countless papers and letters – a great deal of care is needed to specify which Priestley we are talking about, and when.[310] Attempts at a synoptic Priestley cannot yet succeed, for we are only beginning to understand his place in the separate discourses he united in his person. Especially troubling is the failure to account for the implications of his deepening attachment to the associationist argument of David Hartley. There is a world of difference between the defence of liberty, especially intellectual, in the *Essay*, and shorter pieces on toleration, and the thoroughgoing association-driven materialism of the later 1770s.[311] Thus, prior to 1772–4, Priestley could still refer to the 'Newtonian system' with its meta-physical theory of human nature based on the free exercise of reason and supported by the notion of a natural right.[312] Simon Schaffer has argued that the practice of science in eighteenth-century England reflected the Newtonian insistence on the omnipotence and omniscience of the divinity.[313] Priestley's use of association to challenge the system of performance and 'generation of assent' is a sign of his break from its scientific and philosophical implications, as is his repudiation of the possibility of self-motion, or liberty.[314]

Priestley substituted unrestricted freedom of enquiry for constitutional forms, suggesting that complete freedom of thought would

---

[310] Robert E. Schofield, 'Joseph Priestley: Theology, Physics and Metaphysics', *Enlightenment and Dissent*, 2 (1983), 69.

[311] See John G. McEvoy, 'Joseph Priestley: Scientist, Philosopher and Divine', *Proceedings of the American Philosophical Society*, 128 (1984), 195; 'Electricity, Knowledge and the Nature of Progress in Priestley's Thought', *British Journal for the History of Science*, xii (1979), 4; 'Joseph Priestley, "Aerial Philosopher": Metaphysics and Methodology in Priestley's Chemical Thought, from 1772 to 1781', *Ambix*, 25 (1978), 11. Simon Schaffer has sought to stress the different Priestleys that exist ('Measuring Virtue: Eudiometry, Enlightenment and Pneumatic Medicine', in *The Medical Enlightenment of the Eighteenth Century*, ed. Andrew Cunningham and Roger French (Cambridge, 1990), p. 283; 'Priestley and the Politics of Spirit', *Science, Medicine and Dissent: Joseph Priestley (1733–1804)*, ed. R. G. W. Anderson and Christopher Lawrence (London, 1987), p. 46).

[312] Priestley, 'Essay', *Works*, xxii, p. 51.

[313] Schaffer, 'Priestley and the Politics of Spirit', p. 40; 'Natural Philosophy and Public Spectacle in the Eighteenth Century, *History of Science*, 21 (1983), 1–43.

[314] Schaffer, 'Priestley and the Politics of Spirit', pp. 39–45; 'Priestley's Questions: An Historiographic Survey', *History of Science*, 22 (1984), 151–83. His conclusions disrupt Kramnick's assumptions (*Republicanism*, p. 64).

engender a political community in which there would no longer be a need for the traditional political solutions. And where information was free, so were citizens:

By freedom of debate, and writing, the minds of the bulk of any people would in time be enlightened, and their general voice alone would, in a well-regulated state, both command any real useful regulation, and enforce the observance of it when it was made. If the constitution was not a good one, this perfect freedom of debate would be the best method of making it to be so.[315]

It is the debate between Priestley and John Brown which served to generate many of these arguments and so it stands in a prominent position in the development of the alternative political thought formulated by the reformers in the later 1760s and 1770s. In 1768, Priestley published the first edition of his *Essay on First Principles*, declaring in the preface that he was urged by his friends to expand on an earlier and more limited refutation of Brown's arguments. Priestley added that these friends felt that his views were new and more successful because employing 'a more accurate and extensive system of morals and policy, than was adopted by Mr Locke'.[316]

Priestley explicitly challenged Brown's two central claims, that freedom of thought could be restricted in the interests of national security, and that Sparta was an example worthy of emulation. Priestley's alternative political vision sought to meet Brown on his own turf, and so was also articulated in the idiom of classical politics. But in turning ancient Athens into a political metaphor he also was subverting the essential understanding of classical exempla which had previously excluded Athens from consideration.

What Brown lauded as Sparta's greatness was, in fact, her backwardness. Instead, Priestley focused on a different set of human values, one which followed directly from Clarke's formulation of a theory of human nature and which was best demonstrated in Athens:

What advantage did Sparta the constitution of whose government was so much admired by the ancients, (and by many moderns) reap from those institutions which contributed to its longevity, but the longer continuance of what I should not scruple to call the worst government we read of in the

---

[315] Priestley, 'Letters of Advice', *Works*, XXII, p. 455.
[316] Priestley, *Essay* (1768), pp. iii–iv. On Priestley's somewhat distant relationship with Locke, see D. O. Thomas' fine, 'Progress, Liberty and Utility: The Political Philosophy of Joseph Priestley', in *Science, Medicine and Dissent: Joseph Priestley (1733–1804)*, p. 75.

world; a government which secured to a man the fewest of his natural rights, and of which a man who had a taste for life would least of all choose to be a member.

As the 'arts of life' improved elsewhere, Sparta remained immured in her unchanging 'pristine barbarity'. By contrast, the developments in Athens where, despite its 'convulsions', 'life was in some measure enjoyed, and the faculties of body and mind had their proper exercise and gratification, were, in my opinion, far preferable to the savage uniformity of Sparta'.[317] Sparta was rejected as a model because it failed to promote the individual's 'natural rights'. But, for Priestley, the account of what was naturally human diverged from earlier presentations. As humans became more advanced 'in the arts of life' it became possible to imagine no longer being 'servilly governed like brutes' but rather 'governing ourselves like men'.[318] Self-government depended on intellectual development, not simply constitutional arrangement and certainly not indoctrination in the content of virtue.

Priestley's benchmark argument for intellectual liberty was actually constructed in response to Brown's defence of constrained enquiry and against his Spartan model. From where Priestley stood, Brown subordinated the development of the mind and the improvement of knowledge to 'bare security'. He

would raise the terms on which we are to live in society; so that, under his administration, a man could enjoy little more than bare security in the possession of his property, and that upon very hard conditions. The care he would take to shackle men's minds in the first formation of their thinking powers, and to check their exertions when they were formed, would, I apprehend, put an effectual stop to all the noble improvements of which society is capable. Knowledge, particularly of the more sublime kinds, in the sciences of morals and religion, could expect no encouragement. He would have more restrictions laid upon the publication of books. He complains, that, in the late reign, deistical publications proceeded almost without cognizance from the civil magistrate and asserts that there are many opinions or principles tending evidently to the destruction of society or freedom, and which, therefore, ought not to be tolerated in a well-ordered, free community.[319]

Priestley rejected Brown's insinuation that, because of their commitment to rational, private judgment, the dissenters were politically suspect. Rather, it was precisely because of their

[317] Priestley, *Essay*, p. 119.   [318] *Ibid.*, p. 47.   [319] *Ibid.*, pp. 131–2.

commitment to freedom of thought that dissenters were politically incorruptible.[320]

No amount of government intervention could produce truth. Only the free thought of individuals could do that. 'Reason and Authority', wrote Priestley, had generally been diametrically opposed concepts. 'The hand of power, therefore, on the side of any set of principles, cannot but be auspicious circumstance.'[321] To Warburton's and Brown's reliance on an assessment of the public good, Priestley opposed the truth as it appeared to individuals:

Because, whatever utility there may be in ecclesiastical establishments, there is certainly utility in truth, especially moral and religious truth; and truth can never have a fair chance of being discovered, or propagated, without the most perfect freedom of inquiry and debate.[322]

Thus, in the guise of a challenge to Brown's historical interpretation, Priestley was articulating an alternative to the conventional view that individual good could only be achieved in the service of a greater, common good. Because he defined the individual good in terms of precisely those attributes to which the political community could make little contribution, such as thinking and discovering truth, its claim to override the individual in the public interest lost efficacy. One of the passages added to the second edition introducing Priestley's emphasis on a natural right to think places the *Essay* within the horizon of debate on the definition of the common good:

That the happiness of the whole community is the ultimate end of government can never be doubted, and all claims of individuals inconsistent with the public good are absolutely null and void; but there is a real difficulty in determining what general rules, respecting the extent of the power of government, or of governors, are most conducive to the public good.[323]

While Priestley's belief in a single truth upon which all freely enquiring individuals would ultimately converge was not shared by all other dissenters, he remained, perhaps paradoxically, much more steadfastly committed to universal toleration in the meantime. He was prepared to endorse the notion of a heterogeneous, pluralistic society. Precisely because political freedom was dependent upon intellectual freedoms, and human beings had unique souls, the

---

[320] Priestley, 'A View of the Principles and Conduct of the Protestant Dissenters', *Works*, xxii, p. 257.

[321] Priestley, *Essay*, p. 59.   [322] *Ibid.*, p. 89.

[323] *Ibid.*, pp. 56–7. Note also how Priestley sets forth his understanding of civil society and government (pp. 12–13).

particular ends which were to fulfil them were also unique. There could, then, be no single goal or lifestyle for a community of persons: 'The various character of the Athenians was certainly preferable to the uniform character of the Spartans, or to any uniform natural character whatever.'[324] His support for Catholic toleration is explicable on this model. None the less, it must be emphasized that for Priestley this pluralism was a means to secure a common end and not, as for some contemporaries and many followers, the end which had to be secured.

The priority of intellectual enquiry excluded the possibility of political solutions based on a canon of historically deduced maxims. Any attempt to freeze social and political arrangements would soon be undone by the 'progress' of the mind.[325] Again, the image of science and its practice provided Priestley with a ready alternative to Brown's interpretation of history:

> History demonstrates this truth with respect to all the celebrated states of antiquity; and as all things, and particularly what ever depends upon science, has of late years been in a quicker progress towards perfection than ever; we may safely conclude the same with respect to any political state now in being.[326]

Priestley is treated as a theologian, scientist and controversialist, but rarely as a historian. And yet, his first teaching appointment was as tutor in languages and belles-lettres at the dissenting academy at Warrington, where he introduced the study of modern history. The past served Priestley, as it did previous historians, as a storehouse of information with which to guide future conduct.

Knowledge of human nature was the great prize for the student of history: 'Experience and self-examination may assist us in adjusting the general theory of the human mind. But it is in history alone that we can see the strength of its powers, the connexion of its principles, and the variety to which individuals of the species are subject.'[327] It is precisely because political arrangements depended upon the successful organization of groups of people that the study of human nature was a prerequisite to a prospective science of politics. 'Here

---

[324] *Ibid.*, p. 46. Also, Fitzpatrick 'Universal Toleration', p. 10.
[325] 'Were the best formed state in the world to be fixed in its present condition, I make no doubt but that, in a course of time, it would be the very worst' (*A Course of Lectures on the Theory of Language and Universal Grammar* (Warrington, 1762), p. 192).
[326] Priestley, *An Essay on a Course of Liberal Education*, p. 162.
[327] Priestley, *Lectures on History*, p. 445.

observation and experience are the only safe guides' and only the long backward glance of the historian could compensate for the short lifespan of individuals. The theories of Plato, Aristotle, Cicero, More and Harrington were unsuccessful because incompatible with the historical reality.[328]

At Warrington, Priestley was not addressing himself to political theorists, but to young students. His belief that 'the study of History is more or less the employment of all persons of reading and education' reflects a broad commitment to intellectual improvement.[329] Understanding others and self-understanding were both dependent on exempla and so history provided the short-cut to wisdom. In the light of the natural inclination to link reformers with theory, it is wise to attend to Priestley's terribly concrete approach to spiritual, intellectual and political reformation:

We conceive more clearly what true greatness of mind is, at the same time that our hearts are more filled with admiration of it, and burn with a stronger passion for it, by a simple narration of some events in history, than by the most elaborate and philosophically exact description of it.[330]

As a history lecturer, Priestley must have been revolutionary. For sources he drew upon ancient poems, monuments, coins, literary remains, etymology and legal codes, while illustrating his argument with tables, chronologies, maps and other teaching aids. More famous still were the scale models he prepared for lectures on warfare and fortification. His description of proper historical 'method' drew upon his scientific commitment to the concrete, to observation and machines:

Works of fiction resemble those machines which we contrive to illustrate the principles of philosophy, such as globes, and orreries, the uses of which extend no farther than the views of human ingenuity; whereas real history resembles the experiments made by the air-pump, the condensing engine, or electrical machine, which exhibit the operations of nature, and the God of nature himself, whose works are the noblest subject of contemplation to the human mind, and are the ground work and materials of the most extensive and useful theories.[331]

---

[328] *Ibid.*, pp. 11–12. Hence Bolingbroke's lament that 'Experience is doubly defective; we are born too late to see the beginning, and we die too soon to see the end of many things.' The study of history, however, 'supplies both these defects' (Bolingbroke, 'History', *Works*, II, p. 186).

[329] Priestley, *Lectures on History*, p. 1.

[330] *Ibid.*, p. 19. For a similar opinion, see Conyers Middleton's preface to his biography of Cicero, p. xv.

[331] Priestley, *Lectures on History*, p. 5.

While philosophy could describe the principles of human life the way globes described, only history could expose the inner motivations of individuals and so explain their external conduct. Priestley's natural philosophy informed a 'science of politics' that was the successor to the earlier and newly judged 'unscientific' Tacitist attempt to unmask motivations. Explanation mattered to Priestley; he had no time for descriptions, especially as they could be easily manipulated by authorities.

While Brown thought himself the 'true enemy of sedition', the real patriot was actually one who 'proposes, with a manly freedom, whatever he thinks conducive to the greatness and glory of his country'.[332] Priestley redescribed the Roman *gloria e grandezza* to suit the new role of the individual in society. Its content was not war but thought, and its perfection could only result from 'indulging unbounded liberty and even caprice in conducting it'.[333] In this light, Brown's salvation of the polity, itself only an extreme version of the mainstream political thesis, would, in fact, produce its enslavement.[334]

Priestley's position was that 'Unbounded free enquiry upon all kinds of subjects may certainly be attended with some inconvenience, but it cannot be restrained without infinitely greater inconvenience.'[335] The evil that could result from the suppression of freedom of thought provided Priestley with the standard against which to define the realms in which civil intervention proved 'inefficient' and therefore illegitimate. 'For the purpose of finding out truth, individuals are always employed to assist multitudes' because, while greater numbers of enquirers increased the likelihood of discovery, ultimately 'they all act as independent individuals'. The model of intellectual enquiry perfectly illuminated the limits of civil authority:

For, whenever numbers have truth or knowledge for their object, and act as a collective body, that is, authoritatively, so that no single person can have power to determine anything till the majority have been brought to agree to it, the interests of knowledge will certainly suffer; there is so little prospect of the prejudices of the many giving way to the better judgment of an individual. Here there is a case in which society must always be benefited by individuals, as such, and not by numbers, in a collective

---

[332] Priestley, *Essay*, p. 300.   [333] Priestley, *Education*, p. 147.   [334] *Ibid.*, p. 173.
[335] *Ibid.*, p. 177. See, *Essay*, p. 69; *Balguy*, pp. 2, 73.

capacity. It is least of all, therefore, for the advancement of knowledge, that I should be induced to wish for the authoritative interposition of society.[336]

Drawing on this example, Priestley laid down what he hoped would be 'reasonable bounds' on the action of laws and government. Laws were 'defective' when they failed to provide the assistance expected from social living, and oppressive 'that is, injurious to the natural rights and civil liberties of mankind', when they imposed 'unnecessary restrictions' on behaviour. 'Unnecessary' was defined as the public intervention 'in which they can yield him no real assistance'.[337] Elsewhere, Priestley engaged directly with the early modern language of politics: 'As the end of society, and consequently of the institution of magistracy, is *the good of the whole body*; laws, or public regulations, should respect those things in which the wisdom and strength of society can be exerted to the advantage of the members of it.'[338]

In practice, Priestley was no dreamer. He knew that even this principle would get muddied once dipped into the turbid waters of policy-making: 'In some respects, however, it must be acknowledged, that the proper extent of civil government is not easily circumscribed within exact limits.' While Priestley recognized that in social life 'the happiness of the whole community is the ultimate end of government', the 'real difficulty' was in determining the extent to which legal intervention was necessary to serve that public good. Priestley presented a spectrum of opinions. Some thought that legislation should descend to all possible eventualities while others suggested that everything not explicitly affecting civil life should be completely excluded from the purview of the civil establishment. Priestley's preference was for the second, defining the service of the public good in terms of the withdrawal of the public from heretofore vast tracts of social life: 'it is for the advantage of the society, upon the whole, that all those things be left to take their own natural course, and that the legislature cannot interfere in them, without defeating its own great object, the public good'.[339]

Priestley did not despair of a solution. Price had suggested that education offered the only ultimate solution to this problem. Priest-

---

[336] Priestley, *Essay*, pp. 53–4. Note the crucial model of scientific discovery for the assertion of the individual.
[337] *Ibid.*, p. 53.   [338] Priestley, 'The Present State of Liberty', *Works*, XXII, p. 384.
[339] Priestley, *Essay*, pp. 56–7.

ley's suggestion, like his very category of freedom of thought, was modelled on his conception of how science was practised: 'We are so little capable of arguing *a priori* in matters of government, that it should seem, experiments only can determine how far this power of the legislature ought to extend.' At which point, in true eighteenth-century form, Priestley returned, *da capo*, to the claims of 'efficiency':

> and it should likewise seem, that, till a sufficient number of experiments have been made, it becomes the wisdom of the civil magistracy to take as little upon its hands as possible, and never to interfere, without the greatest caution, in things that do not immediately affect the lives, liberty, or property of the members of the community.[340]

He did give some clues as to areas he wished to see excluded from the purview of civil government. His presentation of the issues of education and religious toleration[341] was founded upon the assertion that they benefited least from government intervention. This is Priestley's fundamental insight: the public good does not disappear, but is best served by leaving individuals responsible for what had heretofore been seen as part of the necessary task of government.

Where Priestley employed the language of 'efficiency', we must remember that he gave a specific content to what would otherwise have been, and which in the mouths of his opponents was intended to be, a pragmatic catch-all. Priestley's 'inconvenience' is determined by his view of human nature built around rational free enquiry and natural rights. Thus, because he believed that the object of education was not 'the tranquility of the state, but the forming of wise and virtuous men', Priestley denied the legitimacy of any state interference in the educational process, a necessarily fitful progress of enquiry towards truth.[342]

In the preface to the *Essay* Priestley declared his departure from Locke's account of 'morals and policy'. In the later 'Letter of Advice' to dissenters (1774), Priestley proceeded to spell out his disagreement with Locke's position on individual rights. He admitted to expecting the hail of abuse his writings had generated

---

[340] *Ibid.*, p. 58.

[341] Education: 'This I cannot help thinking to be the shortest, and the best issue upon which we can put every thing in which the civil magistrate pretends to a right of interference' (*ibid.*, p. 77).

Religion: 'The most important question concerning the extent of civil government is whether the civil magistrate ought to extend his authority to matters of religion' (*ibid.*, p. 110).

[342] *Ibid.*, pp. 90–1.

since he 'advanced some new arguments, and of considerable strength, in favour of religious liberty, all preceding writers having, as far as I know, acquiesced in the arguments and limits of Mr Locke ... '.[343] It is as a spokesman for the pre-eminent claim of the security of the community that Priestley found fault with Locke. Even though he was trying to defend the liberty of individuals, he believed that Locke's categories actually provided for the security of the state, first and foremost: 'The foundation of this difficulty seems to me to be laid in an abuse of Mr Locke's great argument for toleration, founded on the distinction between civil and religious rights, and allowing the magistrate to interfere in the former, but not in the latter.'[344]

Priestley's razor opposed to this the claim that state intervention was justified only if the magistrate's action could accomplish more for society's benefit than his inaction.[345] Locke's division into spheres of civil and spiritual all too easily dissolved into the pragmatics of security that enabled Balguy to cite Locke's approval for 'converting christianity into civil policy'.[346] Priestley sought to prevent this kind of wilful misunderstanding by developing an argument 'of a more general and less exceptionable nature, than Mr Locke's ... '.[347] Ultimately, Priestley's verdict on Locke was that he cleared a great swath of dark and forbidding forest, but that he did not succeed in finding the path that led through it:

... we have no occasion to confine ourselves within the bounds of Mr Locke's principles of toleration. His treatise was certainly admirable for the time in which it was written; but it is an argument that we have made a very poor use of it, if we acquiesce in it at this day. It is certainly not adviseable to rest solely upon the authority of any man, as if his sentiments and maxims were the perfect and unalterable standard with respect to it, so as to abide by any conclusion that may be drawn from his doctrine. Mr Locke was staggered at the thought of tolerating Atheism, and for the same reason he might have hesitated to tolerate other opinions, about which a wise civil magistrate would give himself very little concern; and Dr Brown, we know, availed himself of Mr Locke's authority for intolerance in some other cases also.[348]

[343] Priestley, 'Letter of Advice', *Works*, xxii, p. 458.   [344] *Ibid.*, p. 476.
[345] *Ibid.*, p. 476.
[346] Priestley, *Considerations on Church Authority*, p. 21.
[347] Priestley, 'Letter of Advice', *Works*, xxii, pp. 476–7.
[348] *Ibid.*, p. 478.

Priestley believed that Brown's security-based attack on toleration, and especially towards Roman Catholics and atheists, was inspired by Locke's justification of legal intolerance. Though clearly distancing himself from Locke on the fundamental issue of freedom of thought, Priestley did not minimize Locke's role in the development of the argument which came to fruition in the dissenters' position. His historical understanding of the deep changes in European thought set in motion by the new science led Priestley to argue that, just as the pioneers of the Reformation did the best they could but were constrained by the limited conceptual options available to them, Locke's defence of toleration was constrained by the narrower views of the individual characteristic of a less reflective time. By implication, only the intervening years with the increasing power of the scientific model and specific political debates made it possible to defend freedom of thought in a more forthright manner than had Locke. Just as, over a century earlier, Galileo had defended his new world-view against contemporary Aristotelians by contending that if Aristotle were to reappear the two of them would make common cause, Priestley argued against a conservative position anchored in Locke that if the great Mr Locke were to return in 1768 he would join in the dissenters' demand for total freedom of thought.[349]

In scientific experiment diverse modes of enquiry increased the probability that the truth would be discovered. Uniformity, conversely, decreased its likelihood.[350] In addition to science, Robinson suggested that an authentic system of parliamentary representation also illustrated the value of the free exchange of opinions:

Diversity of opinions, if judiciously managed, rather tend to discover than to destroy the truth: Hence that proper advice at opening a general assembly of old, *consider* the fact, *take advice, and speak your minds*: The same notion is conveyed in the very name of the British representation, it is a parliament, that is, an assembly convened to give advice by speaking their minds. If this be a proper method of finding out truth in the state, why not in the church?[351]

Free enquiry was actually a means to social peace and political solidarity since the demise of a persecuting society would 'teach

---

[349] Priestley, *Essay*, pp. 128–9.
[350] Furneaux, *Letter to Blackstone*, pp. 75–6; also, Firebace, *Letters to a Member of Parliament*, p. 59.
[351] Robinson, *Arcana*, p. 49.

contending Sects candidly to unite in the same external Bond of Communion'.[352] Even if toleration did result in the dissolution of some commonly held beliefs, the search for truth could not be suppressed:

> But should free inquiry lead to the destruction of Christianity itself, it ought not, on that account, to be discontinued; for we can only wish for the prevalence of Christianity on the supposition of its being true; and if it fall before the influence of free inquiry, it can only do so in consequence of its not being true.[353]

In other words, the natural right of human beings to think and pursue truth had to be taken as the basis of civil society. There was no other way of describing a common good. And if the individual's pursuit of truth revealed the falsity of the doctrines currently accepted as defining the common good there was only one solution: *fiat iustitia & ruat mundus.*

---

[352] Wyvill, *Thoughts on Our Articles of Religion* (London, 1771), p. 8.
[353] Priestley, 'Free Enquiry', *Works*, xv, p. 78.

CHAPTER 6

'Alternatives' to the common good 1774–1776

The experience of empire had shown that it could not be managed according to the principles that had consolidated control of the state. France, Spain and England had overcome regional diversity because there was enough of an existing coincidence of interest among the regions for the application of power to create a concentrated entity. The union that had made Great Britain in the eighteenth century was less successful; overwhelming force had to persuade people of this community of interest. This was an 'incorporation' of a clearly junior partner. After the Seven Years War, the thirteen colonies in British North America resisted the extension of the dominance of parliament that was such a notable feature of British political life in the eighteenth century. Centralization and sovereignty coincided in the ideology and practice of early modern states. But the attempt to rule the empire as a part of the state was much less successful. The alternative, but rejected, ideology of representation, federalism and commonwealth offered a means of imperial governance that would probably have succeeded in maintaining a union, much as it did for the nineteenth-century British empire.

The search for a common good capable of uniting the efforts of a diverse population had taken on its especially early modern meaning in the context of the sixteenth-century civil wars of religion. Heterodoxy was dangerous, but so was persecution. The policies of the early modern states often oscillated between these poles. Generally, however, civil rulers felt secured by the support of powerful, though not all-powerful and certainly not autonomous, religious establishments. The demand for toleration from those with differing views could easily be seen as a challenge to the infrastructure of the state. The Toleration Act of 1689 and the practice of 'connivance'

349

had made eighteenth-century Britain one of the least persecuting of polities. None the less, or perhaps, as a result, the latitudinarian and dissenting push for toleration of heterodoxy and non-subscription evoked many of the well-worn arguments about the primacy of the state and the needs of the sovereign. The particular argument developed by the dissenters tackled their opponents obliquely; rather than engaging the question of civil security, they argued that the very purpose of government was invalidated by the failure to afford citizens the freedom to think.

The imperial debate, initially couched in terms of a clash between a part of the empire and the whole had, through the debate on representation, come to be seen as pitting the interests of individuals against those of the community. So had the toleration debate. The thematic convergence of these arguments made possible the formulation of a new reforming critique of British government. Simply put, the Revolution that had curbed the aggrandizement of the crown at the expense of the 'people' had been vitiated by the aggrandizement of parliament at the expense of that same 'people'. The crisis within the empire was seen as parliament's doing and this, as James Burgh was to suggest, the consequence of its corrupt insulation from the source of its power. The legislated subordination of dissenters reflected a similar institutionalized inattention to the legitimate claims of individuals to manage their own lives. The political import of the attack on the principles of contemporary political economy was still another indication of disaffection with the management of the conflicting needs of individuals and their community.

PRINCIPLES OF REFORM

Because natural rights arguments are so obviously central to the positions of the reformers in the debates over American representation and freedom of thought it might be worthwhile to review their role. It is easy to assume that in the aftermath of the heroic seventeenth-century 'discovery' and systematization of natural law that these arguments served little use, especially since the assertion by some scholars of an affinity between 'natural jurisprudence' and liberalism led others, eager to banish the bogey of an early modern liberalism, to dismiss the existence of a viable modern natural law tradition in the eighteenth century. The debate over the presence or absence of Locke's *Second Treatise* in Anglo-American political thought, for example, is really about the place of natural law arguments in the eighteenth-century debate. The immediate point to be made is that natural law never disappeared. Rutherforth's Cambridge lectures on Grotius and Blackstone's introductory chapters in the *Commentaries on the Laws of England* offer convincing proof. The identification of natural law with a radical John Locke has obscured its far more usual role in the eighteenth century as support for the existing order. It was, as we saw in chapter 1, precisely the nature of Grotius' endeavour to have joined Cicero's defence of necessity to Cicero's conception of natural law. One consequence was that the threat of 'ruin and destruction', of a threat to physical or communal integrity, triggered the claim of necessity and the revolutionary invocation of *salus populi suprema lex esto*. This was precisely what had occurred in North America between 1764 and 1766. Taxation without consent, coming on the heels of what colonists believed was a substantial effort on behalf of the mother country, led them to feel as if they were being treated differently from other British subjects. An attenuated sense of community, due as much to recent and longer-term developments within colonial society as to metropolitan measures, made the legislated attempt at imperial reform seem like a threat to specifically North American interests. The colonial response in terms of a natural right to self-preservation followed from the basic early modern principles of sovereignty and obligation.

But what helped transform this argument was the attack launched by Protestant dissenters and nonconformists on the Establishment of the Church of England. They drew upon the tradition of intellectual liberty traced back to John Locke and Samuel Clarke, relying on the latter to avoid the more prudential cast of the former's own defence of toleration. A natural right to freedom of thought amounted to an entirely different sense of what made social life meaningful and, therefore, the threshold beyond which communal coercion undermined the purpose of politics. The reformers examined in this chapter went beyond the minimalist account of natural rights that Grotius had assembled from a reading of Cicero and, to be sure, other ancients. Sociability constructed at this level produced what for the early seventeenth century was, indeed, a minimally coercive civil society. But it was the experience of the late eighteenth-century British reformers that it remained far too coercive, on the one hand, and took too dim a view of human capacities, on the other.

The importance of natural rights in the debates over American representation and freedom of thought is seen to best advantage in the writings of leading reformers like John Cartwright, Granville Sharp, James Burgh and Richard Price.[1] In their arguments the metaphysical and epistemological defence of individual liberty honed in the simultaneous toleration debate was joined to the practical political demand for individual consent through representation. At this stage, the two parallel debates were transformed into a single, coherent political discourse. Its importance lies not in its immediate popularity, though James Bradley and others have made this case,[2] nor in its promotion of immediate political change, though it had some notable successes, but in its articulation of a distinctly new perception of the political relationship between individuals and their communities. Individuals, defined by their possession of certain natural rights, were to be sovereign within their political communities.[3] In effect, this amounted to a new way of calculating the 'common' good of a society. J. A. W. Gunn has commented on the fragility and turmoil of British politics in the mid-1770s, and the suggestion of fundamental change occurring in the later eighteenth century is not uncommon.[4] The threat this argument posed to the self-definition of the new British state was acutely felt well before the French Revolution elicited both more radical demands and more fearful rejections.

Cartwright, Sharp and Burgh published their contributions to this extended argument in the course of 1774 and 1775, and Price at

---

[1] These writers were associated with a larger circle of dissenters and political activists who called themselves the 'Club of Honest Whigs' and who met fortnightly, first in St Paul's Churchyard and after 1772 in the London Coffee House on Ludgate Hill (D. O. Thomas, *The Honest Mind: The Thought and Work of Richard Price* (Oxford, 1977), p. 142). Many were members of the Royal Society, highlighting, again, the link between science, and its explicit espousal of freedom of enquiry, and the epistemology of the reformers' political thought in the 1760s and 1770s.

[2] James E. Bradley, *Popular Politics and the American Revolution in England* (Athens, GA, 1986).

[3] The relationship of natural rights to individual sovereignty would explain its *un*importance in the political language of Anglicanism (Clark, *English Society*, p. 50).

[4] J. A. W. Gunn, *Beyond Liberty and Property*, p. 172; Ian R. Christie, 'Party and Politics in the Age of Lord North's Administration', *Parliamentary History*, 6 (1987), 47–68.

the beginning of 1776.[5] Cartwright's treatise[6] and Tucker's *True Interest of Great Britain Set Forth in Regard to the Colonies* were the first to advocate the separation of the colonies from Britain. Cartwright's *American Independence* draws on many of the commonplaces associated with Samuel Clarke's followers. Moral realism, for Cartwright as for Clarke, defined the content of individual natural rights. The standard of truth existed independently of men: 'Truth is not the less truth, though mankind were in ignorance of it until lately.'[7] The renunciation of expedient alternatives constitutes a further re-working of Cicero's heritage. The strict construction of public utility and the constricted scope for prudential considerations was a necessary consequence of the reformers' reliance on truth. They believed that civil society could be constructed so as to accommodate the demands of justice and truth. Thus, as we have seen, Priestley was prepared to risk Christianity if it abused the truth. In the same way, Cartwright was ready to renounce Britain's national status. While 'some politicians' were prepared to claim 'that present expediency is a sufficient justification of any measure', Cartwright was firm: 'though our very existence as a nation, depended on violating the express laws of God, it must not be done'.[8] Price, too, was prepared to risk the empire if it required the suppression of true relations between men: 'If, in order to preserve its unity, one half of it must be enslaved to the other half, let it, in the name of God, want unity.'[9] There is a direct line from Cartwright's defence of an immanent and unimpeachable truth back to the assertion that men had to answer to an inner standard of rectitude.

Close adherence to this metaphysics led Cartwright to repudiate history and precedent in favour of 'the most well-known principles of the English constitution', 'the plain maxims of the law of nature'

---

[5] Cartwright's *American Independence* appeared as letters in the *Public Advertiser* beginning in March 1774; these were collected and published in the summer, as was Sharp's *Declaration of the People's Natural Right*. Only the first of Burgh's three-volume *Political Disquisitions* appeared before the parliamentary elections of 1774, the others were published in 1775. Price began the *Observations* in October of 1775 and the first edition was printed in March of 1776, by which time Cartwright's *Take your Choice!* already existed in a manuscript copy.

[6] The full title captures the range of issues which he saw as appended to the colonial crisis: 'American Independence the Interest and Glory of Great Britain; or, Arguments to prove, that not only in Taxation, but in Trade, Manufactures, and Government, the Colonies are entitled to an entire Independency on the British Legislature; and that it can only be by a formal Declaration of these Rights, and forming there upon a friendly League with them, that the true and lasting Welfare of both countries can be promoted.'

[7] Cartwright, *American Independence*, p. 4.   [8] *Ibid.*, p. 31.

[9] Richard Price, *Observations*, p. 36.

and 'the clearest doctrines of Christianity.'[10] Cartwright's later writings were, in fact, grounded on the principles of Anglo-Saxon and English history. Perhaps the fact that natural rights were part of the American debate led Cartwright in this direction in 1774. He also believed that these natural rights were part of Britain's own constitution and this may explain the later effort to demonstrate the convergence of common and natural law. Nevertheless, at this stage Cartwright's strong defence of human liberty was founded on an appeal to natural rights and was, therefore, free from the midwifery of social contracts or states of nature. Liberty was 'the universal gift of God' and 'inherent and unalienable' in all mankind. Its definition was not to be found 'among mouldy parchments, nor in the cobwebs of a casuist's brain'. Cartwright's understanding of liberty is best appreciated indirectly as the opposite of 'slavery', which was clearly defined as 'an outrageous violation of the rights of mankind; an odious degradation of human nature. It is utterly impossible that any human being can be without a title to liberty, except he himself hath forfeited it by crimes which make him dangerous to society.'[11]

Thus, while it might once have been plausible to maintain British guardianship of still under-age and immature colonies, having reached putative personhood they had to be treated as independent individuals. Here again, the attempt to ascertain the obligations and liberties of individuals towards their community is expressed, in terms of the colonial crisis, in a version of the 'family' metaphor. 'Those who are so fond of placing them metaphorically in the relation of children to a parent state' had to recognize that the 'blind obedience' of childhood did not condone parental 'tyranny'.[12] To speak of Britain and North America 'as *mother* and *daughter*' was 'a delusion and allusion'.[13] Instead, the relationship was closer to that between enlightened spouses: 'I propose that America shall become the wife of Great Britain', though 'I do not mean she shall obey his arbitrary will, nor that he shall have a direct power over her.'[14] The American colonies were 'sister kingdoms', 'separate branches of one great family'.[15] Cartwright also suggested an alternative image, one appropriate to a man of science and industry like himself. The

---

[10] Cartwright, *American Independence*, p. 6.   [11] *Ibid.*, p. 7.   [12] *Ibid.*, p. 8.
[13] Cartwright, 'Letter to Burke', *American Independence*, p. 25.
[14] *Ibid.*, p. 27.
[15] Cartwright, *American Independence*, p. 13. For other uses of the metaphor, see pp. 13, 19, 48, 62–3.

colonies were like 'an industrious and intelligent youth just arriving at a man's estate'. After having served 'a long apprenticeship' he was now entitled either to become a partner or to be released from his contract.[16]

For Cartwright, the metaphysical priority of the individual led him to conclude that no single community centred on Westminster could claim to govern in the best interest of settlers in North America. For 'The rights of sovereignty reside in the people themselves; that is, they have a right to chuse their own governors.'[17] Like Pownall and others attracted by astronomical imagery, Cartwright's vision of the correct relationship between individuals and communities was expressed in the contrast between a Ptolomaic and a Copernican, or Newtonian, cosmos. Contemporary sophists

at once place before our eyes, in an indirect point of view, that multiplicity of wheels within wheels, pulleys upon pulleys, and springs upon springs, which belong to the complicated machines of government and trade, instead of directing our attention to the first principles of motion, and the few master springs, on whose movements all the rest depend in a regular order and subordination.

The alternative was to reformulate the empire on 'Newtonian' principles, reducing everything 'to the first principles of motion'.[18] The size of the empire had militated against acknowledging the sovereignty of the individual so that Britain could no longer both retain an empire and claim to be a just society. If an empire was 'too large' and its various dominions 'too widely separated by immense oceans' to be governed according to the 'principles essentially belonging to all free governments, it is an over-grown empire, and ought to be divided before it fall to pieces'.[19] If an empire or government became too 'wide and unwieldy', then 'by the laws of nature, which are the laws of God, it is no empire, that is to say, not a just empire'.[20]

The government defence of 'virtual representation' had obviously

[16] Cartwright, 'Letter to Burke', *American Independence*, p. 15.
[17] Cartwright, *American Independence*, p. 9.
[18] *Ibid.*, p. 14. It was, no doubt, on this score that Cartwright criticized Burke's famous vision of empire consisting in a parliament and various subordinate spheres moving to their own music ('Letter to Burke', p. 21). Recall Pownall (1768): 'If it should be thought difficult and hazardous, to extend the legislative rights, grievances and preeminences, the true Imperium of government, to wheresoever the dominions of the state extend, – the administration must be content to go on in this ptolomaic system of policy – as long as the various centers and systems shall preserve their due order and subordination' (p. 168).
[19] Cartwright, *American Independence*, p. 15; also, pp. 24, 30.   [20] *Ibid.*, p. 41.

failed to answer the challenge to the unity of the realm posed by the distance and size of the colonies. 'Can any thing be more notorious, than that a great majority of the national representatives are elected by a small majority of indigent and corrupt men, who professedly make a trade of voting, and who, gratify, in the very act, a sordid self-interest, in direct violation of the rights and interests of the nation collectively?'[21] Cartwright had no patience with the claim that what was inadequate for Britain could be satisfactory in the colonies. If liberty became slavery somewhere between London and Boston, then, he mocked, its exact longitude could be discovered. 'What a happy discovery! How the sciences cast light upon one another!'[22] Nor could the government maintain the converse: what was illegitimate in North America could never be just in Great Britain: 'Since a virtual representation in the house of commons was so learnedly argued to extend to three millions of people beyond the Atlantic; we may expect that it will be most unmercifully crammed down the throats of poor Englishmen.'[23]

The first part of *The Declaration of the People's Right to a Share in the Legislature*, the most important colonial tract by the leading abolitionist in Britain, Granville Sharp (1735–1813), flows naturally from the arguments brought against slave-holding. Sharp sought to establish the inalienable sovereignty of the individual. All men were '*equally free* by the law of *Nature*' and therefore 'are *equally* entitled to the same *Natural Rights* that are *essential* for their own preservation'.[24] This sovereignty was expressed politically in terms of representation. The essential principle was that 'no Tax can be levied without manifest *Robbery and Injustice* where this *legal and constitutional Representation* is wanting'.[25] Because this was a privilege which every individual could claim, it was as applicable in North America as in Britain.[26] Sharp perceived the defects of the British system, but, unlike Cartwright, sought to preserve the empire through a colonial representation rather than overthrow it by reformation.[27] He believed that 'even a *defective Representation* is better

---

[21] *Ibid.*, p. 42.   [22] Cartwright, 'Postscript', *American Independence*, p. 20.
[23] Cartwright, *Take your Choice!*, p. 48n. Note that throughout Cartwright uses 'virtual' in its weaker sense ('as if').
[24] Granville Sharp, *A Declaration of the People's Right to a Share in the Legislature* (London, 1774), p. 2.
[25] *Ibid.*, p. 10.   [26] *Ibid.*, p. 20.
[27] Britain was represented 'by the votes of the respective proprietors; since every Freeholder has a Right to vote; so that, in this one respect, the Representation is general' (*Declaration*, p. 5).

than none at all' and that the colonists, therefore, ought not to 'be deprived entirely of their natural Rights and Liberties, merely because our own liberties are not entirely perfect'.[28]

Like other dissenters, James Burgh began his attempt to set forth a new foundation for British politics by seeking the proper relationship between individuals and communities. He thought in terms of a new expression, 'personal liberty', but the fixed point remained consideration of the 'general good':

to determine precisely how far personal liberty is compatible with the general good, and of the propriety of social conduct in all cases, is a matter of great extent, and demands the united wisdom of a whole people. And the consent of the whole people, as far as it can be obtained, is indispensably necessary to every law, by which the whole people are to be bound; else the whole people are to be enslaved to the one, or the few, who frame the laws for them.[29]

Having established the primacy of individuals, Burgh argued for the necessary reform of parliament to bring Britain's system of communal representation into line with the individual source of political power. Burgh believed the colonial dispute 'doubly entitled' to be included in a study of government abuses such as *Political Disquisitions*, 'both as being itself one of the grossest abuses, and also as being particularly the consequence of *parliamentary* corruption'.[30] Though it was 'an established maxim in free states' that the taxed had to authorize their assessors, the Americans were deprived of their property without consent.[31] 'The new method of taxing our colonies in parliament, where they have no representation, adequate or inadequate, is subversive of liberty, annihilates property, is repugnant to the genius of the people' and struck at the root of their charters and liberties as British subjects.[32]

Though the first five books of the *Political Disquisitions* are about parliamentary reform, Burgh did not resume the arguments of the dispute over virtual representation. Thus, when he wrote that parliament could function in the public interest 'as if every inhabitant of the country were to deliberate and vote in person', he added

---

[28] *Ibid.*, pp. 8–9.
[29] Burgh, *Political Disquisitions* (hereafter cited as *PD*), I, pp. 2–3. Alternatively, he wrote that 'Power in the people is like light in the sun, native, original, inherent and unlimited by any thing human. In governors, it may be compared to the reflected light of the moon; for it is only borrowed, delegated and limited by the intention of the people ...' (I, pp. 3–4).
[30] *Ibid.*, II, p. 274.   [31] *Ibid.*, I, p. 37; II, p. 310.   [32] *Ibid.*, II, p. 328.

that 'this supposes parliament free from all indirect influence'.[33] His concern, like that of his British predecessors, was largely with the reform of abuses. Burgh made all the requisite attacks on rotten boroughs, length of parliaments, and pay for public service.[34] Where other reformers had begun to argue that MPs should be paid in order to discourage bribery, Burgh retained the traditional commonwealth view of the nobility of public office. Britain's 'inadequate representation' could not fulfil the purpose of government's institution and was even capable of being the instrument of enslaving the people by governing them 'contrary to their inclination'.[35] Personality played a limited role in Burgh's attack on parliamentary corruption because of his basic confidence that institutional reform remained possible and able to resolve the existing deficiencies. 'And an honest parliament would make all people in public stations honest.'[36]

Burgh believed that there had to be some recognition of the popular origin of power even though he did not insist on any vehicle like 'actual' representation. That Britain was run by a handful of men elected by a slightly larger handful was clearly unjust.[37] He described the prohibition on constituency instructions as 'notorious'. If the government believed their opinions to be worthless 'why', he asked, 'is the choice of members of parliament left to the people? Why should not the ministry nominate them at once?'[38] Ultimately, of course, Burgh's popular sovereignty depended on a theory of human nature that reflected his conception of moral psychology: 'Every man has a life, a personal liberty, a character, a right to his earnings, a right to a religious profession and worship according to his conscience, &c.' Servants and the poor also possessed these rights even if they possessed little else. Why should this 'immense multitude' be 'utterly deprived of all power in determining who shall be the protectors of their lives, their personal liberty, their little property (which though singly considered is of small value yet is upon the whole a very great object) and the chastity of their wives and daughters'?[39] The most powerful and politicized version of this argument was to be made by Cartwright one year later.

Cartwright and Burgh maintained that the existing structure of the empire was inadequate since it was not modelled on the sover-

---

[33] *Ibid.*, I, p. 6.   [34] *Ibid.*, I, p. 72; I, p. 110.   [35] *Ibid.*, I, p. 25.
[36] *Ibid.*, II, p. 319.
[37] *Ibid.*, I, p. 26.   [38] *Ibid.*, I, p. 181.   [39] *Ibid.*, I, p. 37.

eignty of individuals. The unjust political condition manifested itself in a notion of political economy which, like 'virtual' representation, was a theory of the sovereignty of the community with the determination of a common good placed in the hands of an unchosen elite. Those who pressed for the representation of individuals also contended that commercial regulation designed to further the economic well-being of the community had to be a decision of its constituent members. If parliament could by right tell an American, ' "you shall not make a hat to cover your head, nor a shoe to defend your foot; you shall not manufacture a piece of cloth to keep out the cold, nor a knife wherewithal to cut your victuals" ', then there was nothing to prevent parliament from also saying, ' "give us the money out of your pocket" '.[40] Every trade regulation that cost the colonies money was 'in the nature, although it may not come within the precise definition of a tax' and if unassented, then illegal.[41] Burgh argued that colonial customs duties were taxes and that the sum total of restraint on colonial trade 'is taxing them with a vengeance' unsurpassed even by Carthage, widely believed to be the most rapacious of the ancient empires.[42]

Congruent with their view of the need for individual representation, Burgh and Cartwright both suggested that commerce, like politics, had to be founded upon a relation of equality. Cartwright looked back to a non-existent past in which Britain's commercial empire embodied principles of justice:

If we would reap any lasting commercial advantage from, and preserve any durable power over, the American states, it must be by withdrawing, not asserting, our claims to parliamentary Sovereignty; thereby removing every cause of jealousy towards us, and proving that, with regard to them, Great Britain is not a conquering, but a commercial state; not an oppressive ruler, but an equal trader.[43]

Cartwright argued that the commercial status of the 'old' empire was related to the reduced extent of parliamentary sovereignty. Parliament's increasing importance at the core of the eighteenth-century British state had unexamined, but none the less, significant, consequences for the political foundation of the empire.

Cartwright's belief in the natural equality and freedom of commerce was echoed by Burgh: 'nothing brooks constraint so little as

[40] Cartwright, *American Independence*, p. 69.
[41] Cartwright, 'Appendix', *American Independence*, pp. 9–10.
[42] Burgh, *PD*, II, pp. 295–6.   [43] Cartwright, 'Appendix', *American Independence*, p. 13.

commerce: nothing is more delicate, nothing more spontaneous'. Therefore, whatever the metropolis does to 'break in upon the freedom of commerce, [does] defeat the very intention of colonising, and overthrow it to the foundation'.[44] Ultimately, he wrote, 'Nothing requires more to be free and unconfined than commerce.'[45] Cartwright, too, writing with regard to Ireland, specified 'free trade' as the ideal relationship between parts of the empire and the whole. 'Besides the liberty of raising her [Ireland's] own taxes, and that share of legislation which she enjoys in her own parliament, I must confess, I see no reason why her trade should not be as free as that of Great Britain.'[46] Contemporary Italy served Burgh as an object lesson: while its dukedoms were 'wretched beggars', her republics were thriving. 'Lucca, to mention no others at present, is a remarkable instance of the happy effects of liberty.'[47] Hobbes' oft-cited attack on the *Libertas* of Lucca (*Leviathan*, II.21) does not mark the death-knell of the ancients; here we see how the perceived equality of a republic could be transformed into a justification for a free and equal commerce of goods and ideas within a society no longer debating the finer points of classical republicanism.

Perhaps Cartwright's most important contribution to the construction of this alternative to contemporary practice was his reformulation of the principles of empire. He urged that the planting of colonies and the 'extending of empire' ought not be be considered synonymous when colonies were too distant to be governed on 'the principles of justice and freedom'. Where size rendered the notion of 'community' useless and distance made colonial representation impossible there the British empire had to stop.[48] Under no circumstances could the inalienable rights of the individual settlers be encroached upon in the cause of imperial glory. 'Let the *intention* of government, in planting a colony, be what it may, 'tis impossible it should take away an *inherent unalienable* right.'[49] Furthermore, possession of these 'inalienable' rights meant that colonists were, *in potentia*, absolved from metropolitan ties: 'they had therein the rights of independency, whenever they should think proper to assert them'.[50]

---

[44] Burgh, *PD*, II, p. 280. [45] *Ibid.*, II, p. 298.
[46] Cartwright, *American Independence*, p. 17.
[47] Burgh, *PD*, III, p. 399.
[48] 'That the people of America are too far distant from Great-Britain to obtain those ends by her exercising a legislative authority over them, and therefore cannot be subject to such an authority' (Cartwright, 'Letter 12', *American Independence*, p. 10; also p. 22).
[49] Cartwright, *American Independence*, p. 25. [50] *Ibid.*, p. 23.

Cartwright's choice of words is very important. His use of the term 'independence' to describe the legitimate status of the colonies, both here and in the very title of the pamphlet, explicitly challenged the common usage. Montesquieu had distinguished between 'liberty' and 'independence' and this was upheld by defenders of government practice on imperial and ecclesiological matters.

We must have continually present to our minds the difference between independence and liberty. Liberty is a right of doing what ever the laws permit, and if a citizen could do what they forbid he would no longer be possessed of liberty, because all his fellow-citizens would have the same power.[51]

Recall that in his sermon on the 'Education of Women' John Brown had singled out their increasing 'independence' as the source of all moral corruption. Freedom from civil law was no liberty for the spokesmen of civil liberty, while freedom from divine law risked the conflagration of atheism. Here, too, Montesquieu's attack on Pierre Bayle registered with English readers. Bayle had suggested that atheism was to be preferred to idolatry. Montesquieu's critical rejoinder was that the absence of belief in God facilitated an independence that was tantamount to rebellion: 'From the idea of his non-existence immediately follows that of our independence, or, if we cannot conceive this idea, that of disobedience.'[52] Later in this chapter we shall observe that this relationship between independence, religious heterodoxy and rebellion was emphasized by defenders of the government.

Whence did Cartwright draw his notion of independence? That same tradition of moral psychology which provided him with natural rights and a common sense fabric of moral realism, in the person of Samuel Clarke, had linked morality with independence. God's attributes included intelligence, self-existence and self-motion. The subsequent emphasis on metaphysical liberty as a prerequisite for moral agency maintained the impetus of this argument. To this way of thinking, also characteristic of rational dissent writ large, independent and enquiring individuals were more moral and more religious than those who merely obeyed.

Cartwright's demand for colonial 'independency' was consistent with his broader aims. It led him to assert that the British empire

---

[51] Montesquieu, *Spirit of the Laws*, XI.3, p. 150. I thank Neil Robertson for pointing this out to me.
[52] *Ibid.*, XXIV.2, II, p. 28.

ought to be limited to the European islands 'and to the various settlements and manufactories [*sic*] of our trade in the different parts of the world'.[53] Cartwright provocatively restricted the legitimacy of the common good to 'the nation, not the country; the people, not the soil'.[54] The political wishes of individuals, not the bare facts of possession and geography were to determine the limits of the 'realm'. The revolutionary implications of this claim are buried in the modern political device of an absentee ballot. It exists precisely because physical presence within a community no longer constitutes a legitimate qualification for citizenship.

Cartwright's redefinition of the proper extent of a political community based on the rights of individuals not only provided a solution to Pownall's theoretical 'Realm Question', but also to the broader issue of the relationship between size and liberty in its eighteenth-century application to the problem of the territorial state and the legitimate extent of *imperium*. The attempt to redefine liberty to make it consistent with modern, commercial and territorial states was the engine behind much 'sceptical' writing, such as Hume's 'Idea of a Perfect Commonwealth'. In this essay he set forth a system of tiered representative councils, culminating in a senate. Behind this scheme lay the time-honoured belief that large states could never become commonwealths. While agreeing that these were more difficult to form in more extensive territories, he asserted that they endured longer:

In a large government, which is modelled with masterly skill, there is compass and room enough to refine the democracy, from the lower people, who may be admitted into the first elections or first concoction of the commonwealth, to the higher magistrates, who direct all the movements. At the same time, the parts are so distant and remote, that it is very difficult, either by intrigue, prejudice, or passion, to hurry them into any measure against the public interest.[55]

Whether or not engaged directly with Hume, as has been sug-

---

53 This includes Newfoundland, Gibraltar and Minorca. Cartwright was prepared to see the West Indian islands go the way of the continental colonies and either become independent or remain under the sway of parliament, depending on their preference (*American Independence*, pp. 22–3).
54 Cartwright, 'Letter to Burke', *American Independence*, p. 26.
55 Hume, 'Idea of a Perfect Commonwealth', *Essays*, pp. 527–8. This is undercut in a letter written a year before his death in which Hume suggested that only absolute power could rule Britain's extended state (quoted in James Moore, 'Hume's Political Science and the Classical Republican Tradition', *Canadian Journal of Political Science*, 10, (1977), 831).

gested of James Madison,[56] Cartwright's solution to the problem of the West went one step further. He suggested that this vast territory not be reapportioned among the existing colonies, but rather ruled in a 'Grand British League and Confederacy' until such time as the population reached a total of 50,000. At that point its individual inhabitants 'should be entitled and free to erect themselves into an independent political state, and to constitute for their own government such a legislative power as they should judge most proper'.[57] This solution gave priority to the decisions of the affected individuals while simultaneously providing for a freely chosen federation, creating a political community premised upon individual decision.[58] If, as Judith Shklar has maintained, preservation of an extensive republic made adequate representation crucial, Cartwright's point was that in the modern territorial state this reformed representation had to be an expression of self-government.[59] A full ten years later, William Paley was also to come around to a federal solution to the problem of size and liberty, seemingly modelled on the American Confederation. To see to 'what limits such a republic might, without inconvenience, enlarge its dominions, by assuming into the confederacy neighbouring provinces' was something 'which the records of mankind do not authorize us to decide with tolerable certainty. – The experiment is about to be tried in America upon a large scale.'[60] The 'Northwest Ordinance', promulgated by the new United States of America two years later, in 1787, reflected the letter and principle of Cartwright's plan and Paley's discussion. It provided a federal solution to the problem of size and liberty in the early modern territorial state where the examples of the Roman empire and smaller city-republics were of little use. Combined with a reformed representation, this imperial sketch also suggested an alternative to the model of the British state constructed in 1707. Cartwright would, in fact, dedicate his activity over the next half-

---

[56] Douglas Adair, '"That Politics May Be Reduced to a Science": David Hume, James Madison, and the Tenth "Federalist"', *Huntington Library Quarterly*, 20 (1957), 343–60; John Robertson, 'The Scottish Enlightenment at the Limits of the Civic Tradition', in *Wealth and Virtue*, p. 172.

[57] Cartwright, 'Appendix', *American Independence*, p. 42.

[58] 'Nations are most free and happy when their extremities are near enough to the vital seat of government to feel its pervading principle in its full warmth and activity, and by the spring of their own re-action to pour into the heart again full-flowing tides of health, life and vigour' (*ibid.*, p. 43).

[59] Shklar, 'Montesquieu and the New Republicanism', p. 277.

[60] William Paley, *The Principles of Moral and Political Philosophy* (Cambridge, 1785), pp. 461–2.

century to effecting a national reform of this kind within the existing constitutional framework.

The problems addressed by these reformers as well as their categories of enquiry were inherited from the same stock of arguments employed by earlier commonwealthmen. The convergence of opposition and government arguments on party, patriotism and security meant that the later reformers who set themselves against the government's position on these issues effectively repudiated the conclusions of their intellectual ancestors. Burgh's attack on the Polybian metaphor of the cycle of constitutions is an example of this change. He rejected the classical parallel between the natural and political bodies. Organicism provided no common ground since the life of individuals was limited to seventy or eighty years while states could persist far longer. He lampooned the polyannas who cried out that 'States ... have their old age, decay, and death, as individuals. And when the fatal hour is come, the efforts of the physician, and of the patriot, prove equally ineffective.' 'But', wrote Burgh, 'the durations of states regulate by no laws of nature; nor can my inestimable friend Dr Price construct any tables of the physical probabilities of the continuance of kingdoms or commonwealths'.[61] Burgh also overturned the dependent clause, that constitutions rose and fell according to natural laws as inexorable as human growth and decline. Unlike the natural world governed by natural laws, the social world of politics was built by man and capable, therefore, of human renovation.[62] This same argument was made by two other repudiators of received political wisdom, Benjamin Franklin and Josiah Tucker. In 1760 Franklin had distinguished between the human and political bodies because while the former was 'limited by nature to a certain stature, which when attain'd, it cannot, ordinarily, exceed; the other, by better government and more prudent police, as well as by change of manners' was capable of reinvigorating itself.[63] In a tract written in 1758 Tucker had objected to the habit of borrowing terms 'from the state of natural bodies' and applying them to 'political Constitutions'. Unlike the natural body, there was no 'physical Necessity' for the political body to decay and

---

[61] Burgh, *PD*, III, p. 287. He also rejected this parallelism in the *Remarks* (p. 120) and in *Crito* (II, p. 35).

[62] 'The unsteadiness of human affairs is caused either by a constitution originally deficient, and ill-balanced, or by a deviation from the intent and spirit of a constitution originally good' (Burgh, *PD*, III, p. 288).

[63] Franklin, *The Interest of Great Britain*, pp. 24–5.

it could be revived, while the passage of time marked the inexorable doom of natural existence.[64]

Cartwright, Sharp and Burgh were instrumental in making the problem of America an issue for British political thought and they did so by coopting the demand for 'actual' representation into the parliamentary reform movement. Cartwright's contribution dwarfed the others'; it was only in his account that this new theory of representation actually carried the argument. In the second edition of *American Independence* (1775) he emphasized both the inadequacy of colonial representation and the monitory aspect of the American crisis. 'Who can conceive, that a power so very loosely defined, so extremely extensive, and without a counterpoise' could be restrained without some measure of popular control and some degree of American influence.[65] Writing to Burke, Cartwright commented that 'America is become both by precept and example your most faithful monitor, your best instructor, in the only possible means of preserving your own liberties; and of recovering from that state of corruption, of which the constitution is sick at heart.'[66] One year later he published *Take your Choice!*, the opening salvo in his fifty-year campaign for parliamentary reform and the first to employ the language of natural rights and individual representation.

Demands for the reform of parliament stretched back into the seventeenth century. The problem was twofold: the corruption of members both insidiously by royal offers of places and vulgarly with cash, and the deficiencies of the electoral system itself. For most of the eighteenth century the first problem, corruption, tended to exercise passions the more fiercely.[67] Of course, the misshapen nature of the system was itself seen to make corruption inevitable. The size of electorates was very small, with many boroughs controlled by a handful of voters. Only in the aftermath of the colonial crisis did attention swing dramatically towards this second problem. The revived parliamentary reform movement is generally associated with John Wilkes and the Middlesex elections and is easily depicted

---

[64] Tucker, *A Solution of the Important Question, Whether a Poor Country, Where Raw Materials and Provisions Are Cheap, and Wages Low, Can Support the Trade of a Rich Manufacturing Country, Where Raw Materials and Provisions Are Dear, and the Price of Labor High*, in *Four Tracts, Together with Two Sermons on Political and Commercial Subjects*, (Gloucester, 1774), p. 47.

[65] Cartwright, 'Appendix', *American Independence*, pp. 7–8.

[66] Cartwright, 'Letter to Burke', *American Independence*, p. 16.

[67] For an indication of the place of demands for parliamentary reform within opposition ideology see Marie Peters, 'The *Monitor* on the Constitution, 1755–1765: New Light on the Ideological Origins of English Radicalism', *English Historical Review*, 86 (1971), pp. 711–12.

as moving from 'The Wilkites 1769–76' to 'The Beginnings of the Association Movement 1779–80'.[68] Despite the consensus that the arguments of the American crisis affected the articulation of English 'radicalism', little effort has been made to explore the implications of the representation debate on the movement for parliamentary reform.[69] Even if the impact of the American crisis was only felt in the mid-1770s, in other words, subsequent to the Middlesex elections, the fact is that the arguments of the reformers of the 1770s drew directly on the American and not on the Middlesex debate.[70] While the latter was about constitutional manipulation and corruption, the former was about the relationship between individuals and community, between representation and questions of sovereignty – precisely the argument that was to be made by Cartwright, in *Take your Choice!*. Furthermore, this later movement also drew upon the concepts recently forged in the toleration debates. Jonathan Clark has pointed out that 'Parliamentary reform cannot, therefore, be written about in isolation, as modern secular historians have too often done: it must be integrated into, and take its place within, the story of reform in all its varieties.'[71]

The arguments of Joseph Priestley and Obadiah Hulme are representative of the older, but changing, approach to parliamentary reform. Describing the *Present State of Liberty* in 1769, Priestley warned that a pliant and purchased parliament was the worst possible 'engine of oppression' since it facilitated the easy transformation of a republic into a despotism.[72] His proposed cure for these ills was a six-point plan differing from later, nineteenth-century proposals only in that he did not suggest that members be paid a fixed salary. He suggested that placemen and pensioners be excluded, the duration of parliament shortened, small boroughs abolished, elections held by ballot uniformly in the style of the

---

[68] Christie, *Wilkes, Wyvill and Reform*, p. 14; Cannon, *Parliamentary Reform*, pp. 52–4; G. S. Veitch, *The Genesis of Parliamentary Reform* (rpt, London, 1965), pp. 26–7.

[69] Though Arthur Sheps and Colin Bonwick, among others, have drawn attention to the role of America in radical politics (Sheps, 'The American Revolution and the Transformation of English Radicalism', *Historical Reflections / Reflexions Historiques*, 2 (1975), 3–28; Bonwick, *English Radicals and the American Revolution* (Chapel Hill, NC, 1977)), Ian Hampsher-Monk, has sought to examine the radicalism of the 1790s parliamentary reformers in terms of 'civic humanism' ('Civic Humanism and Parliamentary Reform', *Journal of British Studies*, 18 (1979), 70–89).

[70] John Cannon, *Parliamentary Reform*, p. 60.   [71] Clark, *English Society*, p. 278.

[72] Priestley, 'Present State of Liberty', *Works*, xxii, p. 388. Also, p. 385, where representation is called the 'best security' of natural rights.

counties, and oaths against bribery and corruption administered to all Members.[73] Even Priestley's nemesis, Brown, had argued for the need to reform the boroughs, since as constituted 'Power is lodged without annexed Property'.[74] The main target of these reforms was sitting Members of Parliament since as long as British liberty depended 'on the personal Virtues of its Magistrates' it was precariously balanced.[75]

Obadiah Hulme's focus was on the danger of a long-sitting Parliament and he reiterated the old country solution of frequent, even annual, elections. Hulme's central argument was later quarried by both Burgh and Cartwright: 'The first principle of government, that is founded upon the natural rights of mankind, is the principle of annual election. Liberty and election, in this case, are synonymous terms; for where there is no election, there can be no liberty.'[76] Without annual election there was no 'circulatory' pressure to keep the body politic in a healthy state. Hulme feared parliamentary more than royal sovereignty precisely because in it was reposed the power to act for the common good and therefore the power to work its ruin insidiously, under the pretext of legitimate necessity.[77] Other antidotes, in addition to annual election, were the reform of the existing borough system and the assignment of members of constituencies.[78] Unlike Cartwright writing only five years later, whose views on parliamentary reform were driven by a conception of the sovereign rights of individuals, Hulme's thoughts on representation still reflected the classical suspicion of governors and therefore the need to install constitutional obstacles to their aggrandizement: 'To deduce our rights from the principles of equity, justice, and the constitution, is very well; but equity and justice, are no defence against power. You must take your constitutional rights, under your own protection, and that quickly too, or they will be lost for ever.'[79] Yet, even without a metaphysics like Cartwright's, it was Hulme who first made the representation of individuals an issue for British parliamentary reform with his description of the Saxon model. Jean-Louis De Lolme, in the first English edition of his *Constitution of England*, had recognized that the act of voting was a demonstration of political power, but denied that it was an expression of 'liberty'.[80]

[73] *Ibid.*, xxii, p. 392.   [74] Brown, *Thoughts on Civil Liberty*, pp. 57, 170.
[75] Ruffhead, *Ministerial Usurpation Displayed*, p. 55.
[76] Hulme, *Historical Essay*, p. 11.   [77] *Ibid.*, pp. 111, 113, 142.   [78] *Ibid.*, p. 153.
[79] *Ibid.*, p. 143.   [80] De Lolme, *Constitution of England*, p. 226.

As we have seen, James Burgh's concern for the health of parliament also centred on the 'inadequate state of representation, the enormous length of their period, and the ministerial influence prevailing in them'.[81] Catharine Macaulay supported frequent elections for all the seats, following Harrington's ideal of a rotation.[82] In the *History* she praised the 1654 elections for the republican parliament as worthy of emulation. The plan would have eliminated the small, corrupt boroughs and established 'a free representative on this plan'. The House was about to vote on it when 'the act was seized out of the clerk's hand by Cromwell' and with it went the last hope for parliamentary reform.[83] She predicted that the only way to effect any change in the term and election of parliament was to appeal directly to the honest, working and excluded 'multitude'.[84] Without a theoretical justification, however, this could be, and was, dismissed as demagogic levelling.

Cartwright's contribution, at this stage, was vital. By demanding change in the name of natural rights he secured the theoretical high ground for the parliamentary reform movement. The flavour of this new argument, though, can only be properly appreciated by recognizing its dependence on the categories and issues laid down by early theorists of the sovereignty of the community.[85] Cartwright

---

[81] Burgh, *PD*, I, p. xx. In his guide for George III Burgh mentioned the seriously uneven distribution of seats. While the West Country sent a large proportion of all members, cities like Manchester, Newcastle and Birmingham were completely unrepresented. Not only would annual parliaments properly reapportion power, but they were the only effective restraint on corrupt members (*Remarks*, pp. 60–1, 66–8. For another reforming plan, see *Crito*, II, pp. 37–8). A recent assessment of this problem is by Frank O'Gorman, 'The Unreformed Electorate of Hanoverian England: The Mid Eighteenth Century to the Reform Act of 1832', *Social History*, 11 (1986), 33–52.

[82] Catharine Macaulay, *Observations on a Pamphlet, Entitled, 'Thoughts on the Cause of the Present Discontents'* (London, 1770), p. 14.

[83] Catharine Macaulay, *The History of England*, 8 vols. (London, 1763–83), V, p. 140n.

[84] Catharine Macaulay, *An Address to the People of England, Scotland and Ireland, on the Present Important Crisis of Affairs* (Bath, 1775), p. 14.

[85] The title page highlights this relationship. Cartwright foresees a choice between 'Representation and Respect v. Imposition and Contempt', 'Annual Parliaments and Liberty v. Long Parliaments and Slavery'. 'Respect' and 'contempt' are characteristic of individual-oriented politics while 'liberty' and 'slavery' are the reference points for the common good.

The quotations chosen for the page also point up how his natural rights scheme really supervenes on top of a deeply classical debate: 'Where annual election ends, slavery begins' (Hulme). 'A free government, in order to maintain itself free, hath need every day of some new provision in favour of Liberty' (Machiavel). 'I wish the maxim of Machiavel was followed, that of examining a constitution, at certain periods, according to its first principles; this would correct abuses and supply defects' (Lord Camden). 'And now – in the name of all that is holy – let us consider whether a scheme may not be laid down for obtaining the necessary reformation of parliament' (Burgh).

approached his chief concern through the structure left over from the debate over representation: 'The ministers of the present reign have daringly struck at your most sacred rights, have aimed through the sides of America a deadly blow at the life of your constitution, and have shewn themselves hostile, not only to the being, but to the very name of liberty.'[86] The lesson to be learned was classical, the means to attain it distinctly different: 'Trust not, I say, in princes nor in ministers; but trust in YOURSELVES, and in representatives chosen by YOURSELVES alone!'[87] No other strategy could secure the liberty of citizens. As long as the election of members remained unfree, 'the fountain of legislation is poisoned. Every stream, how much soever mixed, as it flows with justice and patriotism, will still have poison in its composition.' Unfair elections made for corrupt parliaments, and corrupt parliaments made a patriotic minister a logical impossibility. The solution of Machiavelli and Bolingbroke had become dependent on the individual exercise of power through representation. Moreover, factions, the bane of classical theorists, would no longer arise since members would rarely be seated long enough to entrench themselves.[88]

Cartwright began by positing the axiomatic quality of metaphysical liberty as a prerequisite for the possibility of moral agency. People 'have, therefore, necessarily been created FREE. Were it otherwise, neither virtue nor vice, right nor wrong, could be ascribed to their actions; and to talk of happiness, would be to talk of nonsense.' If men were not free, they could not live a moral life and could experience no happiness.[89] But, in addition to being free, all men were created equal. And without a natural hierarchy only 'common consent' could elevate one man, or several, above the others. Cartwright's political theory is an instance of natural rights without a contract or state of nature.[90]

Richard Watson, Regius Professor of Divinity at Cambridge and later Bishop of Llandaff, drew a similar political conclusion from the premise of natural equality. Note the pronounced emphasis on 'independence' that followed from Watson's premise:

[86] Cartwright, *Take your Choice!* (London, 1776), pp. xxi–xxii; also, pp. 20–1.
[87] *Ibid.*, p. xxv.
[88] *Ibid.*, pp. ix, xxi–xiii. See also Price, *Additional Observations on the Nature and Value of Civil Liberty, and the War with America*, pp. 45–6.
[89] Cartwright, *Take your Choice!*, p. 2.   [90] *Ibid.*, pp. 2, 4–5, 7.

The natural equality and independence that individuals have contended for, is not only the great source, from which that part of the System of natural law, which explains the duties of all men towards all in their individual capacity, and of all independent States towards each other in their collective capacity, is derived; but is also the surest foundation of all just reasoning concerning the origin and extent of civil Government in every part of the world.[91]

A political society organized in accord with the natural relations between men would be immune to the ills of all commonwealths. Cartwright took the next step and repudiated the Polybian heritage. The political body was 'essentially different' from the natural because, while 'the natural body grows weaker and weaker from the successive attacks of disease' and moves inexorably towards dissolution, a political body may be completely rejuvenated: 'Its natural tendency is consequently towards all the immortality which the duration of this world can afford it.' The implicit rejection of the metaphor was followed by an explicit one: 'Perhaps the careless figurative expression of *body* politic, may have contributed very much to the unphilosophical language commonly used, with regard to the supposed certainty that every state, like a human body, must necessarily perish through infirmities and old age, which I *deny*.'[92] The precepts of revealed and natural religion gave Britain an unprecedented opportunity to build an indestructible society based on true relations between men. The failure of the ancient empires bore no relevance to Christian Britain: 'The idolatry and polytheism of the Assyrians, the Medes, Persians, Greeks and Romans, all perished, as well as their respective empires and constitutions of government. Does it then follow that the religion of the English nation shall also perish? We know it shall not perish.'[93]

For Britain to avoid this dismal fate, however, it had first to bring the instrument of power into line with its actual disposition. The consent of each individual citizen, regardless of the extent of his possessions, was required to give force to the laws of the state: 'The first and most natural idea which will occur to any unprejudiced man, is, that *every individual of them*, whether possessed of what is vulgarly called property, or not, ought to have a vote in sending to parliament those men who are to act as his representatives.' Cart-

---

[91] Richard Watson, *The Principles of the Revolution Vindicated* (Cambridge, 1776), p. 4.
[92] Cartwright, *Take your Choice!*, pp. 15–16.
[93] *Ibid.*, p. 18.

wright's move beyond property qualifications broke from the traditional position and showed that defenders of consent to taxation like Locke and Blackstone were not, in fact, concerned to uphold the rights of individuals *per se*, but only to preserve the sanctity of property:

> Though a man should have neither lands nor gold, nor herds nor flocks; yet he may have parents and kindred, he may possess a wife and an offspring to be solicitous for . . . Shall we add to the unkindness of fortune, the cruelty of oppression and injustice! . . . Their poverty is, surely, the worst of all reasons, for stripping them of their natural rights! Let us rather reconcile to them the many hardships of their condition, by shewing them that it doth not degrade them below the nature of man. If they have not wherewithal to gratify the pride, let them at least retain the dignity of human nature by knowing they are free, and sharing in the privileges inseparable from liberty.[94]

Cartwright believed that the inherent metaphysical and epistemological status of the individual could bring with it substantive political power. Freedom could not be dependent on property of any kind, since 'by adding free-will to rationality' God made men 'accountable for their actions'. 'All are by nature free; all are by nature equal: freedom implies choice; equality excludes degrees in freedom.'[95] Cartwright attacked the prevailing orthodoxy, associated with Blackstone, which subsumed this consideration beneath the overarching claim of property: '. . . *personality* is the sole foundation of the *right* of being *represented*' and therefore '*property* has, in reality, nothing to do in the case'. If property, rather than its possessors, was the subject of representation, then representatives would have 'farms, woods and houses' for constituents, rather than people.[96] The property qualification that prevented 'considering *every* member of the community as a free-man' was purely conventional.[97] Only 'absolute impracticability', therefore, could militate against a reformed and equal representation.[98] As for the scoffers who thought election for approximately 500 MPs impossible, Cartwright pointed out that 32,000 militia officers had been elected throughout the nation.[99]

Cartwright's labours, and those of contemporary campaigners,

---

[94] *Ibid.*, pp. 19–20. It is no wonder that even the bristling and defensive Tucker could not summon up the venom to condemn Cartwright's integrity.
[95] Cartwright, *Take your Choice!*, p. 21.   [96] *Ibid.*, p. 22.   [97] *Ibid.*, p. 36.
[98] *Ibid.*, p. 28.
[99] *Ibid.*, p. 50.

directly continued the demand for actual representation initiated by
the colonists. The program of *Take your Choice!* – annual parliaments,
equal electoral districts, secret ballots, abolition of plural voting,
salaries for MPs and manhood suffrage – became the platform of the
Chartists. Cartwright himself intended this book to be a 'blue-print
for action' and it remained 'the key to his thought and tactics
throughout his career as a parliamentary reformer'.[100] Though it
has been argued that Cartwright's interpretations of historical
precedent and constitutional theory were mistaken, nevertheless
'both enabled him to root the parliamentary reform movement
within a native tradition, and to inculcate in the lower classes a
respect for law and adherence to constitutional methods of agi-
tation'.[101] It is precisely in this realm of action that Cartwright's
catalysation of a movement for the reform of domestic political
representation bridged the gap between the tracts on imperial
reform and practical national politics. Obadiah Hulme had called
for the establishment of associations to absorb rotten boroughs into
county constituencies with the leading association to be based in
London.[102] Burgh, the other great influence on Cartwright, had
envisioned a 'Grand National Association for Restoring the Constitution', to be led by the king. The association would provide, at one
and the same time, both a measure of popular support for change as
well as a vehicle for its implementation.[103] Cartwright's establishment of the 'Society for Constitutional Information' and Christopher Wyvill's of the 'Yorkshire Association' mark the initial
attempts to translate the force of this idea of the sovereign individual
from political theory to political action.

These men saw themselves as reformers not revolutionaries. Burgh
placed the king at the head of his reforming association, while
Cartwright dedicated the second edition of *Take your Choice!* to
George III. Indeed, Burgh denied any wish to 'alter' the constitutional form of king, lords and commons. Instead, his proposal
aimed 'to restore', 'preserve' and 're-establish' a parliament based
on the annual election of an uncorrupted and 'more adequate'
representation. This conservative language of reform employed the
standard description of the purpose of political life to justify its new

---

[100] Naomi H. Churgin, 'Major John Cartwright: A Study in Radical Parliamentary Reform,
     1774–1823', Unpublished Ph.D. thesis (Columbia, 1963), p. 90.
[101] *Ibid.*, p. 3.   [102] Hulme, *Historical Essay*, p. 161.   [103] Burgh, *PD*, III, pp. 428–9.

understanding of sovereignty: 'It is the duty of a prince to consult at all adventures, the greatest good of his people, his *children*; and if the diminution of his prerogative will increase the happiness of his people, the superfluous power of one is certainly to yield to the happiness of millions.'[104] The common good now meant the good of the individual citizens of the state.

The venture of reform was perilous and its progress, reflected in the public career of Major Cartwright, for example, erratic and strewn with disappointments. Still, it would be a mistake to dismiss their politics because of the radical nature of their ideas. It is true that many of them relied on preconditions like belief in a Christian deity to anchor the natural political liberty of individuals. But their petitioning parliament for religious reform did bring real gains in 1779 and 1790 and John Jebb's push for educational reform at Cambridge did succeed in replacing subscription with a short declaration of fidelity in June of 1772, even as subscription was to remain required at Oxford into the middle of the nineteenth century. Finally, the public character of debate over the shape of parliament turned the theoretical ideas generated by the imperial crisis into an agenda for reshaping the state. This campaign was conducted by wary idealists who did not seek revolution and were aware of the inherent difficulty of their project. Nevertheless, they believed that the recovery of the sovereign power warranted certain risks:

I am not speaking of the *prudence* of such a step; nor do I justify a people's proposing to alter their constitution, if such alteration is likely to be followed by worse evils, than it is likely to redress; nor have I any thing to say concerning the difficulty of obtaining the real sense of the majority of a great nation. But I assert, that, saving the laws of prudence, and of morality, the people's mere absolute, sovereign will and pleasure, is a sufficient reason for their making any alteration in their form of government.[105]

RICHARD PRICE AND HIS CRITICS

Richard Price's *Observations on the Nature of Civil Liberty and the War with America* (its full title reflects the mingling of the two discourses)

---

[104] *Ibid.*, p. 299.   [105] *Ibid.*, p. 278.

was one of the most popular[106] and provocative books of the age.[107] It encouraged and enraged because of Price's peculiar commitments. On the one hand, he helped shape private judgment as both a religious and a political concept. On the other hand, he largely retained the heavily classical language used by commonwealthmen. Thus, it was possible for him to be attacked as an enemy of the security of the community by its defenders, and as a political dinosaur by someone of Bentham's persuasion.

Price's quadripartite analysis of liberty was a straightforward assertion of the philosophy underpinning the reformers' position:

By physical liberty I mean that principle of spontaneity, or Self-determination, which constitutes us Agents; or which gives us a command over our actions, rendering them properly ours, and not effects of the operation of any foreign cause.

Moral liberty is the power of following, in all circumstances, our sense of right and wrong; or of acting in conformity to our reflecting and moral principles, without being controuled by any contrary principles.

Religious liberty signifies the power of exercising, without molestation, that mode of religion which we think best; or of making the decisions of our own consciences, respecting religious truth, the rule of our conduct, and not any of the decisions of others.

Civil liberty is the power of a Civil Society or State to govern itself by its own discretion; or by laws of its own making, without being subject to any foreign discretion, or to the impositions of any extraneous will or power.[108]

His fundamental conception of liberty was obviously dependent on the arguments of Samuel Clarke and his followers, and repeats those in his own *Review of the Principal Questions and Difficulties in Morals*. Thus, the four kinds of liberty all shared 'one general idea ... the idea of *Self-direction*, or *Self-government*'.[109] Price stressed this aspect in

---

[106] The first edition sold out its press run of 1,000 copies within three days of publication on 10 February 1776. By May of that year it was being issued in its eleventh edition (Thomas, *Honest Mind*, p. 149) and by the end of 1776 it had gone through six different printings and eighteen editions (Bernard Peach, *Richard Price and the Ethical Foundations of the American Revolution* (Durham, NC, 1977), p. 41) while amassing total sales of 60,000 copies (Schuyler, *Fall of the Old Colonial System*, p. 61).

[107] Thomas R. Adams lists upwards of twenty-six hostile responses to Price's tract in the two years immediately following (*The American Controversy: Bibliography of British Pamphlets on America 1763–1783* (Providence, RI, 1980). Smith's evaluation was fairly common and inaccurate: 'Price's speculations cannot fail to sink into the neglect that they always deserved. I have always considered him as a factious citizen, a most superficial Philosopher and by no means an able calculator' (Letter no. 251, addressed to George Chalmers, 22 December 1785, quoted in *WN*, p. 88).

[108] Price, *Observations*, pp. 3–4.

[109] *Ibid.*, p. 3. Frederick Rosen's accurate distinction between Locke and Price is not concerned with the source of Price's 'more radical' conception of liberty 'in terms of

his vindication, published the following year as the *Additional Observations on Civil Liberty*: 'The Liberty of men as *agents* is that power of self-determination which all agents, as such, possess. – Their Liberty as *moral* agents is their power of self-government in their *moral* conduct.'[110] The subsequent storm of protest and misunderstanding is really evidence for the passing away of a philosophical discourse. If liberty was understood as self-direction, its antithesis was slavery. In the four examples, therefore, that 'force which stands opposed to the agent's own will ... produce servitude'. Physical enslavement was a repudiation of the specifically Newtonian view of liberty since 'the subject of it is a mere passive instrument which never acts, but is always acted upon'. Without physical liberty the individual would be an automaton 'having no principle of motion in himself or command over events; and, therefore, incapable of all merit and demerit'. This was the position Price had argued in the *Review* nearly twenty years before. It was on these grounds that he opposed the decision of the General Body of Protestant Dissenting Ministers to replace subscription with a declaration of faith in the gospel. In his subsequent *Observations* Price described religious enslavement as *'Human Authority* in religion requiring conformity to particular modes of faith and worship, and superseding *private judgment'*. The common thread between the four types of liberty was the notion of 'self-direction' or 'self-government', and the different varieties of slavery all operated by restraining that 'power of Self-government'.[111]

The failure of his critics to recognize that 'slavery' was also part of the terminology of moral psychology and not simply opposition cant led to accusations that Price intentionally abused the definition of liberty in order to justify anarchism. Clarke's definition of liberty as self-government, as it gave a specific content to the claim of private judgment, was denounced. Men do not have 'an indisputable right to express their private judgment of men and measures in whatever terms they please'. The consequence of Price's use of private judgment was a critical stress on independence: 'What they contend for in reality is, That every man may do what is right in his OWN eyes. This, in the opinion of some, is the perfection of civil liberty.'[112] Prior

---

self-determination and self-government' ('The Origin of Liberal Utilitarianism: Jeremy Bentham and Liberty', in *Victorian Liberalism: Nineteenth-Century Political Thought and Practice*, ed. Richard Bellamy (London and New York, 1990), esp. p. 58).

[110] Price, *Additional Observations*, p. 2.   [111] Price, *Observations*, pp. 4–5.

[112] John Martin, *Familiar Dialogues between Americus and Britannicus* (London, 1776), p. 16. Also Shebbeare, *Essay*, p. 65.

to Price, wrote another, 'the term Civil Liberty always implied the degree of relative liberty, which men enjoyed in a state of society under whatever form of government they lived'. It 'is altogether new' to suggest that civil liberty meant, as Price argued, 'the legislative independence of one state in respect to another'.[113] While independence, for Price, was an attribute of human beings created in God's image, for those whose ideas of liberty, like Montesquieu's, were related to security, it was dangerous and to be avoided. Instead, according to Wesley, all British citizens, whatever their place of residence, already possessed civil liberty, understood as 'a liberty to dispose of our lives, persons and fortunes, according to our own choice, and the laws of our country'.[114] It was his broad attack on the sovereignty of state interests that led critics to see rebellion as the end of all Price's arguments.

Harrington, citing Aristotle and Livy, had described government as an 'empire of laws and not of men'. A century later, living with the consequences of the Tiberian corruption of parliament and its exercise of untrammelled supremacy, Price had come to doubt Harrington's faith in law. For a corrupt legislature could not be the instrument for the execution of what Harrington had called 'an art whereby a civil society of men is instituted and preserved upon the foundation of common right or interest'.[115] 'Liberty, therefore,' according to Price, 'is too imperfectly defined when it is said to be "a Government by LAWS, and not by MEN". If the laws are made by one man, or a junto of men in a state, and not by COMMON CONSENT, a government by them does not differ from slavery.'[116] Eighteenth-century British history had shown that laws, without the consent of the governed, could still oppress. Hence, if 'There is nothing that requires more to be watched than power' and parliament was the locus of power, then parliament had to be watched and, resorting to a classical idea, the only trustworthy guardians were the people themselves.[117] Priestley, however, disagreed, restating the basic truth that decisive success consisted in a change of 'rules and administration of government' not 'of governors'.[118]

Unlike Priestley, Price was not prepared to mitigate the individual's direct control of the instruments of power. While they were

---

[113] John Gray, *Dr Price's Notions of the Nature of Civil Liberty* (London, 1777), p. 8.
[114] Wesley, *Some Observations on Liberty Occasioned by a Late Tract* (London, 1776), p. 4.
[115] Harrington, *Oceana*, p. 161.   [116] Price, *Observations*, p. 7.   [117] *Ibid.*, pp. 15, 18.
[118] Priestley, *Essay*, p. 31.

both vilified as anarchic traitors, Price and Priestley had very different attitudes towards politics.[119] While Price was deeply committed to a political life controlled by individual citizens, Priestley, despite his powerful defence of private judgment and freedom of thought, did not extend its full implications to political relations. The American crisis played a surprisingly small role in his intellectual life, generating only two small pamphlets in 1769 and 1774, and the issue of a reformed representation, seemingly fundamental to his world-view, does not command much attention.

In the *Lectures on History*, Priestley followed Grotius' division between personal and public liberty: 'The power which the community leaves him possessed of with respect to his own conduct, may be called his *civil* liberty, whereas the share that he may have in directing the affairs of the society may be called his *political* liberty.'[120] The account in the *Essay* is a more elaborate version of what Priestley had presented in his lectures at Warrington:

> Political liberty, therefore, is equivalent to the right of magistracy, being the claim that any member of the state hath, to have his private opinion or judgment become that of the public, and thereby control the actions of others; whereas civil liberty, extends no farther than to a man's own conduct, and signifies the right he has to be exempt from the control of the society, or its agents; that is the power he has of providing for his own advantage and happiness.

An individual could possess civil liberty, 'power over his own actions', while lacking the 'power over those of another' that constituted political liberty.[121] Moreover, Priestley thought it was possible for 'all the members' of a community to participate in legislation 'and yet those laws may be very oppressive, leaving individuals little power over their own actions'. Nevertheless, Priestley did not dismiss political liberty completely. He conceded that people could possess civil without political liberty, 'But in this case their civil liberties, or *private rights*, will be precarious, being at the mercy of others. Political liberty is therefore the only sure guard of civil liberty, and it is chiefly valuable on that account.'[122] Without the liberty to participate in government there could be 'no *security* for

---

[119] See D. O. Thomas, 'Progress, Liberty and Utility: The Political Philosophy of Joseph Priestley', p. 78.
[120] Priestley, *Lectures on History*, p. 237.   [121] Priestley, *Essay*, pp. 9–10.
[122] Priestley, *Lectures on History*, p. 237.

the continuance of the same laws' that furthered civil liberty.[123] And with 'the Statesman', the stock early modern figure of the prudent politician, Priestley acknowledged that 'the proper object of the civil magistrate is the peace and well being of society' and that anything which disturbed that peace came under his purview.[124] Like Hume, Priestley distinguished between the ancient monarchies, which acted in both executive and judicial capacities, and modern ones which had been deprived of the power of rendering justice. This provided a means of defending against tyrannous aggrandizement, but Priestley went still further, wielding the concept of modern monarchy against republicanism: 'In Italy, where they [executive and judicial power] are united, there is less liberty than in monarchies.'[125] Unlike Burgh, Priestley saw little of value in the persistence of the Lucchese republic.

Other practical elements of Priestley's politics reveal a similarly anti-democratic bias. In the context of the times, his defence of established political economic practice could have been seen, especially in the light of the repudiation of it by Cartwright and Price, as support for the existing unrepresentative principles of imperial governance.[126] Mass political participation was not justified in terms of the natural rights he deployed so frequently elsewhere, but simply as the best means of achieving the security needed to 'encourage a man to make great exertions'.[127] In this account, suffrage is weighted according to income and social class, belying any claim to universal equality. In the catechism at the end of the *Present State*, Priestley asked, rhetorically, whether it was necessary for 'all the people' to vote for their magistrates. He answered that 'it will generally be sufficient if the choice of magistrates be in the majority of those whose circumstances render them above being corrupted, so as to give their voices in an improper manner'.[128] While Priestley was a strong supporter of women's education, this did not cut across class lines; respect for rank remained, as Margaret Canovan has observed, deeply ingrained in Priestley's social and

---

[123] Priestley, *Essay*, p. 60.
[124] *Ibid.*, p. 119. This passage was added in the second edition.
[125] Priestley, *Lectures on History*, p. 240.
[126] See Chuhei Sugiyama, 'The Economic Thought of Joseph Priestley', *Enlightenment and Dissent*, 3 (1984), 77–91.
[127] Priestley, *Lectures on History*, p. 238.
[128] Priestley, 'Present State', *Works*, xxii, p. 385; also *Essay*, pp. 15–17. This passage was added to the second edition.

political thought. She has suggested that he placed the burden of rectifying these problems on Providence.[129] Again we see that this reformation depended on extra-political preconditions like the belief in an active Providence. Perhaps the solvent of this seeming paradox is to be found in Priestley's commitment to intellectuality. Martin Fitzpatrick has suggested that Priestley only endorsed unrestricted individual free enquiry where he believed that people could make use of this freedom. The Americans and Irish could exercise this liberty but the English were too backward. According to him, 'The reservations Dissenters had about the extension to the people of their undoubted right to participate in the political community can thus be traced to their emphasis upon their ideal that that community should be capable of taking enlightened decisions.'[130] Hence William Wood's declaration, in a sermon commemorating the centenary of the Revolution of 1688, that 'Political Liberty never produces its just effect, when it is not subservient to the more important liberty of the mind.'[131]

Price, on the contrary, was committed to private judgment because of a belief in universal equality. He was not a pure republican because he, too, repudiated participation in favour of consent. But the inalienability of individual liberty made it impossible for him to separate the source of sovereignty and the means of its administration: 'A citizen is free when the power of the commanding his own conduct and the quiet possession of his life, person, property and good name are secured to him by being his own legislator ... A government is free when constituted in such a manner as to give this security'.[132]

Price's combination of Clarke's self-government and vestigial classical republican arguments left him exposed to the accusation of having made a series of indefensible claims. The vitriolic John Shebbeare (1709–88), chemist, self-proclaimed doctor and member of the French academy of Sciences (though better known as a government hack), took Price's reworking of the Harringtonian

---

[129] Ruth Watts, 'Priestley and Education', *Enlightenment and Dissent* 2 (1983), 88–9; Margaret Canovan, 'Priestley on Rank', *Enlightenment and Dissent*, 2 (1983), 27–32.

[130] Fitzpatrick, 'Heretical Religion and Radical Political Ideas in Late Eighteenth-Century England', in *The Transformation of Political Culture*, pp. 353–5.

[131] William Wood, *Two Sermons Preached ... on the Celebration of the Hundredth Anniversary of the Happy Revolution* (Leeds, 1788), p. 28, quoted in Fitzpatrick, 'Heretical', p. 356.

[132] Price, *Additional Observations*, pp. 16–17.

formula of 'laws not men' to be an attempt to justify the rule of 'King Mob'. 'I imagine the Doctor is totally mistaken in his definition of civil liberty; for, according to him, that liberty does not consist in the nature of the laws by which men are governed, but in that of the government by which they are formed.' Price was asserting that laws 'made by the majority of a people', howsoever unjust, could never 'annihilate or abridge' a nation's civil liberty.[133]

Characteristic of his metaphysical position (recall Cartwright's similarly grounded disinterest in 'mouldy charters'), Price's argument was devoid of references to charters, parliamentary laws and debates or the common law. Instead, he appealed to reason, common sense and natural rights: 'The question, with all liberal enquirers, ought to be, not what jurisdiction over them, precedents, statutes and charters give, but what reason and equity and the rights of humanity give?'[134] This led him to conclude that individual civil and religious liberty was derived from a shared vision of human nature. Just as private judgment in religion was obviously inalienable 'so neither can any civil societies lawfully surrender their Civil Liberty, by giving up to any extraneous jurisdiction their power of legislating for themselves and disposing their property'.[135] Like Cartwright in the near-simultaneous *Take your Choice!*, Price was explicitly linking the two debates so as to create a new political argument.

The American débâcle demonstrated the inadequacy of the theory behind the politics of the British empire: 'This is a case which is new in the history of mankind; and it is extremely improper to judge of it by the rules of any narrow and partial policy; or to consider it on any other ground than the general one of reason and justice.'[136] Britain's unprecedented acquisition of a distant continental empire raised the risk of her experiencing the wholly Polybian fate of the Roman republic.[137] Refining Pownall's path-clearing argument, Price asserted that the sheer size and distance of the new empire mocked the government assertion of one king, one realm, one confession. Price laid great weight on these practical, logistical concerns:

Were there any distant state which had acquired a sovereignty over this

[133] John Shebbeare, *An Essay on the Origin, Progress and Establishment of National Society* (London, 1776), p. 28.
[134] Price, *Observations*, p. 32.   [135] *Ibid.*, p. 25.   [136] *Ibid.*, p. 33.
[137] *Ibid.*, pp. 24, 59.

country, and exercised the power of making its laws and disposing its property, we should be in the first kind of slavery; and, if not totally depraved by the habit of subjection to such a power, we should think ourselves in a miserable condition; and an advocate for such a power would be considered as insulting us, who should attempt to reconcile us to it by telling us, that we were one community with that distant state, though destitute of a single voice in its legislature; and, on this ground, should maintain, that all resistance to it was no less criminal than any resistance within a state to the authority of that state. – In short, every state, not incorporated with another by an equal representation, and yet subject to its dominion, is enslaved in this sense.

This constituted the slavery of the Roman provinces and those of all provinces which, by definition as we have seen, had no control over their 'taxation and internal legislation'.[138]

While a kingdom was a community with common interests and which could therefore speak with a single parliamentary voice, the early modern British empire was an agglomeration of different communities with different interests. Just forms of governance existed for each, but they were not interchangeable. An empire could not be ruled like a kingdom:

Different communities forming an Empire have no connexions, which produce a necessary reciprocation of interests between them. They inhabit different districts, and are governed by different legislatures. – On the contrary. The different classes of men within a kingdom are all placed on the same ground. Their concerns and interests are the same; and what is done to one part must affect all – These are situations totally different; and a constitution of government that may be consistent with Liberty in one of them, may be entirely inconsistent with it in the other.[139]

Unlike Cartwright and Tucker, Price did not foresee the inevitable disintegration of the British empire, so long as it was administered as an 'empire' and not as a single 'kingdom'. In an empire each member state possessed a free constitution and was autonomous in respect of taxation and internal legislation. Under these circumstances subordination did not militate against it being an 'Empire of Freemen'.[140] The bald assertion of parliamentary sovereignty in lands possessed by force of arms alone could not, however, manufacture a community of interests. This practice was analogous to the claim of religious establishments to doctrinal

---

[138] Price, *Additional Observations*, pp. 5–6. Also, *Observations*, p. 46.
[139] Price, *Observations*, p. 27.
[140] *Ibid.*, p. 28.

hegemony at the expense of the private judgments of those whose
interests did not coincide with those of the church:

> Pleas of this sort have, in all ages, been used to justify tyranny. – They have
> in RELIGION given rise to numberless oppressive claims, and slavish Hier-
> archies. And in the Romish Communion, particularly, it is well known,
> that the POPE claims the title and powers of the supreme head on earth of
> the Christian church, in order to preserve its UNITY.[141]

Britain's attempt to ignore the realities of the situation and enforce
the framework of a single community upon the North American
colonies produced 'civil servitude' akin to that generated by des-
pots.[142]

Richard Price's critics balked at his analysis of empire and
kingdom. While Adam Ferguson acknowledged that 'a republic
extending 1200 miles in one direction, and without any known
bounds in the other, is still an experiment to be made in the history
of mankind', most could not envision the British empire or, indeed,
the concept of sovereignty, as in any way mitigated by spatial
realities.[143] The response of the last Governor of Massachusetts to
Price's claim was typical: parliament possessed 'constitutional authority' over the colonies and could exercise it. When it can no longer
do so '[i]t will then be time enough to inquire whether the power
and authority existing ought to be continued. The question now is a
matter of mere speculation.'[144] Distance proved surprisingly resist-
ant to theory: 'To live beyond a rivulet, or beyond the Atlantic,
makes no exemption; if it be English ground, it is English empire,
and subject to the plenitude of British supremacy.'[145] This sentiment
was not necessarily wrong, just misguided. Many of these authors
were thinking in the conventional early modern terms of community
and cultural bonds and so produced brilliant statements that none
the less reveal how difficult it was to address the peculiar problems of

---

[141] *Ibid.*, p. 36.   [142] *Ibid.*, p. 42.

[143] Adam Ferguson, *Remarks on a Pamphlet Lately Published by Dr Price* (London, 1776), p. 23.
Even Ferguson thought in terms of republics; there was no existing model to help
disentangle the relationship between empire and vast territorial state.

[144] Thomas Hutchinson, *Experience Preferable to Theory. An Answer to Dr Price's Observations*
(London, 1776), p. 38. The title conveys an attitude towards the making of policy that
was characteristic of the political spokesmen of post-Reformation states. One of the most
sophisticated and telling attacks on the politics of necessity and the common good was
levelled by Immanuel Kant in an essay which took this feature as its target: 'On the
Common Saying "This may be true in theory, but it does not apply in practice"' (1793).

[145] *Duty*, p. 16. See also Shebbeare's *Essay*, p. 92; John Lind, *Three Letters to Dr Price*, p. 106.

eighteenth-century empire. 'If the Distances of Places are said to be the Criterion of mutual Interests, Affections and reciprocal Tyes, certainly the French and Dutch ought to be much greater Favorites with us than all the Americans together.'[146] Another writer showed his rejection of this problem by asserting a static interpretation of the 'family metaphor'. If distance were to matter, 'you might as well affirm, that when children are married, all their former friendships, relations, and obligations, are annihilated; or that the collateral branches of a family have no further dependance on, or interest in, the original stock'.[147]

If Price were correct, the only options were inconceivable; either the dissolution or refoundation of empire. His critics could not imagine an empire composed of semi-independent components of differing interests. If this were the case 'they would all be soon divided'. If the claims of the parts became as important as that of the centre it would cease to be an empire.[148] Hutchinson observed that Price's arguments were the same as those which appeared two years before under the title *American Independence*. Both were dangerous to the fortunes of union. Under the pressure of events the defenders of the empire resorted to increasingly blunt and unnuanced assertions of the reason of state: 'The principles laid down will not admit of the subjection of the plantations to the same supreme authority with the kingdom; such an authority is the only bond by which it is possible for them to be held together as one state.'[149]

The problem of the Realm, first made central by Pownall in 1768, had become inescapable in the intervening years. Price's critics believed that upholding the Realm necessarily entailed colonial subordination. Empire could only be defended by a unitary sovereign:

The question is, whether America is part of the British constitution? If not, we have no right to taxation: but if America owns itself our subject – taxation is the only proof of its subordinacy. For that we contend; there can be no medium; America either is, or is not part of the British empire – It admits of no palliation.[150]

---

[146] Anon., *A Letter to the Rev. Dr Price* (London, 1776), p. 45.
[147] [Moir], *Obedience the Best Charter or, Law the Only Sanction of Liberty* (London, 1776), p. 29.
[148] Anon., *Remarks on Dr Price's Observations* (London, 1776), p. 14.
[149] Hutchinson, *Experience Preferable to Theory*, p. 2.
[150] *Remarks on Dr Price's Observations*, p. 27.

The Realm Question was about the relationship between territorial sovereignty and political obligation. 'The colonists either are, or are not the subjects of Great-Britain.' If they are subjects, 'the legislature cannot treat with them while its supremacy is denied'. If, however, they are not subjects of Great Britain, representation is pointless and 'their petitioning its Government is mean'.[151] The status of colonists as subjects was perceived as 'the main Hinge, the grand Axis, on which the whole Chain of Reasoning must turn'.[152]

Price's attempt to invent a language in which to describe his desired political relationship was mocked, as was Pownall's: 'I should be glad to know what you possibly can mean by *Self Direction* or *Self Government?*' The failure to perceive Clarke's heritage is startling. Price's empire was instead likened to some physical body in which appendages and head shared the force of animation and direction. This was either monstrous or purely visionary. 'Or do you mean the British Empire is a mere Phantom or a political Dream, and that every island, Colony or Province is a separate Self-directed State, independent of the great Centre of the Empire.'[153]

The mirroring of the larger debate in the narrower compass of the response to Price is also reflected in his critics' analyses of Greek and Roman colonization. Price's preference for the Greeks was scored as irrelevant to the present case:

> The case of the Syracusans and Greek colonists, mentioned by our author, I fancy, will likewise be found to be as little applicable as that of the Netherlands. I have not at present opportunity to enquire into the nature of the Greek colonies; but I apprehend they are not sent out with a form of laws to the remote dominions of the parent state under her protection; but were sent out, as our first parents were sent out of Paradise, with the world all before them.[154]

Another critic argued that the only antique state that guarded the liberty of its citizens was the Roman and he could 'not conceive how you came to be so partial to the States of Greece'.[155]

The attack on Greek colonization followed from the definition of colonies as subordinate entities ruled for the benefit of the community (understood as the metropolis). The model of ecclesiastical polity served in the colonial debate just as allegations of civil disloyalty dominated the debate on toleration: 'That the supreme

---

[151] Anon., *Honour of Parliament*, p. 14.   [152] Anon., *A Letter to the Rev. Dr Price*, p. 39.
[153] *Ibid.*, pp. 12–13.   [154] Gray, *Doctor Price's Notions*, p. 108.
[155] Anon., *A Letter to the Rev. Dr Price*, p. 19.

power may be duly exercised to secure the great ends of society, and to preserve order and peace, God has commanded all men to be subject to the temporal powers.' The colonists' denial of this supremacy constituted rebellion because 'supremacy naturally includes a right to obedience and support'.[156] Questions of right and wrong were not for individual subjects to determine, but were matters of state: 'This may be *right* or *wrong* according to the principles of *natural* equity; – it is nevertheless fact; it is nevertheless the *Law* and *Constitution* of the British Empire.'[157] In this logic, Price's definition of empire as a collection of self-governing states was identical with rebellion. Contemporaries could neither follow nor accept his distinction between state and empire: 'But the term [empire] does not imply the idea of a "collection of separate states or communities". It implies nothing more than one large united state.'[158]

The governors of this political community had the authority to take action in the name of all its members. Hence the argument of John Lind and Jeremy Bentham that the dispute was not about the authority one community had over another 'but into the authority which one part of the community, called governors, may exercise over another part of that same community, called subjects'. This, obviously, presumed the existence of a single community.[159] Moreover, Price's claim that political authority derived from the representative consent of freely judging individuals was incomprehensible for men who believed in the sovereignty and authority of the community: 'Consent, whether personal, or by delegation, has no more constitutional connection with taxation, than with every other right of the supreme power. But the truth is, the position itself, as understood in this application of it, is destitute of all foundation.'[160] Members of Parliament were believed to stand for the entire commons of Britain, though, according to one writer, the 'nobler character of a member of parliament is that of representative of God himself'.[161] It was precisely because of their adherence to the notion of a community's virtual representation that Price's critics could define the unity of empire in different terms: 'Each representative, as soon as the body, of which he is one member, is formed, is the

---

[156] Anon., *Licentiousness Unmark'd; or Liberty Explained* (London, n.d.), p. 13.
[157] Henry Goodricke, *Observations on Dr Price's Theory and Principles of Civil Liberty and Government* (York, 1776), p. 6.
[158] Lind, *Three Letters to Dr Price*, p. 111. [159] *Ibid.*, p. 112.
[160] Goodricke, *Observations on Dr Price's Observations*, p. 7.
[161] J. Fletcher, *American Patriotism Farther Confronted with Reason* (Shrewsbury, 1776), pp. 66–7.

representative of the whole kingdom; and no more so of that particular part of it, which elected him, than of any other.'[162] On the contrary, the employment of representatives was, according to Lind and Bentham, one of the means to insure 'that the powers of government will be employed to the production of the greatest happiness of the greatest number'. It served this end by providing a check on the power of both people and crown and thus created 'political Security' at the same time that it 'ensured Civil Liberty'.[163] We shall soon turn to their analysis. It was feared that an attempt to remodel the representative would destabilize a successful system. For the defenders of the security of the community change was a sign, not of progress, but of danger.

> The stability of a well regulated legislature is the surest foundation of order and good government; and it is evidently for the advantage of the people, that government, with the reservations above specified, should be considered as a kind of inheritance in the constitution. Anarchy and confusion would be the constant attendants of every government, were it allowable for the people to make a resumption of their power on any other pretences.[164]

The perceived link between freedom of thought, or individual private judgment, and anarchy reflected Britain's recent history: the chaos of 1640–60, the Revolution of 1689 and the Jacobite risings of 1715 and 1745. The resort to natural rights with its implications of natural equality, so typical of Price and his colleagues, was attacked with particular vehemence because it was seen as a means of undermining the security of the community and engendering anarchy. William Stevens drew the connection between equality and that right to resistance which could only generate a military rule 'destructive of all power' and reducing all subjects to 'absolute slavery'. This scenario characterized the 'grand usurpation of the last century'.[165] Natural rights meant natural equality and that meant 'levelling' social distinctions, evoking the precondition of that 'usurpation'. Few arguments could have been more potent: 'On the same levelling principles, however, every species of property is less, or

---

[162] Hutchinson, *Experience Preferable to Theory*, p. 20. See also, Anon., *Cursory Remarks on Dr Price's Observations* (London, 1776), p. 12; *Duty*, p. 9.

[163] Lind, *Three Letters to Dr Price*, pp. 95–6.   [164] Anon., *Honour of Parliament*, p. 5.

[165] W. Stevens, *The Revolution Vindicated, and Constitutional Liberty Asserted* (Cambridge, 1777), p. 51.

more, disputable. And you have the peculiar honour, Sir, by introducing your NATURAL RIGHTS into the very heart of artificial life.'[166] The Americans' declaration that 'all men are created equal' was yet another red flag. Responding to the Declaration of of Independence, Lind commented, 'This surely is a new discovery; now, for the first time, we learn, that a child, at the moment of his birth, has the same quantity of natural power as the parent, the same quantity of political power as the magistrate.'[167] Talk of power from the people and fictional original compacts had obviously worked to 'confound the duties of Rulers and Subjects'. The Americans and their British supporters had, consequent upon their claim of natural equality, 'set up their pretended Natural Rights in Opposition to the positive Laws of the State'.[168] The 'Health of a State requires a regular and due subordination of its Members' to the governors and this was precisely what the claim of equality, backed up by rights, would surely subvert. The reason of a state demanded the preservation of a social hierarchy determining the public good:

Let every man then be contented with his Station, and faithfully discharge its attendant duties. Let every private view be abandoned, as soon as it is found to interfere with the Interest and Honour of the Public. And let it be the earnest endeavour of One and All, to promote internal Peace, Harmony and Unanimity, which are things essentially requisite to public prosperity and national happiness.[169]

Because support for the privately judging individual and support for the security of the community were understood to be mutually exclusive, Shebbeare sought to mould the individual will to create a 'national mind'. His notions left no room for private judgment as a religious or political concept and resemble John Brown's proposals, though shorn of reference to the liberty that was the latter's goal. 'Practical ordinances' were to be promulgated 'to create in each man, tribe and nation, the same sentiments respecting public and private conduct'. The force of this 'national mind' would be power-

---

166 [Moir], *Obedience the Best Charter*, p. 43. Also, 'Admitting the truth of your levelling principle, that in a *state* of *nature* individuals are equal ...' (T.D., *A Letter to the Rev. Dr Richard Price* (London, n.d.), p. 8). Also, [B. Jackson], *Three Dialogues Concerning Liberty* (London, 1776), p. 30: '... relieved from the dread I had of the levelling principles, which at first I thought would have been the consequence of this natural equality'.
167 Lind, *Answer to the Declaration of the American Congress* (London, 1776), p. 120. See also, John Gray, *Doctor Price's Notions*, pp. 15, 20; Goodricke, *Observations on Dr Price's Observations*, p. 10.
168 Myles Cooper, *National Humiliation and Repentence Recommended* (Oxford, 1777), p. 22.
169 *Ibid.*, p. 23.

ful 'in proportion as this *will* approaches to universality'.[170] Like Brown, Shebbeare argued that religion 'effected' the 'unity of sentiments and of will' and thus 'preserved entire' the 'strength and morality of the *whole* community'.[171] Shebbeare turned to a thought experiment and then, specifically, to the issue of religious liberty. If someone were to poison London's water supply, he wrote, there would be a demand for punishment. Why should opinions 'which poison the sources of moral and civil obligation, and alike destroy the felicity of individuals and of the whole community' not be treated similarly? Justification of private judgment at the expense of the destruction of the community, Shebbeare exploded, was an 'Abominable contradiction!'. Freedom of thought, under these conditions, was merely a cover for treason.[172]

An astute, if vicious, polemicist, Shebbeare targeted Price's moral realism as the root of all evil. Clarke's dangerous heritage had been adopted by his fellow Arian and shaped into a deadly political charge. Like Nathaniel Forster in the toleration debate, Shebbeare questioned the social value of emphasizing something upon which few people could ever agree:

But *truth*, it seems, is a thing so hallowed, that its progress, on no occasion, ought to be obstructed. I readily coincide in that sentiment; and yet, I verily believe that the words, *truth, liberty*, and *reason*, have proved to be more pernicious to the *happiness* of individuals and to national society, than all the *exertions* of arbitrary power that ever have existed.

If the Clarkean terms were now being wielded as weapons in a war against the practice of ecclesiastical and imperial polity it could only be as a result of a set of unproved assumptions. Chief among them was the belief that practical political obligations could be derived from a natural law. In the absence of the Analogy, Barbeyrac's question about the relationship between natural law and political obligation remained a haunting one: 'But, what is *truth*? It certainly cannot consist in such conclusions, from the same premises, as every man may form, in consequence of his *own* peculiar *mode* of thinking.'[173]

If the 'truth' of the dissenters and reformers was not some universal accessible to reason, what was it? They had employed a thick account of natural rights in order to trump the government's pru-

---

[170] Shebbeare, *Essay*, p. 21.   [171] *Ibid.*, p. 49.   [172] *Ibid.*, pp. 52–6.
[173] *Ibid.*, pp. 50–1; Nathaniel Forster, *The Establishment of the Church of England*, p. 16.

dential justification of the reason of state. Its defenders, in turn, spelled out still more explicitly the force of post-Reformation Ciceronian policy. Truth, Shebbeare wrote,

consists in the objects of them being adapted to the *utility* of man. By this test alone, the institutes of morality and civil government can be fairly tried, and the truth of them determined. If, therefore, the *truth* of sensible, moral, and legislative objects depend on the *utility* and *rectitude* of them, and on this adaptation to the benefit of *civil* society; those of *faith*, being adapted in an equally useful and beneficial manner, are equally true; and the application of them must be equally *right*. And, as it is justly inferred, from that adaptation and utility to man, that the former are *right* or *true*; by the faculty of reason, the latter are equally intitled to the like approbation. Whatever, then, is *useful*, in all these objects, is equally true.[174]

Natural equality never existed and never could exist. It was not even to be found in the ancient republics, whose liberty was so praised. Athens, which, as we have argued, was an exemplar for defenders of individual rights, was declared no better than modern Britain.[175] Those who rejected a natural right to private judgment for fear that it would legitimate equality among men believed naturally unequal. And since there were natural inequalities it was, therefore, unnatural to presuppose an equality of ability.[176] Because the masses knew liberty as 'lawlessness', their rule could only produce 'Anarchy and confusion'.[177]

Ironically, because Price upheld the completely novel position that the individual remained the acting sovereign in political society, he was often seen as giving democracy as the answer to the classical enquiry about the best form of government. Strong assertions of individualism were assimilated to a strong assertion of popular sovereignty. We have examined this 'slippage' in the case of Locke where, moving in the opposite direction, the individual rights arguments of the 1760s and 1770s were read back into his text. Consequently, it was possible for defenders of the common good to

[174] Shebbeare, *Essay*, p. 52.
[175] Lind, *Three Letters to Dr Price*, p. 49 note 'n'. Additional attacks on the inequality of ancient Greek democracy are found in Hutchinson, *Experience Preferable to Theory*, p. 8; *Remarks on Dr Price's Observations*, pp. 31, 52; Ferguson, *Remarks on a Pamphlet*, p. 9; Gray, *Dr Price's Notions*, p. 21; Shebbeare, *Essay*, pp. 34, 36; *Cursory Remarks*, p. 2. For criticism of Spartan and Roman liberty, see Lind, *Three Letters to Dr Price*, pp. 46, 76–7 and 84.
[176] *Honour of Parliament*, p. 11; [Moir], *Obedience the Best Charter*, p. 17. 'Give the helm into the hands of so many unskilful pilots – The vessel would deviate from its course, and soon be a-ground' (Hutchinson, *Experience Preferable to Theory*, p. 11).
[177] *Remarks on Dr Price's Observations*, pp. 3, 6; *Honour of Parliament*, p. 5.

attack Price's individual rights as an abuse of Locke's meaning. Price had identified his principles with Locke, writing in the preface to the fifth edition of the *Observations* that the principles of his discussion of free states 'are the same with those taught by Mr Locke, and all the writers on Civil Liberty who have been hitherto most admired in this country'. Henry Goodricke denied there to be any theoretical similarity between Price and the esteemed Locke: 'Where does Locke teach such principles, and who are those most admired writers?'[178] The 'Editor's advertisement' in Goodricke's tract had compared Price's *Observations* with Filmer's *Patriarcha* but at the opposite end of the spectrum: 'Between these two are several mediums, which Reason and Experience recommend, and which have the sanction of Mr Locke and of the most esteemed writers on Civil Government.'[179]

There were also general condemnations of the Americans' practice of wrapping themselves in the mantle of Locke. Lind explained that the restrictive regulations governing the colonial charters 'were first made at a time that Mr Locke sat at the Board; that great man, whose arguments the Americans have so tortured, in order to press them into the service of rebellion'.[180] But there were also very perceptive comments, focusing on highly ambiguous points in Locke such as his defence of legislative supremacy and the royal prerogative. Goodricke cited Locke's statement ' "that the Legislative is, IN ALL CASES, whilst the Government subsists, SUPREME" ' as support for parliament's position against Price's assertion that individuals remained supreme in civil society.[181] Shebbeare chimed in that 'those who prate of Locke, respecting his inclination to democracy, have never examined and compared with it, what he says of the prerogative royal: or they never could, with justice, have applied him, to serve their purposes, as they have done'.[182]

If some saw Price as an ungrounded innovator, others attacked him for clinging to old-fashioned English commonwealth ideology. By contending that an independent legislature was a prerequisite for a state being free of another's control, Price seemed to endorse a specific form of government. Moreover, history recorded that those nations which hewed most closely to his definition of liberty, namely republics, all encroached upon the property and personal liberty of

---

[178] Goodricke, *Observations on Dr Price's Theory*, pp. 113–14.   [179] *Ibid.*, sig. |a1|v.
[180] Lind, *Answer to the Declaration of Independence*, p. 86.
[181] *Ibid.*, pp. 37n, 38.   [182] Shebbeare, *Essay*, p. 175.

their citizens.[183] Goodricke played on the substantive difference between Price and Priestley to emphasize the total implausibility of any direct, participatory government: 'I can by no means agree to this sentiment, and think rather with Doctor PRIESTLEY, – that such a pure Democracy is not only not possible, except in exceeding small states, but that, if practicable, it would not be generally for the good of mankind'.[184] Priestley's definition of liberty in the *Essay*, and his convergence on Montesquieu's notion of *sûreté*, was taken up by those critics of Price who saw in his metaphysical support for natural equality political support for participatory democracy:

Give us liberty of property and personal liberty; we mean freedom of person and freedom of action according to the laws, which we formerly enjoyed. We have not time to trouble ourselves about who are the law-makers: we wish only to live under that government where liberty of property and personal liberty are most regarded.[185]

Ferguson rejected Price's implication that liberty and restraint were mutually exclusive. The end of government 'is to give people security from the effect of crimes and disorders, and to preserve the peace of mankind', not to promote liberty. Ferguson's suggestion that freedom from restraint, rather than constituting liberty, actually produced slavery was ultimately based on Montesquieu's distinction between liberty and independence:

The Liberty of any single man, in this sense of a freedom from restraint, would be the servitude of all. In Turkey, perhaps in Brandenburgh, there are persons who pretend to this Liberty; but I believe that no one can devise a more plentiful source of slavery than this. The Liberty of every separate district or corporation in a state would be national independence . . .[186]

This same argument lay behind Wesley's claim that 'The greater share the people have in the government, the less liberty, either civil or religious does the nation in general enjoy.'[187] Where Price believed that liberty was achieved where each person served as his own governor, Ferguson asserted that security was protected by a

---

[183] Gray, *Dr Price's Notions*, pp. 8, 10.
[184] Goodricke, *Observations on Dr Price's Theory*, p. 99.
[185] Gray, *Dr Price's Theory*, p. 12. Priestley had written that 'It is comparatively of small consequence, *who*, or *how many* be our governors, or *how long* their office continues, provided their power be the same while they are in office, and the administration be uniform and certain' (*Essay*, p. 49).
[186] Ferguson, *Remarks on a Pamphlet*, p. 3.   [187] Wesley, *Some Observations on Liberty*, p. 20.

representation composed of those best able to serve the nation. 'It is less material who elects, than it is who may be elected.'[188] Virtue and religion were anchors capable of withstanding 'the greatest Storms and Tempests that can beat upon a State'. Britain's problem was that the current storms were the product of a weak and corrupted religion. Cooper's solution was humiliation and fasting in order to bring about repentance and a changed national 'character'.[189] This certainly reflects Paul Langford's description of the clerical reaction to the perceived threat to the state in the decade subsequent to the outbreak of the American War. Gascoigne has written of a 'clash of principles' in the mid-1770s that was characterized by a rejection of contract theory for more concrete ties of obedience. Bradley, too, has described a 'new authoritarianism' which aimed 'to strengthen respect for government', especially the crown, and 'emphasized trusting the political judgement of social superiors'.[190] An aspect of this response was to strengthen the power of the ecclesiastical establishment in Britain and advocate its extension to North America since the 'peace of the whole empire' also depended on 'the exclusion of dissenters from places of trust'.[191]

Another characteristic of the political debate set in motion by the publication of Price's tract was the introduction of utilitarian political arguments.[192] These occupied a middle ground since they retained a weaker notion of community while stripping away both the metaphysical and rights-based justifications of individual sover-

---

[188] Ferguson, *Remarks on a Pamphlet*, p. 13. Another distinction between Price and Priestley may be usefully elaborated here. Where Price had defended the importance of an alteration of men in order to assure proper measures, Priestley demurred. 'They will, also, consider, that unless their measures be perfectly well laid, and their success decisive, ending in a change, not of *men*, but of *things*; not of governors, but of the rules and administration of government, they will only rivet their chains the faster, and bring upon themselves and their country tenfold ruin' (*Essay*, p. 31).

[189] Cooper, *National Humiliation*, p. 4.

[190] Paul Longford, 'The English Clergy and the American Revolution', *The Transformation of Political Culture*, ed. Eckhart Hellmuth (Oxford, 1990), pp. 275–308; Gascoigne, *Cambridge in the Age of Enlightenment* (Cambridge, 1989), p. 210; Bradley, *Religion*, p. 25; Colley, *Britons*, ch. 4.

[191] Stevens, *Revolution Vindicated*, pp. 67–8.

[192] 'Utilitarianism is a normative theory which holds that moral and legal rules are acceptable to the extent that their acceptance and enforcement promote happiness. It is hostile to doctrines of "natural right", holding that legal rights must be a matter of positive law, and that "moral rights" are explicable as liberties and powers which individuals ought to have in order to promote their most important interests' (Alan Ryan, *Property* (Milton Keynes, 1987), p. 53). This is very different from the arguments about utility in eighteenth-century moral philosophy, which remain bound up with just the sort of metaphysical assumptions that utilitarianism excluded.

eignty and the older discussions of forms of government, leaving only the double-edged, prudential argument about the most efficient operation of government. Cicero's defence of the *utilitas rei publicae* remained anchored by his commitment to the *res publica*; the theorists of the reason of state and science of politics retained this perspective while dispensing with the belief that it was best assured by a particular form of government. In the *Observations* of Richard Hey (1745–1835), Fellow of Sidney Sussex and Magdalene Colleges, Cambridge, essayist and mathematician, the content of the common good had become extremely diluted. On the 'ground of Utility' people had simply to 'submit to the Difficulty and Necessity of human affairs, and content themselves with studying to avoid the greatest Mischief'. This was the purpose of a civil society.[193] Hey believed that most people would be satisfied with Priestley's liberty from invasive government if they could be assured that legislation would be as limited as possible. This solution diminished the need for participatory government and hence cut the ground out from beneath what he believed Price to be articulating. Priestley's concern to limit the intervention of government in areas where its operation was inefficient became, in Hey's language, the standard utilitarian assertion that laws were necessary evils and that the fewer of them the better. The marriage of this view of law and liberty to the older notion of the public good as the measure of social life transformed that conventional discussion of politics:

We seem then to be arrived at one useful principle by which a legislature may guide itself in the formation of laws: To avoid, as much as possible, multiplying restraints upon the Subject. This principle leads to the point of Perfection in Civil Liberty. It is the nature of Society that each member of it can only be allowed to pursue his own happiness in a manner consistent with that of the other members; or we may say, that he ought to procure his private Good through the Medium (as it were) of the public Good. Wherever that does not require him to be curbed, our Principle would leave him as free as he himself can wish or conceive. If he is ambitious of being more free than the public Good will allow, he forgets surely that he is a member of Civil Society.[194]

John Lind's *Three Letters to Dr Price* was begun in collaboration with Jeremy Bentham, but was completed by Lind alone. Not for

[193] Richard Hey, *Observations on the Nature of Civil Liberty, and Principles of Government* (London, 1776), no. 86, p. 49.
[194] *Ibid.*, no. 98, p. 56.

nothing has he been called 'the earliest Benthamite'.[195] Interestingly, it would seem that Bentham's arguments were introduced into
British political discussion largely in response to Price's metaphysical concept of liberty. Lind and Bentham coined the derisory
term 'positive' liberty to describe the employment of Clarke's fundamental notions of 'self-direction' and 'self-government'. 'I think,
that you take liberty, or (as you explain it, or mean to explain it)
spontaneity or self-government, for something positive.'[196] Again,
'The truth is, Sir, you set out with a capital mistake. It is a capital
mistake to suppose liberty to be anything positive.'[197] Price's
'general idea' of 'self-direction or self-government' was the stum-
bling block.[198] This afforded Lind and Bentham a platform to voice
their own concept of liberty as the 'absence of coercion', with
'coercion' defined as the power to constrain or restrain.[199] In a long
footnote Lind attributed this distinction to Bentham, an anonymous, but 'very worthy and ingenious friend':

That liberty is nothing positive, that it means only the absence of restraint,
was an idea first suggested to me by a very worthy and ingenious friend,
whose name I am not now permitted to mention. In turning this idea over
in my mind, I thought the definition imperfect; a man may be compelled to
do as well as to forbear an act; liberty therefore I thought meant the absence
of constraint, as well as of restraint. I mentioned this some time after to my
friend from whom I received the original idea; he had already perceived
the defect, and had substituted the general term of coercion to the partial
one of restraint. it was on many accounts necessary to make this acknow-
ledgement; on one more specially, that this notion of liberty will make a
leading principle in a work which this gentleman means, and I hope soon,
to give the world.[200]

Since both the body and the mind were susceptible of coercion,
liberty constituted the freedom from both physical and mental
coercion.[201] On this account, liberty was neither innate nor a
natural right. For there to be a natural right, there had to be a
natural law, yet Bentham and Lind scoffed at moral realism: 'But

---

[195] Margaret Avery, 'Toryism in the Age of American Revolution: John Lind and John
Shebbeare', *Historical Studies*, 18 (1978), 25.
[196] Lind, *Three Letters to Dr Price*, p. 10.   [197] *Ibid.*, pp. 14, 25.
[198] *Ibid.*, p. 15. The received view is 'that people in the eighteenth century did not distinguish
between what today is termed "positive liberty" and "negative liberty"' (John Phillip
Reid, *The Concept of Liberty in the Age of the American Revolution* (Chicago, 1988), p. 56).
[199] Lind, *Three Letters to Dr Price*, p. 16.   [200] *Ibid.*, p. 16n.
[201] *Ibid.*, p. 18. The definition is repeated at p. 20.

where is the Law of Nature to be found? Who has produced it?'[202]
Lind argued that the phrase had no legal meaning but simply
referred to 'imaginary regulations' which appeared 'expedient'.[203]
How then was it to be derived? Bentham's role here went unacknow-
ledged. Rights to anything, whether liberty, land or possessions,
could only be derived from law:

How is it that a man acquires a right to do, or to forbear any act? By the
declaration of the legislator, that he may do or forbear it; joined to a
promise of the legislator, expressed or implied, that he will restrain every
other person from constraining him to forbear the one or to do the other.[204]

Without the support of natural rights, there could be no shift to
the sovereignty of the individual. Indeed, Lind and Bentham
explicitly contended that the 'utility' and 'happiness' (not the
'rights') of individuals were compatible with the sovereignty of law
and legislators.[205] Some years later, Paley's elaboration of the implications of utilitarian political thought for the contemporary debate
on the relative priority of the community and the individual made
plain the continuing impact of Cicero on the shape of this particular
discussion:

To do what we will is natural liberty; to do what we will, consistently with
the interest of the community to which we belong, is civil liberty; that is to
say, the only liberty to be desired in a state of civil society . . . The definition
of civil liberty above laid down, imports that the laws of a free people
impose no restraint upon the private will of the subject, but what conduce
in a greater degree to the public happiness: by which it is intimated, 1st,
that restraint itself is an evil; 2dly, that this evil ought to be overbalanced
by some public advantage . . .[206]

The Grotian division between the liberty of communities and individuals is supplemented by a new description of law, one also found
in Richard Hey's contemporary tract. Lind and Bentham argued
that there could be no control over the legislators since that implied
the logical impossibility that the makers of sovereign law were
themselves unfree. Law was an expression of the will of the governors and it was neither likely nor possible 'that they should give
liberty against themselves'.[207] Bentham was even to replace Blackstone's traditional notion of unitary sovereignty with a 'habit of

---

[202] *Ibid.*, p. 22.   [203] *Ibid.*, p. 23.   [204] *Ibid.*, p. 21.   [205] *Ibid.*, p. 26.
[206] Paley, *Principles*, pp. 441–2.
[207] Lind, *Three Letters to Dr Price*, p. 69.

obedience'. This can, of course, be seen as a more rigorous application of Hume's destruction of the original contract than Blackstone's
own. What was described as 'sovereignty' reflected only the people's
disposition to obey.[208] With a rare turn to history, Lind and
Bentham asserted that even the slightest amount of popular control
only diminished the actual freedom of individuals:

> The very attempt to do it, I mean directly and openly, would be destruc-
> tive of civil liberty, properly so called; of that liberty, I mean, which we
> have just described, and which only should be called by this name: For the
> truth of this I may appeal to the history of Rome in ancient days, to that of
> Poland in our own. In both these states, in proportion as the power of the
> governors has been openly and directly checked, the civil liberty of the
> subject has been checked with it. The governors, as such, could not indeed
> infringe the liberty of the subject, but then neither could they protect the
> accused against the abuse of power on the part of the magistrate nor the
> feeble against the oppression of the more powerful individual.[209]

If liberty was the absence of coercion and law was the primary
instrument of coercion, then liberty could not be described as
freedom under law, as was customary. Instead of dubious 'liberty',
Lind's citizens possessed 'civil or political security'. This turned the
arguments of Grotius and Montesquieu against the commonwealth
trope evoked by Price's metaphysical liberty. Without security there
was no possibility that individuals could realize any happiness.[210]
The most complete security was the product of the complete identification of the interests of governors and governed. Here the appeal is
to the version of the science of politics promoted by John Campbell
and Hume, among others. Thus, perfect security consisted in the
coincidence of interests and this, in turn, resulted in 'the greatest.
happiness of the greatest number':

> In a free state, besides civil or political liberty, the subject enjoys what is
> often confounded with it, though very different from it; I mean civil or
> political security. This security arises not from any limitation of the
> supreme power, but from such a distribution of the several parts of it, as
> shall best insure the greatest happiness of the greatest number. If this
> distinction could be so made, as to render the interests of the governors and
> governed perfectly undistinguishable, this end would be completely

---

208 Burns, 'Bentham and Blackstone: A Lifetime's Dialectic', *Utilitas*, 1 (1989), 32; H. L. A.
Hart, 'Sovereignty and Legally Limited Government', *Essays on Bentham. Studies in Jurisprudence and Political Theory* (Oxford, 1982), p. 221.
209 Lind, *Three Letters to Dr Price*, pp. 69–70.
210 Rosen, 'Origin of Liberal Utilitarianism', pp. 59–61.

obtained, and the subject would enjoy perfect political security: this security is more or less perfect, as these interests are more or less indistinguishable.[211]

For Lind and Bentham, individuals could be constrained or restrained by law. Those upon whom law did not operate remained free. This was the antithesis of Blackstone's comment that laws were actually 'introductive of liberty'.[212] If liberty could be defined as the residue of legislation, civil or political 'security' was achieved by the actions of the supreme power designed 'to produce the greatest happiness of the greatest number'.[213] If, however, security depended upon the action of magistrates, then Lind and Bentham had to answer the question of resistance. 'How then are the people to be assured that the powers of government will be applied to the production of the greatest happiness of the greatest number?' Lind concluded that the only solution was in the separation of powers and a limit on terms of service.[214] But without any sense of the sovereignty of the rights-bearing individual this was not to be understood as resembling the demands of Price and others nor acknowledging government as a trust. 'The people have not, it is true, the power of controuling the elected class of governors by any positive act of theirs; nor, if they had it, could they ever more properly apply it.'[215] Lind and Bentham seem to have used Price's *Observations on Civil Liberty*, with its justification of civil and religious liberty, as the platform for launching a wide-ranging redefinition of the bases of social life.

William Paley's rigorous attack on Price's line of argument in his Cambridge textbook, *Principles of Moral and Political Philosophy*, based on lectures given at Christ's College from 1768–75, reflects the scepticism about moral realism that suffused the tract of Lind and Bentham and which characterized the early utilitarian writings of Bentham. Clarke's tradition of moral psychology is accurately described, but for the purpose of parody:

Because it is right, says one. – Because it is agreeable to the fitness of things, says another. – Because it is conformable to reason and nature, says a third. – Because it is conformable to truth, says a fourth. – Because it promotes the

---

[211] Lind, *Three Letters to Dr Price*, pp. 72–3. The reader is also referred to Bentham's *Fragment on Government*, ch. 4.
[212] Blackstone, *Commentaries*, I, p. 125.   [213] Lind, *Three Letters to Dr Price*, p. 87.
[214] *Ibid.*, pp. 89–90.
[215] *Ibid.*, p. 93.

public good, says a fifth. – Because it is required by the will of God, concludes a sixth.[216]

Because of his resistance to moral realism Paley rejected the claim of 'those writers who insist upon representation as a natural right'. Since there could be no legitimate appeal to abstract moral entities, the only means of justifying representation was in so far 'as it conduces to public utility; that is, as it contributes to the establishment of good laws, or secures to the people the just administration of these laws'.[217] This standard of measurement rested upon Paley's 'criterion of utility'. Grappling with the fundamental question for those early modern writers who sought to understand and also direct the political force of the new entity of the state, one we have seen encountered by Grotius, Pufendorf, Barbeyrac and the English and Scottish writers, Paley asked, 'Must we admit these actions to be right, which would be to justify assassination, plunder, and perjury, or must we give up our principle, that the criterion of right is utility?' In response, Paley relied on the early modern reading of Cicero, the one challenged by Price in the *Review*: 'these actions after all, are not useful, and for that reason, and that alone, are not right'.[218]

Thus, on the issue of religious toleration, Paley, who had defended his teacher Edmund Law's tolerationist tract in 1774, contended that private judgment could not be defended by reliance on an evanescent natural law. Those, like himself, who doubted the existence of some state of pristine equality and who refused to 'allow an arbitrary fiction to be made the foundation of real rights and of real obligations' had to find another foundation. The utilitarian response to Barbeyrac suggested that the 'general utility' of a community determined the legitimate freedoms of its members:

The reasoning which deduces the authority of civil government from the will of God, and which collects that will from public expediency alone, binds us to the unreserved conclusion, that the jurisdiction of the magistrate is limited by no consideration but that of general utility: In plainer terms, that whatever be the subject to be regulated, it is lawful for him to interfere, whenever his interference, in its general tendency, appears to be conducive to the common interest. There is nothing in the nature of religion, as such, which exempts it from the authority of the legislator, when the safety or welfare of the community require his interposition.[219]

---

[216] Paley, *Principles*, pp. 47–8.   [217] *Ibid.*, p. 487.   [218] *Ibid.*, p. 62.
[219] *Ibid.*, pp. 571.

Paley's assertion that civil intervention in religion was always for temporal reasons helps us perceive the force of Priestley's move to exclude civil intervention on the grounds of inefficiency rather than teleology.

Restraints on liberty are justifiable when they 'conduce in a greater degree to the public happiness'. Paley sketched the implications of this general rule. Because 'restraint itself is an evil' it had 'to be overbalanced by some public advantage'. The legislature was obliged to demonstrate the 'proof of this advantage' since 'it is not enough to say that a law is harmless; its being a law is a harm'. Paley's attitude towards law broke radically with that of Blackstone, who would never have described law, irrespective of content, as an 'evil'.[220]

Rather, following Grotius, Paley defined liberty as security and so distinguished between the liberty of persons and of states (Grotius' 'individual' and 'civil' liberty and Priestley's 'civil' and 'political' liberty). As security, liberty was defined as not merely being free from the 'constraint of useless and noxious laws' but in 'being free from the danger of having any such [useless and noxious laws] hereafter imposed or exercised'. This marked the limit of legitimate invasiveness. He analyses Sweden's loss of liberty in the terms forged by Grotius, Montesquieu and Priestley:

What then have they lost? They have lost the power and functions of their diet; the constitution of their states and orders, whose deliberation and concurrence were required in the formation and establishment of every public law; and thereby have parted with the security they possessed against any attempts of the crown to harrass its subjects, by oppressive and useless exertions of prerogative. The loss of this security we denominate the loss of liberty. They have not changed their laws, but their legislature; not their enjoyment, but their safety; not their present burthens, but their prospects of future grievances: and this we pronounce a change from the condition of freemen to that of slaves.[221]

THE POLITICAL ECONOMY OF THE INDIVIDUAL

The attack on Price sought to preserve the notion of a unitary, metropolitan common good. Adam Smith emerged from a different quarter, but his challenge to the political-economic expression of this underlying premise was to prove devastating. Some of the

---

[220] *Ibid.*, p. 442.   [221] *Ibid.*, pp. 444–5.

reformers, like Cartwright and Burgh, had described commercial regulation as an example of Britain's imperial misrule. Yet, precisely because of their other commitments, this economic insight had little impact on contemporaries. Not so with the powerful criticisms of Smith and Josiah Tucker. According to Smith, England's treasure was not in foreign trade, as had been alleged by the seventeenth-century English counterparts of the Spanish *arbitristas*, but domestic production.[222] Specie was a token of exchange bearing no relation to the domestic capacity for production and having no intrinsic value.[223] Consequently, the importance of a putative 'balance of trade' was chimerical.[224] The policy of competing for trade had often provoked international conflict, derisorily called 'commercial warfare'. Josiah Tucker's condemnation of this type of war was unmatched. The very nature of war made it a counter-productive means of accumulating trade and wealth:

A War, whether crowned with Victory, or branded with Defeats, can never prevent another Nation from being more industrious than you are; and if they are more industrious, they will sell cheaper; and consequently your former Customers will forsake your Shop, and go to theirs; tho' you covered the Ocean with Fleets and the Land with armies: – In short, the Soldier may make Waste, the Privateer, whether successful or unsuccessful, will make Poor; but it is the eternal Law of Providence that the Hand of the Diligent alone can make Rich.[225]

According to Tucker, 'both the conquering and conquered countries, are prodigious Losers' when resorting to warfare, while foreign markets were agnostic about the origin of goods, caring only for cost. The cheapest goods, even if produced by the least glorious nation, would still be purchased first.[226] This 'Trade of War' would, if pushed to its logical conclusion, result in civil anarchy: 'there is no one Argument for inducing Nations to fight for the sake of trade, but which would oblige every Country, Town, Village, nay, and every Shop among ourselves, to be engaged in civil and intestine wars for the same End'.[227]

A characteristic means of enforcing this economic perspective was

---

[222] Smith, *WN*, IV.i.10, p. 435.
[223] *Ibid.*, IV.i.11, p. 435; IV.i.17, p. 438; 'Early Draft', *LJ*, ¶40, p. 578.
[224] Smith, *WN*, IV.iii.a.2, p. 475. He wanted to replace the balance of trade with a balance of production (IV.iii.c.17, p. 497).
[225] Tucker, *Four Tracts*, pp. 41–2.   [226] Tucker, *The Case of Going to War*, pp. 9, 40.
[227] *Ibid.*, p. 34. See also *The Essay on the Times* (London, 1756), pp. 17, 20; *Naked Truth* (London, 1755), pp. 8–10.

through the use of sanctioned monopolies. Even many writers other-wise kindly disposed towards a planned economy rejected the use of monopoly.[228] For them, and for thinkers like Hume and Tucker, monopolies disrupted natural relationships of initiative and com-petition. Monopoly, according to Hume, typified a primitive state of commerce in which nations sought to preserve goods for themselves without recognizing that by hoarding they were actually limiting their future enjoyment. '. . . the more is exported of any commodity, the more will be raised at home, of which they themselves will always have the first offer'.[229] Tucker reviled monopolies for elimi-nating the competition that brought with it improvements in life: 'Where then can be the Motive to excel, when Emulation is stifled, and the idlest Blockhead, if free of a Corporation, is preferred to the most ingenious and industrious Artist that is not free?'[230] Robert Wallace's comment that 'where trade is beneficial to the public, there a monopoly is of the most ruinous consequences' shows how a more individuated conception of 'public' was capable of hoisting an economic conception of security by its own theoretical petard.[231] It was in this context that Pownall formulated a law of supply and demand: 'From the natural state and order of things, I think it may be affirmed, that the worth or price of anything will always be, as the quantity and uses amongst mankind; as the uses directly, and as the quantity reciprocally or inversely.'[232] Pownall expressly linked this to a conception of transcendent, natural laws which guided all fields of human endeavour.

The rules of natural justice flowing from our fixed and unchangeable relations to each other, and the invariable nature and order of things, inforced by the express commands of God, are of eternal and indispensable obligation. No laws, no combinations of human power, customs, usages, or practice, can control or change them.[233]

Smith's attack on monopolies was made against commercial regu-lation, writ large, in the name of 'natural liberty'.[234] The danger of national competition for finite resources was nowhere better

---

[228] Burgh wrote to George III, 'All monopolies are hurtful' (*Remarks*, p. 122. See also *Crito*, I, p. 36). Matthew Decker recognized that 'never yet was a Monopolized Trade extended to the degree of a Free one' (*Essay*, p. 23). See also, Newton, *The Influence of the Improvements*, p. 11.

[229] Hume, 'Of the Balance of Trade', *Essay*, p. 308. Also, *History*, IV, p. 374.

[230] Tucker, *The Elements of Commerce and Theory of Taxes* (Bristol, 1755), p. 85.

[231] Wallace, *A View of the Internal Policy of Great Britain*, p. 275.

[232] Pownall, *Administration* (1768), p. 191.

[233] *Ibid.*, p. 208.   [234] Smith, *WN*, IV.vii.c.88–98, pp. 630–3.

revealed than in its perverse consequences. 'Commerce, which ought naturally to be, among nations, as among individuals, a bond of union and friendship, has become the most fertile source of discord and animosity.'[235] In the *Lectures on Jurisprudence* Smith is recorded as saying that 'all commerce that is carried on betwixt any two countries must necessarily be advantageous to both'. Instead of resorting to commercial warfare, Smith proposed that the enrichment of neighbours should be encouraged. Such a nation could trade for 'a greater value, and to afford a better market . . . As a rich man is likely to be a better customer to the industrious people in his neighbourhood, than a poor, so is likewise a rich nation.' Their wealth also promoted competition, from which 'the great body of the people benefit'. Just as individuals moved to rich towns not poor provinces, richer neighbours were more useful than poorer ones:

> They know, that, where little wealth circulates, there is little to be got, but that where a great deal is in motion, some share of it may fall to them. The same maxims which would in this manner direct the common sense of one, or ten, or twenty individuals, should regulate the judgment of one, or ten, or twenty millions, and should make a whole nation regard the riches of its neighbours, as a probable cause and occasion for itself to acquire riches.[236]

Because Britain's policy towards North America was dominated by older commercial considerations, Smith's attack on the latter took the form of a critical analysis of the former. European colonies in the New World were unique in the entire history of colonization since they weakened rather than strengthened their respective metropoleis.[237] Though the metropoleis benefited from exclusive trading relationships, this, in turn, brought with it all the ills of monopoly. Unlike Pownall, Smith saw nothing advantageous in seizing any monopolistic 'lead'. Though the opening of the Western hemisphere offered the possibility of 'new divisions of labour and improvements of art', it had not happened. The conventional practice of the colonizing nations, namely, decreasing supply and increasing prices, had the effect of actually depressing the standard of living and slowing the progress of improvements. 'It is a dead weight upon the action of one of the great springs which puts into motion a great part of the business of mankind.' Colonies were damaged even more than were their parents.[238] Britain's own mono-

---

[235] *Ibid.*, IV.iii.c.9, p. 493.   [236] *Ibid.*, IV.,iii.c.11, pp. 494-5.
[237] *Ibid.*, IV.vii.c.11-12, p. 593.
[238] *Ibid.*, IV.vii.c.9, p. 592.

poly on colonial trade had 'broken altogether that natural balance' between various British industries and enterprises. In their race for quick profits merchants were directing resources in ways that would come to threaten both their future prosperity and that of Britain: 'Under the present system of management, therefore, Great Britain derives nothing but loss from the dominion which she assumes over her colonies.'[239] The Navigation Acts were the instrument of this disastrous policy. By contrast, progressive relaxation of the Navigation Acts, 'this truly shopkeeper proposal', would restore the trade to its natural, healthy and consequently more productive channels.[240]

Smith described the truculent North American colonies as 'appendages, as a sort of splendid and showy equipage of the empire'. But if the empire could no longer afford 'the expence of keeping up this equipage, it ought certainly to lay it down'. The failure of the colonies to adequately recompense the metropolis for the costs of imperial defence and management effectively disconnected the bonds of polity. 'The rulers of Great Britain have, for more than a century past, amused the people with the imagination that they possessed a great empire on the west side of the Atlantic. This empire, however, has hitherto existed in imagination only.'[241]

Because the move towards a 'free' trade came at the expense of state-managed commerce, it ought to be considered as an aspect of the articulation of an alternative to the prevailing model of the sovereignty of the community. Early modern political economy grew out of the effort to further the power and wealth of the state and critics of the economics tended to reject the overarching political theory as well. Free trade was explicitly linked to the political status of individuals.

Now any Trade may be said to be FREE, in which every Person may ingage if he pleases: And consequently those Trades are really confined, where the Liberty of exercising them is denied to some, tho' granted to others; or where the expence and Difficulties of obtaining this Liberty, are a great Burden and Discouragement.[242]

Burke described Grenville's efforts as a middle way between this individual-directed trade and the received mercantilist strategy: 'He conceived, and many conceived along with him, that the flourishing

---

[239] *Ibid.*, IV.vii.c.65, p. 616. Also, IV.vii.c.19, p. 595; IV.vii.c.43, pp. 604–6.
[240] *Ibid.*, IV.vii.c.44, p. 606; IV.vii.c.63, p. 614.
[241] *Ibid.*, v.iii, pp. 946–7.   [242] Tucker, *Elements of Commerce*, p. 80.

trade of this country was greatly owing to law and institution, and not quite so much to liberty; for but too many are apt to believe regulation to be commerce and taxes to be revenue.'[243] Priestley's emphasis on efficiency worked to vitiate government intervention in the personal and economic lives of its citizens. He suggested that as a rule 'no restrictions upon commerce are useful but such as obliged people to increase their own labour, and extend and improve their own manufactures'.[244] For Tucker, a version of the 'market' provided the 'efficient' self-regulating mechanism. Natural imbalances of goods and persons would correct themselves naturally over time, 'For such is the Rotation of human Affairs, Dearness begets Cheapness, and Cheapness Dearness.'[245]

Natural trading relations in economics, like natural rights for individuals in politics, provided the only legitimate first principles. Because Britain's policy towards her North American colonies was governed by the inadequate precepts dictated by a no longer common good, the economic and political aspects of their relationship were in crisis.[246] In this light, Smith's discussion of a reformed colonial trade could not but stress the resonant contemporary concepts of 'natural' and 'free' in both their political and economic sense:

> The effect of the colony trade in its *natural* and *free* state, is to open a great, though distant market for such parts of British Europe, and of the countries which lie round the Mediterranean sea. In its *natural* and *free* state, the colony trade, without drawing from those markets any part of the produce which had ever been sent to them, encourages Great Britain to increase the surplus continually, by continually presenting new equivalents to be exchanged for it. In its *natural* and *free* state, the colony trade tends to increase the quantity of productive labour ... In the *natural* and *free* state of the colony trade, the competition of all other nations would hinder the rate of profit from rising above the common level whether in the new market, or in the new employment.[247]

Smith's model for this kind of metropolis-colony relationship was none other than that of Greek colonization. Instead of competing economically and politically, mother and child parted 'good friends'

---

[243] Burke's speech on American taxation, quoted in Christie and Labaree, *Empire or Independence?*, p. 27.

[244] Priestley, *Lectures on History*, p. 332.   [245] Tucker, *Elements of Commerce*, p. 87.

[246] *Ibid.*, p. 99; Tucker, *A Brief Essay on the Advantages and Disadvantages which Respectively Attend France and Great Britain with Regard to Trade* (2nd edn, London, 1753), p. 56; *Instructions for Travellers* (London, 1757), pp. 13–14.

[247] Smith, *WN*, IV.vii.c.48, p. 608, emphasis added.

so that, in time, perhaps, 'the same sort of parental affection on the one side, and filial respect on the other, might revive between Great Britain and her colonies, which used to subsist between those of ancient Greece and the mother city from which they descended'. In the contemporary debate in which the defenders of British economic policy and its complementary political principles opted for Roman-style colonization, Smith's preference for the Greek might well have registered as favouring the individual over the community in matters of commerce and politics.[248]

Josiah Tucker and Adam Smith, the two most acute commentators on the economics of managing the North American colonies, offered their views on the proper metropolis–colony relationship in the context of analyses of human nature. The deep philosophical unity between free trade economics and individual rights-based politics is brought out most clearly in their conceptual equation of freedom of trade and freedom of thought.

Tucker maintained that among the fruits of a free commerce was free thought and that both, in turn, were incompatible with an interventionist central authority since 'Trade and Industry naturally create an independent Turn of Thinking' antithetical to arbitrary power.[249] The symbiosis of commerce and free thought also manifested itself, according to Tucker, in the relationship between religious persecution and commerce. Liberty of conscience, such as was possessed by all Englishmen, was ever conducive to the growth of trade, while history showed 'that Bigotry and Industry, Manufactures and Persecution' were mutually repulsive.[250] Like the free exchange of ideas, commerce speeded the perfection of the arts, a process Benjamin Newton termed the 'enlightening of the mind'.[251]

Tucker offered a lengthy deduction of the argument for free trade from certain principles of moral psychology. Humans first joined into societies to reap the benefits of mutual assistance and support. But, while solving certain problems, social life also introduced a new set of specifically social needs. Their pursuit was made necessary, according to Tucker, by the 'self-love' in all men. These desires often led to exclusive combinations aimed at procuring specific goods.

---

[248] *Ibid.*, IV.vii.c.66, p. 617.

[249] Tucker, *Elements of Commerce*, p. 151. This relationship led Benjamin Newton to describe the merchant as 'the philosopher, a citizen of the world', distributing ideas as well as goods, across the globe (*Another Dissertation*, p. 13).

[250] Tucker, *Elements of Commerce*, p. 81.

[251] Newton, *The Influence of the Improvements*, p. 9.

Tucker borrowed his description from the language of contemporary economic and political thought, likening this to the formation
of monopolies 'under the ridiculous and absurd pretence of the
Public Good, when, in Fact, private Advantage is the only Point
aimed at'.[252] The only way to correct that 'pretence of the Public
Good' was by individuals employing reason to channel 'self-love' in
useful directions. This created a real common good built from the
authentic interests of individuals: 'Consequently, the main Point to
be aimed at, is neither to extinguish nor enfeeble Self-Love, but to
give it such a Direction, that it may promote the public Interest by
pursuing its own.' In such a system individuals would pursue their
ends and serve the 'Good of the Whole' at the same time.[253] In
Tucker's argument, Campbell's own redefinition of the science of
politics is itself redefined according to the standard of individual,
rather than national, interest. Thus, legislators seeking to further the
nation's commerce could do no better than 'by a prudent Direction
of the Passion of self-Love to its proper Objects'. Policy-making
in this key would inexorably and unwittingly unite the interests of
individual and community without diminishing either one:

The Passion of Self-Love therefore must be taken hold of by some Method
or other; and so trained or guided in its Operations, that its Activity may
never be mischievous, but always productive of the public Welfare. When
Things are brought to that pass, the Consequence will be, that every
Individual (whether he intend it or not) will be promoting the Good of his
Country, and of Mankind in general, while he is pursuing his own private
Interest.[254]

Tucker's plan to 'remove those Obstructions' which blocked the
useful deployment of self-love implied granting a wider scope to
individual action, 'to set Mankind and Nature FREE: – Free, I mean,
in that Sense in which consists our true Liberty'.[255]

This same recognition of the free individual as the fundamental
datum of political and social thought was elaborated in the two
sermons appended to the *Four Tracts* (1774). There he observed that
the 'great End' of government was to promote the 'Good and
Happiness' of the governed. This was accomplished 'by causing each
Individual to conduct himself in such a Manner, as shall contribute
to the general good'. The common good was not perceived to be

252 Tucker, *Elements of Commerce*, p. 6.   253 *Ibid.*, p. 7.   254 *Ibid.*, p. 9.
255 Thus, he suggested manipulating self-love and not 'multiplying Laws relating to Commerce' (*ibid.*, p. 78).

secured in the first place either by good laws or by good institutions, but by individual action.

Tucker made the maxims of free trade the anchor for an entire philosophy of private life. The 'leading Idea' of commerce was that 'every Man should be allowed, and even encouraged to be industrious in all such Ways as will serve himself and the Public together'. This 'Freedom of Commerce' was the basis 'of private Industry' and also 'of national Prosperity and universal Plenty'.[256] Furthermore, the same 'Freedom of Commerce' also animated the proper organization of religion. 'For when you apply this Maxim to Religion, you will find, that it both keeps the Thoughts and Time of Mankind properly employed (an affair of infinite Consequence to Morality and Virtue) and also enables Men to do Good to others, whilst they are doing Good to themselves.'[257] Finally, he applied these conclusions about individuals and free trade to ascertaining the legitimate purview of government itself. Completely overturning the view that the citizen's first obligation was to serve the common, public good, Tucker argued that political communities only flourished as a consequence of the flourishing of their citizens.

Lastly, should you apply the same leading Idea to the Concerns of Government, you must see, you cannot help observing, that Government cannot make any tolerable Figure upon any other Plan. For Government is the Union of the interests of all the Individuals in one common Center; and if one Part of the Society is restrained by the other from being useful to the Community, the whole must suffer; and Tyranny and Oppression, Poverty and Slavery, more or less, must unavoidably take place.[258]

Tucker's search for a new organizing principle for society explicitly rejected the alternative proposed by the reformers. In his long-announced attack on Locke and those perceived to be his followers, Tucker recognized that demands for consent in politics and private judgment in religion were one and the same. Both elevated the role of the enquiring, deliberating individual to a position of pre-eminence at the expense of an undemocratically declared common good.

While many of his contemporaries saw this as an effect of religious heterodoxy alone, Tucker blamed Locke for these pernicious developments. Seeing that the government interfered in the affairs of religion far more than was necessary for its success, Locke had

---

[256] Tucker, 'Sermon I', *Four Tracts*, p. 14.   [257] *Ibid.*, p. 12.   [258] *Ibid.*, p. 14.

articulated a strong defence of the sphere of private judgment based on the 'ends' of civil society.[259] The problem was that he applied his conclusions to the realm of political thought. Could the claim of private judgment, with all that was packed into it, be accommodated to the nuance of political obligation? This was the issue for Tucker, who argued that 'the whole Merits of the Question depend on the single Point, whether the cases are parallel, or not'. If people could choose for themselves in religion they could choose for themselves in politics. But this extended the destabilizing effects of the toleration debate, itself a problem for Tucker (he favoured civil establishments for security reasons), to the even more precarious questions of politics. Locke had generalized

those Ideas, which were true only in what concerns Religion, to Matters of a mere civil nature, and even to the Origin of civil Government itself; – as if there had been the same Plea for Liberty of Conscience in disobeying the civil Laws of one's Country, as for not conforming to a Church Establishment, or an Ecclesiastical Institution; – and that the Rights of private Judgment (I mean the open and public Exercise of those Rights) were equally unalienable and indefeasible in both Respects. Indeed, it must be confessed, that, had the Cases been truly parallel, a Non-conformist in the one Case ought to have been tolerated equally with a Non-conformist in the other.[260]

Tucker credited Locke with first applying private judgment to political life and so creating the concept of freedom of thought. This, however, offered the possibility of nearly unlimited social dissent, for if there was an inalienable right to freedom of thought then all the ties of political obligation were undone.[261] Price's defence of 'self-Government' served as a lightning-rod for Tucker's critique, as it had for those who responded to him in 1776:

And then what is the Consequence? Necessarily this, That if the Cases between Religion and Civil Government be similar, as the Doctor supposes them to be, no one Individual can appoint another to judge for him, what Laws shall be propounded, what Taxes shall be raised, or what is to be done at Home or Abroad, in Peace, or in War: – But every Person, who has this indefeasible, this unalienable, incommunicable, and untransferable

---

[259] 'He saw the Rights of private Judgment exposed to continual Vexations; and he saw likewise, that the interests of the State were not at all concerned in maintaining that rigid, universal Conformity in Religion, for which the Bigots of those Times so fiercely contended; ... And hence he inferred, and very justly, that every Man had a Right not only to think, but even to act for himself, in all such religious Matters as did not oppose, or clash with the Interests of civil Society' (Tucker, *Treatise*, p. 30).

[260] *Ibid.*, pp. 30–1. [261] *Ibid.*, p. 33.

Right of voting, judging, and fighting, must vote, judge, and fight for himself.[262]

Tucker also saw that the new demands for parliamentary reform rested on this same conceptual foundation. Like many subsequent writers, he conflated Clarke's moral psychology and Locke's political philosophy, seemingly unaware that the rights-based political arguments of his contemporary 'Lockians' were actually founded on the metaphysical and epistemological concepts of the former: 'This Notion of the Necessity of an equal Representation, is grounded on that Lockian Idea of the *unalienable Right of each Individual to be Self-governed*; Notions, which I hope, have been sufficiently confuted.'[263]

Tucker recognized that the consequences of private judgment and consent amounted to a reworking of the familiar equation of liberties and obligations. 'So that the great Good of political Liberty, and the intolerable evil of political Slavery, are according to this blessed Doctrine, resolved at last into the single Words – CONSENT, or not consent.'[264] We know that the dissenters found Locke's views on religious liberty lacking, and that their enemies found support in Locke for their view of non-consensual politics.[265] Tucker is, then, a most important source for the identification of Locke with the program of the eighteenth-century reformers.

The turn to free trade economics was part of the broader discomfort with the overwhelming logic of the preservation and security of the state in the years following the Seven Years War. In a free, unmonopolized market, economic success depended on convincing individuals to buy a product, not on assertions of the common good. Hence Smith's dictum that 'Consumption is the sole end and purpose of all production; and the interest of the producer ought to be attended to, only so far as it may be necessary for promoting that

---

[262] *Ibid.*, p. 38.   [263] *Ibid.*, pp. 257–8.   [264] *Ibid.*, p. 140.
[265] The extent of Tucker's ahistoricity – and perhaps, by extension, that of subsequent scholars who followed in his assessment of Locke – is made indubitably clear in Joseph Towers' rebuttal of the attack on Locke. Towers was a dissenting supporter of the reformist cause, and saw Locke as an intellectual ancestor, but rejected Tucker's assertion that Locke had forged the liberal connection between private judgment and consent: 'Nor does it appear to have been the sentiment of Mr. Locke, that civil and religious rights were equally unalienable and indefeasible. It may, perhaps, be admitted, that there is some difference between civil and religious rights, and that a man may with less criminality sacrifice the former than the latter: and I know not that Mr. Locke has advanced any thing contrary to this opinion' (*A Vindication of the Political Purposes of Mr Locke* (London, 1782), pp. 42–3).

of the consumer.' Smith thought this self-evident, but recognized that in contemporary theory and practice things were upside-down: 'the interest of the consumer is almost constantly sacrificed to that of the producer'.[266] Smith noted that mercantilist economics was singularly incompatible with this new orientation. Instead, 'the boasted liberty of the subject' was routinely 'sacrificed to the futile interests of our merchants and manufacturers'.[267] While a freer trade increased the wealth and happiness of a state, centralized economic policy artificially elevated the price of goods and depressed individuals' happiness.[268] Smith stressed that economic prosperity sponsored by a freer trade increased the political 'freedom and independency' of the population.[269]

In a highly felicitous phrasing, Smith linked the 'savage patriotism' of the ancients, one of the most criticized characteristics of classical politics, to their narrow vision of the common good. Smith's analysis of modern European political thought set his emphasis on the primacy of the individual into stark relief. In antiquity, Cato the elder's *Carthago delenda est* reflected 'the savage patriotism of a strong but coarse mind', while Scipio Nasica's opposition 'was the liberal expression of a more enlarged and enlightened mind'. In modern times, however, Scipio's logic had more to recommend it:

France and England may each of them have some reason to dread the increase of the naval and military power of the other; but for either of them to envy the internal happiness and prosperity of the other, the cultivation of its lands, the advancement of its manufactures, the increase of its commerce, the security and number of its ports and harbours, its proficiency in all the liberal arts and sciences, is surely beneath the dignity of two such great nations. These are real improvements of the world we live in. Mankind are benefited, human nature is ennobled by them. In such improvements each nation ought, not only to endeavour itself to excel, but from the love of mankind, to promote, instead of obstructing the excellence of its neighbours.[270]

Smith's next step was crucial. By appropriating the concept of the 'natural' for his view of the true relationship between individuals and political communities, Smith forged a bond between economic

---

[266] Smith, *WN*, IV.viii.49, p. 660.   [267] *Ibid.*, IV.viii.47, p. 660.
[268] Smith, *LJ*, I, VI.84, p. 362.
[269] *Ibid.*, I, VI.6, p. 333. This is contrasted with the political oppression of the barons, those ruthless implementers of monopoly supporting their version of a 'common good' (*WN*, III.iv.4, p. 412).
[270] Smith, *The Theory of Moral Sentiments*, VI.ii.2.3, p. 228.

thought and the new view of human nature. Beyond the great irony of Smith's making even indirect common cause with the political reformers he so loathed, it is clear that, however disliked, the reformers were not intellectually isolated but must be seen as operating within the broader currents of political argument. Tucker and Smith could condemn the implications of their politics, but their arguments differ only in degree, while their common opposition to the philosophy underpinning government policy reflected substantial agreement. Smith suggested that citizens ought to be allowed their 'natural liberty of exercising what species of industry they please'.[271] To the individual natural right of political sovereignty, Smith added economic independence: 'To prohibit a great people, however, from making all that they can of every part of their own produce, or from employing their stock and industry in the way that they judge most advantageous to themselves, is a manifest violation of the most *sacred* rights of mankind ...[272] Just as he had equivocated on the matter of the Navigation Acts, here too, Smith was forced to admit that necessity was a natural law which knew no others: 'To hinder, besides, the farmer from sending his goods at all times to the best market, is evidently to sacrifice the ordinary laws of justice to an idea of publick utility, to a sort of reason of state; an act of legislative authority which ought to be exercised only, which can be pardoned only, in cases of most urgent necessity.'[273] Still, the great difference between Smith and those writers on political economy who addressed these questions over a century before is how limited are the conditions in which he was prepared to acknowledge that these reasons of state could be invoked. Twenty years before, Tucker had also asserted that the 'Monopolists themselves are violating the NATURAL RIGHTS of Mankind every Day ....[274] He, too, had isolated the key difference as the relative weight and power of the community's decision-making as against that of the individual. 'For, in Fact, the whole Difference consists in the Persons, that are to execute' the laws.[275]

Without the additional dimension presented by natural liberty, Smith's critique of what he called 'mercantilism', like Priestley's of sanctioned religious interventionism, would have been conducted in purely prudential terms. Like Priestley, Smith contended that the

---

[271] Smith, *WN*, IV.ii.42, p. 470.   [272] *Ibid.*, IV.vii.b.44, p. 582.
[273] *Ibid.*, IV.v.b.39, p. 530.
[274] Tucker, *Elements of Commerce*, p. 124.   [275] *Ibid.*, p. 81.

interventions of government planners had hampered, rather than increased its efficiency.[276] But it was by providing his defence of the individual with the sanction of nature that Smith, like Priestley, was to render his argument less vulnerable to the ideologists of the common good:

All systems either of preference or of restraint, therefore, being thus completely taken away, the obvious and simple system of natural liberty establishes itself of its own accord. Every man, as long as he does not violate the laws of justice, is left perfectly free to pursue his own interest his own way, and to bring both his industry and capital into competition with those of any other man, or order of men.[277]

And if Smith protected the individual by the attribution of natural rights, he explicitly and commensurately excluded the power of the public authority from those duties for 'which no human wisdom or knowledge could ever be sufficient': directing the interests of private citizens. Smith saw only three tasks for the civil ruler '[a]ccording to the system of natural liberty', defence against foreign invasion, the enforcement of justice and maintenance of selected public works.[278]

Smith used Colbert to distinguish his own system of 'natural liberty' from the latter's mercantilism. Smith described this system of natural relationships centred on the individual and not the community as 'liberal': 'instead of allowing every man to pursue his own interest his own way, upon the liberal plan of equality, liberty and justice, he bestowed upon certain branches of industry extraordinary privileges, while he laid others under extraordinary restraints'.[279] 'Generosity', in this political context, was to acquire more defined connotations. National wealth was best achieved by recognizing the individuals' capacity for innovation and initiative. Thus, another of the characteristics of the new political thought of the 1770s was defined: free trade.[280]

---

[276] Smith, *WN*, iv.ix.50, p. 687.   [277] *Ibid.*, iv.ix.51, p. 687.

[278] '... the duty of erecting and maintaining certain publick works and certain publick institutions, which it can never be for the interest of any individual, or small number of individuals, to erect and maintain; because the profit could never repay the expence of any individual, or small number of individuals, though it may frequently do much more than repay it to a great society' (*WN*, iv.ix.51, pp. 687–8).

[279] *Ibid.*, iv.ix.3, p. 664.

[280] 'According to this liberal and generous system, therefore, the most advantageous method in which a landed nation can raise up artificers, manufacturers and merchants of its own, is to grant the most perfect freedom of trade to the artificers, manufacturers and merchants of all other nations' (*ibid.*, iv.viii.24, p. 671).

Conclusion

The post-Reformation state, a political entity characterized by the need to keep joined necessity and morality in the formulation of policy and the practice of governing disparate political communities only recently united under a single head, did not die in 1776. Not in Britain and not on the Continent. But the revolutionary epoch that began in the 1770s and continued for the next fifty years does, indeed, mark the end of its creative, vital period. The profusion of a literature on the 'reason' of state accompanied the appearance in the sixteenth century of these powerful new entities which have, therefore, usually been assigned a causal role in its generation. But the problem of necessity preceded the early modern state by several thousand years. What changed was the emphasis on a certain aspect of politics, one which, I have argued, was intimately linked with the needs of post-Reformation states. With the focus on the competing claims of public and private utility Cicero returned to a new kind of prominence, no longer as the teacher of rectitude held up by the Church Fathers, nor the republican hero of the Quattrocento, but as the teacher of a moral prudence to be distinguished from the purely calculating Tacitean variety prevalent at this time. It was believed that the causes of conflict could be resolved by demonstrating that social life was itself impossible without the voluntary subordination of private aims to the claims of public utility. Individual self-preservation and, by extension, the preservation of the political communities which secured the lives of their inhabitants became the touchstone of political practice and its theoretical justifications. This is what was meant when writers on politics and politicians did homage to the common, or public, good.

But this entire argument remained contingent on their being a single community whose good, or utility, was clearly being served by the actions of the established government. Thus, the logic of the state placed limits on its spatial and emotional dimensions. The eighteenth-century clash of British state and British empire revealed the constraints of this framework for governance. It was now suggested that the determination of the common good had to be altered so as to include the far-flung and diverse interests of the vast expanse of empire. No one sought to 'eliminate' the common good because civil society was inconceivable without some centre in which individuals cohered. None the less, the development of a notion of the individual that demanded more of governors, or rather, demanded that governors stay clear of more of peoples' lives, and implicitly denied the political nature of much personal belief and practice, constituted a dramatically new definition of it. This new view of the individual's relation to his community is illustrated by the attempt to institutionalize individual representation and consent, which at once recognized the practical political sovereignty of the individual and at the same time placed him at one remove from the *vita activa*.

This was a debate internal to British culture. While Britain's imperial penumbra extended eastwards, southwards and further northwards, only the inhabitants of some of the western colonies could have made the arguments they did, because only they grew up in a tradition in which the contest to limit sovereignty was part of national myth. Even those whose birthplace was in one of the hundreds of distant parts from which flowed voyagers to the West had, by the later eighteenth century, come to feel enough a part of the British world to resent the British government's transparent attempt to seize their property. Moreover, the periodic conflicts and the ideological dimension of this contest between sovereign and citizens can be employed to mark the *longue durée* of state-building in Britain. Thus, the eighteenth-century revival of natural rights arguments by constitutional reformers and later by supporters of the French Revolution provoked accusations of 'levelling' that harked back to an earlier episode in the construction of the sovereign.

The ending of our story is, I recognize, a bit of a deceptive cadence. For the kind of state whose conceptual foundation was discussed in the first chapter and whose eighteenth-century British lifespan unfolded in the subsequent ones did not magically come to an end all at once. Even the seamlessness of historical change cannot, however, obscure two direct points of contact between the older and newer notions of individual and community.

Hugo Grotius had made the conflict between states and citizens central to his discussion of both personal morality and the law of nations. Necessity was nowhere more insistent than on the field of battle. The logic of self and national preservation could legitimately, but also ruthlessly, encroach upon the claims of other men, or states. It was common for statesmen and their spokesmen, even as they affirmed that nothing base could be either honest or useful, to note that, all the same, there were separate standards of morality for individuals in their private and public capacities. While acknowledging this fact, Grotius admonished those leaders never to assume invincibility, for 'there is no state so powerful that it may not some time need the help of others outside itself'.[1]

The Ciceronian discussion of *honestum* and *utile* was valuable precisely because it sketched the problem faced by governors of a composite state with official religions whose brief was both to conserve and to augment its power and wealth. The problems of international and domestic order were inextricably linked; aside from obvious reciprocal financial and social pressures, the conceptual foundation on which rested the Reformation state did not distinguish between them. As Grotius recognized, a strong state in a community of states, like a physically powerful individual living in a community, was still better off united with others. The colonial crisis and demand for toleration as a natural right challenged the principle of community which animated this conception of social life. Not only did Richard Price introduce the valuable distinction between *empire* and *kingdom*, he also showed how a reformed representation made possible a confederacy of states capable of covering the largest territory while preserving the liberty of individuals. He foresaw possibilities not only in the new American lands, but in Europe itself. Where it was now divided 'into a great number of independent kingdoms whose interests are continually clashing' and producing 'war and carnage', a confederal, representative senate offered the possibility of 'universal peace'.[2]

In the papers they produced in the wake of a convention designed to create the legal blue-print for this new type of state, Alexander Hamilton, John Jay and James Madison confronted the politics of necessity head-on and drew new conclusions about how best to secure this end. Jay, writing in *Federalist* no. 3, acknowledged that 'Among the many objects to which a wise and free people find it

---

[1] Grotius, 'Preliminary Discourse', *De Iure Belli*, xxi, p. xvii.
[2] Price, *Observations*, pp. 12–13.

necessary to direct their attention, that of providing for their *safety* seems to be the first.' Still, it was necessary to give a more precise definition if the historically double-edged character of this claim was to be avoided.[3] Jay limited it to 'security for the preservation of peace and tranquility' against foreign and domestic aggression. He continued by arguing that the creation of a single federal state was much more likely to eliminate the causes for the prosecution against the United States of a just war, while in the subsequent paper he also argued that the elimination of competing jurisdictions would reduce the occasions for foreign meddling and unjust wars. The argument for the structure of an American union employed the language of reason of state. 'As the safety of the whole is the interest of the whole, and cannot be provided for without government', the only question was whether one or many governments best delivered that security.[4] The analysis of union and security was based on a thorough appreciation of recent European history. Jay began the fifth *Federalist* with a discussion of Queen Anne's letter of 1 July 1706 to the Scottish parliament supporting the Anglo–Scottish Union. Union would provide 'the solid foundation of lasting peace' and, in addition to its social and commercial benefits, would enable the island 'to resist all its enemies'. Those who opposed it were enemies of Scotland and England, seeking to block the most 'effectual way to secure our present and future happiness'.[5] Interestingly, like Pownall so many years before, Jay also argued that political union followed inexorably from the convergence of existing 'interests' shared by seemingly distinct communities. Only the meddling of other nations had forestalled the earlier culmination of this process.[6]

Where Jay had focused on the danger of external aggression prompted by dissension within the confederacy, Alexander Hamilton followed by emphasizing the still more immediate risks of civil warfare. He denounced as 'far gone in Utopian speculation' those who believed that the independent states could live side by side without there arising the kind of squabbles that, speaking historically and in terms of human nature, frequently degenerated into armed conflict: 'But not withstanding the concurring testimony of

---

[3] 'The *safety* of the people has a relation to a great variety of circumstances and considerations, and consequently affords great latitude to those who wish to define it precisely and comprehensively' (*The Federalist Papers*, ed. Clinton Rossiter (New York, 1961), no. 3, p. 42).
[4] *Ibid.*, no. 4, p. 47. See also Lucio Levi, 'Il "Federalist" e la teoria della ragion di stato', *Il Pensiero Politico*, 21 (1988), 5–25.
[5] *The Federalist papers*, no. 5, p. 50.   [6] *Ibid.*, no. 5, pp. 50–1.

experience, in this particular, there are still to be found visionary or designing men, who stand ready to advocate the paradox of perpetual peace between the States, though dismembered and alienated from each other.' As in the account of Grotius two centuries earlier, the very neediness of human beings in their desperate struggle for self-preservation provided a model for the possible relations between states.[7] Just as warfare in a putative state of nature made the attainment of a 'good' life well nigh impossible, the consequences of international warfare imperilled the rule of law and the pursuit of happiness within states. The voice of necessity always spoke loudest:

Safety from external danger is the most powerful director of national conduct. Even the ardent love of liberty will, after a time, give way to its dictates. The violent destruction of life and property incident to war, the continual effort and alarm attendant on a state of continual danger, will compel nations the most attached to liberty to resort for repose and security to institutions which have a tendency to destroy their civil and political rights. To be more safe, they at length become willing to run the risk of being less free.[8]

Like many of his fellows, Hamilton was a student of modern European history. In the familiar scenario he sketched, 'The military state becomes elevated above the civil' and the preservation of those liberties so ardently sought after is fatally compromised.[9] The citizenship created by the American Revolution could only endure if the security of the community – never disregarded – could be maintained without recourse to the kind of intellectual and pragmatic defences that characterized the literature and action of early modern statecraft. The American union and the constitution which elaborated its shape was an institutional response to this problem. As Madison wrote in the paper that followed Hamilton's analysis of confederation, one could not count on statesmen 'to adjust these clashing interests and render them all subservient to the public good'.[10] However much the writers on prudence and statecraft had tried, they had failed to create a more peaceful, more prosperous and more free world for the inhabitants of Europe. With the inevitability of clashing interests and the resultant production of factions, some alternative to the enlightened statesman had to be sought.

Immanuel Kant, writing in the backwash of the French Revolution, drew many of the same conclusions as *Publius*. He, too,

[7] *Ibid.*, no. 6, pp. 54–9.   [8] *Ibid.*, no. 8, p. 67.   [9] *Ibid.*, no. 8, p. 70.
[10] *Ibid.*, no. 10, p. 80.

appears to posterity as one of the profound thinkers who engaged
with, and transformed, the debate about necessity and the reason of
state. Kant observed that 'The increasing culture of the states,
along with their growing tendency to aggrandise themselves by
cunning or violence at the expense of the others, must make wars
more frequent.' And, as historians of early modern Europe like
Helmut Koenigsberger, John Elliott and Conrad Russell have
shown, this dramatically increased the fiscal stress on government
and sucked resources from other healthier corners of the national
economy. The creation of a national debt could put an end to this
monetary crunch, but only, as Istvan Hont has observed, at the risk
of an even more deadly collapse (what Kant termed 'an ultimately
self-defeating expedient'). Speaking more prescriptively than
descriptively, Kant argued that the crisis provoked by the politicians of necessity and communal security would, eventually,
produce its own remedy. Each state, he wrote, 'must be organised
internally in such a way that the head of state, for whom the war
actually costs nothing (for he wages it at the expense of others, i.e.
the people), must no longer have the deciding vote on whether war
is to be declared or not, for the people who pay for it must
decide'.[11]

Precisely because both domestic and international policy was
conducted in pursuit of the security of the community, which was
usually described as the common good, any attempt to alleviate
the depressing scenario of warfare and economic collapse required
a readjustment of the constitution of that political community.
Statecraft alone was no solution. Kant, like Madison, mocked the
failures of the statesman, that stock figure of the reason of state
literature, who 'tends to look down with great complacency' upon
theorists of politics but whose own achievements were themselves so
checkered.[12]

But it was equally true that reform of the civil constitution was
purely utopian in a world in which nations fought without surcease
and at the merest provocation. Hence, Kant wrote, 'The problem
of establishing a perfect civil constitution is subordinate to the
problem of a law-governed external relationship with other states,

---

[11] Immanuel Kant, 'On the Common Saying: "This may be true in theory, but it does not
   apply in practice"', in *Kant: Political Writings*, ed. and intro. Hans Reiss, tr. H. B. Nisbet
   (2nd edn, Cambridge, 1991), pp. 90–1.
[12] Kant, 'Perpetual Peace: A Philosophical Sketch', in *Political Writings*, p. 93.

and cannot be solved unless the latter is also solved.'[13] Like Grotius, Price, Jay and Hamilton, Kant argued from the uncertain fate of individuals in a state of nature that states shared a similar fate unless joined in some kind of political community – like individuals. The Americans addressed themselves to the practical task of a North American union; Kant spoke of 'a cosmopolitan system of general political security'.[14]

Kant's twinned goals of cosmopolitan security and the establishment of public right transformed the conceptual foundation of the post-Reformation state. He acknowledged the 'disagreement between morals and politics' in contemporary international relations but denied that the *honestum* and *utile* were mutually exclusive. 'It is true, alas, that the saying "Honesty is the best policy" embodies a theory which is frequently contradicted by practice. Yet the equally theoretical proposition "Honesty is better than any policy" infinitely transcends all objections.' Where Grotius cited approvingly Cicero's dictum that Jupiter sanctioned the precept that 'All things salutary to the commonwealth are to be regarded as legitimate and just', Kant fired back that 'The god of morality does not yield to Jupiter, the custodian of violence.'[15] Kant endorsed the actions of the 'moral politician', 'someone who conceives of the principles of political expediency in such a way that they can co-exist with morality', but repudiated the 'political moralist', who articulated moral principles 'to suit his own advantage as a statesman'.[16] Because of the structural injustice and absence of 'public right' in the post-Reformation state, its strategists ended up sounding like 'political moralists' despite their ostensible desire to uphold the same union of morality and expediency that Kant set as his objective. The difference between Kant and the similar-sounding writers on statecraft is in his notion of public right. In the conclusion to part II of *Theory and Practice*, a treatise engaged directly with the Ciceronian argument, he contended that the idea of an original contract, understood as 'a coalition of the wills of all private individuals in a nation to form a common, public will for the purposes of rightful legislation', constituted the standard of justice in a political

[13] Kant, 'Idea for a Universal History with a Cosmopolitan Purpose', in *Political Writings*, p. 47.
[14] *Ibid.*, p. 49.
[15] Grotius, *De Iure Praedae*, ch. 2, p. 20 (cited in ch. 1, p. 61); Kant, 'Perpetual Peace', Appendix I, p. 116.
[16] *Ibid.*, Appendix I, p. 18.

community. Even with the status of an idea it could 'oblige every legislator to frame his laws in such a way that they could have been produced by the united will of a whole nation, and to regard each subject, in so far as he can claim citizenship, as if he had consented within the general will. This is the test of the rightfulness of every public law.'[17] The primacy of the individual in establishing public priorities was Kant's answer to the practice and consequences of early modern *arcana imperii*. Like the British reformers, he argued that the just needs of the community had to be built out of the confluence of private wills. 'The proverbial saying *fiat iustitia, pereat mundus* (i.e. let justice reign, even if all the rogues in the world must perish) may sound somewhat inflated, but it is nonetheless true. It is a sound principle of right, which blocks up all the devious paths followed by cunning or violence.' The only sure means of achieving this end was with 'an internal constitution organized in accordance with pure principles of right', and relations with other political communities organized in 'something analogous to a universal state', neither of which characterized the history of the post-Reformation state.

If the concept of 'public right', built on an assessment of the individual as citizen, could provide a means of insuring that what was declared *honestum* was, indeed, moral, it could also be used to distinguish between the truly useful and mere happiness, or expediency. Kant's effort to demonstrate the union of *honestum* and *utile* bespoke a centuries-old concern. The difference is that his solution overthrew the primacy of the security of the community, which had, until then, structured all prior arguments:

And this is the highest principle from which all maxims relating to the commonwealth must begin and which cannot be qualified by any other principles. No generally valid principle of legislation can be based on happiness. For both the current circumstances and the highly conflicting and variable illusions as to what happiness is (and no-one can prescribe to others how they should attain it) make all fixed principles impossible, so that happiness alone can never be a suitable principle of legislation. The doctrine that *salus publica suprema civitatis lex est* retains its value and authority undiminished; but the public welfare which demands *first* consideration lies precisely in that legal consideration which guarantees everyone his freedom within the law, so that each remains free to seek his happiness in what ever way he thinks best, so long as he does not violate the lawful freedom and rights of his fellow subjects at large.[18]

[17] Kant, 'Theory and Practice', p. 79.   [18] *Ibid.*, p. 80.

In the *Metaphysics of Morals* Kant stressed that the *salus reipublicae* was not to be identified with the 'well-being and happiness' of citizens since these could be assured under despotic government. On the contrary, he wrote, 'the welfare of the state should be seen as that condition in which the constitution most closely approximates to the principles of right'.[19]

It followed from this definition, then, that the ruler's pursuit of the *salus populi*, what has been called statecraft, was a means 'of securing the rightful state, especially against external enemies of the people'. The choice of measures and legislation was a matter of prudence in which, as in all things human, there was scope for error. But there was no deviating from the public right, which at all times marked the limit of policy.[20] Finally, the double-edged claim of necessity which had been wielded so mercilessly by governors and governed was ruled out-of-bounds: 'Nor can a right of necessity (*ius in casu necessitatis*) be invoked here as a means of removing the barriers which restrict the power of the people, for it is monstrous to suppose that we can have a right to do wrong in the direst necessity.'[21]

The web of ideas captured in the assertion of a common or public good is an important part of the fabric of social life. Neither *Publius* nor Kant wished to, nor could, discard them. The great historical significance of the ideas of these and other late eighteenth-century thinkers examined in this book was their reassessment of the concept at the heart of the contemporary discussion. The British reformers, the Americans and Kant put the individual citizen in the position of determining the goals of the community. The revolutionary ideas of representation and federation redefined the very understanding of community that had guided the early modern statesman. 'Necessity', '*salus populi*' and 'common good' remain part of the language of politics, but they serve a different master.

---

[19] Kant, 'The Metaphysics of Morals', in *Political Writings*, p. 143.
[20] Kant, 'Theory and Practice', p. 80.
[21] *Ibid.*, p. 81.

Bibliography

PRIMARY MATERIAL

Abercromby, James, *Magna Charta for America: James Abercromby's 'An Examination of the Acts of Parliament Relative to the Trade and Government of our American Colonies' (1752) and 'De Jure et Gubernatione Coloniarum, or An Inquiry into the Nature, and the Rights of Colonies, Ancient, and Modern' (1774)*, ed. Jack P. Greene, Charles F. Mullett and Edward C. Papenfuse Jr, Philadelphia, 1986

Acta Pacis Westphalicae, Der Französischen Korrespondenzen, Band 1 1644, *Acta Pacis Westphalicae*, ed. Ursula Irsigler, Münster, 1979

Protokolle Band 6, *Die Beratungen der Städtekurie Osnabrück 1645–1649*, *Acta Pacis Westphalicae* ed. Günter Buchstab, Münster, 1981

Addison, Joseph, *Selections from the 'Tatler' and 'Spectator'*, ed. Robert J. Alter, New York, 1957

Alamos de Barrientos, Balthasar, *Advertencias políticos sobre lo particular y público de esta monarchia*, Hispanic Society of America, mss HC 380/80

Almon, John, ed., *A Collection of Tracts, on the Subjects of Taxing the British Colonies in America and Regulating their Trade*, London, 1773

A Collection of Interesting, Authentic Papers, Relative to the Dispute between Great Britain and America; shewing the causes and progress of that Misunderstanding, from 1764 to 1775, 4 vols., London, 1777

Alvord, C. V., and Carter, C. E., eds., *The New Regime 1765–1767*, Springfield, IL, 1916

Trade and Politics 1767–1769, Springfield, IL, 1921

Anon., *An Appeal to the Justice and Interests of the People of Great Britain, in the Present Disputes with America*, London, 1766

Anon., *An Application of Some General Political Rules, to the Present State of Great Britain, Ireland and America*, London, 1766

Anon., *An Argument in Defense of the Exclusive Right Claimed by the Colonies to Tax themselves, with a Review of the Laws of England, Relative to Representation and Taxation*, London, 1774

Anon., *A Candid and Fair Examination of the Remarks on the Letter to Two Great Men*, 2nd edn, London, 1760

422

Anon., *The Conduct of the Opposition, and the Tendency of Modern Patriotism* ... , London, 1734

Anon., *Considerations on the American Stamp Act and on the Conduct of the Minister Who Planned It*, London, 1766

Anon., *Considerations Relative to the North American Colonies*, London, 1765

Anon., *The Constitutional Right of the Legislature of Great Britain, to Tax the British Colonies in America, Impartially Stated*, London, 1765

Anon., *The Crisis. Or, a Full Defence of the Colonies*, London, 1765

Anon., *Cursory Observations upon Dr Price's Essay on Civil Liberty, Particularly Relating to Specie and Paper Currency*, London, 1766

Anon., *A Detection of False Reasons and Facts*, London, 1761

Anon., *The Detector Detected: or, the Danger to Which our Constitution Now Lies Exposed, Set in a True and Manifest Light*, London, 1743

Anon., *Essays Commercial and Political, on the Real and Relative Interests of Imperial and Dependent States. Particularly Those of Great Britain and her Dependencies*, London, 1777

Anon., *An Essay on the Times*, London, 1756

Anon., *An Examination of the Rights of the Colonies, upon the Principles of Law*, London, 1766

Anon., *The Foundations of Religious Liberty Explained*, London, 1755

Anon., *Free Remarks on a Sermon, Entitled, The Requisition of Subscription to the Thirty Nine Articles and Liturgy of the Church of England not Inconsistent with Christian Liberty*, London, 1772

Anon., *The General Opposition of the Colonies to the Payment of the Stamp Duty*, London, 1766

Anon., *The Honour of Parliament and the Justice of the Nation Vindicated. In a Reply to Dr Price's Observations on the Nature of Civil Liberty*, London, 1776

Anon., *An Inquiry into the Nature and Causes of the Present Disputes between the British Colonies in America and the Mother-Country*, London, 1765

Anon., *The Justice and Necessity of Taxing the American Colonies Demonstrated*, London, 1776

Anon., *The Late Occurrences in North America, and Policy of Great Britain, Considered*, London, 1766

Anon., *A Letter to the Members of the New Association for Altering the Articles and Liturgy of the Church of England*, London, 1772

Anon., *A Letter to the People of England on the Necessity of Putting an Immediate End to the War; and the means of Obtaining an Advantageous Peace*, Dublin, 1760

Anon., *A Letter to the Rev. Dr Cooper, on the Origin of Civil Government in Answer to his Sermon* ... , London, 1772

Anon., *A Letter to the Rev. Dr Price FRS. Wherein his Observations on the Nature of Civil Liberty, the Principles of Government, &c. are Candidly Examined; his Fundamental Principles Refuted, and the Fallacy of his Reasoning from these Principles Detected*, London, 1776

Anon., *Letters to a Young Nobleman*, London, 1762

Anon., *A Letter to the Right Hon. the Earl of Hillsborough, on the Present State of Affairs in America ... An Appendix in Answer to the Pamphlet Intituled, 'The Constitutional Right of Great-Britain to Tax the Colonies'*, London, 1769

Anon., *The Naked Truth*, London, 1755

Anon., *A Plain and Seasonable Address to the Freeholders of Great Britain*, London, 1766

Anon., *The Political Balance. In Which the Principles and Conduct of the Two Parties are Weighed*, London, 1765

Anon., *Propositions for Improving the Manufactures, Agriculture and Commerce of Great Britain*, London, 1763

Anon., *Protest against the Bill to Repeal the American Stamp Act*, London, 1766

Anon., *Reasons for Keeping Guadeloupe at a Peace, Preferable to Canada*, London, 1761

Anon., *Reflections on Government, with Respect to America*, London, 1766

Anon., *Reflexions on Representation in Parliament: being an Attempt to shew the equity and practicability, not only of establishing a more equal representation throughout Great Britain, but also of admitting the Americans to a share in the legislature*, London, 1766

Anon., *Remarks on Dr Price's Observations on the Nature of Civil Liberty*, London, 1766

Anon., *Remarks upon Certain Proposals for an Application to Parliament, for Relief in the Matter of Subscription to the Liturgy and the Thirty-Nine Articles of the Established Church of England*, London, 1771

Anon., *Remonstrance salutaire aux rebelles de Montauban, & de la Rochelle ... sur leur desobeyssance & resistance au Roy*, Paris, 1621

Anon., *The Right of the British Legislature to Tax the American Colonies Vindicated*, London, 1774

Anon., *The Rights of Parliament Vindicated on Occasion of the Late Stamp Act*, London, 1766

Anon., *The Rights of the British Colonies Considered. The Administration and Regulation of the Colonies Exploded. And the Best Means Recommended to Make the Colonies Most Useful to the Mother Country*, London, 1765

Anon., *Salus populi, &c., or the Case of King and People*, London, 1681

Anon., *Salus populi suprema lex. Or, the Free Thoughts of a Well Wisher, for a Good Settlement ... n.p.*, 1689

Anon., *The State of Subscription to the Articles and Liturgy of the Church of England, towards the Close of the Year 1773*, London, 1774

Anon., *The State of the British and French Colonies in North America*, London, 1755

Anon., *Thoughts on a Question of Importance Proposed to the Public, Whether it is Probable that the Immense Extent of Territory Acquired by this Nation at the Late Peace, Will Operate towards the Prosperity, or the Ruin of the Island of Great-Britain?*, London, 1765

Anon., *Three Essays on the Populousness, Trade, &c. of Africa*, London, 1764

Anon., *A Translation of the Memorial to the Sovereigns of Europe ...*, London, 1781

Anon., *The True Constitutional Means for Putting an End to the Disputes between Great-Britain and the American Colonies*, London, 1769

Anon., *Two Papers on the Subject of Taxing the British Colonies in America*, London, 1739; rpt 1767

[Arnall, William], *Clodius and Cicero. With other Examples and Reasonings, in Defence of Just Measures against Faction and Obloquy, Suited to the Present Conjuncture* [London, 1727]

Ashley, John, *Memoirs and Considerations Concerning the Trade and Revenues of the British Colonies in America. With Proposals for Rendering those Colonies More Beneficial to Great Britain*, London, 1740

Balguy, Thomas, *Discourses on Various Subjects; and Charges Delivered to the Clergy of the Archdeaconry of Winchester*, ed. James Drake, 2 vols., Cambridge, 1822.

   A Sermon Preached at Lambeth Chapel, on the Consecration of the Right Rev. Jonathan Shipley, DD, Lord Bishop of Landaff, February 12, 1769, London, 1769

[Bancroft, Edward], *Remarks on the Review of the Controversy between Great Britain and her Colonies*, London, 1769

Barbeyrac, Jean, *An Historical and Critical Account of the Science of Morality, and the Progress it Has Made in the World, from the Earliest Times down to the Publication of this Work*, tr. Carew, in Samuel Pufendorf, *The Law of Nature and Nations*, Tr. B. Kennet, London, 1749

Barron, Richard, ed., *The Pillars of Priestcraft and Orthodoxy Shaken*, 4 vols., London, 1766

Barron, William, *History of the Colonization of the Free States of Antiquity, Applied to the Present Contest between Great Britain and her American Colonies. With Reflections Concerning the Future Settlement of these Colonies*, London, 1777.

Beattie, James, *Essays on Poetry and Music, on Laughter and Ludicrous Composition & on the Utility of Classical Learning*, Edinburgh, 1776

   An Essay on the Nature and Immutability of Truth, in Opposition to Sophistry and Scepticism, 4th edn, London, 1773

Bendelowe, Phillip, *Animadversions on an Essay in Religious Establishments, and on Three Letters to the Author of the 'Confessional'*, London, 1769

Bentham, Jeremy, *A Comment on the Commentaries and A Fragment on Government*, ed. J. H. Burns and H. L. A. Hart, London, 1977

Bernard, Francis, 'Principles of Law and Polity, Applied to the Government of the British Colonies in America' (1764), *Select Letters on the Trade and Government of America*, London, 1774

Béthune, Philippe de, *Le conseiller d'estat, ou Recueil des plus générales considerations servant au maniment des affaires publiques*, Paris, 1631

Biographia Britannica: or, the Lives of the Most Eminent Persons Who Have Flourished in Great Britain and Ireland, 7 vols., London, 1757

Blackburne, Francis, *The Confessional; or, a Full and Free Inquiry into the Right, Utility, Edification, and Success, of Establishing Systematical Confessions of Faith and Doctrine in Protestant Churches*, London, 1766

The Works, Theological and Miscellaneous, ed. Francis Blackburne the Younger, 7 vols., Cambridge, 1804

Blackburne, Francis, ed., *A Collection of Letters and Essays in Favour of Publick Liberty*, 3 vols., London, 1774

Blackstone, William, *Commentaries on the Laws of England* (1768), 15th edn, 4 vols., London, 1809

   A Reply to Dr Priestley's Remarks on the Fourth Volume of the 'Commentaries', London, 1769

Bland, Richard, *An Enquiry into the Rights of the British Colonies; Intended as an Answer to 'The Regulations Lately Made'*, Williamsburg; rpt, London, 1769

Bolingbroke, *Works*, 4 vols., London, 1844; rpt, 1967

Bollan, William, *Coloniae anglicanae illustratae; or, the Acquest of Dominion, and the Plantation of Colonies made by the English in America, with the Rights of the Colonists Examined, Stated and Illustrated*, London, 1762

   The Mutual Interest of Great Britain and the American Colonies Considered, London, 1765

   A Succinct View of the Origin of our Colonies, with their Civil State . . ., London, 1766

Botero, Giovanni, *The Reason of State*, (1589), tr. P. J. and D. P. Waley, London, 1956

The Briton

Brown, John, *On Liberty: A Poem*, Cambridge, 1749

   Essays on the Characteristicks, 2nd edn, London, 1751

   An Estimate of the Manners and Principles of the Times, 2 vols., London, 1757–8

   An Additional Dialogue of the Dead, London, 1761

   On Religious Liberty. Preached at St Paul's . . ., London, 1763

   Sermons on Various Subjects, London, 1764

   'An Appendix Relative to a Proposed Code of Education', *Thoughts on the Education of Women*, London, 1765

   Thoughts on Civil Liberty, on Licentiousness and Faction, Dublin, 1765

Burgh, James, *The Dignity of Human Nature. Or, a Brief Account of the certain and Established Means for Attaining the True End of our Existence*, London, 1754

   Remarks Historical and Political, Collected from Books and Observations Humbly Presented to the King's Most Excellent Majesty, BL, King's MSS 433, 1762

   [van Neck], *An Account of the First Settlement, Laws, Form of Government and Police of the Cessares*, London, 1759

   Crito. Or, Essays on Various Subjects, 2 vols., London, 1766–7

   Political Disquisitions: or, an Enquiry into Public Errors, Defects, and Abuses. Illustrated by, and established upon facts and remarks extracted from a variety of authors, ancient and modern. Calculated to draw the timely attention of government and people to a due consideration of the necessity, and the means, of reforming those errors, defects, and abuses; of restoring the constitution and saving the state, 3 vols., London, 1774–5

Burke, Edmund, *A Vindication of Natural Society*, 2nd edn, London, 1757
  Observations on the Present State of the Nation, London, 1769
  *Speech of Edmund Burke, Esq. on moving his resolutions for conciliation with the
  Colonies, March 22, 1775*, London, 1775
  Speeches on the American War and Letters to the Sheriffs of Bristol, ed. A. J.
  George, Boston, 1972
Burke, Edmund and William, *An Account of the European Settlements in
  America*, 2 vols., London, 1757
[Burke, William], *Remarks on the Letter Addressed to Two Great Men in a Letter
  to the Author of that Piece*, London, 1760
[Burke, ?William], *An Examination of the Commercial Principles of the Late
  Negotiation between Great Britain and France*, London, 1762
[Bushe, Gervase Parker], *Case of Great-Britain and America*, 3rd edn, Dublin,
  1769
Butler, Joseph, *The Analogy of Religion, Natural and Revealed, to the Constitution
  and Course of Nature. To which are added two brief dissertations: I. Of
  Personal Identity. II. Of the Nature of Virtue*, London, 1736
Campbell, John, *The Present State of Europe; explaining the interests, connections,
  political and commercial views of its several powers, comprehending also, a clear
  and consise history of each country, so far as to shew the nature of their present
  constitutions*, 4th edn, London, 1753
  Candid and Impartial Considerations on the Nature of the Sugar Trade, London,
  1763
[Campbell, John], *Liberty and Right: or, an Essay, Historical and Political, on the
  Constitution and Administration of Great Britain*, London, 1747
Campion, Nicolas de, *Entretiens sur divers sujets d'histoire, de politique et de
  morale*, Paris, 1704
[Canning, George], *A Letter to the Right Honourable Earl of Hillsborough, on the
  Connection between Great Britain and her American Colonies*, London, 1768
Cartwright, John, *American Independence The Interest and Glory of Great Britain;
  or, arguments to prove, that not only in taxation, but in trade, manufactures, and
  government, the colonies are entitled to an entire independency of the British
  legislature; and that it can only be by a formal declaration of these rights, and
  forming thereupon a friendly league with them, that the true and lasting welfare
  of both countries can be promoted*, 2nd edn, London, 1775
  Take Your Choice!, London, 1776
Charron, Pierre, *Of Wisdome*, (1604), London, 1651
Cicero, *De Inventione*, tr. H. M. Hubbell, Cambridge, MA, and London
  1976; 1st edn, 1949
  De Officiis, tr. Walter Miller, Cambridge, MA, and London, 1976; 1st
  edn, 1913
  In Catilinam, tr. and ed. C. Macdonald, Cambridge, MA, 1977
  In Vatinium, tr. R. Gardiner, Cambridge, MA, and London, 1966
  Letters to Atticus, tr. E. O. Winstedt, 3 vols., Cambridge, MA, and
  London, 1980, 1984

Pro Murena, tr. and ed. C. Macdonald, Cambridge, MA, 1977

Pro Plancio and Pro Milone, tr. N. H. Watts, Cambridge, MA, and London, 1979

Pro Sestio, tr. R. Gardiner, Cambridge, MA, and London, 1966

Clarendon, *The History of the Rebellion* ..., 6 vols., Oxford, 1888

Clarke, Samuel, *A Demonstration of the Being and Attributes of God: More Particularly in Answer to Mr Hobbs, Spinoza, and their Followers. Wherein the Notion of Liberty is Stated, and the Possibility and Certainty of it Proved, in Opposition to Necessity and Fate*, London, 1705

   A Discourse Concerning the Unchangeable Obligations of Natural Religion, and the Truth and Certainty of the Christian Revelation, London, 1706

   A Collection of Papers which Passed between the Late Learned Mr Leibnitz, and Dr Clarke, in the Years 1715 and 1716. Relating to the Principles of Natural Philosophy and Religion. To which are added Letters from Cambridge and a response to a book entitled, A Philosophical Enquiry concerning Human Liberty, London, 1717

A Collection of Scarce and Interesting Tracts on Commerce and Economics 1763–1770, 4 vols., London, 1787

A Collection of State Tracts Publish'd on Occasion of the Late Revolution of 1688, and during the Reign of King William III, 3 vols., London, 1705

Collins, Anthony, *A Philosophical Inquiry Concerning Human Liberty*, London, 1727

The Con-Test

Cooper, Anthony Ashley, Third Earl of Shaftesbury, *Characteristics of Men, Manners, Opinions, Times*, Indianapolis, 1964

Cooper, Myles, *National Humiliation and Repentence Recommended, and the Causes of the Present Rebellion in America Assigned, in a Sermon* ..., Oxford, 1777

The Crisis, No. 1, 1775

The Critical Review, vol. 7, March 1759

Cumberland, Richard, *A Philosophical inquiry into the Laws of Nature* ..., in *A Treatise on the Laws of Nature*, intro. and tr. John Maxwell, London, 1727

   Traité philosophique des loix naturelles ..., tr. and commentary J. Barbeyrac, Amsterdam, 1744

Cumberland, Richard, *The Banishment of Cicero*, London, 1761

Davenant, Charles, *The Political and Commercial Works*, ed. Charles Whitworth, 5 vols., London, 1771

Dawson, Benjamin, *A Short and Safe Expedient for Terminating the Present Debates about Subscriptions, Occasioned by a Celebrated Performance, Intitled, 'The Confessional'*, London, 1769

   A Free and Candid Disquisition on Religious Establishments in General, and the Church of England in Particular, London, 1771

   A Letter to the Clergy of the Archdeaconry of Winchester. Being a Vindication of the Petition Presented the Last Sessions of Parliament to the Legislature, for the

Removal of Subscription to Human Formularies of Religious Faith and Doctrine. London, 1773

De Lolme, Jean-Louis, *The Constitution of England; or, an Account of the English Government; in Which it is Compared Both with the Republican Form of Government, and the Other Monarchies in Europe*, London, 1772; rpt, 1800

De Witt, John [Pieter de la Court], *Political Maxims of the State of Holland*, intro. and tr. John Campbell, London, 1743

Decker, Matthew, *An Essay on the Causes of the Decline of Foreign Trade*, London, 1744

Defoe, Daniel, *A Collection of the Writings of the Author of the True-Born Englishman*, London, 1703

Desaguliers, J. T., *The Newtonian System of the World the Best Model of Government*, London, 1728

Dickinson, John, *Letters from a Farmer in Pennsylvania*, Philadelphia; rpt London, 1768

Douglass, William, *A Summary, Historical and Political, of the First Planting, Progressive Improvements, and Present State of the British Settlements in North-America*, 2nd edn, London, 1755; 1st edn, 1749–50

[Douglass, John], *A Letter Addressed to Two Great Men on the Prospect of Peace and on the Terms Necessary to Be Insisted upon in the Negotiation*, 2nd edn, London, 1760

Eliot, John, *De Jure Maiestatis, or a Political Treatise of Government*, ed. A. B. Grosart, 2 vols., London, 1882

The Monarchie of Man, ed. A. B. Grosart, 2 vols, London, 1882

[Ellis, Henry], 'Hints Relative to the Division and Government of the Conquered and Newly Acquired Countries in America', ed. Verner M. Crane, *Mississippi Valley Historical Review*, 8 (1922), 367–73.

Entick, John, *The General History of the Late War: Containing its Rise, Progress, and Event, in Europe, Asia, Africa and America* ..., 5 vols., London, 1763

Essay on the Times, London, 1756

Estwick, Samuel, *A Letter to the Rev. Josiah Tucker*, London, 1776

[Evans, Caleb], *British Constitutional Liberty. A Sermon* ..., Bristol, [1775]

[Evans, Caleb], *A Letter to the Rev. Mr John Wesley Occasioned by his Calm Address to the American Colonies*, London, 1775

[Evans, Caleb], *A Reply to the Rev. Mr Fletcher's Vindication of Mr Wesley's Calm Address*, Bristol, [1776]

Faret, Nicolas, ed., *Recueil de lettres nouvelles*, Paris, 1627

Fawcett, Benjamin, *The Encouraging Prospect that Religious Liberty Will Be Enlarged*, Shrewsbury, 1773

The Federalist Papers, ed. Clinton Rossiter, New York, 1961

Ferguson, Adam, *Remarks on a Pamphlet Lately Published by Dr Price*, London, 1776

Fielding, Henry, *The True Patriot and Related Writings*, ed. W. B. Coley, Oxford, 1987

Filmer, Robert, *Observations on Aristotle's Politiques, Touching Forms of Government*, London, 1652

Filmer, Robert, *The Anarchy of a Limited or Mixed Monarchy*, n.p., 1689
The Necessity of the Absolute Power of All Kings: And in Particular of the King of England, London, 1648

Firebrace, John, *A Further Defence of the Present Scheme of Petitioning the Parliament for Relief in the Matter of Subscription*, London, 1771
A Letter to the Rev. James Ibbetson . . . , London, 1771
Letters to a Member of Parliament, in Which the Present Design of Removing Subscription to Human Articles of Faith is Vindicated, London, 1772

Fleming, Caleb, *Civil Establishments in Religion, a Ground of Infidelity*, London, 1767

Fletcher, J., *American Patriotism farther Confronted with Reason, Scripture, and the Constitution*, Shrewsbury, 1776

Forster, Nathaniel, *The Establishment of the Church of England Defended upon the Principles of Religious Liberty*, London, 1770

Fothergill, John, *Considerations Relative to the North American Colonies*, London, 1765

Fownes, Joseph, *An Enquiry into the Principles of Toleration*, 2nd edn, Shrewsbury, 1773

Franklin, Benjamin, *The Interest of Great Britain Considered, with Regard to her Colonies, and the Acquisition of Canada and Guadaloupe . . .* , London, 1760

Furneaux, Phillip, *Letters to his Honourable Mr Justice Blackstone, Concerning his Exposition of the Act of Toleration, and Some Positions Relative to Religious Liberty*, London, 1769
An Essay on Toleration: with a Particular View to the Late Application of the Protestant Dissenting Ministers to Parliament, London, 1773

(Gage, Thomas), *The Correspondence of General Thomas Gage with the Secretaries of State and with the War Office and Treasury*, ed. C. E. Carter, 2 vols., New Haven, 1931–3

Galileo Galilei, 'Third Letter on Sunspots', *The Discoveries and Opinions of Galileo*, ed. Stillman Drake, New York, 1951

Gay, John, *A Dissertation Concerning the Principle and Criterion of Virtue and the Origins of the Passions*, in William King, *De Origine Mali*, ed. Edmund Law, Cambridge, 1731

Gentillet, Innocent, *Discours, sur le moyens de bien gouverner et maintenir en bonne paix un royaume ou autre principauté*, n.p., 1576

Gibbon, Edward, *The Decline and Fall of the Roman Empire*, 6 vols., New York, n.d.

Glover, Phillip, *An Inquiry Concerning Virtue and Happiness*, London, 1751

Godwin, William, *Enquiry Concerning Political Justice and its Influence on Modern Morals and Happiness* (1793), ed. Isaac Kramnick, Harmondsworth, 1976

Goldsmith, Oliver, 'Citizen of the World', *Collected Works*, ed. Arthur Friedman, 4 vols., Oxford, 1966

Goodricke, Henry, *Observations on Dr Price's Theory and Principles of Civil Liberty and Government*, York, 1776

Gordon, Thomas, *The Works of Tacitus. To Which are Prefixed, Political Discourses*, 2nd edn, London, 1737

The Works of Sallust . . . with Political Discourses upon that Author, London, 1744

A Cordial for Low Spirits, London, 1763

Gordon, Thomas, and Trenchard, John, *Cato's Letters. Essays on Liberty, Civil and Religious*, 4 vols., 4th edn, London, 1737

Gray, John, *Doctor Price's Notions of the Nature of Civil Liberty, Shewn to be Contradictory to Reason and Scripture*, London, 1777

Grotius, Hugo, *The Freedom of the Seas, or the Right Which Belongs to the Dutch to Take Part in the East Indian Trade* (1609), tr. Ralph van Deman Magoffin, ed. and intro. James Brown Scott, New York, 1916

The Laws of War and Peace . . . to Which Are Added, All the large Notes of Mr J. Barbeyrac (1625), London, 1738

De Iure Praedae Commentarius, ed. and tr. G. L. Williams, Oxford, 1950

Guez de Balzac, Jean-Louis, *Œuvres complètes*, 2 vols., Paris, 1665

Guicciardini, Francesco, *Ricordi*, ed. Emilio Pasquini, Milan, 1984; 1st edn, 1975

Hall, John, *Of Government and Obedience, as They Stand Directed and Determined by Scripture and Reason*, London, 1654

Hampton, James, *Reflections on Ancient and Modern History*, Oxford, 1746

Harrington, James, *The Political Works of James Harrington*, ed. J. G. A. Pocock, Cambridge, 1976

Harris, J., *Observations on National Establishments in Religion in General and on the Establishment of Christianity in Particular*, London, 1767

Harris, James, *Hermes*, London, 1751

Harris, Joseph, *An Essay upon Money and Coins*, 2 vols., London, 1757–8

Hartley, David, *Observations on Man, his Frame, his Duty, and his Expectations*, 2 vols., London, 1749

[Lord Hervey], *Ancient and Modern Liberty Stated and Compar'd*, London, 1734

Hey, Richard, *Observations on the Nature of Civil Liberty, and Principles of Government*, London, 1776

Hoadly, Benjamin, *The Works of Benjamin Hoadly*, ed. John Hoadly, 3 vols., London, 1773

Hobbes, Thomas, *Leviathan* (1651), ed. C. B. Macpherson, Harmondsworth, 1968

Horsley, William, *A Treatise on Maritime Affairs*, London, 1744

Hulme, Obadiah, *An Historical Essay on the English Constitution*, London, 1770

Hume, David, *A Treatise of Human Nature*, ed. Selby-Bigge; 2nd edn, ed. P. H. Nidditch, Oxford, 1978

Enquiries Concerning Human Understanding and Concerning the Principles of Morals, ed. P. H. Nidditch, 3rd edn, Oxford, 1975

Essays, ed. Eugene Miller, Indianapolis, 1985
History of England, 6 vols., Indianapolis, 1983
Hunter, Thomas, *Observations on Tacitus*, London, 1752
Hunton, Philip, *A Treatise of Monarchy*, London, 1648
Hutcheson, Francis, *An Inquiry into the Original of our Ideas of Beauty and Virtue*, 2nd edn, London, 1726
   An Essay on the Nature and Conduct of the Passions and Affections with Illustrations on the Moral Sense, London, 1728
   A Short Introduction to Moral Philosophy (1747), 3rd edn, Glasgow, 1764
   A System of Moral Philosophy, 2 vols., Glasgow, 1754–5
Hutchinson, Thomas, *Experience Preferable to Theory. An Answer to Dr Price's Observations*, London, 1776
Ibbetson, James, *A Plea for the Subscription of the Clergy to the Thirty-Nine Articles of Religion*, 2nd edn, London, 1767
Ibbot, Benjamin, *The Nature and Extent of the Office of the Civil Magistrate; Considered in a Discourse Preached before the Right. Hon. Sir George Thorold, Knt, Lord-Mayor of the City of London*, London, 1720
J. M., *The Legislative Authority of the British Parliament, with Respect to North America, and the Privileges of the Assemblies There, Briefly Considered*, London, 1766
[Jackson, B.], *Three Dialogues Concerning Liberty*, London, 1776
Jackson, John, *The Grounds of Civil and Ecclesiastical Government Briefly Considered*, London, 1718
   A Vindication of Humane Liberty: in Answer to a Dissertation on Liberty and Necessity; Written by Ac, Esq., London, 1727
   A Defense of Human Liberty, in Answer to the Principal Arguments Which Have Been Alledged Against It; and Particularly to CATO's Letters on that Subject, 2nd edn, London, 1730
Jebb, John, *The Works. Theological, Medical, Political and Miscellaneous of John Jebb*, ed. J. Disney, London and Cambridge, 1787
Jenyns, Soame, *A Free Inquiry into the Nature and Origins of Evil*, London, 1757
   The Objections to the Taxation of our American Colonies, London, 1765
Johnson, Samuel, *A Dictionary of the English Language*, London, 1755
   Samuel Johnson's Political Writings, ed. Donald J. Greene, New Haven and London, 1977
Jones, John, *Free and Candid Disquisitions Relating to the Church of England*, 2nd edn, London, 1750
Jones, William, *An Essay on the First Principles of Natural Philosophy*, Oxford, 1762
Jonson, Ben, *The Complete Poems*, ed. George Parfitt, Harmondsworth, 1988; 1st edn 1975
Jortin, John, *Remarks on Ecclesiastical History*, 5 vols., London, 1751–73
Kant: Political Writings, ed. and intro. Hans Reiss, tr. H. B. Nisbet, 2nd edn, Cambridge, 1991

Kennedy, Archibald, *Serious Considerations on the Present State of the Affairs of the Northern Colonies*, London, 1754

King, Dr William, *An Essay on the Origin of Evil*, tr. with notes by Edmund Law, 3rd edn, London, 1739

Kippis, Andrew, *A Vindication of the Late Protestant Dissenting Ministers, with Regard to their Late Application to Parliament*, 2nd edn, London, 1773

[Knox, William], *A Letter to a Member of Parliament, Wherein the Power of the British Legislature, and the Case of the Colonies are Briefly and Impartially Considered*, London, 1765

[Knox, William], *The Claim of the Colonies to an Exemption from Internal Taxes Imposed by Parliament, Examined*, London, 1765

[Knox, William], *The Present State of the Nation*, Dublin, 1768

[Knox, William], *The Controversy between Great Britain and her Colonies Reviewed*, London, 1769

[Knox, William], *The Interest of the Merchants and Manufacturers of Great Britain, in the Present Contest with the Colonies, Stated and Considered*, London, 1774

[Knox, William], *Thoughts on the Act for Making More Effectual Provision for the Government of the Province of Quebec*, London, 1774

[Langrische, Sir Hercules], *Considerations on the Dependencies of Great Britain. With Observations on a Pamphlet, Intitled 'The Present State of the Nation'*, Dublin, 1769

Law, Edmund, *Considerations on the Theory of Religion*, 5th edn, Cambridge, 1765

Lawson, George, *An Examination of the Political Part of Mr Hobbs his Leviathan*, London, 1657

Politica Sacra & Civilis. Or, a Model of Civil and Ecclesiastical Government, London, 1660

Lind, John, *An Answer to the Declaration of the American Congress*, London, 1776

Three Letters to Dr Price Containing Remarks on his Observations on the Nature of Civil Liberty, London, 1776

Lipsius, Justus, *Six Bookes of Politickes or Civil Doctrines*, tr. William Jones, London, 1594

Lloyd, Charles, *The Conduct of the Late Administration Examined*, London, 1766

Locke, John, *An Essay Concerning Human Understanding* (1689), ed. P. H. Nidditch, Oxford, 1975

A Letter Concerning Toleration (1689), ed. James Tully, Indianapolis, 1983

Two Treatises of Government (1689), ed. Peter Laslett, New York, 1965

Works, ed. Edmund Law, 4th edn, 4 vols., London, 1768

Lyttleton, George Lloyd, *Dialogues of the Dead*, Dublin, 1760

Maarten, Henry, *Familiar Letters to his Lady of Delight*, London, 1663

Macaulay, Catharine, *The History of England*, 8 vols., London, 1763–83.

Observations on a Pamphlet, Entitled, 'Thoughts on the Cause of the Present Discontents', London, 1770

An Address to the People of England, Scotland, and Ireland, on the Present Important Crisis of Affairs, Bath, 1775

Loose Remarks on Certain Positions to be Found in Mr Hobbes' Philosophical Rudiments on Government and Society with a Short Sketch of a Democratical Form of Government in a Letter to Signor Paoli, London, 1775

McCulloh, Henry, *A Miscellaneous Essay Concerning the Courses pursued by Great Britain in the Affairs of her Colonies*, London, 1755

The Wisdom and Policy of the French in the Construction of the Great Offices, London, 1755

Miscellaneous Representations Relative to our Concerns in America (1761), London, 1905

MacLaurin, Colin, *An Account of Sir Isaac Newton's Philosophical Discoveries*, London, 1748

Macpherson, James, *The Rights of Great Britain Asserted against the Claims of America: Being an Answer to the Declaration of the General Congress*, 2nd edn, London, 1775

Mandeville, Bernard, *The Fable of the Bees*, ed. F. B. Kaye, 2 vols. Oxford, 1924

Manwaring, Roger, *Religion and Allegiance: In Two Sermons* (1628), London, 1709

Marquez, Juan, *El governador cristiano, deducido de las vidas de Moysen y Josue, príncipes del pueblo de Dios*, Salamanca, 1612

Martin, Benjamin, *A Plain and Familiar Introduction to the Newtonian Philosophy*, London, 1751

Martin, John, *Familiar Dialogues between Americus and Britannicus; in Which the Right of Private Judgment; the Exploded Doctrines of Infallibility, Passive Obedience, and Non-Resistance: With the Leading Sentiments of Dr Price, on the Nature of Civil Liberty, &c, Are Particularly Considered*, London, 1776

Maseres, Francis, *Considerations on the Expediency of Admitting Representatives from the American Colonies in the British House of Commons*, London, 1770

Massie, Joseph, *A Representation Concerning the Knowledge of Commerce as a National Concern*, London, 1760

Mauduit, Israel, *Considerations on the Present German War*, 2nd edn, London, 1760

Occasional Thoughts on the Present German War, 2nd edn, London, 1761

The Case of the Dissenting Ministers, 3rd edn, London, 1773

Maxwell, John, *Sacro-sancta regum majestas: or, the Sacred and Royall Prerogative of Christian Kings*, Oxford, 1644

Meister, Christopher Friedrich George, *Bibliotheca Iuris Naturae et Gentium*, Gottingen, 1757

Middleton, Conyers, *The History of the Life of Marcus Tullius Cicero*, 2 vols., London, 1742

Mitchell, John, *The Contest in America between Great Britain and France*, London, 1757

[Moir, John], *Obedience the Best Charter; or, Law the Only Sanction of Liberty. In a Letter to the Rev. Dr Price*, London, 1776

Molesworth, Robert, *An Account of Denmark*, London, 1694

Molinier, E., *A Mirrour for Christian States: or, a Table of Politick Vertues Considerable amongst Christians*, tr. William Tyruuhit, London, 1635

Montagu, Edward Wortley, Jr., *Reflections on the Rise and Fall of the Antient Republicks. Adapted to the Present State of Great Britain*, 2nd edn, London, 1759

Montesquieu, *Considerations on the Greatness and Decline of the Romans* (1738), tr. David Lowenthal, Ithaca, 1968

Spirit of the Laws (1748), tr. Thomas Nugent, New York, 1959

Morgan, John, *et al. Four Dissertations, on the Reciprocal Advantages of a Perpetual Union between Great-Britain and her American Colonies*, Philadelphia, 1766

Moyle, Walter, 'An Essay upon the Lacedemonian Government', *A Select Collection of Tracts*, Dublin, 1728

Muret, Marc-Antoine, *Opera Omnia*, ed. David Rutinken, 4 vols., Leiden, 1789

The Naked Truth, No. 1, 2nd edn, London, 1755

Nalson, John, *The Common Interest of King and People*, London, 1677

Naudé, Gabriel, *Considerations sur les coups d'estat* (1639) [Leiden], 1679

Navarette, Pedro Fernandez, *Conservación de monarquías ... discursos políticos*, Madrid, 1626

Nedham, Marchmont, *Interest Will Not Lie. Or, a View of England's True Interest*, London, n.d.

The Excellencie of a Free State, ed. Richard Barron, London, 1767, rpt.

Neville, Henry, *Plato Redivivus*, in *Two English Republican Tracts*, ed. Caroline Robbins, Cambridge, 1969

Newton, Benjamin, *Another Dissertation on the Mutual Support of Trade and Civil Liberty*, London, 1756

The Influence of the Improvements of Life on the Moral Principle, Considered, Cambridge, 1758

Norman, Henry, *Two Letters on the Subject of Subscription to the Liturgy and Thirty-Nine Articles of the Church of England*, Winchester, 1773

Otis, James, *The Rights of the British Colonies*, 2nd edn, London, 1764

Considerations on Behalf of the Colonies, 2nd edn, London, 1766

Paley, William, *A Defence of the 'Considerations on the Propriety of Requiring a Subscription to Articles of Faith'*, London, 1774

The Principles of Moral and Political Philosophy, Cambridge, 1785

Palmer, Samuel, *The Protestant Dissenter's Catechism ...*, 4th edn, Belfast, 1773

Parker, Henry, *The Case of Ship-Money Briefly Discoursed*, London, 1640

Observation on His Majesties Late Answers and Expresses, London, 1642

Contra-Replicant, London, 1643

Pease, Theodore, ed., *Anglo-French Border Disputes in the West 1749–1763*, Springfield, IL, 1936

Pemberton, Henry, *A View of Sir Isaac Newton's Philosophy*, London, 1728

[Perceval, John, Earl of Egmont], *Things As They Are*, London, 1758

Faction Detected by the Evidence of Facts, London, 1743

[Phelps, Richard], *The Rights of the Colonies and the Extent of the Legislative Authority of Great-Britain*, London, 1769

Polybius, *The Rise of the Roman Republic*, tr. Ian Scott-Kilvert, Harmondsworth, 1979

The History of Polybius, tr. Henry Shears, 3 vols., London, 1693–8

A Fragment out of the Sixth Book of Polybius, tr. and ed. Edward Spelman, London, 1743

Two Extracts from the Sixth Book of the General History of Polybius, tr. and ed. James Hampton, London, 1764

The General History of Polybius, tr. Hampton, 2 vols., London, 1756–72

Postlethwayt, Malachi, *The Universal Dictionary of Trade and Commerce*, 2 vols., London, 1751–5

Great Britain's True System, London, 1757

Great Britain's Commercial Interest Explained and Improved, 2nd edn, London, 1759

Powell, W. S., *A Defence of the Subscriptions Required in the Church of England*, London, 1758

Pownall, Thomas, *A Treatise on Government: Being a Review of the Doctrine of an Original Contract More Particularly As It Respects the Rights of Government and the Duty of Allegiance*, London, 1750

Principles of Polity, Being the Grounds and Reasons of Civil Empire in Three Parts, London, 1752

The Administration of the Colonies, London, 1764; 2nd edn, 1765; 3rd edn, 1766; 4th edn, 1768; 5th edn, 1775

The Right, Interest, and Duty of the State As Concerned in the Affairs of the East Indies, London, 1773

Administration of the Colonies. Part II, Wherein a Line of Government between the Supreme Jurisdiction of Great Britain and the Rights of the Colonies, is Drawn and a Plan of Pacification Is Suggested, London, 1775

Letter to Adam Smith, London, 1776

A Memorial Addressed to the Sovereigns of America, London, 1783

[Pownall, Thomas], *State of the Constitution of the Colonies*, [London], [1769]

[Pownall, Thomas], *A Memorial, Most Humbly Addressed to the Sovereigns of Europe . . .*, London, 1780

Price, Richard, *Britain's Happiness and the Proper Improvement of It, Represented in a Sermon Preach'd at Newington-Green*, London, 1759

A Review of the Principal Questions and Difficulties in Morals (1759), 2nd edn, London, 1769

The Nature and Dignity of the Human Soul. A Sermon Preached at St Thomas's, January the First, 1766, London, 1766

The Vanity, Misery and Infamy of Knowledge without Suitable Practice, London, 1770

Observations on the Nature of Civil Liberty, the Principles of Government and the Justice and Policy of the War with America, London, 1776

Additional Observations on the Nature and Value of Civil Liberty, and the War with America: Also Observations on Schemes for Raising Money by Public Loans; an Historical Deduction and Analysis of the National Debt; and a Brief Account of the Debts and Resources of France, Dublin, 1777

Four Dissertations, Dublin, 1777

Priestley, Joseph, *An Essay on a Course of Liberal Education for Civil and Active Life to Which Are Added Remarks on a Code of Education Proposed by Dr Brown,* London, 1765

Essay on the First Principles of Government, London, 1768; 2nd edn, 1771

Considerations on Church Authority; Occasioned by Dr Balguy's Sermon, London, 1769

Institutes of Natural and Revealed Religion, 3 vols., London, 1772–4

An Examination of Dr Reid's 'Inquiry into the Human Mind on the Principles of Common Sense', Dr Beattie's 'Essay on the Nature and Immutability of Truth', and Dr Oswald's 'Appeal to Common Sense on Behalf of Religion', London, 1774

Hartley's Theory of the Human Mind, on the Principle of the Association of Ideas, London, 1775

A Free Discussion of the Doctrines of Materialism, and Philosophical Necessity, in a Correspondence between Dr Price and Dr Priestley, London, 1778

Lectures on History, Warrington, 1788

Essays on Political and Religious Liberty, *Works,* ed. J. T. Rutt, xxii, London, 1823

Proceedings and Debates of the British Parliaments Respecting North America 1754–1783, ed. R. C. Simmons and P. D. G. Thomas, 6 vols., White Plains, NY, 1981–7

Pufendorf, Samuel, *Elementorum Jurisprudentiae Universalis Libri Duo (1659),* tr. William Abbot Oldfather, Oxford, 1931

The Law of Nature and Nations (1672), tr. Basil Kennet, London, 1717

On the Duty of Man and Citizen According to Natural Law (1673), ed. and intro. James Tully and tr. Michael Silverthorne, Cambridge, 1991

The Compleat History of Sweden from its Origin to this Time, (1682), London, 1702

An Introduction to the History of the Principal Kingdoms and States of Europe (1682), London, 1707

Commentariorum de Rebus Suecicis, Nuremberg, 1686

A Discourse by M. Samuel Pufendorf upon the Alliances between Sweden and France, (1708), tr. J. Ozell, London, 1709

Ramsay, Allan, *Thoughts on the Origin and Nature of Government,* London, 1769 .

Randolph, Rev. Dr Thomas, *An Answer to the Pamphlet, entituled Consider-ations on the Propriety of Requiring a Subscription to Articles of Faith*, Oxford, 1774
The Reasonableness of Requiring Subscription to Articles of Religion from Persons to be Admitted to Holy Orders, Oxford, 1771
Rees, Abraham, *Acceptable Religion Illustrated and Recommended. A Sermon . . .*, London, 1770
Rivadeneira, Pedro, de, *Tratado de la religion y virtudes que debe tener el príncipe cristiano para gobernar y conservar sus estados*, in *Obras Escogidas*, (Madrid, 1868)
Robinson, Robert, *Arcana: or the Principles of the Late Petitioners to Parliament for Relief in Subscription*, Cambridge, 1774
Robinson-Morris, Matthew, *Considerations of the Measures Carrying on with Respect to the British Colonies in North America*, London, 1774
Ross, John, *A Discourse Delivered before the University of Cambridge*, Cambridge, 1756
Rossaeus, Gulielmus, *De iusta reipublicae christianae in reges impios et hereticos*, Paris, 1590
Rotheram, John, *An Essay on Establishments in Religion. With Remarks on the 'Confessional'*, London, 1766
Ruffhead, Owen, *Ministerial Usurpation Displayed*, London, 1760
Considerations on the Present Dangerous Crisis, London, 1763
Rutherforth, Thomas, *A System of Natural Philosophy*, 2 vols., Cambridge, 1748
An Essay on the Nature and Obligations of Virtue, Cambridge, 1754
Institutes of Natural Law. Being the Substance of a Course of Lectures on Grotius 'De jure belli ac pacis', 2 vols., Cambridge, 1754–6
Saavedra Fajardo, Diego de, *Idea de un Príncipe Político-Christiano Repre-sentada en Cien Empresas* (1640), Murcia, 1985
Sacheverell, Henry, *The Political Union: A Discourse Shewing the Dependence of Government on Religion in General; and of the English Monarchy on the Church of England in Particular*, Oxford, 1710; 1st edn, 1702
The Perils of False Brethren, Both in Church and State, London, 1709
Sancroft, William, *Modern Policies, Taken from Machiavel, Borgia, and Other Choice Authors, by an Eye Witnesse*, 4th edn, London, 1653
Savile George, *The Complete Works of George Savile*, ed. and intro. Walter Raleigh, Oxford, 1912
s'Gravesande, Willem Jakob Storm van, *Mathematical Elements of Natural Philosophy Confirm'd by Experiments*, London, 1720
Sharpe, Granville, *A Declaration of the People's Natural Right to a Share in the Legislature, Which is the Fundamental Principal of the British Constitution of State*, London, 1774
A Tract on the Law of Nature and Principles of Action in Man, London, 1777
Shebbeare, John, *An Essay on the Origin, Progress and Establishment of National Society*, London, 1776

Sidney, Algernon, *Discourses on Liberty*, ed. Thomas G. West, Indianapolis, 1990

Sirmond, Jean, *Le coup d'estat de Louis XIII*, Paris, 1631

Smith, Adam, *The Theory of Moral Sentiments* (1759), ed. D. D. Raphael and A. L. Macfie, Indianapolis, 1982

An Inquiry into the Nature and Causes of the Wealth of Nations (1776), ed. R. H. Campbell, A. S. Skinner and W. B. Todd, Indianapolis, 1982

Essays on Philosophical Subjects, ed. W. P. D. Wrightman and J. C. Bryce, Indianapolis, 1982

Lectures on Jurisprudence, ed. R. L. Meek, D. D. Raphael and P. G. Stein, Indianapolis, 1982

Lectures on Rhetoric and Belles-Lettres, ed. J. C. Boyce, Indianapolis, 1985

State Trials, ed. W. Cobett and T. H. Howell, 33 vols., London, 1809–26

[Steele, Joshua], *An Account of a Late Conference on the Occurrences in America*, London, 1766

Steele, Richard, *The Tatler*, ed. and intro. Donald F. Bond, 3 vols., Oxford, 1987

Sterne, Laurence, *Tristram Shandy*, ed. Howard Anderson, New York, 1980

[Stevens, W.], *The Revolution Vindicated, and Constitutional Liberty Asserted. In Answer to Dr Watson's Accession Sermon*, Cambridge, 1777

Stevenson, John, *Letters in Answer to Dr Price's Two Pamphlets on Civil Liberty*, 2nd edn, London, 1777

Sturges, J., *A Letter to a Bishop Occasioned by the Late Petition to Parliament*, 2nd edn, London, 1773

Sykes, Arthur Ashley, *The Principles and Connexion of Natural and Revealed Religion Distinctly Considered* London, 1740

T. D., *A Letter to the Rev. Dr Price*, London, 1776

Temple, Sir Richard, *An Account of Government*, Bod. MS, Eng. Hist. C.20.1

Theveneau, Jean, *Les Morales*, Paris, 1607

Thomson, James, *Liberty*, London, 1735

Thucydides, *History of the Peloponnesian War*, tr. Rex Warner, Harmondsworth, 1972

Thuillerio, Gaspar, *Il soldato svezzese: historia della guerra tra Ferdinando II imperatore, e Gustavo Adolfo re di Suetia*, tr. Pompeo Bellanda il Vecchio, Venice, 1634

Tindall, Matthew, *An Essay Concerning Obedience to the Supreme Powers, and the Duty of Subjects in All Revolutions*, London, 1694

Toulmin, Joshua, *The American War Lamented. A Sermon ...*, London, 1776

Towers, Joseph, *A Dialogue between Two Gentlemen, Concerning the Late Application to Parliament for Relief in the Matter of Subscription*, London, 1772

A Letter to Dr Samuel Johnson: Occasioned by his late Political Publications, London, 1776

A Vindication of the Political Principles of Mr Locke: in Answer to the Objections of the Rev. Dr Tucker, London, 1782

Tucker, Josiah, *A Brief Essay on the Advantages and Disadvantages Which Perspectively Attend France and Great Britain with Regard to Trade*, 2nd edn, London, 1753

The Elements of Commerce and Theory of Taxes, Bristol, 1755

Instructions for Travellers, London, 1757

The Case of Going to War for the Sake of Procuring, Enlarging, or Securing of Trade, Considered in a New Light, Being a Fragment of a Greater Work, London, 1763

An Apology for the Present Church of England as by Law Established, Gloucester, 1772

Letters to the Rev. Dr. Kippis, Gloucester, 1773

A Brief and Dispassionate View of the Difficulties Attending the Trinitarian, Arian and Socinian Systems, Gloucester, 1774

Four Tracts, Together with Two Sermons on Political and Commercial Subjects, Gloucester, 1774

Tract V. The Respective Pleas and Arguments of the Mother Country and of her Colonies, Distinctly Set Forth, Gloucester, 1775

A Letter to Edmund Burke, Gloucester, 1775

A Treatise Concerning Civil Government, London, 1781

Tunstall, James, *Lectures on Natural and Revealed Religion, Read in the Chapel of St John's College, Cambridge*, London, 1765

The Universal History. The Modern Part, London, 1759–64

Vera y Figueroa, Juan de, *El Enbaxador*, Seville, 1620

Vieusseux, André, *Essays on Liberalism*, London, 1823

Villareal, Fernandez, *El político cristiano o discursos políticos*, Pamplona, 1642; translated as: *Le Politique très-chrestien ou Discours politiques sur les actions principales de la vie de seu Monr L'Eminentissime Cardinal duc de Richelieu*, Paris, 1647

Voltaire, *The Elements of Sir Isaac Newton's Philosophy*, tr. John Hanna, London, 1738

Wallace, Robert, *Characteristics of the Present Political State of Great Britain*, 2nd edn, London, 1758

A View of the Internal Policy of Great Britain, London, 1764

Wallin, Benjamin, *The Popular Concern in the Choice of the Representatives. A Sermon . . .*, London, 1774

Warburton, William, *The Alliance between Church and State, or the Necessity and Equity of an Established Religion and a Test-Law, Demonstrated, from the Essence and End of Civil Society, upon the Fundamental Principles of the Law of Nature and Nations*, London, 1756

Watson, Richard, *A Brief State of the Principles of Church Authority*, London, 1773

The Principles of the Revolution Vindicated. In a Sermon . . ., Cambridge, 1776

Watts, Isaac, 'An Essay on the Freedom of the Will in God and in Creatures', *Works*, VI London, 1753

'A New Essay on Civil Power in Things Sacred: or, An Enquiry after an

Established Religion, Consistent with the Just Liberties of Mankind, and Practicable under Every Form of Civil Government', *Works*, VI, London, 1753

Webb, Daniel, *An Inquiry into the Beauties of Painting*, London, 1760

Wesley, John, *A Calm Address to our American Colonies*, London, 1775
   Some Observations on Liberty: Occasioned by a late Tract, London, 1776

Whately, Thomas, *The Regulations Lately Made Concerning the Colonies and the Taxes Imposed on Them*, London, 1765

[Wheelock, Matthew], *Reflections Moral and Political on Great Britain and her Colonies*, London, 1770

Whiston, William, *Astronomical Principles of Religion, Natural and Revealed*, London, 1717

White, Thomas, *The Grounds of Obedience and Government*, London, 1655

Willan, Leonard, *The Exact Politician*, London, 1678

Williams, David, *Essays on Public Worship*, London, 1773
   Letter to the Body of Protestant Dissenters, London, 1777

Wilton, Samuel, *An Apology for the Removal of an Application to Parliament by the Protestant Dissenting Ministers*, London, 1773

Winder, Henry, *A Critical and Chronological History of the Rise, Progress, Declension and Revival of Knowledge, Chiefly Religious*, 2nd edn, London, 1766

Wollaston, William, *The Religion of Nature Delineated*, London, 1724

Wyvill, Christopher, *Thoughts on our Articles of Religion, with Respect to their Supposed Utility to the State*, London, 1771

Wyvill, Christopher, *A Defense of Dr Price and the Reformers of England* London, 1792

Wyvill, Christopher, ed., *A Collection of the Letters Which Have Been Addressed to the Volunteers of Ireland on the Subject of a Parliamentary Reform, by the Earl of Effingham, Dr Price, Major Cartwright, Dr Jebb and the Rev. Mr Wyvill*, London, 1783

Yorke, Philip, *The Life and Correspondence of Philip Yorke, Earl of Hardwicke*, ed. Philip C. Yorke, 3 vols., Cambridge, 1913

Young, Arthur, *Political Essays Concerning the Present State of the British Empire*. London, 1772

Young, William, *Considerations Which May Tend to Promote the Settlement of our New W. India Colonies by Encouraging Individuals to Embark in the Undertaking*, London, 1764

The Spirit of Athens, London, 1777

SECONDARY MATERIAL

PUBLISHED SOURCES

Abbattista, Guido, *Commercio, colonie e impero alla vigilia della rivoluzione americana: John Campbell pubblicista e storico nell'Inghilterra del sec. XVIII*, Florence, 1990

Adair, Douglas, '"That Politics May Be Reduced to a Science": David Hume, James Madison, and the Tenth "Federalist"', *Huntington Library Quarterly*, 20 (1957), 343–60.

Adams, Thomas R., *The American Controversy: Bibliography of British Pamphlets on America 1763–1783*, Providence, RI, 1980

Agresto, John T., 'Liberty, Virtue, and Republicanism, 1776–1787', *The Review of Politics*, 39 (1977), 473–505

Alexander, Peter, 'Boyle and Locke on Primary and Secondary Qualities', in *Locke on Human Understanding. Selected Essays*, ed. I. C. Tipton, Oxford, 1977, pp. 62–76

Ideas, Qualities and Corpuscles: Locke and Boyle on the External World, Cambridge, 1985

Alvord, Clarence Walworth, *The Mississippi Valley in British Politics. A Study of the Trade, Land Speculation, and Experiments in Imperialism Culminating in the American Revolution*, 2 vols., Cleveland, OH, 1917

Andrews, Charles M., 'England's Commercial and Colonial Policy', *The Colonial Period of American History*, vol. IV, New Haven, 1938

Andrews, Kenneth R., *Trade, Plunder and Settlement: Maritime Enterprises and the Genesis of the British Empire 1480–1630*, Cambridge, 1984

Ships, Money and Politics: Seafaring and Naval Enterprise in the Reign of Charles I, Cambridge, 1991

Appleby, Joyce O., 'Republicanism in Old and New Contexts', *William and Mary Quarterly*, 3rd ser. 43 (1986), 20–34

Ashcraft, Richard, 'Latitudinarianism and Toleration: Historical Myth Versus Political History', in *Philosophy, Science and Religion in England 1640–1700*, ed. Richard Kroll, Richard Ashcraft and Perez Zagorin, Cambridge, 1992, pp. 151–77

Ashton, Robert, 'From Cavalier to Roundhead Tyranny, 1642–9', *Reactions to the English Civil War 1642–1649*, ed. John Morrill, London, 1982, pp. 185–207

Avery, Margaret, 'Toryism in the Age of the American Revolution: John Lind and John Shebbeare', *Historical Studies*, 18 (1978), 24–36.

Axtell, James L., 'Locke, Newton and the Two Cultures', *John Locke: Problems and Perspectives*, ed. John Yolton, Cambridge, 1969, pp. 165–82.

Bailyn, Bernard, *The Ideological Origins of the American Revolution*, Cambridge, MA, 1967

Faces of Revolution: Personalities and Themes in the Struggle for American Independence, New York, 1990

The Peopling of British North America: An Introduction, New York, 1986

Voyagers to the West: A Passage in the Peopling of America on the Eve of the Revolution, New York, 1986

Bailyn, Bernard, ed., *Pamphlets of the American Revolution. Volume I 1750–1765*, Cambridge, MA, 1965

Bailyn, Bernard, and Morgan, Philip D., eds., *Strangers within the Realm: Cultural Margins of the First British Empire*, Chapel Hill, NC, 1991

Ball, Terence, '"A Republic – If You Can Keep It"', in *Conceptual Change and the Constitution*, ed. J. G. A. Pocock and T. Ball, Lawrence, KA, 1988, pp. 137–64

Barlow, Richard Burgess, *Citizenship and Conscience*, Philadelphia, 1962

Barrow, Thomas C., 'Background to the Grenville Program 1757–1763', *William and Mary Quarterly*, 3rd ser., 22 (1965), 93–104

Trade and Empire. The British Customs Service in Colonial America, Cambridge, MA, 1967

Baugh, Daniel A., 'Great Britain's "Blue-Water" Policy, 1689–1815', *International History Review*, 10 (1988), 33–58

Baumgartner, F. J., *Radical Reactionaries: The Political Thought of the French Catholic League*, Geneva, 1975

Beer, George Louis, *British Colonial Policy 1754–1765*, New York, 1907

Bellot, Leland, *William Knox: The Life and Thought of an Eighteenth-Century Imperialist*, Austin, TX, 1977

Berkowitz, David S., 'Reason of State in England and the Petition of Right, 1603–29', *Staatsrason*, ed. Roman Schnur, Berlin, 1975, pp. 165–213

Birley, Robert, *The Counter-Reformation Prince: Anti-Machiavellism or Catholic Statecraft in Early Modern Europe*, Chapel Hill, NC, 1990

Black, Antony, *Political Thought in Europe, 1250–1450*, Cambridge, 1992

Black, Jeremy, *British Foreign Policy in the Age of Walpole*, Edinburgh, 1985

Natural and Necessary Enemies: Anglo-French Relations in the Eighteenth Century, London, 1986

'Mid-Eighteenth Century Conflict with Particular Reference to the Wars of the Polish and Austrian Successions', in *The Origins of War in Early Modern Europe*, ed. Jeremy Black, Edinburgh, 1987, pp. 210–41

Bond, W. H., *Thomas Hollis of Lincoln's Inn: A Whig and his Books*, Cambridge, 1990

Bonwick, Colin, *English Radicals and the American Revolution*, Chapel Hill, NC, 1977

'Joseph Priestley: Emigrant and Jeffersonian', *Enlightenment and Dissent*, 2, (1983), 3–22

Boulton, James T., *The Language of Politics in the Age of Wilkes and Burke*, London and Toronto, 1963

Bouwsma, William, 'Two Faces of Renaissance Humanism', in *Itinerarium Italicum: The Profile of the Italian Renaissance in the Mirror of its European Transformations*, ed. Heiko A. Oberman with Thomas A. Brady, Jr Leiden, 1975, pp. 3–60

Bradley, James E., *Popular Politics and the American Revolution in England*, Athens, GA, 1986

Religion, Revolution and English Radicalism: Non-Conformity in Eighteenth-Century Politics and Society, Cambridge, 1990

Brewer, John, *Party Ideology and Popular Politics at the Accession of George III*, Cambridge, 1976

'English Radicalism in the Age of George III', in *Three British Revolutions*, ed. J. G. A. Pocock, Princeton, 1980, pp. 323–67

The Sinews of Power, London, 1989

Brown, Peter, *The Chathamites. A Study in the Relationship between Personalities and Ideas in the Second Half of the Eighteenth Century*, London, 1967

Browning, Reed, *The Political and Constitutional Ideas of the Court Whigs*, Baton Rouge, LA, 1982

Bullion, John L., *A Great and Necessary Measure: George Grenville and the Origins of the Stamp Act*, Columbia, MO, 1982

'Securing the Peace: Lord Bute, the Plan for the Army, and the Origins of the American Revolution', in *Lord Bute: Essays in the Re-Interpretation*, ed. Karl W. Schweizer, Leicester, 1988, pp. 176–40

Burke, Peter, 'Tacitism', *Tacitus*, ed. T. A. Dorey, London, 1969, pp. 149–71

Burns, J. H., 'Bentham and Blackstone: A Lifetime's Dialect', *Utilitas*, 1 (1989), pp. 22–40

'Utilitarianism and Reform: Social Theory and Social Change, 1750–1800', *Utilitas*, 1 (1989), 211–25

Cairns, John W., 'Blackstone, an English Institutionalist: Legal Literature and the Rise of the Nation State', *Oxford Journal of Legal Studies*, 4 (1984), 318–60

Cannon, John, *Parliamentary Reform 1640–1832*, Cambridge, 1973

Canovan, Margaret, 'Priestley on Rank', *Enlightenment and Dissent*, 2 (1983), 27–32

Cassirer, Ernst, *The Philosophy of the Enlightenment*, tr. Fritz C. A. Koelln and James P. Pettegrove, Princeton, 1951

Champion, Justin, *The Pillars of Priestcraft Shaken: The Church of England and its Enemies 1660–1730*, Cambridge, 1992

Christie, Ian R., *Wilkes, Wyvill and Reform. The Parliamentary Reform Movement in British Politics 1760–1785*, London, 1962

Crisis of Empire. Great Britain and the American Colonies 1754–1783, London, 1966

Stress and Stability in Late Eighteenth-Century Britain. Reflections on the British Avoidance of Revolution, Oxford, 1984

'Party and Politics in the Age of Lord North's Administration', *Parliamentary History*, (1987), 47–68

Christie, Ian R., and Labaree, Charles, *Empire or Independence?*, London, 1976

Church, William F., *Richelieu and Reason of State*, Princeton, 1972

Clark, G. N., *The Seventeenth Century*, London, 1947

Clark, J. C. D., *The Dynamics of Change: The Crisis of the 1750s and English Party Systems*, Cambridge, 1982

English Society: 1688–1832, Cambridge, 1985

Clayton, T. R., 'The Duke of Newcastle, the Earl of Halifax, and the American Origins of the Seven Years' War', *Historical Journal*, 24 (1981), 571–603

Colish, Marcia, 'Cicero's *De Officiis* and Machiavelli's *Prince*, *The Sixteenth-Century Journal*, 9 (1978), 80–93
The Stoic Tradition from Antiquity to the Early Middle Ages, 2 vols., Leiden, 1990; 1st edn 1985
Colley, Linda, 'Eighteenth-Century English Radicalism before Wilkes', *Transactions of the Royal Historical Society*, 5th ser., 31 (1981), 1–25
In Defiance of Oligarchy, Cambridge, 1983
Britons: Forging the Nation 1707–1837, New Haven and London, 1992
Collins, Robert J., 'Montaigne's Rejection of Reason of State in "De l'utile et de l'honneste", *Sixteenth-Century Journal*, 23 (1992), 71–94
Comperat, André, *Amor et verité: Sebon, Vives et Montaigne*, Paris, 1983
Condren, Conal, *George Lawson' 'Politica' and the English Revolution*, Cambridge, 1990
Conquest, Robert, 'The State and Commercial Expansion: England in the Years 1642–1688', *Journal of European Economic History*, 14 (1985), 155–72
Coussin, Pierre, 'The Stoicism of the New Academy', in *The Skeptical Tradition*, ed. Myles Burnyeat, Berkeley, Los Angeles and London, 1983, pp. 31–65
Cragg, Gerald, R., *Reason and Authority in the Eighteenth Century*, Cambridge, 1964
Croll, Maurice, *Style, Rhetoric, and Rhythm*, ed. J. Max Patrick and Robert O. Evans, with John M. Wallace and R. J. Schoeck, Princeton, 1966
Crossland, Maurice, 'The Image of Science as a Threat: Burke Versus Priestley and the "Philosophic Revolution"', *British Journal for the History of Science*, 20 (1987), 277–308
Cunningham, Hugh, 'The Language of Patriotism, 1750–1914', *History Workshop*, 12 (1981), 8–33
Cust, Richard, *The Forced Loan and English Politics 1626–1628*, Oxford, 1987
Cust, Richard, and Hughes, Ann, eds., *Conflict in Early Stuart England: Studies in Religion and Politics 1603–1642*, London, 1989
d'Addio, Mario, *Il pensiero politico di Gaspare Scioppio e il machiavellismo del seicento*, Milan, 1962
Davie, Donald, *A Gathered Church. The Literature of the English Dissenting Interest, 1700–1930*, London, 1978
Davis, G. A., 'The Influence of Justus Lipsius on Juan de Vera y Figueroa's *Embaxador* (1620)', *Bulletin of Hispanic Studies*, 42 (1965), 160–73
de Maddalena, Aldo, 'Il mercantilismo', in *Storia delle idee politiche, economiche e sociali*, vol. iv *L'età moderna*, ed. Luigi Firpo, Turin, 1980, pp. 637–706
de Mattei, Rodolfo, *Dal premachiavellismo all'antimachiavellismo*, Florence, 1969
Il problema della 'ragion di stato' nell'età della controriforma, Milan and Naples, 1979
Il pensiero politico italiano nell'età della controriforma, 2 vols. Milan and Naples, 1982

Dean, Winton, *Handel's Dramatic Oratorios and Masques*, Oxford, 1959, rpt. 1990

Dickerson, Oliver M., *The Navigation Acts and the American Revolution*, Philadelphia, 1951

Dickinson, H. T., *Liberty and Property: Political Ideology in Eighteenth-Century Britain*, London, 1977

Dinwiddy, J. R., 'Utility and Natural Law in Burke's Thought: A Reconsideration', *Studies in Burke and his Time*, 16 (1974–5), 105–28

Ditchfield, G. M., 'The Subscription Issue in British Parliamentary Politics, 1772–9', *Parliamentary History*, 7 (1988), 45–80

'The Parliamentary Struggle over the Repeal of the Test and Corporation Acts, 1787–1790', *English Historical Review*, 89 (1974), 551–77

Donaldson, William, *Machiavelli and the Mysteries of State*, Cambridge, 1989

Doufor, Alfred, 'Pufendorf', in *Cambridge History of Political Thought, 1450–1700* ed. J. H. Burns and Mark Goldie, Cambridge, 1991, pp. 561–88

Dunn, John, 'Consent in the Political Theory of John Locke', *Historical Journal*, 10 (1967), 153–82

'The Politics of Locke in England and America in the Eighteenth Century', in *John Locke: Problems and Perspectives*, ed. John Yolton, Cambridge, 1969, pp. 45–80

The Political Thought of John Locke. An Historical Account of the Argument of the 'Two Treatises of Government', Cambridge, 1969

'From Applied Theology to Social Analysis: The Break between John Locke and the Scottish Enlightenment', in *Wealth and Virtue*, ed. Istvan Hont and Michael Ignatieff, Cambridge, 1983, pp. 119–35

'The Claim to Freedom of Conscience: Freedom of Speech, Freedom of Thought, Freedom of Worship?', in *From Persecution to Toleration: The Glorious Revolution and Religion in England*, ed. O. P. Grell, J. I. Israel, N. Tyacke, Oxford, 1991, pp. 171–94

Dybikowski, J., 'David Williams and the Eighteenth-Century Distinction between Civil and Political Liberty', *Enlightenment and Dissent*, 3 (1984), 15–40

Egnal, Marc, *A Mighty Empire: The Origins of the American Revolution*, Ithaca, 1988

Elkana, Yehuda, 'Newtonianism in the Eighteenth Century', *British Journal of the Philosophy of Science*, 22 (1971), 297–306

Elliott, J. H., *The Revolt of the Catalans*, Cambridge, 1984; 1st edn, 1963

The Count-Duke of Olivares: The Statesman in an Age of Decline, New Haven and London, 1986

'The Spanish Monarchy and the Kingdom of Portugal 1580–1640', in *Conquest and Coalescence*, ed. Barry Greengrass, London, 1991, pp. 48–67

'A Europe of Composite Monarchies', *Past and Present*, 137 (1992), 48–71

Emerson, Roger L., 'Science and Moral Philosophy in the Scottish Enlightenment', in *Studies in the Philosophy of the Scottish Enlightenment*, ed. M. A. Stewart, Oxford, 1990, pp. 11–36

Ericson, Fred J., 'British Motives for Expansion in 1763: Territory, Commerce, or Security', *Papers of the Michigan Academy of Science, Arts, and Letters*, 27 (1941), 481–594

Evans, R. J. W., *The Making of the Habsburg Monarchy 1550–1700*, Oxford, 1979, rpt, 1991

'The Habsburg Monarchy and Bohemia, 1526–1848', in *Conquest and Coalescence: The Shaping of the State in Early Modern Europe*, ed. Mark Greengrass, London, 1991, pp. 134–54

Evans, R. W., *Warburton and the Warburtonians: A Study in Some Eighteenth-Century Controversies*, Oxford, 1932

Fenlon, Iain, and Miller, Peter N., *The Song of the Soul: Understanding 'Poppea'*, London, 1992

Ferguson, J. P., *An Eighteenth-Century Heretic: Dr Samuel Clarke*, Kenton, 1976

Fieldhouse, D. K., 'British Imperialism in the Late Eighteenth Century', *Essays in Imperial Government*, ed. K. Robinson and F. Madden, Oxford, 1963, pp. 23–46

Finley, M. I., 'Colonies – An Attempt of a Typology', *Transactions of the Royal Historical Society*, 5th ser., 26 (1976), 167–88

Finnis, John M., 'Blackstone's Theoretical Intentions', *Natural Law Forum*, 13 (1967), 163–82

Natural Law and Natural Rights, Oxford, 1980

Fitzpatrick, Martin, 'Joseph Priestley and the Cause of Universal Toleration', *The Price-Priestley Newsletter*, 1 (1977), 3–30

'Toleration and Truth', *Enlightenment and Dissent*, 1 (1982), 3–32

'Science and Society in the Enlightenment', *Enlightenment and Dissent*, 4 (1985), 83–106

'Joseph Priestley and the Millenium', in *Science, Medicine and Dissent: Joseph Priestley (1733–1804)*, ed. R. G. W. Anderson and Christopher Lawrence, London, 1987, pp. 29–38

'Heretical Religion and Radical Political Ideas in Late Eighteenth-Century England', in *The Transformation of Political Culture: England and Germany in the Late Eighteenth Century*, ed. Eckhart Hellmuth, Oxford, 1990, pp. 339–74

Forbes, Duncan, *Hume's Philosophical Politics*, Cambridge, 1975

Fornara, Charles W., *The Nature of History in Ancient Greece and Rome*, Berkeley, Los Angeles and London, 1983

Francis, Mark, and Morrow, John, 'After the Ancient Constitution: Political Theory and English Constitutional Writings, 1765–1832', *History of Political Thought*, 9 (1988), 283–302

Franklin, Julian, *John Locke and the Theory of Sovereignty*, Cambridge, 1978

Freudenthal, Gideon, *Atom and Individual in the Age of Newton. On the Genesis of the Mechanical World View*, Dordrecht, 1986

Fruchtman, Jack Jr, *The Apocalyptic Politics of Richard Price and Joseph Priestley*, in *Transactions of the American Philosophical Society*, Philadelphia, 1983

Funkenstein, Amos, *Theology and the Scientific Imagination from the Middle Ages to the Seventeenth Century*, Princeton, 1986

Fussell, Paul, *The Rhetorical World of Augustan Humanism. Ethics and Imagery from Swift to Burke*, Oxford, 1965

Gascoigne, John, 'Anglican Latitudinarianism and Political Radicalism in the Late Eighteenth Century', *History*, 71 (1986), 22–38

'From Bentley to the Victorians: The Rise and Fall of British Newtonian Natural Theology', *Science in Context*, 2 (1988), 219–56

Cambridge in the Age of Enlightenment, Cambridge, 1989

Gaudemet, J., '*Utilitas publica*', *Revue historique de droit français et étranger*, 29 (1951), 465–99

Gawlick, Günter, 'Cicero and the Enlightenment', *Studies on Voltaire and the Eighteenth Century*, 25 (1963), 657–82

Gay, John, 'Matter and Freedom in the Thought of Samuel Clarke', *Journal of the History of Ideas*, 24 (1963), 85–105

Gipson, Lawrence Henry, *The British Empire before the American Revolution*, XIII, pt 2, New York, 1967

Gipson, Lawrence P., 'The American Revolution as an Aftermath of the Great War for the Empire, 1754–1763', *Political Science Quarterly*, 65 (1950), 86–104

Goldie, Mark, 'The Revolution of 1689 and the Structure of Political Argument', *Bulletin of Research in the Humanities*, 83 (1980), 473–564

'The Scottish Catholic Enlightenment', *Journal of British Studies*, 30 (1991), 20–62

Goumarre, Pierre J., 'La morale et la politique: Montaigne, Cicero et Machiavel', *Italica*, 50 (1973), 285–98

Grafton, Anthony, *New Worlds, Ancient Texts: The Power of Tradition and the Shock of Discovery*, Cambridge, MA, 1992

Graham, A. J., *Colony and Mother City in Ancient Greece*, 2nd edn, Chicago, 1983

Graham, Jenny, 'Revolutionary Philosopher: The Political Ideas of Joseph Priestley (1733–1804), Part One', *Enlightenment and Dissent*, 8 (1989), 43–68

Grampp, William D., 'The Liberal Elements in English Mercantilism', *The Quarterly Journal of Economics*, 66 (1952), 465–501

Grant, W. L., 'Canada Versus Guadaloupe, an Episode of the Seven Years War', *American Historical Review*, 17 (1912), 735–43

Gray, John, *Liberalism*, Milton Keynes, 1986

Greenberg, Janelle, 'The Confessor's Law and the Radical Face of the English Constitution', *English Historical Review*, 412 (1989), 610–37

Greene, Jack P., 'William Knox's Explanation for the American Revolution', *William and Mary Quarterly*, 3rd ser., 30 (1973), 293–306

'The Seven Years' War and the American Revolution: the Causal Relationship Reconsidered', *The British Atlantic Empire before the American Revolution* ed. Peter Marshall and Glynn Williams, London, 1980, pp. 85–105

Peripheries and Center. Constitutional Development in the Extended Polities of the British Empire and the United States, 1607–1788, Athens, GA, 1986
Gunn, J. A. W. '"Interest Will Not Lie": A Seventeenth-Century Political Maxim', *Journal of the History of Ideas*, 39 (1968), 551–64
Politics and the Public Interest in the Seventeenth Century, London and Toronto, 1969
Factions No More: Attitudes to Party in Government and Opposition in Eighteenth-Century England, London, 1972
Beyond Liberty and Property: The Process of Self-Recognition in Eighteenth-Century Political Thought, Kingston and Montreal, 1983
Guttridge, G. H., 'Thomas Pownall's "Administration of the Colonies": The Six Editions', *William and Mary Quarterly*, 3rd ser., 26 (1969), 31–46
Haakonssen, Knud, 'Hugo Grotius and the History of Political Thought', *Political Theory*, 13 (1985), 239–65
'Natural Jurisprudence in the Scottish Enlightenment: Summary of an Interpretation', in *Enlightenment, Rights and Revolution: Essays in Legal and Social Philosophy*, ed. Neil MacCormick and Zenon Bankowski, Aberdeen, 1989, pp. 36–49
'Natural Law and Moral Realism: The Scottish Synthesis', in *Studies in the Philosophy of the Scottish Enlightenment*, ed. M. A. Stewart, Oxford, 1990, pp. 61–86
Hale, David George, *The Body Politics: A Political Metaphor in English Renaissance Literature*, The Hague, 1971
Hall, A. Rupert, *From Galileo to Newton*, New York, 1963
Halsband, Robert, *Lord Hervey: Eighteenth-Century Courtier*, Oxford, 1973
Halstead, David, 'Distance, Dissolution and Neo-Stoic Ideals: History and Self-Definition in Lipsius', *Humanistica Lovaniensia*, 40 (1991), 262–74
Hampsher-Monk, Ian, 'Civic Humanism and Parliamentary Reform: The Case of the Society of the Friends of the People', *Journal of British Studies*, 18 (1979), 70–89
Harlow, Vincent T., *The Founding of the Second British Empire 1763–1793*, vol. I, London 1952
Harré, Rom, 'Knowledge', in *The Ferment of Knowledge. Studies in the Historiography of Eighteenth-Century Science*, ed. Roy Porter, Cambridge, 1980, pp. 11–54
Hart, H. L. A., 'Sovereignty and Legally Limited Government', *Essays on Bentham. Studies in Jurisprudence and Political Theory*, Oxford, 1982, pp. 220–42
Hay, Carla H., *James Burgh, Spokesman for Reform in Hanoverian England*, Washington, DC, 1979
Heckscher, Eli, *Mercantilism*, tr. Mendel Shapiro. 2 vols., London, 1935
Heimann, P. M., 'Newtonian Natural Philosophy and the Scientific Revolution', *History of Science*, 11 (1973), 1–7
'Nature as a Perpetual Worker: Newton's Aether and Eighteenth-Century Natural Philosophy', *Ambix*, 20 (1973), 1–25

'Voluntarism and Immanence: Conceptions of Nature in Eighteenth-Century Thought', *Journal of the History of Ideas*, 39 (1978), 271–83

Hellmuth, Eckhart, '"The Palladium of All Other English Liberties": Reflections on the Liberty of the Press in England during the 1760s and 1770s', in *The Transformation of Political Culture: England and Germany in the Late Eighteenth Century*, ed. E. Hellmuth, Oxford, 1990, pp. 467–502

Hirshman, Albert, *The Passions and the Interests*, Princeton, 1977

Hoecker, James J., 'Joseph Priestley and Utilitarianism in the Age of Reason', *Enlightenment and Dissent*, 3 (1984), 55–64

Holmes, Geoffrey, *The Trial of Doctor Sacheverell*, London, 1973

Hont, Istvan, 'Free Trade and the Economic Limits to National Politics: Neo-Machiavellian Political Economy Reconsidered', in *The Economic Limits to Modern Politics*, ed. John Dunn, Cambridge, 1990, pp. 41–120

'Commercial Society and Political Theory in the Eighteenth Century: The Problem of Authority in David Hume and Adam Smith', Paper presented to the Seminar on Cultural History of the University of Amsterdam, June, 1991

'The Rhapsody of Public Debt: David Hume and Voluntary State Bankruptcy', in *Political Discourse in Early Modern Britain*, ed. Nicholas Phillipson and Quentin Skinner, Cambridge, 1993, pp. 321–48

Horn, David Bayne, *Great Britain and Europe in the Eighteenth Century*, Oxford, 1967

Horne, Thomas, 'Politics in a Corrupt Society: William Arnall's Defense of Robert Walpole', *Journal of the History of Ideas*, 41 (1980), 601–14

Horrocks, J. W., *A Short History of Mercantilism*, London, 1925

Houston, Alan, *Algernon Sidney and the Republican Heritage in England and America*, Princeton, 1991

Hudson, W. D. *Reason and Right: A Critical Examination of Richard Price's Moral Philosophy*, London, 1970

Humphreys, R. A., 'Lord Shelburne and the Proclamation of 1763', *English Historical Review*, 49 (1934), 241–64

Hutchinson, Terence, *Before Adam Smith: The Emergence of Political Economy, 1662–1776*, Oxford, 1988

Hyam, Ronald, 'Imperial Interests and the Peace of Paris (1763)', *Reappraisals in British Imperial History*, ed. Ged Martin and Ronald Hyam, London, 1975, pp. 21–43

Innes, Joanna, 'Politics and Morals: The Reformation of Manners Movement in Later Eighteenth-Century England', in *The Transformation of Political Culture*, ed. Eckhart Hellmuth, Oxford, 1990, pp. 57–118

Israel, Jonathan I., *The Dutch Republic and the Hispanic World, 1606–1661*, Oxford, 1986; 1st edn, 1982

'Spain, the Spanish Embargoes, and the Struggle for the Mastery of World Trade, 1585–1660', in *Empires and Entrepôts: The Dutch, the Spanish Monarchy and the Jews, 1585–1713*, London and Ronceverte, 1990, pp. 189–212

Jacob, Margaret, *The Newtonians and the English Revolution: 1689–1720*, Ithaca, 1976
'Newtonianism and the Origin of the Enlightenment: A Reappraisal', *Eighteenth Century Studies*, 11 (1977), 1–25
'Scientific Culture in the Early English Enlightenment: Mechanisms, Industry, and Gentlemanly Facts', *Anticipations of Enlightenment in England, France and Germany*, ed. Paul J. Korskin and Alan Charles Kors, Philadelphia, 1987, pp. 134–64
Jehasse, Jean, *La renaissance de la critique*, Paris, 1976
Jezierski, John J., 'Parliament or People: James Wilson and Blackstone on the Nature and Location of Sovereignty', *Journal of the History of Ideas*, 32 (1971), 95–106
Jones, Peter, *Hume's Sentiments: Their Ciceronian and French Context*, Edinburgh, 1982
Jossa, Giorgio, 'L'*utilitas rei publicae* nel pensiero de Cicerone', *Studi romani*, 12 (1964), 269–88
Jover, José Maria, *1635: Historia de una polémica y semblanza de una generación*, Madrid, 1949
Judson, Margaret, *The Crisis of the Constitution*, New York, 1980; 1st edn, 1949
Kammen, Michael, *Empire and Interest: The American Colonies and the Politics of Mercantilism*, Philadelphia, 1970
Kelley, Donald R., *The Beginning of Ideology*, Cambridge, 1981
Kelley, Patrick, 'Locke and Molyneux: Anatomy of a Friendship', *Hermathena*, 126 (1979), 38–54
Kenyon, J. P., *Revolution Principles: The Politics of Party 1689–1720*, Cambridge, 1977; rpt, 1990
Keohane, Nannerl, *Philosophy and the State of France*, Princeton, 1980
Knollenberg, Bernhard, *Origin of the American Revolution 1759–1766*, New York, 1966
Knorr, K., *British Colonial Theories 1570–1850*, Toronto, 1944
Koebner, Richard, *Empire*, Cambridge, 1961
Koenigsberger, H. G., '*Dominium regale* or *Dominium politicum et regale*: Monarchies and Parliaments in Early Modern Europe', in *Politicians and Virtuosi: Essays in Early Modern History*, London and Ronceverte, 1986, pp. 1–25.
'Composite States, Representative Institutions and the American Revolution', *Historical Research*, 62 (1989), 135–54
'Epilogue: Central and Western Europe', in *Crown, Church and Estates: Central European Politics in the Sixteenth and Seventeenth Centuries*, ed. R. J. W. Evans and T. V. Thomas, London, 1991, pp. 300–10
Kramnick, Isaac, *Republicanism and Bourgeois Radicalism: Political Ideology in Late Eighteenth-Century England and America*, Ithaca, 1990
Landesman, Ned, 'The Legacy of the British Union for the North American Colonies: Provincial Perspectives on the Problem of Imperial Union',

in *A Union for Empire: The Union of 1707 in the History of British Political Thought*, ed. John Robertson. Cambridge, forthcoming

Langford, Paul, 'William Pitt and Public Opinion, 1757', *English Historical Review*, 88 (1973), 54–80

'Old Whigs, Old Tories and the American Revolution', *Journal of Imperial and Commonwealth History*, 8: 2 (1980), 106–30

A Polite and Commercial People. England 1727–1783, Oxford, 1989

'The English Clergy and the American Revolution', in *The Transformation of Political Culture: England and Germany in the Late Eighteenth Century*, ed. Eckhart Hellmuth, Oxford, 1990, pp. 275–308

Public Life and the Propertied Englishman, Oxford, 1991

Larraz, José, *La epoca del mercantilismo en Castilla 1500–1700*, Madrid, 1963

Laudan, L. L., 'Thomas Reid and the Newtonian Turn of British Methodological Thought', *The Methodological Heritage of Newton*, ed. Robert Butts and Jon W. Davis, Toronto, 1970, pp. 101–31

Lawson, Philip, '"The Irishman's Prize": Views of Canada from the British Press, 1760–1774', *Historical Journal*, 28 (1985), 575–96

'The Missing Link: The Imperial Dimension in Understanding Hanoverian Britain', *Historical Journal*, 29 (1986), 747–51

The Imperial Challenge: Quebec and Britain in the Age of the American Revolution, Montreal, Kingston and London, 1989

Lepore, Ettore, *Il princeps ciceroniano e gli ideali politici della tarda repubblica*, Naples, 1954

Levi, Lucio, 'Il *Federalist* e la teoria della ragion di stato', *Il pensiero politico*, 21 (1988), 5–25

Lieberman, David, *The Province of Legislation Determined: Legal Theory in Eighteenth-Century Britain*, Cambridge, 1989

Lincoln, Anthony, *Some Political and Social Ideas of English Dissent 1763–1800*, Cambridge, 1938

Long, Douglas G., *Bentham on Liberty: Jeremy Bentham's Idea of Liberty in Relation to his Utilitarianism*, Toronto, 1977

'"Utility" and the "Utility Principle": Hume, Smith, Bentham, Mill', *Utilitas*, 2, (1990), 12–39

Loomie, Albert J., 'The *Conducteur des ambassadeurs* of Seventeenth Century France and Spain', *Revue belge de philologie et d'histoire*, 53 (1975), 333–56

Lynd, Staughton, *Intellectual Origins of American Radicalism*, London, 1973

McCrea, Adriana, 'Reason's Muse; Andrew Marvell, R. Fletcher, and the Politics of Poetry in the Engagement Debate', *Albion*, 23 (1991), 655–80

McEvoy, J. G., 'Joseph Priestley, "Aerial Philosopher": Metaphysics and Methodology in Priestley's Chemical Thought, from 1772 to 1781', *Ambix*, 25 (1978), 1–55, 93–116, 153–75

'Enlightenment and Dissent in Science: Joseph Priestley and the Limits of Theoretical Reasoning', *Enlightenment and Dissent*, 2 (1983), 47–68

'Causes and Laws, Powers and Principles: The Metaphysical Foundations of Priestley's Concept of Phlogiston', in *Science, Medicine and Dissent: Joseph Priestley (1733–1804)*, ed. R. G. W. Anderson and Christopher Lawrence, London, 1987, pp. 55–72

McEvoy, J. G., and McGuire, J. E., 'God and Nature: Priestley's Way of Rational Dissent', *Historical Studies in the Physical Sciences*, 6 (1975), 325–404

McGuire, J. E., 'Newton and the "Pipes of Pan"', *Notes and Records of the Royal Society of London*, 21 (1966), 108–43

'Force, Active Principles and Newton's Invisible Realm', *Ambix*, 15 (1968), 154–208

'The Origin of Newton's Doctrine of Essential Qualities', *Centaurus*, 12 (1968), 233–60

'Existence, Actuality and Necessity: Newton on Space and Time', *Annals of Science*, 35 (1978), 463–508

McGuire, J. E., and Heimann, P. M., 'Newtonian Forces and Lockean Powers: Concepts of Matter in Eighteenth-Century Thought', *Historical Studies in the Physical Sciences*, 3 (1971), 233–306

McGuire, J. E., and Tamny, Martin, *Certain Philosophical Questions: Newton's Trinity Notebook*, Cambridge, 1983

Marshall, P. J., 'The First and Second British Empires: A Question of Demarcation', *History*, 49 (1964), 13–23

'The British Empire in the Age of the American Revolution. Problems of Interpretation', *The American Revolution: Changing Perspectives*, ed. William M. Fowler Jr and Wallace Coyle, Boston, 1979, pp. 182–212

Marshall, Peter, 'The Incorporation of Quebec in the British Empire, 1763–1774', in *Of Mother Country and Plantations*, ed. V. V. Platt and D. C. Skaggs, Bowling Green, OH, 1971, pp. 42–61

Marston, Jerrilyn Greene, *The Transfer of Political Legitimacy, 1774–1776*, Princeton, 1987

Mason, Cathy, and Onuf, Peter, 'Toward a Republican Empire: Interest and Ideology in Revolutionary America', *American Quarterly*, 37 (1985), 496–531

Mattingly, Garret, *Renaissance Diplomacy*, Boston, 1955

Meehan, Michael, *Liberty and Poetics in Eighteenth-Century England*, London, 1986

Meinecke, Friedrich, *Machiavellism. The Doctrine of Raison d'Etat and its Place in Modern History*, tr. Douglas Scott, Boulder, CO, 1984; 1st edn, 1957

Middendorf, John H., 'Dr Johnson and Mercantilism', *Journal of the History of Ideas*, 21 (1960), 66–83

Middleton, Richard, *The Bells of Victory. The Pitt-Newcastle Ministry and the Conduct of the Seven Years' War, 1757–1762*, Cambridge, 1985

Momigliano, Arnaldo, 'Polybius' Reappearance in Western Europe', *Entretiens sur l'antiquité classique*, Geneva, 1974, pp. 345–72

Polybius between the English and the Turks, Oxford, 1974
'The Origins of Universal History', *On Pagans, Christians and Jews*, Middletown, CT, 1987, pp. 31–57
Moore, James, 'Hume's Political Science and the Classical Republican Tradition', *Canadian Journal of Political Science*, 10 (1977), 809–39
'Natural Law and the Pyrrhonian Controversy', in *Philosophy and Science in the Scottish Enlightenment*, ed. P. Jones, Edinburgh, 1988, pp. 20–38
'The Two Systems of Francis Hutcheson: On the Origins of the Scottish Enlightenment', in *Studies in the Philosophy of the Scottish Enlightenment*, ed. M. A. Stewart, Oxford, 1990, pp. 37–60
'Theological Politics: A Study of the Reception of Locke's *Two Treatises of Government* in England and Scotland in the *Early Eighteenth Century*', *John Locke and / und Immanuel Kant: Historical Reception and Contemporary Relevance*, ed. Martyn P. Thompson, Berlin, 1991, pp. 62–82
Morford, Paul, *Stoics and Neostoics: Rubens and the Circle of Lipsius*, Princeton, 1991
Murrin, John M., 'Self-Interest Conquers Patriotism: Republicans, Liberals, and Indians Reshape the Nation', *The American Revolution: Its Character and Limits*, ed. Jack P. Greene, New York, 1987, pp. 224–9
Namier, Sir Lewis, *England in the Age of the American Revolution*, 2nd edn, London, 1961
Namier, Sir Lewis, and Brooke, John, *The House of Commons 1754–1790*, 3 vols., London, 1964
Nangle, B. C., '*The Monthly Review*', First Series 1749–89: Indexes of Contributors and Articles*, Oxford, 1955
Nevo, Ruth, *The Dial of Virtue: A Study of Poems on Affairs of State in the Seventeenth Century*, Princeton, 1963
Newman, A. N., 'Leicester House Politics, 1748–1751', *English Historical Review*, 76 (1961), 577–89
Nicgorski, Walter, 'Cicero's Paradoxes and his Idea of Utility', *Political Theory*, 12 (1984), 557–78
Oestreich, Gerhard, *Neostoicism and the Early Modern State*, Cambridge, 1982
Ogden, H. V. S., 'The State of Nature and the Decline of Lockian Political Theory in England, 1760–1800', *American Historical Review*, 46 (1940), 21–44
O'Gorman, Frank, 'The Unreformed Electorate of Hanoverian England: The Mid Eighteenth Century to the Reform Act of 1832', *Social History*, 11 (1986), 33–52
Olson, Alison Gilbert, *Anglo-American Politics 1660–1775*, Oxford, 1973
Making the Empire Work: London and American Interest Groups 1690–1790, Cambridge, MA, 1992
Oxford English Dictionary, 2nd edn, Oxford, 1989
Pares, Richard, *War and Trade in the West Indies 1739–1763*, Oxford, 1936

'American or Continental Warfare, 1739–63', *English Historical Review*, 51 (1936), 429–65

Parker, Geoffrey, *Europe in Crisis 1598–1648*, London, 1979

The Military Revolution, Cambridge, 1988

Parry, Keith, *British Politics and the American Revolution*, London, 1990

Peach, Bernard, *Richard Price and the Ethical Foundations of the American Revolution*, Durham, NC, 1977

'Human Nature and the Foundation of Ethics', *Enlightenment and Dissent*, 4 (1985), 13–34

Pearson, D. N., 'Merchants and States', in *The Political Economy of Merchant Empires*, ed. James D. Tracy, Cambridge, 1991, pp. 41–116

Peters, Marie, 'The *Monitor* on the Constitution, 1755–1765: New Light on the Ideological Origins of English Radicalism', *English Historical Review*, 86 (1971), 706–27

Pitt and Popularity. The Patriot Minister and London Opinion during the Seven Years' War, Oxford, 1980

'"Names and Cant": Party Labels in English Political Propaganda c. 1755–1765', *Parliamentary History*, 3 (1984), 103–27

Philip, Mark, 'Rational Religion and Political Radicalism', *Enlightenment and Dissent*, 4 (1985), 35–46

Godwin's 'Political Justice', Ithaca, 1988

'Enlightenment, Toleration and Liberty, *Enlightenment and Dissent*, 9 (1990), 47–62

Phillipson, Nicholas, 'Adam Smith as a Civic Moralist', *Wealth and Virtue*, ed. I. Hont and M. Ignatieff, Cambridge, 1983, pp. 179–202

Pincus, S. C. A., 'Popery, Trade and Universal Monarchy: The Ideological Context of the Outbreak of the Second Anglo-Dutch War', *English Historical Review*, 105 (1992), 1–29

'The English Debate on Universal Monarchy', *A Union for Empire: The Union of 1707 in the History of British Political Thought*, ed. John Robertson, Cambridge, forthcoming

Protestantism and Patriotism: Ideology and the Making of English Foreign Policy 1650–1668, Cambridge, forthcoming

Pitkin, Hanna F., *The Concept of Representation*, Berkeley and Los Angeles, 1967

Pocock, J. G. A., *The Machiavellian Moment. Atlantic Political Thought and the Florentine Republican Tradition*, Princeton, 1975

'The Limits and Divisions of British History', *Studies in Public Policy*, 31 (1979) University of Strathclyde

'The Myth of John Locke and the Obsession with Liberalism', *John Locke*, ed. Richard Ashcraft and J. G. A. Pocock, Los Angeles, 1980

'Cambridge Paradigms and Scotch Philosophers', *Wealth and Virtue*, ed. I. Hont and M. Ignatieff, Cambridge, 1983, pp. 235–52

'Clergy and Commerce. The Conservative Enlightenment in England', in *L'eta dei lumi. Studi storici sul settecento Europeo in onore di Franco Venturi*, ed. R. Ajello, E. Cortese and V. Diano Mortes, Turin, 1985, pp. 525–62

Virtue, Commerce and History, Cambridge, 1985

'States, Republics and Empires: The American Founding in Early Modern Perspective', in *Conceptual Change and the Constitution*, ed. Terence Ball and J. G. A. Pocock, Lawrence, KA, 1988, pp. 55–77

The Politics of Extent and the Problem of Freedom, Colorado Springs, 1988

'Conservative Enlightenment and Democratic Revolution: The American and French Cases in British Perspective', *Government and Opposition*, 24 (1989), 81–105

Pole, J. R., *Political Representation in England and the Origins of the American Revolution*, Berkeley, Los Angeles and London, 1966

Polisensky, J. V., *The Thirty Years War*, tr. R. J. W. Evans, London, 1971

Porter, Roy, 'The English Enlightenment', *The Enlightenment in National Context*, ed. Roy Porter and Miklaus Teich, Cambridge, 1981

Pownall, Charles A. W., *Thomas Pownall*, London, 1908

Price, Jacob, 'The Transatlantic Economy', in *Colonial British America*, ed. J. R. Pole and Jack P. Greene, Baltimore, 1984, pp. 18–42

Rashed, Zenab E., *The Treaty of Paris 1763*, Liverpool, 1951

Rawson, Elizabeth, *The Spartan Tradition in European Thought*, Oxford, 1969

Reeve, L. J., *Charles I and the Road to Personal Rule*, Cambridge, 1989

Reid, John Philip, *The Concept of Liberty in the Age of the American Revolution*, Chicago, 1987

The Concept of Representation in the Age of the American Revolution, Chicago, 1990

Richardson, Patrick, *Empire and Slavery*, London, 1968

Richey, Russell E., 'Joseph Priestley: Worship and Theology', *Transactions of the Unitarian Historical Society*, 15 (1972), 41–53, 98–104

'The Origins of British Radicalism: The Changing Rationale for Dissent', *Eighteenth-Century Studies*, 7 (1974), 179–92

Ricuperati, G., '*Universal History*: storia di un progetto europeo. Impostori, storici ed editori, nella *Ancient Part*', *Studi settecenteschi*, 1 (1981), 7–90

Robbins, Caroline, *The Eighteenth-Century Commonwealthman*, Cambridge, MA, 1959

Absolute Liberty: A Selection from the Articles and Papers of Caroline Robbins, ed. Barbara Taft, Hamden, CT, 1982

Roberts, Michael, *Gustavus Adolphus: A History of Sweden 1611–1632*, 2 vols., London, 1958

'The Political Objectives of Gustav Adolf in Germany, 1630–2', in *Essays in Swedish History*, London, 1967

'Oxenstierna in Germany, 1633–1636', *Scandia*, 48 (1982), 61–105

Roberts, Michael, ed., *Sweden as a Great Power 1611–1697: Government, Society, Foreign Policy*, London, 1968

Robertson, John, 'The Scottish Enlightenment at the Limits of the Civic

Tradition', in *Wealth and Virtue*, ed. I. Hont and M. Ignatieff, Cambridge, 1983, pp. 137–78

'Universal Monarchy and the Liberties of Europe: David Hume's Critique of an English Whig Doctrine', in *Political Discourse in Early Modern Britain*, ed. N. Phillipson and Q. Skinner, Cambridge, 1993

Rogers, G. A. J., 'Locke's "Essay" and Newton's "Principia"', *Journal of the History of Ideas*, 37 (1978), 217–32

'Locke, Newton, and the Cambridge Platonists on Innate Ideas', *Journal of the History of Ideas*, 40 (1979), 191–206

'The Empiricism of Locke and Newton', in *Philosophers of the Enlightenment*, ed. S. C. Brown, Sussex, 1979, pp. 1–30

'The System of Locke and Newton', *Contemporary Newtonian Research*, ed. Zvi Beckler, Haifa, 1982, pp. 215–38

Romilly, Jacqueline de, *The Rise and Fall of States According to Greek Authors*, Ann Arbor, 1977

Rosen, Frederick, 'The Origin of Liberal Utilitarianism: Jeremy Bentham and Liberty', in *Victorian Liberalism: Nineteenth-Century Political Thought and Practice*, ed. Richard Bellamy, London and New York, 1990, pp. 58–70

Rostvig, Maren, *The Happy Man*, Oslo, 1954

Rupp, Gordon, *Religion in England 1688–1791*, Oxford, 1986

Russell, Colin A., *Science and Social Change 1700–1900*, London 1985

Russell, Conrad, 'Monarchies, Wars and Estates in England, France and Spain, c.1580–c.1640', *Legislative Studies Quarterly*, 7 (1982), 205–20

The Fall of the British Monarchies 1637–42, Oxford, 1991

Ryan, Alan, *Property*, Milton Keynes, 1987

Salmon, J. H. M., 'Cicero and Tacitus in Sixteenth-Century France', *American Historical Review*, 85 (1980), 307–31

'Rohan and the Interest of State', *Renaissance and Revolt*, Cambridge, 1987, pp. 98–116

Schaffer, Simon, 'Natural Philosophy', in *The Ferment of Knowledge. Studies in the Historiography of Eighteenth-Century Science*, ed. Roy Porter and G. S. Rousseau, Cambridge, 1980, pp. 55–92

'Natural Philosophy and Public Spectacle in the Eighteenth Century, *History of Science*, 21 (1983), 1–43

'Priestley's Questions: An Historiographic Survey', *History of Science*, 22 (1984), 151–83

'Priestley and the Politics in Spirit', in *Science, Medicine and Dissent: Joseph Priestley (1733–1804)*, ed. R. G. W. Anderson and Christopher Lawrence, London, 1987, pp. 39–54

'Measuring Virtue: Eudiometry, Enlightenment and Pneumatic Medicine', in *The Medical Enlightenment of the Eighteenth Century*, ed. Andrew Cunningham and Roger French, Cambridge, 1990, pp. 281–318

Schellhase, Kenneth C., *Tacitus in Renaissance Political Thought*, Chicago, 1976

Schmoller, Gustav, *The Mercantile System and its Historical Significance. Illustrated Chiefly from Prussian History*, New York, 1931; 1st edn., 1895

Schneewind, J. B., 'Pufendorf's Place in the History of Ethics', *Synthèse*, 72 (1987), 123–55

Schofield, Robert E., *Mechanism and Materialism: British Natural Philosophy in an Age of Reason*, Princeton, 1970

  'An Evolutionary Taxonomy of Eighteenth-Century Newtonianisms', *Studies in Eighteenth-Century Culture*, 7 (1978), 175–92

  'Joseph Priestley: Theology, Physics and Metaphysics', *Enlightenment and Dissent*, 2 (1983), 69–82

Schutz, John A., *Thomas Pownall British Defender of American Liberty*, Glendale, CA, 1951

Schuyler, Robert Livingston, *The Fall of the Old Colonial System. A Study in British Free Trade 1770–1870*, Oxford, 1945

Schweizer, Karl, 'The Seven Years War: A System Perspective', in *The Origins of War in Early Modern Europe*, ed. Jeremy Black, Edinburgh, 1987, pp. 242–60

Scott, H. M., *British Foreign Policy in the Age of the American Revolution*, Oxford, 1990

Scott, Jonathan, *Algernon Sidney and the English Republic, 1623–1677*, Cambridge, 1988

Seed, John, 'Gentlemen Dissenters: The Social and Political Meanings of Rational Dissent in the 1770s and 1780s', *Historical Journal*, 28 (1985), 299–325

Shapin, Steven, 'Social Uses of Science', in *The Ferment of Knowledge. Studies in the Historiography of Eighteenth-Century Science*, Roy Porter, Cambridge, 1980, pap. 93–142

  'Of Gods and Kings: Natural Philosophy and Politics in the Leibniz–Clarke disputes', *Isis*, 72 (1981), 187–215

Shapin, Steven, and Shaffer, Simon, *Leviathan and the Air-Pump*, Princeton, 1985

Sheps, Arthur, 'The American Revolution and the Transformation of English Radicalism', *Historical Reflections / Reflexions Historiques*, 2 (1975), 3–28

Shklar, Judith, 'Montesquieu and the New Republicanism', in *Machiavelli and Republicanism*, ed. Gissela Bock, Quentin Skinner and Maurizio Viroli, Cambridge, 1990, pp. 265–79

Shy, John, *Toward Lexington: The Role of the British Army in the Coming of the American Revolution*, Princeton, 1965

  A People Numerous and Armed, Oxford, 1976

Skinner, Andrew S., *A System of Social Science: Papers Relating to Adam Smith*, Oxford, 1979

Skinner, Quentin, 'The Principles and Practice of Opposition: The Case of Bolingbroke Versus Walpole', in *Historical Perspectives*, ed. Neil McKendrick, London, 1974, pp. 93–128

The Foundations of Modern Political Thought, 2 vols., Cambridge, 1978
'Machiavelli on the Maintenance of Liberty', *Politics*, 18 (1983), 3–15
'The Idea of Negative Liberty: Philosophical and Historical Perspectives', in *Philosophy in History*, ed. Richard Rorty, J. B. Schneewind and Quentin Skinner, Cambridge, 1984, pp. 193–221
'The Paradoxes of Political Liberty', *The Tanner Lectures on Human Values*, VII, 1986, ed. Sterling M. McMurrin, Cambridge, 1986, pp. 225–50
'Ambrogio Lorenzetti: The Artist as Political Philosopher', *Proceedings of the British Academy*, 72 (1986), 1–56
'The State', in *Political Innovation and Conceptual Change*, ed. Terence Ball, Cambridge, 1989, pp. 90–131
'The Republican Ideal of Liberty', in *Machiavelli and Republicanism*, eds. G. Bock, Q. Skinner and M. Viroli, Cambridge, 1990, pp. 293–309
Smith, R. J., *The Gothic Bequest*, Cambridge, 1987
Sommerville, Johann, *Politics and Ideology 1603–42*, London, 1988
'Ideology, Property and the Constitution', in *Conflict in Early Stuart England: Studies in Religion and Politics 1603–1642*, ed. R. Cust and A. Hughes, London, 1989, pp. 47–71
Sosin, Jack, *Whitehall and the Wilderness. The Middle West in British Colonial Policy, 1760–1775*, Lincoln, NB, 1961
Spadafora, David, *The Idea of Progress in Eighteenth-Century Britain*, New Haven and London, 1990
Spector, Margaret Marion, *The American Department of the British Government 1768–1782*, New York, 1940
Spector, Robert Donald, *English Literary Periodicals and the Climate of Opinion during the Seven Years' War*, The Hague, 1966
Steele, Ian K., *The English Atlantic 1675–1740. An Exploration of Communication and Community*, Oxford, 1986
Stegmann, André, 'La place de la praxis dans la notion de "Raison d'état"', in *Théorie et Pratique Politiques à la Renaissance*, ed. Stegmann, Paris, 1977, pp. 483–503
Stephens, John, 'The London Ministers and Subscription, 1772–1779', *Enlightenment and Dissent*, 1 (1982), 43–73
'The Epistemological Strategy of Richard Price's "Review of Morals"', *Enlightenment and Dissent*, 5 (1986), 39–50
'Price, Providence and the *Principia*', *Enlightenment and Dissent*, 6 (1987), 77–93
Stewart, Larry, 'Samuel Clarke, Newtonianism, and the Factions of Post-Revolutionary England', *Journal of the History of Ideas*, 42 (1981), 53–72
Stewart, M. A., 'The Stoic Legacy in the Early Scottish Enlightenment', in *Atoms, "Pneuma", and Tranquillity: Epicurean and Stoic Themes in European Thought*, ed. Margaret J. Osler, Cambridge, 1991, 273–96
Stromberg, Roland, N., *Religious Liberalism in Eighteenth-Century England*, Oxford, 1954

Sutcliffe, F. E., *Guez de Balzac et son temps*, Paris, 1957
Tarcov, Nathan, *Locke's Education for Liberty*, Chicago, 1984
Taylor, Stephen, 'William Warburton and the Alliance of Church and State', *Journal of Ecclesiastical History*, 43 (1972), 271–86
Thomas, D. O., *The Honest Mind: The Thought and Work of Richard Price*, Oxford, 1977
  'Progress, Liberty and Utility: The Political Philosophy of Joseph Priestley', in *Science, Medicine and Dissent: Joseph Priestley (1733–1804)*, ed. R. G. W. Anderson and Christopher Lawrence, London, 1987, pp. 73–80
Thomas, Keith, *Man and the Natural World. Changing Attitudes in England, 1500–1700*, London, 1983
Thomas, Peter D. G., *The Stamp Act Crisis*, Oxford, 1975
  The Townshend Duties Crisis. The Second Phase of the American Revolution 1767–1773, Oxford, 1987
Thuau, Etienne, *Raison d'état et pensée politique a l'époque de Richelieu*, Paris, 1966
Toffanin, Giuseppe, *Machiavelli e il 'Tacitismo'*, Naples, 1972; 1st edn, 1921
Toohey, Robert, *Liberty and Empire: British Radical Solutions to the American Problem*, Lexington, KY, 1978
Tuck, Richard, *Natural Rights Theories*, Cambridge, 1979
  '"The Ancient Law of Freedom": John Selden and the Civil War', in *Reactions to the English Civil War 1642–1649*, ed. John Morrill, London, 1982, pp. 137–62
  'Grotius, Carneades and Hobbes', *Grotiana*, new ser., 4 (1983), 43–62
  'The Modern Theory of Natural Law', in *The Languages of Political Thought in Early Modern Europe*, ed. Anthony Pagden, Cambridge, 1987, pp. 99–119
  'Scepticism and Toleration in the Seventeenth Century', in *Justifying Toleration*, ed. Susan Mendus, Cambridge, 1988, pp. 21–36
  Hobbes, Oxford, 1989
  Philosophy and Government 1580–1715, Cambridge, 1993
Tucker, Robert W., and Hendrickson, David C., *The Fall of the First British Empire*, Baltimore, 1982
Tully, James, *A Discourse on Property: John Locke and his Adversaries*, Cambridge, 1980
  'Locke on Liberty', in *Conceptions of Liberty in Political Philosophy*, ed. Z. Pelczynski and J. Gray, London, 1984, pp. 57–82
  'Governing Conduct', in *Conscience and Casuistry in Early Modern Europe*, ed. Edmund Leites, Cambridge, 1988, pp. 3–71
  'Locke', in *Cambridge History of Political Thought*, ed. J. H. Burns with Mark Goldie, Cambridge, 1991, pp. 589–649
Turner, Frank M., 'Why the Greeks and not the Romans in Victorian Britain?', *Rediscovering Hellenism: The Hellenistic Inheritance and the English Imagination*, ed. G. W. Clarke, Cambridge, 1989

Valenté, P. Milton, *L'éthique stoicienne chez Cicéron*, Paris, 1957

Veitch, George Stead, *The Genesis of Parliamentary Reform*, London, 1965, rpt

Viner, Jacob, 'English Theories of Foreign Trade before Adam Smith', *Journal of Political Economy*, 38 (1930), 249–301 , 404–57

'Power Versus Plenty as Objectives of Foreign Policy in the Seventeenth and Eighteenth Centuries', *World Politics*, 1 (1949), 1–29

Wallerstein, Immanuel, *The Modern World System. II. Mercantilism and the Consolidation of the World Economy 1600–1750*, New York, 1980

Ward, Addison, 'The Tory View of Roman History', *Studies in English Hisrtory* 4, (1964), 413–56

Watts, Ruth, 'Joseph Priestley and Education', in *Enlightenment and Dissent*, 2 (1983), pp. 83–100

Wickwire, Franklin B., 'John Pownall and British Colonial Policy', *William and Mary Quarterly*, 3rd ser., 20 (1963), 534–54

Wilde, C., 'Hutchinsonians, Natural Philosophy and Religious Controversy in Eighteenth-Century England', *History of Science*, 18 (1980), 1–24

Willman, Robert, 'Blackstone and the "Theoretical Perfection" of English Law in the Reign of Charles II', *Historical Journal*, 26 (1983), 39–70

Wilson, Charles, 'The Other Face of Mercantilism', in *Revisions in Mercantilism*, ed. D. C. Coleman, London, 1969, pp. 118–30

Winch, Donald, *Adam Smith's Politics: An Essay in Historiographical Revision*, Cambridge, 1978

Wirszubski, Chaim, *The Idea of Libertas in Rome*, Cambridge, 1947

Wood, Gordon, *The Creation of the American Republic 1776–1787*, New York, 1975, rpt

'Ideology and the Origins of Liberal America', *William and Mary Quarterly*, 3rd ser., 44 (1987), 628–40

The Radicalism of the American Revolution, New York, 1992

Wootton, David, *Paolo Sarpi. Between Renaissance and Enlightenment*, Cambridge, 1983

'John Locke: Socinian or Natural Law Theorist?', in *Religion, Secularization and Political Thought: Thomas Hobbes to J. S. Mill*, ed. James E. Crimmins, London, 1989, pp. 39–67

UNPUBLISHED DISSERTATIONS

Churgin, Naomi Helen, 'Major John Cartwright: A Study in Radical Parliamentary Reform, 1774–1824' Columbia (1963)

de Sousa, Norberto, '"Societas Civilis": Classical Roman Republican Theory on the Theme of Justice', Cambridge (1992)

Ditchfield, Grayson McClure, 'Some Aspects of Unitarianism and Radicalism', Cambridge (1968)

Drinkwater-Lunn, David, 'John Carwright: Political Education and English Radicalism', Oxford, (1970)

Fitzpatrick, Martin Hugh, 'Rational Dissent in the Late Eighteenth

Century with Particular Reference to the Growth of Toleration', Aberystwyth (1982)

Goldie, Mark, 'Tory Political Thought, 1689–1714', Cambridge (1978)

Leslie, Margaret Evelyn, 'The Social and Political Thought of Joseph Priestley', Cambridge (1966)

Marshall, John, 'John Locke in Context: Religion, Ethics and Politics', The Johns Hopkins University (1990)

Ohmori, Yuhtaro, '"The artillery of Mr Locke": The use of Locke's "Second Treatise" in pre-Revolutionary America, 1764–1776', The Johns Hopkins University (1988)

Pincus, S. C. A., 'Protestantism and Patriotism: Ideology and the Making of English Foreign Policy 1650–1665', Harvard University (1990)

Schaffer, Simon John, 'Newtonian Cosmology and the Steady State', Cambridge (1980)

Taylor, Stephen J. C., 'Church and State in England in the Mid-Eighteenth Century: The Newcastle Years 1742–1762', Cambridge (1987)

Thomas, P. J., 'Imperial Issues in the British Press', Oxford, (1982)

Walsh-Atkins, P. G., 'Shelburne and America', Oxford, (1971)

Zebrowsky, Martha Kaderly, 'One Cato Is Not enough; Or, How James Burgh Found Nature's Duty and Real Authority and Secured the Dignity of Human Nature against All Manner of Public Abuse, Iniquitous Practice, Corruption, Vice, and Irreligion', Columbia (1982)

Index

IDEAS IN CONTEXT

Edited by Quentin Skinner (general editor), Lorraine Daston, Wolf Lepenies, Richard Rorty and J.B. Schneewind